THE THIRTEEN PRINCIPAL UPANISHADS

TRANSLATED FROM THE SANSKRIT

THE THIRTEEN PRINCIPAL UPANISHADS

TRANSLATED FROM THE SANSKRIT

WITH AN OUTLINE OF
THE PHILOSOPHY OF THE UPANISHADS
AND AN ANNOTATED BIBLIOGRAPHY

BY

ROBERT ERNEST HUME

PH.D., D.THÉOL.

Professor of the History of Religions,
Union Theological Seminary, New York

WITH A LIST OF
RECURRENT AND PARALLEL PASSAGES

BY

GEORGE C. O. HAAS, PH.D.

SECOND EDITION, REVISED

DELHI
OXFORD UNIVERSITY PRESS
BOMBAY CALCUTTA MADRAS

Oxford University Press, Great Clarendon Street, Oxford OX2 6DP

Oxford New York
Athens Auckland Bangkok Calcutta
Cape Town Chennai Dar es Salaam Delhi
Florence Hong Kong Istanbul Karachi
Kuala Lumpur Madrid Melbourne Mexico City
Mumbai Nairobi Paris Singapore
Taipei Tokyo Toronto

and associates in

Berlin Ibadan

First published in England 1921
Second edition, revised 1931
Reprinted in India 1949
Seventh impression 1968
First Indian paperback edition 1983
Oxford India paperback 1995
Fourth impression 1998

ISBN 0 19563743 7

Printed in India at Wadhwa International, New Delhi
and published by Manzar Khan, Oxford University Press
YMCA Library Building, Jai Singh Road, New Delhi 110 001

TO MY COUSIN

JANE PORTER WILLIAMS

IN LOVE AND GRATITUDE

The One who, himself without color, by the manifold application of his power
Distributes many colors in his hidden purpose,
And into whom, its end and its beginning, the whole world dissolves—He is God!
May He endow us with clear intellect!

—Śvetāśvatara Upanishad, 4. 1 (p. 402).

PREFACE

In the long history of man's endeavor to grasp the fundamental truths of being, the metaphysical treatises known as the Upanishads[1] hold an honored place. They represent the earnest efforts of the profound thinkers of early India to solve the problems of the origin, the nature, and the destiny of man and of the universe, or—more technically—the meaning and value of 'knowing' and 'being'. Though they contain some fanciful ideas, naïve speculations, and inadequate conclusions, yet they are replete with sublime conceptions and with intuitions of universal truth.[2]

Here are found intimations of the inadequacy of mere nature-worship and of the falsity of an empty ceremonialism. Here are expressed the momentous discoveries that the various gods of polytheistic belief are but numerous special manifestations of the One Power of the universe, and that the supreme object of worship is this variously revealed, partially elusive, all-comprehending unitary Reality. Still more momentous are the discernments that man is of more significance than all the forces of Nature; that man himself is the interpretation as well as the interpreter of Nature, because he is akin to the reality at the heart of the universe; indeed, that the One God, the great intelligent Person who is immanent in the universe, is to be found most directly in the heart of man. Here in the Upanishads are set forth, in concrete example as well as in dogmatic instruction, two opposing theories of life: an ignorant, narrow, selfish way of life which seeks temporary, unsatisfying, unreal ends; and a way of life which seeks to relate itself to the Supreme Reality of the universe, so as to escape from the needless misery of ordinary existence into undying bliss.

These important texts, the earliest of which can hardly

[1] According to the derivation of the word, they are 'sessions close to [a preceptor]'; in the actual usage of the Upanishads themselves, 'mystic teachings'. For various other meanings of the word, see the Sanskrit Index, s.v.

[2] For various modern estimates of the Upanishads, both in India and in the West, see the comments cited on pages 2–4 and in the Bibliography.

have taken form later than the seventh century B.C.,[1] are still attracting devoted readers, as they have during the past twenty-five centuries. The student of the history of philosophy who desires to know some of the earliest answers reached in India for the ever insistent problems of man and the universe and for the ideals of the highest existence; the special student of India who strives to understand the essence as well as the externals of its culture; the religious teacher and worker in East and West who seeks to apprehend the aspirations and spiritual ideals of the Hindu soul; the educated English-speaking Hindu who feels a special affection for, and interest in, the sacred writings of his native land; and the deep thinker who searches in arcane texts for clues to the solution of life's mysteries—all of these students will turn constantly to the Upanishads as an authoritative compendium of Indian metaphysical teachings. It has been my aim to prepare for such students and readers a faithful rendering of the original Sanskrit texts—a translation which will show exactly what the revered Upanishads say.

It is hardly necessary to dwell here on the difficulties and perplexities that confront anyone engaged on such a task; texts such as these are among the hardest to present adequately in another language, and a completely satisfying translation is wellnigh unattainable. I trust that I have succeeded at least in being literal without becoming cryptic, and in attaining clearness without exegetical accretions. Further remarks on the plan and arrangement of the translation will be found on subsequent pages (pp. xii–xiv).

In presenting this new version I would first pay due respect to Professor F. Max Müller, that eminent figure of an earlier generation of Sanskrit scholars, who, in volumes I and XV of the *Sacred Books of the East* (1879, 1884), published an English translation of twelve of the Upanishads. It is no unappreciative aspersion to assert that the same work can be done better now. Indeed, Max Müller himself predicted such improvement.[2]

[1] 'The earliest of them can hardly be dated later than 600 B.C.'—Macdonell, *History of Sanskrit Literature*, p 226.

[2] 'I have no doubt that future translators will find plenty of work to do.'

PREFACE

Among previous translators my indebtedness is greatest to the late Professor Paul Deussen, of the University of Kiel. No Western scholar has made a more thorough study of the Upanishads, both in themselves and in their relation to the wide field of Sanskrit philosophy. As a philosophical interpreter as well as an exact translator of the Upanishads, Deussen has no equal. I most gladly and gratefully acknowledge the help derived from constant reference to his German translation, *Sechzig Upanishad's des Veda*,[1] as well as the stimulus of personal association with him, many years ago, at his home in Kiel.

It is a pleasure to express here the debt of gratitude that I owe to Professor E. Washburn Hopkins, of Yale University. Under his supervision the introductory essay and part of the translation originally took form, and he has since been good enough to revise the entire work in manuscript. His instruction and encouragement have been of the greatest assistance, and many a passage has been clarified as a result of his helpful comments and constructive suggestions.

This volume has also had the benefit of the scholarship and technical skill of my friend Dr. George C. O. Haas, who not only revised the entire manuscript before it originally went to the printers, securing consistency of style and treatment and solving problems of typographical arrangement, but also saw both the first edition and the present one through the press. In the present edition he has enabled me to reprint as an appendix his very useful paper on 'Recurrent and Parallel Passages in the Principal Upanishads and the Bhagavad-Gītā'. For his generous assistance extending over a long series of years I feel deeply and sincerely grateful.

My thanks are due also to Mr. James Southgate, of the Department of Oriental Books and Manuscripts of the British Museum, who went through the Bibliography and furnished some corrections and additional titles.

(*Lectures on the Vedânta Philosophy*, p. 119.) 'Each one [of the previous translators] has contributed something, but there is still much left to be improved. In these studies everybody does the best he can; and scholars should never forget how easy it is to weed a field which has once been ploughed, and how difficult to plough unbroken soil.' (*Sacred Books of the East*, vol. 1, American ed., preface, p. f.)

[1] See the Bibliography, p. 464 below.

A word must be said, too, in appreciation of the unfailing courtesy and helpfulness of the Oxford University Press, whose patient co-operation in the production of both the first edition and the second deserves hearty recognition.

In conclusion I would add a reverent salutation to India, my native land, mother of more religions than have originated or flourished in any other country of the world. In the early years of childhood and later in the first period of adult service, it was the chief vernacular of the Bombay Presidency which furnished a medium, along with the English language, for intercourse with the wistful people of India, among whom are still many of my dearest friends. It has been a satisfaction that some part of the preparation of this book, begun in the West, could be carried on in the land that gave these Upanishads to the world. Many of the pages have been worked over in conjunction with native scholars in Calcutta, Lahore, and Bombay, and I wish to acknowledge especially the patient counsels of Mahâmahopâdhyâya Hara Prasâd Shâstri and some of his group of pandits.

It is a satisfaction to find that the call for the book has been sufficient to exhaust the first edition in a fairly brief period of years. The preparation of this second edition has given me an opportunity to make a number of trivial corrections, to add recent publications to the Bibliography, and to include, as an appendix, the list of recurrent and parallel passages compiled by Dr. George C. O. Haas.

May this volume, in its improved form, continue to serve as a means of bringing about a wider knowledge of the contents of these venerated texts and a discriminating appreciation of their sublime teachings!

ROBERT ERNEST HUME.

UNION THEOLOGICAL SEMINARY,
NEW YORK.
September 15, 1930.

CONTENTS

REMARKS CONCERNING THE TRANSLATION
ITS METHOD AND ARRANGEMENT

Principles observed in the translation

It has been the aim of the translator to prepare a rendering that represents, as faithfully as possible, the form and meaning of the Sanskrit text. A literal equivalent, even though lacking in fluency or grace of expression, has been preferred throughout to a fine phrase which less exactly reproduces the original. The version has been made in accordance with philological principles, with constant and comprehensive comparison of recurrent words and phrases, and due attention has been paid to the native commentaries as well as to the work of previous scholars in East and West.

The text on which it is based

The text of the Upanishads here translated may be said to be in fairly good condition, and the readings of the printed editions could in the main be followed. Occasional adoption of variants or conjectural emendations is mentioned and explained in the footnotes (as on pp. 207, 226, 455). In the Bṛihad-Āraṇyaka Upanishad the text of the Kāṇva recension has been used as the basis; some of the variations of the Mādhyaṁdina recension are noted at the foot of the page. In the Kaushītaki Upanishad the principal divergencies between the Bibliotheca Indica edition and that in the Ānandāśrama Series are set forth in the notes.

Order of the Upanishads in this volume

The traditional sequence of the ten principal Upanishads is that given in the following useful *versus memorialis*:—

īśā-kena-kaṭha-praśna-muṇḍa-māṇḍūkya-tittiri
aitareyaṁ ca chāndogyaṁ bṛhadāraṇyakaṁ tathā.[1]

In the present volume, which adds the Maitri Upanishad to the usual group of twelve, they are arranged in the presumable order of their original composition. Though the determination of this order is

[1] Muktikā Upanishad, 1. 30.

difficult and at best conjectural, yet a careful study of the style and contents of these texts points to a relative sequence nearly like that first formulated by Deussen.[1] The only departure in this volume from Deussen's order consists in placing the Svetasvatara in the later group with the Maitri, rather than in the earlier group before the Muṇḍaka.[2]

Treatment of metrical portions

Metrical portions of the text are indicated by the use of type of a smaller size and by an arrangement that suggests verse form to the eye. The meter of each stanza is shown by the width of the margin: a margin of moderate width denotes the 11-syllable *triṣṭubh*, whereas a wider margin denotes the familiar *śloka*, or 8-syllable *anuṣṭubh.* The number of lines accords with the number of verses in the original, and wherever possible the translation follows the text line for line. It has frequently been possible to attain in English the same number of syllables as in the Sanskrit, though no attempt has been made to produce a consistently metrical translation to the detriment of the sense.

Use of square brackets

Matter in square brackets is matter not actually expressed in the words of the Sanskrit text. It comprises—

(a) the English equivalent of a word or words omitted or to be understood in the Sanskrit (as at Ait, 4. 6, p. 300; Kaṭha 4.3, p. 354);

(b) words added by the translator to complete or improve the English grammatical structure (as at Chānd. 5. 3. 3, p. 230);

(c) explanations added by the translator to make clear the import of the passage (as at Praśna 5. 3–5, p. 388; Maitri 6. 14, p. 433).

Square brackets are used also to enclose the section number whenever a new section begins *within* a sentence, in order to shut off the section number from the regular flow of the thought (as at Tait. 1. 11. 3 and 4, p. 282).

[1] See Deussen, *Die Philosophie der Upanishad's*, pp. 22–25; English tr., pp. 22–26 (cf. the Bibliography, p. 503 below). See also Macdonell *History of Sanskrit Literature*, London, 1900, p. 226.

[2] See Hopkins, 'Notes on the Çvetāçvatara, etc.,' *JAOS.* 22 (1901), pp. 380-387, where he controverts Deussen on this very point.

CONCERNING THE TRANSLATION

Use of parentheses

Matter in parentheses is always identical in meaning with the preceding word or words. It comprises—

(a) translations or equivalents of proper names or other designations, as: 'the Golden Germ (Hiraṇyagarbha)';

(b) Sanskrit words in italics, immediately after their English translation as: 'peace (*śānti*).'

Parentheses are used also to enclose variant section numbers occurring in text editions other than those whose system of numbering is regularly followed in this work (as at Chānd. 6. 1. 4, p. 240).

Use of italics

Sanskrit words have been quoted freely in italics enclosed in parentheses—

(a) to aid the special student in his search for the exact shade of meaning by giving the original of which the word or phrase immediately preceding is a translation;

(b) to render evident to the eye the play on words or the etymological explanation that frequently occurs in the exposition or argumentation of the Upanishads (cf. Chānd. 1. 2. 10–12, p. 179).

Nouns and adjectives are usually given in their uninflected stem-form; occasionally, however, an inflected form is used for the sake of clearness (as at Chānd. 8. 3. 3, p. 265).

Transliteration of Sanskrit words

The transliteration of Sanskrit words *in italics* follows the current usage of Western Oriental scholars. In *roman type*, as part of the English translation, however, proper names (as of divinities, persons, texts, and ceremonies) are given in a slightly less technical transliteration, with some concession to popular usage; the vowel *ṛ* is represented by 'ṛi' (except in 'Rig', 'Rig-Veda'), and the sibilant *ṣ* by 'sh.'

Headings in heavy-face type

The headings in heavy-face type have been inserted by the translator to summarize the contents of the ensuing sections and to interpret, as far as possible in a few words, the development of thought in the text.

LIST OF ABBREVIATIONS

A . . . the recension of Kaush. published in the Ānandāśrama Sanskrit Series.
Ait. . . Aitareya Upanishad.
Ait. Br. . Aitareya Brāhmaṇa.
AJP. . *American Journal of Philology.*
Āśv. . . Āśvalāyana (Gṛihya Sūtra).
AV. . . Atharva-Veda.
AVTr. . Atharva-Veda Translation, by Whitney and Lanman, in the Harvard Oriental Series, vols. 7 and 8, Cambridge, Mass., 1905.
B . . . the recension of Kaush. published in the Bibliotheca Indica.
BhG. . . Bhagavad-Gītā.
BR. . . Böhtlingk and Roth's great Sanskrit Dictionary, 7 vols., St. Petersburg, 1855–1875.
Bṛih. . . Bṛihad-Āraṇyaka Upanishad.
BWb. . Böhtlingk's shorter Sanskrit Dictionary, 7 parts, St. Petersburg, 1879–1889.
C. . . . Calcutta edition of the Mahābhārata.
Chānd. . Chāndogya Upanishad.
com. . . commentator, commentators.
D. . . . Deussen, *Sechzig Upanishad's des Veda*, Leipzig, 1897 (second edition, 1905; reprinted 1921).
ed. . . edited, edition.
JAOS. . *Journal of the American Oriental Society.*
K . . Kāṇva recension of Bṛih.
Kaush. . Kaushītaki Upanishad.
l.c. . . (*loco citato*), at the place cited.
M . . . Mādhyaṁdina recension of Bṛih. [= Śat. Br. 10. 6. 4–5; 14. 4–9], ed. and tr. O. Böhtlingk, St. Petersburg, 1889.
MBh. . Mahābhārata.
Mahānār. Mahānārāyaṇa Upanishad.
Māṇḍ. . Māṇḍūkya Upanishad.
MS. . . Maitrāyaṇī Saṁhitā.

LIST OF ABBREVIATIONS

Muṇḍ. .	Muṇḍaka Upanishad.
MW. .	Monier-Williams's Sanskrit Dictionary, 2d edition, Oxford, 1899.
Pār. . .	Pāraskara (Gṛihya Sūtra).
RV. . .	Rig-Veda.
Śat. Br. .	Śatapatha Brāhmaṇa.
SBE. .	*Sacred Books of the East.*
SV. . .	Sāma-Veda.
s.v. . .	(*sub verbo*), under the word.
Śvet. . .	Śvetāśvatara Upanishad.
TA. . .	Taittirīya Āraṇyaka.
Tait. . .	Taittirīya Upanishad.
tr. . . .	translated, translation.
TS. . .	Taittirīya Saṁhitā.
VS. . .	Vājasaneyi Saṁhitā.
ZDMG. .	*Zeitschrift der Deutschen Morgenländischen Gesellschaft.*

AN OUTLINE OF THE PHILOSOPHY OF THE UPANISHADS

CHAPTER I

THE PLACE OF THE UPANISHADS IN THE HISTORY OF PHILOSOPHY

ALMOST contemporaneous with that remarkable period of active philosophic and religious thought the world over, about the sixth century B.C., when Pythagoras, Confucius, Buddha, and Zoroaster were promulgating new philosophies and inaugurating great religions, there was taking place, in the land of India, a quiet philosophic movement which has exercised a continuous influence upon the entire subsequent thought of that country and which has also made itself felt in the West.

The early Aryan invaders of Hindustan, after having conquered the territory and gained an undisputed foothold, betook themselves to the consideration of those mighty problems which thrust themselves upon every serious and thoughtful person—the problems of the meaning of life and the world and of the relation of the individual to the great unseen forces of the universe. They sought earnestly for a satisfactory solution of these profound questions. Thus we read in the Śvetāśvatara Upanishad (I. 1):—

'What is the cause? Brahma? Whence are we born?
Whereby do we live? And on what are we established?
Overruled by whom, in pains and pleasures,
Do we live our various conditions, O ye theologians?'

In a seemingly childlike manner, like the early Greek cosmologists, they advanced now one thing and now another as an image of the primary material out of which the whole world is made. Yet, again like the early Greek philosophers and also with the subtlety of genuine philosophic insight, they were always aware of the underlying unity of all being. Out of this penetrating intuition those early Indian thinkers elaborated a system of intelligent monism which has been accepted as most illuminating and inherently true by their descendants throughout the centuries. If there is any one intellectual tenet which, explicitly or implicitly, is held by the people of India, furnishing a fundamental presupposition of all their thinking, it is this doctrine of universal immanence, of an intelligent monism.

The Upanishads are the first recorded attempts of the Hindus at systematic philosophizing. These ancient documents constitute the earliest written presentation of their efforts to construe the world of experience as a rational whole. Furthermore, they have continued to be the generally accepted authoritative statements with which every subsequent orthodox philosophic formulation has had to show itself in accord, or at least not in discord. Even the materialistic Cārvākas, who denied the Vedas, a future life, and almost every sacred doctrine of the orthodox Brahmans, avowed respect for these Upanishads. That interesting later epitome of the Vedānta, the Vedānta-sāra,[1] shows how these Cārvākas and the adherents of the Buddhistic theory and also of the ritualistic Pūrva-mīmāṁsā and of the logical Nyāya appealed to the Upanishads in support of their varying theories. Even the dualistic Sāṁkhya philosophers claimed to find scripture authority in the Upanishads.[2] For the orthodox Vedānta, of course, the Upanishads, with Bādarāyana's Vedānta-Sūtras and Śaṅkara's Commentary on them, have been the very text-books.

Not only have they been thus of historical importance in the past development of philosophy in India, but they are of present-day influence. 'To every Indian Brahman today the Upanishads are what the New Testament is to the Christian.'[3] Max Müller calls attention to the fact that more new editions of the Upanishads and Śaṅkara are being published in India

[1] Translated by Col. Jacob in his *Manual of Hindu Pantheism*, London, 1891, pp. 76–78. Text published by him in Bombay, 1894, and by Bohtlingk in his *Sanskrit-Chrestomathie*.

[2] See the Sarva-darśana-saṁgraha, a later summary of the various philosophers, translated by Cowell and Gough, p. 227 (2nd ed., London, 1894).

[3] Deussen, *The Philosophy of the Upanishads*, tr. by Geden, p. viii, Edinburgh, 1906.

than of Descartes and Spinoza in Europe.[1] Especially now, in the generally admitted inadequacy of the degraded form of popular Hinduism, the educated Hindus are turning to their old Scriptures and are finding there much which they confidently stake against the claims of superiority of any foreign religion or philosophy. It is noteworthy that the significant movement indicated by the reforming and theistic Samājas of modern times was inaugurated by one who was the first Hindu to prepare an English translation of the Upanishads. Rammohun Roy expected to restore Hinduism to its pristine purity and superiority through a resuscitation of Upanishadic philosophy with an infusion of certain eclectic elements.

They have also been taken up by the theosophists, who recognize in them the sources of deep mystic knowledge and look upon this group of texts 'as a world-scripture, that is to say, a scripture appealing to the lovers of religion and truth in all races and at all times, without distinction.'[2] And occultists of many lands find in these treatises numerous hints of things hidden from ordinary sight and clues to progress on the pathway of spiritual attainment.

Not only have the Upanishads thus furnished the regnant philosophy for India from their date up to the present time and proved illuminating to mystics outside of India, but their philosophy presents many interesting parallels and contrasts to the elaborate philosophizings of Western lands. And Western professional students of philosophy, as well as literary historians, have felt and expressed the importance of the Upanishads. In the case of Arthur Schopenhauer, the chief of modern pantheists of the West, his philosophy is unmistakably transfused with the doctrines expounded in the Upanishads, a fact that might be surmised from his oft-quoted eulogy: 'It [i.e. Anquetil du Perron's Latin translation of a Persian rendering of the Upanishads] is the most rewarding and the most elevating reading which (with the exception of

[1] Max Müller, *Lectures on the Vedânta Philosophy*, p. 39.

[2] *The Upanishads*, by Mead and Chaṭṭopādhyāya, p. 5, London, Theosophical Publishing Society, 1896. See also *The Theosophy of the Upanishads* (anonymous), London, Theosophical Publishing Society, 1896, and *The Upanishads with Śankara's Commentary*, a translation made by several Hindus, published by V. C. Seshacharri, Madras, 1898.

the original text) there can possibly be in the world. It has been the solace of my life and will be of my death.' [1]

Professor Deussen, the late professor of philosophy in the University of Kiel (Germany), always regarded his thorough study of the Upanishads and of the Vedānta philosophy as a reward in itself, apart from the satisfaction of contributing so largely to our understanding of its teachings. For in the Upanishads he found Parmenides, Plato, and Kant in a nutshell, and on leaving India in 1893, in an address before the Bombay Branch of the Royal Asiatic Society,[2] he gave it as his parting advice that 'the Vedānta, in its unfalsified form, is the strongest support of pure morality, is the greatest consolation in the sufferings of life and death. Indians, keep to it!'

Professor Royce of Harvard University deemed the philosophy of the Upanishads sufficiently important to expound it in his Gifford Lectures,[3] before the University of Aberdeen, and to introduce some original translations especially made by his colleague Professor Lanman.

The Upanishads undoubtedly have great historical and comparative value, but they are also of great present-day importance. No one can thoroughly understand the workings and conclusions of the mind of an educated Hindu of today who does not know something of the fountain from which his ancestors for centuries past have drunk, and from which he too has been deriving his intellectual life. The imagery under which his philosophy is conceived, the phraseology in which it is couched, and the analogies by which it is supported are largely the same in the discussions of today as are found in the Upanishads and in Śaṅkara's commentaries on them and on the Sūtras. Furthermore, although some elements are evidently of local interest and of past value, it is evident that the monism of the Upanishads has exerted and will continue to exert an influence on the monism of the West, for it contains certain elements which penetrate deeply into the truths

[1] *Parerga*, 2, § 185 (*Werke*, 6. 427).

[2] Printed as a pamphlet, Bombay, 1893, and also contained in his *Elements of Metaphysics*, English translation, p. 337, London, 1894.

[3] Royce, *The World and the Individual*, 1. 156–175, New York, 1900.

which every philosopher must reach in a thoroughly grounded explanation of experience.

The intelligent and sympathetic discrimination of these elements will constitute a philosophic work of the first importance. As a preliminary step to that end, the mass of unorganized material contained in the Upanishads has been culled and the salient ideas here arranged in the following outline.

CHAPTER II

THE UPANISHADS AND THEIR PLACE IN INDIAN PHILOSOPHY

THE older Upanishads are religious and philosophical treatises, forming part of the early Indian Vedas.[1] The preceding portions are the Mantras, or Hymns to the Vedic gods, and the Brāhmaṇas, or directories on and explanations of the sacrificial ritual. Accordingly these three divisions of the Śruti, or 'Revelation,' may be roughly characterized as the utterances successively of poet, priest, and philosopher. The distinction, of course, is not strictly exclusive; for the Upanishads, being integral parts of the Brāhmaṇas,[2] are continuations of the sacrificial rules and discussions, but they pass over into philosophical considerations. Much that is in the Upanishads, particularly in the Bṛihad-Āraṇyaka and in the Chāndogya, might more properly be included in the Brāhmaṇa portion, and some that is in the Brāhmaṇas is Upanishadic in character. The two groups are closely interwoven.

[1] 'That which is hidden in the secret of the Vedas, even the Upanishads.'—Śvetāśvatara Upanishad 5. 6.

[2] Technically, the older Upanishads (with the exception of the Īśā, which is the last chapter of the Saṁhitā of the White Yajur-Veda) form part of the Āraṇyakas, 'Forest Books,' which in turn are part of the Brāhmaṇas, the second part of the Vedas.

Later a distinct class of independent Upanishads arose, but even of several of the classical Upanishads the connection with the Brāhmaṇas has been lost. Only the thirteen oldest Upanishads, which might be called classical, have been translated in this volume and are here discussed.

This fact, along with the general lack of data in Sanskrit literature for chronological orientation, makes it impossible to fix any definite dates for the Upanishads. The Śatapatha Brāhmaṇa, of which the Bṛihad-Āraṇyaka Upanishad forms the conclusion, is believed to contain material that comes down to 300 B. C. The Upanishads themselves contain several references to writings which undoubtedly are much later than the beginnings of the Upanishads. The best that can be done is to base conjectures upon the general aspect of the contents compared with what may be supposed to precede and to succeed. The usual date that is thus assigned to the Upanishads is around 600 B. C., just prior to the rise of Buddhism.

Yet evidences of Buddhist influences are not wanting in them. In Bṛih. 3. 2. 13 it is stated that after death the different parts of a person return to the different parts of Nature from whence they came, that even his soul (*ātman*) goes into space and that only his *karma*, or effect of work, remains over. This is out and out the Buddhist doctrine. Connections in the point of dialect may also be shown. *Sarvāvat* is 'a word which as yet has not been discovered in the whole range of Sanskrit literature, except in Śatapatha Brāhmaṇa 14. 7. 1. 10 [= Bṛih. 4. 3. 9] and in Northern Buddhist writings.'[1] Its Pāli equivalent is *sabbāvā*. In Bṛih. 4. 3. 2–6 *r* is changed to *l*, i. e. *paly-ayate* for *pary-ayate*—a change which is regularly made in the Pāli dialect in which the books of Southern Buddhism are written. It may be that this is not a direct influence of the Pāli upon the Sanskrit, but at least it is the same tendency which exhibits itself in Pāli, and here the two languages are close enough together to warrant the assumption of contact and synchronous origin. Somewhat surer evidence, however, is the use of the second person plural ending *tha* for *ta*. Müller pointed out in connection with the word *ācaratha* (Muṇḍ. 1. 2. 1) that this irregularity looks suspiciously Buddhistic. There are, however, four other similar instances. The word *saṃvatsyatha* (Praśna 1. 2) might be explained as a future indicative (not an imperative), serving as a mild future imperative. But *pṛcchatha* (Praśna 1. 2), *āpadyatha* (Praśna 2. 3), and *jānatha* and *vimuñcatha* (Muṇḍ. 2. 2. 5) are evidently meant

[1] Kern, *SBE.* 21, p. xvii.

as imperatives, and as such are formed with the Pāli instead of with the regular Sanskrit ending. It has long been suspected that the later Śiva sects, which recognized the Atharva-Veda as their chief scripture, were closely connected with the Buddhistic sects. Perhaps in this way the Buddhistic influence [1] was transmitted to the Praśna and Muṇḍaka Upanishads of the Atharva-Veda.

This shows that the Upanishads are not unaffected by outside influences. Even irrespective of these, their inner structure reveals that they are heterogeneous in their material and compound in their composition. The Bṛihad-Āraṇyaka, for instance, is composed of three divisions, each of which is concluded, as if it were a complete whole, by a *vaṁśa,* or genealogy of the doctrine (that is, a list of teachers through whom the doctrine there taught had originally been received from Brahma and handed down to the time of writing). The first section, entitled 'The Honey Section,' contains a dialogue between Yājñavalkya and Maitreyī which is almost verbally repeated in the second section, called 'The Yājñavalkya Section.' It seems quite evident that these two pieces could not have been parts of one continuous writing, but that they were parts of two separate works which were mechanically united and then connected with the third section, whose title, 'Supplementary Section,' is in accord with the heterogeneous nature of its contents.

Both the Bṛihad-Āraṇyaka and the Chandogya are very composite in character. Disconnected explanations of the sacrificial ritual, legends, dialogues, etymologizings (which now appear absurd, but which originally were regarded as important explanations),[2] sayings, philosophical disquisitions, and so forth are, in the main, merely mechanically juxtaposed. In the shorter and later Upanishads there is not room for such a collection ; but in them, more and more, quotations from the earlier Upanishads and from the Vedas are inserted. Many of these can be recognized as such. There are also certain passages, especially in the Kaṭha and Śvetāśvatara, which,

[1] See on this point the interesting testimony adduced by Foucher, *Étude sur l'iconographie bouddhique de l'Inde,* Paris, 1900.

[2] Such as Bṛih. 1. 2. 7 ; 1. 3. 22 ; 1. 4. 1 ; 3. 9. 8–9 ; Chānd. 1. 2. 10–12 ; 6. 8. 1.

though not referable, are evidently quotations, since they are not grammatically construable in the sentence, but contain a thought which seems to be commented upon in the words immediately following.

Not only are the Upanishads thus heterogeneous in point of structure, but they also contain passages which set forth the dualistic Sāṁkhya philosophy, which has been the chief antithesis of the monistic Vedānta. Of the earlier Upanishads the Chāndogya, in 6. 4, explains all existing objects as a composition of three elements, a reduction which has an analogue in the Sāṁkhya with its three qualities. In Kaṭha 4. 7, the *prakṛti* or 'Nature' of the Sāṁkhya is described. In Kaṭha 3. 10–13, and similarly in 6. 7–8, there is a gradation of psychical principles in the order of their emanation from the Unmanifest (*avyakta*) which agrees closely with the Sāṁkhya order; but a difference is added when that Unmanifest, instead of being left as the ultimate, is subordinated to the Person of the world-ground. Somewhat similar are the genealogies of Muṇḍ. 1. 1. 8; 2. 1. 3; and Praśna 6. 4. In Praśna 4. 8 is a combined Sāṁkhya and Vedānta list, the major part of which, up to *citta*, 'thought and what can be thought,' is Sāṁkhyan. The term *buddhi*, 'intellect,' is an important Sāṁkhyan word. It is noticeable that it does not occur until the Kaṭha, where other Sāṁkhyan similarities are first prominent and where this word is found four times.

In the Śvetāśvatara the Sāṁkhya is mentioned by name in the last chapter, and the statement is made that it reasons in search of the same object as is there being expounded. The references in this Upanishad to the Sāṁkhya are unmistakable. The enumerations of 1. 4–5 are distinctly non-Vedāntic and quite Sāṁkhyan. The passage at 6. 1, where *svabhāva*, 'the nature of things,' evidently means *prakṛti*, the 'Nature' of the Sāṁkhya, denounces that theory as the utterance of deluded men. Similarly 1. 3 contradicts the Sāṁkhyan doctrine in placing the *guṇas*, or 'qualities,' in God and in attributing to him 'self-power.' But more numerous are the instances where the Vedānta theory is interpreted in Sāṁkhyan terms, as in 4. 10, where the *prakṛti* of the Sāṁkhya is identified with the *māyā* of the Vedānta. The passage 4. 5, where the explanation of experience is sensually analogized, is thoroughly Sāṁkhyan. The relation of the Vedānta to the Sāṁkhya has not yet been satisfactorily made out. Perhaps, as Professor Cowell maintained,[1] 'the Śvetāśvatara Upanishad is the most direct attempt to reconcile the Sāṁkhya and the Vedānta.' The Maitri is even more evidently pervaded by Sāṁkhyan influences, especially the explicit references to the *guṇas*, or 'qualities,' with the enumeration of their effects (3. 5) and the explanation of their origin (5. 2).

Even with due allowance made for a supposititious period when the terms of philosophy may have existed without distinction of systems, such as are known afterwards as Vedānta and Sāṁkhya, it is nevertheless improbable that so complete a Sāṁkhyan vocabulary as meets us in the Śvetāśvatara and the Maitri Upanishads could belong to such a period. They seem rather to belong to a period when systems were not only recognized as such, but as antithetic.

These remarks have made it clear that the Upanishads are no homogeneous products, cogently presenting a philosophic theory, but that they are compilations from different sources recording the 'guesses at truth' of the early Indians. A single, well articulated system cannot be deduced from them; but underlying all their expatiations, apparent inconsistencies, and unordered matter there is a general basis of a developing monism which will now be placed in exposition.

CHAPTER III

FIRST ATTEMPTS AT THE CONCEPTION OF A UNITARY WORLD GROUND

AMONG the early Indians, as among the early Greeks, an explanation of the beginnings of the world, its original substance, and its construction, formed the first and most interesting subject of philosophical speculation. In the Vedas such speculation had gone on to some extent and had produced the

[1] In his notes to Colebrooke's *Miscellaneous Essays*, 1. 257, London, 1873. But see more especially Professor Hopkins, *JAOS.* 22. 380–387.

famous Creation Hymn, RV. 10. 129, as well as others (such as RV. 10. 121; 10. 81; 10. 72; 10. 90) in which the origin of the world was pictured under architectural, generative, and sacrificial analogies. In the Brāhmaṇas speculation continued further along the same lines. When the period of the Upanishads arrived, the same theme had not grown old—and when will it? The quotation from Śvet. 1. 1 already cited (page 1) shows how this theme was still discussed and indicates the alternatives that were offered late in the period. But among the early Upanishads these first cosmogonic theories had not yet been superseded.

Prominent among these is one which was advanced among the early Greeks by Thales and which was also a widely prevailing Semitic idea, namely, that the original stuff of the world was Water. Thus in Bṛih. 5. 5 we find it stated that 'in the beginning this world was just Water.' 'It is just Water solidified that is this earth, that is the atmosphere, that is the sky, that is gods and men, that is animals and birds, grass and trees, beasts, together with worms, flies, and ants; all these are just Water solidified' (Chānd. 7. 10. 1). Gārgī in Bṛih. 3. 6. 1 opens a discussion with the philosopher Yājña-valkya by asking for an explanation of the popular theory that 'all this world is woven, warp and woof, on water.'

In the later Kaṭha a more philosophic theory of the world-ground was added on to this older theory that water was the primal entity: '[Ātman], who was born of old from the waters' (4. 6). Somewhat similar combinations of the earlier and later theories are made in Ait. 1. 1. 3, where Atman, after creating the waters, 'from the waters drew forth and shaped a person,' from whose members the different parts of the world and of man emanated; and in Kaush. 1. 7, where Brahma declares 'the waters, verily, indeed, are my world.'

In a little more philosophic fashion Space also was posited as the ultimate ground of the world. At Chānd. 1. 8–9 three men are represented as having a discussion over the origin (or 'what it goes to,' *gati*) of the Sāman, 'Chant,' of the sacrificial ritual. One of the group traced it back to sound, to breath, to food, to water, to yonder world. When pressed as to what 'yonder world goes back to,' he replied: 'One should not lead beyond the heavenly world. We establish the Sāman upon the heavenly world, for the Sāman is praised as heaven.' The second member of the group taunted the first that his Sāman had no foundation, and when challenged himself to declare the origin of that world, replied 'this world'; but he was immediately brought to the limit of his knowledge as regards the origin of this world. 'One should not lead beyond the world-support. We establish the Sāman upon the world as a support, for the Sāman is praised as a support.' Then the third member put in his taunt: 'Your Sāman comes to an end,' said he. It is noticeable that he, who was the only one of the three not a Brahman, or professional philosopher, was able to explain: 'Verily, all things here arise out of space. They disappear back into space, for space alone is greater than these; space is the final goal.'

With still greater abstraction the origin of the world is traced back, as in the early Greek speculations and as in RV. 10. 72. 2–3 and AV. 17. 1. 19, to Non-being (*a-sad*).

> 'In the beginning, verily, this [world] was non-existent.
> Therefrom, verily, Being was produced.' (Tait. 2. 7.)

In Chānd. 3. 19 the same theory is combined with another theory, which is found among the Greeks and which was popular among the Indians, continuing even after the time of Manu, namely, that of the cosmic egg. 'In the beginning this world was merely non-being (*a-sad*). It was existent. It developed. It turned into an egg. It lay for the period of a year. It was split asunder. One of the two eggshell-parts became silver, one gold. That which was of silver is this earth. That which was of gold is the sky. What was the outer membrane is the mountains. What was the inner membrane is cloud and mist. What were the veins are the rivers. What was the fluid within is the ocean.'

This theory of the Rig-Veda, of the Atharva-Veda, of the Taittirīya, and of the early part of the Chāndogya is expressly referred to and combated at Chānd. 6. 2. 'In the beginning, my dear, this world was just Being, one only, without a second. To be sure, some people say: "In the beginning this world was just Non-being, one only, without a second; from that

Non-being Being was produced." But verily, my dear, whence could this be? How from Non-being could Being be produced? On the contrary, my dear, in the beginning this world was Being, one only, without a second. It bethought itself: "Would that I were many! Let me procreate myself!" It emitted heat.' Similarly the heat procreated water, and the water food. Out of these three elements, after they had been infused by the original existent with name and form (i. e. a principle of individuation), all physical objects and also the organic and psychical nature of man were composed.

Still more abstract than the space-theory, but connected with it, is the cosmological speculation offered by Yājñavalkya to Gārgī, who confronted him with two supposedly unanswerable questions. 'That which is above the sky, that which is beneath the earth, that which is between these two, sky and earth, that which people call the past and the present and the future —across what is that woven, warp and woof?' 'Across space,' was Yājñavalkya's reply. 'Across what then, pray, is space woven?' 'That, O Gārgī, Brahmans call the Imperishable,' answers Yājñavalkya, but he does not attempt to describe this, since it is beyond all earthly distinctions. However, with a directness and a grand simplicity that call to mind the Hebrew account of the creation by the mandatory word of the Divine Being, there follows an account of the governances of the world by that world-ground. 'Verily, O Gārgī, at the command of that Imperishable the sun and moon stand apart. Verily, O Gārgī, at the command of that Imperishable the earth and the sky stand apart. Verily, O Gārgī, at the command of that Imperishable the moments, the hours, the days, the nights, the fortnights, the months, the seasons, and the years stand apart. Verily, O Gārgī, at the command of that Imperishable some rivers flow from the snowy mountains to the east, others to the west, in whatever direction each flows' (Bṛih. 3. 8. 3–9).

These searchings for the origin and explanation of the world of phenomena, first in a phenomenal entity like water and space, and then in a super-phenomenal entity like non-being, being, or the Imperishable, had even in the Rig- and Atharva-

Vedas reached the conception of a necessarily unitary basis of the world and even the beginnings of monism. Thus:—

'Brahmanaspati like a smith
Did forge together all things here.' (RV. 10. 72. 2.)

Viśvakarman (literally, the 'All-maker'), the one God, established all things (RV. 10. 81). From the sacrificial dismemberment of Purusha, the World-Person, all things were formed (RV. 10. 90). Again, in RV. 10. 121. 1:—

'In the beginning arose Hiraṇyagarbha,
The earth's begetter, who created heaven.'

So also in RV. 10. 129. 1, 2, the Creation Hymn: –

'There was then neither being nor non-being. . . .
Without breath breathed by its own power That One.'

So also RV. 1. 164. 6:—

'I, unknowing, ignorant, here
Ask the wise sages for the sake of knowledge:
What was That One, in the form of the unborn,
Who established these six worlds?'

A glimpse into monism is seen in RV. 1. 164. 46:—

'Him who is the One existent, sages name variously.'

Various, indeed, were the conjectures regarding the world-ground. Four—Brahmaṇaspati, Viśvakarman, Purusha, and Hiraṇyagarbha—besides the indefinite That One, have just been cited from the Rig-Veda. Another, Prajāpati (literally 'Lord of creatures') began to rise towards the end of the Vedic period, increased in prominence through the Brahmanic, and continued on into the Upanishadic. But the conception which is the ground-work of the Vedānta, which overthrew or absorbed into itself all other conceptions of the world-ground, was that of Brahma. Emerging in the Brāhmaṇas, it obtained in the Upanishads a fundamental position which it never lost. Indeed, the philosophy of the Upanishads is sometimes called Brahma-ism from its central concept.

PHILOSOPHY OF THE UPANISHADS

CHAPTER IV

THE DEVELOPMENT OF THE CONCEPTION OF BRAHMA

As the early cosmologies started with one thing and another, but always one particular thing, posited as the primal entity, so in Bṛih. 1. 4. 10–11 and again in Maitri 6. 17 we find the statement: 'Verily, in the beginning this world was Brahma.' And as in the old cosmologies, especially in the Rig-Veda and in the Brāhmaṇas, so also in the Upanishads procreation was adopted as the specific analogy for world-production. Thus: 'He desired: "Would that I were many! Let me procreate myself!" He performed austerity. Having performed austerity, he created this whole world, whatever there is here' (Tait. 2. 6). It should be noticed that consciousness, which was absent in the water- and space-cosmologies, is here posited for the production of the world; also that the creation of the world, as in the Purusha Hymn, RV. 10. 90, and all through the Brāhmaṇas, is an act of religious significance accompanied by ceremonial rites.

This last fact is not unnatural when the situation is considered. Every undertaking of importance had to be preceded by sacrifices and austerities in order to render it auspicious. The greater the importance of the affair, such as beginning a war or going on a journey, the greater was the need of abundant sacrifice. And if sacrifice was so essential and efficacious for human affairs, would it not be equally necessary and efficacious for so enormous an undertaking as the creation of the world?

These considerations probably had the greater weight in view of the meaning and historical importance of the word *brahma*, which now and henceforth was to be employed as the designation of the world-ground.

In the Rig-Veda *brahma* seems to have meant first 'hymn,' 'prayer,' 'sacred knowledge,' 'magic formula.' In this very sense it is used in the Upanishads, e.g. Tait. 3. 10. 4, as well as in compounds such as *brahmavat*, 'possessed of magic formulas,' and *brahma-varcasa*, 'superiority in sacred knowledge.' It also signified the power that was inherent in the hymns, prayers, sacred formulas, and sacred knowledge. This latter meaning it was that induced the application of the word to the world-ground—a power that created and pervaded and upheld the totality of the universe.

Yet how difficult it was to preserve the penetrating philosophical insight which discerned that efficiency, that power, that *brahma* underlying the world—an insight which dared to take the word from its religious connection and to infuse into it a philosophical connotation—will be shown in the recorded attempts to grasp that stupendous idea, all of which fell back, because of figurative thinking, into the old cosmologies which this very Brahma-theory itself was intended to transcend.

The unknown character of this newly discovered Being and the idea that only by its will do even the gods perform their functions, is indicated in a legend contained in the Kena Upanishad. Brahma appeared to the gods, but they did not understand who it was. They deputed Agni, the god of fire, to ascertain its identity. He, vaunting of his power to burn, was challenged to burn a straw, but was baffled. Upon his unsuccessful return to the gods, Vāyu, the god of wind, was sent on the same mission. He, boasting of his power to blow anything away, was likewise challenged to blow a straw away and was likewise baffled. To Indra, the next emissary, a beautiful woman, allegorized by the commentator as Wisdom, explained that the incognito was Brahma, through whose power the gods were exalted and enjoyed greatness.

In Bṛih. 3. 9. 1–9 Yājñavalkya was pressed and further pressed by Śākalya to state the real number of the gods. Unwillingly he reduced, in seven steps, the popular number of 3306 gods to one, and that one was Brahma, the only God.

But apart from legend and apart from religion it was difficult for the ordinary person to understand who or what this Brahma was.

Gārgī, one of the two women in the Upanishads who philosophize, takes up the old water-cosmology and asks Yājñavalkya, the most prominent philosopher of the Upanishads (Bṛih. 3. 6): 'On what, pray, is the water woven, warp and woof?' He replies, 'The atmosphere-worlds.' On being asked again, 'On what then, pray, are the atmosphere-worlds woven, warp and woof?' he says, 'The Gandharva-world [or world of spirits].' The regressus has been entered, and Yājñavalkya plays somewhat the part of an early protagonist to Locke's 'Indian [i.e. American Indian] philosopher' with his tortoise, and elephant, and so forth, as the world's last standing-ground. Here he takes Gārgī back to the worlds of the sun upon which the Gandharva-worlds are woven, and then in turn to the worlds of the moon, the worlds of the stars, the worlds of the gods, the worlds of Indra, the worlds of Prajāpati, the worlds of Brahma. 'On what then, pray, are the worlds of Brahma woven, warp and woof?' 'Gārgī, do not question too much, lest your head fall off. In truth you are questioning too much about a divinity about which further questions cannot be asked. Gārgī, do not over-question.' Thereupon Gārgī ceased to question.

It is a remnant of the old space-cosmology joined with the Brahma-theory when in Bṛih. 5. 1 it is stated that 'Brahma is ether—the ether primeval, the ether that blows.' A little more is added when it is said that 'Brahma is life. Brahma is joy. Brahma is the void' (Chānd. 4. 10. 5). The abundance and variousness of being in that world-ground which must also be the ground of the physical and of the mental life of persons is approached in Tait. 3, where the instruction is successively given that Brahma is food, breath, mind, understanding, and bliss, since out of each of those, as from the world-ground, things are born, by those they live, unto those they enter on departing hence.

There are four other passages where attempts are expressly made to define Brahma.

In Bṛih. 2. 1 the renowned Brahman Gārgya Bālāki came to Ajātaśatru, king of Benares, and volunteered to tell him of Brahma. The wealthy king, in emulation of the lavish Janaka, offered a thousand cows for such an exposition. Gārgya explained that he venerated the person in the sun as Brahma. 'Talk not to me about such a Brahma,' Ajātaśatru protested. He venerated as Brahma the Supreme Head and King of all beings. Then Gārgya said that he also venerated the person in the moon as Brahma. Ajātaśatru again protested against the inadequacy of such a conception of Brahma. He venerated It as the great white-robed king Soma (i.e. the person vivifying the moon). Again Gārgya gave another definition of Brahma, namely, as the person in the lightning; and again Ajātaśatru condemned his statement as inadequate by declaring that he venerated as Brahma the Brilliant One, the principle of brilliancy, not only in the lightning but in all brilliant things. So the two converse back and forth, Gārgya successively giving new definitions and Ajātaśatru declaring their inadequacy with a broader conception which included and went beyond Gārgya's, and at the same time deducing a practical benefit to any who held such a conception. Gārgya's conception of Brahma as the person in space was supplemented by the conception of Brahma as the Full, the non-active; the person in the wind, by Indra, the terrible, and the unconquered army; the person in the fire, by the Vanquisher; the person in water, by the Counterpart (of all phenomenal objects); the person in the mirror, by the Shining One; the sound which follows after one, by Life; the person in the quarters of heaven, by the Inseparable Companion; the person consisting of shadow, by Death; the person in the body, by the Embodied One—in all, twelve[1] conceptions of Brahma, which exhaust Gārgya Bālāki's speculation on the subject. He, the challenger, the professional philosopher, then requests instruction from his vanquisher, who, it may be noticed again, was not a Brahman, but a Kshatriya (i.e. a man belonging to the second caste). Ajātaśatru called attention to the anomaly of a Brahman's coming to a Kshatriya for instruction, but consented to make him know clearly this comparatively new and not fully comprehended conception of Brahma. 'He, verily, O Bālāki, who is the maker of all these persons [whom you have mentioned in succession], of whom,

[1] In Kaush. 4, which is evidently another version of the same dialogue, there are sixteen conceptions, 'the person in the quarters of heaven' being omitted from the Bṛihad-Āraṇyaka list and there being added the person in thunder, in the echo, the conscious self by whom a sleeping person moves about in dreams, the person in the right eye, and the person in the left eye—conceptions which are supplemented respectively by the soul of sound, the inseparable companion, Yama (king of the dead), the soul of name, of fire, of light, and the soul of truth, of lightning, of splendor.

verily, this is the work—he, verily, should be known' (Kaush. 4.19). With the illustration at hand of a man awaking from sleep, Ajātaśatru shows that finally Brahma is to be conceived of as that into which one goes to sleep and from which one wakes again. The conclusion is: 'As a spider might come out with his thread, as small sparks come forth from the fire, even so from this Soul come forth all vital energies, all worlds, all gods, all beings. The mystic meaning (*upaniṣad*) thereof is "the Real of the real"' (Bṛih. 2. 1. 20).

This is the most important passage, for it is the first in the Upanishads where the conception of Brahma is subjected to a regressive analysis leading to a conclusion which obtains throughout the remainder of the Upanishads, except as it is further supplemented. In it the following points are to be noticed. The old cosmologies, according to which the world-ground was to be discovered in some particular phenomenal object or substance, are still clung to insofar as Brahma, the newly postulated world-ground, is to be found in one and another individual object, such as the sun, the moon, lightning, space, fire, water, and so forth; they are transcended, however, insofar as those objects are not regarded as themselves of the stuff out of which the world was fashioned, but are looked upon only as a habitation of the world-ground, which is also a person, locally lodged. Such a conception of the first disputant is corrected by the second's pointing out that the world-ground cannot be the substrate of only certain particular phenomena; that the several principles must be referred back to a single one, 'who is the maker of these persons, of whom this [universe] is the work' (Kaush. 4. 19), and (more important still) that if one would come close to the apprehension of this world-ground, it is chiefly to be known as the upholder of his own psychical existence through the period of sleep; that it is a Soul (*Ātman*) and that this Soul is the source of all existing things, vital energies, worlds, gods, all beings, which are actual, to be sure, but actual only because It is their Real.

A very great advance in the conception of the world-ground is here made, and a doctrine is reached of which most of the later dialogues are further explications. There are two other dialogues, however, which by a similar succession of definitions and corrections arrive at the same fundamental conception of Brahma.

In Bṛih. 4. 1–2 Janaka, at Yājñavalkya's request, states the various philosophical theories that have been propounded to him. Six different conceptions of Brahma, taught by different teachers, are thus elicited. First, that Brahma is speech. This was self-evident, replied Yājñavalkya, but it was saying no more than that one had a mother, or a father, or a teacher; without explaining the seat and support of speech, such a Brahma was one-legged. Yājñavalkya then supplied the deficiency by explaining that its seat was speech, its support space, and it should be reverenced as intelligence, for by speech all things were known. Similarly, the theory that Brahma was breath was approved as true, but condemned as inadequate, and supplemented by the explanation that breath was its seat, space its support, and it should be reverenced as dear, since the breath of life is dear. So Brahma is sight, the eye its seat, space its support; and it should be reverenced as truthfulness, since the eyes see truly. Brahma is hearing, the ear its seat, space its support; and it should be reverenced as the endless, for the quarters of heaven from which one hears are endless. Brahma is mind, its seat is mind, its support is space; and it should be reverenced as the blissful, for with the mind one experiences bliss. Brahma is the heart, its seat is the heart, its support is space; and it should be reverenced as the steadfast, for the heart is a steadfast support. The conclusion is not clearly connected with the dialogue; at 4. 2. 4 there seems to be a break in the text. But it ends with the description of the Ātman (Soul, or Spirit), which is without describable limits.

Here it is to be noticed that Brahma is postulated as manifest in a person's psychical activities; that It has its seat in the sense-organs and in the mental organs; that It has various qualities, such as the quality of intelligence, truthfulness, endlessness, blissfulness, steadfastness; and that It turns out to be a Self, without any limiting qualities. All these statements are of importance, both as indicating the development of the conception of Brahma and as contrasted with later modifications.

The only other dialogue where an extended attempt is made

to arrive at a conception of Brahma, exhibits in philosophy the henotheistic religious tendency of the Indian mind, which elevates the god or the concept immediately concerned to the highest position and accepts it as supreme and complete, only to turn to another and repeat the process. In Chānd. 7. 1 Nārada, in search of saving knowledge, comes to Sanatkumāra with the request 'Teach me, Sir!' (*adhīhi bhagavo*). [It is probable that this should be 'Sir, declare Brahma!' (*adhīhi bhagavo brahma*), the same request that Bhṛigu Vāruṇi put to his father in a similar progressive definition of Brahma (Tait. 3. 1, referred to on page 16).] The latter, being bidden to declare his learning, enumerates seventeen books and sciences, but is informed that they all teach such knowledge as is only a name—not however worthless, since a name is part of Brahma and should be revered as Brahma. Indeed, he who does so venerate names as Brahma has free sway so far as a name covers the nature of Brahma, which, however, is only to a slight extent. But there is more than a name, viz. speech. That, too, is a manifestation of Brahma, because it makes everything manifest—all the sciences, all objects, all distinctions. But there is more than speech, viz. the mental organ, or mind (*manas*), for that embraces both speech and name. The self is mind. The world is mind. Brahma is mind. But there is something more than mind or ideation. There is will (*saṁkalpa*, the constructive faculty). It is through will that everything comes into existence. Again, though will defines a phase of Brahma, there is something greater, viz. thought. Verily, when one thinks, then he wills and performs all the previously named processes. So there is given a successive advance over each previous conception of Brahma, and usually some reason for the dependence of the preceding upon the succeeding. After thought follows meditation, understanding, strength, food, water, heat, space, memory, hope, and breath, or life; everything is breath. Further, by a circuitous route, the author leads to the immortal, unrestricted, undifferenced, self-supported plenum which is below, above, before, behind, to the right, to the left, which is the whole world itself. The next thought seems to be that since it is a spirit for whom there is a below and above, a before and behind, a right and a left, a spirit for whom a whole world exists, therefore all these are themselves spirit, or the Spirit (*Ātman*). So Spirit alone is below, above, before, behind, to the right, to the left. This whole world is Spirit. Out of Spirit arise hope, memory, space, heat, water, appearance and disappearance, food, strength, understanding, meditation, thought, will, mind, speech, name, sacred verses, religious work—which previously were defined as parts of Brahma. Indeed, this whole world arises out of Spirit (*Ātman*).

One more reference will show the manner of progress in the development of the conception of Brahma which has now been reached, namely that It is the one great reality, present both in objective phenomena and in the self's activities (Chānd. 3. 18. 1–2). 'One should reverence the mind as Brahma. Thus with reference to the self (*ātman*). Now with reference to the divinities [who operate the different departments of nature]. One should reverence space as Brahma. . . . That Brahma has four quarters. One quarter is speech. One quarter is breath. One quarter is the eye. One quarter is the ear. Thus with reference to the self. Now with reference to the divinities. One quarter is Agni (Fire). One quarter is Vāyu (Wind). One quarter is Āditya (the Sun). One quarter is the quarters of heaven. This is the twofold instruction with reference to the self and with reference to the divinities.'

Two stages are analyzable in the progress thus far: (1) the necessity for a universal, instead of a particular, world-ground led to a theory which postulated a world-ground that embraced all phenomena as parts of it, and so which gradually identified everything with the world-ground; (2) it was felt that this world-ground was in some sense a Soul, co-related with the finite ego. These two tendencies will now be further traced.

According to the earlier theory of Brahma, in which It was the primal entity which procreated the world, the world was somehow apart from Brahma. Thus, 'having created it, into it he entered' (Tait. 2. 6). Or, as Chānd. 6. 3 speaks of the originally Existent, after it had procreated heat, water, and food: 'That divinity thought to itself: "Come! Let me enter these three divinities [i.e. heat, water, and food] with this living Soul, and separate out name and form."'

With the development of the concept of Brahma away from its earliest form (i.e. from the influence of the early cosmogonies), the thought of pervading-all, mentioned in the previous paragraph, and the general enlargement and universalizing of the concept, led to the thought of being-all. So the world was identified with Brahma, in a different sense from what is implied in 'Verily, in the beginning this world was Brahma' (Bṛih. 1. 4. 10). The world, according to this developed conception, is not the emanation of the original Being that was called Brahma, nor is it strictly the past construct of an artificer Brahma (Kaush. 4. 19). Nor yet is it to be regarded as pervaded by Brahma as by something not itself, as in: 'He entered in here, even to the fingernail-tips, as a razor would be hidden in a razor-case, or fire in a fire-holder [i.e. the fire-wood]' (Bṛih. 1. 4. 7). But here and now 'verily, this whole world is Brahma' (Chānd. 3. 14). The section of the Chāndogya just quoted is the first clear statement of the pantheism which had been latent in the previous conception of Brahma and of the relation of the world to It. Later that pantheism is made explicit and remains so through the rest of the Upanishads, where the thought recurs that Brahma actually is everything.[1] Thus:—

'The swan [i.e. the sun] in the clear, the Vasu in the atmosphere,
The priest by the altar, the guest in the house,
In man, in broad space, in the right (*ṛta*), in the sky,
Born in water, born in cattle, born in the right, born in rock,
is the Right, the Great.' (Kaṭha 5. 2.)

'Brahma, indeed, is this immortal. Brahma before,
Brahma behind, to right and to left.
Stretched forth below and above,
Brahma, indeed, is this whole world, this widest extent.'
(Muṇḍ. 2. 2. 11.)

'For truly, everything here is Brahma' (Māṇḍ. 2).

Thus far, in the exposition of the development of the pantheistic conception of the world, the merging of all objective

[1] Brihad-Āraṇyaka, Chāndogya, Taittirīya, Aitareya, Kaushītaki, and Kena 14-34 (the prose portion) are regarded as forming the group representative of the earlier Upanishadic philosophy. The others are later and dogmatic, presupposing a considerable development of thought and not infrequently quoting the earlier ones.

phenomena into a unitary world-ground has been the process emphasized; for this seems to have been its first stage. Objective phenomena are the ones which first arrest the attention and demand explanation. But, as the Śvetāśvatara, at its beginning (1. 2), in recounting the various speculative theories, states explicity, there is another important factor, namely 'the existence of the soul (*ātman*),' which cannot be lumped in with material objects, but presents another and more difficult fact for the philosopher who would find a unitary ground that shall include the diverse objective and subjective.

This leads over to what was stated on page 21 as the second stage in the development of the conception of Brahma as the world-ground, namely, that It is in some sense a Soul co-related with the finite ego.

CHAPTER V

THE DEVELOPMENT OF THE CONCEPTION OF THE ĀTMAN AND ITS UNION WITH BRAHMA

IN the dialogue in Bṛih. 2. 1 (and its longer recension, Kaush. 4), where a progressive attempt was made to conceive of Brahma, it was admitted that Brahma was to be found not only in the not-self, but also in the self; that It was not only the essence of cosmical phenomena, but also of the organic and mental functions of the human person.

This probably was an outgrowth of the macrocosmic conception of the world-ground as an enormous human person, graphically portrayed in the 'Hymn of the Cosmic Person,' RV. 10. 90. The sun came out of his eye, the moon from his mind, Indra and Agni (fire) from his mouth, Vāyu (the wind) from his breath, the air from his navel, the sky from his head, the earth from his feet, and so forth.

In the Atharva-Veda (10. 7. 32–34) the earth is the base of the highest Brahma, the air his belly, the sky his head, the sun and moon his eyes, fire his mouth, the wind his breaths.

In the cosmology in Bṛih. 1. 2 fire is the semen of the

demiurge Death, the east is his head, the south-east and north-east his arms, the west his hinder part, the south-west and the north-west his thighs, the south and north his sides, the sky his back, the atmosphere his belly, the earth his chest.

According to Aitareya 1, there proceeded from the mouth of the world-person fire, from his nostrils the wind, from his eyes the sun, from his ears the quarters of heaven, from his skin plants and trees, from his heart the moon, from his navel death, from his male generative organ water. But here the important thought is added that not only are the bodily parts of this cosmic person to be observed in the external world, but they are also correlated with the functions of the individual person. So, in the sequel of the Aitareya account, fire became speech and entered in the mouth of the individual; wind became breath and entered in his nose; the sun, sight in his eyes; the quarters of heaven, hearing in his ears; plants and trees, hairs in his skin; the moon, mind in the heart; Death, semen in the generative organ.

This is perhaps the first detailed mention of a correspondence between the microcosm and the macrocosm. Glimpses of it there have been before, as in Chānd. 3. 18. 2, where Brahma, selfwise, is fourfold: speech, breath, eye, ear; and with regard to nature, is implicitly corresponding, also fourfold: fire, wind, sun, quarters. A correspondence between four parts of the bodily self and of the world is as old as the Cremation Hymn of the Rig-Veda (10. 16. 3), where the deceased is addressed: 'Let thine eye go to the sun, thy breath to wind,' a notion of dissolution at death which recurs in Īśā 17, 'My breath to the immortal wind,' and more fully in Bṛih. 3. 2. 13: 'The voice of a dead man goes into fire, his breath into wind, his eye into the sun, his mind into the moon, his hearing into the quarters of heaven, his body into the earth, his soul (*ātman*) into space, the hairs of his head into plants, the hairs of his body into trees, and his blood and semen into water.'

After the correspondence between the parts of the bodily self and the cosmic phenomena was firmly in mind, the next step with the development of abstract thought was probably to conceive of the world as really a Soul (*Ātman*), a universal

Soul of which the individual self or soul is a miniature. This was a great step in advance. A sign of the dawning of the philosophical self-consciousness and of a deeper insight into the nature and meaning of the self is given in Bṛih. 1. 4. 7: 'One's self (*ātman*), for therein all these become one. That same thing, namely, this self, is the trace of this All; for by it one knows this All. Just as, verily, one might find by a footprint.' This thought recurs in Śvet. 2. 15:—

'When with the nature of the self, as with a lamp,
A practiser of Yoga beholds here the nature of Brahma.'

Still crude and figurative, it is nevertheless of deep philosophical significance, yielding a concept which is of equal importance to that of Brahma. Its development may in the same way be traced now, remembering that this Atman theory was not in all probability a development subsequent to that of Brahma, which has already been traced, though its beginnings certainly were posterior to the beginnings of the Brahma theory. The two, it would seem, progressed simultaneously and influenced each other until their final union. For the sake of clearness in exposition, however, they are here analyzed and followed separately.

In the second movement, Ātman being postulated as the world-ground, attempts were made to conceive of him as was the case with Brahma. Thus there was an early theory of procreation, Bṛih. 1. 4. 1–5, but much coarser than the similar theory with Brahma. Although by a recognized mistake he was stricken by fear at first and overcame it, Ātman was possessed by a feeling of loneliness in his primeval solitariness and wished: 'Would that I had a wife, then I would procreate' (Bṛih. 1. 4. 17). By an act of self-bifurcation which, etymologically interpreted, explains the existence and complementary nature of husband and wife, he produced a female principle by union with which, the pair continually converting themselves into different species, all the different kinds of animals were born. Then, by the usual method of attrition and blowing, he made fire. This crude myth, near the beginning of the earliest Upanishad, is based on the primitive idea that the same empirical methods which man uses for productive purposes, especially the one which is the most mysterious and which accounts for his own production, may be held accountable analogously for the production of the world. It is in the old Brahmanic style and is somewhat misplaced in an Upanishad. The idea does not recur again.

A more serious attempt to conceive of Ātman is the dialogue in Chānd. 5. 11–18, which again resembles similar attempts with Brahma. Five learned householders came together and discussed: 'Who is our Ātman? What is Brahma?' (a collocation which shows that the two theories of the world-ground were being connected; in this passage they are not, however, identified, as they are to be later). These five decided to resort to another who had the reputation of understanding that universal Ātman, but even he dared not expound him and answer all questions concerning him. The six then repair to the famed Aśvapati for instruction. He, in genuine Socratic manner, first elicits from each of them his present conception of the universal Ātman. One says that he venerates the sky as the universal Ātman. Asvapati commends the conception and gives assurance that he is shining like the sky, but a great deal more. The sky would be only his head. The others in turn contribute their conceptions, all of which are accepted as true, but as only partially true, and in essence false. The universal Ātman is indeed the sun, and like it all-formed; but the sun is only his eye. He is indeed the wind, and like it moving in various paths; but the wind is only his breath. The universal Ātman is indeed space, and like it expanded; but space is only his body. He is indeed water, and like it abundant; but water is only his bladder. The universal Ātman is indeed the earth, and like it a support; but the earth is only his feet. The six Brahmans, as they learned from Aśvapati, in spite of having thus grasped partial truth, had made a most serious error in conceiving of Ātman as something apart from themselves. This universal Ātman, or Soul, is best referred to as in oneself.

Important steps in the development of the Ātman doctrine are here taken. In the figurative manner of speculation, from which Indian philosophy as well as all philosophy proceeded, Ātman, like Brahma, is first conceived under the form of particular objects of nature. The truth there contained is appreciated and, better than in the Brahma-dialogues, commended by being immediately universalized. All the great nature-gods, mentioned as henotheistically venerated for the philosophical world-ground, are indeed the Ātman, but only parts of him. They may, by an accommodation to the learner's standpoint of sense-thought, be regarded as his bodily parts. But by transcending this lower plane of attention directed to objectively observed facts, Aśvapati directed them, in their search for ultimate reality, to an inclusive cosmic Self, which must be conceived of after the analogy of a human self and with which the human self must be identified.

A new line of thought is here entered upon, namely introspection, which always follows after extrospection, but which marks the beginnings of a deeper philosophic thought. What it finally led on to will be described after an exposition of certain developments and conjunctions of the concept of Ātman.

The world-ground being Ātman, an objective Soul, which was known by the analogy of the soul, but which externally included the soul, certain closer relations were drawn between the not-self and the self, of both of which that Ātman was the ground. On pages 23–24 citations were made illustrating the notion of correspondences between parts of the world as a cosmic corporeal person and of the individual's bodily self. That notion occurs also in the first chapter of the Chāndogya. 'This [breath in the mouth] and that [sun] are alike. This is warm. That is warm. People designate this as sound (*svara*), that as sound (*svara*) [an approximation to *svar*, light] and as the reflecting (*pratyasvara*)' (Chānd. 1. 3. 2). 'The form of this one is the same as that [Person seen in the sun]' (Chānd. 1. 7. 5). But now with the doctrine of a universal Ātman immanent both in the subjective and in the objective, it is no longer similarities, but parts of a unity or identities. 'Both he who is here in a person and he who is yonder in the sun—he is one' (Tait. 2. 8; 3. 10. 4). 'He who is in the fire, and he who is here in the heart, and he who is yonder in the sun—he is one' (Maitri 6. 17; 7. 7). 'He who is yonder, yonder Person (*puruṣa*)—I myself am he!' (Bṛih. 5. 15; Īśā 16). 'Verily, what the space outside of a person is—that is the same as what the space within a person is. Verily, what the space within a person is—that is the same as what the space here within the heart is. That is the Full, the Non-moving' (Chānd. 3. 12. 7–9).

Longer descriptions of Ātman as the basis of the unity implied in the usual correlations of the not-self and the self, are the two following: Ātman is the person in the earth and the person in the body; in the waters and in the semen; in fire and in speech; in wind and in breath; in the sun and in the eye; in the quarters and in the ear and in the echo; in the moon and in the mind; in lightning and in heat; in thunder and in sound; in space and in the space of the heart; in law and in virtuousness; in truth and in truthfulness; in humanity and in a human; in the Self and in the self. All these are just Ātman (Bṛih. 2. 5). Bṛih. 3. 9. 10–17 similarly presents this idea of the one Person immanent in and including the self and the not-self: the person in the earth and in fire is also the person in the body; the person in the sun is also the person in appearances and in the eye; the person in space is also the person in the ear and in hearing; the person in darkness and in the shadow is also the person in the heart; the person in the waters is also the person in semen and in the heart. And finally he is Ātman, the Self, the Soul.

So, as Yājñavalkya explained to Ushastas: 'He who breathes in with your breathing in is the Soul (Ātman) of yours which is in all things. He who breathes out with your breathing out is the Soul of yours which is in all things. He who breathes about with your breathing about is the Soul of yours which is in all things. He who breathes up with your breathing up is the Soul of yours which is in all things' (Bṛih. 3. 4. 1). The inner essence, then, of the objective and the subjective is one Being, and that, too, of the nature of a Self, by reason of the reality of the directly known self which necessarily constitutes a part of that ground of all being.

But by a different course of speculation and (as was natural with the earlier) one which had regard more especially to the objective, the conception of a single world-ground and then of the actual being of the world itself had been that of Brahma. An objective entity though this Brahma was, the unity of being which it was intended to signify could not disregard the existence and activities of the self, which surely were as real as the sun, moon, waters, space, and so forth that had been the prominent facts to be grounded in the unitary being of the world of Brahma. An approachment to Brahma as underlying the self also was being made, as was shown in the exposition of the development of the conception of Brahma. But, differently from the realistic procedure with Brahma, a more personal and self-like ground was necessary for effecting the union of the psychologically viewed subjective and objective. For this purpose the old conception of a cosmic Person was more serviceable; and it was developed away from its first materialistic and corporeal connections to that of a more spiritual Ātman, who is immanent in self and not-self and who constitutes the unity expressed in their correlation.

Yet finally these two world-grounds, Brahma and Ātman, are not different and separate. Their essential oneness, as aspects of the same great Being, was at first only hinted at, but was later explicitly stated. The suspicion that these two theories, which were becoming current and which people desired to understand more fully, were both of the same Being, was manifested by the form in which learners who came to recognized philosophers for instruction put their questions. Thus, Ushastas came to Yājñavalkya and said: 'Explain to me him who is the Brahma, present and not beyond our ken, him who is the Soul (Ātman) in all things' (Bṛih. 3. 4. 1). Likewise the five householders who came to Aśvapati were first discussing among themselves 'Who is our Ātman (Soul)? What is Brahma'? (Chānd. 5. 11. 1).

Then we find it directly stated: 'Verily, that great unborn Soul, undecaying, undying, immortal, fearless, is Brahma' (Bṛih. 4. 4. 25). 'He [i.e. Ātman] is Brahma' (Ait. 5. 3). 'Him [i.e. Brahma] alone know as the one Soul (Ātman). Other words dismiss' (Muṇḍ. 2. 2. 5). 'The Soul (Atman), which pervades all things . . . , this is Brahma' (Śvet. 1. 16). Before the identification of Brahma and Ātman was formally made, the two terms were hovering near each other as designations of the ultimate world-ground, as in Bṛih. 2. 5. 1, where to emphasize a point the phrases are used in succession: 'This Soul (Ātman), this Immortal, this Brahma, this All.' After the identification was made the two became interchangeable terms, as in Chānd. 8. 14. 1 : '. . . Brahma, that is the immortal, that is the Soul (Ātman),' and Muṇḍ. 2.2.9 : 'Brahma, that which knowers of the Soul (Ātman) do know' (through the whole of this section, where the Imperishable is being described, the terms Brahma and Ātman are used indifferently). So the two great conceptions—Brahma, reached first realistically, the unitary cosmic ground, with outreachings towards a cosmo-anthropic ground ; and Ātman, the inner being of the self and the not-self, the great world-spirit—were joined, the former taking over to itself the latter conception and the two being henceforth to a considerable degree synonymous. Here the quest for the real,[1] for the unity of the diversified world, for the key to the universe, reached a goal. That which Śvetaketu did not know, though he had been away from home studying twelve years and had studied all the Vedas and thought himself learned, even that 'whereby what has not been heard of becomes heard of, what has not been thought of becomes thought of, what has not been understood becomes understood' (Chānd. 6. 1. 1–3) ; that for instruction in which Śaunaka, the great householder, came to Aṅgiras (Muṇḍ. 1. 1. 3) ; that which Nārada knew not, though he knew eighteen books and sciences, and for lack of the knowledge of which he was sorrowing (Chānd. 7. 1. 1–2) ; that for complete instruction in which Indra remained with Prajāpati as a pupil for one hundred and one years—that supreme object is just this Brahma, this Ātman, who is in the world, who is the great Self, the ground of oneself. He is the highest object of knowledge, whom one should desire to know.

> 'By knowing Him only, a wise
> Brahman should get for himself intelligence.' (Bṛih. 4. 4. 21.)

He is the key to all knowledge. 'Verily, with the seeing of, with the hearkening to, with the thinking of, and with the under-

[1] Beautifully expressed, in a different connection, by the three verses of Bṛih. 1. 3. 28 :—

> 'From the unreal lead me to the real.
> From darkness lead me to light.
> From death lead me to immortality.'

The earnestness of the search for truth is one of the delightful and commendable features of the Upanishads.

standing of the Soul, this world-all is known' (Bṛih. 2. 4. 5). 'Verily, he who knows that thread and the so-called Inner Controller knows Brahma, he knows the worlds, he knows the gods, he knows the Vedas, he knows created things, he knows the Soul, he knows everything' (Bṛih. 3. 7. 1). 'This is the knowledge the Brahmans know. Thereby I know what is to be known' (Bṛih. 5. 1. 1). 'As, when a drum is being beaten, one would not be able to grasp the external sounds, but by grasping the drum or the beater of the drum the sound is grasped; as, when a conch-shell is being blown, one would not be able to grasp the external sounds, but by grasping the conch-shell or the blower of the conch-shell the sound is grasped; as, when a lute is being played, one would not be able to grasp the external sounds, but by grasping the lute or the player of the lute the sound is grasped'—so by comprehending Ātman or Brahma everything is comprehended (Bṛih. 2. 4. 7–9).

So the unity which has been searched for from the beginning of Indian speculation was reached. 'As all the spokes are held together in the hub and felly of a wheel, just so in this Soul all things, all gods, all worlds, all breathing things, all selves are held together' (Bṛih. 2. 5. 15). Monism now is the ruling conception of the world, for the world is identical with Ātman. 'Ātman alone is the whole world' (Chānd. 7. 25. 2). 'This Brahmanhood, this Kshatrahood, these worlds, these gods, these beings, everything here is what this Soul is' (Bṛih. 2. 4. 6; 4. 5. 7). 'Who is this one?' is asked in Ait. 5. 1, and the reply is: 'He is Brahma; he is Indra; he is Prajāpati; [he is] all the gods here; and these five gross elements, namely earth, wind, space, water, light; these things and those which are mingled of the fine, as it were; origins of one sort or another: those born from an egg, and those born from a womb, and those born from sweat, and those born from a sprout; horses, cows, persons, elephants; whatever breathing thing there is here—whether moving or flying, and what is stationary.' As the later metrical Śvetāśvatara expresses the thought:—

'That God faces all the quarters of heaven.
Aforetime was he born, and he it is within the womb.
He has been born forth. He will be born.' (Śvet. 2. 16.)

And again, with more indefiniteness, concerning the monistic 'That':—

'That surely is Agni (fire). That is Āditya (the sun).
That is Vāyu (the wind), and That is the moon.
That surely is the pure. That is Brahma.
That is the waters. That is Prajāpati (Lord of Creation).

Thou art woman. Thou art man.
Thou art the youth and the maiden too.
Thou as an old man totterest with a staff.
Being born, thou becomest facing in every direction.

Thou art the dark-blue bird and the green [parrot] with red eyes.
Thou hast the lightning as thy child. Thou art the seasons and the seas.
Having no beginning, thou dost abide with all-pervadingness,
Wherefrom all beings are born.' (Śvet. 4. 2–4.)

And most important of all, as Uddālaka nine times repeated to Śvetaketu (Chānd. 6. 8–16): 'That art thou.'

CHAPTER VI

THE REALISTIC CONCEPTION OF THE ULTIMATE UNITY, AND THE DOCTRINE OF ILLUSION

What, now, is the nature of that single all-encompassing monistic Being that has been discovered? It must possess as many qualities as there are in the whole of the real world which it constitutes. This attribution of all possible qualities to the Being of the world is made in the famous Śāṇḍilya section of the Chāndogya (3. 14). 'Verily, this whole world is Brahma . . . He who consists of mind, whose body is life, whose form is light, whose conception is truth, whose soul (*ātman*) is space, containing all works, containing all desires, containing all odors, containing all tastes, encompassing this whole world, the unspeaking, the unconcerned, . . . smaller than a grain of rice, or a barley-corn, or a mustard-seed, or a grain of millet, or the kernel of a grain of millet, . . . [yet] greater than the earth, greater than the atmosphere, greater than the sky, greater than these worlds.' It must also be capable of all contraries:—

'Unmoving, the One is swifter than the mind.
The sense-powers reached not It, speeding on before.
Past others running, This goes standing.
In It Mātariśvan places action.

It moves. It moves not.
It is far, and It is near.
It is within all this,
And It is outside of all this.' (Īśā 4–5.)

'Sitting, he proceeds afar.
Lying, he goes everywhere.' (Kaṭha 2. 21.)

The diverse identification and constitution of this monistic Being are further expressed in the verses:—

'As fire (Agni), he warms. He is the sun (Sūrya).
He is the bountiful rain (Parjanya). He is the wind (Vāyu).
He is the earth, matter, God,
Being and Non-being, and what is immortal.' (Praśna 2. 5.)

'What that is, know as Being and Non-being.'
(Muṇḍ. 2. 2. 1.)

This necessity of postulating in the substrate itself of the world the whole store of materials and qualities which exist in the world, led to the summary contained in Bṛih. 4. 4. 5, where Brahma is described as 'made of knowledge, of mind, of breath, of seeing, of hearing, of earth, of water, of wind, of space, of energy and of non-energy, of desire and of non-desire, of anger and of non-anger, of virtuousness and of non-virtuousness. It is made of everything. This is what is meant by the saying "made of this, made of that."'

But such a realistic conception of Brahma as a conglomerate was subversive of the very idea of unity which the concept of Brahma fundamentally signified. All those diverse material objects, psychical functions, and mental states as such could not be regarded as the materials composing the structure of a unitary world-ground. Yet there is diversity and manifoldness in the being of the world which cannot be regarded as existing apart from the world-ground. How account for them?

In one of the old cosmologies (Tait. 2. 6), where Brahma

wished that he were many, performed austerities, procreated himself, and ejected this whole world from himself, it is stated that he entered into it with a double nature. 'He became both the actual and the yon, both the defined and the undefined, both the based and the non-based, both the conscious and the unconscious, both the real and the false.' Here is perhaps the first emergence of the thought which is the solution to the question put above. It is the distinction made between the so-called phenomenal and noumenal, between the sensuously perceived and that which cannot be thus brought into consciousness, but can only be thought. This notion that there is much of reality which is not within the sphere of the senses, or within the world of what is called common-sense experiences, expresses itself here and there in the early part of the Upanishads, as in Chānd. 3. 12. 6:—

> 'All beings are one-fourth of him;
> Three-fourths, the immortal in the sky.'

Also in Bṛih. 1. 4. 7: 'Him they see not, for [as seen] he is incomplete.' And later also, more like clarified conceptions of immanence and transcendence, as in Bṛih. 3. 7. 3: 'He who, dwelling in the earth, yet is other than the earth, . . . whose body the earth is, who controls the earth from within,' and similarly of twenty other objects.

> 'As the one wind has entered the world
> And becomes corresponding in form to every form,
> So the one Inner Soul of all things
> Is corresponding in form to every form, and yet is outside.' (Kaṭha 5. 10.)

But it is by the distinction between the noumenal and the phenomenal that the apparent conflict between the One and the many is solved. In a noteworthy passage, Bṛih. 1. 6. 3, it is declared that 'Life (*prāṇa*, 'breath') [a designation of the Ātman], verily, is the Immortal. Name and form [the usual phrase signifying individuality] are the actual. By them this Life is veiled.' Similarly in Bṛih. 2. 1. 20: 'The mystic meaning (*upanisad*) thereof is the "Real of the real." Breathing creatures, verily, are the real. He is their Real.' Bṛih. 2. 3. 1 makes the distinction explicit by affirming that 'there are, assuredly, two forms of Brahma.' It is the same thought, for the section closes with the words of Bṛih. 2. 1. 20, just cited; but the effort to express the great truth finds itself halting and falling back directly upon the early sensuous conceptions which it endeavored to rise above.

These two forms of Brahma are the formed and the unformed, the mortal and the immortal, the stationary and the moving, the actual and the yon. As regards the Vedic nature-gods, the unformed, immortal, moving, yonder Brahma is the wind and the atmosphere. The essence of that is the person in the sun-disk. The formed, the mortal, the stationary, the actual Brahma is what is different from the wind and the atmosphere. Its essence is the sun which gives forth heat. As regards the self, the unformed, immortal, moving, yonder Brahma is the breath and the space in the heart. Its essence is the person in the right eye. The formed, mortal, stationary, and actual Brahma is what is different from the breath and the intracardiac space. Its essence is the eye (this being typical of the senses by which the phenomenal is perceived). The glorious, brilliant nature of the higher Brahma is then represented by similes of the bright and shining—a saffron-colored robe, white wool, a red beetle, a flame of fire, a white lotus flower, a sudden flash of lightning. But immediately there follows the warning that the noumenal Brahma cannot be represented to the senses, indeed cannot be defined by any positive characteristics. '*Neti, neti*: Not thus! Not so!' (Bṛih. 2. 3. 6; 3. 9. 26). Nevertheless it is the reality of the individual phenomenal actualities. Though starting with and making use of sense data and accepting a strange pair of differentia, namely the stationary and the moving, for the actual and the yon, or for the phenomenal and the noumenal Brahmas, this section nevertheless advances toward the final idealistic conception of reality, to which the monism of the Upanishads led.

The two Brahmas are described again in Maitri 6. 15. 'There are, assuredly, two forms of Brahma: Time and the Timeless. That which is prior to the sun is the Timeless (*a-kāla*) without parts (*a-kala*). But that which begins with the sun is Time, which has parts.'

The thought begins to appear that if all is One, the manifold differences that seem so real in experience are not constitutive of the inner being of that One; they must be only an appearance, a phenomenon. So again the two Brahmas are described in Maitri 6. 22: 'Verily there are two Brahmas to be meditated upon: sound and non-sound. Now non-sound is revealed only by sound. . . . Of it there is this sevenfold comparison: like rivers, a bell, a brazen vessel, a wheel, the croaking of frogs, rain, as when one speaks in a sheltered place. Passing beyond this variously characterized [sound-Brahma], men disappear in the supreme, the non-sound, the unmanifest Brahma.'

These two Brahmas, the one manifold with sense qualities, and the other a superphenomenal unity, were accepted as both real, though in different ways. They were 'both the higher and the lower' of Muṇḍ. 2. 2. 8 and Praśna 5. 2; the two forms of Śvet. 1. 13. They formed the subject-matter of the 'two knowledges to be known—as indeed the knowers of Brahma are wont to say: a higher and a lower.' The lower knowledge is of various sciences, but 'the higher is that whereby that Imperishable is apprehended' (Muṇḍ. 1. 1. 4-5). Their importance in a complete knowledge of Brahma is affirmed by Kaṭha 6. 13, for

'He can indeed be comprehended by the thought "He is"
And by [admitting] the real nature of both [his comprehensibility and his incomprehensibility].'

But this dualizing of the world-ground, this postulating of two Brahmas when the fundamental and repeated axiom of the whole Upanishadic speculation was that 'there is only one Brahma, without a second,' induced by way of correction the further development of the previous conception of phenomenality.[1] Reality is One. Diversity and manifoldness are only an appearance.

'There is on earth no diversity.
He gets death after death,
Who perceives here seeming diversity.
As a unity only is It to be looked upon—
This indemonstrable, enduring Being.' (Bṛih. 4. 4. 19–20.)

[1] Thus Śaṅkara reconciled the opposition between the two Brahmas and the one Brahma, at the end of his commentary on the Vedānta-Sūtras, 4. 3. 14.

'The seer sees not death,
Nor sickness, nor any distress.
The seer sees only the All,
Obtains the All entirely.' (Chānd. 7. 26. 2.)

That is the real Brahma, the undifferenced unity. The lower Brahma of sense-manifoldness, in which everything appears as a self-subsistent entity, is merely an appearance due to a person's ignorance that all is essentially one; that is, it is an illusion. So Maitri 6. 3 says plainly of the two Brahmas: 'There are, assuredly, two forms of Brahma: the formed and the formless. Now, that which is the formed is unreal; that which is the formless is real.'

The distinction between the phenomenal and the super-phenomenal was, as has been described, made quite early in the Upanishadic thought. First, the phenomenal, though admittedly a part of the reality of the world, is only a fragment of its totality. 'Him they see not, for [as seen] he is incomplete.... Whoever worships one or another of these [individual manifestations]—he knows not; for he is incomplete with one or another of these' (Bṛih. 1. 4. 7). It is mere ignorance (*avidyā*) on one's own part, then, that allows him to rest in the things of sense as the ultimate being of the world; but this ignorance, or non-knowledge, is remediable under instruction concerning the underlying unity.

But soon the conception arose that the error is attributable not so much to oneself, as to that Other which hides its unitary nature. 'There is nothing by which he is not covered, nothing by which he is not hid' (Bṛih. 2. 5. 18). Poetically expressed, 'Life, verily, is the Immortal. Name and form are the real. By them that Life is veiled' (Bṛih. 1. 6. 3). He who is essentially one,

'The Inner Soul (*antarātman*) of all things . . . ,
Who makes his one form manifold' (Katha 5. 12),

is performing a piece of supernatural magic in appearing as many.

'He became corresponding in form to every form.
This is to be looked upon as a form of him.
Indra by his magic powers (*māyā*) goes about in many forms;
Yoked are his ten-hundred steeds.' (Bṛih. 2. 5. 19.)

This is the first occurrence in the Upanishads of the word *māyā* —in the plural, be it noticed, and as a quotation from Rig-Veda 6. 47. 18, where it occurs many times in the meaning of 'supernatural powers' or 'artifices.' It is this thought which is developed into the theory of cosmic illusion and which is expressed in Śvet. 4. 9-10, the favorite proof-text in the Upanishads of the later Māyā doctrine.

> 'This whole world the illusion-maker projects out of this [Brahma].
> And in it by illusion the other is confined.
> Now, one should know that Nature is illusion,
> And that the Mighty Lord is the illusion-maker.'

Such was the beginning of that which became a prominent doctrine of the later Vedānta, the doctrine of Māyā or the inevitable illusoriness of all human cognition. In its early development it did not base itself in any way upon what was a chief source of the early Greek scepticism, namely illusions of sense. The sole reference to them in the Upanishads, Kaṭha 5. 11—

> 'As the sun, the eye of the whole world,
> Is not sullied by the external faults of the eyes'—

is not used as an argument for illusion, though Śaṅkara in his Commentary *ad locum* explains it by the stock simile of the later Vedānta in which the piece of rope lying by the wayside appears in the twilight as a snake to the belated traveler.[1] On the contrary, sight is to the philosophers of the Upanishads the symbol of truth. 'Sight is truthfulness, for when they say to a man who sees with his eyes "Have you seen?" and he says "I have seen," that is the truth' (Bṛih. 4. 1. 4; similarly also in Bṛih. 5. 14. 4).

The doctrine of illusion, then, was the speculative outcome of the conflict between the phenomenal and the super-phenomenal, between the lower and the higher Brahma. It was the logical

[1] Gough, in his *Philosophy of the Upanishads*, maintains, in my judgment, an erroneous position, viz. that the Upanishads teach the pure Vedāntism of Śaṅkara, who flourished at least a thousand years after their date. Gough's book is filled with explanations bringing in the similes of the rope and snake, the distant post seeming to be a man, the mirage on the sand, the reflection of the sun on the water, etc., all of which are drawn from Śaṅkara and even later Hindu philosophers, and not from the Upanishads.

conclusion of the abstract presupposition as to the nature and possibilities of the pure unity which these thinkers conceived of as the essence of reality and to which they pressed on as the great goal of all their speculations. The manifold world of sense furnished no such unity and therefore had to be abandoned as illusory and unreal, in favor of that undifferenced unity to which they were driven as the basis underlying the illusory and which, just because it is beyond all sense-qualities, distinctions, or limitations of any kind, is the real Brahma.

> 'As a unity only is It to be looked upon—
> This indemonstrable, enduring Being.' (Bṛih. 4. 4. 20.)

The attempts to describe this pure unity of being are numerous. 'This Brahma is without an earlier and without a later, without an inside and without an outside' (Bṛih. 2. 5. 19). 'For him east and the other directions exist not, nor across, nor below, nor above.... [He is] unlimited' (Maitri 6. 17). 'It is not coarse, not fine, not short, not long, not glowing, not adhesive, without shadow and without darkness, without air and without space, without stickiness, (intangible), odorless, tasteless, without eye, without ear, without voice, without mind, without energy, without breath, without mouth, (without personal or family name, unaging, undying, without fear, immortal, stainless, not uncovered, not covered), without measure, without inside and without outside. It consumes nothing soever. No one soever consumes it' (Bṛih. 3. 8. 8).

> 'What is soundless, touchless, formless, imperishable,
> Likewise tasteless, constant, odorless,
> Without beginning, without end, higher than the great.'
> (Kaṭha 3. 15.)

'That which is invisible, ungraspable, without family, without caste—without sight or hearing is It, without hand or foot, eternal' (Muṇḍ. 1. 1. 6). He is apart from all moral, causal, or temporal relations. One must put Him aside as possessed of qualities and take Him as the subtile only (Kaṭha 2. 13–14). The ultimate is void of any mark (*a-liṅga*) whatever (Kaṭha 6. 8; Śvet. 6. 9); without qualities (*nir-guṇa*) (Śvet. 6. 11). About this higher Brahma 'there is the teaching "Not thus! Not so!" (*neti, neti*), for there is nothing higher than this [negative definition]' (Brih. 2. 3. 6; 3. 9. 26; 4. 2. 4). 'Indefinable,' 'inconceivable,' mere negative statements are all that can be asserted of this pure being, which *ex hypothesi* is incapable of the qualification, determination, and diversity implied in descriptive attribution. This is exactly the conclusion which Spinoza reached with his in many respects similar pantheism —the famous dictum 'Omnis determinatio negatio est.'[1]

How now is this kind of real Brahma to be known? The practical method, stated in Kaṭha 2. 8–9 and frequently elsewhere, that if one were taught by a competent *guru*, or teacher, he might find Brahma, is of course superseded. The progress of speculation had taken Brahma to that far-off, transcendent realm where it is a question whether it may be reached or known at all. Certainly—

'Not above, not across,
Not in the middle has one grasped Him.
There is no likeness of Him
Whose name is Great Glory.

His form is not to be beheld.
No one soever sees Him with the eye.
They who know Him with heart and mind
As abiding in the heart, become immortal.' (Śvet. 4. 19–20.)

But no! that higher Brahma is not accessible to knowledge by sense or by thought or by instruction:—

'There the eye goes not;
Speech goes not, nor the mind.
We know not, we understand not
How one would teach it.' (Kena 3.)

'Wherefrom words turn back,
Together with the mind, not having attained.'
(Tait. 2. 4, 9.)

No more than its bare existence can be postulated.

'Not by speech, not by mind,
Not by sight can He be apprehended.
How can He be comprehended
Otherwise than by one's saying "He is!"?' (Kaṭha 6. 12.)

But even here the real point is dodged.

[1] 'All determining (describing or qualifying) is a negating.'

'He who rules the ignorance and the knowledge is another.' (Śvet. 5. 1.)

'[Brahma is] higher than understanding.' (Muṇḍ. 2. 2. 1.)

'Other indeed is It than the known,
And moreover above the unknown.' (Kena 3.)

'Into blind darkness enter they
That worship ignorance;
Into darkness greater than that, as it were,
That delight in knowledge.

Other indeed, they say, than knowledge!
Other, they say, than non-knowledge!
—Thus have we heard from the wise
Who to us have explained It.' (Īśā 9–10.)

Utterly inconceivable is this supreme Brahma. The very attempt to conceive of it indicates that one does not know the essential fact about it. There follows the paradox:—

'It is conceived of by him by whom It is not conceived of.
He by whom It is conceived of, knows It not.
It is not understood by those who [say they] understand It.
It is understood by those who [say they] understand It not.' (Kena 11.)

Such is the outcome of a long circuitous journey to reach that ultimate unity of reality which was dimly foreseen long before in the Rig-Veda and which had been the goal of all the succeeding speculations. What is it—we pause and ask—that has now been reached? On the one hand an illusory world and on the other hand an unknowable reality. Honestly and earnestly had the thinkers of the Upanishads sought to find the true nature of this world of experience and of a beyond which constantly lured them on, but it had proved to be an *ignis fatuus*. Yet they did not give up in the despair of agnosticism or in the disappointment of failure. The glimpses which they had had of that final unity had frequently suggested that the self must be accounted for in the unity of being. They had found an underlying basis for the subjective and objective in the great Ātman, the world-soul, like unto the self-known soul and inclusive of that, but in itself external to it. And they had found that the great Ātman was identical with the great Brahma, the power or efficacy that actuates the world. But in the explanation of the phenomenal and the noumenal that Brahma had fallen apart and vanished, one part into the illusory and the other into the unknowable.

CHAPTER VII

IDEALISM AND THE CONCEPTION OF PURE UNITY

THE former glimpses of that nearest of known facts, the self, showed the thinkers of the Upanishads that the path they had been following, the path of realism, had logically led them to an unsatisfying conclusion. The unity for which they had been searching as if it were something outside of and apart from the self, could never be reached. For there still remains the stubborn dualism of self and not-self, however deeply the two might be set into a monistic frame which should embrace them both in an external grasp. Epistemological idealism must henceforth be the path traveled in order to reach the goal of an absolute unity.

This was a wonderful discovery, intuitions of which had flashed out here and there, but which was forced upon them for adoption by the limit which they had reached along the line of epistemological realism. The final unity could not and would not, then, be found outside of self, but in it. In truth, the self is the unity that they had been looking for all along, 'for therein all these [things] become one' (Bṛih. 1. 4. 7), and only in it, i.e. in one's own consciousness, do things exist. 'As far, verily, as this world-space extends, so far extends the space within the heart. Within it, indeed, are contained both heaven and earth, both fire and wind, both sun and moon, lightning and stars, both what one possesses here and what one does not possess; everything here is contained within it' (Chānd. 8. 1. 3).

Realistic monism has been changed into epistemological idealism. All existence is for, and in, the self. 'This whole world is Brahma.... This Soul of mine within the heart ...' (Chānd. 3. 14. 1, 3). 'He is the world-protector. He is the world-sovereign. He is the lord of all. He is my self' (Kaush. 3. 8). 'I am Brahma!' (Bṛih. 1. 4. 10). Thus that world-ground, that unity of being which was being searched for realistically outside of the self, and which, as it was being approached, seemed to recede back into the illusory and into the unknowable, is none other than the self, which had eluded cognition for the reason that, as the subject of consciousness, it could not become an object. 'He is the unseen Seer, the unheard Hearer, the unthought Thinker, the ununderstood Understander' (Bṛih. 3. 7. 23). 'You could not see the seer of seeing. You could not hear the hearer of hearing. You could not think the thinker of thinking. You could not understand the understander of understanding' (Bṛih. 3. 4. 2). 'Wherewith would one understand him with whom one understands this All? Lo, wherewith would one understand the understander?' (Bṛih. 2. 4. 14).

The world, which by the simile of birds supported on a tree as their roost had been realistically explained (in Praśna 4. 7) as supported on that which, with unforeseen insight, was called Ātman, a Self, because I, a self, am also a part of It—that world is none other than my self.

> 'He who has found and has awakened to the Soul (Self) . . .
> The world is his; indeed, he is the world itself.'
>
> (Bṛih. 4. 4. 13.)

'One should reverence the thought "I am the world-all!"' (Chānd. 2. 21. 4). 'I alone am this whole world' (Chand. 7. 25. 1). 'When he imagines . . . "I am this world-all," that is his highest world. This, verily, is that form of his which is beyond desires, free from evil, without fear' (Bṛih. 4. 3. 20–21).

Rather, instead of being identified with my consciousness, this world of sense is the product of my constructive imagination, as is evident in sleep, when one 'himself tears it apart, himself builds it up, and dreams by his own brightness, by his own light. . . . There are no chariots there, no spans, no roads. But he projects from himself chariots, spans, roads. There are no blisses there, no pleasures, no delights. But he projects from himself blisses, pleasures, delights. There are no tanks there, no lotus-pools, no streams. But he projects from himself tanks, lotus-pools, streams. For he is a creator. . . .

In the state of sleep going aloft and alow,
A god, he makes many forms for himself.'

(Bṛih. 4. 3. 9, 10, 13.)

Such a theory is distinctly idealistic metaphysics.[1]

Here, then, is the source of that manifold diversity which has seemed to contradict the pure unity of being. It all is the thought-product of the larger real Self, apart from whom neither it nor I have any existence whatever. 'He who knows "Let me smell this," "Let me utter this," "Let me hear this," "Let me think this," is the Self' (Chānd. 8. 12. 4–5).

The ego does not perform those activities. 'Assuredly, the Soul (Ātman) of one's soul is called the Immortal Leader. As perceiver, thinker, goer, evacuator, begetter, doer, speaker, taster, smeller, seer, hearer—and he touches—the All-pervader has entered the body' (Maitri 6. 7). The real illusion is not strictly the trick of the other, the great magician, but my own persistence in the vain belief that I and the world exist apart from, or are in any sense other than, the pure, undifferenced unity of the Self—or, according to the theory of realistic monism, the one world-all Brahma.[2]

In either case knowledge of the truth banishes the illusion and restores the identity which was only temporarily sundered by ignorance. 'Whoever thus knows "I am Brahma!" becomes this All; even the gods have not power to prevent his becoming thus, for he becomes their self' (Bṛih. 1. 4. 10). Knowledge of the real nature of Brahma in general effects an assimilation of the knower of it. 'Verily, Brahma is fearless. He who knows this becomes the fearless Brahma' (Bṛih. 4. 4. 25). 'He, verily, who knows that supreme Brahma, becomes very Brahma' (Muṇḍ. 3. 2. 9). 'He who recognizes that shadowless, bodiless, bloodless, pure Imperishable, arrives at the Imperishable itself. He, knowing all, becomes the All' (Praśna 4. 10). 'Brahma-knowers become merged in Brahma' (Śvet. 1. 7).

In the Ātman-theory the great desideratum is union with

[1] This is an ancient foreshadowing of the modern theory of the 'project.'

[2] 'In this Brahma-wheel the soul (*haṁsa*) flutters about, thinking that itself and the Actuator are different' (Śvet. 1. 6).

Ātman, the inner, real, unitary Self—who in truth am I, if I but knew it and could realize it. That is 'the Self which is free from evil, ageless, deathless, sorrowless, hungerless, thirstless, whose desire is the Real, whose conception is the Real' (Chānd. 8. 7. 1; Maitri 7. 7). In the Brahma-theory also it is complete unqualified unity that is the ideal. 'An ocean, a seer alone without duality, becomes he whose world is Brahma. This is a man's highest path. . . . This is his highest bliss' (Bṛih. 4. 3. 32). For 'verily, a Plenum is the same as Pleasure. There is no Pleasure in the small. Only a Plenum is Pleasure.' (Chānd. 7. 23. 1.) This path, however, from the troubled consciousness with its limitations, sorrows, and pains, to that state of unalloyed beatitude and unbounded bliss—

> 'A sharpened edge of a razor, hard to traverse,
> A difficult path is this—poets declare!' (Kaṭha 3. 14.)

'Verily, there are just two conditions of this person: the condition of being in this world and the condition of being in the other world. There is an intermediate third condition, namely, that of being in sleep' (Bṛih. 4. 3. 9). Going to it, as a fish goes over to the other side of a river and back, one may have an actual experience of that reality of bliss in contrast with which the waking life is but a bad dream (Bṛih. 4. 3. 18).

It is noteworthy how the dominant realistic monism of the Upanishads is frequently overridden by the idealistic tendency which rejects the world of the waking consciousness as the the real world and which adopts the state of dreamless sleep or of ecstatic meditation as grasping the absolute unity and reality. So Prajāpati described the real Self, after futile attempts to satisfy Indra with the lower conceptions such as the person who is seen in the eye and the reflected image in a vessel of water, as follows: 'He who moves about happy in dream—he is the Self' (Chānd. 8. 10. 1). But Indra perceived the failure on Prajāpati's part to instruct him about a Self which is free from evil and from sorrow, for even in dreams one has most unpleasant experiences, such as being struck and cut to pieces.[1]

[1] Bṛih. 4. 3. 20 meets the same difficulty—that in a person's dreaming sleep people seem to be killing him, they seem to be overpowering him, an elephant seems to be tearing him to pieces, he seems to be falling into a hole—with the

Admitting the inadequacy of the state of dreaming sleep as furnishing a cognition of the supreme blissful Self, Prajāpati gives it as his final instruction that 'When one is sound asleep, composed, serene, and knows no dream—that is the Self' (Chānd. 8. 11. 1). But Indra found no satisfaction in such a Self, for in that condition a man does not really know himself so that he can say 'This is I,' nor does he know other things. The objection is not fairly met by Prajāpati's reply that pleasure and pain are due to the self's connection with the body; that the highest condition is when in sleep the serene one, rising out from this body, no longer thinks of the appendage of the body, but goes around laughing, sporting, taking delight with women or chariots or relatives. For the explanation is a relapse into the state of dreaming sleep, which, however pleasant it may be at times, had nevertheless been condemned by Prajāpati himself as faulty, because it is a conscious condition and therefore liable to all the vicissitudes of waking consciousness.

In contrast with the unsatisfactory conclusion of this dialogue, Yājñavalkya, in Bṛih. 2. 4. 14 and 4. 5. 15, gave to Maitreyī—who, like Indra, had been perplexed by the similar instruction that the highest stage of the one Self is unconscious—a more philosophical explanation of why it can not be conscious. 'Where there is a duality, as it were, there one sees another; there one smells another; there one tastes another; there one speaks to another. . . . But where everything has become just one's own self, then whereby and whom would one see? then whereby and whom would one smell? then whereby and to whom would one speak? then whereby and whom would one hear? then whereby and of whom would one think? then whereby and whom would one touch? then whereby and whom would one understand?'[1] 'Knowledge is only of a second.' Consciousness means consciousness of an object; but in that consciousness where all things become one (Kaush. 3. 4), in that unbounded ocean-like

explanation that 'he is imagining through ignorance the very fear which he sees when awake' and which by implication is illusory.

[1] There is another almost identical occurrence of a part of this passage in Bṛih. 4. 3. 31.

pure unity of the real Self (Bṛih. 4. 3. 32), the duality and limitation of the subject-object relation are obliterated. In it, therefore, consciousness is an impossibility.

The conception of this pure unity of being and of the blissful union with self was not clearly defined and consistently held. Maitri 6. 7 suggests the reason. 'Now, where knowledge is of a dual nature [i.e. subjective-objective], there, indeed, one hears, sees, smells, tastes, and also touches; the soul knows everything. Where knowledge is not of a dual nature, being devoid of action, cause, or effect, unspeakable, incomparable, indescribable—what is that? It is impossible to say!' It is strictly inconceivable:—

'Wherefrom words turn back,
Together with the mind, not having attained—
The bliss of Brahma.' (Tait. 2. 4.)

It may only be affirmed as approximately conceived:—

'"This is it"—thus they recognize
The highest, indescribable happiness.' (Kaṭha 5. 14.)

There was consequently vacillation and indefiniteness in the statements regarding it. Prajāpati, when pressed to justify it as unconsciousness, fell back upon the notion of pleasant dreams. The Taittirīya Upanishad, where by arithmetical computation that perfect bliss is declared equal to octillion blisses of the most favored man on earth, states in closing that the aspirant, having reached the 'self which consists of bliss,' goes up and down these worlds, eating what he will and assuming what forms he will, and sits singing the song of universal unity which begins with 'Oh, wonderful! Oh, wonderful! Oh, wonderful!' (Tait. 3. 10. 5).

The limitation of the not-self certainly would be absent in that plenary bliss. 'Where one sees nothing else, hears nothing else, understands nothing else—that is a Plenum. But where one sees something else—that is the small.' 'Verily, a Plenum is the same as Pleasure. There is no Pleasure in the small. Only a Plenum is Pleasure' (Chānd. 7. 23-24). One passage, Bṛih. 4. 3. 23-30 (the only one of its kind in the Upanishads), attempts, contrary to the prevailing conception of the condition of union with the Self, to make qualified provision for sense-activity by a sort of paradox, which is more intelligible in the Mādhyaṁdina than in the Kāṇva recension. 'Verily, while he does not there see, he is verily seeing, though he does not see what is [usually] to be seen; for there is no cessation of the seeing of a seer, because of his imperishability. It is not, however, a second thing, other than himself and separate, that he may see.' Similarly he continues to smell, taste, speak, hear, think, touch, and know, though not a second thing other than himself and separate.

A striking image to illustrate the nature of that bliss is found in Bṛih. 4. 3. 21, according to which the condition of union with the Self is conscious, but void of content either subjectively or objectively referrent, a mere state of bliss. 'As a man, when in the embrace of a beloved wife, knows nothing within or without, so this person when in the embrace of the intelligent Soul knows nothing within or without.' In Māṇḍ. 5 that bliss is found in deep sleep as such.

The true conception of the bliss of union with the Self, then, would seem to be that it is strictly an unconscious condition; but with the attempt to conceive of that condition, which indeed was asserted to be inconceivable, recourse is had to sensual experiences and to balmy sleep.

Strictly it is the state of dreamless sleep which is taken as typifying the attainment of the real. 'Therefore they say of him "he sleeps," for he has gone to his own' (Chānd. 6. 8. 1). This is true both in the Brahma theory and in the Ātman theory. 'So, just as those who do not know the spot might go over a hid treasure of gold again and again, but not find it, even so all creatures here go to that Brahma-world [in deep sleep] day by day, but do not find it' (Chānd. 8. 3. 2)—a doctrine alluded to in Praśna 4. 4. 'Now, that serene one [the soul in sleep] who, rising up out of this body, reaches the highest light and appears with his own form—He is the Soul! That is the immortal, the fearless. That is Brahma. The name, verily, of that Brahma is the Real. . . . Day by day, verily, he who knows this goes to the heavenly world' (Chānd. 8. 3. 4–5).

The pleasant dreams of sleep, rather than the hampered waking consciousness, were, according to some of the passages which have been quoted, tentatively accepted as characteristic of the unlimited Self; but, because of the fact of unpleasant dreams, they were rejected in favor of the bliss of dreamless sleep, where even the duality of subject and object that is foreign to the essential nature of the unitary Self is melted away.

But even that condition of profound sleep from which one wakes refreshed—back, however, into diversity and into the limitation of the waking consciousness—seems too near the unreality of the illusory egohood which is conscious of falsely apparent objects and subjects. In the Māṇḍūkya, therefore, there is put, above the waking consciousness and the dreaming sleep and the dreamless sleep, a fourth stage. 'Not inwardly cognitive, not outwardly cognitive, not bothwise cognitive, not a cognition-mass, not cognitive, not non-cognitive, unseen, with which there can be no dealing, ungraspable, having no distinctive mark, non-thinkable, that cannot be designated, the essence of the assurance of which is the state of being one with the Self' (Māṇḍ. 7). Another later Upanishad, the Maitri, speaks of these same four states of consciousness and denominates the fourth and highest state *turīya* (7. 11).

Not only in sleep and in a superconscious condition deeper than profound sleep does one reach that unity with the Self. He does so also in death, the consummation of unification, for then the diversity and illusoriness of sense-knowledge and separateness are overcome. 'When this self comes to weakness and to confusedness of mind, as it were, then the breaths gather around him. He takes to himself those particles of energy and descends into the heart. When the person in the eye turns away, back [to the sun], then one becomes non-knowing of forms. "He is becoming one," they say; "he does not see." "He is becoming one," they say; "he does not smell." "He is becoming one," they say; "he does not taste." "He is becoming one," they say; "he does not speak." "He is becoming one," they say; "he does not hear." "He is becoming one," they say; "he does not think." "He is becoming one," they say; "he does not touch." "He is becoming one," they say; "he does not know." . . . He becomes one with intelligence' (Bṛih. 4. 4. 1–2). Similarly in Chānd. 6. 8. 6

and 6. 15 death is only the process of absorption into the Real, into the Self. Of a dying person it is said: 'His voice goes into his mind; his mind into his breath; his breath into heat; the heat into the highest divinity. That which is the finest essence—the whole world has that as its soul. That is Reality. That is Ātman. That art thou, Śvetaketu.' And, it might be added, only ignorance and persistence in the thought of a separate self keep one from actually being It. Death is truly the loosing of the cords of the heart which bind one to an illusory life and to the thought of a separate self-existence.

'Gone are the fifteen parts according to their station,
Even all the sense-organs in their corresponding divinities!
One's work and the soul that consists of understanding—
All become unified in the supreme Imperishable.'
(Muṇd. 3. 2. 7.)

It is evident that this pure unity of the self, the really Existent, union with which is effected in sleep and in death, is unconscious, because it is void of all limitations or distinctions whatsoever, being 'the Person all-pervading and without any mark whatever' (Kaṭha 6. 8).

And therein even the possible distinction that 'this is I' (loss of which represented a condition which seemed so abhorrent to Indra and which Prajāpati did not succeed in justifying) is impossible, just because the duality and limitations of the subject-object relation are impossible in that plenary unity. Thus, from the empirical point of view which regards the waking consciousness as the real, a man does in this way 'go straight to destruction'; but to the philosopher, who understands the falsity of ordinary standards and the illusoriness of the ego to which men fondly cling, the loss of finite individuality in the real Self that is unlimited is the supreme achievement. This doctrine is set forth in parables from nature in the 'That-art-thou' section of the Chāndogya. 'As the bees, my dear, prepare honey by collecting the essences of different trees and reducing the essence to a unity, as they are not able to discriminate "I am the essence of this tree," "I am the essence of that tree"—even so, indeed, my dear, all creatures here, though they reach Being, know not "We have reached Being." . . . These rivers, my dear, flow, the eastern toward the east, the western toward the west. They go just from the ocean to the ocean. They become the ocean itself. As there they know not "I am this one," "I am that one"—even so, indeed, my dear, all creatures here, though they have come forth from Being, know not "We have come forth from Being"' (Chānd. 6. 9–10). It is the very consciousness of 'this' and of 'I' which is the limitation that separates one from the unlimited. And individuality and self-consciousness must be lost ere one reach that infinite Real. 'As these flowing rivers that tend toward the ocean, on reaching the ocean, disappear, their name and form [or individuality] are destroyed, and it is called simply "the ocean"—even so of this spectator these sixteen parts that tend toward the Person, on reaching the Person, disappear, their name and form are destroyed, and it is called simply "the Person"' (Praśna 6. 5).

Thus the ultimate unity of reality which has been the search throughout the Upanishads is finally reached. On the epistemological basis of the common-sense realism which views all things as really existing just as they are seen to exist, and in continuation of the cosmologies of the Rig-Veda, the Upanishads started by positing various primeval entities, out of which by various processes the manifold world was produced. Then Brahma, a power such as that inherent in the ritual and sacrifice whereby rain and the forces of nature were controlled, was postulated as the one world-producer and controller. This conception of Brahma gradually developed into a monism. Simultaneously speculation regarding the nature of the unity in which the self and objects are joined developed the conception of Ātman, a great Self, after the analogy of the individual self. The Ātman-theory and the Brahma-theory became merged together in an absolute pantheism. An apparent conflict between the many and the One led to the distinction between phenomenon and noumenon. Those two under further speculation turned out to be respectively an illusory world and an unknowable reality. The theory of epistemological idealism which had been intuited previously on occasions and which had been led up to by the failure of realism, was then developed. The manifold world was seen to be the construction of the imagination, and the supreme unity was found in one's own Self from which the ego is falsely sundered by the life of waking consciousness. That pure unity with the Real which is actually effected in sleep and in death is a blissful state of consciousness in which individuality and all distinctions are overcome.

Thus far chiefly the metaphysical doctrines of the Upanishads have been treated. There remain important ethical and practical corollaries to the main propositions here laid down, and these will be considered in the following chapters.

CHAPTER VIII

THE OUTCOME ON RELIGION AND ON THE DOCTRINE OF KARMA

In the Vedic period punctilious performance of the ritual was the one means of satisfying the gods and of obtaining salvation. In the Brahmanic period a change took place similar to that in the Greek religion. That very efficacy of the sacrifice for the appeasement of the gods whereby men had been kept in subjection, turned out to be an instrument in their hands for controlling the gods, who now became the dependents and received their sustenance from such sacrifice as men might give. In the Upanishads a still further change occurred. The development of a monistic philosophy removed altogether the necessity of believing in the various Vedic or Brahmanic gods to superintend and operate the different departments of nature or to be coerced into man's service. The beginning of this subordination to the one world-all and of the later displacement of the gods as philosophic conceptions (although in popular religion the gods have continued to hold sway) is evidenced in the latter part of the Kena Upanishad. The first half of this Upanishad, by reason of its advanced position on the unknowability of Brahma, must belong to a late period in the Upanishadic philosophy, while the last part of it, which represents Brahma as a new and unknown Being, must belong to the period of the first speculations about that conception. There Agni (Fire) and Vāyu (Wind) discover that their power is not independent, but is subject to the will of the world-ruler Brahma. However, by their knowledge of Brahma they attained a pre-eminence over the other gods; and 'he, verily, who knows it thus, striking off evil, becomes established in the most excellent, endless, heavenly world—yea, he becomes established' (Kena 34).

That last paragraph of the Kena states the radically new standard of religion and of ethics. No longer is worship or sacrifice or good conduct the requisite of religion in this life, or of salvation in the next. Knowledge secures the latter and disapproves of the former. The whole religious doctrine of different gods and of the necessity of sacrificing to the gods is seen to be a stupendous fraud by the man who has acquired metaphysical knowledge of the monistic unity of self and of the world in Brahma or Ātman. 'This that people say, "Worship this god! Worship that god!"—one god after another—this is his creation indeed! And he himself is all the gods' (Bṛih. 1. 4. 6). 'So whoever worships another divinity [than his Self], thinking "He is one and I another," he knows not. He is like a sacrificial animal for the gods. Verily, indeed, as many animals would be of service to a man, even so each single person is of service to the gods. If even one animal is taken away, it is not pleasant. What, then, if many? Therefore it is not pleasing to those [gods] that men should know this [i.e. that the gods are only a phase of Brahma and that an individual man may himself become Brahma by knowing himself to be such]' (Bṛih. 1. 4. 10). Sacrifice and works of merit towards hypostatized divinities are, in the light of metaphysical knowledge, seen to be futile. On the other hand, the very same knowledge conserves all the efforts of the knower who may care to worship and to do religious acts. 'Verily, even if one performs a great and holy work, but without knowing this [i.e. that the whole world is Brahma or the Self, and that I am Brahma or the Self], that work of his merely perishes in the end. One should worship the Self alone as his [true] world. The work of him who worships the Self alone as his [true] world does not perish' (Bṛih. 1. 4. 15).

Thus religious piety is renounced as unnecessary, and knowledge of that fact, or metaphysical knowledge in general, replaces religiosity in worth and alone renders efficacious any religious or meritorious act which anyone, for the sake of conformity to popular custom, may choose to perform. 'If one offers the Agnihotra sacrifice without knowing this [i.e. that the cosmic process itself is a continuous Agnihotra]—that would be just as if he were to remove the live coals and pour the offering on ashes. But if one offers the Agnihotra sacrifice knowing it thus, his offering is made in all worlds, in all beings, in all selves' (Chānd. 5. 24. 1–2). 'This that people say, "By offering with milk for a year one escapes repeated death"—one should know that this is not so, since on the very day that he makes the offering he who knows escapes repeated death' (Bṛih. 1. 5. 2).

This last quotation leads to a topic which holds an important place in the practical religion of India today, namely, the doctrine of *karma* (literally 'action'), the theory that according to one's good or bad actions in this life one passes at death into the body of a higher or a lower being. It is noteworthy that in the Rig-Veda there is no mention of metempsychosis.[1] This fact is interestingly confirmed in the Upanishads at Chānd. 5. 3, where neither Śvetaketu (who, according to Chānd. 6. 1. 2, had spent twelve years in studying the Vedas) nor his father and instructor, Gautama, had heard of the doctrine; but when they are instructed in it, it is expressly stated that the doctrine had always belonged to the Kshatriyas, the military class, and was then for the first time divulged to one of the Brahman class. In the Rig-Veda the eschatology consisted of a belief in a personal immortality in the paradise of the gods. After 'a preliminary sign of the doctrine of metempsychosis in the Atharva-Veda,'[2] the notion first makes its definite appearance in the Śatapatha Brāhmaṇa. In the Upanishads it had not yet become what it became in later times, a belief which Monier Williams

[1] The native commentator of later times thought he discovered a reference to it in RV. 1. 164. 32, *bahu-prajaḥ*, interpreting the word as 'subject to many births.' For a refutation see Monier Williams, *Brahmanism and Hinduism*, p. 18, note 2.

[2] Hopkins, *Religions of India*, p. 175.

has aptly characterized in the following severe statement: 'Transmigration, or metempsychosis, is the great bugbear —the terrible nightmare and daymare—of Indian philosophers and metaphysicians. All their efforts are directed to the getting rid of this oppressive scare. The question is not, What is the truth? The one engrossing problem is, How is the man to break this iron chain of repeated existences?'[1]

How this doctrine of *karma* and reincarnation came to be so thoroughly accepted in India, is uncertain: whether from the Indigenes whom the invading Aryans found in India (as Gough conjectures[2]) or whether as the most plausible philosophic explanation of the phenomena of instinctive knowledge (as in Bṛih. 4. 4. 2) and of dreaming and remembrance of things not experienced in this life, as well as of sin (according to Śaṅkara on Bṛih. 4. 3. 9). (In passing be it noted that these are exactly the considerations which led philosophers like Plato, and Christian theologians like Origen and Julius Müller to the belief in an existence prior to the present life.) At any rate, the belief in a person's renewed existence in another body after death is present in the Upanishads, but not as a burden of despair. It is only the belief that the thoughts and deeds of one earthly life will have their fruition in a subsequent embodiment in the physical world (after an interval in excarnate existence). 'Accordingly, those who are of pleasant conduct here—the prospect is, indeed, that they will enter a pleasant womb, either the womb of a Brahman, or the womb of a Kshatriya, or the womb of a Vaiśya. But those who are of stinking conduct here—the prospect is, indeed, that they will enter a stinking womb, either the womb of a dog, or the womb of a swine, or the womb of an outcast' (Chānd. 5. 10. 7).

'According unto his deeds the embodied one successively
Assumes forms in various conditions.
Coarse and fine, many in number,
The embodied one chooses forms according to his own qualities.

[1] Monier Williams, *Brahmanism and Hinduism*, p. 41.

[2] In the first chapter of his *Philosophy of the Upanishads*, where he cites the prevalence of the belief among semi-savage peoples, connected with animism.

[Each] subsequent cause of his union with them is seen to be
Because of the quality of his acts and of himself.'

(Śvet. 5. 11–12.)

The character which is thus determinative of one's position in the next life is formed not only by action but also by knowledge. 'Either as a worm, or as a moth, or as a fish, or as a bird, or as a snake, or as a tiger, or as a person, or as some other in this or that condition, he is born again here according to his deeds, according to his knowledge' (Kaush. 1. 2).

'Some go into a womb
For the embodiment of a corporeal being.
Others go into a stationary thing
According to their deeds, according to their knowledge.'

(Kaṭha 5. 7.)

In some passages we find a fuller elucidation of the process of *saṁsāra*, according to which a span of life here on earth is followed by a period of excarnate existence, with enjoyment as the result of good deeds, whereupon the inexorable law of rebirth leads to a subsequent life in the physical world :—

'Unsafe boats, however, are these sacrificial forms,
The eighteen, in which is expressed the lower work [i.e. the Vedas and the sciences of subsidiary rules].
Since doers of deeds do not understand, because of passion,
Therefore, when their worlds are exhausted, they sink down wretched.
Thinking sacrifice and merit is the chiefest thing,
Naught better do they know—deluded!
Having had enjoyment on the top of the heaven won by good works,
They re-enter this world, or a lower.' (Muṇḍ. 1. 2. 7, 9, 10.)

As in the matter of religion, so as regards this theological tenet, the Upanishads offer the philosophical knowledge which was the result of their own speculations and which was assessed at a very high value as the means of escape. 'Now, whether they perform the cremation obsequies in the case of such a person [i. e. a person who knows] or not, they [i. e. the dead] pass over into a flame; from a flame, into the day; from the day, into the half-month of the waxing moon; from the half-month of the waxing moon, into the six months during which the sun moves northwards; from the months, into the year; from the year, into the sun; from the sun, into the moon; from the moon, into lightning. There there is a person who is non-human. He leads them on to Brahma. This is the way to the gods, the way to Brahma. They who proceed by it return not to the human condition here!' (Chānd. 4. 15. 5–6). In Bṛih. 6. 2, where the same transmigration theory is discussed, the conclusion is that 'those who know this [namely, the stages of transmigration]' go to the Brahma-worlds. 'Of these there is no return' (Bṛih. 6. 2. 15).

There are several other passages which emphasize the efficaciousness over *karma* and rebirth of that knowledge, the bringing forth of which formed the travails of the Upanishads and the laborious attainment of which induced an exceedingly high estimate of its value:—

> 'What is soundless, touchless, formless, imperishable,
> Likewise tasteless, constant, odorless,
> Without beginning, without end, higher than the great, stable—
> By discerning That, one is liberated from the mouth of death.'
> (Kaṭha 3. 15.)

> 'And one's deeds (*karman*) cease
> When He is seen—both the higher and the lower.'
> (Muṇḍ. 2. 2. 8.)

> 'By knowing what is therein, Brahma-knowers
> Become merged in Brahma, intent thereon, liberated from the womb [i.e. from rebirth].' (Śvet. 1. 7.)

> 'By knowing God there is a falling off of all fetters;
> With distresses destroyed, there is cessation of birth and death.' (Śvet. 1. 11.)

'But they who seek the Ātman by austerity, chastity, faith, and knowledge . . . they do not return' (Praśna 1. 10).

CHAPTER IX

THE OUTCOME ON PRACTICAL LIFE AND ON MORALS

KNOWLEDGE—not 'much learning,' but the understanding of metaphysical truths—was the impelling motive of the thinkers of the Upanishads. Because of the theoretical importance of knowledge in that period of speculative activity, and also because of the discrediting of the popular polytheistic religion by philosophical reasoning, there took place in India during the times of the Upanishads a movement similar to that which produced the Sophists in Greece, namely, a re-adjustment of the accepted ethics and a substitution of philosophic insight for traditional morality. Knowledge was the one object of supreme value, the irresistible means of obtaining one's ends. This idea of the worth and efficacy of knowledge is expressed again and again throughout the Upanishads not only in connection with philosophical speculation, but also in the practical affairs of life. 'That Udgātṛi priest who knows this—whatever desire he desires, either for himself or for the sacrificer, that he obtains by singing. This, indeed, is world-conquering' (Bṛih. 1. 3. 28). 'This whole world, whatever there is, is fivefold. He obtains this whole world who knows this' (Bṛih. 1. 4. 17). 'He [Indra] is without a rival. . . . He who knows this has no rival' (Bṛih. 1. 5. 12). 'Whoever strives with one who knows this, dries up and finally dies' (Bṛih. 1. 5. 21). 'He who knows this [the etymology of Atri (eater)] becomes the eater of everything; everything becomes his food' (Bṛih. 2. 2. 4). 'He who knows that wonderful being as the first-born —namely, that Brahma is the Real—conquers these worlds. Would he be conquered who knows thus that great spirit as the first-born—namely, that Brahma is the Real?' (Bṛih. 5. 4). 'As a lump of clay would fall to pieces in striking against a solid stone, so falls to pieces he who wishes evil to one who knows this, and he, too, who injures him. Such a one is a solid stone' (Chānd. 1. 2. 8).

'He who knows Brahma as the real, as knowledge, as the infinite . . . ,
He obtains all desires.' (Tait. 2. 1.)

'He who knows that food which is established on food, becomes established. He becomes an eater of food, possessing food. He becomes great in offspring, in cattle, in the splendor of sacred knowledge, great in fame' (Tait. 3. 7). 'Whatever conquest is Brahma's, whatever attainment—that conquest he conquers, that attainment he attains who knows this' (Kaush. 1. 7). 'Verily, indeed, if upon one who knows this both mountains should roll themselves forth—both the southern and the northern—desiring to lay him low, indeed they would not lay him low. But those who hate him and those whom he himself hates—these all die around him' (Kaush. 2. 13). 'He, verily, who knows that supreme Brahma . . . in his family no one ignorant of Brahma arises' (Muṇḍ. 3. 2. 9). So frequent are the statements describing the invulnerability and omnipotence of him who is possessed of this magic talisman, that *ya evaṁ veda*, 'he who knows this,' becomes the most frequently recurring phrase in all the Upanishads.

Besides this practical value of knowledge and the speculative value, previously described, for attainment of the ideal unity with the Real,[1] knowledge also had a marked ethical value.

[1] It is noteworthy how the extreme valuation put upon both these kinds of knowledge produced a reaction within the period of the Upanishads themselves. The license to override the prescriptive usages of religion and custom which the possessor of knowledge claimed for himself, is distinctly denied in Maitri 4. 3, on the point of the four customary stages in the life of every orthodox Hindu, through disregard of which the revenues of the priests were seriously diminished.

As regards speculative knowledge of Ātman, its apprehension by means of human knowledge is opposed by the doctrine of *prasāda*, or 'Grace', in Kaṭha 2. 20 (and, with a slight verbal change, in Śvet. 3. 20): 'Through the grace of the Creator he beholds the greatness of Ātman.' It is by means of this grace, according to Śvet. 1. 6, that an individual obtains release from illusion and reaches immortality:—

'In this Brahma-wheel the soul flutters about,
Thinking that itself and the Actuator are different.
When favored by Him, it attains immortality.'

An even more explicit denial of the knowledge-doctrine is found at Kaṭha 2. 23 (= Muṇḍ. 3. 2. 3), where a strict Calvinistic doctrine of election is anticipated:—

'This Soul is not to be obtained by instruction,
Nor by intellect, nor by much learning.
He is to be obtained only by the one whom He chooses.
To such a one that Soul reveals his own person.'

The possessor of knowledge is freed even now from all his evil deeds as well as from the later metempsychosical results of doing any deeds at all. 'Verily, indeed, even if they lay very much [wood] on a fire, it burns it all. Even so one who knows this, although he commits very much evil, consumes it all and becomes clean and pure, ageless and immortal' (Bṛih. 5. 14. 8). 'Brahma is lightning (*vidyut*), they say, because of unloosing (*vidāna*). Lightning unlooses him from evil who knows this, that Brahma is lightning' (Bṛih. 5. 7).

'The plunderer of gold, the liquor-drinker,
The invader of a teacher's bed, the Brahman-killer—
These four sink downward in the scale,
And, fifth, he who consorts with them.

But he who knows these five fires [i.e. the five-fire doctrine, *pañcāgnividyā*] thus, is not stained with evil, even though consorting with those people. He becomes pure, clean, possessor of a pure world, who knows this—yea, he who knows this' (Chānd. 5. 10. 9–10). 'As a rush-reed laid on a fire would be burned up, even so are burned up all the evils of him who offers Agnihotra sacrifice knowing it thus' (Chānd. 5. 24. 3). 'He who understands me [Indra is the speaker, representing Ātman]—by no deed whatsoever of his is his world injured, not by stealing, not by killing an embryo, not by the murder of his mother, not by the murder of his father; if he has done any evil, the dark color departs not from his face' (Kaush. 3. 1). This ethical theory has been compared with the Socratic doctrine of the identity of knowledge and virtue. There is a wide difference, however, between the Upanishadic theory and the theory of the Greek sages that the man who has knowledge should thereby become virtuous in character, or that the result of teaching should be a virtuous life. Here the possession of metaphysical knowledge actually cancels all past sins and even permits the knower unblushingly to continue in 'what seems to be much evil,' with perfect impunity, although such acts are heinous crimes and are disastrous in their effect for others who lack that kind of knowledge.

But this unrestricted freedom of the earlier Upanishads could not long continue. It probably went to excess, for in the middle of the period it is sternly denounced. Good conduct was declared to be an equal requisite with knowledge.

'He who has not understanding,
Who is unmindful and ever impure,
Reaches not the goal,
But goes on to transmigration.

He, however, who has understanding,
Who is mindful and ever pure,
Reaches the goal
From which he is born no more.' (Kaṭha 3. 7–8.)

'Not he who has not ceased from bad conduct . . .
Can obtain Him by intelligence.' (Kaṭha 2. 24.)

The earlier conception that the knower was able to continue in evil unharmed was true only so far as it expressed the idea that knowledge exempts from evil.

'One should be familiar with it. By knowing it,
One is not stained by evil action.' (Bṛih. 4. 4. 23.)

'As water adheres not to the leaf of a lotus-flower, so evil action adheres not to him who knows this [that the Self is Brahma]' (Chānd. 4. 14. 3). This thought recurs at Maitri 3. 2, and, with another simile, at Praśna 5. 5: 'As a snake is freed from its skin, even so, verily, is he [who knows this] freed from sin.' Still another simile is used to drive home this same thought:—

'As to a mountain that's enflamed
Deer and birds do not resort—
So, with the Brahma-knowers, faults
Do never any shelter find.' (Maitri 6. 18.)[1]

The consistent monistic conception, however, of the relation of knowledge and moral evil is that knowledge exempts from both good and evil, and elevates the knower altogether from the region of moral distinctions to the higher one where they are not operative. 'Such a one, verily, the thought does not torment: "Why have I not done the good? Why have I done the evil?" He who knows this, saves himself from

[1] The similes contained in this and the three preceding passages are excellent illustrations of a method of instruction characteristic of the Upanishads and of the Hindu mind in general. Analogies from nature that serve to illustrate a proposition are used to give forceful expression to an argument.

these [thoughts]. For truly, from both of these he saves himself—he who knows this!' (Tait. 2. 9). 'Him [who knows this] these two do not overcome—neither the thought "Hence I did wrong," nor the thought "Hence I did right." Verily he overcomes them both. What he has done and what he has not done do not affect him' (Bṛih. 4. 4. 22).

'When a seer sees the brilliant
Maker, Potentate, Person, the Brahma-source,
Then, being a knower, shaking off good and evil,
Stainless, he attains supreme identity [with Him].'
(Muṇḍ. 3. 1. 3.)

For this emancipation, an emancipation from the unreal and an entrance into the real, the reason is that to the knower good and evil are conceptions of partial knowledge which can no longer hold in the light of full knowledge. They are only verbal distinctions. 'Verily, if there were no speech, neither right nor wrong would be known, neither true nor false, neither good nor bad, neither pleasant nor unpleasant. Speech, indeed, makes all this known' (Chānd. 7. 2. 1).

The world of reality, the Brahma-world to which the true knower is admitted, is devoid of all distinctions, pleasant and unpleasant, which are empirically real, but transcendentally unreal. Accordingly that world is free also from the ethical distinction of good and evil. 'Over that bridge there cross neither day, nor night, nor old age, nor death, nor sorrow, nor well-doing, nor evil-doing. All evils turn back therefrom, for that Brahma-world is freed from evil' (Chānd. 8. 4. 1–2). 'He goes to the world that is without heat, without cold. Therein he dwells eternal years' (Bṛih. 5. 10).

'When there is no darkness, then there is no day or night,
Nor being, nor non-being, only the Kindly One alone.'
(Śvet. 4. 18.)

'He, ... a knower of Brahma, unto Brahma goes on.... He comes to the river Vijarā ('Ageless'). This he crosses with his mind alone. There he shakes off his good deeds and his evil deeds. His dear relatives succeed to the good deeds; those not dear, to the evil deeds. Then, just as one driving a chariot looks down upon the two chariot-wheels [which in their revolutions do not touch him], thus he looks down upon day and night, thus upon good deeds and evil deeds, and upon all the pairs of opposites. This one, devoid of good deeds, devoid of evil deeds, a knower of Brahma, unto very Brahma goes on' (Kaush. 1. 4).

The same ethical position is held in the Ātman-theory. The world-ground, the great Ātman, in itself is—

> 'Apart from the right and apart from the unright,
> Apart from both what has been done and what has not been done here,
> Apart from what has been and what is to be.'
>
> (Kaṭha 2. 14.)

> 'As the sun, the eye of the whole world,
> Is not sullied by the external faults of the eyes,
> So the one Inner Soul of all things
> Is not sullied by the evil in the world, being external to it.'
>
> (Kaṭha 5. 11.)

> 'The bright, the bodiless, the scatheless,
> The sinewless, the pure, unpierced by evil.' (Īśā 8.)

This idea that the Ātman-world is 'free from evil or sin, free from impurity, blameless, spotless,' which is expressed in numerous epithets and detached phrases, also receives an etymological justification. 'In the beginning this world was Soul (*Ātman*) alone in the form of a Person (*puruṣa*). . . . Since before (*pūrva*) all this world he burned up (√*uṣ*) all evils, therefore he is a person (*pur-uṣ-a*)' (Bṛih. 1. 4. 1).[1]

The Ātman thus being void of all ethical distinctions, the Ātman-knower who by his knowledge becomes Ātman likewise transcends them in his union with Him. 'As a man when in the embrace of a beloved wife knows nothing within or without, so this person when in the embrace of the intelligent Soul knows nothing within or without. Verily, that is his [true] form. . . . There a father becomes not a father; a mother, not a mother; the worlds, not the worlds; the gods, not the gods; the Vedas, not the Vedas; a thief, not a thief.

[1] In spite of this non-attributability of moral qualities to the world-ground by theoretical reason, the affirmation of the practical reason in postulating a moral order at the heart of the universe is to be observed in two passages in the Upanishads, Chānd. 6. 16 and Śvet. 6. 6.

. . . He is not followed by good, he is not followed by evil, for then he has passed beyond all sorrows of the heart' (Bṛih. 4. 3. 21–22).[1]

The ethical theory thus far presented, which was based on the epistemological realism of the Upanishads, did not, like the theory of reality, suffer any change by the transition to idealism, but rather was confirmed by it. The illusion of an external world and of an external Soul that needs to be reached by effort of will served only to prove illusory all activity whatever, even the good and evil deeds making up such activity. Sleep is the nearest approach to real existence, an individual in sleep only 'appearing to think, appearing to move about' (Bṛih. 4. 3. 7). 'In this state of sleep, having traveled around and seen good and bad, he hastens again, according to the entrance and place of origin, back to the state of waking. Whatever he sees there [i.e. in dreaming sleep], he is not followed by it, for this person is without attachments' (Bṛih. 4. 3. 16). He there actually reaches the Real and therefore is not affected by the ethical distinctions which are alien to its nature.[2] 'Now, when one is thus sound asleep, composed, serene, he knows no dream . . .; so no evil touches him, for then he has reached the Bright Power' (Chānd. 8. 6. 3).

So the final goal of metaphysical speculation and the practical attainment of supreme and imperishable value was the Soul, the larger Soul which was the ground of the individual soul and of all existence. 'That self is dearer than a son, is dearer than wealth, is dearer than all else, since this self is nearer' (Bṛih. 1. 4. 8). 'He should be searched out, Him one should desire to understand' (Chānd. 8. 7. 1).

[1] Among the many Kantian ideas which Deussen finds in the Upanishads there is a striking one in this connection, namely, that the final goal and perfect condition of the human soul is autonomy. See *svarāj* at Chānd. 7. 25. 2 and *svārājya* at Tait. 1. 6. 2. But the conception of autonomy there held is very different from the idea that an autonomous person is in such full control of self that he never by passion disobeys the moral law. As is indicated in the following sentence, 'He has unchecked sway in all the worlds,' the idea of autonomy is that of unhindered liberty to do what one wills, the same as the condition of perfect bliss described at Tait. 3. 10. 5—a condition in which the successful aspirant 'goes up and down these worlds, eating what he desires, assuming what form he desires.' Cf. also Chānd. 8. 1. 6.

[2] An idea possibly based on the psychological fact that in sleep the moral sense appears greatly weakened.

However beautiful such a doctrine was in theory, it might very easily be misunderstood and misapplied in practice, as indeed it was by Virocana, who is said to have lived as a pupil with Prajāpati for thirty-two years. After receiving instruction about 'the Self which is free from evil, ageless, deathless, sorrowless, hungerless, thirstless, whose desire is the Real, whose conception is the Real,' he went forth and declared the following doctrine: 'Oneself is to be made happy here on earth. Oneself is to be waited upon. He who makes merely himself happy here on earth, who waits upon himself, obtains both worlds, this world and the yonder.' Such utter selfishness is forthwith condemned by the author, who comments: 'Therefore even now here on earth they say of one who is not a giver, who is not a believer, who is not a sacrificer, "Oh! devilish!" for such is the doctrine of the devils.' And Prajāpati also regretfully declared: 'Whosoever shall have such a doctrine—be they gods or be they devils—shall perish' (Chānd. 8. 7–8).

The same mistaken ethical theory might be gathered from Yājñavalkya's advice to Maitreyī, Bṛih. 2. 4 and 4. 5, if Ātman were translated by 'self' or 'ego.' 'Not for love of the wife is a wife dear, but for love of the Soul a wife is dear.' Similarly, not for love of sons, wealth, the Brahman class, the Kshatriya class, the worlds, the gods, things, any thing, are they dear, but for love of the Soul they are dear.

This is not the modern psychological doctrine that we do not desire anything in itself, but only the pleasantness or self-advantage which the possession of that thing yields to us; nor is Yājñavalkya advocating the utilitarian doctrine that all love and apparent altruism are and should be self-love and selfishness. The central idea is rather that all those objects are not separate entities, in themselves of value to us; but that they all are phases of the world-self and that in the common, every-day experience of having affection for others we find illustrated the great doctrine of the individual self finding his selfhood grounded in, and reaching out towards, that larger Self which embraces all individuals and all things.

With this liberal interpretation, Yājnavalkya's advice to Maitreyī, so far as it contains ethical theory, represents the high-water mark in the Upanishads. The practical ethics are certainly not as high. The general teaching is that already presented, namely, that moral distinctions do not obtain for the man who has metaphysical knowledge. This is the influence effected on the Bhagavad-Gītā, the popular book of religious meditation, in which (at 2. 19) Kṛishṇa, the divine incarnation, quells the scruples of Arjuna over the murdering of his enemies by this Upanishadic assurance :—

'If the slayer think to slay,
If the slain think himself slain,
Both these understand not.
This one slays not, nor is slain.' (Kaṭha 2. 19.)

CHAPTER X

THE VOLUNTARY METHOD OF UNITY IN RENUNCIATION AND IN YOGA

As the absolute unity of the Ātman was the final goal of speculative thought, so absolute unity with the Ātman was regarded as the supreme actual attainment. Though this is theoretically accomplishable by mere metaphysical knowledge, it is as a matter of fact accomplished only after death or during sleep. Therefore for the period while one is still alive and not sleeping some other method than knowledge must be provided.

That was found to be what in Muṇḍ. 3. 2. 1 was joined with knowledge as the means of escaping transmigration :—

'They who, being without desire, worship the Person
And are wise, pass beyond the seed [of rebirth] here.'

After knowledge has informed a person that he is Brahma or Ātman, he should strictly have no more desires, for 'he who has found and has awakened to the Soul . . . the world is his' (Bṛih. 4. 4. 13).

'If a person knew the Soul
With the thought "I am He!"
With what desire, for love of what
Would he cling unto the body?' (Bṛih. 4. 4. 12.)

'Verily, because they knew this, the ancients desired not

offspring, saying: "What shall we do with offspring, we whose is this Soul, this home?" They, verily, rising above the desire for sons and the desire for wealth and the desire for worlds, lived the life of a mendicant' (Bṛih. 4. 4. 22; cf. 3. 5. 1).

In actual experience, however, desires do still continue and harass one. But by harboring desires and resorting to activity to satisfy them, one is only admitting and emphasizing to the mind a lack or limitation, and thereby preventing assimilation to and union with the desireless, blissful plenum of the Soul. The entertaining of any desires whatsoever, and the resulting activity, are conditions which from the point of view of knowledge are sheer ignorance; these react in dulling the understanding (cf. Muṇḍ. 1. 2. 9), blind one to the limitation of existence in the world, cause the series of rebirths, and maintain the person's false separation from the real Brahma or Ātman:—

> 'He who in fancy forms desires,
> Because of his desires is born [again] here and there.'
>
> (Muṇḍ. 3. 2. 2.)

The psychology and praxis of this doctrine are set forth in a notable passage, Bṛih. 4. 4. 5–7. 'A person is made of desires only. As is his desire, such is his resolve; as is his resolve, such the action he performs; what action (*karma*) he performs, that he procures for himself. On this point there is this verse:—

> Where one's mind is attached—the inner self
> Goes thereto with action, being attached to it alone.
>
> Obtaining the end of his action,
> Whatever he does in this world,
> He comes again from that world
> To this world of action.

So the man who desires. Now the man who does not desire. He who is without desire, who is freed from desire, whose desire is satisfied, whose desire is the Soul—his breaths do not depart. Being very Brahma, he goes to Brahma. On this point there is this verse:—

> When are liberated all
> The desires that lodge in one's heart,

Then a mortal becomes immortal!
Therein he reaches Brahma!'[1]

But if the metaphysical knowledge of the essential oneness of the individual soul (*ātman*) and the universal Soul (*Ātman*) did not procure the blissful union with that Soul, neither does this theory of the avoidance of limiting desires; for they inevitably rise up in the ordinary life of activity. The final solution of the practical problem which the Upanishads offer, namely Yoga, is the outcome of that conception of strict unity which started the speculations of the Upanishads and which urged them on from cosmology to intelligent monism, and from an external to an internal unity. That unity—under which it is the aim of every philosophy which has ever existed rationally to bring experience—the early Indian thinkers found in Brahma, and then in the objective Soul (*Ātman*), and then in one's own soul, wherein the manifoldness of thought itself and the limitation of the distinctions of object and subject and all sorrows of the heart are merged into an undifferentiated unitary blissful plenum. 'To the unity of the One goes he who knows this [i. e. that all is one]. The precept for effecting this [unity] is this: restraint of the breath, withdrawal of the senses [from objects], meditation, concentration, contemplation, absorption' (Maitri 6. 17, 18). This is Yoga (from the root *yuj*, meaning to 'join,' 'yoke,' 'harness'), a harnessing of the senses and mind from the falsely manifold objects and thoughts, and at the same time a union with the unitary blissful Self.

'When cease the five
[Sense-]knowledges, together with the mind,
And the intellect stirs not—
That, they say, is the highest course.'
(Kaṭha 6. 10; Maitri 6. 30.)

The practical application, the ethics, and the offers of this

[1] It is interesting to note the opposition between this theory that desires are limitations, and the earlier theory in which one of the strongest practical inducements to knowledge was the sure means of obtaining all desires. Cf. Chānd. 1. 1. 7; 5. 1. 4; 7. 10. 2; 8. 2. 10; Bṛih. 1. 3. 28; 6. 1. 4; Tait. 2. 1; Kaṭha 2. 16. Similarly the former method of obtaining Brahma was to know Brahma; now it is to quench all desires. The change on this point is another instance of that transition from epistemological realism to idealism which has been previously traced.

theory of the union with the Self are set forth in Maitri 6. 20. According to that—

'By tranquillity of thought
Deeds, good and evil, one destroys!
With soul serene, stayed on the Soul,
Delight eternal one enjoys!'

The final exhortation of the Upanishads is well expressed in the following words connected with the Brahma-theory:—

'Taking as a bow the great weapon of the Upanishad,
One should put upon it an arrow sharpened by meditation.
Stretching it with a thought directed to the essence of That,
Penetrate that Imperishable as the mark, my friend.

The mystic syllable *Om*[1] is the bow. The arrow is the soul.
Brahma is said to be the mark.
By the undistracted man is It to be penetrated.
One should come to be in It, as the arrow [in the mark].' (Muṇḍ. 2. 2. 3-4.)

CHAPTER XI

CONCLUDING ESTIMATE

SUCH is the philosophy of the Upanishads in what may very probably have been its order of development. Many tendencies made up the process; and perhaps centuries elapsed between the first and last of the speculations recorded, from the Bṛihad-Āraṇyaka and the Chāndogya to the Maitri. The thinkers were earnest in their search for truth, and they unhesitatingly abandoned conclusions which had been reached, when in the light of further reasonings and new considerations they were proved inadequate. The changes from the first realistic materialism to the final speculative idealism form an interesting chapter in the history of philosophy. Their intuitions of

[1] The sacred syllable used in meditation generally and as a special means for attaining the superconscious ecstatic state. For a Western discussion of the mystic union with God, see Evelyn Underhill, *Mysticism*, 3d ed., New York, 1912, esp. pp. 427-452 ('Ecstasy and Rapture'); cf. R. M. Bucke, *Cosmic Consciousness*, 4th ed., New York, 1923.

deep truths are subtile with the directness and subtlety of new seekers after truth. In a few passages the Upanishads are sublime in their conception of the Infinite and of God, but more often they are puerile and groveling in trivialities and superstitions. As Hegel, a keen appreciator and thorough student of the history of philosophy, estimated it, 'If we wish to get the so-called pantheism in its poetic, most elevated, and, if one will, its coarsest form, we must look for it in the Eastern poets; and the largest expositions of it are found among the Indians.'

As it was suggested before, so it must be emphasized again that, although at first the order of exposition here followed was in all probability the historical order in the progress of thought in the early Hindu philosophy, yet there are not the chronological data in the Upanishads upon which an unquestioned order can be maintained throughout. The Bṛihad-Āraṇyaka, Chāndogya, Taittirīya, Aitareya, Kaushītaki and Kena 14–34, from their structure and literary characteristics, as well as from their contents, are quite certainly assigned to the earlier group of the Upanishads. But even in them there is a variety of philosophical doctrines which are not in the same stage of development. The heterogeneity and unordered arrangement and even apparent contradictions of the material make it difficult, indeed impossible, to set forth in systematic exposition a single system of philosophy. The purpose has been, therefore, to discern the different tendencies that are undoubtedly present in the philosophy of the Upanishads and to present them in what seems to be the most probable order of development. For the purposes of exposition there have been followed out and connected with each other certain lines of thought which in the actual development of the philosophy were, of course, interacting and interwoven.

The thought of any people and of any generation is exceedingly complex, consciously or unconsciously containing certain elements from the past, which are being gradually discarded, and also certain presentiments of truth which are only later fully recognized. Yet in it all there is a dominant tendency which may readily be discerned. So in the Upanishadic period there were symbolic cosmologies inherited and accepted, whose influence continued long after they had logically been superseded by more philosophical theories. In the main, however, there was an appreciation of idealism. This, having seen in the psychic self the essence of the whole world, and having identified it with Brahma, reacted against the realistic philosophy which had produced the concept of Brahma; and then it carried the Ātman, or the purely psychical, element over into the extreme of philosophical idealism.

Intelligent monism it may, in general, be called; for, although very different types of philosophy have been shown to be represented in the Upanishads, monism is their most prevalent type and the one which has constituted their chief heritage. Still, even as monism, it is hardly the monism of the West, nor is it the monism that is based upon science. It is like the simple intuition of the early Greek philosopher Xenophanes, who (after a prior course of cosmological theorizings similar to those in the Upanishads) 'looked up into the expanse of heaven and declared, "The One is God."' (Aristotle's *Metaphysics*, 1. 5.) Can such faith in such form, although it has laid hold of the profound truths of ultimate unity and spirituality, furnish the highly inspiring religion of progress and the elaborately articulated philosophy, correlated with science, which modern India demands?

Before that question can be answered, it will be necessary to find out exactly what the revered Upanishads do actually say. Sanskritists, historians, philosophers, religionists—all who are interested in India's past and concerned about India's future may find here something of what each is already seeking in his separate line. In particular, there will be found by the sympathetic reader throughout these thirteen principal Upanishads the records of that eager quest which India has been pursuing through the centuries, which is tersely expressed in the Bṛihad-Āraṇyaka Upanishad in its first division (at 1. 3. 28):—

> 'From the unreal lead me to the real.
> From darkness lead me to light.
> From death lead me to immortality.'

The Upanishads have indubitably exercised, and in the revival of Sanskrit learning and of the Indian national consciousness will continue to exercise, a considerable influence[1] on the religion and philosophy of India. To present their actual contents by a faithful philological translation, and to furnish a clue to their unsystematic expositions by a brief outline of the development of their philosophical concepts, is one of the needs of the time and has been the aim in the preparation of this volume.

[1] Evidenced, for example, in the recent establishment by a Hindu of Bombay of a valuable annual prize for the best exposition and defence of some doctrine of the Upanishads or of Śaṅkara.

BṚIHAD-ĀRAṆYAKA UPANISHAD

FIRST ADHYĀYA

FIRST BRĀHMAṆA[1]

The world as a sacrificial horse[2]

1. *Om!* Verily, the dawn is the head of the sacrificial horse; the sun, his eye; the wind, his breath; universal fire (Agni Vaiśvānara), his open mouth. The year is the body (*ātman*) of the sacrificial horse; the sky, his back; the atmosphere, his belly; the earth, the under part of his belly; the quarters, his flanks; the intermediate quarters, his ribs; the seasons, his limbs; the months and half-months, his joints; days and nights, his feet; the stars, his bones; the clouds, his flesh. Sand is the food in his stomach; rivers are his entrails. His liver and lungs are the mountains; plants and trees, his hair. The orient is his fore part; the occident, his hind part. When he yawns, then it lightens. When he shakes himself, then it thunders. When he urinates, then it rains. Voice, indeed, is his voice.

2. Verily, the day arose for the horse as the sacrificial vessel which stands before. Its place is the eastern sea.

Verily, the night arose for him as the sacrificial vessel which stands behind. Its place is the western sea. Verily, these two arose on both sides of the horse as the two sacrificial vessels.[3]

[1] This Brāhmaṇa occurs also as Śat. Br. 10. 6. 4.

[2] The Aśva-medha, 'Horse-sacrifice,' the most elaborate and important of the animal sacrifices in ancient India (described at length in Śat. Br. 13. 1–5), is interpreted, in this and the following Brāhmaṇa, as of cosmic significance—a miniature reproduction of the world-order. In the liturgy for the Horse-sacrifice (contained in VS. 22–25) there is a similar apportionment of the parts of the animal to the various parts of the world. Compare also a similar elaborate cosmic correlation of the ox at AV. 9. 7.

[3] The vessels used to hold the libations at the Aśva-medha. Here they are symbolized cosmically by the Bay of Bengal and the Indian Ocean.

Becoming a steed, he carried the gods; a stallion, the Gandharvas; a courser, the demons; a horse, men.[1] The sea, indeed, is his relative. The sea is his place.

SECOND BRĀHMAṆA[2]

The creation of the world, leading up to the institution of the horse-sacrifice

1. In the beginning nothing whatsoever was here. This [world] was covered over with death, with hunger—for hunger is death.

Then he made up his mind (*manas*): 'Would that I had a self!'[3]

So he went on (*acarat*) praising (*arcan*). From him, while he was praising, water was produced. 'Verily, while I was praising, I had pleasure (*ka*)!' thought he. This, indeed, is the *arka*-nature of what pertains to brightness (*arkya*). Verily, there is pleasure for him who knows thus that *arka*-nature of what pertains to brightness.

2. The water, verily, was brightness.

That which was the froth of the water became solidified. That became the earth.

On it he [i.e. Death] tortured himself (√*śram*). When he had tortured himself and practised austerity, his heat (*tejas*) and essence (*rasa*) turned into fire.

3. He divided himself (*ātmānam*) threefold: [fire (*agni*) one third], the sun (*āditya*) one third, wind (*vāyu*) one third. He also is Life (*prāṇa*) divided threefold.

The eastern direction is his head. Yonder one and yonder one[4] are the fore quarters. Likewise the western direction is his tail. Yonder one and yonder one[5] are the hind quarters. South and north are the flanks. The sky is the back. The atmosphere is the belly. This [earth] is the chest. He stands firm in the waters. He who knows this, stands firm wherever he goes.

[1] Different names for, and aspects of, this cosmic carrier.
[2] This Brāhmaṇa is found also as a part of Śat. Br. 10. 6. 5.
[3] Or 'a body,' *ātman-vin*.
[4] Explained by Śaṅkara as northeast and southeast respectively.
[5] Explained by Śaṅkara as northwest and southwest respectively.

4. He desired: 'Would that a second self of me were produced!' He—death, hunger—by mind copulated with speech (*vāc*). That which was the semen, became the year. Previous to that there was no year. He bore him for a time as long as a year. After that long time he brought him forth. When he was born, Death opened his mouth on him. He cried '*bhāṇ!*' That, indeed, became speech.

5. He bethought himself: 'Verily, if I shall intend against him, I shall make the less food for myself.' With that speech, with that self he brought forth this whole world, whatsoever exists here: the Hymns (*ṛc*) [i.e. the Rig-Veda], the Formulas (*yajus*) [i.e. the Yajur-Veda], the Chants (*sāman*) [i.e. the Sāma-Veda], meters, sacrifices, men, cattle.

Whatever he brought forth, that he began to eat. Verily, he eats (√*ad*) everything: that is the *aditi*-nature of Aditi (the Infinite). He who knows thus the *aditi*-nature of Aditi, becomes an eater of everything here; everything becomes food for him.

6. He desired: 'Let me sacrifice further with a greater sacrifice (*yajña*)!' He tortured himself. He practised austerity. When he had tortured himself and practised austerity, glory and vigor went forth. The glory and vigor, verily, are the vital breaths. So when the vital breaths departed, his body began to swell. His mind, indeed, was in his body (*śarīra*).

7. He desired: 'Would that this [body] of mine were fit for sacrifice! Would that by it I had a self (*ātmanvin*)!' Thereupon it became a horse (*aśva*), because it swelled (*aśvat*). 'It has become fit for sacrifice (*medhya*)!' thought he. Therefore the horse-sacrifice is called Aśva-medha. He, verily, knows the Aśva-medha, who knows it thus.

He kept him [i.e. the horse] in mind without confining him.[1] After a year he sacrificed him for himself. [Other] animals he delivered over to the divinities. Therefore men sacrifice the victim which is consecrated to Prajāpati as though offered unto all the gods.

[1] Even as in the regular Aśva-medha the consecrated horse is allowed to range free for a year.

Verily, that [sun] which gives forth heat is the Aśva-medha. The year is its embodiment (*ātman*).

This [earthly] fire is the *arka*.[1] The worlds are its embodiments. These are two, the *arka* sacrificial fire and the Aśva-medha sacrifice. Yet again they are one divinity, even Death. He [who knows this] wards off repeated death (*punarmṛtyu*), death obtains him not, death becomes his body (*ātman*), he becomes one of these deities.

Third Brāhmaṇa

The superiority of breath among the bodily functions

1. The gods (*deva*) and the devils (*asura*) were the twofold offspring of Prajāpati. Of these the gods were the younger, the devils the older. They were struggling with each other for these worlds.

The gods said: 'Come, let us overcome the devils at the sacrifice with the Udgītha.'[2]

2. They said to Speech: 'Sing for us the Udgītha.'

'So be it,' said Speech, and sang for them. Whatever pleasure there is in speech, that it sang for the gods; whatever good one speaks, that for itself.

They [i.e. the devils] knew: 'Verily, by this singer they will overcome us.' They rushed upon it and pierced it with evil. That evil was the improper thing that one speaks. That was the evil.

3. Then they [i.e. the gods] said to the In-breath (*prāṇa*) 'Sing for us the Udgītha.'

'So be it,' said the In-breath, and sang for them. Whatever pleasure there is in the in-breath, that it sang for the gods; whatever good one breathes in, that for itself.

They [i.e. the devils] knew: 'Verily, by this singer they will overcome us.' They rushed upon it and pierced it with evil. That evil was the improper thing that one breathes in. This, truly, was that evil.

4. Then they [i.e. the gods] said to the Eye: 'Sing for us the Udgītha.'

[1] That is, the fire in the Horse-sacrifice.

[2] The important Loud Chant in the ritual.

'So be it,' said the Eye, and sang for them. Whatever pleasure there is in the eye, that it sang for the gods; whatever good one sees, that for itself.

They [i.e. the devils] knew: 'Verily, by this singer they will overcome us.' They rushed upon it and pierced it with evil. That evil was the improper thing that one sees. This, truly, was that evil.

5. Then they [i.e. the gods] said to the Ear: 'Sing for us the Udgītha.'

'So be it,' said the Ear, and sang for them. Whatever pleasure there is in the ear, that it sang for the gods; whatever good one hears, that for itself.

They [i.e. the devils] knew: 'Verily, by this singer they will overcome us.' They rushed upon it and pierced it with evil. That evil was the improper thing that one hears. This, truly, was that evil.

6. Then they [i.e. the gods] said to the Mind: 'Sing for us the Udgītha.'

'So be it,' said the Mind, and sang for them. Whatever pleasure there is in the mind, that it sang for the gods; whatever good one imagines, that for itself.

They [i.e. the devils] knew: 'Verily, by this singer they will overcome us.' They rushed upon him and pierced him with evil. That evil was the improper thing that one imagines. This, truly, was that evil.

And thus they let out upon these divinities with evil, they pierced them with evil.

7. Then they [i.e. the gods] said to this Breath in the mouth: 'Sing for us the Udgītha.'

'So be it,' said this Breath, and sang for them.

They [i.e. the devils] knew: 'Verily, by this singer they will overcome us.' They rushed upon him and desired to pierce him with evil. As a clod of earth would be scattered by striking on a stone, even so they were scattered in all directions and perished. Therefore the gods increased, the demons became inferior. He increases with himself, a hateful enemy becomes inferior for him who knows this.

8. Then they said, 'What, pray, has become of him who stuck to us thus?' 'This one here (*ayam*) is within the mouth

(*asya*)!' He is called Ayāsya Āṅgirasa, for he is the essence (*rasa*) of the limbs (*aṅga*).

9. Verily, that divinity is Dūr by name, for death is far (*dūram*) from it. From him who knows this, death is far.

10. Verily, that divinity having struck off the evil of these divinities, even death, made this go to where is the end of the quarters of heaven. There it set down their evils. Therefore one should not go to [foreign] people, one should not go to the end [of the earth], lest he fall in with evil, with death.

11. Verily, that divinity by striking off the evil, the death, of those divinities carried them beyond death.

12. Verily, it carried Speech over as the first. When that was freed from death, it became fire. This fire, when it has crossed beyond death, shines forth.

13. Likewise it carried Smell across. When that was freed from death, it became wind. This wind, when it has crossed beyond death, purifies.

14. Likewise it carried the Eye across. When that was freed from death, it became the sun. That sun, when it has crossed beyond death, glows.

15. Likewise it carried the Ear across. When that was freed from death, it became the quarters of heaven. These quarters of heaven have crossed beyond death.

16. Likewise it carried the Mind across. When that was freed from death, it became the moon. That moon, when it has crossed beyond death, shines.

Thus, verily, that divinity carries beyond death him who knows this.

17. Then it [i.e. breath] sang out food for itself, for whatever food is eaten is eaten by it. Hereon one is established.

18. Those gods said: 'Of such extent, verily, is this universe as food. You have sung it into your own possession. Give us an after-share in this food.'

'As such, verily, do ye enter into me.'

'So be it.' They entered into him from all sides. Therefore whatever food one eats by this breath, these are satisfied by it. Thus, verily, his people come to him, he becomes the supporter of his people, their chief, foremost leader, an eater of food, an overlord—he who knows this. And whoever among his people desires to be the equal of him who has this knowledge suffices not for his dependents. But whoever follows after him and whoever, following after him, desires to support his dependents, he truly suffices for his dependents.

19. He is Ayāsya Āṅgirasa, for he is the essence (*rasa*) of the limbs (*aṅga*). Verily, breath is the essence of the limbs, for verily breath is the essence of the limbs. Therefore from whatever limb the breath departs, that indeed dries up, for it is verily the essence of the limbs.

20. And it is also Bṛihaspati. The Bṛihatī[1] is speech. He is her lord (*pati*), and is therefore Bṛihaspati.

21. And it is also Brahmaṇaspati. Prayer (*brahman*),[2] verily, is speech. He is her lord (*pati*), and is therefore Brahmaṇaspati.

A glorification of the Chant as breath

22. And it is also the Sāma-Veda. The Chant (*sāman*), verily, is speech. It is *sā* (she) and *ama* (he). That is the origin of the word *sāman*.

Or because it is equal (*sama*) to a gnat, equal to a fly, equal to an elephant, equal to these three worlds, equal to this universe, therefore, indeed, it is the Sāma-Veda. He obtains intimate union with the Sāman, he wins its world who knows thus that Sāman.

23. And it is also the Udgītha. The breath verily is up (*ut*), for by breath this whole world is upheld (*ut-tabdha*). Song (*gītha*), verily, is speech; *ut* and *gītha*—that is Udgītha.

24. As also Brahmadatta Caikitāneya, while partaking of King [Soma], said: ' Let this king cause this man's[3] head to fall off, if Ayāsya Āṅgirasa sang the Udgītha with any other means than that, for,' said he, ' only with speech and with breath did he sing the Udgītha.'

25. He who knows the property of that Sāman has that property. Its property, truly, is tone. Therefore let him who is about to perform the duties of an Ṛitvij priest desire a good

[1] Name of a meter used in the Rig-Veda. Here it signifies the Rig-Veda itself.

[2] Here referring particularly to the Yajur-Veda.

[3] That is, ' my.'—Com.

tone in his voice. Being possessed of such a voice, let him perform the duties of the Ṛitvij priest. Therefore people desire to see at the sacrifice one who has a good tone, as being one who has a possession. He has a possession who knows thus the property of the Sāman.

26. He who knows the gold of that Sāman comes to have gold. The tone (*svara*), verily, is its gold. He comes to have gold who knows thus that gold of the Sāman.

27. He who knows the support of that Sāman is indeed supported. Voice, verily, is its support, for when supported on voice the breath sings. But some say it is supported on food.

Prayers to accompany an intelligent performance of the Chant

28. Now next, the praying of the purificatory formulas (*pavamāna*).—

The Prastotṛi priest (Praiser), verily, begins to praise with the Chant (*sāman*). When he begins to praise, then let [the sacrificer] mutter the following :—

'From the unreal (*asat*) lead me to the real (*sat*)!
From darkness lead me to light!
From death lead me to immortality!'

When he says 'From the unreal lead me to the real,' the unreal, verily, is death, the real is immortality. 'From death lead me to immortality. Make me immortal'—that is what he says.

'From darkness lead me to light'—the darkness, verily, is death, the light is immortality. 'From death lead me to immortality. Make me immortal'—that is what he says.

'From death lead me to immortality'—there is nothing there that seems obscure.

Now whatever other verses there are of a hymn of praise (*stotra*), in them one may win food for himself by singing. And, therefore, in them he should choose a boon, whatever desire he may desire. That Udgātṛi priest who knows this—whatever desire he desires, either for himself or for the sacrificer, that he obtains by singing. This, indeed, is world-conquering. There is no prospect of his being without a world who knows thus this Sāman.

Fourth Brāhmaṇa

The creation of the manifold world from the unitary Soul

1. In the beginning this world was Soul (*Ātman*) alone in the form of a Person. Looking around, he saw nothing else than himself. He said first: 'I am.' Thence arose the name 'I.' Therefore even today, when one is addressed, he says first just 'It is I' and then speaks whatever name he has. Since before (*pūrva*) all this world he burned up (√*uṣ*) all evils, therefore he is a person (*pur-uṣ-a*). He who knows this, verily, burns up him who desires to be ahead of him.

2. He was afraid. Therefore one who is alone is afraid. This one then thought to himself: 'Since there is nothing else than myself, of what am I afraid?' Thereupon, verily, his fear departed, for of what should he have been afraid? Assuredly it is from a second that fear arises.

3. Verily, he had no delight. Therefore one alone has no delight. He desired a second. He was, indeed, as large as a woman and a man closely embraced. He caused that self to fall (√*pat*) into two pieces. Therefrom arose a husband (*pati*) and a wife (*patnī*). Therefore this [is true]: 'Oneself (*sva*)[1] is like a half-fragment,' as Yājñavalkya used to say. Therefore this space is filled by a wife. He copulated with her. Therefrom human beings were produced.

4. And she then bethought herself: 'How now does he copulate with me after he has produced me just from himself? Come, let me hide myself.' She became a cow. He became a bull. With her he did indeed copulate. Then cattle were born. She became a mare, he a stallion. She became a female ass, he a male ass; with her he copulated, of a truth. Thence were born solid-hoofed animals. She became a she-goat, he a he-goat; she a ewe, he a ram. With her he did verily copulate. Therefrom were born goats and sheep. Thus, indeed, he created all, whatever pairs there are, even down to the ants.

5. He knew: 'I, indeed, am this creation, for I emitted it all from myself.' Thence arose creation. Verily, he who has this knowledge comes to be in that creation of his.

[1] Less likely is Deussen's interpretation: 'Therefore is this [body] by itself (*sva* = *sve* = *ātmani*) like . . .'

6. Then he rubbed thus.[1] From his mouth as the fire-hole (*yoni*) and from his hands he created fire (*agni*). Both these [i.e. the hands and the mouth] are hairless on the inside, for the fire-hole (*yoni*) is hairless on the inside.

This that people say, 'Worship this god! Worship that god!'—one god after another—this is his creation indeed! And he himself is all the gods.

Now, whatever is moist, that he created from semen, and that is Soma. This whole world, verily, is just food and the eater of food.

That was Brahma's super-creation: namely, that he created the gods, his superiors; likewise that, being mortal, he created the immortals. Therefore was it a super-creation. Verily, he who knows this comes to be in that super-creation of his.

7. Verily, at that time the world was undifferentiated. It became differentiated just by name and form, as the saying is: 'He has such a name, such a form.' Even today this world is differentiated just by name and form, as the saying is: 'He has such a name, such a form.'

He entered in here, even to the fingernail-tips, as a razor would be hidden in a razor-case, or fire in a fire-holder.[2] Him they see not, for [as seen] he is incomplete. When breathing, he becomes breath (*prāṇa*) by name; when speaking, voice; when seeing, the eye; when hearing, the ear; when thinking, the mind: these are merely the names of his acts. Whoever worships one or another of these—he knows not; for he is

[1] The adverb is here used deictically.

[2] Such is the traditional interpretation. If that is correct, the passage presents the earliest occurrence of a favorite simile of the later Vedānta; cf. for example, Śaṅkara on the Brahma-Sūtras 3. 2. 6: 'as fire is latent in firewood or in covered embers.' But the meaning of *viśvambhara* is uncertain. Etymologically the word is a compound signifying 'all-bearing.' As such it is an unambiguous appellation of the earth at AV. 12. 1. 6. The only other occurrence of its adjectival use that is cited in *BR.* is AV. 2. 16. 5, where the commentator substantiates his rendering 'fire' by quoting the present passage. In both of these passages Whitney rejects the meaning 'fire' (*AV. Tr.* p. 60-61), and in his criticism of Böhtlingk's translation of this Upanishad (*AJP.* 11. 432) suggests that '*viśvambhara* may perhaps here mean some kind of insect, in accordance with its later use,' and 'since the point of comparison is the invisibility of the things encased' proposes the translation 'or as a *viśvambhara* in a *viśvambhara*-nest.' But Professor Lanman adds to Whitney's note on AV. 2. 16. 5 (*AV. Tr.* p. 60-61): 'I think, nevertheless, that fire may be meant.' The same simile recurs at Kaush. 4. 20.

incomplete with one or another of these. One should worship with the thought that he is just one's self (*ātman*), for therein all these become one. That same thing, namely, this self, is the trace (*padanīya*) of this All, for by it one knows this All. Just as, verily, one might find by a footprint (*pada*), thus—.[1] He finds fame and praise who knows this.

8. That self is dearer than a son, is dearer than wealth, is dearer than all else, since this self is nearer.

If of one who speaks of anything else than the self as dear, one should say, 'He will lose what he holds dear,' he would indeed be likely to do so. One should reverence the self alone as dear. He who reverences the self alone as dear—what he holds dear, verily, is not perishable.

9. Here people say: 'Since men think that by the knowledge of Brahma they become the All, what, pray, was it that Brahma knew whereby he became the All?'

10. Verily, in the beginning this world was Brahma.

It knew only itself (*ātmānam*): 'I am Brahma!' Therefore it became the All. Whoever of the gods became awakened to this, he indeed became it; likewise in the case of seers (*ṛṣi*), likewise in the case of men. Seeing this, indeed, the seer Vāmadeva began:—

I was Manu and the sun (*Sūrya*)![2]

This is so now also. Whoever thus knows 'I am Brahma!'

[1] In the above translation *evam* ('thus') is regarded as the complete apodosis of the sentence whose protasis is introduced by *yathā* ('just as'). This arrangement of clauses involves an ellipsis, which, if supplied in full, might be: 'Just as, verily, one might find [cattle, the commentator explains] by a footprint, thus one finds this All by its footprint, the self (*ātman*).'

Another possible grouping would connect that protasis with the preceding sentence merely as an added simile, *evam* ('thus') being regarded as a resumptive introduction for the following sentence. The translation of the words thus grouped would be: 'That very thing is the trace of this All—even this self (*ātman*); for by it one knows this All, just as, verily, one might find by a footprint. Thus he finds fame and praise who knows this.'

Neither arrangement of the clauses is entirely satisfactory. Of the two, the latter, however, would appear to be the less probable, for the reason that it prevents the concluding sentence from assuming the exact form—permitted by the arrangement adopted above—of the customary formula announcing the reward of knowing the truths which have been expounded.

[2] RV. 4. 26. 1 a.

becomes this All; even the gods have not power to prevent his becoming thus, for he becomes their self (*ātman*).

So whoever worships another divinity [than his Self], thinking 'He is one and I another,' he knows not. He is like a sacrificial animal for the gods. Verily, indeed, as many animals would be of service to a man, even so each single person is of service to the gods. If even one animal is taken away, it is not pleasant. What, then, if many? Therefore it is not pleasing to those [gods] that men should know this.

11. Verily, in the beginning this world was Brahma, one only. Being one, he was not developed. He created still further[1] a superior form, the Kshatrahood, even those who are Kshatras (rulers)[2] among the gods: Indra, Varuṇa, Soma, Rudra, Parjanya, Yama, Mṛityu, Īśāna. Therefore there is nothing higher than Kshatra. Therefore at the Rājasūya ceremony[3] the Brahman sits below the Kshatriya. Upon Kshatrahood alone does he confer this honor. This same thing, namely Brahmanhood (*brahma*), is the source of Kshatrahood. Therefore, even if the king attains supremacy, he rests finally upon Brahmanhood as his own source. So whoever injures him [i.e. a Brahman] attacks his own source. He fares worse in proportion as he injures one who is better.

12. He was not yet developed. He created the Vis (the commonalty), those kinds of gods that are mentioned in numbers: the Vasus, the Rudras, the Ādityas, the Viśvadevas, the Maruts.

13. He was not yet developed. He created the Sudra caste (*varṇa*), Pūshan.[4] Verily, this [earth] is Pūshan, for she nourishes (√*puṣ*) everything that is.

14. He was not yet developed. He created still further a better form, Law (*dharma*). This is the power (*kṣatra*) of the Kshatriya class (*kṣatra*), viz. Law. Therefore there is nothing higher than Law. So a weak man controls a strong man by Law, just as if by a king. Verily, that which is Law is truth. Therefore they say of a man who speaks the truth,

[1] *aty-asṛjata*: 'super-created.'

[2] *kṣatra*: abstractly, power or dominion; specifically, temporal power: used to designate the military and princely class, as contrasted with the priestly class of Brahmans. See page 98, note 2.

[3] The ceremonial anointing of a king.

[4] Another Vedic divinity.

'He speaks the Law,' or of a man who speaks the Law, 'He speaks the truth.' Verily, both these are the same thing.

15. So that Brahma [appeared as] Kshatra, Viś, and Śūdra. So among the gods Brahma appeared by means of Agni, among men as a Brahman, as a Kshatriya by means of the [divine] Kshatriya, as a Vaiśya by means of the [divine] Vaisya, as a Śūdra by means of the [divine] Śūdra. Therefore people desire a place among the gods in Agni, among men in a Brahman, for by these two forms [pre-eminently] Brahma appeared.

Now whoever departs from this world [i. e. the world of the Ātman] without having recognized it as his own, to him it is of no service, because it is unknown, as the unrecited Vedas or any other undone deed [do not help a man].

Verily, even if one performs a great and holy work, but without knowing this, that work of his merely perishes in the end. One should worship the Self alone as his [true] world. The work of him who worships the Self alone as his world does not perish, for out of that very Self he creates whatsoever he desires.[1]

16. Now this Self, verily, is a world of all created things. Insofar as a man makes offerings and sacrifices, he becomes the world of the gods. Insofar as he learns [the Vedas], he becomes the world of the seers (*ṛṣi*). Insofar as he offers libations to the fathers and desires offspring, he becomes the world of the fathers. Insofar as he gives lodging and food to men, he becomes the world of men. Insofar as he finds grass and water for animals, he becomes the world of animals. Insofar as beasts and birds, even to the ants, find a living in his houses, he becomes their world. Verily, as one would desire security for his own world, so all creatures wish security for him who has this knowledge. This fact, verily, is known when it is thought out.

17. In the beginning this world was just the Self (*Ātman*), one only. He wished: 'Would that I had a wife; then I would procreate. Would that I had wealth; then I would offer sacrifice.' So great, indeed, is desire. Not even if one desired, would he get more than that. Therefore even today when one is lonely one wishes: 'Would that I had a wife, then

[1] Cf. Chānd. 8. 2, where this thought is developed in detail.

I would procreate. Would that I had wealth, then I would offer sacrifice.' So far as he does not obtain any one of these, he thinks that he is, assuredly, incomplete. Now his completeness is as follows: his mind truly is his self (*ātman*); his voice is his wife; his breath is his offspring; his eye is his worldly wealth, for with his eye he finds; his ear is his heavenly [wealth], for with his ear he hears it; his body (*ātman*), indeed, is his work, for with his body he performs work.

The sacrifice is fivefold. The sacrificial animal is fivefold. A person is fivefold. This whole world, whatever there is, is fivefold. He obtains this whole world who knows this.

Fifth Brāhmaṇa

The threefold production of the world by Prajāpati as food for himself

1. When the Father produced by intellect
And austerity seven kinds of food,
One of his [foods] was common to all,
Of two he let the gods partake,
Three he made for himself,
One he bestowed upon the animals.
On this [food] everything depends,
Both what breathes and what does not.
How is it that these do not perish
When they are being eaten all the time?
He who knows this imperishableness—
He eats food with his mouth (*pratīka*),
He goes to the gods,
He lives on strength.

Thus the verses.

2. 'When the Father produced by intellect and austerity seven kinds of food'—truly by intellect and austerity the Father did produce them.

'One of his [foods] was common to all.' That of his which is common to all is the food that is eaten here. He who worships that, is not turned from evil, for it is mixed [i. e. common, not selected].

'Of two he let the gods partake.' They are the *huta* (fire-sacrifice) and the *prahuta* (offering). For this reason one sacrifices and offers to the gods. People also say that these two are the new-moon and the full-moon sacrifices. Therefore one should not offer sacrifice [merely] to secure a wish.

'One he bestowed upon the animals'—that is milk, for at first both men and animals live upon milk. Therefore they either make a new-born babe lick butter or put it to the breast. Likewise they call a new-born calf 'one that does not eat grass.'

'On this [food] everything depends, both what breathes and what does not'—for upon milk everything depends, both what breathes and what does not. This that people say, 'By offering with milk for a year one escapes repeated death (*punarmṛtyu*)'—one should know that this is not so, since on the very day that he makes the offering he who knows escapes repeated death, for he offers all his food to the gods.

'How is it that these do not perish when they are being eaten all the time?' Verily, the Person is imperishableness, for he produces this food again and again.

'He who knows this imperishableness'—verily, a person is imperishableness, for by continuous meditation he produces this food as his work. Should he not do this, all the food would perish.

'He eats food with his mouth (*pratīka*).' The *pratīka* is the mouth. So he eats food with his mouth.

'He goes to the gods, he lives on strength'—this is praise.

3. 'Three he made for himself.' Mind, speech, breath—these he made for himself.

People say: 'My mind was elsewhere; I did not see. My mind was elsewhere; I did not hear. It is with the mind, truly, that one sees. It is with the mind that one hears. Desire, imagination, doubt, faith, lack of faith, steadfastness, lack of steadfastness, shame, meditation, fear—all this is truly mind.[1] Therefore even if one is touched on his back, he discerns it with the mind.

Whatever sound there is, it is just speech. Verily, it comes to an end [as human speech]; verily, it does not [as the heavenly voice].

The in-breath, the out-breath, the diffused breath, the up-breath, the middle-breath—all this is just breath.

[1] This and the two preceding sentences are quoted at Maitri 6. 30.

Verily, the self (*ātman*) consists of speech, mind, and breath.

4. These same are the three worlds. This [terrestrial] world is Speech. The middle [atmospheric] world is Mind. That [celestial] world is Breath.

5. These same are the three Vedas. The Rig-Veda is Speech. The Yajur-Veda is Mind. The Sāma-Veda is Breath.

6. The same are the gods, Manes, and men. The gods are Speech. The Manes are Mind. Men are Breath.

7. These same are father, mother, and offspring. The father is Mind. The mother is Speech. The offspring is Breath.

8. These same are what is known, what is to be known, and what is unknown.

Whatever is known is a form of Speech, for Speech is known. Speech, having become this, helps him [i. e. man].

9. Whatever is to be known is a form of Mind, for mind is to be known. Mind, having become this, helps him.

10. Whatever is unknown is a form of Breath, for Breath is unknown. Breath, having become this, helps him.

11. Of this Speech the earth is the body. Its light-form is this [terrestrial] fire. As far as Speech extends, so far extends the earth, so far this fire.

12. Likewise of that Mind the sky is the body. Its light-form is yon sun. As far as Mind extends, so far extends the sky, so far yon sun.

These two [the fire and the sun] entered sexual union. Therefrom was born Breath. He is Indra. He is without a rival. Verily, a second person is a rival. He who knows this has no rival.

13. Likewise of that Breath, water is the body. Its light-form is yon moon. As far as Breath extends, so far extends water, so far yon moon.

These are all alike, all infinite. Verily he who worships them as finite wins a finite world. Likewise he who worships them as infinite wins an infinite world.

One's self identified with the sixteenfold Prajāpati

14. That Prajāpati is the year. He is composed of sixteen parts. His nights, truly, are fifteen parts. His

sixteenth part is steadfast. He is increased and diminished by his nights alone. Having, on the new-moon night, entered with that sixteenth part into everything here that has breath, he is born thence on the following morning [as the new moon]. Therefore on that night one should not cut off the breath of any breathing thing, not even of a lizard, in honor of that divinity.

15. Verily, the person here who knows this, is himself that Prajāpati with the sixteen parts who is the year. The fifteen parts are his wealth. The sixteenth part is his self (*ātman*). In wealth alone [not in self] is one increased and diminished.

That which is the self (*ātman*) is a hub; wealth, a felly.[1] Therefore even if one is overcome by the loss of everything, provided he himself lives, people say merely: 'He has come off with the loss of a felly!'

The three worlds and how to win them

16. Now, there are of a truth three worlds—the world of men, the world of the fathers, and the world of the gods. This world of men is to be obtained by a son only, by no other means; the world of the fathers, by sacrifice; the world of the gods, by knowledge. The world of the gods is verily the best of worlds. Therefore they praise knowledge.

A father's transmission to his son

17. Now next, the Transmission.[2]—

When a man thinks he is about to depart, he says to his son: 'Thou art holy knowledge. Thou art sacrifice. Thou art the world.' The son replies: 'I am holy knowledge. I am sacrifice. I am the world.' Verily, whatever has been learned [from the Vedas], the sum of all this is expressed by the word 'knowledge' (*brahma*). Verily, whatever sacrifices have been made, the sum of them all is expressed by the word 'sacrifice.' Whatever worlds there are, they are all comprehended under the word 'world.' So great, verily, is this all.

[1] In the analogy of a wheel.

[2] Another description of a dying father's benediction and bestowal upon his son occurs at Kaush. 2. 15.

'Being thus the all, let him assist me from this world,' thus [the father considers]. Therefore they call 'world-procuring' a son who has been instructed.[1] Therefore they instruct him.

When one who has this knowledge departs from this world, he enters into his son with these vital breaths [i. e. faculties: Speech, Mind, and Breath]. Whatever wrong has been done by him, his son frees him from it all. Therefore he is called a son (*putra*).[2] By his son a father stands firm in this world. Then into him [who has made over to his son his mortal breaths] enter those divine immortal breaths.

18. From the earth and from the fire the divine Speech enters him. Verily, that is the divine Speech whereby whatever one says comes to be.

19. Out of the sky and out of the sun the divine Mind enters him. Verily, that is the divine Mind whereby one becomes blissful and sorrows not.

20. Out of the water and out of the moon the divine Breath enters him. Verily, that is the divine Breath which, whether moving or not moving, is not perturbed, nor injured.

He who knows this becomes the Self of all beings. As is that divinity [i. e. Prajāpati], so is he. As all beings favor that divinity, so to him who knows this all beings show favor. Whatever sufferings creatures endure, these remain with them. Only good goes to him. Evil, verily, does not go to the gods.

Breath, the unfailing power in a person: like the unwearying world-breath, wind

21. Now next, a Consideration of the Activities.—Prajāpati created the active functions (*karma*). They, when they had been created, strove with one another. 'I am going

[1] The sense of this and the following paragraph seems to involve a play upon the double meaning of a word, a procedure characteristic of the Upanishads. The word *lokya* may here be translated 'world-wise' or 'world-procuring.' When properly instructed, a son is 'world-wise' in his own attainment of the world through knowledge. He is also 'world-procuring' for his father, in that he is able, through the discharge of appointed filial duties, to help the departed spirit of his father to attain a better world than would otherwise be possible.

[2] Cf. Mānava-Dharma-Śāstra 9. 138: 'Because a son delivers (*trāyate*) his father from the hell called Put, therefore he is called *putra* (son) [i. e. deliverer from hell].'

to speak,' the voice began. 'I am going to see,' said the eye. 'I am going to hear,' said the ear. So spake the other functions, each according to his function. Death, appearing as weariness, laid hold and took possession of them; and, taking possession of them, Death checked them. Therefore the voice becomes weary, the eye becomes weary, the ear becomes weary. But Death did not take possession of him who was the middle breath. They sought to know him. They said: 'Verily, he is the best of us, since whether moving or not moving, he is not perturbed, nor perishes. Come, let us all become a form of him.' Of him, indeed, they became a form. Therefore they are named 'vital breaths' after him. In whatever family there is a man who has this knowledge, they call that family after him. Whoever strives with one who knows this, dries up and finally dies.—So much with reference to the self.

22. Now with reference to the divinities.—

'Verily, I am going to blaze,' began the Fire. 'I am going to give forth heat,' said the Sun. 'I am going to shine,' said the Moon. So said the other divinities, each according to his divine nature. As Breath holds the central position among the vital breaths [or functions], so Wind among these divinities; for the other divinities have their decline, but not Wind. The Wind is that divinity which never goes to rest

23. There is this verse on the subject:—

> From whom the sun rises
> And in whom it sets—

in truth, from Breath it rises, and in Breath it sets—

> Him the gods made law (*dharma*);
> He only today and tomorrow will be.

Verily, what those [functions] undertook of old, even that they accomplish today. Therefore one should practise but one activity. He should breathe in and breathe out, wishing, 'May not the evil one, Death, get me.' And the observance which he practises he should desire to fulfil to the end. Thereby he wins complete union with that divinity [i. e. Breath] and residence in the same world.

Sixth Brāhmaṇa

The entire actual world a threefold appearance of the unitary immortal Soul

1. Verily, this world is a triad—name, form, and work. Of these, as regards names, that which is called Speech is their hymn of praise (*uktha*), for from it arise (*ut-thā*) all names. It is their Sāman (chant), for it is the same (*sama*) as all names. It is their prayer (*brahman*), for it supports (√*bhar*) all names.

2. Now of forms.—That which is called the Eye is their hymn of praise (*uktha*), for from it arise (*ut-thā*) all forms. It is their Sāman (chant), for it is the same (*sama*) as all forms. It is their prayer (*brahman*), for it supports (√*bhar*) all forms.

3. Now of works.—That which is called the Body (*ātman*) is their hymn of praise (*uktha*), for from it arise (*ut-thā*) all actions. It is their Sāman (chant), for it is the same (*sama*) as all works. It is their prayer (*brahman*), for it supports (√*bhar*) all works.

Although it is that triad, this Soul (*Ātman*) is one. Although it is one, it is that triad. That is the Immortal veiled by the real (*satya*). Life (*prāṇa*, 'breath') [a designation of the Ātman], verily, is the Immortal. Name and form are the real. By them this Life is veiled.

SECOND ADHYĀYA

First Brāhmaṇa[1]

Gārgya and Ajātaśatru's progressive definition of Brahma as the world-source, entered in sleep

1. Dṛiptabālāki was a learned Gārgya. He said to Ajātaśatru, [king] of Benares: 'I will tell you about Brahma.' Ajātaśatru said: 'We will give a thousand [cows] for such a speech. Verily, people will run hither, crying, "A Janaka! a Janaka!"'[2]

[1] Compare the similar conversation in Kaush. 4.

[2] A very learned and liberal king.

2. Gārgya said: 'The Person who is yonder in the sun—him, indeed, I worship as Brahma!'

Ajātaśatru said: 'Talk not to me about him! I worship him as the pre-eminent, the head and king of all beings. He who worships him as such becomes pre-eminent, the head and king of all beings.'

3. Gārgya said: 'The Person who is yonder in the moon—him, indeed, I worship as Brahma!'

Ajātaśatru said: 'Talk not to me about him! I worship him as the great, white-robed king Soma. He who worships him as such, for him soma is pressed out and continually pressed out day by day. His food does not fail.'

4. Gārgya said: 'The Person who is yonder in lightning—him, indeed, I worship as Brahma!'

Ajātaśatru said: 'Talk not to me about him! I worship him, verily, as the Brilliant. He who worships him as such becomes brilliant indeed. His offspring becomes brilliant.'

5. Gārgya said: 'The Person who is here in space—him, indeed, I worship as Brahma!'

Ajātaśatru said: 'Talk not to me about him! I worship him, verily, as the Full, the non-active. He who worships him as such is filled with offspring and cattle. His offspring goes not forth from this earth.'

6. Gārgya said: 'The Person who is here in wind—him, indeed, I worship as Brahma!'

Ajātaśatru said: 'Talk not to me about him! Verily, I worship him as Indra, the terrible (*vaikuṇṭha*), and the unconquered army. He who worships him as such becomes indeed triumphant, unconquerable, and a conqueror of adversaries.'

7. Gārgya said: 'The Person who is here in fire—him, indeed, I worship as Brahma!'

Ajātaśatru said: 'Talk not to me about him! I worship him, verily, as the Vanquisher. He who worships him as such becomes a vanquisher indeed. His offspring become vanquishers.'

8. Gārgya said: 'The Person who is here in water—him, indeed, I worship as Brahma!'

Ajātaśatru said: 'Talk not to me about him! I worship him, verily, as the Counterpart [of phenomenal objects]. His counterpart comes to him [in his children], not that which is not his counterpart. His counterpart is born from him.'

9. Gārgya said: 'The Person who is here in a mirror—him, indeed, I worship as Brahma!'

Ajātaśatru said: 'Talk not to me about him! I worship him, verily, as the Shining One. He who worships him as such becomes shining indeed. His offspring shine. He outshines all those with whom he goes.'

10. Gārgya said: 'The sound here which follows after one as he goes—him, indeed, I worship as Brahma!'

Ajātaśatru said: 'Talk not to me about him! I worship him, verily, as Life (*asu*). To him who worships him as such there comes a full length of life (*āyu*) in this world. Breath (*prāṇa*) leaves him not before the time.'

11. Gārgya said: 'The Person who is here in the quarters of heaven—him, indeed, I worship as Brahma!'

Ajātaśatru said: 'Talk not to me about him! I worship him, verily, as the Inseparable Companion. He who worships him as such has a companion. His company is not separated from him.'

12. Gārgya said: 'The Person here who consists of shadow—him, indeed, I worship as Brahma!'

Ajātaśatru said: 'Talk not to me about him! I worship him, verily, as Death. To him who worships him as such there comes a full length of life in this world. Death does not come to him before the time.'

13. Gārgya said: 'The Person here who is in the body (*ātman*)—him, indeed, I worship as Brahma!'

Ajātaśatru said: 'Talk not to me about him! I worship him, verily, as the Embodied One (*ātmanvin*). He who worships him as such becomes embodied indeed. His offspring becomes embodied.'

Gārgya became silent.

14. Ajātaśatru said: 'Is that all?'

Gārgya said: 'That is all.'

Ajātaśatru said: 'With that much [only] it is not known.'

Gārgya said: 'Let me come to you as a pupil.'

15. Ajātaśatru said: 'Verily, it is contrary to the course of things that a Brahman should come to a Kshatriya, thinking

"He will tell me Brahma." However, I shall cause you to know him clearly.'

He took him by the hand and rose. The two went up to a man who was asleep. They addressed him with these words: 'Thou great, white-robed king Soma!' He did not rise. He [i.e. Ajātaśatru] woke him by rubbing him with his hand. That one arose.

16. Ajātaśatru said: 'When this man fell asleep thus, where then was the person who consists of intelligence (*vijñāna*)? Whence did he thus come back?'

And this also Gārgya did not know.

17. Ajātaśatru said: 'When this man has fallen asleep thus, then the person who consists of intelligence, having by his intelligence taken to himself the intelligence of these senses (*prāṇa*), rests in that place which is the space within the heart. When that person restrains the senses, that person is said to be asleep. Then the breath is restrained. The voice is restrained. The eye is restrained. The ear is restrained. The mind is restrained.

18. When he goes to sleep, these worlds are his. Then he becomes a great king, as it were. Then he becomes a great Brahman, as it were. He enters the high and the low, as it were. As a great king, taking with him his people, moves around in his own country as he pleases, even so here this one, taking with him his senses, moves around in his own body (*śarīra*) as he pleases.

19. Now when one falls sound asleep (*suṣupta*), when one knows nothing whatsoever, having crept out through the seventy-two thousand channels called *hitā*, which lead from the heart to the pericardium, one rests in the pericardium. Verily, as a youth or a great king or a great Brahman might rest when he has reached the summit of bliss, so this one now rests.

20. As a spider might come out with his thread, as small sparks come forth from the fire, even so from this Soul come forth all vital energies (*prāṇa*), all worlds, all gods, all beings. The mystic meaning (*upaniṣad*) thereof is 'the Real of the real (*satyasya satya*).[1] Vital energies, verily, are the real. He is their Real.'

[1] Part of this paragraph recurs at Maitri 6. 32.

SECOND BRĀHMAṆA

The embodiment of Breath in a person

1. Verily, he who knows the new-born infant with his housing, his covering, his post, and his rope, keeps off seven hostile relatives.

Verily, this infant is Breath (*prāṇa*) in the middle. Its housing is this [body]. Its covering is this [head]. Its post is breath (*prāṇa*). Its rope is food.

2. Seven imperishable beings stand near to serve him. Thus there are these red streaks in the eye. By them Rudra is united with him. Then there is the water in the eye. By it Parjanya is united with him. There is the pupil of the eye. By it the sun is united with him. By the black of the eye, Agni; by the white of the eye, Indra; by the lower eyelash, Earth is united with him; by the upper eyelash, Heaven. He who knows this—his food does not fail.

3. In connection herewith there is this verse:—

> There is a cup with its mouth below and its bottom up.
> In it is placed every form of glory.
> On its rim sit seven seers.
> Voice as an eighth is united with prayer (*brahman*).[1]

'There is a cup having its mouth below and its bottom up'—this is the head, for that is a cup having its mouth below and its bottom up. 'In it is placed every form of glory'—breaths, verily, are the 'every form of glory' placed in it; thus he says breaths (*prāṇa*). 'On its rim sit seven seers'—verily, the breaths are the seers. Thus he says breaths. 'Voice as an eighth is united with prayer'—for voice as an eighth is united with prayer.

4. These two [sense-organs] here [i. e. the ears] are Gotama and Bharadvāja. This is Gotama and this is Bharadvāja. These two here [i. e. the eyes] are Viśvāmitra and Jamadagni. This is Viśvāmitra. This is Jamadagni. These two here [i. e. the nostrils] are Vasishṭha and Kaśyapa. This is Vasishṭha. This is Kaśyapa. The voice is Atri, for by the voice food is eaten (√*ad*). Verily, eating (*at-ti*) is the same as the name

[1] A very similar stanza is found at AV. 10. 8. 9.

Atri. He who knows this becomes the eater of everything; everything becomes his food.

THIRD BRĀHMAṆA

The two forms of Brahma

1. There are, assuredly, two forms of Brahma: the formed (*mūrta*) and the formless,[1] the mortal and the immortal, the stationary and the moving, the actual (*sat*) and the yon (*tya*).

2. This is the formed [Brahma]—whatever is different from the wind and the atmosphere. This is mortal; this is stationary; this is actual. The essence of this formed, mortal, stationary, actual [Brahma] is yonder [sun] which gives forth heat, for that is the essence of the actual.

3. Now the formless [Brahma] is the wind and the atmosphere. This is immortal, this is moving, this is the yon. The essence of this unformed, immortal, moving, yonder [Brahma] is the Person in that sun-disk, for he is the essence of the yon. —Thus with reference to the divinities.

4. Now, with reference to the self.—

Just that is the formed [Brahma] which is different from breath (*prāṇa*) and from the space which is within the self (*ātman*). This is mortal, this is stationary, this is actual. The essence of this formed, mortal, stationary, actual [Brahma] is the eye, for it is the essence of the actual.

5. Now the formless [Brahma] is the breath and the space which is within the self. This is immortal, this is moving, this is the yon. The essence of this unformed, immortal, moving, yonder [Brahma] is this Person who is in the right eye, for he is the essence of the yonder.

6. The form of this Person is like a saffron-colored robe, like white wool, like the [red] Indragopa beetle, like a flame of fire, like the [white] lotus-flower, like a sudden flash of lightning. Verily, like a sudden lightning-flash is the glory of him who knows this.

Hence, now, there is the teaching 'Not thus! not so!' (*neti, neti*), for there is nothing higher than this, that he is thus. Now the designation for him is 'the Real of the real.' Verily, breathing creatures are the real. He is their Real.

[1] Thus far the sentence recurs at Maitri 6. 3.

Fourth Brāhmaṇa

The conversation of Yājñavalkya and Maitreyī concerning the pantheistic Soul

1. 'Maitreyī!' said Yājñavalkya, 'lo, verily, I am about to go forth from this state.[1] Behold! let me make a final settlement for you and that Kātyāyanī.'

2. Then said Maitreyī: 'If now, sir, this whole earth filled with wealth were mine, would I be immortal thereby?'

'No,' said Yājñavalkya. 'As the life of the rich, even so would your life be. Of immortality, however, there is no hope through wealth.'

3. Then said Maitreyī: 'What should I do with that through which I may not be immortal? What you know, sir—that, indeed, tell me!'

4. Then said Yājñavalkya: 'Ah (*bata*)! Lo (*are*), dear (*priyā*) as you are to us, dear is what you say! Come, sit down. I will explain to you. But while I am expounding, do you seek to ponder thereon.'

5. Then said he: 'Lo, verily, not for love of the husband is a husband dear, but for love of the Soul (*Ātman*) a husband is dear.

Lo, verily, not for love of the wife is a wife dear, but for love of the Soul a wife is dear.

Lo, verily, not for love of the sons are sons dear, but for love of the Soul sons are dear.

Lo, verily, not for love of the wealth is wealth dear, but for love of the Soul wealth is dear.

Lo, verily, not for love of Brahmanhood[2] (*brahma*) is Brahmanhood dear, but for love of the Soul Brahmanhood is dear.

Lo, verily, not for love of Kshatrahood[2] (*kṣatra*) is Kshatrahood dear, but for love of the Soul Kshatrahood is dear.

[1] Instead of the general meaning 'place,' *sthāna* in this context probably has this more technical meaning, designating 'stage in the life of a Brahman' (*āśrama*); i.e. from being a 'householder' (*gṛhastha*) he is going on to be an 'anchorite' (*vanaprastha*) in the order of the 'four stages.'

[2] From the more simple, general conception of *brahma* as 'devotion' and 'sanctity' there became developed a more specific, technical application, 'the

Lo, verily, not for love of the worlds are the worlds dear, but for love of the Soul the worlds are dear.

Lo, verily, not for love of the gods are the gods dear, but for love of the Soul the gods are dear.

Lo, verily, not for love of the beings (*bhūta*) are beings dear, but for love of the Soul beings are dear.

Lo, verily, not for love of all is all dear, but for love of the Soul all is dear.

priesthood' or 'the Brahman class.' Likewise from the more simple, general conception of *kṣatra* as 'rule' was developed a more specific, technical application, 'the ruling power' or 'the Kshatriya class.'

The trend of this process is discernible in the Rig-Veda at 1. 157. 2, the earliest instance where the two words are associated. Various stages may be noted in other passages where the two words are connected. In the Atharva-Veda at 12. 5. 8 they would seem to be used (unless, indeed, figuratively) in the primary, non-technical sense, for they are mentioned along with other qualities of a Kshatriya. But the technical significance is evident in AV. 2. 15. 4 and 15. 10. 2–11; while in AV. 9. 7. 9 the social classes as such are unmistakably emphasized. Similarly in the Vājasaneyi-Saṁhitā :—in 19. 5 the primary meaning is dominant; in 5. 27; 6. 3; 7. 21; 14. 24; 18. 38 the more technical meaning is evident; while *brahma* and *kṣatra* are mentioned along with other caste terms at 10. 10–12 (with *viś*, 'the people'); 18. 48; 20. 17, 25; 26. 2; 30. 5 (with *vaiśya* and *śūdra*). Similarly in the Aitareya Brāhmaṇa where the two words are associated :—at 3. 11 and 7. 21, with the primary meaning dominant, there seems to be a touch of the technical significance; at 7. 22, 24 the social classes are designated, although it comes out clearly that they are such because characterized by the abstract qualities *brahma* and *kṣatra* respectively; they are mentioned as distinct classes at 2. 33 (along with the *viś*) and at 7. 19 (along with *vaiśya* and *śūdra*). Similarly in the Śatapatha Brāhmaṇa where the two words are associated :—the primary conceptions are apparent in 11. 4. 3. 11–13, where *brahma* and *kṣatra* are qualities or characteristics co-ordinated with other objects desired in prayer; but these qualities are felt as characteristic of certain social classes, as also of certain gods (Bṛihaspati and Mitra respectively) correlated therewith (in 10. 4. 1. 5 Indra and Agni, in 5. 1. 1. 11 Bṛihaspati and Indra, in 4. 1. 4. 1–4 Mitra and Varuṇa respectively); *brahma* and *kṣatra* are also simply technical designations of the social classes in 1. 2. 1. 7; 3. 5. 2. 11; 4. 2. 2. 13; 9. 4. 1. 7–11; 12. 7. 3. 12; 13. 1. 5. 2. Still further advanced class differentiation is evidenced by the use of *brahma* and *kṣatra* along with *viś* as designations of the 'priesthood,' 'nobility,' and 'people' respectively at 2. 1. 3. 5–8; 2. 1. 4. 12; 10. 4. 1. 9; 11. 2. 7. 14–16.

This conspectus of usage furnishes corroboration to the inherent probability that here (in the Upanishad which forms the conclusion of the Śatapatha Brāhmaṇa), especially in § 6, the words *brahma* and *kṣatra* are class-designations, pregnant, however, with the connotation of the respective qualities. Accordingly, the (hybrid) word 'Brahmanhood' can perhaps best express both 'the Brahman class' and the quality of 'devotion' or 'sanctity' characterizing the priesthood. Similarly the word 'Kshatrahood' is used to designate both 'the Kshatriya class' and the quality of 'warrior-rule' characterizing the nobility.

Lo, verily, it is the Soul (*Ātman*) that should be seen, that should be hearkened to, that should be thought on, that should be pondered on, O Maitreyī. Lo, verily, with the seeing of, with the hearkening to, with the thinking of, and with the understanding of the Soul, this world-all is known.

6. Brahmanhood has deserted[1] him who knows Brahmanhood in aught else than the Soul.

Kshatrahood has deserted[1] him who knows Kshatrahood in aught else than the Soul.

The worlds have deserted him who knows the worlds in aught else than the Soul.

The gods have deserted him who knows the gods in aught else than the Soul.

Beings have deserted him who knows beings in aught else than the Soul.

Everything has deserted him who knows everything in aught else than the Soul.

This Brahmanhood, this Kshatrahood, these worlds, these gods, these beings, everything here is what this Soul is.

7. It is—as, when a drum is being beaten, one would not be able to grasp the external sounds, but by grasping the drum or the beater of the drum the sound is grasped.

8. It is—as, when a conch-shell is being blown, one would not be able to grasp the external sounds, but by grasping the conch-shell or the blower of the conch-shell the sound is grasped.

9. It is—as, when a lute is being played, one would not be able to grasp the external sounds, but by grasping the lute or the player of the lute the sound is grasped.

10. It is—as, from a fire laid with damp fuel, clouds of smoke separately issue forth, so, lo, verily, from this great Being (*bhūta*) has been breathed forth that which is Rig-Veda, Yajur-Veda, Sāma-Veda, [Hymns] of the Atharvans and Aṅgirases,[2] Legend (*itihāsa*), Ancient Lore (*purāṇa*), Sciences (*vidyā*), Mystic Doctrines (*upaniṣad*), Verses (*śloka*), Aphorisms (*sūtra*),

[1] If this aorist is gnomic, the meaning would be simply 'deserts' or 'would desert'; so also in all the following similar sentences. Cf. Bṛih. 4. 5. 7.

[2] A designation of the Atharva-Veda.

Explanations (*anuvyākhyāna*), and Commentaries (*vyākhyāna*). From it, indeed, are all these breathed forth.[1]

11. It is—as of all waters the uniting-point is the sea, so of all touches the uniting-point is the skin, so of all tastes the uniting-point is the tongue, so of all smells the uniting-point is the nostrils, so of all forms the uniting-point is the eye, so of all sounds the uniting-point is the ear, so of all intentions (*saṁkalpa*) the uniting-point is the mind (*manas*), so of all knowledges the uniting-point is the heart, so of all acts (*karma*) the uniting-point is the hands, so of all pleasures (*ānanda*) the uniting-point is the generative organ, so of all evacuations the uniting-point is the anus, so of all journeys the uniting-point is the feet, so of all the Vedas the uniting-point is speech.

12. It is—as a lump of salt cast in water would dissolve right into the water; there would not be [any][2] of it to seize forth, as it were (*iva*), but wherever one may take, it is salty indeed—so, lo, verily, this great Being (*bhūta*), infinite, limitless, is just a mass of knowledge (*vijñāna-ghana*).

Arising out of these elements (*bhūta*), into them also one vanishes away. After death there is no consciousness (*na pretya saṁjñā 'sti*). Thus, lo, say I.' Thus spake Yājñavalkya.

13. Then spake Maitreyī: 'Herein, indeed, you have bewildered me, sir—in saying (*iti*): "After death there is no consciousness"!'

Then spake Yājñavalkya: 'Lo, verily, I speak not bewilderment (*moha*). Sufficient, lo, verily, is this for understanding.

14. For where there is a duality (*dvaita*), as it were (*iva*), there one sees another; there one smells another; there one hears another; there one speaks to another; there one thinks of another; there one understands another. Where, verily, everything has become just one's own self, then whereby and whom would one smell? then whereby and whom would one see? then whereby and whom would one hear? then whereby and to whom would one speak? then whereby and on whom would one think? then whereby and

[1] This section recurs, with slight variations, at Maitri 6. 32.

[2] Or the ellipsis might be construed: 'It would not be [possible] to seize it forth . . .'

whom would one understand? Whereby would one understand him by whom one understands this All? Lo, whereby would one understand the understander?'

Fifth Brāhmaṇa

The co-relativity of all things cosmic and personal, and the absoluteness of the immanent Soul

1. This earth is honey for all creatures, and all creatures are honey for this earth. This shining, immortal Person who is in this earth, and, with reference to oneself, this shining, immortal Person who is in the body—he, indeed, is just this Soul (*Ātman*), this Immortal, this Brahma, this All.

2. These waters are honey for all things, and all things are honey for these waters. This shining, immortal Person who is in these waters, and, with reference to oneself, this shining, immortal Person who is made of semen—he is just this Soul, this Immortal, this Brahma, this All.

3. This fire is honey for all things, and all things are honey for this fire. This shining, immortal Person who is in this fire, and, with reference to oneself, this shining, immortal Person who is made of speech—he is just this Soul, this Immortal, this Brahma, this All.

4. This wind is honey for all things, and all things are honey for this wind. This shining, immortal Person who is in this wind, and, with reference to oneself, this shining, immortal Person who is breath—he is just this Soul, this Immortal, this Brahma, this All.

5. This sun is honey for all things, and all things are honey for this sun. This shining, immortal Person who is in this sun, and, with reference to oneself, this shining, immortal Person who is in the eye—he is just this Soul, this Immortal, this Brahma, this All.

6. These quarters of heaven are honey for all things, and all things are honey for these quarters of heaven. This shining, immortal Person who is in these quarters of heaven, and, with reference to oneself, this shining, immortal Person who is in the ear and in the echo—he is just this Soul, this Immortal, this Brahma, this All.

7. This moon is honey for all things, and all things are honey for this moon. This shining, immortal Person who is in this moon, and, with reference to oneself, this shining, immortal Person consisting of mind—he is just this Soul, this Immortal, this Brahma, this All.

8. This lightning is honey for all things, and all things are honey for this lightning. This shining, immortal Person who is in this lightning, and, with reference to oneself, this shining, immortal Person who exists as heat—he is just this Soul, this Immortal, this Brahma, this All.

9. This thunder is honey for all things, and all things are honey for this thunder. This shining, immortal Person who is in thunder, and, with reference to oneself, this shining, immortal Person who is in sound and in tone—he is just this Soul, this Immortal, this Brahma, this All.

10. This space is honey for all things, and all things are honey for this space. This shining, immortal Person who is in this space, and, with reference to oneself, this shining, immortal Person who is in the space in the heart—he is just this Soul, this Immortal, this Brahma, this All.

11. This Law (*dharma*) is honey for all things, and all things are honey for this Law. This shining, immortal Person who is in this Law, and, with reference to oneself, this shining, immortal Person who exists as virtuousness—he is just this Soul, this Immortal, this Brahma, this All.

12. This Truth is honey for all things, and all things are honey for this Truth. This shining, immortal Person who is in this Truth, and, with reference to oneself, this shining, immortal Person who exists as truthfulness—he is just this Soul, this Immortal, this Brahma, this All.

13. This mankind (*mānuṣa*) is honey for all things. and all things are honey for this mankind. This shining, immortal Person who is in this mankind, and, with reference to oneself, this shining, immortal Person who exists as a human being—he is just this Soul, this Immortal, this Brahma. this All.

14. This Soul (*Ātman*) is honey for all things, and all things are honey for this Soul. This shining, immortal Person who is in this Soul, and, with reference to oneself, this shining,

immortal Person who exists as Soul—he is just this Soul, this Immortal, this Brahma, this All.

15. Verily, this Soul is the overlord of all things, the king of all things. As all the spokes are held together in the hub and felly of a wheel, just so in this Soul all things, all gods, all worlds, all breathing things, all these selves are held together.

The honey-doctrine taught in the Vedas

16. This, verily, is the honey which Dadhyañc Ātharvaṇa declared unto the two Aśvins. Seeing this, the seer spake:—

'That mighty deed of yours, O ye two heroes, [which ye did] for gain,
I make known, as thunder [makes known the coming] rain,
Even the honey which Dadhyañc Ātharvaṇa to you
Did declare by the head of a horse.'[1]

17. This, verily, is the honey which Dadhyañc Ātharvaṇa declared unto the two Aśvins. Seeing this, the seer spake:—

'Upon Dadhyañc Ātharvaṇa ye Aśvins
Did substitute a horse's head.
He, keeping true, declared to you the honey
Of Tvashṭri, which is your secret, O ye mighty ones.'[2]

18. This, verily, is the honey which Dadhyañc Ātharvaṇa declared unto the two Aśvins. Seeing this, the seer spake:—

'Citadels with two feet he did make.
Citadels with four feet he did make.
Into the citadels he, having become a bird—
Into the citadels (*puras*) the Person (*puruṣa*) entered.'

This, verily, is the person (*puruṣa*) dwelling in all cities (*puri-śaya*). There is nothing by which he is not covered, nothing by which he is not hid.

19. This, verily, is the honey which Dadhyañc Ātharvaṇa declared unto the two Aśvins. Seeing this, the seer spake:—

[1] RV. 1. 116. 12. The two Aśvins desired instruction from Dadhyañc. But the latter was loath to impart it, for Indra had threatened Dadhyañc that if he ever told this honey-doctrine to anyone else, he (Indra) would cut his head off. To avoid this untoward result, the Aśvins took off Dadhyañc's head and substituted a horse's head. Then, after Dadhyañc had declared the honey-doctrine in compliance with their request and Indra had carried out his threat, the Aśvins restored to Dadhyañc his own head. The episode shows the extreme difficulty with which even gods secured the knowledge originally possessed by Indra.

[2] RV. 1. 117. 22.

He became corresponding in form to every form.
This is to be looked upon as a form of him.
Indra by his magic powers (*māyā*) goes about in many forms;
Yoked are his ten-hundred steeds.'[1]

He [i. e. the Soul, *Ātman*], verily, is the steeds. He, verily, is tens and thousands, many and endless. This Brahma is without an earlier and without a later, without an inside and without an outside. This Soul is Brahma, the all-perceiving.—Such is the instruction.

Sixth Brāhmaṇa

The teachers of this doctrine

1. Now the Line of Tradition (*vaṁśa*).—

Pautimāshya [received this teaching] from Gaupavana,
Gaupavana from Pautimāshya,
Pautimāshya from Gaupavana,
Gaupavana from Kauśika,
Kauśika from Kauṇḍinya,
Kauṇḍinya from Śāṇḍilya,
Śāṇḍilya from Kauśika and Gautama,
Gautama [2] from Āgniveśya,
Āgniveśya from Śāṇḍilya and Ānabhimlāta,
Ānabhimlāta from Ānabhimlāta,
Ānabhimlāta from Ānabhimlāta,
Ānabhimlāta from Gautama,
Gautama from Saitava and Prācīnayogya,
Saitava and Prācīnayogya from Pārāśarya,
Pārāśarya from Bhāradvāja,
Bhāradvāja from Bhāradvāja and Gautama,
Gautama from Bhāradvāja,
Bhāradvāja from Pārāśarya,
Pārāśarya from Vaijavāpāyana,
Vaijavāpāyana from Kauśikāyani,
Kauśikāyani [3] from Ghṛitakauśika,
Ghṛitakauśika from Pārāśaryāyaṇa,
Pārāśaryāyaṇa from Pārāśarya,
Pārāśarya from Jātūkarṇya,

[1] RV. 6. 47. 18.

Jātūkarṇya from Āsurāyaṇa and Yāska,
Āsurāyaṇa from Traivani,
Traivani from Aupajandhani,
Aupajandhani from Āsuri,
Āsuri from Bhāradvāja,
Bhāradvāja from Ātreya,
Ātreya from Māṇṭi,
Māṇṭi from Gautama,
Gautama from Gautama,
Gautama from Vātsya,
Vātsya from Śāṇḍilya,
Śāṇḍilya from Kaiśorya Kāpya,
Kaiśorya Kāpya from Kumārahārita,
Kumārahārita from Gālava,
Gālava from Vidarbhīkauṇḍinya,
Vidarbhīkauṇḍinya from Vatsanapād Bābhrava,
Vatsanapād Bābhrava from Panthāḥ Saubhara,
Panthāḥ Saubhara from Ayāsya Āṅgirasa,
Ayāsya Āṅgirasa from Ābhūti Tvāshṭra,
Ābhūti Tvāshṭra from Viśvarūpa Tvāshṭra,
Viśvarūpa Tvāshṭra from the two Aśvins,
the two Aśvins from Dadhyañc Ātharvaṇa,
Dadhyañc Ātharvaṇa from Atharvan Daiva,
Atharvan Daiva from Mṛityu Prādhvaṁsana,
Mṛityu Prādhvaṁsana from Pradhvaṁsana,
Pradhvaṁsana from Eka Ṛishi,
Eka Ṛishi from Vipracitti,
Vipracitti from Vyashṭi,
Vyashṭi from Sanāru.
Sanāru from Sanātana,
Sanātana from Sanaga,
Sanaga from Parameshṭin,
Parameshṭin from Brahma.

Brahma is the Self-existent (*svayam-bhū*). Adoration to Brahma!

THIRD ADHYĀYA

First Brāhmaṇa

Concerning sacrificial worship and its rewards

1. Janaka, [king] of Videha, sacrificed with a sacrifice at which many presents were distributed. Brahmans of the Kurupañcālas were gathered together there. In this Janaka of Videha there arose a desire to know which of these Brahmans was the most learned in scripture. He enclosed a thousand cows. To the horns of each ten *pādas* [of gold] were bound.

2. He said to them: 'Venerable Brahmans, let him of you who is the best Brahman drive away these cows.'

Those Brahmans durst not.

Then Yājñavalkya said to his pupil: 'Sāmaśravas, my dear, drive them away.'

He drove them away.

The Brahmans were angry. 'How can he declare himself to be the best Brahman among us?'

Now there was Aśvala, the Hotṛi-priest of Janaka, [king] of Videha. He asked him: 'Yājñavalkya, are you now the best Brahman among us?'

He replied: 'We give honor to the best Brahman. But we are really desirous of having those cows.'

Thereupon Aśvala, the Hotṛi-priest, began to question him.

3. 'Yājñavalkya,' said he, 'since everything here is overtaken by death, since everything is overcome by death, whereby is a sacrificer liberated beyond the reach of death?'

'By the Hotṛi-priest, by fire, by speech. Verily, speech is the Hotṛi of sacrifice. That which is this speech is this fire, is the Hotṛi. This is release (*mukti*), this is complete release.'

4. 'Yājñavalkya,' said he, 'since everything here is overtaken by day and night, since everything is overcome by day and night, whereby is a sacrificer liberated beyond day and night?'

'By the Adhvaryu-priest, by the eye, by the sun. Verily, the eye is the Adhvaryu of sacrifice. That which is this eye is yonder sun, is the Adhvaryu. This is release, this is complete release.'

5. 'Yājñavalkya,' said he, 'since everything here is over-

taken by the waxing and waning moon, by what means does a sacrificer obtain release from the waxing and waning moon?'

'By the Udgātṛi-priest, by the wind, by breath. Verily, breath is the Udgātṛi of the sacrifice. That which is this breath is wind, is the Udgātṛi. This is release, this is complete release.'

6. 'Yājñavalkya,' said he, 'since this atmosphere does not afford a [foot]hold, as it were, by what means of ascent does a sacrificer ascend to the heavenly world?

'By the Brahman-priest, by the mind, by the moon. Verily, the mind is the Brahman of the sacrifice. That which is this mind is yonder moon, is the Brahman. This is release, this is complete release.'—Thus [concerning] liberation.

Now the acquirements.—

7. 'Yājñavalkya,' said he, 'how many Ṛig verses will the Hotṛi make use of today in this sacrifice?'

'Three.'

'Which are those three?'

'The introductory verse, the accompanying verse, and the benediction as the third.'

'What does one win by these?'

'Whatever there is here that has breath.'

8. 'Yājñavalkya,' said he, 'how many oblations will the Adhvaryu pour out today in this sacrifice?'

'Three.'

'Which are those three?'

'Those which when offered flame up, those which when offered flow over, those which when offered sink down.'

'What does one win by these?'

'By those which when offered flame up, one wins the world of the gods, for the world of the gods gleams, as it were. By those which when offered flow over (*ati-nedante*), one wins the world of the fathers, for the world of the fathers is over (*ati*), as it were. By those which when offered sink down (*adhiśerate*) one wins the world of men, for the world of men is below (*adhas*), as it were.'

9. 'Yājñavalkya,' said he, 'with how many divinities does the Brahman protect the sacrifice on the right today?'

'With one.'

'Which is that one?'

'The mind. Verily, endless is the mind. Endless are the All-gods. An endless world he wins thereby.'

10. 'Yājñavalkya,' said he, 'how many hymns of praise will the Udgātṛi chant today in this sacrifice?'

'Three.'

'Which are those three?'

'The introductory hymn, the accompanying hymn, and the benediction hymn as the third.'

'Which are those three with reference to the self?'

'The introductory hymn is the in-breath (*prāṇa*). The accompanying hymn is the out-breath (*apāna*). The benediction hymn is the diffused breath (*vyāna*).'

'What does one win by these?'

'One wins the earth-world by the introductory hymn, the atmosphere-world by the accompanying hymn, the sky-world by the benediction hymn.'

Thereupon the Hotṛi-priest Aśvala held his peace.

Second Brāhmaṇa

The fettered soul, and its fate at death

1. Then Jāratkārava Ārtabhāga questioned him. 'Yājñavalkya,' said he, 'how many apprehenders are there? How many over-apprehenders?'

'Eight apprehenders. Eight over-apprehenders.'

'Those eight apprehenders and eight over-apprehenders—which are they?'

2. 'Breath (*prāṇa*), verily, is an apprehender. It is seized by the out-breath (*apāna*) as an over-apprehender, for by the out-breath one smells an odor.

3. Speech, verily, is an apprehender. It is seized by name as an over-apprehender, for by speech one speaks names.

4. The tongue, verily, is an apprehender. It is seized by taste as an over-apprehender, for by the tongue one knows tastes.

5. The eye, verily, is an apprehender. It is seized by appearance as an over-apprehender, for by the eye one sees

6. The ear, verily, is an apprehender. It is seized by sound as an over-apprehender, for by the ear one hears sounds.

7. The mind, verily, is an apprehender. It is seized by desire as an over-apprehender, for by the mind one desires desires.

8. The hands, verily, are an apprehender. It is seized by action as an over-apprehender, for by the hands one performs action.

9. The skin, verily, is an apprehender. It is seized by touch as an over-apprehender, for by the skin one is made to know touches.'

10. 'Yājñavalkya,' said he, 'since everything here is food for death, who, pray, is that divinity for whom death is food?'

'Death, verily, is a fire. It is the food of water (*āpas*). He wards off (*apa-jayati*) repeated death [who knows this].'[1]

11. 'Yājñavalkya,' said he, 'when a man dies, do the breaths go out of him, or no?'

'No,' said Yājñavalkya. 'They are gathered together right there. He swells up. He is inflated. The dead man lies inflated.'

12. 'Yājñavalkya,' said he, 'when a man dies, what does not leave him?'

'The name. Endless, verily, is the name. Endless are the All-gods. An endless world he wins thereby.'

13. 'Yājñavalkya,' said he, 'when the voice of a dead man goes into fire, his breath into wind, his eye into the sun, his mind into the moon, his hearing into the quarters of heaven, his body into the earth, his soul (*ātman*) into space, the hairs of his head into plants, the hairs of his body into trees, and his blood and semen are placed in water, what then becomes of this person (*puruṣa*)?'

'Ārtabhāga, my dear, take my hand. We two only will know of this. This is not for us two [to speak of] in public.'

The two went away and deliberated. What they said was *karma* (action). What they praised was *karma*. Verily, one becomes good by good action, bad by bad action.

Thereupon Jāratkārava Ārtabhāga held his peace.

[1] Supplying *ya evaṁ veda*, as in 3. 3. 2 and 1. 2. 7.

THIRD BRĀHMAṆA

Where the offerers of the horse-sacrifice go

1. Then Bhujyu Lāhyāyani questioned him. 'Yājñavalkya,' said he, 'we were traveling around as wanderers among the Madras. As such we came to the house of Patañcala Kāpya. He had a daughter who was possessed by a Gandharva. We asked him: "Who are you?" He said: "I am Sudhanvan, a descendant of Aṅgiras." When we were asking him about the ends of the earth, we said to him: "What has become of the Pārikshitas? What has become of the Pārikshitas?"— I now ask you, Yājñavalkya. What has become of the Pārikshitas?'

2. He said: 'That one doubtless said, "They have, in truth, gone whither the offerers of the horse-sacrifice go."'

'Where, pray, do the offerers of the horse-sacrifice go?'

'This inhabited world, of a truth, is as broad as thirty-two days [i.e. days' journeys] of the sun-god's chariot. The earth, which is twice as wide, surrounds it on all sides. The ocean, which is twice as wide, surrounds the earth on all sides. Then there is an interspace as broad as the edge of a razor or the wing of a mosquito. Indra, taking the form of a bird, delivered them [i.e. the Pārikshitas] to Wind. Wind, placing them in himself, led them where the offerers of the horse-sacrifice were. Somewhat thus he [i.e. Sudhanvan] praised Wind. Therefore Wind alone is individuality (*vyaṣṭi*). Wind is totality (*samaṣṭi*). He who knows this wards off repeated death.'

Thereupon Bhujyu Lāhyāyani held his peace.

FOURTH BRĀHMAṆA

The theoretical unknowability of the immanent Brahma

1. Then Ushasta Cākrāyaṇa questioned him. 'Yājñavalkya, said he, 'explain to me him who is the Brahma present and not beyond our ken, him who is the Soul in all things.'

'He is your soul (*ātman*), which is in all things.'

'Which one, O Yājñavalkya, is in all things?'

'He who breathes in with your breathing in (*prāṇa*) is the

Soul of yours, which is in all things. He who breathes out with your breathing out (*apāna*) is the Soul of yours, which is in all things. He who breathes about with your breathing about (*vyāna*) is the Soul of yours, which is in all things. He who breathes up with your breathing up (*udāna*) is the Soul of yours, which is in all things. He is your soul, which is in all things.'

2. Ushasta Cākrāyaṇa said: 'This has been explained to me just as one might say, "This is a cow. This is a horse." Explain to me him who is just the Brahma present and not beyond our ken, him who is the Soul in all things.'

'He is your soul, which is in all things.'

'Which one, O Yājñavalkya, is in all things?'

'You could not see the seer of seeing. You could not hear the hearer of hearing. You could not think the thinker of thinking. You could not understand the understander of understanding. He is your soul, which is in all things. Aught else than Him [or, than this] is wretched.'

Thereupon Ushasta Cākrāyaṇa held his peace.

Fifth Brāhmaṇa

The practical way of knowing Brahma—by renunciation

Now Kahola Kaushītakeya questioned him. 'Yājñavalkya,' said he, 'explain to me him who is just the Brahma present and not beyond our ken, him who is the Soul in all things.'

'He is your soul, which is in all things.'

'Which one, O Yājñavalkya, is in all things?'

'He who passes beyond hunger and thirst, beyond sorrow and delusion, beyond old age and death—Brahmans who know such a Soul overcome desire for sons, desire for wealth, desire for worlds, and live the life of mendicants. For desire for sons is desire for wealth, and desire for wealth is desire for worlds, for both these are merely desires. Therefore let a Brahman become disgusted with learning and desire to live as a child. When he has become disgusted both with the state of childhood and with learning, then he becomes an ascetic (*muni*). When he has become disgusted both with the non-ascetic state and with the ascetic state, then he becomes a Brahman.'

'By what means would he become a Brahman?'

'By that means by which he does become such a one. Aught else than this Soul (*Ātman*) is wretched.'

Thereupon Kahola Kaushītakeya held his peace.

SIXTH BRĀHMAṆA

The regressus to Brahma, the ultimate world-ground

Then Gārgī Vācaknavī questioned him. 'Yājñavalkya,' said she, 'since all this world is woven, warp and woof, on water, on what, pray, is the water woven, warp and woof?'

'On wind, O Gārgī.'

'On what then, pray, is the wind woven, warp and woof?'

'On the atmosphere-worlds, O Gārgī.'

'On what then, pray, are the atmosphere-worlds woven, warp and woof?'

'On the worlds of the Gandharvas, O Gārgī.'

'On what then, pray, are the worlds of the Gandharvas woven, warp and woof?'

'On the worlds of the sun, O Gārgī.'

'On what then, pray, are the worlds of the sun woven, warp and woof?'

'On the worlds of the moon, O Gārgī.'

'On what then, pray, are the worlds of the moon woven, warp and woof?'

'On the worlds of the stars, O Gārgī.'

'On what then, pray, are the worlds of the stars woven, warp and woof?'

'On the worlds of the gods, O Gārgī.'

'On what then, pray, are the worlds of the gods woven, warp and woof?'

'On the worlds of Indra, O Gārgī.'

'On what then, pray, are the worlds of Indra woven, warp and woof?'

'On the worlds of Prajāpati, O Gārgī.'

'On what then, pray, are the worlds of Prajāpati woven, warp and woof?'

'On the worlds of Brahma, O Gārgī.'

'On what then, pray, are the worlds of Brahma woven, warp and woof?'

Yājñavalkya said: 'Gārgī, do not question too much, lest your head fall off. In truth, you are questioning too much about a divinity about which further questions cannot be asked. Gārgī, do not over-question.'

Thereupon Gārgī Vācaknavī held her peace.

SEVENTH BRĀHMAṆA

Wind, the string holding the world together; the immortal immanent Soul, the Inner Controller

1. Then Uddālaka Āruṇi questioned him. 'Yājñavalkya,' said he, 'we were dwelling among the Madras in the house of Patañcala Kāpya, studying the sacrifice. He had a wife possessed by a spirit (*gandharva*). We asked him: "Who are you?" He said: "I am Kabandha Ātharvaṇa." He said to Patañcala Kāpya and to us students of the sacrifice: "Do you know, O Kāpya, that thread by which this world and the other world and all things are tied together?" Patañcala Kāpya said: "I do not know it, sir." He said to Patañcala Kāpya and to us students of the sacrifice: "Pray do you know, O Kāpya, that Inner Controller who from within controls this world and the other world and all things?" Patañcala Kāpya said: "I do not know him, sir." He said to Patañcala Kāpya and to us students of the sacrifice: "Verily, Kāpya, he who knows that thread and the so-called Inner Controller knows Brahma, he knows the worlds, he knows the gods, he knows the Vedas, he knows created things, he knows the Soul, he knows everything." Thus he [i. e. the spirit] explained it to them. And I know it. If you, O Yājñavalkya, drive away the Brahma-cows without knowing that thread and the Inner Controller, your head will fall off.'

'Verily, I know that thread and the Inner Controller, O Gautama.'

'Anyone might say "I know, I know." Do you tell what you know.'

2. He [i. e. Yājñavalkya] said: 'Wind, verily, O Gautama,

is that thread. By wind, verily, O Gautama, as by a thread, this world and the other world and all things are tied together. Therefore, verily, O Gautama, they say of a deceased person, "His limbs become unstrung," for by wind, O Gautama, as by a thread, they are strung together.'

'Quite so, O Yājñavalkya. Declare the Inner Controller.'

3. 'He who, dwelling in the earth, yet is other than the earth, whom the earth does not know, whose body the earth is, who controls the earth from within—He is your Soul, the Inner Controller, the Immortal.

4. He who, dwelling in the waters, yet is other than the waters, whom the waters do not know, whose body the waters are, who controls the waters from within—He is your Soul, the Inner Controller, the Immortal.

5. He who, dwelling in the fire, yet is other than the fire, whom the fire does not know, whose body the fire is, who controls the fire from within—He is your Soul, the Inner Controller, the Immortal.

6. He who, dwelling in the atmosphere, yet is other than the atmosphere, whom the atmosphere does not know, whose body the atmosphere is, who controls the atmosphere from within—He is your Soul, the Inner Controller, the Immortal.

7. He who, dwelling in the wind, yet is other than the wind, whom the wind does not know, whose body the wind is, who controls the wind from within—He is your Soul, the Inner Controller, the Immortal.

8. He who, dwelling in the sky, yet is other than the sky, whom the sky does not know, whose body the sky is, who controls the sky from within—He is your Soul, the Inner Controller, the Immortal.

9. He who, dwelling in the sun, yet is other than the sun, whom the sun does not know, whose body the sun is, who controls the sun from within—He is your Soul, the Inner Controller, the Immortal.

10. He who, dwelling in the quarters of heaven, yet is other than the quarters of heaven, whom the quarters of heaven do not know, whose body the quarters of heaven are, who controls the quarters of heaven from within—He is your Soul, the Inner Controller, the Immortal.

11. He who, dwelling in the moon and stars, yet is other than the moon and stars, whom the moon and stars do not know, whose body the moon and stars are, who controls the moon and stars from within—He is your Soul, the Inner Controller, the Immortal.

12. He who, dwelling in space, yet is other than space, whom space does not know, whose body space is, who controls space from within—He is your Soul, the Inner Controller, the Immortal.

13. He who, dwelling in the darkness, yet is other than the darkness, whom the darkness does not know, whose body the darkness is, who controls the darkness from within—He is your Soul, the Inner Controller, the Immortal.

14. He who, dwelling in the light, yet is other than the light, whom the light does not know, whose body the light is, who controls the light from within—He is your Soul, the Inner Controller, the Immortal.

—Thus far with reference to the divinities. Now with reference to material existence (*adhi-bhūta*).—

15. He who, dwelling in all things, yet is other than all things, whom all things do not know, whose body all things are, who controls all things from within—He is your Soul, the Inner Controller, the Immortal.

—Thus far with reference to material existence. Now with reference to the self.—

16. He who, dwelling in breath, yet is other than breath, whom the breath does not know, whose body the breath is, who controls the breath from within—He is your Soul, the Inner Controller, the Immortal.

17. He who, dwelling in speech, yet is other than speech, whom the speech does not know, whose body the speech is, who controls the speech from within—He is your Soul, the Inner Controller, the Immortal.

18. He who, dwelling in the eye, yet is other than the eye, whom the eye does not know, whose body the eye is, who controls the eye from within—He is your Soul, the Inner Controller, the Immortal.

19. He who, dwelling in the ear, yet is other than the ear, whom the ear does not know, whose body the ear is, who

controls the ear from within—He is your Soul, the Inner Controller, the Immortal.

20. He who, dwelling in the mind, yet is other than the mind, whom the mind does not know, whose body the mind is, who controls the mind from within—He is your Soul, the Inner Controller, the Immortal.

21. He who, dwelling in the skin, yet is other than the skin, whom the skin does not know, whose body the skin is, who controls the skin from within—He is your Soul, the Inner Controller, the Immortal.

22. He who, dwelling in the understanding, yet is other than the understanding, whom the understanding does not know, whose body the understanding is, who controls the understanding from within—He is your Soul, the Inner Controller, the Immortal.

23. He who, dwelling in the semen, yet is other than the semen, whom the semen does not know, whose body the semen is, who controls the semen from within—He is your Soul, the Inner Controller, the Immortal.

He is the unseen Seer, the unheard Hearer, the unthought Thinker, the ununderstood Understander. Other than He there is no seer. Other than He there is no hearer. Other than He there is no thinker. Other than He there is no understander. He is your Soul, the Inner Controller, the Immortal.'

Thereupon Uddālaka Āruṇi held his peace.

EIGHTH BRĀHMAṆA

The ultimate warp of the world—the unqualified Imperishable

1. Then [Gārgī] Vācaknavī said: 'Venerable Brahmans, lo, I will ask him [i.e. Yājñavalkya] two questions. If he will answer me these, not one of you will surpass him in discussions about Brahma.'

'Ask, Gārgī.'

2. She said: 'As a noble youth of the Kāśis or of the Videhas might rise up against you, having strung his unstrung bow and taken two foe-piercing arrows in his hand, even so, O Yājñavalkya, have I risen up against you with two questions. Answer me these.'

Yājñavalkya said: 'Ask, Gārgī.'

3. She said: 'That, O Yājñavalkya, which is above the sky, that which is beneath the earth, that which is between these two, sky and earth, that which people call the past and the present and the future—across what is that woven, warp and woof?'

4. He said: 'That, O Gārgī, which is above the sky, that which is beneath the earth, that which is between these two, sky and earth, that which people call the past and the present and the future—across space is that woven, warp and woof.'

5. She said: 'Adoration to you, Yājñavalkya, in that you have solved this question for me. Prepare yourself for the other.'

'Ask, Gārgī.'

6. She said: 'That, O Yājñavalkya, which is above the sky, that which is beneath the earth, that which is between these two, sky and earth, that which people call the past and the present and the future—across what is that woven, warp and woof?'

7. He said: 'That, O Gārgī, which is above the sky, that which is beneath the earth, that which is between these two, sky and earth, that which people call the past and the present and the future—across space alone is that woven, warp and woof.'

'Across what then, pray, is space woven, warp and woof?'

8. He said: 'That, O Gārgī, Brahmans call the Imperishable (*akṣara*). It is not coarse, not fine, not short, not long, not glowing [like fire], not adhesive [like water], without shadow and without darkness, without air and without space, without stickiness, (intangible),[1] odorless, tasteless, without eye, without ear, without voice, without wind, without energy, without breath, without mouth, (without personal or family name, unaging, undying, without fear, immortal, stainless, not uncovered, not covered),[1] without measure, without inside and without outside.

It consumes nothing soever.
No one soever consumes it.

9. Verily, O Gārgī, at the command of that Imperishable the sun and the moon stand apart. Verily, O Gārgī, at the command of that Imperishable the earth and the sky stand

[1] A Mādhyaṁdina addition.

apart. Verily, O Gārgī, at the command of that Imperishable the moments, the hours, the days, the nights, the fortnights, the months, the seasons, and the years stand apart. Verily, O Gārgī, at the command of that Imperishable some rivers flow from the snowy mountains to the east, others to the west, in whatever direction each flows. Verily, O Gārgī, at the command of that Imperishable men praise those who give, the gods are desirous of a sacrificer, and the fathers [are desirous] of the Manes-sacrifice.

10. Verily, O Gārgī, if one performs sacrifices and worship and undergoes austerity in this world for many thousands of years, but without knowing that Imperishable, limited indeed is that [work] of his. Verily, O Gārgī, he who departs from this world without knowing that Imperishable is pitiable. But, O Gārgī, he who departs from this world knowing that Imperishable is a Brahman.

11. Verily, O Gārgī, that Imperishable is the unseen Seer, the unheard Hearer, the unthought Thinker, the ununderstood Understander. Other than It there is naught that sees. Other than It there is naught that hears. Other than It there is naught that thinks. Other than It there is naught that understands. Across this Imperishable, O Gārgī, is space woven, warp and woof.'

12. She said: 'Venerable Brahmans, you may think it a great thing if you escape from this man with [merely] making a bow. Not one of you will surpass him in discussions about Brahma.'

Thereupon [Gārgī] Vācaknavī held her peace.

NINTH BRĀHMAṆA

Regressus of the numerous gods to the unitary Brahma

1. Then Vidagdha Śākalya questioned him. 'How many gods are there, Yājñavalkya?'

He answered in accord with the following *Nivid* (invocationary formula): 'As many as are mentioned in the *Nivid* of the Hymn to All the Gods, namely, three hundred and three, and three thousand and three [=3306].'

'Yes,' said he, 'but just how many gods are there, Yājñavalkya?'

'Thirty-three.'

'Yes,' said he, 'but just how many gods are there, Yājñavalkya?'

'Six.'

'Yes,' said he, 'but just how many gods are there, Yājñavalkya?'

'Three.'

'Yes,' said he, 'but just how many gods are there, Yājñavalkya?'

'Two.'

'Yes,' said he, 'but just how many gods are there, Yājñavalkya?'

'One and a half.'

'Yes,' said he, 'but just how many gods are there, Yājñavalkya?'

'One.'

'Yes,' said he, 'which are those three hundred and three, and those three thousand and three?'

2. He [i. e. Yājñavalkya] said: 'Those are only their powers (*mahiman*). There are just thirty-three gods.'

'Which are those thirty-three?'

'Eight Vasus, eleven Rudras, twelve Ādityas. Those are thirty-one. Indra and Prajāpati make thirty-three.'

3. 'Which are the Vasus?'

'Fire, earth, wind, atmosphere, sun, sky, moon, and stars. These are Vasus, for upon them this excellent (*vasu*) world is set, (for they give a dwelling (*vāsayante*) to the world).[1] Therefore they are called Vasus.'

4. 'Which are the Rudras?'

'These ten breaths in a person, and the self as the eleventh. When they go out from this mortal body, they make us lament. So, because they make us lament (√*rud*), therefore they are Rudras.'

5. 'Which are the Ādityas?'

'Verily, the twelve months of the year. These are Ādityas, for they go carrying along this whole world. Since they go

[1] A Mādhyaṁdina addition. Cf. Chānd. 3. 16. 1.

(*yanti*) carrying along (*ā-dā*) this whole world, therefore they are called Ādityas.'

6. 'Which is Indra? Which is Prajāpati?'

'The thunder, verily, is Indra. The sacrifice is Prajāpati.'

'Which is the thunder?'

'The thunderbolt.'

'Which is the sacrifice?'

'The sacrificial animals.'

7. 'Which are the six [gods]?'

'Fire, earth, wind, atmosphere, sun, and sky. These are the six, for the whole world is these six.'

8. 'Which are the three gods?'

'They, verily, are the three worlds, for in them all these gods exist.'

'Which are the two gods?'

'Food and breath.'

'Which is the one and a half?'

'This one here who purifies [i. e. the wind].'

9. Then they say: 'Since he who purifies is just like one, how then is he one and a half?'

'Because in him this whole world did prosper (*adhyārdhnot*). Therefore he is one and a half (*adhyardha*).'

'Which is the one god?'

'Breath,' said he. 'They call him Brahma, the Yon (*tya*).'

Eight different Persons and their corresponding divinities

10. [Śākalya said:] 'Verily, he who knows that Person whose abode is the earth, whose world is fire, whose light is mind, who is the last source of every soul—he, verily, would be a knower, O Yājñavalkya.'

[Yājñavalkya said:] 'Verily, I know that Person, the last source of every soul, of whom you speak. This very person who is in the body is He. Tell me, Śākalya, who is his god?'

'The Immortal,' said he.

11. [Śākalya said:] 'Verily, he who knows that Person whose abode is desire, whose world is the heart, whose light is mind, who is the last source of every soul—he, verily, would be a knower, O Yājñavalkya.'

[Yājñavalkya said:] 'Verily, I know that Person, the last

source of every soul, of whom you speak. This very person who is made of desire is He. Tell me, Śākalya, who is his god?'

'Women,' said he.

12. [Śākalya said:] 'Verily, he who knows that Person whose abode is forms (*rūpa*), whose world is the eye, whose light is mind, who is the last source of every soul—he, verily, would be a knower, O Yājñavalkya.'

'Verily, I know that Person, the last source of every soul, of whom you speak. That very person who is in the sun is He. Tell me, Śākalya, who is his god?'

'Truth,' said he.

13. [Śākalya said:] 'Verily, he who knows that Person whose abode is space (*ākāśa*), whose world is the ear, whose light is mind, who is the last source of every soul—he, verily, would be a knower, O Yājñavalkya.'

'Verily, I know that Person, the last source of every soul, of whom you speak. This very person who is in hearing and who is in the echo is He. Tell me, Śākalya, who is his god?'

'The quarters of heaven,' said he.

14. [Śākalya said:] 'Verily, he who knows that Person whose abode is darkness (*tamas*), whose world is the heart, whose light is mind, who is the last source of every soul—he, verily, would be a knower, O Yājñavalkya.'

'Verily, I know that Person, the last source of every soul, of whom you speak. This very person who is made of shadow is He. Tell me, Śākalya, who is his god?'

'Death,' said he.

15. [Śākalya said:] 'Verily, he who knows that Person whose abode is forms (*rūpa*), whose world is the eye, whose light is mind, who is the last source of every soul—he, verily, would be a knower, O Yājñavalkya.'

'Verily, I know that Person, the last source of every soul, of whom you speak. This very person who is in the mirror is He. Tell me, Śākalya, who is his god?'

'Life (*asu*),' said he.

16. [Śākalya said:] 'Verily, he who knows that Person whose abode is water, whose world is the heart, whose light is mind, who is the last source of every soul—he, verily, would be a knower, O Yājñavalkya.'

'Verily, I know that Person, the last source of every soul, of whom you speak. This very person who is in the waters is He. Tell me, Śākalya, who is his god?'

'Varuṇa,' said he.

17. [Śākalya said:] 'Verily, he who knows that Person whose abode is semen, whose world is the heart, whose light is mind, who is the last source of every soul—he, verily, would be a knower, O Yājñavalkya.'

'Verily, I know that Person, the last source of every soul, of whom you speak. This very person who is made of a son is He. Tell me, Śākalya, who is his god?'

'Prajāpati,' said he.

18. 'Śākalya,' said Yājñavalkya, 'have those Brahmans made you their coal-remover?'[1]

Five directions in space, their regent gods, and their bases

19. 'Yājñavalkya,' said Śākalya, 'by knowing what Brahma is it that you have talked down the Brahmans of the Kuru-pañcālas?'

'I know the quarters of heaven together with their gods and their bases.'

'Since you know the quarters of heaven together with their gods and their bases, [20] what divinity have you in this eastern quarter?'

'The sun.'

'That sun—on what is it based?'

'On the eye.'

'And on what is the eye based?'

'On appearance, for with the eye one sees appearances.'

'And on what are appearances based?'

'On the heart,' he said, 'for with the heart one knows appearances, for on the heart alone appearances are based.'

'Quite so, Yājñavalkya.'

21. [Śākalya said:] 'What divinity have you in this southern (*dakṣiṇa*) quarter?'

'Yama.'

'That Yama—on what is he based?'

'On sacrifice.'

[1] Literally, 'remover of burning coals'; 'a cat's-paw,' as Müller suggests.

'And on what is sacrifice based?'

'On gifts to the priests (*dakṣiṇā*).'

'And on what are the gifts to the priests based?'

'On faith, for when one has faith, then one gives gifts to the priests. Verily, on faith the gifts to the priests are based.'

'On what is faith based?'

'On the heart,' he said, 'for with the heart one knows faith. Verily, on the heart alone faith is based.'

'Quite so, Yājñavalkya.'

22. [Śākalya said:] 'What divinity have you in this western quarter?'

'Varuṇa.'

'That Varuṇa—on what is he based?'

'On water.'

'And on what is water based?'

'On semen.'

'And on what is semen based?'

'On the heart. Therefore they say of a son who is just like his father, "He has slipped out from his heart, as it were. He is built out of his heart." For on the heart alone semen is based.'

'Quite so, Yājñavalkya.'

23. [Śākalya said:] 'What divinity have you in this northern quarter?'

'Soma.'

'That Soma—on what is he based?'

'On the Dīkshā [initiatory] rite.'

'And on what is the Dīkshā rite based?'

'On truth. Therefore they say to one who is initiated, "Speak the truth!" For on truth alone the Dīkshā rite is based.'

'And on what is truth based?'

'On the heart,' he said, 'for with the heart one knows truth. Verily, on the heart alone truth is based.'

'Quite so, Yājñavalkya.'

24. [Śākalya said:] 'What divinity have you in this fixed quarter [i. e. the zenith]?'

'The god Agni.'

'That Agni—on what is he based?'

'On speech.'

'And on what is speech based?'

'On the heart.'

'And on what is the heart based?'

25. 'You idiot,' said Yājñavalkya, 'that you will think that it could be anywhere else than in ourselves! for if it were anywhere else than in ourselves, the dogs might eat it, or the birds might tear it to pieces.'

The Soul, the Person taught in the Upanishads

26. 'On what are you and your soul (*ātman*) based?'

'On the in-breath (*prāṇa*).'

'And on what is the in-breath based?'

'On the out-breath (*apāna*).'

'And on what is the out-breath based?'

'On the diffused breath (*vyāna*).'

'And on what is the diffused breath based?'

'On the up-breath (*udāna*).'

'And on what is the up-breath based?'

'On the middle [or equalizing] breath (*samāna*).'

'That Soul (*Ātman*) is not this, it is not that (*neti, neti*). It is unseizable, for it is not seized. It is indestructible, for it is not destroyed. It is unattached, for it does not attach itself. It is unbound. It does not tremble. It is not injured.

These[1] are the eight abodes, the eight worlds, the eight gods, the eight persons. He who plucks apart and puts together these persons and passes beyond them—that is the Person taught in the Upanishads about whom I ask you.

If him to me ye will not tell,
Your head indeed will then fall off.'

But him Śākalya did not know,
And so indeed his head fell off.

Indeed, robbers carried off his bones, thinking they were something else.

Man, a tree growing from Brahma

27. Then he [i.e. Yājñavalkya] said: 'Venerable Brahmans, let him of you that desires question me. Or do ye all question

[1] That is, those mentioned in sections 10–17.

me. Or I will question him of you that desires [to be questioned]; or I will question all of you.'

Those Brahmans, however, durst not.

28. Then he [i. e. Yājñavalkya] questioned them with these verses:—

As a tree of the forest,
Just so, surely, is man.
His hairs are leaves,
His skin the outer bark.
From his skin blood,
Sap from the bark flows forth.
From him when pierced there comes forth
A stream, as from the tree when struck.

His pieces of flesh are under-layers of wood.
The fibre is muscle-like, strong.
The bones are the wood within.
The marrow is made resembling pith.

A tree, when it is felled, grows up
From the root, more new again;
A mortal, when cut down by death—
From what root does he grow up?[1]

Say not 'from semen,'
For that is produced from the living,
As the tree, forsooth, springing from seed,
Clearly arises without having died.

If with its roots they should pull up
The tree, it would not come into being again
A mortal, when cut down by death—
From what root does he grow up?

When born, indeed, he is not born [again].
Who would again beget him?

Brahma is knowledge, is bliss,
The final goal of the giver of offerings,
Of him, too, who stands still and knows It.

[1] For a similar comparison in Hebrew literature see Job 14. 7–10

FOURTH ADHYĀYA

First Brāhmaṇa

King Janaka instructed by Yājñavalkya: six partial definitions of Brahma

1. Janaka, [king] of Videha, was seated. Yājñavalkya came up. To him he said: 'Yājñavalkya, for what purpose have you come? Because you desire cattle or subtle disputations?'

'Indeed, for both, your Majesty,' he said.

2. 'Let us hear what anybody may have told you,' [continued Yājñavalkya].

'Jitvan Śailini told me: "Brahma, verily, is speech (*vāc*),"' [said Janaka].

'As a man might say that he had a mother, that he had a father, that he had a teacher,[1] so did that Śailini say, "Brahma, verily, is speech." For he might have thought (*iti*), "What can one have who cannot speak?" But did he tell you Its seat and support?'

'He did not tell me.'

'Forsooth, your Majesty, that is a one-legged [Brahma].'

'Verily, Yājñavalkya, do you here tell us.'

'Its seat is just speech; Its support, space (*ākāśa*). One should worship It as intelligence (*prajñā*).'

'What is Its quality of intelligence, Yājñavalkya?'

'Just speech, your Majesty,' said he. 'Verily, by speech, your Majesty, a friend is recognized. By speech alone, your Majesty, the Rig-Veda, the Yajur-Veda, the Sāma-Veda, the [Hymns] of the Atharvans and Aṅgirases,[2] Legends (*itihāsa*), Ancient Lore (*purāṇa*), Sciences (*vidyā*), Mystic Doctrines (*upaniṣad*), Verses (*śloka*), Aphorisms (*sūtra*), Explanations (*anuvyākhyāna*), Commentaries (*vyākhyāna*), what is offered in sacrifice and as oblation, food and drink, this world and the other, and all beings are known. The highest Brahma, your Majesty, is in truth speech. Speech does not desert him

[1] That is, what is self-evident, what anyone might know. This rendering, it should be noted, takes the active *brūyāt* as if it were middle voice—a late epic usage.

[2] A designation of the Atharva-Veda.

who, knowing this, worships it as such. All things run unto him. He, having become a god, goes even to the gods.'

'I will give you a thousand cows with a bull as large as an elephant,' said Janaka, [king] of Videha.

Yājñavalkya replied: 'My father thought that without having instructed one should not accept.'

3. 'Let us hear what anybody may have told you,' [continued Yājñavalkya].

'Udaṅka Śaulbāyana told me: "Brahma, verily, is the breath of life (*prāṇa*)."'

'As a man might say that he had a mother, that he had a father, that he had a teacher, so did that Śaulbāyana say, "Brahma is the breath of life." For he might have thought, "What can one have who is without the breath of life?" But did he tell you Its seat and support?'

'He did not tell me.'

'Forsooth, your Majesty, that is a one-legged [Brahma].'

'Verily, Yājñavalkya, do you here tell us.'

'Its seat is just the breath of life; Its support, space. One should worship It as the dear (*priya*).'

'What is Its dearness, Yājñavalkya?'

'The breath of life itself, your Majesty,' said he. 'Verily, out of love for the breath of life, your Majesty, one has sacrifice offered for him for whom one should not offer sacrifice, one accepts from him from whom one should not accept. Out of love of just the breath of life, your Majesty, there arises fear of being killed wherever one goes. The highest Brahma, your Majesty, is in truth the breath of life. The breath of life leaves not him who, knowing this, worships it as such. All things run unto him. He, having become a god, goes even to the gods.'

'I will give you a thousand cows with a bull as large as an elephant,' said Janaka, [king] of Videha.

Yājñavalkya replied: 'My father thought that without having instructed one should not accept.'

4. 'Let us hear what anybody may have told you,' [continued Yājñavalkya].

'Barku Vārshṇa told me: "Brahma, verily, is sight."'

'As a man might say that he had a mother, that he had

a father, that he had a teacher, so did that Vārshṇa say, "Brahma is sight (*cakṣu*)." For he might have thought, "What can one have who cannot see?" But did he tell you Its seat and support?'

'He did not tell me.'

'Forsooth, your Majesty, that is a one-legged [Brahma].'

'Verily, Yājñavalkya, do you here tell us.'

'Its seat is just sight; Its support, space. One should worship It as the true (*satya*).'

'What is Its truthfulness, Yājñavalkya?'

'Sight alone, your Majesty,' said he. 'Verily, your Majesty, when they say to a man who sees with his eyes, "Have you seen?" and he says, "I have seen," that is the truth. Verily, your Majesty, the highest Brahma is sight. Sight leaves not him who, knowing this, worships it as such. All things run unto him. He, becoming a god, goes to the gods.'

'I will give you a thousand cows with a bull as large as an elephant,' said Janaka, [king] of Videha.

Yājñavalkya replied: 'My father thought that without having instructed one should not accept.'

5. 'Let us hear what anybody may have told you,' [continued Yājñavalkya].

'Gardabhīvipīta Bhāradvāja told me: "Brahma, verily, is hearing."'

'As a man might say that he had a mother, that he had a father, that he had a teacher, so did that Bhāradvāja say, "Brahma is hearing." For he might have thought, "What can one have who cannot hear?" But did he tell you Its seat and support?

'He did not tell me.'

'Forsooth, your Majesty, that is a one-legged [Brahma].'

'Verily, Yājñavalkya, do you here tell us.'

'Its seat is just hearing; Its support, space. One should worship It as the endless (*ananta*).'

'What is Its endlessness, Yājñavalkya?'

'Just the quarters of heaven, your Majesty,' said he. 'Therefore, verily, your Majesty, to whatever quarter one goes, he does not come to the end of it, for the quarters of heaven are endless. Verily, your Majesty, the quarters of heaven are hearing. Verily, your Majesty, the highest Brahma is hearing. Hearing does not desert him who, knowing this, worships it as such. All things run unto him. He, becoming a god, goes to the gods.'

'I will give you a thousand cows with a bull as large as an elephant,' said Janaka, [king] of Videha.

Yājñavalkya replied: 'My father thought that without having instructed one should not accept.'

6. 'Let us hear what anybody may have told you,' [continued Yājñavalkya].

'Satyakāma Jābāla told me: "Brahma, verily, is mind."'

'As a man might say that he had a mother, that he had a father, that he had a teacher, so did that Jābāla say, "Brahma is mind." For he might have thought, "What can one have who is without a mind?" But did he tell you Its seat and support?'

'He did not tell me.'

'Forsooth, your Majesty, that is a one-legged [Brahma].'

'Verily, Yājñavalkya, do you here tell us.'

'Its seat is just the mind; Its support, space. One should worship It as the blissful (*ānanda*).'

'What is Its blissfulness, Yājñavalkya?'

'Just the mind, your Majesty,' said he. 'Verily, your Majesty, by the mind one betakes himself to a woman. A son like himself is born of her. He is bliss. Verily, your Majesty, the highest Brahma is mind. Mind does not desert him who, knowing this, worships it as such. All things run unto him. He, becoming a god, goes to the gods.'

'I will give you a thousand cows with a bull as large as an elephant,' said Janaka, [king] of Videha.

Yājñavalkya replied: 'My father thought that without having instructed one should not accept.'

7. 'Let us hear what anybody may have told you,' [continued Yājñavalkya].

'Vidagdha Śākalya told me: "Brahma, verily, is the heart."'

'As a man might say that he had a mother, that he had a father, that he had a teacher, so did that Śākalya say, "Brahma is the heart." For he might have thought, "What can one have who is without a heart?" But did he not tell you Its seat and support?'

'He did not tell me.'

'Forsooth, your Majesty, that is a one-legged [Brahma].'

'Verily, Yājñavalkya, do you here tell us.'

'Its seat is just the heart; Its support, space. One should worship It as the steadfast (*sthiti*).'

'What is Its steadfastness, Yājñavalkya?'

'Just the heart, your Majesty,' said he. 'Verily, your Majesty, the heart is the seat of all things. Verily, your Majesty, the heart is the support (*pratiṣṭhā*) of all things, for on the heart alone, your Majesty, all things are established (*pratiṣṭhita*). Verily, your Majesty, the highest Brahma is the heart. The heart does not leave him who, knowing this, worships it as such. All things run unto him. He, becoming a god, goes to the gods.'

'I will give you a thousand cows with a bull as large as an elephant,' said Janaka, [king] of Videha.

Yājñavalkya replied: 'My father thought that without having instructed one should not accept.'

SECOND BRĀHMANA

Concerning the soul, its bodily and universal relations

1. Janaka, [king] of Videha, descending from his cushion and approaching, said: 'Adoration to you, Yājñavalkya. Do you instruct me.'

He [i.e. Yājñavalkya], said: 'Verily, as a king about to go on a great journey would prepare a chariot or a ship, even so you have a soul (*ātman*) prepared with these mystic doctrines (*upaniṣad*). So, being at the head of a troop, and wealthy, learned in the Vedas, and instructed in mystic doctrines, whither, when released hence, will you go?'

'That I know not, noble sir—whither I shall go.'

'Then truly I shall tell you that—whither you will go.'

'Tell me, noble sir.

2. 'Indha (i.e. the Kindler) by name is this person here in the right eye. Him, verily, who is that Indha people call "Indra"

cryptically, for the gods are fond of the cryptic, as it were, and dislike the evident.[1]

3. Now that which has the form of a person in the left eye is his wife, Virāj. Their meeting-place [literally, their common praise, or concord] is the space in the heart. Their food is the red lump in the heart. Their covering is the net-like work in the heart. The path that they go is that channel which goes upward from the heart. Like a hair divided a thousandfold, so are the channels called *hitā*, which are established within the heart. Through these flows that which flows on [i. e. the food]. Therefore that [soul which is composed of Indha and Virāj] is, as it were, an eater of finer food than is this bodily self.[2]

4. The eastern breaths are his eastern quarter. The southern breaths are his southern quarter. The western breaths are his western quarter. The northern breaths are his northern quarter. The upper breaths are his upper quarter [i. e. the zenith]. The lower breaths are his lower quarter [i. e. the nadir]. All the breaths are all his quarters.

But the Soul (*Ātman*) is not this, it is not that (*neti*, *neti*). It is unseizable, for it cannot be seized. It is indestructible, for it cannot be destroyed. It is unattached, for it does not attach itself. It is unbound. It does not tremble. It is not injured.

Verily, Janaka. you have reached fearlessness.'—Thus spake Yājñavalkya.

Janaka, [king] of Videha, said: 'May fearlessness come unto you, noble Sir, you who make us to know fearlessness. Adoration to you! Here are the Videhas, here am I [as your servants].'

THIRD BRĀHMAṆA

The light of man is the soul

1. Yājñavalkya came to Janaka, [king] of Videha. He thought to himself: 'I will not talk.'[3]

[1] This same etymological explanation occurs at Śat. Br. 6. 1. 1. 2 (cf. 11).

[2] The connection seems to be broken here and the following paragraph appears to refer to the supreme Soul.

[3] Dvivedaganga and Böhtlingk adopt the ingenious reading *sam enena*, 'I will talk with him' (instead of the text as translated, *sa mene na*). But the historical

But [once][1] when Janaka, [king] of Videha, and Yājñavalkya were discussing together at an Agnihotra, Yājñavalkya granted the former a boon. He chose asking whatever question he wished. He granted it to him. So [now] the king, [speaking] first, asked him:

2. 'Yājñavalkya, what light does a person here have?'

'He has the light of the sun, O king,' he said, 'for with the sun, indeed, as his light one sits, moves around, does his work, and returns.'

'Quite so, Yājñavalkya.

3. But when the sun has set, Yājñavalkya, what light does a person here have?'

'The moon, indeed, is his light,' said he, 'for with the moon, indeed, as his light one sits, moves around, does his work, and returns.'

'Quite so, Yājñavalkya.

4. But when the sun has set, and the moon has set, what light does a person here have?'

'Fire, indeed, is his light,' said he, 'for with fire, indeed, as his light one sits, moves around, does his work, and returns.'

'Quite so, Yājñavalkya.

5. But when the sun has set, Yājñavalkya, and the moon has set, and the fire has gone out, what light does a person here have?'

'Speech, indeed, is his light,' said he, 'for with speech, indeed, as his light one sits, moves around, does his work, and returns. Therefore, verily, O king, where one does not discern even his own hands, when a voice is raised, then one goes straight towards it.'

'Quite so, Yājñavalkya.

6. But when the sun has set, Yājñavalkya, and the moon has set, and the fire has gone out, and speech is hushed, what light does a person here have?'

'The soul (*ātman*), indeed, is his light,' said he, 'for with the soul, indeed, as his light one sits, moves around, does his work, and returns.'

situation referred to in Śat. Br. (see the following foot-note) explains Janaka's forwardness in asking questions.

[1] In the episode culminating at Śat. Br. 11. 6. 2. 10.

The various conditions of the soul

7. 'Which (*katama*) is the soul?'

'The person here who among the senses is made of knowledge, who is the light in the heart. He, remaining the same, goes along both worlds, appearing to think, appearing to move about, for upon becoming asleep he transcends this world and the forms of death.

8. Verily, this person, by being born and obtaining a body, is joined with evils. When he departs, on dying, he leaves evils behind.

9. Verily, there are just two conditions of this person: the condition of being in this world and the condition of being in the other world. There is an intermediate third condition, namely, that of being in sleep. By standing in this intermediate condition one sees both those conditions, namely being in this world and being in the other world. Now whatever the approach is to the condition of being in the other world, by making that approach one sees the evils [of this world] and the joys [of yonder world].

The state of dreaming

When one goes to sleep, he takes along the material (*mātrā*) of this all-containing world, himself tears it apart, himself builds it up, and dreams by his own brightness, by his own light. Then this person becomes self-illuminated.

10. There are no chariots there, no spans, no roads. But he projects from himself chariots, spans, roads. There are no blisses there, no pleasures, no delights. But he projects from himself blisses, pleasures, delights. There are no tanks there, no lotus-pools, no streams. But he projects from himself tanks, lotus-pools, streams. For he is a creator.

11. On this point there are the following verses:—

Striking down in sleep what is bodily,
Sleepless he looks down upon the sleeping [senses].
Having taken to himself light, there returns to his place
The golden person, the one spirit (*haṁsa*).

12. Guardling his low nest with the breath,
The Immortal goes forth out of the nest.
He goes where'er he pleases—the immortal,
The golden person, the one spirit (*haṁsa*).

13. In the state of sleep going aloft and alow,
A god, he makes many forms for himself—
Now, as it were, enjoying pleasure with women,
Now, as it were, laughing, and even beholding fearful sights.

14. People see his pleasure-ground;
Him no one sees at all.

"Therefore one should not wake him suddenly," they say. Hard is the curing for a man to whom He does not return.

Now some people say: "That is just his waking state, for whatever things he sees when awake, those too he sees when asleep." [This is not so, for] there [i. e. in sleep] the person is self-illuminated.'

[Janaka said:] 'I will give you, noble sir, a thousand [cows]. Declare what is higher than this, for my release [from re-incarnation].'

15. 'Having had enjoyment in this state of deep sleep, having traveled around and seen good and bad, he hastens again, according to the entrance and place of origin, back to sleep. Whatever he sees there [i. e. in the state of deep sleep], he is not followed by it, for this person is without attachments.'

[Janaka said:] 'Quite so, Yājñavalkya. I will give you, noble sir, a thousand [cows]. Declare what is higher than this, for my release.'

16. 'Having had enjoyment in this state of sleep, having traveled around and seen good and bad, he hastens again, according to the entrance and place of origin, back to the state of waking. Whatever he sees there [i. e. in dreaming sleep], he is not followed by it, for this person is without attachments.'

[Janaka said:] 'Quite so, Yājñavalkya. I will give you, noble sir, a thousand [cows]. Declare what is higher than this, for my release.'

17. 'Having had enjoyment in this state of waking, having traveled around and seen good and evil, he hastens again,

according to the entrance and place of origin, back to dreaming sleep.[1]

18. As a great fish goes along both banks of a river, both the hither and the further, just so this person goes along both these conditions, the condition of sleeping and the condition of waking.

The soul in deep, dreamless sleep

19. As a falcon, or an eagle, having flown around here in space, becomes weary, folds its wings, and is borne down to its nest, just so this person hastens to that state where, asleep, he desires no desires and sees no dream.

20. Verily, a person has those channels called *hitā* ; as a hair subdivided a thousandfold, so minute are they, full of white, blue, yellow, green, and red. Now when people seem to be killing him, when they seem to be overpowering him, when an elephant seems to be tearing him to pieces,[2] when he seems to be falling into a hole—in these circumstances he is imagining through ignorance the very fear which he sees when awake. When, imagining that he is a god, that he is a king, he thinks "I am this world-all," that is his highest world.

21. This, verily, is that form of his which is beyond desires, free from evil, without fear. As a man, when in the embrace of a beloved wife, knows nothing within or without, so this person, when in the embrace of the intelligent Soul, knows nothing within or without. Verily, that is his [true] form in which his desire is satisfied, in which the Soul is his desire, in which he is without desire and without sorrow.

22. There a father becomes not a father ; a mother, not a mother ; the worlds, not the worlds ; the gods, not the gods ; the Vedas, not the Vedas ; a thief, not a thief. There the destroyer of an embryo becomes not the destroyer of an embryo[3] ; a Cāṇḍāla [the son of a Śūdra father and a Brahman mother] is not a Cāṇḍāla ; a Paulkasa [the son of a Śūdra father and a Kshatriya mother] is not a Paulkasa ; a mendicant

[1] This section is lacking in the Mādhyaṁdina recension.

[2] Taking *vicchāyayanti* from *vi* + √*chā*. If from √*vich*, it means 'pressing him hard.' Com. says 'chase.' Cf. Chānd. 8. 10. 2 and note.

[3] Cf. Kaush. 3. 1.

is not a mendicant; an ascetic is not an ascetic. He is not followed by good, he is not followed by evil, for then he has passed beyond all sorrows of the heart.

23. Verily, while he does not there see [with the eyes], he is verily seeing, though he does not see (what is [usually] to be seen)[1]; for there is no cessation of the seeing of a seer, because of his imperishability [as a seer]. It is not, however, a second thing, other than himself and separate, that he may see.

24. Verily, while he does not there smell, he is verily smelling, though he does not smell (what is [usually] to be smelled)[1]; for there is no cessation of the smelling of a smeller, because of his imperishability [as a smeller]. It is not, however, a second thing, other than himself and separate, that he may smell.

25. Verily, while he does not there taste, he is verily tasting, though he does not taste (what is [usually] to be tasted)[1]; for there is no cessation of the tasting of a taster, because of his imperishability [as a taster]. It is not, however, a second thing, other than himself and separate, that he may taste.

26. Verily, while he does not there speak, he is verily speaking, though he does not speak (what is [usually] to be spoken)[1]; for there is no cessation of the speaking of a speaker, because of his imperishability [as a speaker]. It is not, however, a second thing, other than himself and separate, to which he may speak.

27. Verily, while he does not there hear, he is verily hearing, though he does not hear (what is [usually] to be heard)[1]; for there is no cessation of the hearing of a hearer, because of his imperishability [as a hearer]. It is not, however, a second thing, other than himself and separate, which he may hear.

28. Verily, while he does not there think, he is verily thinking, though he does not think (what is [usually] to be thought)[1]; for there is no cessation of the thinking of a thinker, because of his imperishability [as a thinker]. It is not, however, a second thing, other than himself and separate, of which he may think.

29. Verily, while he does not there touch, he is verily touching, though he does not touch (what is [usually] to be touched)[1]; for there is no cessation of the touching of a toucher, because of his imperishability [as a toucher]. It is not, however, a second thing, other than himself and separate, which he may touch.

[1] An addition in the Mādhyaṁdina text.

30. Verily, while he does not there know, he is verily knowing, though he does not know (what is [usually] to be known)[1]; for there is no cessation of the knowing of a knower, because of his imperishability [as a knower]. It is not, however, a second thing, other than himself and separate, which he may know.

31. Verily, where there seems to be another, there the one might see the other; the one might smell the other; the one might taste the other; the one might speak to the other; the one might hear the other; the one might think of the other; the one might touch the other; the one might know the other.[2]

32. An ocean, a seer alone without duality, becomes he whose world is Brahma, O King!'—thus Yājñavalkya instructed him. 'This is a man's highest path. This is his highest achievement. This is his highest world. This is his highest bliss. On a part of just this bliss other creatures have their living.

33. If one is fortunate among men and wealthy, lord over others, best provided with all human enjoyments—that is the highest bliss of men. Now a hundredfold the bliss of men is one bliss of those who have won the fathers' world. Now a hundredfold the bliss of those who have won the fathers' world is one bliss in the Gandharva-world. A hundredfold the bliss in the Gandharva-world is one bliss of the gods who gain their divinity by meritorious works. A hundredfold the bliss of the gods by works is one bliss of the gods by birth and of him who is learned in the Vedas, who is without crookedness, and who is free from desire. A hundredfold the bliss of the gods by birth is one bliss in the Prajāpati-world and of him who is learned in the Vedas, who is without crookedness, and who is free from desire. A hundredfold the bliss in the Prajāpati-world is one bliss in the Brahma-world and of him who is learned in the Vedas, who is without crookedness, and who is free from desire. This truly is the highest world. This is the Brahma-world, O king.'—Thus spake Yājñavalkya.

[Janaka said:] 'I will give you, noble sir, a thousand [cows]. Speak further than this, for my release.'

[1] An addition in the Mādhyaṁdina text.

[2] This section is lacking in the Mādhyaṁdina recension.

Then Yājñavalkya feared, thinking: 'This intelligent king has driven me out of every corner.'[1]

34. [He said:] 'Having had enjoyment in this state of sleep, having traveled around and seen good and bad, he hastens again, according to the entrance and place of origin, back to the state of waking.[2]

The soul at death

35. As a heavily loaded cart goes creaking, just so this bodily self, mounted by the intelligent Self, goes groaning when one is breathing one's last.

36. When he comes to weakness—whether he come to weakness through old age or through disease—this person frees himself from these limbs just as a mango, or a fig, or a berry releases itself from its bond; and he hastens again, according to the entrance and place of origin, back to life.

37. As noblemen, policemen, chariot-drivers, village-heads wait with food, drink, and lodgings for a king who is coming, and cry: "Here he comes! Here he comes!" so indeed do all things wait for him who has this knowledge and cry: "Here is Brahma coming! Here is Brahma coming!"

38. As noblemen, policemen, chariot-drivers, village-heads gather around a king who is about to depart, just so do all the breaths gather around the soul at the end, when one is breathing one's last.

FOURTH BRĀHMAṆA

1. When this self comes to weakness and to confusedness of mind, as it were, then the breaths gather around him. He takes to himself those particles of energy and descends into the heart. When the person in the eye turns away, back [to the sun], then one becomes non-knowing of forms.

2. "He is becoming one," they say; "he does not see." "He is becoming one," they say; "he does not smell." "He is becoming one," they say; "he does not taste." "He is becoming one," they say; "he does not speak." "He is becoming one,"

[1] Or, 'has driven me to extremities.'

[2] This paragraph is probably an intrusion. It is not contained in the Mādhyamdina text and does not fit in well with the context. Cf. 4. 3. 16.

they say; "he does not hear." "He is becoming one," they say; "he does not think." "He is becoming one," they say; "he does not touch." "He is becoming one," they say; "he does not know." The point of his heart becomes lighted up. By that light the self departs, either by the eye, or by the head, or by other bodily parts. After him, as he goes out, the life (*prāṇa*) goes out. After the life, as it goes out, all the breaths (*prāṇa*) go out. He becomes one with intelligence. What has intelligence departs with him. His knowledge and his works and his former intelligence [i.e. instinct] lay hold of him.

The soul of the unreleased after death

3. Now as a caterpillar, when it has come to the end of a blade of grass, in taking the next step draws itself together towards it, just so this soul in taking the next step strikes down this body, dispels its ignorance, and draws itself together [for making the transition].

4. As a goldsmith, taking a piece of gold, reduces it to another newer and more beautiful form, just so this soul, striking down this body and dispelling its ignorance, makes for itself another newer and more beautiful form like that either of the fathers, or of the Gandharvas, or of the gods, or of Prajāpati, or of Brahma, or of other beings.

5. Verily, this soul is Brahma, made of knowledge, of mind, of breath, of seeing, of hearing, of earth, of water, of wind, of space, of energy and of non-energy, of desire and of non-desire, of anger and of non-anger, of virtuousness and of non-virtuousness. It is made of everything. This is what is meant by the saying "made of this, made of that."

According as one acts, according as one conducts himself, so does he become. The doer of good becomes good. The doer of evil becomes evil. One becomes virtuous by virtuous action, bad by bad action.

But people say: "A person is made [not of acts, but] of desires only." [In reply to this I say:] As is his desire, such is his resolve; as is his resolve, such the action he performs; what action (*karma*) he performs, that he procures for himself.[1]

[1] Or, 'into that does he become changed.'

6. On this point there is this verse:—

Where one's mind is attached—the inner self
Goes thereto with action, being attached to it alone.

Obtaining the end of his action,
Whatever he does in this world,
He comes again from that world
To this world of action.[1]

—So the man who desires.

The soul of the released

Now the man who does not desire.—He who is without desire, who is freed from desire, whose desire is satisfied, whose desire is the Soul—his breaths do not depart. Being very Brahma, he goes to Brahma.

7. On this point there is this verse:—

When are liberated all
The desires that lodge in one's heart,
Then a mortal becomes immortal!
Therein he reaches Brahma![2]

As the slough of a snake lies on an ant-hill, dead, cast off, even so lies this body. But this incorporeal, immortal Life (*prāṇa*) is Brahma indeed, is light indeed.'

'I will give you, noble sir, a thousand [cows],' said Janaka, [king] of Videha.

8. [Yājñavalkya continued:] 'On this point there are these verses:—

The ancient narrow path that stretches far away
Has been touched by me, has been found by me.
By it the wise, the knowers of Brahma, go up
Hence to the heavenly world, released.

9. On it, they say, is white and blue
And yellow and green and red.
That was the path by Brahma found;
By it goes the knower of Brahma, the doer of right (*puṇya-kṛt*), and every shining one.

[1] Or 'for action,' or 'because of his action.'
[2] This stanza is found also at Kaṭha 6. 14.

10. Into blind darkness enter they
That worship ignorance;
Into darkness greater than that, as it were, they
That delight in knowledge.[1]

11. Joyless are those worlds called,[2]
Covered with blind darkness.
To them after death go those
People that have not knowledge, that are not awakened.[3]

12. If a person knew the Soul (*Ātman*),
With the thought "I am he!"
With what desire, for love of what
Would he cling unto the body?

13. He who has found and has awakened to the Soul
That has entered this conglomerate abode—
He is the maker of everything, for he is the creator of all;
The world is his: indeed, he is the world itself.

14. Verily, while we are here we may know this.
If you have known it not, great is the destruction.
Those who know this become immortal,
But others go only to sorrow.

15. If one perceives Him
As the Soul, as God (*deva*), clearly,
As the Lord of what has been and of what is to be—
One does not shrink away from Him.[4]

16. That before which the year
Revolves with its days—
That the gods revere as the light of lights,
As life immortal.

17. On whom the five peoples
And space are established—
Him alone I, the knowing, I, the immortal,
Believe to be the Soul, the immortal Brahma.

18. They who know the breathing of the breath,
The seeing of the eye, the hearing of the ear,
(The food of food),[5] the thinking of the mind—
They have recognized the ancient, primeval Brahma.

[1] This stanza is identical with Īśā 9.
[2] Compare Kaṭha 1. 3 a.
[3] A variation of this stanza is found at Īśā 3.
[4] Compare Kaṭha 4. 5 c, d; 4. 12 c, d; Īśā 6 d.
[5] An addition in the Mādhyaṃdina text.

19. By the mind alone is It to be perceived.
There is on earth no diversity.
He gets death after death,
Who perceives here seeming diversity.

20. As a unity only is It to be looked upon—
This indemonstrable, enduring Being,
Spotless, beyond space,
The unborn Soul, great, enduring.

21. By knowing Him only, a wise
Brahman should get for himself intelligence;
He should not meditate upon many words,
For that is a weariness of speech.

22. Verily, he is the great, unborn Soul, who is this [person] consisting of knowledge among the senses. In the space within the heart lies the ruler of all, the lord of all, the king of all. He does not become greater by good action nor inferior by bad action. He is the lord of all, the overlord of beings, the protector of beings. He is the separating dam for keeping these worlds apart.

Such a one the Brahmans desire to know by repetition of the Vedas, by sacrifices, by offerings, by penance, by fasting. On knowing him, in truth, one becomes an ascetic (*muni*). Desiring him only as their home, mendicants wander forth.

Verily, because they know this, the ancients desired not offspring, saying: "What shall we do with offspring, we whose is this Soul, this world?" They, verily, rising above the desire for sons and the desire for wealth and the desire for worlds, lived the life of a mendicant. For the desire for sons is the desire for wealth, and the desire for wealth is the desire for worlds; for both these are desires.

That Soul (*Ātman*) is not this, it is not that (*neti, neti*). It is unseizable, for it cannot be seized. It is indestructible, for it cannot be destroyed. It is unattached, for it does not attach itself. It is unbound. It does not tremble. It is not injured.

Him [who knows this] these two do not overcome—neither the thought "Hence I did wrong," nor the thought "Hence I did right." Verily, he overcomes them both. What he has done and what he has not done do not affect him.

23. This very [doctrine] has been declared in the verse :—

This eternal greatness of a Brahman
Is not increased by deeds (*karman*), nor diminished.
One should be familiar with it. By knowing it,
One is not stained by evil action.

Therefore, having this knowledge, having become calm, subdued, quiet, patiently enduring, and collected, one sees the Soul just in the soul. One sees everything as the Soul. Evil does not overcome him ; he overcomes all evil. Evil does not burn him ; he burns all evil. Free from evil, free from impurity, free from doubt, he becomes a Brahman.

This is the Brahma-world, O king,' said Yājñavalkya.

[Janaka said :] 'I will give you, noble sir, the Videhas and myself also to be your slave.'

24. [Yājñavalkya continued :] 'This is that great, unborn Soul, who eats the food [which people eat], the giver of good. He finds good who knows this.

25. Verily, that great, unborn Soul, undecaying, undying, immortal, fearless, is Brahma. Verily, Brahma is fearless. He who knows this becomes the fearless Brahma.'

FIFTH BRĀHMAṆA [1]

The conversation of Yājñavalkya and Maitreyī concerning the pantheistic Soul

1. Now then, Yājñavalkya had two wives, Maitreyī and Kātyāyanī. Of the two, Maitreyī was a discourser on sacred knowledge [2] (*brahma-vādinī*) ; Kātyāyanī had just (*eva*) a woman's knowledge in that matter (*tarhi*).

Now then, Yājñavalkya was about to commence another mode of life.[3]

2. 'Maitreyī!' said Yājñavalkya, 'lo, verily, I am about to wander forth [4] from this state. Behold! Let me make a final settlement for you and that Kātyāyanī.'

[1] Another version, probably a secondary recension, of the same episode at 2. 4.

[2] Besides this general meaning, *brahma* may also contain pregnantly something of the technical philosophical meaning of 'Brahma.'

[3] For the exact meaning, consult the footnote on 2. 4. 1, page 98, note 1.

[4] *pra-vraj*, the verb from which are formed the technical terms, *pravrājin*, *pravrājaka*, *pravrajita*, for 'a religious mendicant.'

3. Then spake Maitreyī: 'If now, sir, this whole earth filled with wealth were mine, would I now thereby be immortal?'

'No, no!' said Yājñavalkya. 'As the life of the rich, even so would your life be. Of immortality, however, there is no hope through wealth.'

4. Then spake Maitreyī: 'What should I do with that through which I may not be immortal? What you know, sir—that, indeed, explain to me.'

5. Then spake Yājñavalkya: 'Though, verily, you, my lady, were dear to us, you have increased your dearness. Behold, then, lady, I will explain it to you. But, while I am expounding, do you seek to ponder thereon.'

6. Then spake he: 'Lo, verily, not for love of the husband is a husband dear, but for love of the Soul (*Ātman*) a husband is dear.

Lo, verily, not for love of the wife is a wife dear, but for love of the Soul a wife is dear.

Lo, verily, not for love of the sons are sons dear, but for love of the Soul sons are dear.

Lo, verily, not for love of the wealth is wealth dear, but for love of the Soul wealth is dear.

Lo, verily, not for love of the cattle are cattle dear, but for love of the Soul cattle are dear.

Lo, verily, not for love of Brahmanhood is Brahmanhood dear, but for love of the Soul Brahmanhood is dear.

Lo, verily, not for love of Kshatrahood is Kshatrahood dear, but for love of the Soul Kshatrahood is dear.

Lo, verily, not for love of the worlds are the worlds dear, but for love of the Soul the worlds are dear.

Lo, verily, not for love of the gods are the gods dear, but for love of the Soul the gods are dear.

Lo, verily, not for love of the Vedas are the Vedas dear, but for love of the Soul the Vedas are dear.

Lo, verily, not for love of the beings (*bhūta*) are beings dear, but for love of the Soul beings are dear.

Lo, verily not for love of all is all dear, but for love of the Soul all is dear.

Lo, verily, it is the Soul (*Ātman*) that should be seen, that should be hearkened to, that should be thought on, that should be pondered on, O Maitreyī.

Lo, verily, in the Soul's being seen, hearkened to, thought on, understood, this world-all is known.

7. Brahmanhood deserts him who knows Brahmanhood in aught else than the Soul. Kshatrahood deserts him who knows Kshatrahood in aught else than the Soul. The worlds desert him who knows the worlds in aught else than the Soul. The gods desert him who knows the gods in aught else than the Soul. The Vedas desert him who knows the Vedas in aught else than the Soul. Beings desert him who knows beings in aught else than the Soul. Everything deserts him who knows everything in aught else than the Soul. This Brahmanhood, this Kshatrahood, these worlds, these gods, these Vedas, all these beings, everything here is what this Soul is.

8. It is—as, when a drum is being beaten, one would not be able to grasp the external sounds, but by grasping the drum or the beater of the drum the sound is grasped.

9. It is—as, when a conch-shell is being blown, one would not be able to grasp the external sounds, but by grasping the conch-shell or the blower of the conch-shell the sound is grasped.

10. It is—as, when a lute is being played, one would not be able to grasp the external sounds, but by grasping the lute or the player of the lute the sound is grasped.

11. It is—as, from a fire laid with damp fuel, clouds of smoke separately issue forth, so, lo, verily, from this great Being (*bhūta*) has been breathed forth that which is Rig-Veda Yajur-Veda, Sāma-Veda, [Hymns] of the Atharvans and Aṅgirases,[1] Legend (*itihāsa*), Ancient Lore (*purāṇa*), Sciences (*vidyā*), Mystic Doctrines (*upaniṣad*), Verses (*śloka*), Aphorisms (*sūtra*), Explanations (*anuvyākhyāna*), Commentaries (*vyākhyāna*), sacrifice, oblation, food, drink, this world and the other, and all beings. From it, indeed, have all these been breathed forth.

12. It is—as the uniting-place of all waters is the sea, likewise the uniting-place of all touches is the skin; likewise the uniting-place of all tastes is the tongue; likewise the uniting-place of all odors is the nose; likewise the uniting-place of all forms is the eye; likewise the uniting-place of all sounds is the ear; likewise the uniting-place of all intentions is the mind;

[1] A designation of the Atharva-Veda.

likewise the uniting-place of all knowledges is the heart; likewise the uniting-place of all actions is the hands; likewise the uniting-place of all pleasures is the generative organ; likewise the uniting-place of all evacuations is the anus; likewise the uniting-place of all journeys is the feet; likewise the uniting-place of all Vedas is speech.

13. It is—as is a mass of salt, without inside, without outside, entirely a mass of taste, even so, verily, is this Soul, without inside, without outside, entirely a mass of knowledge.

Arising out of these elements, into them also one vanishes away. After death there is no consciousness (*saṁjñā*). Thus, lo, say I.' Thus spake Yājñavalkya.

14. Then said Maitreyī: 'Herein, indeed, you have caused me, sir, to arrive at the extreme of bewilderment. Verily, I understand It [i.e. this *Ātman*] not.'

Then said he: 'Lo, verily, I speak not bewilderment. Imperishable, lo, verily, is this Soul, and of indestructible quality.

15. For where there is a duality, as it were, there one sees another; there one smells another; there one tastes another; there one speaks to another; there one hears another; there one thinks of another; there one touches another; there one understands another. But where everything has become just one's own self, then whereby and whom would one see? then whereby and whom would one smell? then whereby and whom would one taste? then whereby and to whom would one speak? then whereby and whom would one hear? then whereby and of whom would one think? then whereby and whom would one touch? then whereby and whom would one understand? whereby would one understand him by means of whom one understands this All?

That Soul (*Ātman*) is not this, it is not that (*neti, neti*). It is unseizable, for it cannot be seized; indestructible, for it cannot be destroyed; unattached, for it does not attach itself; is unbound, does not tremble, is not injured.

Lo, whereby would one understand the understander?

Thus you have the instruction told to you, Maitreyī. Such, lo, indeed, is immortality.'

After speaking thus, Yājñavalkya departed.

Sixth Brāhmaṇa

The teachers of this doctrine

1. Now the Line of Tradition (*vaṁśa*).—
(We [received this teaching] from Pautimāshya),[1]
Pautimāshya from Gaupavana,
Gaupavana from Pautimāshya,
Pautimāshya from Gaupavana,
Gaupavana from Kauśika,
Kauśika from Kauṇḍinya,
Kauṇḍinya from Śāṇḍilya,
Śāṇḍilya from Kauśika and Gautama,
Gautama [2] from Āgniveśya,
Āgniveśya from Gārgya,
Gārgya from Gārgya,
Gārgya from Gautama,
Gautama from Saitava,
Saitava from Pārāśaryāyaṇa,
Pārāśaryāyaṇa from Gārgyāyaṇa,
Gārgyāyaṇa from Uddālakāyana,
Uddālakāyana from Jābālāyana,
Jābālāyana from Mādhyaṁdināyana,
Mādhyaṁdināyana from Saukarāyaṇa,
Saukarāyaṇa from Kāshāyaṇa,
Kāshāyaṇa from Sāyakāyana,
Sāyakāyana from Kauśikāyani,
Kauśikāyani [3] from Ghṛitakauśika,
Ghṛitakauśika from Pārāśaryāyaṇa,
Pārāśaryāyaṇa from Pārāśarya,
Pārāśarya from Jātūkarṇya,
Jātūkarṇya from Āsurāyaṇa and Yāska,
Āsurāyaṇa from Traivani,
Traivani from Aupajandhani,
Aupajandhani from Āsuri,
Āsuri from Bhāradvāja,
Bhāradvāja from Ātreya,
Ātreya from Māṇṭi,

[1] So the Mādhyaṁdina text begins the list.

Māṇṭi from Gautama,
Gautama from Gautama,
Gautama from Vātsya,
Vātsya from Śāṇḍilya,
Śāṇḍilya from Kaiśorya Kāpya,
Kaiśorya Kāpya from Kumārahārita,
Kumārahārita from Gālava,
Gālava from Vidarbhīkauṇḍinya,
Vidarbhīkauṇḍinya from Vatsanapāt Bābhrava,
Vatsanapāt Bābhrava from Pathin Saubhara,
Pathin Saubhara from Ayāsya Āṅgirasa,
Ayāsya Āṅgirasa from Ābhūti Tvāshṭra,
Ābhūti Tvāshṭra from Viśvarūpa Tvāshṭra,
Viśvarūpa Tvāshṭra from the two Aśvins,
the two Aśvins from Dadhyañc Ātharvaṇa,
Dadhyañc Ātharvaṇa from Atharvan Daiva,
Atharvan Daiva from Mṛityu Prādhvaṁsana,
Mṛityu Prādhvaṁsana from Pradhvaṁsana,
Pradhvaṁsana from Eka Ṛishi,
Eka Ṛishi from Vipracitti,
Vipracitti from Vyashṭi,
Vyashṭi from Sanāru,
Sanāru from Sanātana,
Sanātana from Sanaga,
Sanaga from Parameshṭhin,
Parameshṭhin from Brahma.

Brahma is the Self-existent (*svayam-bhū*). Adoration to Brahma!

FIFTH ADHYĀYA

First Brāhmaṇa

The inexhaustible Brahma

Om!

The yon is fulness; fulness, this.
From fulness, fulness doth proceed.
Withdrawing fulness's fulness off,
E'en fulness then itself remains.[1]

[1] This stanza occurs with variations in AV. 10. 8. 29.

Om!

'Brahma is the ether (*kha*)—the ether primeval, the ether that blows.' Thus, verily, was the son of Kauravyāyanī wont to say.

This is the knowledge (*veda*) the Brahmans know. Thereby I know (*veda*) what is to be known.

SECOND BRĀHMAṆA

The three cardinal virtues

1. The threefold offspring of Prajāpati—gods, men, and devils (*asura*)—dwelt with their father Prajāpati as students of sacred knowledge (*brahmacarya*).

Having lived the life of a student of sacred knowledge, the gods said: 'Speak to us, sir.' To them then he spoke this syllable, '*Da.*' 'Did you understand?' 'We did understand,' said they. 'You said to us, "Restrain yourselves (*damyata*)."' 'Yes (*Om*)!' said he. 'You did understand.'

2. So then the men said to him: 'Speak to us, sir.' To them then he spoke this syllable, '*Da.*' 'Did you understand?' 'We did understand,' said they. 'You said to us, "Give (*datta*)."' 'Yes (*Om*)!' said he. 'You did understand.'

3. So then the devils said to him: 'Speak to us, sir.' To them then he spoke this syllable, '*Da.*' 'Did you understand?' 'We did understand,' said they. 'You said to us, "Be compassionate (*dayadhvam*)."' 'Yes (*Om*)!' said he. 'You did understand.'

This same thing does the divine voice here, thunder, repeat: *Da! Da! Da!* that is, restrain yourselves, give, be compassionate. One should practise this same triad: self-restraint, giving, compassion.

THIRD BRĀHMAṆA

Brahma as the heart

The heart (*hṛdayam*) is the same as Prajāpati (Lord of Creation). It is Brahma. It is all.

It is trisyllabic—*hṛ-da-yam.*

hṛ is one syllable. Both his own people and others bring (√*hṛ*) offerings unto him who knows this.

da is one syllable. Both his own people and others give (√*dā*) unto him who knows this.

yam is one syllable. To the heavenly world goes (*eti* [pl. *yanti*]) he who knows this.

FOURTH BRĀHMAṆA

Brahma as the Real

This, verily, is That. This, indeed, was That, even the Real. He who knows that wonderful being (*yakṣa*) as the first-born—namely, that Brahma is the Real—conquers these worlds. Would he be conquered who knows thus that great spirit as the first-born—namely, that Brahma is the Real? [No!] for indeed, Brahma is the Real.

FIFTH BRĀHMAṆA

The Real, etymologically and cosmologically explained

1. In the beginning this world was just Water. That Water emitted the Real—Brahma [being] the Real—; Brahma, Prajāpati; Prajāpati, the gods. Those gods reverenced the Real (*satyam*). That is trisyllabic: *sa-ti-yam—sa* is one syllable, *ti* is one syllable, *yam* is one syllable. The first and last syllables are truth (*satyam*).[1] In the middle is falsehood (*anṛtam*).[2] This falsehood is embraced on both sides by truth; it partakes of the nature of truth itself. Falsehood does not injure him who knows this.

2. Yonder sun is the same as that Real. The Person who is there in that orb and the Person who is here in the right eye—these two depend the one upon the other. Through his rays that one depends upon this one; through his vital breaths this one upon that. When one is about to decease, he sees that orb quite clear [i. e. free from rays]; those rays come to him no more.

3. The head of the person who is there in that orb is *Bhūr*—there is one head, this is one syllable. *Bhuvar* is the arms—there are two arms, these are two syllables. *Svar* is the feet

[1] 'Truth' is another meaning (beside 'the Real') of the word *satyam*.

[2] Because, as the Commentator explains, the sound *ti* is contained in the word *anṛtam*.

—there are two feet, these are two syllables (*su-ar*). The mystic name (*upaniṣad*) thereof is 'Day' (*ahan*). He slays (√*han*) evil, he leaves it behind (√*hā*), who knows this.

4. The head of the person who is here in the right eye is *Bhūr*—there is one head, this is one syllable. *Bhuvar* is the arms—there are two arms, these are two syllables. *Svar* is the feet—there are two feet, these are two syllables (*su-ar*). The mystic name (*upaniṣad*) thereof is 'I' (*aham*). He slays (√*han*) evil, he leaves it behind (√*hā*), who knows this.

Sixth Brāhmaṇa

The individual person, monistically explained

This person (*puruṣa*) here in the heart is made of mind, is of the nature of light, is like a little grain of rice, is a grain of barley. This very one is ruler of everything, is lord of everything, governs this whole universe, whatsoever there is.

Seventh Brāhmaṇa

Brahma as lightning, etymologically explained

Brahma is lightning (*vidyut*), they say, because of unloosing (*vidāna*). Lightning unlooses (*vidyati*) him from evil who knows this, that Brahma is lightning—for Brahma is indeed lightning.

Eighth Brāhmaṇa

The symbolism of speech as a cow

One should reverence Speech as a milch-cow. She has four udders: the *Svāhā* (Invocation), the *Vashaṭ* (Presentation), the *Hanta* (Salutation), the *Svadhā* (Benediction).[1] The gods subsist upon her two udders, the *Svāhā* and the *Vashaṭ*; men, upon the *Hanta*; the fathers, upon the *Svadhā*. The breath is her bull; the mind, her calf.

Ninth Brāhmaṇa [2]

The universal fire and the digestive fire

This is the universal fire which is here within a person, by means of which the food that is eaten is cooked. It is the

[1] Four exclamations in the sacrificial ritual.
[2] Recurs entire in Maitri 2. 6.

noise thereof that one hears on covering the ears thus.[1] When one is about to depart, one hears not this sound.

TENTH BRĀHMAṆA

The course to Brahma after death

Verily, when a person (*puruṣa*) departs from this world he goes to the wind. It opens out there for him like the hole of a chariot-wheel. Through it he mounts higher.

He goes to the sun. It opens out there for him like the hole of a drum. Through it he mounts higher.

He goes to the moon. It opens out for him there like the hole of a kettle-drum. Through it he mounts higher.

He goes to the world that is without heat, without cold.[2] Therein he dwells eternal years.

ELEVENTH BRĀHMAṆA

The supreme austerities

Verily, that is the supreme austerity which a sick man suffers. The supreme world, assuredly, he wins who knows this.

Verily, that is the supreme austerity when they carry a dead man into the wilderness. The supreme world, assuredly, he wins who knows this.

Verily, that is the supreme austerity when they lay a dead man on the fire. The supreme world, assuredly, he wins who knows this.

TWELFTH BRĀHMAṆA

Brahma as food, life, and renunciation

'Brahma is food'—thus some say. This is not so. Verily, food becomes putrid without life (*prāṇa*).

'Brahma is life'—thus some say. This is not so. Verily, life dries up without food. Rather, only by entering into a unity do these deities reach the highest state.

Now it was in this connection that Prātṛida said to his father:

[1] The word is here used deictically.

[2] The words *aśokam ahimam* may also be translated 'without sorrow, without snow.'

'What good, pray, could I do to one who knows this? What evil could I do to him?'[1]

He then said, with [a wave of] his hand: 'No, Prātṛida. Who reaches the highest state [merely] by entering into a unity with these two?'

And he also spoke to him thus: '*vi*'—verily, *vi* is food, for all beings here enter (√*viś*) into food; and '*ram*'—verily, *ram* is life, for all beings here delight (√*ram*) in life. Verily, indeed, all beings enter into him, all beings delight in him who knows this.[2]

THIRTEENTH BRĀHMAṆA

Life represented in the officiating priest and in the ruler

1. The *Uktha*[3]: Verily, the Uktha is life (*prāṇa*), for it is life that causes everything here to rise up (*ut-thā*). From him there rises up an Uktha-knowing son, he wins co-union and co-status with the Uktha, who knows this.

2. The *Yajus*[4]: Verily, the Yajus is life (*prāṇa*), for in life are all beings here united (√*yuj*). United, indeed, are all beings for his supremacy, he wins co-union and co-status with the Yajus, who knows this.

3. The *Sāman*[5]: Verily, the Sāman is life (*prāṇa*), for in life are all beings here combined (*samyañci*). Combined, indeed, are all beings here serving him for his supremacy, he wins co-union and co-status with the Sāman, who knows this.

4. The *Kshatra*: Verily, rule is life (*prāṇa*), for verily, rule is life. Life protects (√*trā*) one from hurting (*kṣaṇitos*). He attains a rule that needs no protection (*a-tra*), he wins co-union and co-status with the Kshatra,[6] who knows this.

[1] That is:—Is not he who has this knowledge of the nature of Brahma and food and life quite superior to benefit or injury from any other individual?

[2] Namely, that the ultimate unity in which food and life are involved is renunciation, since the meaning of the compound verb *vi-ram* is 'to renounce.'

[3] The Recitation portion of the sacrificial ritual.

[4] The prose portion of the sacrificial ritual.

[5] The Chant.

[6] The word *kṣatra* seems to be used in this paragraph in two meanings: abstractly, as 'rule,' and, specifically, as the 'ruler,' referring to the second or ruling class. In connection therewith, the first three items treated in this section may refer to the priestly class of Brahmans, who alone performed the ritual.

Fourteenth Brāhmaṇa

The mystical significance of the sacred Gāyatrī prayer

1. *bhū-mir* (earth), *an-ta-ri-kṣa* (interspace), *dy-aur* (sky)—eight syllables. Of eight syllables, verily, is one line of the Gāyatrī. And that [series], indeed, is that [line] of it. As much as there is in the three worlds, so much indeed does he win who knows thus that line of it.

2. *ṛ-cas* (verses),[1] *ya-jūṁ-ṣi* (sacrificial formulas),[2] *sā-mā-ni* (chants)[3]—eight syllables. Of eight syllables, verily, is one line of the Gāyatrī. And that [series], indeed, is that [line] of it. As much as is this threefold knowledge, so much indeed does he win who knows thus that line of it.

3. *prā-ṇa* (in-breath), *ap-ā-na* (out-breath), *vy-ā-na* (diffused breath)—eight syllables. Of eight syllables, verily, is one line of the Gāyatrī. And that [series], indeed, is that [line] of it. As much breathing as there is here, so much indeed does he win who knows thus that line of it.

That is its fourth, the sightly, foot, namely the one above-the-darksome who glows yonder.[4] This fourth is the same as the Turīya. It is called the 'sightly (*darśataṁ*) foot,' because it has come into sight (*dadṛśe*), as it were. And he is called 'above-the-darksome' (*paro-rajas*), because he glows yonder far above everything darksome. Thus he glows with luster and glory who knows thus that foot of it.

4. This Gāyatrī is based upon that fourth, sightly foot, the one above-the-darksome. That is based upon truth (*satya*). Verily, truth is sight, for verily, truth is sight. Therefore if now two should come disputing, saying 'I have seen!' 'I have heard!' we should trust the one who would say 'I have seen.'

Verily, that truth is based on strength (*bala*). Verily, strength is life (*prāṇa*). It is based on life. Therefore they say, 'Strength is more powerful than truth.'

[1] Referring to the Rig-Veda by designating the principal character of its contents.

[2] Similarly referring to the Yajur-Veda.

[3] Similarly referring to the Sāma-Veda.

[4] That is, the Sun.

Thus is that Gāyatrī based with regard to the Self (*adhyātmam*). It protects the house-servants. Verily, the house-servants are the vital breaths (*prāṇa*). So it protects the vital breaths. Because it protects (√*trā*) the house-servants (*gaya*), therefore it is called Gāyatrī. That Sāvitrī stanza [1] which one repeats is just this. For whomever one repeats it, it protects his vital breaths.

5. Some recite this Sāvitrī stanza as Anushṭubh meter,[2] saying: 'The speech is Anushṭubh meter. We recite the speech accordingly.' One should not do so. One should recite the Sāvitrī stanza as Gāyatrī meter.[3] Verily, even if one who knows thus receives very much, that is not at all in comparison with one single line of the Gāyatrī.

6. If one should receive these three worlds full, he would receive that first line of it [i. e. the Gāyatrī]. If one should receive as much as is this threefold knowledge, he would receive that second line of it. If one should receive as much as there is breathing here, he would receive that third line of it. But that fourth (*turīya*), sightly foot, the one above-the-darksome, who glows yonder, is not obtainable by anyone whatsoever. Whence, pray, would one receive so much!

7. The veneration of it: 'O Gāyatrī, you are one-footed, two-footed, three-footed, four-footed. You are without a foot, because you do not go afoot. Adoration to your fourth, sightly foot, the one above-the-darksome!—Let not so-and-so obtain such-and-such!'—namely, the one whom one hates. Or, 'So-and-so—let not his wish prosper!'—Indeed, that wish is not prospered for him in regard to whom one venerates thus. Or, 'Let me obtain such-and-such!'

8. On this point, verily, Janaka, [king] of Videha, spoke as follows to Buḍila Āśvatarāśvi: 'Ho! Now if you spoke of yourself thus as a knower of the Gāyatrī, how then have you come to be an elephant and are carrying?'

'Because, great king, I did not know its mouth,' said he.

Its mouth is fire. Verily, indeed, even if they lay very much

[1] RV. 3. 62. 10: On this, of Savitṛi the god,
The choicest glory let us think.
Our thoughts may he himself inspire!

[2] Consisting of four eight-syllable lines.

[3] Consisting of three eight-syllable lines.

on a fire, it burns it all. Even so one who knows this, although he commits very much evil, consumes it all and becomes clean and pure, ageless and immortal.

FIFTEENTH BRĀHMAṆA[1]

A dying person's prayer

With a golden vessel
The Real's face is covered o'er.
That do thou, O Pūshan, uncover
For one whose law is the Real (*satya-dharma*) to see.

O Nourisher (*Pūṣan*), the sole Seer, O Controller (*Yama*), O Sun, offspring of Prajāpati, spread forth thy rays! Gather thy brilliance! What is thy fairest form—that of thee I see. He who is yonder, yonder Person (*puruṣa*)—I myself am he!

[My] breath (*vāyu*) to the immortal wind (*anilam amṛtam*)! This body then ends in ashes! *Om!*

O Purpose (*kratu*), remember! The deed (*kṛta*) remember!
O Purpose, remember! The deed remember!

General prayer of petition and adoration

O Agni, by a goodly path to prosperity (*rai*) lead us,
Thou god who knowest all the ways!
Keep far from us crooked-going sin (*enas*)!
Most ample expression of adoration to thee would we render.[2]

SIXTH ADHYĀYA

FIRST BRĀHMAṆA

The characteristic excellence of six bodily functions, and the value of the knowledge thereof[3]

1. *Om*! Verily, he who knows the chiefest and best, becomes the chiefest and best of his own [people].

Breath (*prāṇa*), verily, is chiefest and best. He who knows this becomes the chiefest and best of his own [people] and even of those of whom he wishes so to become.

[1] This section recurs again as Īśā 15–18. See further footnotes there.
[2] This stanza = RV. 1. 189. 1 (the famous Cremation Hymn).
[3] A parallel passage in simpler form is Chānd. 5. 1. 1–5.

2. Verily, he who knows the most excellent becomes the most excellent of his own [people].

Speech, verily, is the most excellent. He who knows this becomes the most excellent of his own [people] and even of those of whom he wishes so to become.

3. Verily, he who knows the firm basis (*prati-ṣṭhā*) has a firm basis (verb *prati-ṣṭhā*) on even ground, has a firm basis on rough ground.

The Eye, verily, is a firm basis, for with the eye both on even ground and on rough ground one has a firm basis. He has a firm basis on even ground, he has a firm basis on rough ground, who knows this.

4. Verily, he who knows attainment—for him, indeed, is attained what wish he wishes.

The Ear, verily, is attainment, for in the ear all these Vedas are attained. The wish that he wishes is attained for him who knows this.

5. Verily, he who knows the abode becomes the abode of his own [people], an abode of folk.

The Mind, verily, is an abode. He becomes an abode of his own [people], an abode of folk, who knows this.

6. Verily, he who knows procreation (*prajāti*) procreates himself with progeny and cattle.

Semen, verily, is procreation. He procreates himself with progeny and cattle, who knows this.

The contest of the bodily functions for superiority, and the supremacy of breath [1]

7. These vital Breaths (*prāṇa*), disputing among themselves on self-superiority, went to Brahma. Then they said: 'Which of us is the most excellent?'

Then he said: 'The one of you after whose going off this body is thought to be worse off, he is the most excellent of you.'

8. Speech went off. Having remained away a year, it came back and said: 'How have you been able to live without me?'

[1] Compare the other accounts of this episode at Chānd. 5. 1. 6–5. 2. 2; Kaush. 3. 3.

They said: 'As the dumb, not speaking with speech, but breathing with breath, seeing with the eye, hearing with the ear, knowing with the mind, procreating with semen. Thus have we lived.' Speech entered in.

9. The Eye went off. Having remained away a year, it came back and said: 'How have you been able to live without me?'

They said: 'As the blind, not seeing with the eye, but breathing with breath, speaking with speech, hearing with the ear, knowing with the mind, procreating with semen. Thus have we lived.' The eye entered in.

10. The Ear went off. Having remained away a year, it came back and said: 'How have you been able to live without me?'

They said: 'As the deaf, not hearing with the ear, but breathing with breath, speaking with speech, seeing with the eye, knowing with the mind, procreating with semen. Thus have we lived.' The ear entered in.

11. The Mind went off. Having remained away a year, it came back and said: 'How have you been able to live without me?'

They said: 'As the stupid, not knowing with the mind, but breathing with breath, speaking with speech, seeing with the eye, hearing with the ear, procreating with semen. Thus have we lived.' The mind entered in.

12. The Semen went off. Having remained away a year, it came back and said: 'How have you been able to live without me?'

They said: 'As the emasculated, not procreating with semen, but breathing with breath, speaking with speech, seeing with the eye, hearing with the ear, knowing with the mind. Thus have we lived.' The semen entered in.

13. Then Breath was about to go off. As a large fine horse of the Indus-land might pull up the pegs of his foot-tethers together, thus indeed did it pull up those vital breaths together. They said: 'Sir, go not off! Verily, we shall not be able to live without you!'

'If such I am, make me an offering.'

'So be it.'

14. Speech said: 'Verily, wherein I am the most excellent, therein are you the most excellent.'

'Verily, wherein I am a firm basis, therein are you a firm basis,' said the eye.

'Verily, wherein I am attainment, therein are you attainment,' said the ear.

'Verily, wherein I am an abode, therein are you an abode,' said the mind.

'Verily, wherein I am procreation, therein are you procreation,' said the semen.

'If such I am, what is my food? what is my dwelling?'

'Whatever there is here, even to dogs, worms, crawling and flying insects—that is your food. Water is your dwelling.'

Verily, what is not food is not eaten; what is not food is not taken by him who thus knows that [i. e. water] as the food (*anna*) of breath (*ana*). Those who know this, who are versed in sacred learning (*śrotriya*), when they are about to eat, take a sip; after they have eaten, they take a sip. So, indeed, they think they make that breath (*ana*) not naked (*anagna*).

SECOND BRĀHMAṆA

The course of the soul in its incarnations[1]

1. Verily, Śvetaketu Āruṇeya went up to an assembly of Pañcālas. He went up to Pravāhaṇa Jaibali while the latter was having himself waited upon. He, looking up, said unto him, 'Young man!'

'Sir!' he replied.

'Have you been instructed by your father?'

'Yes,' said he.

2. 'Know you how people here, on deceasing, separate in different directions?'

'No,' said he.

'Know you how they come back again to this world?'

'No,' said he.

'Know you why yonder world is not filled up with the many who continually thus go hence?'

'No,' said he.

[1] A parallel account is found in Chānd. 5. 3-10.

'Know you in which oblation that is offered the water becomes the voice of a person, rises up, and speaks?'

'No,' said he.

'Know you the access of the path leading to the gods, or of the one leading to the fathers? by doing what, people go to the path of the gods or of the fathers? for we have heard the word of the seer:—

> Two paths, I've heard—the one that leads to fathers,
> And one that leads to gods—belong to mortals.
> By these two, every moving thing here travels,
> That is between the Father and the Mother.'[1]

'Not a single one of them do I know,' said he.

3. Then he addressed him with an invitation to remain. Not respecting the invitation to remain, the boy ran off. He went to his father. He said to him: 'Verily, aforetime you have spoken of me, sir, as having been instructed!'

'How now, wise one?'

'Five questions a fellow of the princely class (*rājanya-bandhu*) has asked me. Not a single one of them do I know.'

'What are they?'

'These'—and he repeated the topics.

4. He said: 'You should know me, my dear, as such, that whatsoever I myself know, I have told all to you. But, come! Let us go there and take up studentship.'

'Go yourself, sir.'

So Gautama[2] went forth to where [the place] of Pravāhaṇa Jaibali was.

He brought him a seat, and had water brought; so he made him a respectful welcome. Then he said to him: 'A boon we offer to the honorable Gautama!'

5. Then he said: 'The boon acceptable to me is this:— Pray tell me the word which you spoke in the presence of the young man.'

6. Then he said: 'Verily, Gautama, that is among divine boons. Mention [one] of human boons.'

7. Then he said: 'It is well known that I have a full share of gold, of cows and horses, of female slaves, of rugs, of apparel.

[1] That is, between Father Heaven and Mother Earth.

[2] That is, Gautama Āruṇi, the father.

Be not ungenerous toward me, Sir, in regard to that which is the abundant, the infinite, the unlimited.'

'Then, verily, O Gautama, you should seek in the usual manner.'

'I come to you, sir, as a pupil!'—with [this] word, verily, indeed, men aforetime came as pupils.—So with the acknowledgment of coming as a pupil he remained.

8. Then he said: 'As truly as this knowledge has never heretofore dwelt with any Brahman (*brāhmaṇa*) whatsoever, so truly may not you and your grandfathers injure us. But I will tell it to you, for who is able to refuse you when you speak thus!' He continued (*iti*):

9. 'Yonder world, verily, is a sacrificial fire, O Gautama. The sun, in truth, is its fuel; the light-rays, the smoke; the day, the flame; the quarters of heaven, the coals; the intermediate quarters, the sparks. In this fire the gods offer faith (*śraddhā*). From this oblation King Soma arises.

10. A rain-cloud, verily, is a sacrificial fire, O Gautama. The year, in truth, is its fuel; the thunder-clouds, the smoke; the lightning, the flame; the thunder-bolts, the coals; the hail-stones, the sparks. In this fire the gods offer King Soma. From this oblation rain arises.

11. This world, verily, is a sacrificial fire, O Gautama. The earth, in truth, is its fuel; fire, the smoke; night, the flame; the moon, the coals; the stars, the sparks. In this fire the gods offer rain. From this oblation food arises.

12. Man (*puruṣa*), verily, is a sacrificial fire, O Gautama. The open mouth, verily, is its fuel; breath (*prāṇa*), the smoke; speech, the flame; the eye, the coals; the ear, the sparks. In this fire the gods offer food. From this oblation semen arises.

13. Woman, verily, is a sacrificial fire, O Gautama. The sexual organ, in truth, is its fuel; the hairs, the smoke; the vulva, the flame; when one inserts, the coals; the feelings of pleasure, the sparks. In this oblation the gods offer semen. From this oblation a person (*puruṣa*) arises.

He lives as long as he lives. Then when he dies, [14] then they carry him to the fire.[1] His fire, in truth, becomes the fire, fuel, the fuel; smoke, the smoke; flame, the flame;

[1] That is, to the funeral pyre.

coals, the coals; sparks, the sparks. In this fire the gods offer a person (*puruṣa*). From this oblation the man arises, having the color of light.

15. Those who know this, and those too who in the forest truly worship (*upāsate*) faith (*śraddhā*), pass into the flame [of the cremation-fire]; from the flame, into the day; from the day, into the half month of the waxing moon; from the half month of the waxing moon, into the six months during which the sun moves northward; from these months, into the world of the gods (*deva-loka*); from the world of the gods, into the sun; from the sun, into the lightning-fire. A Person (*puruṣa*) consisting of mind (*mānasa*) goes to those regions of lightning and conducts them to the Brahma-worlds. In those Brahma-worlds they dwell for long extents. Of these there is no return.

16. But they who by sacrificial offering, charity, and austerity conquer the worlds, pass into the smoke [of the cremation-fire]; from the smoke, into the night; from the night, into the half month of the waning moon; from the half month of the waning moon, into the six months during which the sun moves southward; from those months, into the world of the fathers; from the world of the fathers, into the moon. Reaching the moon, they become food. There the gods—as they say to King Soma, "Increase! Decrease!"—even so feed upon them there. When that passes away for them, then they pass forth into this space; from space, into air; from air, into rain; from rain, into the earth. On reaching the earth they become food. Again they are offered in the fire of man. Thence they are born in the fire of woman. Rising up into the world, they cycle round again thus.

But those who know not these two ways, become crawling and flying insects and whatever there is here that bites.'

THIRD BRĀHMAṆA

Incantation and ceremony for the attainment of a great wish[1]

1. Whoever may wish, 'I would attain something great!'—in the northern course of the sun, on an auspicious day of the

[1] Compare the ceremony for the 'procuring of a special prize' at Kaush. 2. 3 (2),

half month of the waxing moon, having performed the Upasad ceremony for twelve days, having collected in a dish of the wood of the sacred fig-tree (*udambara*), or in a cup, all sorts of herbs including fruits, having swept around,[1] having smeared around, having built up a fire, having strewn it around,[2] having prepared the melted butter according to rule, having compounded the mixed potion under a male star, he makes an oblation, saying :—

'However many gods in thee, All-knower,[3]
Adversely slay desires of a person,
To them participation I here offer!
Let them, pleased, please me with all desires!
Hail!
Whoever lays herself adverse,
And says, "I the deposer am!"
To thee, O such appeasing one,
With stream of ghee I sacrifice.
Hail!'

2. 'To the chiefest, hail! To the best, hail!'—he makes an oblation in the fire, and pours off the remainder in the mixed potion. A Hail to breath (*prāṇa*)!

'To the most excellent, hail!'—he makes an oblation in the fire and pours off the remainder in the mixed potion. A Hail to speech!

'To the firm basis, hail!'—he makes an oblation in the fire and pours off the remainder in the mixed potion. A Hail to the eye!

'To attainment, hail!'—he makes an oblation in the fire and pours off the remainder in the mixed potion. A Hail to the ear!

'To the abode, hail!'—he makes an oblation in the fire and pours off the remainder in the mixed potion. A Hail to the mind!

where some of the same directions occur. Another parallel passage is Chānd. 5. 2. 4—5. 9. 2.

[1] A part of the elaborate ceremonies which occur also at Āśvalāyana Gṛihya Sūtras 1. 3. 1 and at Pāraskara Gṛihya Sūtras 1. 1. 2.

[2] With sacrificial grass—a part of the usual procedure in the sacrificial ceremony. So AV. 7. 99. 1; Śat. Br. 1. 1. 1. 22; 1. 7. 3. 28; Āśvalāyana Gṛihya Sūtras 2. 5. 2; Gobhila Gṛihya Sūtras 1. 7. 9; Kātyāyana Śrauta Sūtras 2. 3. 6.

[3] This word, *jātavedas*, is a name for fire.

'To procreation, hail!'—he makes an oblation in the fire and pours off the remainder in the mixed potion. A Hail to the semen!

Thus he makes an oblation in the fire and pours off the remainder in the mixed potion.

3. 'To Agni (fire), hail!'—he makes an oblation in the fire and pours off the remainder in the mixed potion.

'To Soma, hail!'—he makes an oblation in the fire and pours off the remainder in the mixed potion.

'O Earth (*bhūr*), hail!'—he makes an oblation in the fire and pours off the remainder in the mixed potion.

'O Atmosphere (*bhuvas*), hail!'—he makes an oblation in the fire and pours off the remainder in the mixed potion.

'O Sky (*svar*), hail!'—he makes an oblation in the fire and pours off the remainder in the mixed potion.

'O Earth, Atmosphere, and Sky, hail!'—he makes an oblation in the fire and pours off the remainder in the mixed potion.

'To the Brahmanhood, hail!'—he makes an oblation in the fire and pours off the remainder in the mixed potion.

'To the Kshatrahood, hail!'—he makes an oblation in the fire and pours off the remainder in the mixed potion.

'To the past, hail!'—he makes an oblation in the fire and pours off the remainder in the mixed potion.

'To the future, hail!'—he makes an oblation in the fire and pours off the remainder in the mixed potion.

'To everything, hail!'—he makes an oblation in the fire and pours off the remainder in the mixed potion.

'To the All, hail!'—he makes an oblation in the fire and pours off the remainder in the mixed potion.

'To Prajāpati, hail!'—he makes an oblation in the fire and pours off the remainder in the mixed potion.

4. Then he touches it, saying: 'Thou art the moving. Thou art the glowing. Thou art the full. Thou art the steadfast. Thou art the sole resort. Thou art the sound *hiṅ* that is made. Thou art the making of the sound *hiṅ*.[1] Thou art the Loud Chant (*udgītha*). Thou art the chanting. Thou art that which is proclaimed. Thou art that which is proclaimed

[1] That is, in the preliminary vocalizing of the ritual.

in the antiphon. Thou art the flaming in the moist. Thou art the pervading. Thou art surpassing. Thou art food. Thou art light. Thou art destruction. Thou art the despoiler.'

5. Then he raises it, saying: 'Thou thinkest. Think of thy greatness![1] He is, indeed, king and ruler and overlord. Let the king and ruler make me overlord.'

6. Then he takes a sip, saying:—

'On this choicest [glory] of Savitṛi[2]—
'Tis sweetness, winds for pious man—
'Tis sweetness, too, the streams pour forth.
Sweet-filled for us let be the herbs![3]
To Earth (*bhūr*), hail!
[On this choicest] glory of the god let us meditate.[4]
Sweet be the night and morning glows!
Sweet be the atmosphere of earth!
And sweet th' Heaven-father (*dyaus pitā*) be to us![5]
To Atmosphere (*bhuvas*), hail!
And may he himself inspire our thoughts![6]
The tree be full of sweet for us!
And let the sun be full of sweet!
Sweet-filled the cows become for us![7]
To the Sky (*svar*), hail!'

He repeats all the Sāvitrī Hymn and all the 'Sweet-verses,' and says: 'May I indeed become this world-all! O Earth (*bhūr*) and Atmosphere (*bhuvas*) and Sky (*svar*)! Hail!"

Finally, having taken a sip, having washed his hands, he lies down behind the fire, head eastward. In the morning he worships the sun, and says: 'Of the quarters of heaven thou art the one lotus-flower![8] May I of men become the one lotus-flower!'[8]

[1] This may be the meaning of *āmaṁsi āmaṁhi te mahi.* The words seem to bear some resemblance to the phrase which involves a play on words in the corresponding passage in Chānd. 5. 2. 6, *amo nāmā 'si amā hi te sarvam idam,* 'Thou art He (*ama*) by name, for this whole world is at home (*amā*) in thee.'

[2] The first line of the famous Sāvitrī Hymn, RV. 3. 62. 10 a.

[3] These three lines are found at RV. 1. 90. 6 and VS. 13. 27.

[4] The second line of the Sāvitrī Hymn, RV. 3. 62. 10 b.

[5] These three lines are found at RV. 1. 90. 7 and VS. 13. 28.

[6] The third line of the Sāvitrī Hymn, RV. 3. 62. 10 c.

[7] These last three lines are found at RV. 1. 90. 8 and VS. 13. 29.

[8] A symbolic expression for 'pre-eminent.'

Then he goes back the same way that he came, and, seated behind the fire, mutters the Line of Tradition (*vaṁśa*).[1]

7. This, indeed, did Uddālaka Āruṇi tell to his pupil Vājasaneya Yājñavalkya, and say: 'Even if one should pour this on a dry stump, branches would be produced and leaves would spring forth.'

8. This, indeed, did Vājasaneya Yājñavalkya tell to his pupil Madhuka Paiṅgya, and say: 'Even if one should pour this on a dry stump, branches would be produced and leaves would spring forth.'

9. This, indeed, did Madhuka Paiṅgya tell to his pupil Cūla Bhāgavitti, and say: 'Even if one should pour this on a dry stump, branches would be produced and leaves would spring forth.'

10. This, indeed, did Cūla Bhāgavitti tell to his pupil Jānaki Āyasthūṇa, and say: 'Even if one should pour this on a dry stump, branches would be produced and leaves would spring forth.'

11. This, indeed, did Jānaki Āyasthūṇa tell to his pupil Satyakāma Jābāla, and say: 'Even if one should pour this on a dry stump, branches would be produced and leaves would spring forth.'

12. This, indeed, did Satyakāma Jābāla tell to his pupils, and say: 'Even if one should pour this on a dry stump, branches would be produced and leaves would spring forth.'

One should not tell this to one who is not a son or to one who is not a pupil.[2]

13. Fourfold is the wood of the sacred fig-tree [in the ceremony]: the spoon (*sruva*) is of the wood of the sacred fig-tree; the cup is of the wood of the sacred fig-tree; the fuel is of the wood of the sacred fig-tree; the two mixing-sticks are of the wood of the sacred fig-tree. There are ten cultivated grains [used]: rice and barley, sesamum and beans, millet and panic, and wheat, and lentils, and pulse, and vetches. These, when they have been ground, one sprinkles with curdled milk, honey, and ghee; and one makes an oblation of melted butter.

[1] That is, the tradition through the successive teachers.

[2] A similar prohibition against promulgating esoteric knowledge occurs at Śvet. 6. 22 and Maitri 6. 29.

Fourth Brāhmaṇa

Incantations and ceremonies for procreation

1. Verily, of created things here earth is the essence; of earth, water; of water, plants; of plants, flowers; of flowers, fruits; of fruits, man (*puruṣa*); of man, semen.

2. Prajāpati ('Lord of creatures') bethought himself: 'Come, let me provide him a firm basis!' So he created woman. When he had created her, he revered her below.—Therefore one should revere woman below.—He stretched out for himself that stone which projects. With that he impregnated her.

3. Her lap is a sacrificial altar; her hairs, the sacrificial grass; her skin, the soma-press. The two labia of the vulva are the fire in the middle. Verily, indeed, as great as is the world of him who sacrifices with the Vājapeya ('Strength-libation') sacrifice, so great is the world of him who practises sexual intercourse, knowing this; he turns the good deeds of women to himself. But he who practises sexual intercourse without knowing this—women turn his good deeds unto themselves.

4. This, verily, indeed, it was that Uddālaka Āruṇi knew when he said:—

This, verily, indeed, it was that Nāka Maudgalya knew when he said:—

This, verily, indeed, it was that Kumārahārita knew when he said: 'Many mortal men, Brahmans by descent, go forth from this world, impotent and devoid of merit, namely those who practise sexual intercourse without knowing this.'

[If] even this much[1] semen is spilled, whether of one asleep or of one awake, [5] then he should touch it, or [without touching] repeat:—

'What semen has of mine to earth been spilt now,
Whate'er to herb has flowed, whate'er to water—
This very semen I reclaim!
Again to me let vigor come!
Again, my strength; again, my glow!
Again the altars and the fire
Be found in their accustomed place!'

[1] Deictically used.

Having spoken thus, he should take it with ring-finger and thumb, and rub it on between his breasts or his eye-brows.

6. Now, if one should see himself in water, he should recite over it the formula: 'In me be vigor, power, beauty, wealth, merit!'

This, verily, indeed, is loveliness among women: when she has removed the clothes of her impurity. Therefore when she has removed the clothes of her impurity and is beautiful, one should approach and invite her.

7. If she should not grant him his desire, he should bribe her. If she still does not grant him his desire, he should hit her with a stick or with his hand, and overcome her, saying: 'With power, with glory I take away your glory!' Thus she becomes inglorious.

8. If she should yield to him, he says: 'With power, with glory I give you glory!' Thus they two become glorious.

9. The woman whom one may desire with the thought, 'May she enjoy love with me!'—after inserting the member in her, joining mouth with mouth, and stroking her lap, he should mutter:—

'Thou that from every limb art come,
That from the heart art generate,
Thou art the essence of the limbs!
Distract this woman here in me,
As if by poisoned arrow pierced!'

10. Now, the woman whom one may desire with the thought, 'May she not conceive offspring!'—after inserting the member in her and joining mouth with mouth, he should first inhale, then exhale, and say: 'With power, with semen, I reclaim the semen from you!' Thus she comes to be without seed.

11. Now, the woman whom one may desire with the thought, 'May she conceive!'—after inserting the member in her and joining mouth with mouth, he should first exhale, then inhale, and say: 'With power, with semen, I deposit semen in you!' Thus she becomes pregnant.

12. Now, if one's wife have a paramour, and he hate him, let him put fire in an unannealed vessel, spread out a row of reed arrows in inverse order, and therein sacrifice in inverse

order those reed arrows, their heads smeared with ghee, saying:—

'You have made a libation in my fire! I take away your in-breath and out-breath (*prāṇāpānau*)—you, so-and-so!

You have made a libation in my fire! I take away your sons and cattle[1]—you, so-and-so!

You have made a libation in my fire! I take away your sacrifices and meritorious deeds[1]—you, so-and-so!

You have made a libation in my fire! I take away your hope and expectation[1]—you, so-and-so!'

Verily, he whom a Brahman who knows this curses—he departs from this world impotent and devoid of merit. Therefore one should not desire dalliance with the spouse of a person learned in sacred lore (*śrotriya*) who knows this, for indeed he who knows this becomes superior.[2]

13. Now, when the monthly sickness comes upon anyone's wife, for three days she should not drink from a metal cup, nor put on fresh clothes. Neither a low-caste man nor a low-caste woman should touch her. At the end of the three nights she should bathe and should have rice threshed.

14. In case one wishes, 'That a white son be born to me! that he be able to repeat a Veda! that he attain the full length of life!'—they two should have rice cooked with milk and should eat it prepared with ghee. They two are likely to beget [him].

15. Now, in case one wishes, 'That a tawny son with reddish-brown eyes be born to me! that he be able to recite two Vedas! that he attain the full length of life!'—they two should have rice cooked with sour milk and should eat it prepared with ghee. They two are likely to beget [him].

16. Now, in case one wishes, 'That a swarthy son with red eyes be born to me! that he be able to repeat three Vedas! that he attain the full length of life!'—they two should have rice boiled with water and should eat it prepared with ghee. They two are likely to beget [him].

[1] These same items recur (though not altogether verbatim) in Kaṭha 1. 8 as possessions of which an offender is to be deprived by an offended Brahman.

[2] This prohibition recurs verbatim in Pāraskara Gṛihya Sūtras 1. 11. 6; the last phrase also in Śat. Br. 1. 6. 1. 18.

17. Now, in case one wishes, 'That a learned (*paṇḍita*) daughter be born to me! that she attain the full length of life!'—they two should have rice boiled with sesame and should eat it prepared with ghee. They two are likely to beget [her].

18. Now, in case one wishes, 'That a son, learned, famed, a frequenter of council-assemblies, a speaker of discourse desired to be heard, be born to me! that he be able to repeat all the Vedas! that he attain the full length of life!'—they two should have rice boiled with meat and should eat it prepared with ghee. They two are likely to beget [him], with meat, either veal or beef.

19. Now, toward morning, having prepared melted butter in the manner of the Sthālīpāka,[1] he takes of the Sthālīpāka and makes a libation, saying: 'To Agni, hail! To Anumati,[2] hail! To the god Savitṛi ('Enlivener,' the Sun), whose is true procreation[3] (*satya-prasava*), hail!' Having made the libation, he takes and eats. Having eaten, he offers to the other [i.e. to her]. Having washed his hands, he fills a vessel with water and therewith sprinkles her thrice, saying:—

'Arise from hence, Viśvavasu![4]
Some other choicer maiden seek!
This wife together with her lord—'[5]

20. Then he comes to her and says:—

'This man (*ama*) am I; that woman (*sā*), thou!
That woman, thou; this man am I!
I am the Sāman; thou, the Rig!
I am the heaven; thou, the earth!
Come, let us two together clasp!
Together let us semen mix,
A male, a son for to procure!'

[1] 'Pot-of-cooked-food,' one of the prescribed forms of oblation, namely a mess of barley or rice cooked with milk.

[2] Originally and in general, the feminine personification of 'Divine Favor,' as in RV. 10. 59. 6; 10. 167. 3; VS. 34. 8, 9; AV. 1. 18. 2; 5. 7. 4; Śat. Br. 5. 2. 3. 2, 4. Specifically invoked, as here, to favor procreation at AV. 6. 131. 2; 7. 20 (21). 2. In the ritual, associated with the day of the full moon, Ait. Br. 7. 11.

[3] Such is the meaning especially applicable in this context. Elsewhere, e.g. VS. 10. 28; Śat. Br. 5. 3. 3. 2; 13. 4. 2. 12, this epithet of Savitṛi is usually taken as from another √*sū*, with the meaning 'whose is true impelling.'

[4] A lecherous demon.

[5] A loose quotation of RV. 10. 85. 22 a, c, d.

21. Then he spreads apart her thighs, saying: 'Spread yourselves apart, heaven and earth!' Inserting the member in her and joining mouth with mouth, he strokes her three times as the hair lies, saying:—

'Let Vishṇu make the womb prepared!
Let Tvashṭṛi shape the various forms!
Prajāpati—let him pour in!
Let Dhātṛi place the germ for thee!

O Sinīvālī, give the germ;
O give the germ, thou broad-tressed dame!
Let the Twin Gods implace thy germ—
The Aśvins, crowned with lotus-wreaths!

22. With twain attrition-sticks of gold
The Aśvin Twins twirl forth a flame;
'Tis such a germ we beg for thee,
In the tenth month to be brought forth.[1]

As earth contains the germ of Fire (*agni*),
As heaven is pregnant with the Storm (*indra*),
As of the points the Wind (*vāyu*) is germ,
E'en so a germ I place in thee,
So-and-so!'

23. When she is about to bring forth, he sprinkles her with water, saying:—

'Like as the wind doth agitate
A lotus-pond on every side,
So also let thy fetus stir.
Let it come with its chorion.

This fold of Indra's has been made
With barricade enclosed around.
O Indra, cause him to come forth—
The after-birth along with babe!'[2]

24. When [the son] is born, he [i.e. the father] builds up a fire, places him on his lap, mingles ghee and coagulated milk in a metal dish, and makes an oblation, ladling out of the mingled ghee and coagulated milk, and saying:—

[1] The above three quatrains are a loose quotation of the hymn RV. 10. 184. The first quatrain occurs also at AV. 5. 25. 5; the second (with slight alterations) at AV. 5. 25. 3.

[2] Compare with this the invocation for successful parturition at RV. 5. 78. 7–8.

'In this son may I be increased,
And have a thousand in mine house!
May nothing rob his retinue
Of offspring or of animals!
Hail!

The vital powers (*prāṇa*) which are in me, my mind, I offer in you.

Hail!
What in this rite I overdid,
Or what I have here scanty made—
Let Agni, wise, the Prosperer,
Make fit and good our sacrifice!
Hail!'

25. Then he draws down to the child's right ear and says 'Speech! Speech!' three times. Then he mingles coagulated milk, honey, and ghee and feeds [his son] out of a gold [spoon] which is not placed within [the mouth],[1] saying: 'I place in you *Bhūr*! I place in you *Bhuvas*! I place in you *Svar*! *Bhūr, Bhuvas, Svar*—everything[2] I place in you!'

26. Then he gives him a name, saying: 'You are Veda.'[3] So this becomes his secret name.[4]

27. Then he presents him to the mother and offers the breast, saying:—

'Thy breast which is unfailing and refreshing,
Wealth-bearer, treasure-finder, rich bestower,
With which thou nourishest all things esteemèd—
Give it here, O Sarasvatī, to suck from.'[5]

28. Then he addresses the child's mother:—

'You are Iḷā,[6] of the lineage of Mitra and Varuṇa!
O heroine! She has borne a hero![7]
Continue to be such a woman abounding in heroes—
She who has made us abound in a hero!'

[1] See the similar directions at Mānava-Dharma-Śāstra 2. 29.

[2] Interpreted by the commentators as earth, atmosphere, and heaven, i. e. the world-all; or as Rig-Veda, Yajur-Veda, and Sāma-Veda, i. e. all knowledge.

[3] Possibly with an added connotation, as *vedo* may be the nominative form also of *vedas*, 'property, wealth.'

[4] In later works this sacred ceremony of naming is found considerably elaborated. See Āsvalāyana Gṛihya Sūtras 1. 15. 3–8; Pāraskara Gṛihya Sūtras 1. 17. 1–4; Gobhila Gṛihya Sūtras 2. 8. 14–17; and Mānava-Dharma-Śāstra 2. 30–33.

[5] RV. 1. 164. 49 with lines b and c transposed.

[6] Or Iḍā, goddess of refreshment in the Rig-Veda.

[7] Or, 'To a hero she has borne a hero.'

Of such a son, verily, they say: 'Ah, you have gone beyond your father! Ah, you have gone beyond your grandfather!'

Ah, he reaches the highest pinnacle of splendor, glory, and sacred knowledge who is born as the son of a Brahman who knows this!

Fifth Brāhmaṇa

The tradition of teachers in the Vājasaneyi school

1. Now the Line of Tradition (*vaṁśa*).—

The son of Pautimāshī [received this teaching] from the son of Kātyāyanī,

the son of Kātyāyanī from the son of Gautamī,
the son of Gautamī from the son of Bhāradvājī,
the son of Bhāradvājī from the son of Pārāśarī,
the son of Pārāśarī from the son of Aupasvastī,
the son of Aupasvastī from the son of Pārāśarī,
the son of Pārāśarī from the son of Kātyāyanī,
the son of Kātyāyanī from the son of Kauśikī,
the son of Kauśikī from the son of Alambī and the son of Vaiyāghrapadī,
the son of Vaiyāghrapadī from the son of Kāṇvī and the son of Kāpī,
the son of Kāpī [2] from the son of Ātreyī,
the son of Ātreyī from the son of Gautamī,
the son of Gautamī from the son of Bhāradvājī,
the son of Bhāradvājī from the son of Pārāśarī,
the son of Pārāśarī from the son of Vātsī,
the son of Vātsī from the son of Pārāśarī,
the son of Pārāśarī from the son of Vārkāruṇī,
the son of Vārkāruṇī from the son of Vārkāruṇī,
the son of Vārkāruṇī from the son of Ārtabhāgī,
the son of Ārtabhāgī from the son of Śauṅgī,
the son of Śauṅgī from the son of Sāṅkṛitī,
the son of Sāṅkṛitī from the son of Ālambāyanī,
the son of Ālambāyanī from the son of Ālambī,
the son of Ālambī from the son of Jāyantī,
the son of Jāyantī from the son of Māṇḍūkāyanī,
the son of Māṇḍūkāyanī from the son of Māṇḍūkī,

the son of Māṇḍūkī from the son of Śāṇḍilī,
the son of Śāṇḍilī from the son of Rāṭhītarī,
the son of Rāṭhītarī from the son of Bhālukī,
the son of Bhālukī from the two sons of Krauñcikī,
the two sons of Krauñcikī from the son of Vaidṛibhatī,
the son of Vaidṛibhatī from the son of Kārśakeyī,
the son of Kārśakeyī from the son of Prācīnayogī,
the son of Prācīnayogī from the son of Sāñjīvī,
the son of Sāñjīvī from the son of Prāśnī, the Āsurivāsin,
the son of Prāśnī from Āsurāyaṇa,
Āsurāyaṇa from Āsuri,
Āsuri [3] from Yājñavalkya,
Yājñavalkya from Uddālaka,
Uddālaka from Aruṇa,
Aruṇa from Upaveśi,
Upaveśi from Kuśri,
Kuśri from Vājaśravas,
Vājaśravas from Jihvāvant Vādhyoga,
Jihvāvant Vādhyoga from Asita Vārshagaṇa,
Asita Vārshagaṇa from Harita Kaśyapa,
Harita Kaśyapa from Śilpa Kaśyapa,
Silpa Kaśyapa from Kaśyapa Naidhruvi,
Kaśyapa Naidhruvi from Vāc (Speech),
Vāc from Ambhiṇī,
Ambhiṇī from Āditya (the Sun).

These white[1] sacrificial formulas (*yajus*) which come from Āditya are declared by Yājñavalkya of the Vājasaneyi school.

The line of tradition from Brahma

4. Up to the son of Sāñjīvī it is the same.[2]
The son of Sāñjīvī from Māṇḍūkāyani,
Māṇḍūkāyani from Māṇḍavya,
Māṇḍavya from Kautsa,
Kautsa from Māhitthi,
Māhitthi from Vāmakakshāyaṇa,

[1] That is, pure, unmingled (with Brāhmaṇa portions), orderly. Thus the White Yajur-Veda is distinguished from the Black Yajur-Veda.

[2] As in the previous list.

Vāmakakshāyaṇa from Śāṇḍilya,
Śāṇḍilya from Vātsya,
Vātsya from Kuśri,
Kuśri from Yajñavacas Rājastambāyana,
Yajñavacas Rājastambāyana from Tura Kāvasheya,
Tura Kāvasheya from Prajāpati,
Prajāpati from Brahma.

Brahma is the Self-existent (*svayam-bhū*). Adoration to Brahma!

CHĀNDOGYA UPANISHAD

FIRST PRAPĀṬHAKA

A Glorification of the Chanting of the Sāma-Veda[1]

FIRST KHAṆḌA

The Udgītha identified with the sacred syllable 'Om'

1. *Om*! One should reverence the Udgītha (Loud Chant) as this syllable, for one sings the loud chant (*ud* + √*gī*) [beginning] with '*Om*.'[2]

The further explanation thereof [is as follows].—

2. The essence of things here is the earth.
The essence of the earth is water.
The essence of water is plants.
The essence of plants is a person (*puruṣa*).
The essence of a person is speech.
The essence of speech is the Rig ('hymn').
The essence of the Rig[3] is the Sāman ('chant').
The essence of the Sāman[4] is the Udgītha ('loud singing').

3. This is the quintessence of the essences, the highest, the supreme, the eighth—namely the Udgītha.

4. 'Which one is the Rig? Which one is the Sāman? Which one is the Udgītha?'—Thus has there been a discussion.

5. The Rig is speech. The Sāman is breath (*prāṇa*). The Udgītha is this syllable '*Om*.'

Verily, this is a pair—namely speech and breath, and also the Rig and the Sāman.

[1] The Sāma-Veda is the Veda to which this Chāndogya Upanishad is attached.

[2] The word *Om*, with which every recital of the Vedas begins, is here set forth as a symbol representing the essence and acme of the entire 'loud singing' (*udgītha*).

[3] Specifically, the Rig-Veda, the 'Veda of Hymns.'

[4] Specifically, the Sāma-Veda, the 'Veda of Chants.'

6. This pair is joined together in this syllable '*Om.*'

Verily, when a pair come together, verily, the two procure each the other's desire.

7. A procurer of desires, verily, indeed, becomes he who, knowing this thus, reverences the Udgītha as this syllable.

8. Verily, this syllable is assent; for whenever one assents to anything he says simply '*Om.*'[1] This, indeed, is fulfilment —that is, assent is.

A fulfiller of desires, verily, indeed, becomes he who, knowing this thus, reverences the Udgītha as this syllable.

9. This threefold knowledge[2] proceeds with it: saying '*Om,*' one[3] calls forth; saying '*Om*' one[4] recites; saying '*Om,*' one[5] sings aloud, to the honor of that syllable, with its greatness, with its essence.

10. He who knows this thus and he who knows not, both perform with it. Diverse, however, are knowledge and ignorance. What, indeed, one performs with knowledge, with faith (*śraddhā*), with mystic doctrine (*upaniṣad*)—that, indeed, becomes the more effective.

—Such is the further explanation of this syllable.

Second Khaṇḍa

The Udgītha identified with breath

1. Verily, when the gods (Devas) and the devils (Asuras), both descendants of Prajāpati, contended with each other, the gods took unto themselves the Udgītha, thinking: 'With this we shall overcome them!'[6]

2. Then they reverenced the Udgītha as the breath in the nose. The devils afflicted that with evil. Therefore with it

[1] With its meaning of 'yes' compare 'Amen.'

[2] Concerning the sacrificial procedure, which is conducted by three orders of priests employing selections from the three Vedas.

[3] That is, the Adhvaryu priest of the Yajur-Veda.

[4] That is, the Hotṛi priest of the Rig-Veda.

[5] That is, the Udgātṛi priest of the Sāma-Veda. With the general reference to the sacrificial ritual here compare the more definite description at Tait. 1. 8.

[6] A similar story, but with a different purport, occurs at Bṛih. 1. 3. There are numerous other episodes in the strife of the gods and the devils, e.g. Śat. Br. 3. 4. 4. 3 and Ait. Br. 1 23.

one smells both the sweet-smelling and the ill-smelling, for it is afflicted with evil.

3. Then they reverenced the Udgītha as speech. The devils afflicted that with evil. Therefore with it one speaks both the true and the false, for it is afflicted with evil.

4. Then they reverenced the Udgītha as the eye. The devils afflicted that with evil. Therefore with it one sees both the sightly and the unsightly, for it is afflicted with evil.

5. Then they reverenced the Udgītha as the ear. The devils afflicted that with evil. Therefore with it one hears both what should be listened to and what should not be listened to, for it is afflicted with evil.

6. Then they reverenced the Udgītha as the mind. The devils afflicted that with evil. Therefore with it one imagines both what should be imagined and what should not be imagined, for it is afflicted with evil.

7. Then they reverenced the Udgītha as that which is the breath in the mouth. When the devils struck that, they fell to pieces, as one would fall to pieces in striking against a solid stone.

8. As a lump of clay would fall to pieces in striking against a solid stone, so falls to pieces he who wishes evil to one who knows this, and he, too, who injures him. Such a one is a solid stone.

9. With this [breath] one discerns neither the sweet-smelling nor the ill-smelling, for it is free from evil. Whatever one eats with this, whatever one drinks with this, he protects the other vital breaths. And not finding this [breath in the mouth], one finally deceases; one finally leaves his mouth open.

10. Aṅgiras reverenced this as the Udgītha. People think that it is indeed Aṅgiras, because it is the essence (*rasa*) of the limbs (*aṅga*)—for that reason.

11. Bṛihaspati reverenced this as the Udgītha. People think that it is indeed Bṛihaspati, because speech is great (*bṛhatī*) and it is the lord (*pati*) thereof—for that reason.

12. Ayāsya reverenced this as the Udgītha. People think that it is indeed Ayāsya, because it goes (*ayate*) from the mouth (*āsya*)—for that reason.

13. Baka Dālbhya knew it. He became Udgātri priest of the people of Naimisha. He used to sing to them their desires.

14. An effective singer of desires, verily, indeed, becomes he who, knowing this thus, reverences the syllable as the Udgītha. —Thus with reference to the self.

Third Khaṇḍa

Various identifications of the Udgītha and of its syllables

1. Now with reference to the divinities.—

Him who glows yonder [i.e. the sun] one should reverence as an Udgītha. Verily, on rising (*ud-yan*), he sings aloud (*ud-gāyati*) for creatures. On rising, he dispels darkness and fear. He, verily, who knows this becomes a dispeller of fear and darkness.

2. This [breath in the mouth] and that [sun] are alike. This is warm. That is warm. People designate this as sound (*svara*), that as sound (*svara*)[1] and as the reflecting (*pratyā-svara*). Therefore, verily, one should reverence this and that as an Udgītha.

3. But one should also reverence the diffused breath (*vyāna*) as an Udgītha. When one breathes in—that is the in-breath (*prāṇa*). When one breathes out—that is the out-breath (*apāna*). The junction of the in-breath and the out-breath is the diffused breath. Speech is the diffused breath. Therefore one utters speech without in-breathing, without out-breathing.

4. The Ṛic is speech. Therefore one utters the Ṛic without in-breathing, without out-breathing. The Sāman is the Ṛic. Therefore one sings the Sāman without in-breathing, without out-breathing. The Udgītha is the Sāman. Therefore one chants the Udgītha without in-breathing, without out-breathing.

5. Whatever other actions than these there are that require strength, like the kindling of fire by friction, the running of a race, the bending of a stiff bow—one performs them without in-breathing, without out-breathing. For this reason one should reverence the diffused breath as an Udgītha.

[1] An approximation to *svar*, 'light.'

6. But one should also reverence the syllables of the Udgītha —*ud*, *gī*, *tha*. *ud* is breath, for through breath one arises (*ut-tiṣṭhati*); *gī* is speech, for people designate speeches as words (*giras*); *tha* is food, for upon food this whole world is established (*sthita*).

7. *ud* is heaven; *gī* is atmosphere; *tha* is the earth.

ud is the sun; *gī* is wind; *tha* is fire.

ud is Sāma-Veda; *gī* is Yajur-Veda; *tha* is Rig-Veda.

Speech yields milk—that is, the milk of speech itself—for him, he becomes rich in food, an eater of food, who knows and reverences these syllables of the Udgītha thus: *ud*, *gī*, *tha*.

8. Now then, the fulfilment of wishes.—

One should reverence the following as places of refuge.

One should take refuge in the Sāman with which he may be about to sing a Stotra.[1]

9. One should take refuge in the Ṛic in which it was contained, in the Ṛishi who was the poet, in the divinity unto whom he may be about to sing a Stotra.

10. One should take refuge in the meter with which he may be about to sing a Stotra. One should take refuge in the hymn-form with which he may be about to sing a Stotra for himself.

11. One should take refuge in the quarter of heaven toward which he may be about to sing a Stotra.

12. Finally, one should go unto himself and sing a Stotra, meditating carefully upon his desire. Truly the prospect is that the desire will be fulfilled for him, desiring which he may sing a Stotra—yea, desiring which he may sing a Stotra!

FOURTH KHAṆḌA

'Om,' superior to the three Vedas, the immortal refuge

1. *Om*! One should reverence the Udgītha as this syllable, for one sings the loud chant [beginning] with '*Om*.'

The further explanation thereof [is as follows].—

2. Verily, the gods, when they were afraid of death, took

[1] A Hymn of Praise in the Hindu ritual.

refuge in the threefold knowledge [i.e. the three Vedas]. They covered (*acchādayan*) themselves with meters. Because they covered themselves with these, therefore the meters are called *chandas*.

3. Death saw them there, in the Ṛic, in the Sāman, in the Yajus, just as one might see a fish in water. When they found this out, they arose out of the Ṛic, out of the Sāman, out of the Yajus, and took refuge in sound.

4. Verily, when one finishes an Ṛic, he sounds out '*Om*'; similarly a Sāman; similarly a Yajus. This sound is that syllable.[1] It is immortal, fearless. By taking refuge in it the gods became immortal, fearless.

5. He who pronounces the syllable, knowing it thus, takes refuge in that syllable, in the immortal, fearless sound. Since the gods became immortal by taking refuge in it, therefore he becomes immortal.

FIFTH KHAṆḌA

The Udgītha identified with the sun and with breath

1. Now then, the Udgītha is *Om*; *Om* is the Udgītha. And so, verily, the Udgītha is yonder sun, and it is *Om*, for it is continually sounding '*Om*.'

2. 'I sang praise unto it alone; therefore you are my only [son],' spake Kaushītaki unto his son. 'Reflect upon its [various] rays. Verily, you will have many [sons].'

—Thus with reference to the divinities.

3. Now with reference to the self.—

One should reverence the Udgītha as that which is the breath in the mouth, for it is continually sounding '*Om*.'

4. 'I sang praise unto it alone; therefore you are my only [son],' spake Kaushītaki unto his son. 'Sing praise unto the breaths as a multitude. Verily, you will have many [sons].'

5. Now then, the Udgītha is *Om*; *Om* is the Udgītha. With this thought, verily, from the seat of a Hotṛi priest one puts in order again the Udgītha which has been falsely chanted—yea, puts it in order again.

[1] Perhaps a double meaning is intended here, for the word *akṣara*, which means 'syllable,' also means 'imperishable.'

Sixth Khaṇḍa

The cosmic and personal interrelations of the Udgītha

1. The Ṛic is this [earth]; the Sāman is fire. This Sāman rests upon that Ṛic. Therefore the Sāman is sung as resting upon the Ṛic.[1] *sā* is this [earth]; *ama* is fire. That makes *sāma.*

2. The Ṛic is the atmosphere; the Sāman is the wind. This Sāman rests upon that Ṛic. Therefore the Sāman is sung as resting upon the Ṛic. *sā* is the atmosphere; *ama* is the wind. That makes *sāma.*

3. The Ṛic is heaven; the Sāman is the sun. This Sāman rests upon that Ṛic. Therefore the Sāman is sung as resting upon the Ṛic. *sā* is heaven; *ama* is the sun. That makes *sāma.*

4. The Ṛic is the lunar mansions; the Sāman is the moon. This Sāman rests upon that Ṛic. Therefore the Sāman is sung as resting upon the Ṛic. *sā* is the lunar mansions; *ama* is the moon. That makes *sāma.*

5. Now, the Ṛic is the white shining of the sun; the Sāman is the dark, the ultra-black. This Sāman rests upon that Ṛic. Therefore the Sāman is sung as resting upon the Ṛic.

6. Now, *sā* is the white shining of the sun; *ama* is the dark, the ultra-black. That makes *sāma.*

Now, that golden Person who is seen within the sun has a golden beard and golden hair. He is exceedingly brilliant, all, even to the fingernail tips.

7. His eyes are even as a Kapyāsa lotus-flower. His name is High (*ud*). He is raised high above all evils. Verily, he who knows this rises high above all evils.

8. His songs (*geṣṇau*) are the Ṛic and the Sāman. Therefore [they are called] the Udgītha. Therefore also the Udgātṛi priest [is so called], for he is the singer (*gātṛ*) of this [High (*ud*)]. He is the lord of the worlds which are beyond yonder sun, and also of the gods' desires.

—Thus with reference to the divinities.

[1] The fact that the Sāma-Veda is composed chiefly of extracts from the Rig-Veda is held in mind throughout this and the following sections which deal with the Ṛic and the Sāman.

SEVENTH KHAṆḌA

1. Now with reference to the self.—

The Ṛic is speech ; the Sāman is breath. This Sāman rests upon that Ṛic. Therefore the Sāman is sung as resting upon the Ṛic. *sā* is speech ; *ama* is breath. That makes *sāma*.

2. The Ṛic is the eye ; the Sāman is the soul (*ātman*). This Sāman rests upon that Ṛic. Therefore the Sāman is sung as resting upon the Ṛic. *sā* is the eye ; *ama* is the soul. That makes *sāma*.

3. The Ṛic is the ear ; the Sāman is the mind. This Sāman rests upon that Ṛic. Therefore the Sāman is sung as resting upon the Ṛic. *sā* is the ear ; *ama* is the mind. That makes *sāma*.

4. Now, the Ṛic is the bright shining of the eye ; the Sāman is the dark, the ultra-black. This Sāman rests upon that Ṛic. Therefore the Sāman is sung as resting upon the Ṛic. *sā* is the bright shining of the eye ; *ama* is the dark, the ultra-black. That makes *sāma*.

5. Now, this person who is seen within the eye is the hymn (*ṛc*), is the chant (*sāman*), is the recitation (*uktha*), is the sacrificial formula (*yajus*), is the prayer (*brahman*).

The form of this one is the same as the form of that [Person seen in the sun]. The songs of the former are the songs of this. The name of the one is the name of the other.

6. He is lord of the worlds which are under this one, and also of men's desires. So those who sing on the lute sing of him. Therefore they are winners of wealth.

7. Now, he who sings the Sāman, knowing it thus, sings of both ; through the former he wins the worlds which are beyond the former, and also the gods' desires.

8. Through the latter he wins the worlds which are under the latter, and also men's desires. Therefore an Udgātṛi priest who knows this may say : [9] 'What desire may I win for you by singing ?' For truly he is lord of the winning of desires by singing, who, knowing this, sings the Sāman—yea, sings the Sāman !

EIGHTH KHAṆḌA

The Udgītha identified with the ultimate, i. e. space

1. There were three men proficient in the Udgītha: Śilaka Śālāvatya, Caikitāyana Dālbhya, and Pravāhaṇa Jaivali. These said: 'We are proficient in the Udgītha. Come! Let us have a discussion on the Udgītha!'

2. 'So be it,' said they, and sat down together. Then Pravāhaṇa Jaivali said: 'Do you two, sirs, speak first. While there are two Brahmans speaking, I will listen to their word.'[1]

3. Then Śilaka Śālāvatya said to Caikitāyana Dālbhya: 'Come! Let me question you.'

'Question,' said he.

4. 'To what does the Sāman go back?'

'To sound,' said he.

'To what does sound go back?'

'To breath,' said he.

'To what does breath go back?'

'To food,' said he.

'To what does food go back?'

'To water,' said he.

5. 'To what does water go back?'

'To yonder world,' said he.

'To what does yonder world go back?'

'One should not lead beyond the heavenly world,' said he. 'We establish the Sāman upon the heavenly world, for the Sāman is praised as heaven.'

6. Then Śilaka Śālāvatya said to Caikitāyana Dālbhya: 'Verily, indeed, your Sāman, O Dālbhya, is unsupported. If some one now were to say "Your head will fall off," your head would fall off.'

7. 'Come! Let me learn this from you, sir.'

'Learn,' said he.

'To what does yonder world go back?'

'To this world,' said he.

[1] The implication is that Pravāhaṇa was not a Brahman. In 5. 3. 5 he is spoken of as one of the princely class (*rājanya*).

'To what does this world go back?'

'One should not lead beyond the world-support,' said he. 'We establish the Sāman upon the world as a support, for the Sāman is praised as a support.'

8. Then Pravāhaṇa Jaivali said to him: 'Verily, indeed, your Sāman, O Śālāvatya, comes to an end. If some one now were to say "Your head will fall off," your head would fall off.'

'Come! Let me learn this from you, sir.'

'Learn,' said he.

Ninth Khaṇḍa

1. 'To what does this world go back?'

'To space,' said he. 'Verily, all things here arise out of space. They disappear back into space, for space alone is greater than these; space is the final goal.

2. This is the most excellent Udgītha. This is endless. The most excellent is his, the most excellent worlds does he win, who, knowing it thus, reverences the most excellent Udgītha.

3. When Atidhanvan Saunaka told this Udgītha to Udaraśāṇḍilya, he also said: "As far as they shall know this Udgītha among your offspring, so far will they have the most excellent life in this world, [4] and likewise a world in yonder world." He who knows and reverences it thus has the most excellent life in this world, and likewise a world in yonder world—yea, a world in yonder world.'

Tenth Khanda

The divinities connected with the three parts of the Chant

1. Among the Kurus, when they were struck by hailstorms, there lived in the village of a rich man a very poor man, Ushasti Cākrāyaṇa, with his wife Āṭikī.

2. He begged of the rich man while he was eating beans. The latter said to him: 'I have no others than these which are set before me.'

3. 'Give me some of them,' said he.

He gave them to him and said: 'Here is drink.'

'Verily, that would be for me to drink leavings!' said he.

4. 'Are not these [beans] also leavings?'

'Verily, I could not live, if I did not eat those,' said he. 'The drinking of water is at my will.'

5. When he had eaten, he took what still remained to his wife. She had already begged enough to eat. She took these and put them away.

6. On the morrow he arose and said: 'Oh, if we could get some food, we might get a little money! The king over there is going to have a sacrifice performed for himself. He might choose me to perform all the priestly offices.'

7. His wife said to him: 'Here, my lord, are the beans.' He ate them and went off to that sacrifice, which had already been begun.

8. There he approached the Udgātṛi priests as they were about to sing the Stotra in the place for the singing. Then he said to the Prastotṛi priest: [9] 'Prastotṛi priest, if you shall sing the Prastāva (Introductory Praise) without knowing the divinity which is connected with the Prastāva, your head will fall off.'

10. Similarly also he said to the Udgātṛi priest: 'Udgātṛi priest, if you shall chant the Udgītha (Loud Chant) without knowing the divinity which is connected with the Udgītha, your head will fall off.'

11. Similarly also he said to the Pratihartṛi priest: 'Pratihartṛi priest, if you shall take up the Pratihāra (Response) without knowing the divinity which is connected with the Pratihāra, your head will fall off.'

Then they ceased and quietly seated themselves.

Eleventh Khaṇḍa

1. Then the institutor of the sacrifice said to him: 'Verily, I would wish to know you, sir.'

'I am Ushasti Cākrāyaṇa,' said he.

2. Then he [i. e. the institutor] said: 'Verily, I have been searching around for you, sir, for all these priestly offices. Verily, not finding you, sir, I have chosen others. [3] But do you, sir, perform all the priestly offices for me.'

'So be it,' said he (*iti*). 'But in this matter (*tarhi*) let these indeed, being permitted, sing the Stotra; but you should give me as much money as you would give them.'

'So be it,' said the institutor of the sacrifice.

4. Then the Prastotṛi priest approached him and said: 'You, sir, said unto me: "Prastotṛi priest, if you shall sing the Prastāva without knowing the divinity which is connected with the Prastāva, your head will fall off." Which is that divinity?'

5. 'Breath (*prāṇa*),' said he. 'Verily, indeed, all beings here enter [into life] with breath and depart [from life] with breath. This is the divinity connected with the Prastāva. If you had sung the Prastāva without knowing it, your head would have fallen off, after you had been told so by me.'

6. Then the Udgātṛi priest approached him and said: 'You, sir, said unto me: "Udgātṛi priest, if you shall chant the Udgītha without knowing the divinity which is connected with the Udgītha, your head will fall off." Which is that divinity?'

7. 'The Sun,' said he. 'Verily, indeed, all beings here sing (*gāyanti*) of the sun when he is up (*uccais*). This is the divinity connected with the Udgītha. If you had chanted the Udgītha without knowing it, your head would have fallen off, after you had been told so by me.'

8. Then the Pratihartṛi priest approached him and said: 'You, sir, said unto me: "Pratihartṛi priest, if you shall take up the Pratihāra without knowing the divinity which is connected with the Pratihāra, your head will fall off." Which is that divinity?'

9. 'Food,' said he. 'Verily, indeed, all beings here live by taking up to themselves (*pratiharamāṇa*) food. This is the divinity connected with the Pratihāra. If you had taken up the Pratihāra without knowing it, your head would have fallen off, after you had been told so by me.'

Twelfth Khaṇḍa

A satire on the performances of the priests (?)

1. Now next, the Udgītha of the Dogs.—

So Bāka Dālbhya—or Glāva Maitreya—went forth for Veda-study.

2. Unto him there appeared a white dog. Around this one

other dogs gathered and said: 'Do you, sir, obtain food for us by singing. Verily, we are hungry.'

3. Then he said to them: 'In the morning you may assemble unto me here at this spot.' So Bāka Dālbhya—or Glāva Maitreya—kept watch.

4. Then, even as [priests] here, when they are about to chant with the Bahishpavamāna Stotra, glide hand in hand, so did they glide on. Then they sat down together and performed the preliminary vocalizing (*hiṅkāra*).

5. They sang: '*Om*! Let us eat. *Om*! Let us drink. *Om*! May the god Varuṇa, Prajāpati, and Savitṛi bring food here! O Lord of food, bring food here!—yea, bring it here! *Om*!'

THIRTEENTH KHAṆḌA[1]

The mystical meaning of certain sounds in the Chant

1. Verily, the sound *hā-u* is the world, [for this interjectional trill occurs in the Rathantara Sāman, which is identified with the earth].

The sound *hā-i* is wind, [for this interjectional trill occurs in the Vāmadevya Sāman, which has for its subject the origin of wind and water].

The sound *atha* is the moon, [for on food (*anna*) everything is established (*sthita*), and the moon consists of food].

The sound *iha* is oneself, [for oneself is here (*iha*)].

The sound *ī* is Agni, [for all Sāmans sacred to Agni end with the sound *ī*].

2. The sound *ū* is the sun, [for people sing of the sun when it is up (*ū-rdhvam*)].

The sound *e* is the Invocation, [for people call with 'Come! (*e-hi*)'].

The sound *au-ho-i* is the Viśvadeva gods, [for this interjectional trill occurs in the Sāman to the Viśvadeva gods].

The sound *hiṅ* is Prajāpati, [for Prajāpati is undefined, and the sound *hiṅ* also is indistinct].

[1] In order that this section may convey some meaning, the commentator Śaṅkara's explanation of the basis of this series of identifications is added in brackets. For a discussion of the translation and interpretation of this section see B. Faddegon, *Acta Orientalia* 5. 177–196.

svara (sound) is breath, [for that is the source of sound].

yā is food, [for everything here moves (*yati*) through the help of food].

vāc is Virāj, [for this interjectional trill occurs in the Sāman to Virāj].

3. The sound *hum*, the variable thirteenth interjectional trill, is the Undefined.

4. Speech yields milk—that is, the milk of speech itself—for him, he becomes rich in food, an eater of food,[1] who knows thus this mystic meaning (*upaniṣad*) of the Sāmans—yea, who knows the mystic meaning!

SECOND PRAPĀTHAKA

The significance of the Chant in various forms

First Khaṇḍa

The Chant, good in various significances

1. *Om*! Assuredly, the reverence of the Sāman entire (*samasta*) is good (*sādhu*). Assuredly, anything that is good, people call *sāman* (abundance); anything that is not good, *a-sāman* (deficiency).

2. So also people say: 'He approached him with *sāman* (kindliness[2])'; that is, they say: 'He approached him with good manner (*sādhu*).'—'He approached him with no *sāman*'; that is, they say: 'He approached him with no good manner.'

3. So also, further, people say: 'Oh! we have *sāman* (goods[3])!' if it is something good (*sādhu*); that is, they say: 'Oh! good!'—'Oh! we have no *sāman*!' if it is not good; that is, they say: 'Oh! no good!'

4. He who, knowing this, reverences the Sāman as good—truly the prospect is that good qualities will come unto him and attend him.

[1] The preceding words of this section are a recurrent stereotyped expression found also at 1. 3. 7 and 2. 8. 3.

[2] Still another meaning of the word *sāman*.

[3] A third distinct meaning of the word *sāman*.

SECOND KHAṆḌA

Some analogies to the fivefold Chant

1. In the worlds one should reverence a fivefold Sāman (Chant).

The earth is a Hiṅkāra (Preliminary Vocalizing).
Fire is a Prastāva (Introductory Praise).
The atmosphere is an Udgītha (Loud Chant).
The sun is a Pratihāra (Response).
The sky is a Nidhana (Conclusion).[1]

—Thus in their ascending order.

2. Now in their reverse order.—

The sky is a Hiṅkāra.
The sun is a Prastāva.
The atmosphere is an Udgītha.
Fire is a Pratihāra.
The earth is a Nidhana.

3. The worlds, both in their ascending order and in their reverse order, serve him who, knowing this thus, reverences a fivefold Sāman in the worlds.

THIRD KHAṆḌA

1. In a rain-storm one should reverence a fivefold Sāman.

The preceding wind is a Hiṅkāra.
A cloud is formed—that is a Prastāva.
It rains—that is an Udgītha.
It lightens, it thunders—that is a Pratihāra.

2. It lifts—that is a Nidhana.[2]

It rains for him, indeed, he causes it to rain, who, knowing this thus, reverences a fivefold Sāman in a rainstorm.

FOURTH KHAṆḌA

1. In all waters one should reverence a fivefold Sāman.

When a cloud gathers—that is a Hiṅkāra.
When it rains—that is a Prastāva.

[1] These are the five divisions of the fivefold Sāman.
[2] Compare the similar identifications at AV. 9. 6. 47.

Those [waters] which flow to the east—they are an Udgītha.
Those which flow to the west—they are a Pratihāra.
The ocean is a Nidhana.

2. He perishes not in water, he becomes rich in water, who, knowing this thus, reverences a fivefold Sāman in all waters.

Fifth Khaṇḍa

1. In the seasons one should reverence a fivefold Sāman.
The spring is a Hiṅkāra.
The summer is a Prastāva.
The rainy season is an Udgītha.
The autumn is a Pratihāra.
The winter is a Nidhana.

2. The seasons serve him, he becomes rich in seasons, who, knowing this thus, reverences a fivefold Sāman in the seasons.

Sixth Khaṇḍa

1. In animals one should reverence a fivefold Sāman.
Goats are a Hiṅkāra.
Sheep are a Prastāva.
Cows are an Udgītha.
Horses are a Pratihāra.
Man is a Nidhana.

2. Animals come into his possession, he becomes rich in animals, who, knowing this thus, reverences a fivefold Sāman in animals.

Seventh Khaṇḍa

1. In the vital breaths (*prāṇa*) one should reverence the most excellent fivefold Sāman.
Breath is a Hiṅkāra.
Speech is a Prastāva.
The eye is an Udgītha.
The ear is a Pratihāra.
The mind is a Nidhana.
Verily, these are the most excellent.

2. The most excellent becomes his, he wins the most

excellent worlds, who, knowing this thus, reverences the most excellent fivefold Sāman in the vital breaths.

—So much for the fivefold.

EIGHTH KHAṆḌA

Some analogies to the sevenfold Chant

1. Now for the sevenfold.—

In speech one should reverence a sevenfold Sāman.

Whatsoever of speech is *hum*—that is a Hiṅkāra (Preliminary Vocalizing).

Whatsoever is *pra*—that is a Prastāva (Introductory Praise).

Whatsoever is *ā*—that is an Ādi (Beginning).

2. Whatsoever is *ud*—that is an Udgītha (Loud Chant).

Whatsoever is *prati*—that is a Pratihāra (Response).

Whatsoever is *upa*—that is an Upadrava (Approach to the End).

Whatsoever is *ni*—that is a Nidhana (Conclusion).[1]

3. Speech yields milk—that is, the milk of speech itself—for him, he becomes rich in food, an eater of food,[2] who knowing this thus, reverences a sevenfold Sāman in speech.

NINTH KHAṆḌA

1. Now, verily, one should reverence yonder sun as a sevenfold Sāman. It is always the same (*sama*); therefore it is a Sāman. It is the same with everyone, since people think: 'It faces me! It faces me!' Therefore it is a Sāman.

2. One should know that all beings here are connected with it.

When it is before sunrise—that is a Hiṅkāra (Preliminary Vocalizing). Animals are connected with this [part] of it. Therefore they perform preliminary vocalizing. Truly, they are partakers in the Hiṅkāra of that Sāman.

3. Now, when it is just after sunrise—that is a Prastāva (Introductory Praise). Men are connected with this [part] of

[1] These are the names of the members of a sevenfold Sāman chant.

[2] The preceding words of this section are a recurrent stereotyped expression found also at 1. 3. 7 and 1. 13. 4.

it. Therefore they are desirous of praise (*prastuti*), desirous of laudation. Truly, they are partakers in the Prastāva of that Sāman.

4. Now, when it is the cowgathering-time—that is an Ādi (Beginning). The birds are connected with this [part] of it. Therefore they support (*ādāya*) themselves without support (*an-ārambaṇa*) in the atmosphere and fly around. Truly, they are partakers in the Ādi of that Sāman.

5. Now, when it is just at mid-day—that is an Udgītha (Loud Chant). The gods are connected with this [part] of it. Therefore they are the best of Prajāpati's offspring. Truly, they are partakers in the Udgītha of that Sāman.

6. Now, when it is past mid-day and before [the latter part of] the afternoon—that is a Pratihāra (Response). Fetuses are connected with this [part] of it. Therefore they are taken [or, held] up (*pratihṛta*) and do not drop down. Truly, they are partakers in the Pratihāra of that Sāman.

7. Now, when it is past afternoon and before sunset—that is an Upadrava (Approach to the end). Wild beasts are connected with this [part] of it. Therefore when they see a man, they approach (*upadravanti*) a hiding-place as their hole. Truly, they are partakers in the Upadrava of that Sāman.

8. Now, when it is just after sunset—that is the Nidhana (Conclusion). The fathers are connected with this [part] of it. Therefore people lay aside (*ni* + √*dhā*) the fathers. Truly, they are partakers in the Nidhana of that Sāman.

TENTH KHAṆḌA

The mystical significance of the number of syllables in the parts of a sevenfold Chant

1. Now then, one should reverence the Sāman, measured (*sammita*) in itself, as leading beyond death.

hiṅkāra has three syllables. *prastāva* has three syllables. That is the same (*sama*).

2. *ādi* has two syllables. *pratihāra* has four syllables. One from there, here—that is the same.

3. *udgītha* has three syllables. *upadrava* has four syllables.

Three and three—that is the same, one syllable left over. Having three syllables—that is the same.

4. *nidhana* has three syllables. That is the same, too. These are twenty-two syllables.

5. With the twenty-one one obtains the sun. Verily, the sun is the twenty-first from here.[1] With the twenty-two one wins what is beyond the sun. That is heaven (*nākam*). That is the sorrowless.[2]

6. He obtains the victory of the sun, indeed, a victory higher than the victory of the sun is his, who, knowing this thus, reverences the sevenfold Sāman, measured in itself, as leading beyond death—yea, who reverences the Sāman!

Eleventh Khaṇḍa

The analogical bases of the ten species of the fivefold Chant

1. The mind is a Hiṅkāra.
Speech is a Prastāva.
The eye is an Udgītha.
The ear is a Pratihāra.
The breath is a Nidhana.

This is the Gāyatrī Sāman as woven upon the vital breaths (*prāṇa*).

2. He who knows thus this Gāyatrī Sāman as woven upon the vital breaths becomes possessor of vital breaths, reaches a full length of life, lives long, becomes great in offspring and in cattle, great in fame. One should be great-minded. That is his rule.

Twelfth Khaṇḍa

1. One rubs the fire-sticks together—that is a Hiṅkāra.
Smoke is produced—that is a Prastāva.
It blazes—that is an Udgītha.
Coals are formed—that is a Pratihāra.

[1] The commentator gives the explanation through the following curious calculation of the distance separating the sun from the earth: 12 months, 5 seasons, 3 world-spaces—then the sun is the twenty-first.

[2] The word *nākam* is made to yield the epithet 'sorrowless' by an etymological pun, *na-a-kam*, 'no lack of desire.'

It becomes extinct—that is a Nidhana.
It becomes completely extinct—that is a Nidhana.
This is the Rathantara Sāman as woven upon fire.

2. He who knows thus this Rathantara Sāman as woven upon fire becomes an eater of food, eminent in sacred knowledge, reaches a full length of life, lives long, becomes great in offspring and in cattle, great in fame. One should not take a sip and spit toward fire. That is his rule.

Thirteenth Khaṇḍa

1. One summons—that is a Hiṅkāra.
He makes request—that is a Prastāva.
Together with the woman he lies down—that is an Udgītha.
He lies upon the woman—that is a Pratihāra.
He comes to the end—that is a Nidhana.
He comes to the finish—that is a Nidhana.[1]
This is the Vāmadevya Sāman as woven upon copulation.

2. He who knows thus this Vāmadevya Sāman as woven upon copulation comes to copulation, procreates himself from every copulation, reaches a full length of life, lives long, becomes great in offspring and in cattle, great in fame. One should never abstain from any woman. That is his rule.

Fourteenth Khaṇḍa

1. The rising sun is a Hiṅkāra.
The risen sun is a Prastāva.
Mid-day is an Udgītha.
Afternoon is a Pratihāra.
When it is set—that is a Nidhana.
This is the Bṛihad Sāman as woven upon the sun.

2. He who knows thus this Bṛihad Sāman as woven upon the sun becomes a brilliant eater of food, reaches a full length of life, lives long, becomes great in offspring and in cattle, great in fame. One should not find fault with it when it is hot. That is his rule.

[1] For a somewhat different, but less probable, rendering see Whitney, *AJP*. 11. 413.

Fifteenth Khaṇḍa

1. Mists come together—that is a Hiṅkāra.
A cloud is formed—that is a Prastāva.
It rains—that is an Udgītha.
It lightens and thunders—that is a Pratihāra.
It holds up—that is a Nidhana.

This is the Vairūpa Sāman as woven upon rain (*pārjanya*).

2. He who knows thus this Vairūpa Sāman as woven upon rain acquires cattle both of various form (*vi-rūpa*) and of beautiful form (*su-rūpa*), reaches a full length of life, lives long, becomes great in children and in cattle, great in fame. One should not find fault with it when it rains. That is his rule.

Sixteenth Khaṇḍa

1. Spring is a Hiṅkāra.
Summer is a Prastāva.
The rainy season is an Udgītha.
Autumn is a Pratihāra.
Winter is a Nidhana.

This is the Vairāja Sāman as woven upon the seasons.

2. He who knows thus this Vairāja Sāman as woven upon the seasons shines like a king (*virajati*) with offspring, cattle, and eminence in sacred knowledge, reaches a full length of life, lives long, becomes great in offspring and cattle, great in fame. One should not find fault with the seasons. That is his rule.

Seventeenth Khaṇḍa

1. The earth is a Hiṅkāra.
The atmosphere is a Prastāva.
The sky is an Udgītha.
The regions of the compass are a Pratihāra.
The ocean is a Nidhana.

These are the verses of the Śakvarī Sāman as woven upon the worlds.

2. He who knows thus these verses of the Śakvarī Sāman as woven upon the worlds becomes possessor of a world,

reaches a full length of life, lives long, becomes great in offspring and in cattle, great in fame. One should not find fault with the worlds. That is his rule.

Eighteenth Khaṇḍa

1. Goats are a Hiṅkāra.
Sheep are a Prastāva.
Cows are an Udgītha.
Horses are a Pratihāra.
Man is a Nidhana.

These are the verses of the Revatī Sāman as woven upon animals.

2. He who knows thus these verses of the Revatī Sāman as woven upon animals becomes possessor of animals, reaches a full length of life, lives long, becomes great in offspring and in cattle, great in fame. One should not find fault with animals. That is his rule.

Nineteenth Khaṇḍa

1. Hair is a Hiṅkāra.
Skin is a Prastāva.
Flesh is an Udgītha.
Bone is a Pratihāra.
Marrow is a Nidhana.

This is the Yajñāyajñīya Sāman as woven upon the members of the body.

2. He who knows thus this Yajñāyajñīya Sāman as woven upon the members of the body becomes possessor of the members of his body, does not become defective in any member of the body, reaches a full length of life, lives long, becomes great in offspring and in cattle, great in fame. One should not eat of marrow for a year. That is his rule. Rather, one should not eat of marrow at all.

Twentieth Khaṇḍa

1. Agni (Fire) is a Hiṅkāra.
Váyu (Wind) is a Prastāva.
Āditya (Sun) is an Udgītha.
The Nakshatras (Stars) are a Pratihāra.

Candrama (Moon) is a Nidhana.
This is the Rājana Sāman as woven upon the divinities.

2. He who knows thus this Rājana Sāman as woven upon the divinities goes to the same world, to equality and to complete union (*sāyujya*) with those very divinities, reaches a full length of life, lives long, becomes great in offspring and in cattle, great in fame. One should not find fault with the Brahmans.[1] That is his rule.

TWENTY-FIRST KHAṆḌA

The Sāman itself based on the world-all

1. The triple knowledge[2] is a Hiṅkāra.
The three worlds[3] here are a Prastāva.
Agni, Vāyu, and Āditya[4] are an Udgītha.
Stars, birds, and light-rays are a Pratihāra.
Serpents, Gandharvas, and the Fathers are a Nidhana.
This is the Sāman as woven upon the world-all.

2. He who knows thus this Sāman as woven upon the world-all becomes the world-all itself.

3. On this point there is this verse:—

Whatever triple things are fivefold—
Than these things there is nothing better, higher.
4. Who knows this fact, he knows the world-all;
All regions of the compass bring him tribute.

One should reverence the thought 'I am the world-all!' That is his rule. That is his rule!

TWENTY-SECOND KHAṆḌA

Seven different modes of singing the chant, characteristic of different gods

1. 'I choose the roaring, animal-like form of the Sāman'—such is the Udgītha belonging to Agni. The indistinct form belongs to Prajāpati; the distinct, to Soma; the soft and smooth, to Vāyu; the smooth and strong, to Indra; the

[1] Inasmuch as they are the human representatives of divinity.

[2] That is, Rig-Veda, Sāma-Veda, and Yajur-Veda.

[3] That is, earth, atmosphere, and sky.

[4] Fire, Wind, and Sun, regarded as regents of the three worlds. For another example of the collocation of this triad see 3. 15. 6.

heron-like, to Bṛihaspati; the ill-sounding, to Varuṇa. One may practise all these, but one should avoid that belonging to Varuṇa.

Various desired results of chanting

2. 'Let me obtain immortality for the gods by singing'—thus should one obtain with his singing. 'Let me obtain oblation for the fathers by singing, hope for men, grass and water for cattle, a heavenly world for the sacrificer, food for myself (*ātman*)'—one should sing the Stotra carefully, meditating these things in mind.

The various sounds in the chant under the protection of different gods

3. All vowels are embodiments (*ātman*) of Indra. All spirants are embodiments of Prajāpati. All [other] consonants are embodiments of Mṛityu (Death).

If one should reproach a person on his vowels, let him say to that one: 'I have been a suppliant to Indra for protection. He will answer you.'

4. So, if one should reproach him on his spirants, let him say to that one: 'I have been a suppliant to Prajāpati for protection. He will thrash you.'

So, if one should reproach him on his [other] consonants, let him say to that one: 'I have been a suppliant to Mṛityu (Death) for protection. He will burn you up.'

5. All the vowels should be pronounced strong and sonant, with the thought: 'To Indra let me give strength.' All the spirants should be pronounced well open, without being slurred over, without being elided, with the thought: 'To Prajāpati let me entrust myself.' All the [other] consonants should be pronounced slowly, without being merged together, with the thought: 'From Mṛityu (Death) let me withdraw myself (*ātman*).'

TWENTY-THIRD KHAṆḌA

Different modes of religious life

1. There are three branches of duty. Sacrifice, study of the Vedas, alms-giving—that is the first. (2) Austerity, in-

deed, is the second. A student of sacred knowledge (*brahmacārin*) dwelling in the house of a teacher, settling himself permanently in the house of a teacher, is the third.

All these become possessors of meritorious worlds. He who stands firm in Brahma attains immortality.

The syllable 'Om,' the acme of the cosmogony

2 (3). Prajāpati brooded upon the worlds. From them, when they had been brooded upon, issued forth the threefold knowledge.[1] He brooded upon this. From it, when it had been brooded upon, issued forth these syllables: *bhūr*, *bhuvaḥ*, *svar*.[2]

3 (4). He brooded upon them. From them, when they had been brooded upon, issued forth the syllable *Om*. As all leaves are held together by a spike, so all speech is held together by *Om*. Verily, *Om* is the world-all. Verily, *Om* is this world-all.

TWENTY-FOURTH KHAṆḌA

Earth, atmosphere, and sky the reward for performers of the morning, noon, and evening oblations

1. The expounders of sacred knowledge (*brahmavādin*) say: 'Since to the Vasus belongs the morning Soma-libation, to the Rudras the mid-day Soma-libation, to the Ādityas and the Viśvadevas the third Soma-libation, [2] where, then (*tarhi*), is the sacrificer's world?'

If one knows not, how can he perform [the sacrifice with success]? So let him who knows perform.

3. Before the commencement of the morning litany he sits down behind the Gārhapatya fire, facing the north, and sings forth the Sāman to the Vasus:—

4. 'Open the door to thy world,
And let us see thee,
For the obtaining of
The sovereignty!'[3]

[1] That is, the three Vedas.

[2] Representing earth, atmosphere, and sky.

[3] The four stanzas contained in this Khaṇḍa are adapted to the purposes of the chant by the special prolongation (plutation) of some of the vowels and the occasional insertion of the interjectional words *hum* and *ā*.

5. So he offers the oblation and says: 'Adoration to Agni, earth-inhabiting, world-inhabiting! Find a world for me, the sacrificer! Verily, that is the sacrificer's world! I will go [6] thither, I, the sacrificer, after life. Hail! Thrust back the bar!' Thus having spoken, he rises. At the same time the Vasus bestow upon him the morning Soma-libation.

7. Before the commencement of the mid-day Soma-libation he sits down behind the Āgnīdhrīya fire, facing the north, and sings forth the Sāman to the Rudras:—

8. 'Open the door to thy world,
And let us see thee,
For the obtaining of
Wide sovereignty!'

9. So he offers the libation and says: 'Adoration to Vāyu, atmosphere-inhabiting, world-inhabiting! Find a world for me, the sacrificer! Verily, that is the sacrificer's world! I will go [10] thither, I, the sacrificer, after life. Hail! Thrust back the bar!' Thus having spoken, he rises. At the same time the Rudras bestow upon him the mid-day Soma-libation.

11. Before the commencement of the third Soma-libation he sits down behind the Āhavanīya fire, facing the north, and sings forth the Sāman to the Ādityas and the Viśvadevas:—

12. 'Open the door to thy world,
And let us see thee,
For the obtaining of
Chief sovereignty!'

13. Thus the [Sāman] to the Ādityas. Now the [Sāman] to the Viśvadevas:—

'Open the door to thy world,
And let us see thee,
For the obtaining of
Full sovereignty!'

14. So he offers the oblation and says: 'Adoration to the Ādityas and to the Viśvadevas, sky-inhabiting, world-inhabiting! Find a world for me, the sacrificer! [15] Verily, that is the sacrificer's world! I will go thither, I, the sacrificer, after life. Hail! Thrust back the bar!' Thus having spoken, he rises. At the same time the Ādityas and the Viśvadevas bestow upon him the third Soma-libation.

Verily, he knows the fulness of the sacrifice who knows this —yea, who knows this!

THIRD PRAPĀṬHAKA

Brahma as the sun of the world-all

FIRST KHAṆḌA

The sun as the honey extracted from all the Vedas

1. Verily, yonder sun is the honey of the gods. The cross-beam[1] for it is the sky. The honeycomb is the atmosphere. The brood are the particles of light.

2. The eastern rays of that sun are its eastern honey-cells. The bees are the Rig verses. The flower is the Rig-Veda. The drops of nectar fluid [arose as follows].

Verily, these Rig verses [3] brooded upon that Rig-Veda; from it, when it had been brooded upon, there was produced as its essence splendor, brightness, power, vigor, and food.

4. It flowed forth. It repaired to the sun. Verily, that is what that red appearance of the sun is.

SECOND KHAṆḌA

1. So its southern rays are its southern honey-cells. The bees are the Yajus formulas. The flower is the Yajur-Veda. The drops of nectar fluid [arose as follows].

2. Verily, these Yajus formulas brooded upon that Yajur-Veda; from it, when it had been brooded upon, there was produced as its essence splendor, brightness, power, vigor, and food.

3. It flowed forth. It repaired to the sun. Verily, that is what that white appearance of the sun is.

THIRD KHAṆḌA

1. So its western rays are its western honey-cells. The bees are the Sāman chants. The flower is the Sāma-Veda. The drops of nectar fluid [arose as follows].

[1] The beam from which the honeycomb hangs.

2. Verily, those Sāman chants brooded upon that Sāma-Veda; from it, when it had been brooded upon, there was produced as its essence splendor, brightness, power, vigor, and food.

3. It flowed forth. It repaired to the sun. Verily, that is what that dark appearance of the sun is.

Fourth Khaṇḍa

1. So its northern rays are its northern honey-cells. The bees are the [Hymns] of the Atharvans and Aṅgirases.[1] The flower is Legend and Ancient Lore (*itihāsa-purāṇa*). The drops of nectar fluid [arose as follows].

2. Verily, those [Hymns] of the Atharvans and Aṅgirases brooded upon that Legend and Ancient Lore; from it, when it had been brooded upon, there was produced as its essence splendor, brightness, power, vigor, and food.

3. It flowed forth. It repaired to the sun. Verily, that is what that exceedingly dark appearance of the sun is.

Fifth Khaṇḍa

1. So its upward rays are its upper honey-cells. The bees are the Hidden Teachings [i. e. the Upanishads]. The flower is Brahma. The drops of nectar fluid [arose as follows].

2. Verily, those Hidden Teachings brooded upon that Brahma; from it, when it had been brooded upon, there was produced as its essence splendor, brightness, power, vigor, and food.

3. It flowed forth. It repaired to the sun. Verily, that is what seems to tremble in the middle of the sun.

4. Verily, these are the essences of the essences, for the Vedas are essences and these are their essences. Verily, these are the nectars of the nectars, for the Vedas are nectars and these are their nectars.

Sixth Khaṇḍa

The knower of the cosmic significance of the sacred scriptures advances to the world-sun, Brahma

1. The Vasus live upon that which is the first nectar [i.e. the

[1] A designation of the Atharva-Veda.

Rig-Veda] through Agni as their mouth. Verily, the gods neither eat nor drink. They are satisfied merely with seeing that nectar.

2. These enter that [red] form of the sun and come forth from that form.

3. He who knows thus that nectar becomes one of the Vasus themselves and through Agni as his mouth is satisfied merely with seeing that nectar. He enters that very form and comes forth from that form.

4. As long as the sun shall rise in the east and set in the west, so long will he compass the overlordship and the chief sovereignty (*svārājya*) of the Vasus.

Seventh Khaṇḍa

1. Now, the Rudras live upon what is the second nectar [i. e. the Yajur-Veda] through Indra as their mouth. Verily, the gods neither eat nor drink. They are satisfied merely with seeing that nectar.

2. These enter that [white] form and come forth from that form.

3. He who knows thus that nectar becomes one of the Rudras themselves and through Indra as his mouth is satisfied merely with seeing that nectar. He enters that very form and comes forth from that form.

4. As long as the sun shall rise in the east and set in the west, twice so long will it rise in the south and set in the north, and just that long will he compass the overlordship and the chief sovereignty of the Rudras.

Eighth Khaṇḍa

1. Now, the Ādityas live upon what is the third nectar [i. e. the Sāma-Veda] through Varuṇa as their mouth. Verily, the gods neither eat nor drink. They are satisfied merely with seeing that nectar.

2. These enter that [dark] form and come forth from that form.

3. He who knows thus that nectar becomes one of the Ādityas themselves and through Varuṇa as his mouth is

satisfied merely with seeing that nectar. He enters that very form and comes forth from that form.

4. So long as the sun shall rise in the south and set in the north, twice so long will it rise in the west and set in the east, and just that long will he compass the overlordship and the chief sovereignty of the Ādityas.

NINTH KHAṆḌA

1. Now, the Maruts live upon what is the fourth nectar [i. e. the Atharva-Veda] through Soma as their mouth. Verily, the gods neither eat nor drink. They are satisfied merely with seeing that nectar.

2. These enter that [exceedingly dark] form and come forth from that form.

3. He who knows thus that nectar becomes one of the Maruts themselves and through Soma as his mouth is satisfied merely with seeing that nectar. He enters that very form and comes forth from that form.

4. As long as the sun shall rise in the west and set in the east, twice so long will it rise in the north and set in the south, and just that long will he compass the overlordship and the chief sovereignty of the Maruts.

TENTH KHAṆḌA

1. Now, the Sādhyas live upon what is the fifth nectar [i. e. the Upanishads] through Brahma as their mouth. Verily, the gods neither eat nor drink. They are satisfied merely with seeing that nectar.

2. These enter that form [which seems to tremble in the middle of the sun] and come forth from that form.

3. He who knows thus that nectar becomes one of the Sādhyas themselves and through Brahma as his mouth is satisfied merely with seeing that nectar. He enters that very form and comes forth from that form.

4. As long as the sun shall rise in the north and set in the south, twice so long will it rise in the zenith and set in the nadir, and just that long will he compass the overlordship and the chief sovereignty of the Sādhyas.

ELEVENTH KHAṆḌA

1. Henceforth, after having risen in the zenith, it will no more rise nor set. It will stand alone in the middle. On this point there is this verse:—

> 2. In yonder sphere it has not set,[1]
> Nor even has it risen up;
> And by the truth of this, ye gods,
> Of Brahma let me not be robbed.

3. Verily, it neither rises nor sets for him, it is evermore day for him, who knows thus this mystic doctrine (*upaniṣad*) of Brahma.

4. Brahma told this to Prajāpati; Prajāpati, to Manu; Manu, to his descendants. To Uddālaka Āruṇi, as being the eldest son, his father declared this Brahma.

5. Verily, a father may teach this Brahma to his eldest son or to a worthy pupil, [6] [but] to no one else at all. Even if one should offer him this [earth] that is encompassed by water and filled with treasure, [he should say]: 'This, truly, is more than that! This, truly, is more than that!'

TWELFTH KHAṆḌA

The Gāyatrī meter as a symbol of all that is

1. Verily, the Gāyatrī meter is everything here that has come to be, whatsoever there is here. Verily, the Gāyatrī is speech. Verily, speech both sings of (*gāyati*) and protects (*trāyate*) everything here that has come to be.

2. Verily, what this Gāyatrī is—that is the same as what this earth is; for on it everything here that has come to be is established. It does not extend beyond it.

3. Verily, what this earth is—that is the same as what the body in man here is; for in it these vital breaths are established. They do not extend beyond it.

4. Verily, what the body in man is—that is the same as what the heart within man here is; for on it these vital breaths are established. They do not extend beyond it.

[1] Adopting Böhtlingk's emendation, *nimumloca*, for the impossible *na nimloca*.

5. This is the four-quartered sixfold Gāyatrī. With reference to it a Rig verse states:—

> 6. His greatness is of such extent,
> Yet Purusha is greater still.
> All beings are one-fourth of him;
> Three-fourths, the immortal in the sky.[1]

7. Verily, what is called Brahma—that is the same as what the space outside of a person is. Verily, what the space outside of a person is—[8] that is the same as what the space within a person is. Verily, what the space within a person is—[9] that is the same as what the space here within the heart is. That is the Full, the Non-active.[2] Full, non-active prosperity he obtains who knows this.

THIRTEENTH KHAṆḌA

The five doorkeepers of the heavenly world

1. Verily, indeed, this heart here has five openings for the gods.

As for its eastern opening—that is the Prāṇa breath, that is the eye, that is the sun. One should reverence that as glow and as food. He becomes glowing and an eater of food who knows this.

2. Now, as for its southern opening—that is the Vyāna breath, that is the ear, that is the moon. One should reverence that as prosperity and splendor. He becomes prosperous and splendid who knows this.

3. Now, as for its western opening—that is the Apāna breath, that is speech, that is fire. One should reverence that as eminence in sacred knowledge and as food. He becomes eminent in sacred knowledge and an eater of food who knows this.

4. Now, as for its northern opening—that is the Samāna breath, that is mind, that is the rain-god (Parjanya). One should reverence that as fame and beauty. He becomes famous and beauteous who knows this.

5. Now as for its upper opening—that is the Udāna breath,

[1] RV. 10. 90. 3, with slight variations.
[2] This same characterization is found at Bṛih. 2. 1. 5.

that is wind, that is space. One should reverence that as vigor and greatness. He becomes vigorous and great who knows this.

6. Verily, these same are five Brahma-men, doorkeepers of the heavenly world. Who knows these thus as five Brahma-men, as doorkeepers of the heavenly world, in his family a hero is born. He reaches the heavenly world who knows these thus as five Brahma-men, doorkeepers of the heavenly world.

The ultimate exists within oneself

7. Now, the light which shines higher than this heaven, on the backs of all, on the backs of everything, in the highest worlds, than which there are no higher—verily, that is the same as this light which is here within a person.

There is this seeing of it—[8] when one perceives by touch this heat here in the body. There is this hearing of it—when one closes his ears and hears as it were a sound, as it were a noise, as of a fire blazing. One should reverence that light as something that has been seen and heard. He becomes one beautiful to see, one heard of in renown, who knows this—yea, who knows this!

FOURTEENTH KHAṆḌA[1]

The individual soul identical with the infinite Brahma

1. 'Verily, this whole world is Brahma. Tranquil, let one worship It as that from which he came forth, as that into which he will be dissolved, as that in which he breathes.[2]

Now, verily, a person consists of purpose (*kratu-maya*). According to the purpose which a person has in this world, thus does he become on departing hence. So let him form for himself a purpose.

2. He who consists of mind, whose body is life (*prāṇa*), whose form is light, whose conception is truth, whose soul (*ātman*) is space, containing all works, containing all desires, containing all odors, containing all tastes, encompassing this

[1] This section, which occurs also as Śat. Br. 10. 6. 3, constitutes the famous *Śāṇḍilya-vidyā*, or Doctrine of Śāṇḍilya.

[2] Thus Śaṅkara explains the threefold mystic epithet *taj-ja-lān*.

whole world, the unspeaking, the unconcerned—[3] this Soul of mine within the heart is smaller than a grain of rice, or a barley-corn, or a mustard-seed, or a grain of millet, or the kernel of a grain of millet; this Soul of mine within the heart is greater than the earth, greater than the atmosphere, greater than the sky, greater than these worlds.

4. Containing all works, containing all desires, containing all odors, containing all tastes, encompassing this whole world, the unspeaking, the unconcerned—this is the Soul of mine within the heart, this is Brahma. Into him I shall enter on departing hence.

If one would believe this, he would have no more doubt.—Thus used Sāṇḍilya to say—yea, Śāṇḍilya!

Fifteenth Khaṇḍa

The universe as a treasure-chest and refuge

1. The chest whose space is atmosphere,
With earth for bottom, ne'er decays.
Its corners are the poles of heaven.
Its upper opening is the sky.
This chest is one containing wealth.
Within it everything here rests.

2. Its eastern quarter is named Sacrificial Ladle (*juhū*).[1] Its southern quarter is named Overpowering.[2] Its western quarter is named Queen (*rājñī*).[3] Its northern quarter is named Wealthy.[4] The wind is the child of these quarters of heaven. He who knows this wind thus as the child of the quarters of heaven mourns not for a son.

'I here know this wind thus as the child of the quarters of heaven. Let me not mourn for a son.'

3. 'I take refuge in the imperishable chest with this one, with this one, with this one.'[5]

[1] For one faces the east when one offers a sacrifice for oneself (*juhute*).

[2] For it is the region of Yama, the god of the dead.

[3] For it is the region of King (*rājan*) Varuṇa, or because of the red (*rāga*) of twilight.

[4] For it is the region presided over by Kubera, the god of wealth.—These are Śaṅkara's explanations of the four epithets.

[5] Śaṅkara explains that the son's name is here to be said three times.

'I take refuge in breath (*prāṇa*)[1] with this one, with this one, with this one.'

'I take refuge in *bhūr* with this one, with this one, with this one.'

'I take refuge in *bhuvas* with this one, with this one, with this one.'

'I take refuge in *svar* with this one, with this one, with this one.'

4. When I said, 'I take refuge in breath'—breath, verily, is everything here that has come to be, whatsoever there is. So it was in this I took refuge.

5. So when I said, 'I take refuge in *bhūr*,' what I said was: 'I take refuge in earth; I take refuge in atmosphere; I take refuge in sky.'

6. So when I said, 'I take refuge in *bhuvas*,' what I said was: 'I take refuge in Agni (Fire); I take refuge in Vāyu (Wind); I take refuge in Āditya (Sun).'

7. So when I said, 'I take refuge in *svar*,' what I said was: 'I take refuge in the Rig-Veda; I take refuge in the Yajur-Veda; I take refuge in the Sāma-Veda.' That was what I said.

Sixteenth Khaṇḍa

A person's entire life symbolically a Soma-sacrifice

1. Verily, a person is a sacrifice. His [first] twenty-four years are the morning Soma-libation, for the Gāyatrī meter has twenty-four syllables and the morning Soma-libation is offered with a Gāyatrī hymn. The Vasus are connected with this part of the sacrifice. Verily, the vital breaths (*prāṇa*) are the Vasus, for they cause everything here to continue (√*vas*).

2. If any sickness should overtake him in this period of life, let him say: 'Ye vital breaths, ye Vasus, let this morning libation of mine continue over to the mid-day libation. Let not me, the sacrifice, be broken off in the midst of the vital breaths, of the Vasus.' He arises from it; he becomes free from sickness.

3. Now the [next] forty-four years are the mid-day libation,

[1] That is, in wind, the breath of the world-all.

for the Trishṭubh meter has forty-four syllables and the mid-day libation is offered with a Trishṭubh hymn. The Rudras are connected with this part of the sacrifice. Verily, the vital breaths are the Rudras, for [on departing] they cause everything here to lament (√*rud*).[1]

4. If any sickness should overtake him in this period of life, let him say: 'Ye vital breaths, ye Rudras, let this mid-day libation of mine continue over to the third libation. Let not me, the sacrifice, be broken off in the midst of the vital breaths, of the Rudras.' He arises from it; he becomes free from sickness.

5. Now, the [next] forty-eight years are the third libation, for the Jagatī meter has forty-eight syllables and the third libation is offered with a Jagatī hymn. The Ādityas are connected with this part of the sacrifice. Verily, the vital breaths are the Ādityas, for [on departing] they take everything to themselves (*ādadate*).

6. If any sickness should overtake him in this period of life, let him say: 'Ye vital breaths, ye Ādityas, let this third libation of mine continue to a full length of life. Let not me, the sacrifice, be broken off in the midst of the vital breaths, of the Ādityas.' He arises from it; he becomes free from sickness.

7. Verily, it was this that Mahidāsa Aitareya knew when he used to say: 'Here, why do you afflict me with this sickness—me, who am not going to die with it?' He lived a hundred and sixteen years. He lives to a hundred and sixteen years who knows this.[2]

Seventeenth Khanda

1. When one hungers and thirsts and does not enjoy himself—that is a Preparatory Consecration Ceremony (*dīkṣā*).

2. When one eats and drinks and enjoys himself—then he joins in the Upasada ceremonies.[3]

[1] This same etymological explanation occurs at Bṛih. 3. 9. 4.

[2] That is, who knows this doctrine of the 24 + 44 + 48 years.

[3] The ceremonies which constitute a part of the *Jyotiṣṭoma* (Praise of Light) form of the Soma sacrifice and during which the sacrificer is allowed a certain amount of food.

3. When one laughs and eats and practises sexual intercourse —then he joins in the Chant and Recitation (*stuta-śastra*).

4. Austerity, alms-giving, uprightness, harmlessness, truthfulness—these are one's gifts for the priests.

5. Therefore they say: 'He will procreate (*soṣyati*)! He has procreated (*asoṣṭa*)!'[1]—that is his rebirth (*punar-utpādana*). Death is an ablution after the ceremony.

6. When Ghora Āṅgirasa explained this to Kṛishṇa, the son of Devakī, he also explained—for he had become free from desire—'In the final hour one should take refuge in these three thoughts: "You are the Indestructible; you are the Unshaken; you are the very essence of life (*prāṇa*)."' On this point there are these two Rig verses:—

7. Proceeding from primeval seed,
[The early morning light they see,
That gleameth higher than the heaven].[2]

From out of darkness all around,
We, gazing on the higher light—
Yea, gazing on the higher light—
To Sūrya, god among the gods,
We have attained—the highest light!
—yea, the highest light![3]

EIGHTEENTH KHAṆḌA

The fourfold Brahma in the individual and in the world

1. One should reverence the mind as Brahma.—Thus with reference to the self.

Now with reference to the divinities.—One should reverence space as Brahma.

—This is the twofold instruction with reference to the self and with reference to the divinities.

2. That Brahma has four quarters.[4] One quarter is speech.

[1] In this exposition of the similarities between man and the sacrifice these two words are used in a double signification. They mean also, in relation to the sacrifice: 'He will press out [the Soma juice]! He has pressed [it] out!'

[2] SV. 1. 1. 10, varying slightly from RV. 8. 6. 30.

[3] VS. 20. 21, varying slightly from RV. 1. 50. 10.

[4] Referring to RV. 10. 90. 3, already quoted at Chānd. 3. 12. 5.

One quarter is breath. One quarter is the eye. One quarter is the ear.—Thus with reference to the self.

Now with reference to the divinities.—One quarter is Agni (Fire). One quarter is Vāyu (Wind). One quarter is Āditya (the Sun). One quarter is the quarters of heaven.

—This is the twofold instruction with reference to the self and with reference to the divinities.

3. Speech, truly, is a fourth part of Brahma. It shines and glows with Agni as its light. He shines and glows with fame, with splendor, and with eminence in sacred knowledge who knows this.

4. Breath, truly, is a fourth part of Brahma. It shines and glows with Vāyu as its light. He shines and glows with fame, with splendor, and with eminence in sacred knowledge who knows this.

5. The eye, truly, is a fourth part of Brahma. It shines and glows with Āditya as its light. He shines and glows with fame, with splendor, and with eminence in sacred knowledge who knows this.

6. The ear, truly, is a fourth part of Brahma. It shines and glows with the quarters of heaven as its light. He shines and glows with fame, with splendor, and with eminence in sacred knowledge who knows this—yea, who knows this!

Nineteenth Khaṇḍa

The cosmic egg

1. The sun is Brahma—this is the teaching. A further explanation thereof [is as follows].

In the beginning this world was merely non-being. It was existent. It developed. It turned into an egg. It lay for the period of a year. It was split asunder. One of the two eggshell-parts became silver, one gold.

2. That which was of silver is this earth. That which was of gold is the sky. What was the outer membrane is the mountains. What was the inner membrane is cloud and mist. What were the veins are the rivers. What was the fluid within is the ocean

3. Now, what was born therefrom is yonder sun. When it was born, shouts and hurrahs, all beings and all desires rose up toward it. Therefore at its rising and at its every return shouts and hurrahs, all beings and all desires rise up toward it.

4. He who, knowing it thus, reverences the sun as Brahma—the prospect is that pleasant shouts will come unto him and delight him—yea, delight him!

FOURTH PRAPĀṬHAKA

Conversational instructions

FIRST KHAṆḌA

The story of Jānaśruti and Raikva: wind and breath as snatchers-unto-themselves

1. *Om*! Now there was Jānaśruti, the great-grandson [of Janaśruta], a pious dispenser, a liberal giver, a preparer of much food. He had rest-houses built everywhere with the thought, 'Everywhere people will be eating of my food.'

2. Now then, one time swans flew past in the night, and one swan spoke to another thus: 'Hey! Ho! Short-sight! Short-sight! The light of Jānasruti, the great-grandson [of Janaśruta], has spread like the sky. Do not touch it, lest it burn you up!'

3. To it the other one then replied: 'Come! Who is that man of whom you speak as if he were Raikva, the man with the cart?'

'Pray, how is it with Raikva, the man with the cart?'

4. 'As the lower throws of dice all go to the highest throw, to the winner, so whatever good thing creatures do, all goes to him. I say the same thing of whoever knows what he knows.'

5. Now Jānaśruti, the great-grandson [of Janaśruta], overheard this. Then when he rose he said to the attendant[1]: 'Lo! you speak [of me] as if I were Raikva, the man with the cart!'

'Pray, how is it with Raikva, the man with the cart?'

[1] Whose custom it is continually to flatter his master.

6. 'As the lower throws of dice all go to the highest throw, to the winner, so to this man, whatever good thing creatures do, all goes to him. I say the same thing of whoever knows what he knows.'

7. Then the attendant, having sought, came back, saying, 'I did not find him.'

Then he said to him: 'Oh! Where one searches for a Brahman, there seek for him.'

8. He approached a man who was scratching the itch underneath a cart, and said to him: 'Pray, sir, are you Raikva, the man with the cart?'

'Oh! I am, indeed,' he acknowledged.

Then the attendant went back, and said: 'I have found him.'

Second Khaṇḍa

1. Then Jānaśruti, the great-grandson [of Janaśruta], took six hundred cows and a gold necklace and a chariot drawn by a she-mule, and went back to him.

He said to him: [2] 'Raikva, here are six hundred cows, and here is a gold necklace, and here is a chariot drawn by a she-mule. Now, sir, teach me that divinity—the divinity which you reverence.'

3. And to him then the other replied: 'Oh! Necklace and carriage along with the cows be yours, O Śūdra!'

And then again Jānaśruti, the great-grandson [of Janaśruta], taking a thousand cows and a gold necklace and a chariot drawn by a she-mule, and his daughter too, went unto him.

4. Then he spoke unto him: 'Raikva, here are a thousand cows, and here is a gold necklace, and here is a chariot drawn by a she-mule, and here is a wife, and here is the village in which you dwell. Pray, sir, do you teach me.'

5. Then, lifting up her face toward himself, he [i. e. Raikva] said: 'He has brought these [cows] along!—Śūdra, merely with this face you would cause me to speak.'

—So those are called the Raikvaparṇa [villages], among the people of the Mahāvṛishas, where at his offer[1] he lived.

Then he said to him:—

[1] Literally, 'for him' (*asmai*).

Third Khaṇḍa

1. 'The Wind (Vāyu), verily, is a snatcher-unto-itself. Verily, when a fire blows out, it just goes to the Wind. When the sun sets, it just goes to the Wind. When the moon sets, it just goes to the Wind.

2. When water dries, goes up, it just goes to the Wind. For the Wind, truly, snatches all here to itself.—Thus with reference to the divinities.

3. Now with reference to oneself.—

Breath (*prāṇa*), verily, is a snatcher-unto-itself. When one sleeps, speech just goes to breath; the eye, to breath; the ear, to breath; the mind, to breath; for the breath, truly, snatches all here to itself.

4. Verily, these are two snatchers-unto-themselves: the Wind among the gods, breath among the vital breaths.

5. Now, once upon a time when Śaunaka Kāpeya and Abhipratārin Kākshaseni were being served with food, a student of sacred knowledge begged of them. They did not give to him.

6. Then he said:—

"One God (*deva*) has swallowed up four mighty beings (*mahātman*).
Who is that world's protector, O Kāpeya?
Him mortal men perceive not, though abiding
In manifolded forms, Abhipratārin.

Verily, this food has not been offered to whom it belongs."

7. Then Śaunaka Kāpeya, considering this, replied:—

"The Self (*ātman*) of gods, of creatures Procreator,
With golden teeth Devourer, truly Wise One—
His mightiness they say is truly mighty;
He eats what is not food, and is not eaten.

Thus, verily, O student of sacred knowledge, do we reverence It.—Give ye him alms."

8. Then they gave to him.

These five[1] and the other five[2] make ten, and that is the

[1] Wind, fire, sun, moon, and water. Cf. 4. 3. 1, 2.

[2] Breath, speech, eye, ear, and mind. Cf. 4. 3. 3.

highest throw in dice. Therefore in all regions ten, the highest throw, is food. That is Virāj[1] and an eater of food. Through it this whole world came to light. The whole world comes to light for him, he becomes an eater of food, who knows this—yea, who knows this.'

Fourth Khaṇḍa

Satyakāma instructed concerning four quarters of Brahma

1. Once upon a time Satyakāma Jābāla addressed his mother Jabālā: 'Madam! I desire to live the life of a student of sacred knowledge. Of what family, pray, am I?'

2. Then she said to him: 'I do not know this, my dear—of what family you are. In my youth, when I went about a great deal serving as a maid, I got you. So I do not know of what family you are. However, I am Jabālā by name; you are Satyakāma by name. So you may speak of yourself as Satyakāma Jābāla.'

3. Then he went to Hāridrumata Gautama, and said: 'I will live the life of a student of sacred knowledge. I will become a pupil of yours, sir.'

4. To him he then said: 'Of what family, pray, are you, my dear?'

Then he said: 'I do not know this, sir, of what family I am. I asked my mother. She answered me: "In my youth, when I went about a great deal serving as a maid, I got you. So I do not know this, of what family you are. However, I am Jabālā by name; you are Satyakāma by name." So I am Satyakāma Jābāla, sir.'

5. To him he then said: 'A non-Brahman (*a-brāhmaṇa*) would not be able to explain thus. Bring the fuel, my dear. I will receive you as a pupil. You have not deviated from the truth.'

After having received him as a pupil, he separated out four hundred lean, weak cows and said: 'Follow these, my dear.'

As he was driving them on, he said: 'I may not return without a thousand.' So he lived away a number of years. When they came to be a thousand,

[1] The name of an early mythological representation of original matter; also the name of a meter of ten syllables.

FIFTH KHAṆḌA

[1] the bull spoke to him, saying: 'Satyakāma!'

'Sir!' he replied.

'We have reached a thousand, my dear. Bring us to the teacher's house. [2] And let me tell you a quarter of Brahma.'

'Tell me, sir.'

To him it then said: 'One sixteenth is the east. One sixteenth is the west. One sixteenth is the south. One sixteenth is the north. This, verily, my dear, is the quarter of Brahma, consisting of four sixteenths, named the Shining.

3. He who, knowing it thus, reverences a quarter of Brahma, consisting of four sixteenths, as the Shining, becomes shining in this world. Then he wins shining worlds who, knowing it thus, reverences a quarter of Brahma, consisting of four sixteenths, as the Shining.

SIXTH KHAṆḌA

1. Fire will tell you a quarter.'

He then, when it was the morrow, drove the cows on. Where they came at evening, there he built a fire, penned in the cows, laid on fuel, and sat down to the west of the fire, facing the east.

2. The fire spoke to him, saying: 'Satyakāma!'

'Sir!' he replied.

3. 'Let me tell you, my dear, a quarter of Brahma.'

'Tell me, sir.'

To him it then said: 'One sixteenth is the earth. One sixteenth is the atmosphere. One sixteenth is the sky. One sixteenth is the ocean. This, verily, my dear, is the quarter of Brahma, consisting of four sixteenths, named the Endless.

4. He who, knowing it thus, reverences a quarter of Brahma, consisting of four sixteenths, as the Endless, becomes endless in this world. Then he wins endless worlds who, knowing it thus, reverences a quarter of Brahma, consisting of four sixteenths, as the Endless.

Seventh Khaṇḍa

1. A swan will tell you a quarter.'

He then, when it was the morrow, drove the cows on. Where they came at evening, there he built a fire, penned in the cows, laid on the fuel, and sat down to the west of the fire, facing the east.

2. A swan flew down to him, and spoke to him, saying: 'Satyakāma!'

'Sir!' he replied.

3. 'Let me tell you, my dear, a quarter of Brahma.'

'Tell me, sir.'

To him it then said: 'One sixteenth is fire. One sixteenth is the sun. One sixteenth is the moon. One sixteenth is lightning. This, verily, my dear, is the quarter of Brahma, consisting of four sixteenths, named the Luminous.

4. He who, knowing it thus, reverences a quarter of Brahma, consisting of four sixteenths, as the Luminous, becomes luminous in this world. Then he wins luminous worlds who, knowing it thus, reverences a quarter of Brahma, consisting of four sixteenths, as the Luminous.

Eighth Khaṇḍa

1. A diver-bird will tell you a quarter.'

He then, when it was the morrow, drove the cows on. Where they came at evening, there he built a fire, penned in the cows, laid on fuel, and sat down to the west of the fire, facing the east.

2. A diver-bird flew down to him, and spoke to him, saying: 'Satyakāma!'

'Sir!' he replied.

3. 'Let me tell you, my dear, a quarter of Brahma.'

'Tell me, sir.'

To him it then said: 'One sixteenth is breath. One sixteenth is the eye. One sixteenth is the ear. One sixteenth is mind. This, verily, my dear, is the quarter of Brahma, consisting of four sixteenths, named Possessing-a-support.

4. He who, knowing it thus, reverences a quarter of Brahma, consisting of four sixteenths, as Possessing-a-support, comes to possess a support in this world. Then he wins worlds possessing a support who, knowing it thus, reverences a quarter of Brahma, consisting of four sixteenths, as Possessing-a-support.'

NINTH KHAṆḌA

1. Then he reached the teacher's house. The teacher spoke to him, saying: 'Satyakāma!'

'Sir!' he replied.

2. 'Verily, my dear, you shine like a Brahma-knower. Who, pray, has instructed you?'

'Others than men,' he acknowledged. 'But do you yourself please speak to me; [3] for I have heard from those who are like you, sir, that the knowledge which has been learned from a teacher best helps one to attain his end.'

To him he then declared it. In it then nothing whatsoever was omitted—yea, nothing was omitted.

TENTH KHAṆḌA

Brahma as life, joy, and the void

1. Now, verily, Upakosala Kāmalāyana dwelt with Satyakāma Jābāla as a student of sacred knowledge. For twelve years he tended his fires. Then, although accustomed to allow other pupils to return home, him he did not allow to return.

2. His wife said to him: 'The student of sacred knowledge has performed his penance. He has tended the fires well. Let not the fires anticipate you in teaching him. Teach him yourself.'

But he went off on a journey without having told him.

3. Then, on account of sickness, he [i. e. Upakosala] took to not eating.

The teacher's wife said to him: 'Student of sacred knowledge, eat. Why, pray, do you not eat?'

Then he said: 'Many and various are the desires here in this man. I am filled up with sicknesses. I will not eat.'

4. So then the fires said among themselves: 'The student of

sacred knowledge has performed his penance. He has tended us well. Come! Let us teach him.'

Then they said to him: [5] 'Brahma is life (*prāṇa*). Brahma is joy. Brahma is the void.'

Then he said: 'I understand that Brahma is life. But joy and void I do not understand.'

They said: 'Joy (*ka*)—verily, that is the same as the Void (*kha*). The Void—verily, that is the same as Joy.' And then they explained to him life and space.

ELEVENTH KHAṆḌA

The same person in the sun, the moon, and lightning as in fire and other objects

1. So then the householder's (Gārhapatya) fire instructed him: 'Earth, fire, food, sun [are forms of me. But] the Person who is seen in the sun—I am he; I am he indeed!'

2. [Chorus of the fires:] 'He who knows and reverences this fire thus, repels evil-doing from himself, becomes possessor of a world, reaches a full length of life, lives long. His descendants do not become destroyed. Both in this world and in the yonder we serve him who knows and reverences this fire thus.'

TWELFTH KHAṆḌA

1. So then the southern sacrificial (Anvāhāryapacana) fire instructed him: 'Water, the quarters of heaven, the stars, the moon [are forms of me. But] the Person who is seen in the moon—I am he; I am he indeed!'

2. [Chorus of the fires:] 'He who knows and reverences this fire thus, repels evil-doing from himself, becomes possessor of a world, reaches a full length of life, lives long. His descendants do not become destroyed. Both in this world and in the yonder we serve him who knows and reverences this fire thus.'

THIRTEENTH KHAṆḌA

1. So then the eastern (Āhavanīya) fire instructed him: 'Breath, space, sky, lightning [are forms of me. But] the Person who is seen in the lightning—I am he; I am he indeed!'

2. [Chorus of the fires:] 'He who knows and reverences this fire thus, repels evil-doing from himself, becomes possessor of a world, reaches a full length of life, lives long. His descendants do not become destroyed. Both in this world and in the yonder we serve him who knows and reverences this fire thus.'

Fourteenth Khaṇḍa

The soul, and its way to Brahma

1. Then the fires said: 'Upakosala dear, you have this knowledge of ourselves and the knowledge of the Soul (Ātman). But the teacher will tell you the way.'

Then the teacher returned. The teacher spoke to him, saying: 'Upakosala!'

2. 'Sir!' he then replied.

'Your face, my dear, shines like a Brahma-knower's. Who, pray, has instructed you?'

'Who, pray, would instruct me, sir?'—Here he denied it, as it were.—'These! They are of this appearance now, but they were of a different appearance!'—Here he alluded to the fires.—

'What, pray, my dear, did they indeed tell you?'

3. 'This—,' he acknowledged.

'Verily, my dear, they did indeed tell you the worlds. But I will tell you something. As water adheres not to the leaf of a lotus-flower, so evil action adheres not to him who knows this.'

'Tell me, sir.'

To him he then said:—

Fifteenth Khaṇḍa

1. 'That Person who is seen in the eye—He is the Self (Ātman),' said he. 'That is the immortal, the fearless. That is Brahma. So even if they pour clarified butter or water on that, it goes away to the edges.

2. They call this "Loveliness-uniter" (*saṁyadvāma*), for all lovely things (*vāma*) come together (*saṁyanti*) unto it. All lovely things come together unto him who knows this.

3. And this is also "Goods-bringer" (*vāmanī*), for it brings

(√*nī*) all goods (*vāma*). He brings all goods who knows this.

4. And this one is also "Light-bringer" (*bhāmanī*), for it shines (√*bhā*) in all worlds. He shines in all worlds who knows this.

5. Now, whether they perform the cremation obsequies in the case of such a person or not, they [i. e. the dead] pass over into a flame; from a flame, into the day; from the day, into the half-month of the waxing moon; from the half-month of the waxing moon, into the six months during which the sun moves northwards; from the months, into the year; from the year, into the sun; from the sun, into the moon; from the moon, into lightning. Then there is a Person (*puruṣa*) who is non-human (*a-mānava*).

6. He leads them on to Brahma. This is the way to the gods,[1] the way to Brahma. They who proceed by it return not to the human condition here—yea, they return not!'

Sixteenth Khaṇḍa

The Brahman priest properly silent at the sacrifice

1. Verily, he who purifies here[2] is a sacrifice. Truly, when he moves, he purifies this whole world. Since when he moves (*yan*) he purifies this whole world, therefore indeed he is a sacrifice (*yajña*).

His two paths are mind and speech.

2. Of these the Brahman priest (*brahmā*) forms one with his mind; the Hotṛi, the Adhvaryu, and the Udgātṛi priests, the other with speech.

In case, after the morning litany has commenced, the Brahman priest interrupts before the concluding verse, [3] he forms only one path. The other becomes discontinued.

As a one-legged man walking, or a chariot proceeding with one wheel, suffers injury, so his sacrifice suffers injury. The institutor of the sacrifice suffers injury after the sacrifice which suffers injury. He becomes worse off by having sacrificed.

[1] This same way is described subsequently at 5. 10. 1–2.

[2] That is, the wind.

4. But in case, after the morning litany has commenced, the Brahman priest does not interrupt before the concluding verse, they form both paths; the other does not become discontinued.

5. As a two-legged man walking, or a chariot proceeding with both wheels, is well supported, so his sacrifice is well supported. The institutor of the sacrifice is well supported after the sacrifice which is well supported. He becomes better off by having sacrificed.

Seventeenth Khaṇḍa

How the Brahman priest rectifies mistakes in the sacrificial ritual

1. Prajāpati brooded upon the worlds. As they were being brooded upon, he extracted their essences: fire from the earth, wind from the atmosphere, the sun from the sky.

2. Upon these three deities he brooded. As they were being brooded upon, he extracted their essences: from the fire, the Rig verses; from the wind, the Yajus formulas; the Sāman chants, from the sun.

3. Upon this threefold knowledge he brooded. As it was being brooded upon, he extracted its essences: *bhūr* from the Rig verses, *bhuvas* from the Yajus formulas, *svar* from the Sāman chants.

4. So if there should come an injury in connection with the Rig verses, one should make an oblation in the householder's (Gārhapatya) fire with the words '*bhūr*! Hail!' So by the essence of the Rig verses themselves, by the power of the Rig verses, he mends the injury to the Rig verses of the sacrifice.

5. Moreover, if there should come an injury in connection with the Yajus formulas, one should make an oblation in the southern (Dakshiṇa) fire with the words '*bhuvas*! Hail!' So by the essence of the Yajus formulas themselves, by the power of the Yajus formulas, he mends the injury to the Yajus formulas of the sacrifice.

6. Moreover, if there should come an injury in connection with the Sāman chants, one should make an oblation in the eastern (Āhavanīya) fire with the words '*svar*! Hail!' So by

the essence of the Sāman chants themselves, by the power of the Sāman chants, he mends the injury to the Sāman chants of the sacrifice.

7. So, as one would mend gold with borax-salt, silver with gold, tin with silver, lead with tin, brass[1] with lead, wood with brass or with leather, [8] even so with the power of those worlds, of those divinities, of that triple knowledge one mends the injury to the sacrifice. Verily, that sacrifice is healed in which there is a Brahman priest who knows this.

9. Verily, that sacrifice is inclined to the north[2] in which there is a Brahman priest who knows this. Verily, there is this song on the Brahman priest who knows this:—

> Whichever way he[3] turns himself,
> In that same way goes [10] common man.
> The Brahman priest alone protects
> The sacrificers[4] like a dog.[5]

Verily, the Brahman priest who knows this guards the sacrifice, the institutor of the sacrifice, and all the priests. Therefore one should make as his Brahman priest one who knows this, not one who does not know this—yea, not one who does not know this.

FIFTH PRAPĀṬHAKA

On breath, the soul, and the Universal Soul

FIRST KHANDA

The rivalry of the five bodily functions, and the superiority of breath

1. *Om*! Verily, he who knows the chiefest and best, becomes the chiefest and best. Breath, verily, is the chiefest and best.

[1] On *loha* see *JAOS.* 48. 264.
[2] That is, auspicious.—Śaṅkara.
[3] The Brahman priest. That is, the Brahman is the leader of mankind. But Śaṅkara interprets: 'Wherever it goes back (i. e. there is a defect in the sacrifice), thither the man (i. e. the Brahman) goes, to mend the defect with his knowledge.' Deussen interprets these lines:

> 'Whichever way one turns himself,
> Thereon a human being goes.'

Max-Müller suggests still another idea.
[4] The word *kurūn* may also mean 'the Kuru people.'
[5] Adopting, as do *BR.* and Deussen, the reading *śvā* instead of *aśvā*, 'a mare.'

2. Verily, he who knows the most excellent, becomes the most excellent of his own [people]. Speech, verily, is the most excellent.

3. Verily, he who knows the firm basis, has a firm basis both in this world and in the yonder. The eye, verily, is a firm basis.

4. Verily, he who knows attainment—for him wishes are attained, both human and divine. The ear, verily, is attainment.

5. Verily, he who knows the abode, becomes an abode of his own [people]. The mind, verily, is the abode.

6. Now, the Vital Breaths (*prāṇa*)[1] disputed among themselves on self-superiority, saying [in turn]: 'I am superior!' 'I am superior!'

7. Those Vital Breaths went to Father Prajāpati, and said: 'Sir! Which of us is the most superior?'

He said to them: 'That one of you after whose going off the body appears as if it were the very worst off—he is the most superior of you.'

8. Speech went off. Having remained away a year, it came around again, and said: 'How have you been able to live without me?'

'As the dumb, not speaking, but breathing with the breath, seeing with the eye, hearing with the ear, thinking with the mind. Thus.'

Speech entered in.

9. The Eye went off. Having remained away a year, it came around again, and said: 'How have you been able to live without me?'

'As the blind, not seeing, but breathing with the breath, speaking with speech, hearing with the ear, thinking with the mind. Thus.'

The Eye entered in.

10. The Ear went off. Having remained away a year, it came around again, and said: 'How have you been able to live without me?'

[1] The word might almost be translated 'Senses'; but 'Functions' would perhaps more accurately represent the quaint old idea in the modern scientific terminology. —Cf. the other accounts of this rivalry at Bṛih. 6. 1. 7-14 and Kaush. 3. 3.

'As the deaf, not hearing, but breathing with the breath, speaking with speech, seeing with the eye, thinking with the mind. Thus.'

The Ear entered in.

11. The Mind went off. Having remained away a year, it came around again, and said: 'How have you been able to live without me?'

'As simpletons, mindless, but breathing with the breath, speaking with speech, seeing with the eye, hearing with the ear. Thus.'

The Mind entered in.

12. Now when the Breath was about to go off—as a fine horse might tear out the pegs of his foot-tethers all together, thus did it tear out the other Breaths all together. They all came to it and said: 'Sir! Remain. You are the most superior of us. Do not go off.'

13. Then Speech said unto that one: 'If I am the most excellent, so are you the most excellent.'

Then the Eye said unto that one: 'If I am a firm basis, so are you a firm basis.'

14. Then the Ear said unto that one: 'If I am attainment, so are you attainment.'

Then the Mind said unto that one: 'If I am an abode, so are you an abode.'

15. Verily, they do not call them 'Speeches,' nor 'Eyes,' nor 'Ears,' nor 'Minds.' They call them 'Breaths' (*prāṇa*), for the vital breath is all these.

Second Khaṇḍa

1. It said. 'What will be my food?'

'Whatever there is here, even to dogs and birds,' they said.

So this, verily, is the food (*anna*) of breath (*ana*). Verily, breath is its evident name. Verily, in the case of one who knows this, there is nothing whatever that is not food.

2. It said: 'What will be my garment?'

'Water,' they said.

Therefore, verily, when people are about to eat, they enswathe it [i. e. the breath] with water both before and after.[1] It is accustomed to receive a garment; it becomes not naked.

3. When Satyakāma Jābāla told this to Gośruti Vaiyāgrapadya, he also said: 'Even if one should tell this to a dried-up stump, branches would be produced on it and leaves would spring forth.'

The 'mixed potion' incantation for the attainment of greatness

4. Now, if one should wish to come to something great, let him on the night of a new moon perform the Preparatory Consecration Ceremony (Dīkshā), and on the night of the full moon mix a mixed potion of all sorts of herbs with sour milk and honey.

'Hail to the chiefest and best!'—with these words he should offer a libation of melted butter in the fire and pour the residue into the potion.

5. 'Hail to the most excellent!'—with these words he should offer a libation of melted butter in the fire and pour the residue into the potion.

'Hail to the firm basis!'—with these words he should offer a libation of melted butter in the fire and pour the residue into the potion.

'Hail to the abode!'—with these words he should offer a libation of melted butter in the fire and pour the residue into the potion.

6. Then, creeping back [from the fire], and taking the potion in his hollowed hands, he mutters: 'Thou art He (*ama*) by name, for this whole world is at home (*amā*) in thee, for thou art pre-eminent and supreme (*śreṣṭha*), king and overlord. Let him bring me to pre-eminence and supremacy (*śraiṣṭhya*), kingship and overlordship! Let me be all this!'[2]

7. Verily, then, with this Rig verse[3] he takes a sip at each hemistich:—

'The food which is god Savitṛi's,'

—here he takes a sip—

[1] By sipping at the commencement of a meal and by rinsing out the mouth at the close of the meal—the familiar custom in India.

[2] Or, 'this world-all.'

[3] RV. 5. 82. 1.

'That for ourselves do we prefer,'

—here he takes a sip—

'The best, the all-refreshing food;'

—here he takes a sip—

'The Giver's strength may we attain!'

—here he takes a sip.

8. After having cleansed the drinking-vessel or goblet, he lies down to the west of the fire either on a skin or on the bare ground with voice restrained and self-possessed. If he should see a woman, he may know that the rite is successful.

9. As to this there is the following verse:—

If during rites done for a wish
One sees a woman in his dream,
Success he there may recognize
In this appearance of his dream
—In this appearance of his dream

THIRD KHANDA[1]

The course of the soul in its reincarnations

1. Śvetaketu Āruṇeya attended an assembly of the Pañcālas. Then Pravāhaṇa Jaibali said to him: 'Young man, has your father instructed you?'

'He has indeed, sir.'

2. 'Do you know unto what creatures go forth hence?'

'No, sir.'

'Do you know how they return again?'

'No, sir.'

'Do you know the parting of the two ways, one leading to the gods and one leading to the fathers?'

'No, sir.'

3. 'Do you know how [it is that] yonder world is not filled up?'

'No, sir.'

'Do you know how in the fifth oblation water comes to have a human voice?'

'No, indeed, sir.'

4. 'Now, pray, how did you say of yourself that you had

[1] With the instruction of Śvetaketu in Khaṇḍas 3-10 compare the parallel account of Bṛih. 6. 2.

been instructed? Indeed, how could one who would not know these things speak of himself as having been instructed?'

Distressed, he then went to his father's place. Then he said to him: 'Verily, indeed, without having instructed me, you, sir, said: "I have instructed you."

5. Five questions a fellow of the princely class (*rājanya-bandhu*) has asked me. I was not able to explain even one of them.'

Then he [i.e. the father] said: 'As you have told them to me here, I do not know even one of them. If I had known them, how would I not have told them to you?'

6. Then Gautama[1] went to the king's place. To him, when he arrived, he [i.e. the king] had proper attention shown. Then on the morrow he went up to the audience-hall. Then he [i.e. the king] said to him: 'Honored Gautama, you may choose for yourself a boon of human wealth.'

Then he said: 'Human wealth be yours, O king! The word which you said in the presence of the young man, even that do you speak to me.'

Then he became troubled.

7. 'Wait a while,' he commanded him. Then he said: 'As to what you have told me, O Gautama, this knowledge has never yet come to Brahmans before you; and therefore in all the worlds has the rule belonged to the Kshatriya only.' Then he said to him:—

Fourth Khaṇḍa

1. 'Yonder world, verily, O Gautama, is a sacrificial fire. In this case the sun is the fuel; the light-rays, the smoke; the day, the flame; the moon, the coals; the stars, the sparks.

2. In this fire the gods offer faith (*śraddhā*). From this oblation arises King Soma.

Fifth Khaṇḍa

1. The rain-cloud, verily, O Gautama, is a sacrificial fire. In this case wind is the fuel; mist, the smoke; lightning, the flame; the thunderbolt, the coals; hailstones, the sparks.

[1] That is, Gautama Aruṇi, the father.

2. In this fire the gods offer King Soma. From this oblation arises rain.

SIXTH KHAṆḌA

1. The earth, verily, O Gautama, is a sacrificial fire. In this case the year is the fuel; space, the smoke; night, the flame; the quarters of heaven, the coals; the intermediate quarters of heaven, the sparks.

2. In this fire the gods offer rain. From this oblation arises food.

SEVENTH KHAṆḌA

1. Man, verily, O Gautama, is a sacrificial fire. In this case speech is the fuel; breath, the smoke; the tongue, the flame; the eyes, the coals; the ear, the sparks.

2. In this fire the gods offer food. From this oblation arises semen.

EIGHTH KHAṆḌA

1. Woman, verily, O Gautama, is a sacrificial fire. In this case the sexual organ is the fuel; when one invites, the smoke; the vulva, the flame; when one inserts, the coals; the sexual pleasure, the sparks.

2. In this fire the gods offer semen. From this oblation arises the fetus.

NINTH KHAṆḌA

1. Thus indeed in the fifth oblation water comes to have a human voice.

After he has lain within for ten months, or for however long it is, as a fetus covered with membrane, then he is born.

2. When born, he lives for as long as is his length of life. When deceased, they carry him hence to the appointed place for the fire from whence indeed he came, from whence he arose.

TENTH KHAṆḌA

1. So those who know this, and those too who worship in a forest with the thought that "Faith is austerity," pass into the flame[1]; from the flame, into the day; from the day, into the half-month of the waxing moon; from the half-month of the waxing moon, into the six months during which the sun moves

[1] That is, into the flame of the cremation fire.

northward; [2] from those months, into the year; from the year, into the sun; from the sun, into the moon; from the moon, into the lightning. There there is a Person (*puruṣa*) who is non-human (*a-mānava*). He leads them on to Brahma. This is the way leading to the gods.[1]

3. But those who in the village reverence a belief in sacrifice, merit, and almsgiving—they pass into the smoke[2]; from the smoke, into the night; from the night, into the latter half of the month; from the latter half of the month, into the six months during which the sun moves southward—these do not reach the year; [4] from those months, into the world of the fathers; from the world of the fathers, into space; from space, into the moon. That is King Soma. That is the food of the gods. The gods eat that.

5. After having remained in it as long as there is a residue [of their good works], then by that course by which they came they return again, just as they came, into space; from space, into wind. After having become wind, one becomes smoke. After having become smoke, he becomes mist.

6. After having become mist, he becomes cloud. After having become cloud, he rains down. They are born here as rice and barley, as herbs and trees, as sesame plants and beans. Thence, verily, indeed, it is difficult to emerge; for only if some one or other eats him as food and emits him as semen, does he develop further.

7. Accordingly, those who are of pleasant conduct here—the prospect is, indeed, that they will enter a pleasant womb, either the womb of a Brahman, or the womb of a Kshatriya, or the womb of a Vaiśya. But those who are of stinking conduct here—the prospect is, indeed, that they will enter a stinking womb, either the womb of a dog, or the womb of a swine, or the womb of an outcast (*caṇḍāla*).

8. But on neither of these ways are the small, continually returning creatures,[3] [those of whom it is said:] "Be born, and die"—theirs is a third state.

Thereby [it comes about that] yonder world is not filled up.

[1] This same way has already been described in 4. 15. 5–6.

[2] That is, into the smoke of the cremation fire.

[3] Such as flies, worms, etc.

Therefore one should seek to guard himself. As to this there is the following verse:—

9. The plunderer of gold, the liquor-drinker,
The invader of a teacher's bed, the Brahman-killer—
These four sink downward in the scale,
And, fifth, he who consorts with them.

10. But he who knows these five fires thus, is not stained with evil, even though consorting with those people. He becomes pure, clean, possessor of a pure world, who knows this —yea, he who knows this!'

Eleventh Khaṇḍa[1]

The Universal Soul

1. Prācīnaśāla Aupamanyava, Satyayajña Paulushi, Indradyumna Bhāllaveya, Jana Śārkarākshya, and Buḍila Āśvatarāśvi—these great householders, greatly learned in sacred lore (*śrotriya*), having come together, pondered: 'Who is our Ātman (Soul)? What is Brahma?'

2. Then they agreed among themselves: 'Verily, sirs, Uddālaka Āruṇi here studies exactly this Universal (*vaiśvānara*) Ātman (Soul). Come, let us go unto him.'

Then unto him they went.

3. Then he agreed with himself: 'These great householders, greatly learned in sacred lore, will question me. I may not be able to answer them everything. Come! Let me direct them to another.'

4. Then he said to them: 'Verily, sirs, Aśvapati Kaikeya studies just this Universal Ātman (Soul). Come! Let us go unto him.'

Then unto him they went.

5. Then to them severally, when they arrived, he had proper attentions shown. He was indeed a man who, on rising, could say[2]:—

'Within my realm there is no thief,
No miser, nor a drinking man,
None altarless, none ignorant,
No man unchaste, no wife unchaste.'

[1] Another version is found at Śat. Br. 10. 6. 1.
[2] Deussen's interpretation.

'Verily, sirs, I am about to have a sacrifice performed. As large a gift as I shall give to each priest, so large a gift will I give to you, sirs. Remain, my sirs.'

6. Then they said: 'With whatever subject a person is concerned, of that indeed he should speak. You know just this Universal Ātman (Soul). Him indeed do you tell to us.'

7. Then he said to them: 'On the morrow will I make reply.' Then with fuel in their hands[1] in the morning they returned. Then, without having first received them as pupils, he spoke to them as follows:—

Twelfth Khaṇḍa

1. 'Aupamanyava, whom do you reverence as the Ātman (Soul)?'

'The heaven indeed, sir, O King,' said he.

'The Universal Ātman (Soul) is, verily, that brightly shining one (*sutejas*) which you reverence as the Ātman (Soul). Therefore Soma is seen pressed out (*suta*) and continually pressed out in your family.

2. You eat food; you see what is pleasing. He eats food; he sees what is pleasing. There is eminence in sacred knowledge in the family of him who reverences the Universal Ātman (Soul) thus. That, however, is only the head of the Ātman (Soul),' said he. 'Your head would have fallen off, if you had not come unto me.'

Thirteenth Khaṇḍa

1. Then he said to Satyayajña Paulushi: 'Prācīnayogya! Whom do you reverence as the Ātman (Soul)?'

'The sun indeed, sir, O King,' said he.

'The Universal Ātman (Soul) is, verily, that manifold one which you reverence as the Ātman (Soul). Therefore much of all sorts is seen in your family, [2] [e.g.] a chariot drawn by a she-mule rolled up [before your door], a female slave, a gold necklace. You eat food; you see what is pleasing. He eats food; he sees what is pleasing. There is eminence in sacred knowledge in the family of him who reverences that Universal

[1] As a token of discipleship. Compare 4. 4. 5.

Ātman (Soul) thus. That, however, is only the eye of the Ātman (Soul),' said he. 'You would have become blind, if you had not come unto me.'

Fourteenth Khaṇḍa

1. Then he said to Indradyumna Bhāllaveya: 'Vaiyāghrapadya! Whom do you reverence as the Ātman (Soul)?'

'The wind indeed, sir, O King,' said he.

'The Universal Ātman (Soul) is, verily, that which possesses various paths, which you reverence as the Ātman (Soul). Therefore offerings come unto you in various ways; rows of chariots follow you in various ways.

2. You eat food; you see what is pleasing. He eats food; he sees what is pleasing. There is eminence in sacred knowledge in the family of him who reverences that Universal Ātman (Soul) thus.

That, however, is only the breath of the Ātman (Soul),' said he. 'Your breath would have departed, if you had not come unto me.'

Fifteenth Khaṇḍa

1. Then he said to Jana: 'Śārkarākṣya! Whom do you reverence as the Ātman (Soul)?'

'Space indeed, sir, O King,' said he.

'The Universal Ātman (Soul) is, verily, that expanded one, which you reverence as the Ātman (Soul). Therefore you are expanded with offspring and wealth.

2. You eat food; you see what is pleasing. He eats food; he sees what is pleasing. There is eminence in sacred knowledge in the family of him who reverences that Universal Ātman (Soul) thus.

That, however, is only the body (*saṁdeha*) of the Ātman (Soul),' said he. 'Your body would have fallen to pieces, if you had not come unto me.'

Sixteenth Khaṇḍa

1. Then he said to Buḍila Āśvatarāśvi: 'Vaiyāghrapadya! Whom do you reverence as the Ātman (Soul)?'

Water indeed, sir, O King,' said he.

'The Universal Ātman (Soul) is, verily, that wealth, which

you reverence as the Ātman (Soul). Therefore you are wealthy and thriving.

2. You eat food; you see what is pleasing. He eats food; he sees what is pleasing. There is eminence in sacred knowledge in the family of him who reverences that Universal Ātman (Soul) thus.

That, however, is only the bladder of the Ātman (Soul),' said he. 'Your bladder would have burst, if you had not come unto me.'

Seventeenth Khaṇḍa

1. Then he said to Uddālaka Āruṇi: 'Gautama! Whom do you reverence as the Ātman (Soul)?'

'The earth indeed, sir, O King,' said he.

'The Universal Ātman (Soul) is, verily, that support, which you reverence as the Ātman (Soul). Therefore you are supported with offspring and cattle.

2. You eat food; you see what is pleasing. He eats food; he sees what is pleasing. There is eminence in sacred knowledge in the family of him who reverences that Universal Ātman (Soul) thus.

That, however, is only the feet of the Ātman (Soul),' said he. 'Your feet would have withered away, if you had not come unto me.'

Eighteenth Khaṇḍa

1. Then he said to them: 'Verily, indeed, you here eat food, knowing this Universal Ātman (Soul) as if something separate. He, however, who reverences this Universal Ātman (Soul) that is of the measure of the span[1]—thus,[2] [yet] is to be measured by thinking of oneself[3]—he eats food in all worlds, in all beings, in all selves.

2. The brightly shining [heaven] is indeed the head of that Universal Ātman (Soul). The manifold [sun] is his eye. That which possesses various paths [i.e. the wind] is his breath. The extended [space] is his body. Wealth [i.e.

[1] From earth to heaven—as Śaṅkara suggests.

[2] Deictically.

[3] *abhi-vi-māna*, a word of not altogether certain meaning, either from √*mā* 'to measure,' or from √*man* 'to think,' like the immediately preceding *prādeśa-mātra*, or perhaps pregnantly referring to both.

water] is indeed his bladder. The support [i.e. the earth] is indeed his feet. The sacrificial area is indeed his breast. The sacrificial grass is his hair. The Gārhapatya fire is his heart. The Anvāhāryapacana fire is his mind. The Āhavanīya fire is his mouth.

Nineteenth Khaṇḍa

The mystical Agnihotra sacrifice to the Universal Soul in one's own self

1. Therefore the first food which one may come to, should be offered. The first oblation which he would offer he should offer with "Hail to the Prāṇa breath!" The Prāṇa breath is satisfied.

2. The Prāṇa breath being satisfied, the eye is satisfied. The eye being satisfied, the sun is satisfied. The sun being satisfied, the heaven is satisfied. The heaven being satisfied, whatever the heaven and the sun rule over is satisfied. Along with the satisfaction thereof, he is satisfied with offspring, with cattle, with food, with the glow of health, and with eminence in sacred knowledge.

Twentieth Khaṇḍa

1. Then the second oblation which he would offer he should offer with "Hail to the Vyāna breath!" The Vyāna breath is satisfied.

2. The Vyāna breath being satisfied, the ear is satisfied. The ear being satisfied, the moon is satisfied. The moon being satisfied, the quarters of heaven are satisfied. The quarters of heaven being satisfied, whatever the moon and the quarters of heaven rule over is satisfied. Along with the satisfaction thereof, he is satisfied with offspring, with cattle, with food, with the glow of health, and with eminence in sacred knowledge.

Twenty-first Khaṇḍa

1. Then the third offering which he would offer he should offer with "Hail to the Apāna breath!" The Apāna breath is satisfied.

2. The Apāna breath being satisfied, speech is satisfied.

Speech being satisfied, fire is satisfied. Fire being satisfied, the earth is satisfied. The earth being satisfied, whatever the earth and fire rule over is satisfied. Along with the satisfaction thereof, he is satisfied with offspring, with cattle, with food, with the glow of health, and with eminence in sacred knowledge.

Twenty-second Khaṇḍa

1. Then the fourth offering which he would offer he should offer with "Hail to the Samāna breath!" The Samāna breath is satisfied.

2. The Samāna breath being satisfied, the mind is satisfied. The mind being satisfied, the rain-god (Parjanya) is satisfied. The rain-god being satisfied, lightning is satisfied. Lightning being satisfied, whatever the rain-god and lightning rule over is satisfied. Along with the satisfaction thereof, he is satisfied with offspring, with cattle, with food, with the glow of health, and with eminence in sacred knowledge.

Twenty-third Khaṇḍa

1. Then the fifth offering which he would offer he should offer with "Hail to the Udāna breath!" The Udāna breath is satisfied.

2. The Udāna breath being satisfied, wind is satisfied.[1] Wind being satisfied, space is satisfied. Space being satisfied, whatever wind and space rule over is satisfied. Along with the satisfaction thereof, he is satisfied with offspring, with cattle, with food, with the glow of health, and with eminence in sacred knowledge.

Twenty-fourth Khaṇḍa

1. If one offers the Agnihotra (fire) sacrifice without knowing this—that would be just as if he were to remove the live coals and pour the offering on ashes.

2. But if one offers the Agnihotra sacrifice knowing it thus, his offering is made in all worlds, in all beings, in all selves.

3. So, as the top of a reed laid on a fire would be burned up,

[1] According to the Poona and Madras editions of the Chāndogya Upanishad the first part of this paragraph would read: 'The Udāna breath being satisfied, the skin is satisfied. The skin being satisfied, wind is satisfied,' etc.

even so are burned up all the evils of him who offers the Agnihotra sacrifice knowing it thus.

4. And therefore, if one who knows this should offer the leavings even to an outcast (*caṇḍāla*), it would be offered in his Universal Ātman (Soul). As to this there is the following verse:—

> As hungry children sit around
> About their mother here in life,
> E'en so all beings sit around
> The Agnihotra sacrifice.'

SIXTH PRAPĀṬHAKA

The instruction of Śvetaketu by Uddālaka concerning the key to all knowledge

First Khaṇḍa

The threefold development of the elements and of man from the primary unitary Being

1. *Om*! Now, there was Śvetaketu Āruṇeya. To him his father said: 'Live the life of a student of sacred knowledge. Verily, my dear, from our family there is no one unlearned [in the Vedas] (*an-ucya*), a Brahman by connection (*brahma-bandhu*), as it were.'

2. He then, having become a pupil at the age of twelve, having studied all the Vedas, returned at the age of twenty-four, conceited, thinking himself learned, proud.

3. Then his father said to him: 'Śvetaketu, my dear, since now you are conceited, think yourself learned, and are proud, did you also ask for that teaching whereby what has not been heard of becomes heard of, what has not been thought of becomes thought of, what has not been understood becomes understood?'

4. 'How, pray, sir, is that teaching?'

(4) 'Just as, my dear, by one piece of clay everything made of clay may be known—the modification is merely a verbal distinction, a name; the reality is just "clay"—

5. Just as, my dear, by one copper ornament everything

made of copper may be known—the modification is merely a verbal distinction, a name; the reality is just "copper"—

6. Just as, my dear, by one nail-scissors everything made of iron may be known—the modification is merely a verbal distinction, a name; the reality is just "iron"—so, my dear, is that teaching.'

7. 'Verily, those honored men did not know this; for, if they had known it, why would they not have told me? But do you, sir, tell me it.'

'So be it, my dear,' said he.

Second Khaṇḍa

1. 'In the beginning, my dear, this world was just Being (*sat*), one only, without a second. To be sure, some people say[1]: "In the beginning this world was just Non-being (*a-sat*), one only, without a second; from that Non-being Being was produced."

2. But verily, my dear, whence could this be?' said he. 'How from Non-being could Being be produced? On the contrary, my dear, in the beginning this world was just Being, one only, without a second.

3. It bethought itself: "Would that I were many! Let me procreate myself!" It emitted heat. That heat bethought itself: "Would that I were many! Let me procreate myself." It emitted water. Therefore whenever a person grieves or perspires from the heat, then water [i.e. either tears or perspiration] is produced.[2]

4. That water bethought itself: "Would that I were many! Let me procreate myself." It emitted food. Therefore whenever it rains, then there is abundant food. So food for eating is produced just from water.

Third Khaṇḍa

1. Now, of these beings here there are just three origins[3]: [there are beings] born from an egg, born from a living thing, born from a sprout.

[1] As, for example, in 3. 19. 1 and Tait. 2. 7.

[2] The translation of this paragraph is discussed by Edgerton, *JAOS*. 35. 240-242.

[3] Literally 'seeds' (*bīja*).

2. That divinity [i.e. Being] bethought itself: "Come! Let me enter these three divinities [i.e. heat, water, and food] with this living Soul (*ātman*), and separate out name and form.[1]

3. Let me make each one of them threefold." That divinity entered into these three divinities with this living Soul, and separated out name and form.

4. It made each of them threefold.

Now, verily, my dear, understand from me how each of these three divinities becomes threefold.

Fourth Khaṇḍa

1. Whatever red form fire has, is the form of heat; whatever white, the form of water; whatever dark, the form of food. The firehood has gone from fire: the modification is merely a verbal distinction, a name. The reality is just "the three forms."

2. Whatever red form the sun has, is the form of heat; whatever white, the form of water; whatever dark, the form of food. The sunhood has gone from the sun: the modification is merely a verbal distinction, a name. The reality is just "the three forms."

3. Whatever red form the moon has, is the form of heat; whatever white, the form of water; whatever dark, the form of food. The moonhood has gone from the moon: the modification is merely a verbal distinction, a name. The reality is just "the three forms."

4. Whatever red form the lightning has, is the form of heat; whatever white, the form of water; whatever dark, the form of food. The lightninghood has gone from the lightning: the modification is merely a verbal distinction, a name. The reality is just "the three forms."

5. Verily, it was just this that the great householders, greatly learned in sacred lore, knew when they said of old[2]: "No one now will bring up to us what has not been heard of, what has not been thought of, what has not been understood." For from these [three forms] they knew [everything].

6. They knew that whatever appeared red was the form of

[1] 'Name and form' is the Sanskrit idiom for 'individuality.'

[2] Compare Muṇḍ. 1. 1. 3.

heat. They knew that whatever appeared white was the form of water. They knew that whatever appeared dark was the form of food.

7. They knew that whatever appeared un-understood is a combination of just these divinities.

Verily, my dear, understand from me how each of these three divinities, upon reaching man, becomes threefold.

Fifth Khaṇḍa

1. Food, when eaten, becomes divided into three parts. That which is its coarsest constituent becomes the feces; that which is medium, the flesh; that which is finest, the mind.

2. Water, when drunk, becomes divided into three parts. That which is its coarsest constituent, becomes the urine; that which is medium, the blood; that which is finest, the breath (*prāṇa*).

3. Heat, when eaten, becomes divided into three parts. That which is its coarsest constituent, becomes bone; that which is medium, the marrow; that which is finest, the voice.

4. For, my dear, the mind consists of food; the breath consists of water; the voice consists of heat.'

'Do you, sir, cause me to understand even more.'

'So be it, my dear,' said he.

Sixth Khaṇḍa

1. 'Of coagulated milk, my dear, when churned, that which is the finest essence all moves upward; it becomes butter.

2. Even so, verily, my dear, of food, when eaten, that which is the finest essence all moves upward; it becomes the mind.

3. Of water, my dear, when drunk, that which is the finest essence all moves upward; it becomes the breath.

4. Of heat, my dear, when eaten, that which is the finest essence all moves upward; it becomes the voice.

5. For, my dear, the mind consists of food; the breath consists of water; the voice consists of heat.'

'Do you, sir, cause me to understand even more.'

'So be it, my dear,' said he.

SEVENTH KHAṆḌA

1. 'A person, my dear, consists of sixteen parts. For fifteen days do not eat; drink water at will. Breath, which consists of water, will not be cut off from one who drinks water.'

2. Then for fifteen days he did not eat. So then he approached him, saying, 'What shall I say, sir?'

'The Rig verses, my dear, the Yajus formulas, the Sāman chants.'

Then he said: 'Verily, they do not come to me, sir.'

3. To him he then said: 'Just as, my dear, a single coal of the size of a fire-fly may be left over from a great kindled fire, but with it the fire would not thereafter burn much—so, my dear, of your sixteen parts a single sixteenth part may be left over, but with it you do not now apprehend the Vedas. (4) Eat; [4] then you will understand from me.'

(4) Then he ate. So then he approached him. Then whatsoever he asked him, he answered everything. (5) To him he then said:—

5. 'Just as, my dear, one may, by covering it with straw, make a single coal of the size of a fire-fly that has been left over from a great kindled fire blaze up, and with it the fire would thereafter burn much—[6] so, my dear, of your sixteen parts a single sixteenth part has been left over. After having been covered with food, it has blazed up. With it you now apprehend the Vedas; for, my dear, the mind consists of food, the breath consists of water, the voice consists of heat.'

Then he understood from him—yea, he understood.

EIGHTH KHAṆḌA

Concerning sleep, hunger and thirst, and dying

1. Then Uddālaka Āruṇi said to Śvetaketu, his son: Understand from me, my dear, the condition of sleep. When a person here sleeps (*svapiti*), as it is called, then, my dear, he has reached Being, he has gone to his own (*svam apīta*). Therefore they say of him "he sleeps"; for he has gone to his own.

2. As a bird fastened with a string, after flying in this direction and in that without finding an abode elsewhere, rests down just upon its fastening—even so, my dear, the mind, after flying in this direction and in that without finding an abode elsewhere, rests down just upon breath; for the mind, my dear, has breath as its fastening.

3. Understand from me, my dear, hunger (*aśanā*) and thirst. When a person here is hungry (*aśiśiṣati*), as it is called, just water is leading off (*nayanti*) that which has been eaten (√*aś*). So, as they speak of "a leader-of-cows" (*go-nāya*), "a leader-of-horses" (*aśva-nāya*), "a leader-of-men" (*puruṣa-nāya*), so they speak of water as "a leader-of-food" (*aśa-nāya*, hunger).

On this point, my dear, understand that this [body] is a sprout which has sprung up. It will not be without a root.

4. What else could its root be than food? Even so, my dear, with food for a sprout, look for water as the root. With water, my dear, as a sprout, look for heat as the root. With heat, my dear, as a sprout, look for Being as the root. All creatures here, my dear, have Being as their root, have Being as their home, have Being as their support.

5. Now, when a person here is thirsty, as it is called, just heat is leading off that which has been drunk. So, as they speak of "a leader-of-cows" (*go-nāya*), "a leader-of-horses" (*aśva-nāya*), "a leader-of-men" (*puruṣa-nāya*), so one speaks of heat as "a leader-of-water" (*uda-nyā*, thirst).

On this point, my dear, understand that this [body] is a sprout which has sprung up. It will not be without a root.

6. Where else could its root be than in water? With water, my dear, as a sprout, look for heat as the root. With heat, my dear, as a sprout, look for Being as the root. All creatures here, my dear, have Being as their root, have Being as their abode, have Being as their support.

But how, verily, my dear, each of these three divinities, upon reaching man, becomes threefold, has previously[1] been said.

When a person here is deceasing, my dear, his voice goes into his mind; his mind, into his breath; his breath, into heat;

[1] In 6. 5. 1-4.

the heat, into the highest divinity. (7) That which is the finest essence—[7] this whole world has that as its soul. That is Reality (*satya*). That is Ātman (Soul). That art thou, Śvetaketu.'[1]

'Do you, sir, cause me to understand even more.'

'So be it, my dear,' said he.

NINTH KHAṆḌA

The unitary World-Soul, the immanent reality of all things and of man

1. 'As the bees, my dear, prepare honey by collecting the essences of different trees and reducing the essence to a unity, [2] as they are not able to discriminate "I am the essence of this tree," "I am the essence of that tree"—even so, indeed, my dear, all creatures here, though they reach Being,[2] know not "We have reached Being."

3. Whatever they are in this world, whether tiger, or lion, or wolf, or boar, or worm, or fly, or gnat, or mosquito, that they become.

4. That which is the finest essence—this whole world has that as its soul. That is Reality. That is Ātman (Soul). That art thou, Śvetaketu.'

'Do you, sir, cause me to understand even more.'

'So be it, my dear,' said he.

TENTH KHAṆḌA

1. 'These rivers, my dear, flow, the eastern toward the east, the western toward the west. They go just from the ocean to the ocean. They become the ocean itself. As there they know not "I am this one," "I am that one"—[2] even so, indeed, my dear, all creatures here, though they have come forth from Being, know not "We have come forth from Being." Whatever they are in this world, whether tiger, or lion, or

[1] In an article entitled 'Sources of the filosofy of the Upaniṣads, *JAOS*. 36 (1916), pp. 197–204, Edgerton translates as follows (p. 200, n. 5): 'What that subtle essence is, a-state-of-having-that(-*aṇimā*)-as-its-essence is this universe, that is the Real, that is the Soul, that art thou, Śvetaketu.'

[2] In deep sleep and in death.

wolf, or boar, or worm, or fly, or gnat, or mosquito, that they become.

3. That which is the finest essence—this whole world has that as its soul. That is Reality. That is Ātman (Soul). That art thou, Śvetaketu.'

'Do you, sir, cause me to understand even more.'

'So be it, my dear,' said he.

ELEVENTH KHAṆḌA

1. 'Of this great tree, my dear, if some one should strike at the root, it would bleed, but still live. If some one should strike at its middle, it would bleed, but still live. If some one should strike at its top, it would bleed, but still live. Being pervaded by Atman (Soul), it continues to stand, eagerly drinking in moisture and rejoicing.

2. If the life leaves one branch of it, then it dries up. It leaves a second; then that dries up. It leaves a third; then that dries up. It leaves the whole; the whole dries up. Even so, indeed, my dear, understand,' said he.

3. 'Verily, indeed, when life has left it, this body dies. The life does not die.

That which is the finest essence—this whole world has that as its soul. That is Reality. That is Ātman (Soul). That art thou, Śvetaketu.'

'Do you, sir, cause me to understand even more.'

'So be it, my dear,' said he.

TWELFTH KHAṆḌA

1. 'Bring hither a fig from there.'

'Here it is, sir.'

'Divide it.'

'It is divided, sir.'

'What do you see there?'

'These rather (*iva*) fine seeds, sir.'

'Of these, please (*aṅga*), divide one.'

'It is divided, sir.'

'What do you see there?'

'Nothing at all, sir.'

2. Then he said to him: 'Verily, my dear, that finest essence which you do not perceive—verily, my dear, from that finest essence this great Nyagrodha (sacred fig) tree thus[1] arises.

3. Believe me, my dear,' said he, (3) 'that which is the finest essence—this whole world has that as its soul. That is Reality. That is Ātman (Soul). That art thou, Śvetaketu.'

'Do you, sir, cause me to understand even more.'

'So be it, my dear,' said he.

Thirteenth Khaṇḍa

1. 'Place this salt in the water. In the morning come unto me.'

Then he did so.

Then he said to him: 'That salt you placed in the water last evening—please bring it hither.'

Then he grasped for it, but did not find it, as it was completely dissolved.

2. 'Please take a sip of it from this end,' said he. 'How is it?'

'Salt.'

'Take a sip from the middle,' said he. 'How is it?'

'Salt.'

'Take a sip from that end,' said he. 'How is it?'

'Salt.'

'Set it aside.[2] Then come unto me.'

He did so, saying, 'It is always the same.'

Then he said to him: 'Verily, indeed, my dear, you do not perceive Being here. Verily, indeed, it is here.

3. That which is the finest essence—this whole world has that as its soul. That is Reality. That is Ātman (Soul). That art thou, Śvetaketu.'

'Do you, sir, cause me to understand even more.'

'So be it, my dear,' said he.

[1] Deictically.

[2] Instead of *abhi-pra-asya* Böhtlingk and Roth (*BR.* 1. 543 s.v.) read *abhi-pra-asya*, 'add more unto it.'

Fourteenth Khaṇḍa

1. 'Just as, my dear, one might lead away from the Gandhāras a person with his eyes bandaged, and then abandon him in an uninhabited place; as there he might be blown forth either to the east, to the north, or to the south, since he had been led off with his eyes bandaged and deserted with his eyes bandaged; [2] as, if one released his bandage and told him, "In that direction are the Gandhāras; go in that direction!" he would, if he were a sensible man, by asking [his way] from village to village, and being informed, arrive home at the Gandhāras—even so here on earth one who has a teacher knows: "I shall remain here only so long as I shall not be released [from the bonds of ignorance]. Then I shall arrive home."[1]

3. That which is the finest essence—this whole world has that as its soul. That is Reality. That is Ātman (Soul). That art thou, Śvetaketu.'

'Do you, sir, cause me to understand even more.'

'So be it, my dear,' said he.

Fifteenth Khaṇḍa

1. 'Also, my dear, around a [deathly] sick person his kinsmen gather, and ask, "Do you know me?" "Do you know me?" So long as his voice does not go into his mind, his mind into his breath, his breath into heat, the heat into the highest divinity—so long he knows.

2. Then when his voice goes into his mind, his mind into his breath, his breath into heat, the heat into the highest divinity[2] —then he knows not.

3. That which is the finest essence—this whole world has that as its soul. That is Reality. That is Ātman (Soul). That art thou, Śvetaketu.'

'Do you, sir, cause me to understand even more.'

'So be it, my dear,' said he.

[1] On the interpretation of this paragraph see Edgerton, *JAOS.* 35. 242-245.

[2] This same statement of the order of the cessation of functions on the approach of death occurs in 6. 8. 6

Sixteenth Khaṇḍa

1. 'And also, my dear, they lead up a man seized by the hand, and call: "He has stolen! He has committed a theft! Heat the ax for him!" If he is the doer thereof, thereupon he makes himself (*ātmānam*) untrue. Speaking untruth, covering himself with untruth, he seizes hold of the heated ax and is burned. Then he is slain.[1]

2. But if he is not the doer thereof, thereupon he makes himself true. Speaking truth, covering himself with truth, he seizes hold of the heated ax and is not burned. Then he is released.

3. As in this case he would not be burned [because of the truth], so this whole world has that [truth] as its soul. That is Reality. That is Ātman (Soul). That art thou, Śvetaketu.'

Then he understood it from him—yea, he understood.

SEVENTH PRAPĀṬHAKA

The instruction of Nārada by Sanatkumāra

Progressive worship of Brahma up to the Universal Soul

First Khaṇḍa

1. *Om*! 'Teach me, sir!'[2]—with these words Nārada came to Sanatkumāra.

To him he then said: 'Come to me with what you know. Then I will tell you still further.'

2. Then he said to him: 'Sir, I know the Rig-Veda, the Yajur-Veda, the Sāma-Veda, the Atharva-Veda as the fourth, Legend and Ancient Lore (*itihāsa-purāṇa*) as the fifth, the Veda of the Vedas [i.e. Grammar], Propitiation of the Manes, Mathematics, Augury (*daiva*), Chronology, Logic, Polity, the Science of the Gods (*deva-vidyā*), the Science of Sacred Knowledge (*brahma-vidyā*), Demonology (*bhūta-vidyā*), the Science

[1] The translation of this passage has been discussed by Edgerton, *JAOS.* 35. 245–246.

[2] This sentence *adhīhi bhagavo* lacks but the word *brahma* to be the same as the request which Bhṛigu Vāruṇi put to his father in a similar progressive definition in Tait. 3. 1: *adhīhi bhagavo brahma*, 'Sir, declare Brahma.'

of Rulership (*kṣatra-vidyā*), Astrology (*nakṣatra-vidyā*), the Science of Snake-charming, and the Fine Arts (*sarpa-deva-jana-vidyā*).[1] This, sir, I know.

3. Such a one am I, sir, knowing the sacred sayings (*mantra-vid*), but not knowing the Soul (Ātman). It has been heard by me from those who are like you, sir, that he who knows the Soul (Ātman) crosses over sorrow. Such a sorrowing one am I, sir. Do you, sir, cause me, who am such a one, to cross over to the other side of sorrow.'

To him he then said: 'Verily, whatever you have here learned, verily, that is mere name (*nāman*).

4. Verily, a Name are the Rig-Veda, the Yajur-Veda, the Sāma-Veda, the Atharva-Veda as the fourth, Legend and Ancient Lore (*itihāsa-purāṇa*) as the fifth, the Veda of the Vedas [i.e. Grammar], Propitiation of the Manes, Mathematics, Augury (*daiva*), Chronology, Logic, Polity, the Science of the Gods (*deva-vidyā*), the Science of Sacred Knowledge (*brahma-vidyā*), Demonology (*bhūta-vidyā*), the Science of Rulership (*kṣatra-vidyā*), Astrology (*nakṣatra-vidyā*), the Science of Snake-charming, and the Fine Arts (*sarpa-devajana-vidyā*). This is mere Name. Reverence Name.

5. He who reverences Name as Brahma—as far as Name goes, so far he has unlimited freedom, he who reverences Name as Brahma.'

'Is there, sir, more than Name?'

'There is, assuredly, more than Name.'

'Do you, sir, tell me it.'

SECOND KHAṆḌA

1. 'Speech (*vāc*), assuredly, is more than Name. Speech, verily, makes known the Rig-Veda, the Yajur-Veda, the Sāma-Veda, the Atharva-Veda as the fourth, Legend and Ancient Lore as the fifth, the Veda of the Vedas [i.e. Grammar], Propitiation of the Manes, Mathematics, Augury, Chronology, Logic, Polity, the Science of the Gods, the Science of Sacred Knowledge, Demonology, the Science of Rulership, Astrology, the Science

[1] With this list, which recurs here and in the seventh Khaṇḍa, compare the somewhat similar enumerations at Bṛih. 2. 4. 10; 4. 1. 2; 4. 5. 11. The translation of this passage has been discussed by B. Faddegon, *Acta Orientalia* 4. 42–54.

of Snake-charming, and the Fine Arts, as well as heaven and earth, wind and space, water and heat, gods and men, beasts and birds, grass and trees, animals together with worms, flies, and ants, right and wrong, true and false, good and bad, pleasant and unpleasant. Verily, if there were no speech, neither right nor wrong would be known, neither true nor false, neither good nor bad, neither pleasant nor unpleasant. Speech, indeed, makes all this known. Reverence Speech.

2. He who reverences Speech as Brahma—as far as Speech goes, so far he has unlimited freedom, he who reverences Speech as Brahma.'

'Is there, sir, more than Speech?'

'There is, assuredly, more than Speech.'

'Do you, sir, tell me it.'

THIRD KHAṆḌA

1. 'Mind (*manas*), assuredly, is more than Speech. Verily, as the closed hand compasses two acorns, or two kola-berries, or two dice-nuts, so Mind compasses both Speech and Name. When through Mind one has in mind "I wish to learn the sacred sayings (*mantra*)," then he learns them; "I wish to perform sacred works (*karma*)," then he performs them; "I would desire sons and cattle," then he desires them; "I would desire this world and the yonder," then he desires them. Truly the self (*ātman*) is Mind. Truly, the world (*loka*) is Mind. Truly, Brahma is Mind.

2. He who reverences Mind as Brahma—as far as Mind goes, so far he has unlimited freedom, he who reverences Mind as Brahma.'

'Is there, sir, more than Mind?'

'There is, assuredly, more than Mind.'

'Do you, sir, tell me it.'

FOURTH KHAṆḌA

1. 'Conception (*saṁkalpa*), assuredly, is more than Mind. Verily, when one forms a Conception, then he has in Mind, then he utters Speech, and he utters it in Name. The sacred sayings (*mantra*) are included in Name, and sacred works in the sacred sayings.

2. Verily, these have Conception as their union-point, have Conception as their soul, are established on Conception. Heaven and earth were formed through Conception. Wind and space were formed through Conception. Water and heat were formed through Conception. Through their having been formed, rain becomes formed. Through rain having been formed, food becomes formed. Through food having been formed, living creatures (*prāṇa*) become formed. Through living creatures having been formed, sacred sayings (*mantra*) become formed. Through sacred sayings having been formed, sacred works (*karma*) become [per]formed. Through sacred works having been [per]formed, the world becomes formed. Through the world having been formed, everything becomes formed. Such is Conception. Reverence Conception.

3. He who reverences Conception as Brahma—he, verily, attains the Conception-worlds; himself being enduring, the enduring worlds; himself established, the established worlds; himself unwavering, the unwavering worlds. As far as Conception goes, so far he has unlimited freedom, he who reverences Conception as Brahma.'

'Is there, sir, more than Conception?'

'There is, assuredly, more than Conception.'

'Do you, sir, tell me it.'

FIFTH KHAṆḌA

1. 'Thought (*citta*), assuredly, is more than Conception. Verily, when one thinks, then he forms a conception, then he has in Mind, then he utters Speech, and he utters it in Name. The sacred sayings (*mantra*) are included in Name, and sacred works in the sacred sayings.

2. Verily, these things have Thought as their union-point, have Thought as their soul, are established on Thought. Therefore, even if one who knows much is without Thought, people say of him: "He is not anybody, whatever he knows! Verily, if he did know, he would not be so without Thought!" On the other hand, if one who knows little possesses Thought, people are desirous of listening to him. Truly, indeed, Thought is the union-point, Thought is the soul (*ātman*), Thought is the support of these things. Reverence Thought.

3. He who reverences Thought as Brahma—he, verily, attains the Thought-worlds; himself being enduring, the enduring worlds; himself being established, the established worlds; himself being unwavering, the unwavering worlds. As far as Thought goes, so far he has unlimited freedom, he who reverences Thought as Brahma.'

'Is there, sir, more than Thought?'

'There is, assuredly, more than Thought.'

'Do you, sir, tell me it.'

SIXTH KHAṆḌA

1. 'Meditation (*dhyāna*), assuredly, is more than Thought. The earth meditates, as it were (*iva*). The atmosphere meditates, as it were. The heaven meditates, as it were. Water meditates, as it were. Mountains meditate, as it were. Gods and men meditate, as it were. Therefore whoever among men here attain greatness—they have, as it were, a part of the reward of meditation. Now, those who are small are quarrelers, tale-bearers, slanderers. But those who are superior—they have, as it were, a part of the reward of Meditation. Reverence Meditation.

2. He who reverences Meditation as Brahma—as far as Meditation goes, so far he has unlimited freedom, he who reverences Meditation as Brahma.'

'Is there, sir, more than Meditation?'

'There is, assuredly, more than Meditation.'

'Do you, sir, tell me it.'

SEVENTH KHAṆḌA

1. 'Understanding (*vijñāna*), assuredly, is more than Meditation. Verily, by Understanding one understands the Rig-Veda, the Yajur-Veda, the Sāma-Veda, the Atharva-Veda as the fourth, Legend and Ancient Lore (*itihāsa-purāṇa*) as the fifth, the Veda of the Vedas [i.e. Grammar], Propitiation of the Manes, Mathematics, Augury (*daiva*), Chronology, Logic, Polity, the Science of the Gods (*deva-vidyā*), the Science of Sacred Knowledge (*brahma-vidyā*), Demonology (*bhūta-vidyā*), the Science of Rulership (*kṣatra-vidyā*), Astrology (*nakṣatra-vidyā*), the Science of Snake-charming, and the Fine Arts (*sarpa-*

devajana-vidyā), as well as heaven and earth, wind and space, water and heat, gods and men, beasts and birds, grass and trees, animals together with worms, flies, and ants, right and wrong, true and false, good and bad, pleasant and unpleasant, food and drink, this world and the yonder—all this one understands just with Understanding. Reverence Understanding.

2. He who reverences Understanding as Brahma—he, verily, attains the worlds of Understanding (*vijñāna*) and of Knowledge (*jñāna*). As far as Understanding goes, so far he has unlimited freedom, he who reverences Understanding as Brahma.'

'Is there, sir, more than Understanding?'

'There is, assuredly, more than Understanding.'

'Do you, sir, tell me it.'

EIGHTH KHAṆḌA

1. 'Strength (*bala*), assuredly, is more than Understanding. Indeed, one man of Strength causes a hundred men of Understanding to tremble. When one is becoming strong, he becomes a rising man. Rising, he becomes an attendant. Attending, he becomes attached as a pupil. Attached as a pupil, he becomes a seer, he becomes a hearer, he becomes a thinker, he becomes a perceiver, he becomes a doer, he becomes an understander. By Strength, verily, the earth stands; by Strength, the atmosphere; by Strength, the sky; by Strength, the mountains; by Strength, gods and men; by Strength, beasts and birds, grass and trees, animals together with worms, flies, and ants. By Strength the world stands. Reverence Strength.

2. He who reverences Strength as Brahma—as far as Strength goes, so far he has unlimited freedom, he who reverences Strength as Brahma.'

'Is there, sir, more than Strength?'

'There is, assuredly, more than Strength.'

'Do you, sir, tell me it.'

NINTH KHAṆḌA

1. 'Food (*anna*), assuredly, is more than Strength. Therefore, if one should not eat for ten days,[1] even though he might

[1] Literally 'nights.'

live, yet verily he becomes a non-seer, a non-hearer, a non-thinker, a non-perceiver, a non-doer, a non-understander. But on the entrance of food he becomes a seer, he becomes a hearer, he becomes a thinker, he becomes a perceiver, he becomes a doer, he becomes an understander. Reverence Food.

2. He who reverences Food as Brahma—he, verily, attains the worlds of Food and Drink. As far as Food goes, so far he has unlimited freedom, he who reverences Food as Brahma.'

'Is there, sir, more than Food?'

'There is, assuredly, more than Food.'

'Do you, sir, tell me it.'

Tenth Khaṇḍa

1. 'Water (*āpas*), verily, is more than Food. Therefore, when there is not a good rain, living creatures (*prāṇa*) sicken with the thought, "Food will become scarce." But when there is a good rain, living creatures become happy with the thought, "Food will become abundant." It is just Water solidified that is this earth, that is the atmosphere, that is the sky, that is gods and men, beasts and birds, grass and trees, animals together with worms, flies, and ants; all these are just Water solidified. Reverence Water.

2. He who reverences Water (*āpas*) as Brahma obtains (*āpnoti*) all his desires and becomes satisfied. As far as Water goes, so far he has unlimited freedom, he who reverences Water as Brahma.'

'Is there, sir, more than Water?'

'There is, assuredly, more than Water.'

'Do you, sir, tell me it.'

Eleventh Khaṇḍa

1. 'Heat (*tejas*), verily, is more than Water. That, verily, seizes hold of the wind, and heats the ether (*ākāśa*). Then people say: "It is hot! It is burning hot! Surely it will rain!" Heat indeed first indicates this, and then lets out water. So, with lightnings darting up and across the sky, thunders roll. Therefore people say: "It lightens! It

thunders! Surely it will rain!" Heat indeed first indicates this, and then lets out water. Reverence Heat.

2. He who reverences Heat as Brahma—he, verily, being glowing, attains glowing, shining worlds freed from darkness. As far as Heat goes, so far he has unlimited Freedom, he who reverences Heat as Brahma.'

'Is there, sir, more than Heat?'

'There is, assuredly, more than Heat.'

'Do you, sir, tell me it.'

TWELFTH KHAṆḌA

1. 'Space (*ākāśa*), assuredly, is more than Heat. In Space, verily, are both sun and moon, lightning, stars and fire. Through Space one calls out; through Space one hears; through Space one answers. In Space one enjoys himself; in Space one does not enjoy himself. In Space one is born; unto Space one is born. Reverence Space.

2. He who reverences Space as Brahma—he, verily, attains spacious, gleaming, unconfined, wide-extending worlds. As far as Space goes, so far he has unlimited freedom, he who reverences Space as Brahma.'

'Is there, sir, more than Space?'

'There is, assuredly, more than Space.'

'Do you, sir, tell me it.'

THIRTEENTH KHAṆḌA

1. 'Memory (*smara*), verily, is more than Space. Therefore, even if many not possessing Memory should be assembled, indeed they would not hear any one at all, they would not think, they would not understand. But assuredly, if they should remember, then they would hear, then they would think, then they would understand. Through Memory, assuredly, one discerns his children; through Memory, his cattle. Reverence Memory.

2. He who reverences Memory as Brahma—as far as Memory goes, so far he has unlimited freedom, he who reverences Memory as Brahma.'

'Is there, sir, more than Memory?'

'There is, assuredly, more than Memory.'

'Do you, sir, tell me it.'

FOURTEENTH KHAṆḌA

1. 'Hope (*āśā*), assuredly, is more than Memory. When kindled by Hope, verily, Memory learns the sacred sayings (*mantra*); [kindled by Hope] one performs sacred works (*karma*), longs for sons and cattle, for this world and the yonder. Reverence Hope.

2. He who reverences Hope as Brahma—through Hope all his desires prosper, his wishes are not unavailing. As far as Hope goes, so far he has unlimited freedom, he who reverences Hope as Brahma.'

'Is there, sir, more than Hope?'

'There is, assuredly, more than Hope.'

'Do you, sir, tell me it.'

FIFTEENTH KHAṆḌA

1. 'Life (*prāṇa*, breath), verily, is more than Hope. Just as, verily, the spokes are fastened in the hub, so on this vital breath everything is fastened. Life (*prāṇa*) goes on with vital breath (*prāṇa*). Vital breath (*prāṇa*) gives life (*prāṇa*); it gives [life] to a living creature (*prāṇa*). One's father is vital breath; one's mother, vital breath; one's brother, vital breath; one's sister, vital breath; one's teacher (*ācārya*), vital breath; a Brahman is vital breath.

2. If one answers harshly, as it were (*iva*), a father, or a mother, or a brother, or a sister, or a teacher, or a Brahman, people say to him: "Shame on you! Verily, you are a slayer of your father! Verily, you are a slayer of your mother! Verily, you are a slayer of your brother! Verily, you are a slayer of your sister! Verily, you are a slayer of your teacher! Verily, you are a slayer of a Brahman!"

3. But if, when the vital breath has departed from them, one should even shove them with a poker and burn up every bit of them,[1] people would not say to him: "You are a slayer of your father," nor "You are a slayer of your mother,"

[1] In the cremation-pile.

nor "You are a slayer of your brother," nor "You are a slayer of your sister," nor "You are a slayer of your teacher," nor "You are a slayer of a Brahman."

4. For indeed, vital breath (*prāṇa*) is all these things. Verily, he who sees this, thinks this, understands this, becomes a superior speaker. Even if people should say to him "You are a superior speaker," he should say "I am a superior speaker." He should not deny it.

Sixteenth Khaṇḍa

But he, verily, speaks superiorly who speaks superiorly with Truth (*satya*).'

'Then I, sir, would speak superiorly with Truth.'

'But one must desire to understand the Truth.'

'Sir, I desire to understand the Truth.'

Seventeenth Khaṇḍa

'Verily, when one understands, then he speaks the Truth. One who does not understand, does not speak the Truth. Only he who understands speaks the Truth. But one must desire to understand Understanding (*vijñāna*).'

'Sir, I desire to understand Understanding.'

Eighteenth Khaṇḍa

'Verily, when one thinks, then he understands. Without thinking one does not understand. Only after having thought does one understand. But one must desire to understand Thought (*mati*).'

'Sir, I desire to understand Thought.'

Nineteenth Khaṇḍa

'Verily, when one has Faith, then he thinks. One who has not Faith does not think. Only he who has Faith thinks. But one must desire to understand Faith (*śraddhā*).'

'Sir, I desire to understand Faith.'

TWENTIETH KHAṆḌA

'Verily, when one grows forth, then he has Faith. One who does not grow forth does not have Faith. Only he who grows forth (*niḥ* + √ *sthā*) has Faith. But one must desire to understand the Growing Forth (*niḥ-ṣṭhā*).'

'Sir, I desire to understand the Growing Forth.'

TWENTY-FIRST KHAṆḌA

'Verily, when one is active, then he grows forth. Without being active one does not grow forth. Only by activity does one grow forth. But one must desire to understand Activity (*kṛti*).'

'Sir, I desire to understand Activity.'

TWENTY-SECOND KHAṆḌA

'Verily, when one gets Pleasure for himself, then he is active. Without getting Pleasure one is not active. Only by getting Pleasure is one active. But one must desire to understand Pleasure (*sukha*).'

'Sir, I desire to understand Pleasure.'

TWENTY-THIRD KHAṆḌA

'Verily, a Plenum is the same as Pleasure. There is no Pleasure in the small. Only a Plenum is Pleasure. But one must desire to understand the Plenum (*bhūman*).'

'Sir, I desire to understand the Plenum.'

TWENTY-FOURTH KHAṆḌA

'Where one sees nothing else, hears nothing else, understands nothing else—that is a Plenum. But where one sees something else—that is the small. Verily, the Plenum is the same as the immortal; but the small is the same as the mortal.'

'That Plenum, sir—on what is it established?'

'On its own greatness—unless, indeed, not on greatness at all.

Here on earth people call cows and horses, elephants and gold, slaves and wives, fields and abodes "greatness." I do not speak thus; I do not speak thus,' said he; 'for [in that case] one thing is established upon another.

Twenty-fifth Khaṇḍa

1. That [Plenum], indeed, is below. It is above. It is to the west. It is to the east. It is to the south. It is to the north. It, indeed, is this whole world.—

Now next, the instruction with regard to the Ego (*ahaṁkārādeśa*).—

I, indeed, am below. I am above. I am to the west. I am to the east. I am to the south. I am to the north. I, indeed, am this whole world.—

2. Now next, the instruction with regard to the soul (*ātmādeśa*).—

The Soul (Ātman), indeed, is below. The Soul is above. The Soul is to the west. The Soul is to the east. The Soul is to the south. The Soul is to the north. The Soul, indeed, is this whole world.

Verily, he who sees this, who thinks this, who understands this, who has pleasure in the Soul, who has delight in the Soul, who has intercourse with the Soul, who has bliss in the Soul—he is autonomous (*sva-rāj*); he has unlimited freedom in all worlds. But they who know otherwise than this are heteronomous (*anya-rājan*); they have perishable worlds; in all worlds they have no freedom.

Twenty-sixth Khaṇḍa

1. Verily, for him who sees this, who thinks this, who understands this, Vital Breath (*prāṇa*) arises from the Soul (Ātman); Hope, from the Soul; Memory, from the Soul; Space (*ākāśa*), from the Soul; Heat, from the Soul; Water, from the Soul; Appearance and Disappearance, from the Soul; Food, from the Soul; Strength, from the Soul; Understanding, from the Soul; Meditation, from the Soul; Thought, from the Soul; Conception, from the Soul; Mind, from the Soul; Speech, from the Soul; Name, from the Soul; sacred sayings (*mantra*), from the Soul; sacred works (*karman*), from the Soul; indeed this whole world, from the Soul.

2. As to this there is the following verse :—

The seer sees not death,
Nor sickness, nor any distress.
The seer sees only the All,
Obtains the All entirely.

That [Soul] is onefold, is threefold, fivefold, sevenfold, and also ninefold ;

Again, declared elevenfold,
And hundred-and-eleven-fold,
And also twenty-thousand-fold.[1]

In pure nourishment (*āhāra-śuddhi*) there is a pure nature (*sattva-śuddhi*). In a pure nature the traditional doctrine (*smṛti*) becomes firmly fixed. In acquiring the traditional doctrine there is release from all knots [of the heart]. To such a one[2] who has his stains wiped away the blessed Sanatkumāra shows the further shore of darkness. People call him Skanda[3]—yea, they call him Skanda.'

EIGHTH PRAPĀṬHAKA

Concerning the nature of the soul

FIRST KHAṆḌA

The universal real Soul, within the heart and in the world

1. *Om*! [The teacher should say :] 'Now, what is here in this city of Brahma,[4] is an abode, a small lotus-flower.[5] Within that is a small space. What is within that, should be searched out ; that, assuredly, is what one should desire to understand.'

2. If they [i.e. the pupils] should say to him : 'This abode,

[1] For this same idea of the indefinite self-individuation of ultimate reality see Maitri 5. 2.

[2] As, for example, Nārada, the instruction of whom by Sanatkumāra forms this entire Seventh Prapāṭhaka up to this point.

[3] Meaning, etymologically, 'the Leaper[-over].' Perhaps the idea of this apparently later addition is, that the teacher of this Upanishadic doctrine, which 'overcomes' darkness, is compared to—indeed, is identified with—Skanda, god of war in later Hinduism, the leader of hosts.

[4] Explained by Śaṅkara as 'the body.'

[5] Explained by Śaṅkara as 'the heart.'

the small lotus-flower that is here in this city of Brahma, and the small space within that—what is there there which should be searched out, which assuredly one should desire to understand?' [3] he should say: 'As far, verily, as this world-space (*ayam ākāśa*) extends, so far extends the space within the heart. Within it, indeed, are contained both heaven and earth, both fire and wind, both sun and moon, lightning and the stars, both what one possesses here and what one does not possess; everything here is contained within it.'

4. If they should say to him: 'If within this city of Brahma is contained everything here, all beings as well as all desires, when old age overtakes it or it perishes, what is left over therefrom?' [5] he should say: 'That does not grow old with one's old age; it is not slain with one's murder. That[1] is the real city of Brahma. In it desires are contained. That is the Soul (Ātman), free from evil, ageless, deathless, sorrowless, hungerless, thirstless, whose desire is the Real, whose conception is the Real.

For, just as here on earth human beings follow along in subjection to command; of whatever object they are desirous, whether a realm or a part of a field, upon that they live dependent[2]—

6. As here on earth the world which is won by work (*karma-jita loka*) becomes destroyed, even so there the world which is won by merit (*punya-jita loka*) becomes destroyed.

Those who go hence without here having found the Soul (Ātman) and those real desires (*satya kāma*)—for them in all the worlds there is no freedom. But those who go hence having found here the Soul and those real desires—for them in all worlds there is freedom.

[1] And not the body.

[2] The apodosis of this comparison seems to be lacking. However, the general idea is doubtless the same as in the following predictions: i. e. they who in this life are slaves to the dictates of desire like the slaves of a ruler, will continue unchanged in the hereafter. Whitney, in his review of 'Böhtlingk's Upanishads' in the *American Journal of Philology*, vol. 11, p. 429, interprets the protasis somewhat differently: '"For just as here subjects (of a king who leads them into a new territory) settle down according to order, [and] whatever direction their desires take them to, what region, what piece of ground, that same they severally live upon"—so, we are to understand, is it also in the other world; one's desires determine his condition there.'

Second Khaṇḍa

1. If he becomes desirous of the world of fathers, merely out of his conception (*saṁkalpa*) fathers arise. Possessed of that world of fathers, he is happy.

2. So, if he becomes desirous of the world of mothers, merely out of his conception mothers arise. Possessed of that world of mothers, he is happy.

3. So, if he becomes desirous of the world of brothers, merely out of his conception brothers arise. Possessed of that world of brothers, he is happy.

4. So, if he becomes desirous of the world of sisters, merely out of his conception sisters arise. Possessed of that world of sisters, he is happy.

5. So, if he becomes desirous of the world of friends, merely out of his conception friends arise. Possessed of that world of friends, he is happy.

6. So, if he becomes desirous of the world of perfume and garlands, merely out of his conception perfume and garlands arise. Possessed of that world of perfume and garlands, he is happy.

7. So, if he becomes desirous of the world of food and drink, merely out of his conception food and drink arise. Possessed of that world of food and drink, he is happy.

8. So, if he becomes desirous of the world of song and music, merely out of his conception song and music arise. Possessed of that world of song and music, he is happy.

9. So, if he becomes desirous of the world of women, merely out of his conception women arise. Possessed of that world of women, he is happy.

10. Of whatever object he becomes desirous, whatever desire he desires, merely out of his conception it arises. Possessed of it, he is happy.

Third Khaṇḍa

1. These same are real desires (*satya kāma*) with a covering of what is false. Although they are real, there is a covering that is false.

For truly, whoever of one's [fellows] departs hence, one does not get him [back] to look at here.

2. But those of one's [fellows] who are alive there, and those who have departed, and whatever else one desires but does not get—all this one finds by going in there [i. e. in the Soul]; for there, truly, are those real desires of his which have a covering of what is false.

So, just as those who do not know the spot might go over a hid treasure of gold again and again, but not find it, even so all creatures here go day by day to that Brahma-world (*brahma-loka*) [in deep sleep], but do not find it; for truly they are carried astray by what is false.

3. Verily, this Soul (Ātman) is in the heart. The etymological explanation (*nirukta*) thereof is this: This one is in the heart (*hṛdy ayam*); therefore it is the heart (*hṛdayam*). Day by day, verily, he who knows this goes to the heavenly world (*svarga loka*).

4. Now, that serene one [1] who, rising up out of this body, reaches the highest light and appears with his own form—he is the Soul (Ātman),' said he [i. e. the teacher]. 'That is the immortal, the fearless. That is Brahma.'

Verily, the name of that Brahma is the Real (*satyam*).

5. Verily, these are the three syllables: *sat-ti-yam.*[2] The *sat* (Being)—that is the immortal. The *ti*—that is the mortal.[3] Now the *yam*—with that one holds the two together. Because with it one holds (√*yam*) the two together, therefore it is *yam*. Day by day, verily, he who knows this goes to the heavenly world.

FOURTH KHAṆḌA

1. Now, the Soul (Ātman) is the bridge [or dam], the separation for keeping these worlds apart. Over that bridge [or dam] there cross neither day, nor night, nor old age, nor death, nor sorrow, nor well-doing, nor evil-doing.

2. All evils turn back therefrom, for that Brahma-world is freed from evil. (2) Therefore, verily, upon crossing that bridge, if one is blind, he becomes no longer blind; if he is sick, he becomes no longer sick. Therefore, verily, upon

[1] That is, the soul in deep sleep.

[2] Another analytic explanation of the word *satyam* occurs at Bṛih. 5. 5. 1.

[3] Perhaps on the ground that the sound *ti* is contained in the word *martya*, meaning 'mortal.'

crossing that bridge, the night appears even as the day, for that Brahma-world is ever illumined.

3. But only they who find that Brahma-world through the chaste life of a student of sacred knowledge (*brahmacarya*)—only they possess that Brahma-world. In all worlds they possess unlimited freedom.

Fifth Khaṇḍa

The true way to the Brahma-world, through a life of abstinent religious study

1. Now, what people call 'sacrifice' (*yajña*) is really the chaste life of a student of sacred knowledge (*brahmacarya*), for only through the chaste life of a student of sacred knowledge does he who is a knower (*ya jñātṛ*) find that [world].

Now, what people call 'what has been sacrificed' (*iṣṭa*) is really the chaste life of a student of sacred knowledge, for only after having searched (*iṣṭvā*) with the chaste life of a student of sacred knowledge does one find the Soul (Ātman).

2. Now, what people call 'the protracted sacrifice' (*sattrā-yaṇa*) is really the chaste life of a student of sacred knowledge, for only through the chaste life of a student of sacred knowledge does one find the protection (*trāṇa*) of the real (*sat*) Soul (Ātman).

Now, what people call 'silent asceticism' (*mauna*) is really the chaste life of a student of sacred knowledge, for only in finding the Soul through the chaste life of a student of sacred knowledge does one [really] think (*manute*).

3. Now, what people call 'a course of fasting' (*an-āśakāyana*[1]) is really the chaste life of a student of sacred knowledge, for the Soul (Ātman) which one finds through the chaste life of a student of sacred knowledge perishes not (*na naśyati*).

Now, what people call 'betaking oneself to hermit life in the forest' (*araṇyāyana*) is really the chaste life of a student of sacred knowledge. Verily, the two seas in the Brahma-world, in the third heaven from here, are *Ara* and *Ṇya*. There is the lake Airaṁmadīya ('Affording Refreshment and Ecstasy');

[1] According to another possible division of the compound word which Śaṅkara seems to have adopted, *a-nāśaka-ayana*, it would mean 'entrance into the unperishing.'

there, the fig-tree Somasavana ('the Soma-yielding'); there, Brahma's citadel, Aparājitā ('the Unconquered'), the golden hall of the Lord (*prabhu*).

4. But only they who find those two seas, Ara and Ṇya, in the Brahma-world through the chaste life of a student of sacred knowledge—only they possess that Brahma-world. In all the worlds they possess unlimited freedom.

Sixth Khaṇḍa

Passing out from the heart through the sun to immortality

1. Now, as for these channels of the heart—they arise from the finest essence, which is reddish brown, white, blue, yellow, and red: so it is said. Verily, yonder sun is reddish brown; it is white; it is blue; it is yellow; it is red.

2. Now, as a great extending highway goes to two villages, this one and the yonder, even so these rays of the sun go to two worlds, this one and the yonder. They extend from yonder sun, and creep into these channels. They extend from these channels, and creep into yonder sun.

3. Now, when one is thus sound asleep, composed, serene, he knows no dream; then he has crept into these channels; so no evil touches him, for then he has reached the Bright Power (*tejas*).

4. Now, when one thus becomes reduced to weakness, those sitting around say: 'Do you know me?' 'Do you know me?' As long as he has not departed from this body, he knows them.

5. But when he thus departs from this body, then he ascends upward with these very rays of the sun. With the thought of *Om*, verily, he passes up. As quickly as one could direct his mind to it, he comes to the sun. That, verily, indeed, is the world-door, an entrance for knowers, a stopping for non-knowers.

6. As to this there is the following verse:—

There are a hundred and one channels of the heart.
One of these passes up to the crown of the head.
Going up by it, one goes to immortality.
The others are for departing in various directions.[1]

[1] This stanza recurs at Kaṭha 6. 16.

Seventh Khaṇḍa

The progressive instruction of Indra by Prajāpati concerning the real self

1. 'The Self (Ātman), which is free from evil, ageless, deathless, sorrowless, hungerless, thirstless, whose desire is the Real, whose conception is the Real—He should be searched out, Him one should desire to understand. He obtains all worlds and all desires who has found out and who understands that Self.'—Thus spake Prajāpati.

2. Then both the gods and the devils (*deva-asura*) heard it. Then they said: 'Come! Let us search out that Self, the Self by searching out whom one obtains all worlds and all desires!'

Then Indra from among the gods went forth unto him, and Virocana from among the devils. Then, without communicating with each other, the two came into the presence of Prajāpati, fuel in hand.[1]

3. Then for thirty-two years the two lived the chaste life of a student of sacred knowledge (*brahmacarya*).

Then Prajāpati said to the two: 'Desiring what have you been living?'

Then the two said: '"The Self (Ātman), which is free from evil, ageless, deathless, sorrowless, hungerless, thirstless, whose desire is the Real, whose conception is the Real—He should be searched out, Him one should desire to understand. He obtains all worlds and all desires who has found out and who understands that Self."—Such do people declare to be your words, sir. We have been living desiring Him.'

4. Then Prajāpati said to the two: 'That Person who is seen in the eye—He is the Self (Ātman) of whom I spoke.[2] That is the immortal, the fearless. That is Brahma.'

'But this one, sir, who is observed in water and in a mirror—which one is he?'

'The same one, indeed, is observed in all these,' said he.

[1] In token of discipleship.

[2] Or the text might be translated: '"That Person who is seen in the eye—He is the Self," said he. "That is the immortal, the fearless. That is Brahma."' Such quite certainly is the translation of the very same words which have already occurred in 4. 15. 1.

Eighth Khaṇḍa

1. 'Look at yourself in a pan of water. Anything that you do not understand of the Self, tell me.'

Then the two looked in a pan of water.

Then Prajāpati said to the two: 'What do you see?'

Then the two said: 'We see everything here, sir, a Self corresponding exactly, even to the hair and fingernails!'

2. Then Prajāpati said to the two: 'Make yourselves well-ornamented, well-dressed, adorned, and look in a pan of water.'

Then the two made themselves well-ornamented, well-dressed, adorned, and looked in a pan of water.

Then Prajāpati said to the two: 'What do you see?'

3. Then the two said: 'Just as we ourselves are here, sir, well-ornamented, well-dressed, adorned—so there, sir, well-ornamented, well-dressed, adorned.'

'That is the Self,' said he. 'That is the immortal, the fearless. That is Brahma.'

Then with tranquil heart (*śānta-hṛdaya*) the two went forth.

4. Then Prajāpati glanced after them, and said: 'They go without having comprehended, without having found the Self (Ātman). Whosoever shall have such a doctrine (*upaniṣad*), be they gods or be they devils, they shall perish.'

Then with tranquil heart Virocana came to the devils. To them he then declared this doctrine (*upaniṣad*): 'Oneself (*ātman*)[1] is to be made happy here on earth. Oneself is to be waited upon. He who makes his own self (*ātman*) happy here on earth, who waits upon himself—he obtains both worlds, both this world and the yonder.'

5. Therefore even now here on earth they say of one who is not a giver, who is not a believer (*a-śraddadhāna*), who is not a sacrificer, 'Oh! devilish (*āsura*)!' for such is the doctrine (*upaniṣad*) of the devils. They adorn the body (*śarīra*) of one deceased with what they have begged, with dress, with ornament, as they call it, for they think that thereby they will win yonder world.

[1] Besides meaning 'oneself,' as it evidently does both in this paragraph and in the beginning of the following paragraph, the word *ātman* may also have the connotation 'one's body,' which seems to be the meaning in the latter half of the following paragraph.

Ninth Khaṇḍa

1. But then Indra, even before reaching the gods, saw this danger: 'Just as, indeed, that one [i. e. the bodily self] is well-ornamented when this body (*śarīra*) is well-ornamented, well-dressed when this is well-dressed, adorned when this is adorned, even so that one is blind when this is blind, lame when this is lame, maimed when this is maimed. It perishes immediately upon the perishing of this body. I see nothing enjoyable in this.'

2. Fuel in hand, back again he came. Then Prajāpati said to him: 'Desiring what, O Maghavan ('Munificent One'), have you come back again, since you along with Virocana went forth with tranquil heart?'

Then he said: 'Just as, indeed, that one [i. e. the bodily self] is well-ornamented when this body is well-ornamented, well-dressed when this is well-dressed, adorned when this is adorned even so it is blind when this is blind, lame when this is lame, maimed when this is maimed. It perishes immediately upon the perishing of this body. I see nothing enjoyable in this.'

3. 'He is even so, O Maghavan,' said he. 'However, I will explain this further to you. Live with me thirty-two years more.'

Then he lived with him thirty-two years more.

To him [i. e. to Indra] he [i. e. Prajāpati] then said:—

Tenth Khaṇḍa

1. 'He who moves about happy in a dream—he is the Self (Ātman),' said he. 'That is the immortal, the fearless. That is Brahma.'

Then with tranquil heart he [i. e. Indra] went forth.

Then, even before reaching the gods, he saw this danger: 'Now, even if this body is blind, that one [i. e. the Self, Ātman] is not blind. If this is lame, he is not lame. Indeed, he does not suffer defect through defect of this. [2] He is not slain with one's murder. He is not lame with one's lameness. Nevertheless, as it were (*iva*), they kill him; as it were, they unclothe[1] him; as it were, he comes to experience what is unpleasant; as it were, he even weeps. I see nothing enjoyable in this.'

3. Fuel in hand, back again he came. Then Prajāpati said to him: 'Desiring what, O Maghavan, have you come back again, since you went forth with tranquil heart?'

Then he said: 'Now, sir, even if this body is blind, that one [i.e. the Self] is not blind. If this is lame, he is not lame. Indeed, he does not suffer defect through defect of this. [4] He is not slain with one's murder. He is not lame with one's lameness. Nevertheless, as it were, they kill him; as it were, they unclothe[1] him; as it were, he comes to experience what is unpleasant; as it were, he even weeps. I see nothing enjoyable in this.'

'He is even so, O Maghavan,' said he. 'However, I will explain this further to you. Live with me thirty-two years more.'

Then he lived with him thirty-two years more.

To him [i.e. to Indra] he [i.e. Prajāpati] then said:—

ELEVENTH KHAṆḌA

1. 'Now, when one is sound asleep, composed, serene, and knows no dream—that is the Self (Ātman),' said he. 'That is the immortal, the fearless. That is Brahma.'

Then with tranquil heart he went forth.

Then, even before reaching the gods, he saw this danger: 'Assuredly, indeed, this one does not exactly know himself (*ātmānam*) with the thought "I am he," nor indeed the things here. He becomes one who has gone to destruction. I see nothing enjoyable in this.'

2. Fuel in hand, back again he came. Then Prajāpati said to him: 'Desiring what, O Maghavan, have you come back again, since you went forth with tranquil heart?'

Then he [i.e. Indra] said: 'Assuredly, this [self] does not exactly know himself with the thought "I am he," nor indeed

[1] Reading *vicchādayanti* with all the texts, from √ *chad*. However, the Com. explains as 'they chase.' The parallel passage in Bṛih. 4. 3. 20 has *vicchāyayati* 'tear to pieces,' from √ *chā*.

the things here. He becomes one who has gone to destruction. I see nothing enjoyable in this.'

3. 'He is even so, O Maghavan,' said he. 'However, I will explain this further to you, and there is nothing else besides this. Live with me five years more.'

Then he lived with him five years more.—That makes one hundred and one years. Thus it is that people say, 'Verily, for one hundred and one years Maghavan lived the chaste life of a student of sacred knowledge (*brahmacarya*) with Prajāpati.'—

To him [i.e. to Indra] he [i.e. Prajāpati] then said:—

Twelfth Khaṇḍa

1. 'O Maghavan, verily, this body (*śarīra*) is mortal. It has been appropriated by Death (Mṛityu). [But] it is the standing-ground of that deathless, bodiless Self (Ātman). Verily, he who is incorporate has been appropriated by pleasure and pain. Verily, there is no freedom from pleasure and pain for one while he is incorporate. Verily, while one is bodiless, pleasure and pain do not touch him.

2. The wind is bodiless. Clouds, lightning, thunder—these are bodiless. Now as these, when they arise from yonder space and reach the highest light, appear each with its own form, [3] even so that serene one (*saṃprasāda*), when he rises up from this body (*śarīra*) and reaches the highest light, appears with his own form. Such a one is the supreme person (*uttama puruṣa*). There such a one goes around laughing, sporting, having enjoyment with women or chariots or friends, not remembering the appendage of this body. As a draft-animal is yoked in a wagon, even so this spirit (*prāṇa*) is yoked in this body.

4. Now, when the eye is directed thus toward space, that is the seeing person (*cākṣuṣa puruṣa*); the eye is [the instrument] for seeing. Now, he who knows "Let me smell this"—that is the Self (Ātman); the nose is [the instrument] for smelling. Now, he who knows "Let me utter this"—that is the Self; the voice is [the instrument] for utterance. Now, he who knows "Let me hear this"—that is the Self; the ear is [the instrument] for hearing.

5. Now, he who knows "Let me think this"—that is the Self; the mind (*manas*) is his divine eye (*daiva cakṣu*). He, verily, with that divine eye the mind, sees desires here, and experiences enjoyment.

6. Verily, those gods who are in the Brahma-world[1] reverence that Self. Therefore all worlds and all desires have been appropriated by them. He obtains all worlds and all desires who has found out and who understands that Self (Ātman).'

Thus spake Prajāpati—yea, thus spake Prajāpati!

Thirteenth Khaṇḍa

A paean of the perfected soul

From the dark I go to the varicolored. From the varicolored I go to the dark. Shaking off evil, as a horse his hairs; shaking off the body (*śarīra*), as the moon releases itself from the mouth of Rāhu[2]; I, a perfected soul (*kṛtātman*), pass into the uncreated Brahma-world—yea, into it I pass!

Fourteenth Khaṇḍa

The exultation and prayer of a glorious learner

Verily, what is called space (*ākāśa*) is the accomplisher of name and form.[3] That within which they are, is Brahma. That is the immortal. That is the Self (Ātman, Soul).

I go to Prajāpati's abode and assembly-hall.

I am the glory of the Brahmans (*brāhmaṇa*), the glory of the princes (*rājan*), the glory of the people (*viś*).

I have attained unto glory.

May I, who am the glory of the glories, not go to hoary and toothless, yea to toothless and hoary and driveling [old age]!

Yea, may I not go to driveling [old age]!

[1] Who received this instruction from Prajāpati through Indra, the chief of the Vedic gods.

[2] Referring to the familiar idea that an eclipse is caused by the dragon Rāhu's attempt to swallow the moon.

[3] 'Name and form' is the Sanskrit expression for the modern term 'individuality.'

Fifteenth Khanda

Final words to the departing pupil

This did Brahmā tell to Prajāpati; Prajāpati, to Manu; Manu, to human beings (*prajā*).

He who according to rule has learned the Veda from the family of a teacher, in time left over from doing work for the teacher; he who, after having come back again, in a home of his own continues Veda-study in a clean place and produces [sons and pupils]; he who has concentrated all his senses upon the Soul (Ātman); he who is harmless (*ahiṁsant*) toward all things elsewhere than at holy places (*tīrtha*)[1]—he, indeed, who lives thus throughout his length of life, reaches the Brahma-world and does not return hither again—yea, he does not return hither again![2]

[1] That is, at animal sacrifices.

[2] That is, in reincarnation.

TAITTIRIYA UPANISHAD

FIRST VALLĪ

(Śikshā Vallī, 'Chapter concerning Instruction')

FIRST ANUVĀKA

Invocation, adoration, and supplication

Om!

Propitious unto us, Mitra! Propitious, Varuṇa!
Propitious unto us let Aryaman be!
Propitious unto us, Indra! Bṛihaspati!
Propitious unto us, Vishṇu, the Wide-strider![1]

Adoration to Brahma! Adoration to thee, Vāyu! Thou, indeed, art the perceptible Brahma. Of thee, indeed, the perceptible Brahma, will I speak. I will speak of the right (*ṛta*). I will speak of the true. Let that favor me! Let that favor the speaker! Let it favor me! Let it favor the speaker!

Om! Peace! Peace! Peace!

SECOND ANUVĀKA

Lesson on Pronunciation

Om! We will expound Pronunciation[2]:
the sound (*varṇa*);
the accent (*svara*);
the quantity (*mātrā*);
the force (*bala*);
the articulation (*sāma*);
the combination (*santāna*).
—Thus has been declared the lesson on Pronunciation.[2]

[1] This stanza = RV. 1. 90. 9, in a hymn to the All-Gods.

[2] In the summary title of the chapter, which includes various instructions, the word *śikṣā* probably has its general meaning of 'Instruction.' But here—as also in Muṇḍ. 1. 1. 5—it has a specialized, technical meaning, 'the Science of Pronunciation.' As the first stage in the 'instruction' concerning the Vedas, this is elaborated as the formal discipline named Śikshā, the first of the six Vedāṅgas ('Limbs of the Veda').

Third Anuvāka

The mystic significance of combinations

1. Glory (*yaśas*) be with us two[1]!

Pre-eminence in sacred knowledge (*brahma-varcasa*) be with us two[1]!

Now next, we will expound the mystic meaning (*upaniṣad*) of combination (*saṁhitā*) in five heads:

with regard to the world;
with regard to the luminaries;
with regard to knowledge;
with regard to progeny;
with regard to oneself.

Now, with regard to the world.—

The earth is the prior form; the heaven, the latter form. Space is their conjunction; [2] wind, the connection.—Thus with regard to the world.

Now, with regard to the luminaries.—

Fire is the prior form; the sun, the latter form. Water is their conjunction; lightning, the connection.—Thus with regard to the luminaries.

Now, with regard to knowledge.—

The teacher is the prior form; [3] the pupil, the latter form. Knowledge is their conjunction; instruction, the connection.—Thus with regard to knowledge.

Now, with regard to progeny.—

The mother is the prior form; the father, the latter form. Progeny is their conjunction; procreation, the connection.—Thus with regard to progeny.

4. Now, with regard to oneself.—

The lower jaw is the prior form; the upper jaw, the latter form. Speech is their conjunction; the tongue, the connection.—Thus with regard to oneself.

These are the great combinations. He who knows these combinations, thus expounded, becomes conjoined with offspring, with cattle, with pre-eminence in sacred knowledge, with food, with the heavenly world.

[1] That is, the teacher and the pupil.

Fourth Anuvāka

A teacher's prayer

1. He who is pre-eminent among the Vedic hymns (*chandas*), who is the all-formed (*viśva-rūpa*),
Who has sprung into being from immortality above the Vedic hymns—
Let this Indra deliver (√*spṛ*) me with intelligence!
O God (*deva*), I would become possessor of immortality!
May my body be very vigorous!
May my tongue be exceeding sweet!
May I hear abundantly with my ears!
Thou art the sheath of Brahma,
With intelligence covered o'er!
Guard for me what I have heard!
[It is Prosperity] who brings, extends,
[2] And long[1] makes her own—
My garments and cows,
And food and drink alway.
Therefore bring me prosperity (*śrī*)
In wool, along with cattle!
Hail!

May students of sacred knowledge (*brahmacārin*) come unto me! Hail!

May students of sacred knowledge come apart unto me! Hail!

May students of sacred knowledge come forth unto me! Hail!

May students of sacred knowledge subdue themselves! Hail!

May students of sacred knowledge tranquillize themselves! Hail!

3. May I become glorious among men! Hail!

May I be better than the very rich! Hail!

Into thee thyself, O Gracious Lord (*bhaga*), may I enter! Hail!

Do thou thyself, O Gracious Lord, enter into me! Hail!

In such a one, a thousandfold ramified—O Gracious Lord, in thee I am cleansed! Hail!

[1] If reading should the be '*ciram* instead of *ciram*, then translate 'shortly.' The two following lines, whose grammatical structure is not evident, seem to interrupt this sentence.

As waters run downward, as months into the year, so, O Establisher (*dhātṛ*), may students of sacred knowledge run unto me from all sides! Hail!

Thou art a refuge! Shine upon me! Come unto me!

Fifth Anuvāka

The fourfold mystic Utterances

1. *Bhūr*! *Bhuvas*! *Suvar*! Verily, these are the three Utterances (*vyāhṛti*). And beside these, too, Māhācamasya made known a fourth, namely *Mahas* (Greatness)! That is Brahma. That is the body (*ātman*); other divinities are the limbs.

Bhūr, verily, is this world; *Bhuvas*, the atmosphere; *Suvar*, yonder world; [2] *Mahas*, the sun. Verily, all worlds are made greater (*mahīyante*) by the sun.

Bhūr, verily, is Agni (Fire); *Bhuvas*, Vāyu (Wind); *Suvar*, Āditya (Sun); *Mahas*, the moon. Verily, all lights are made greater by the moon.

Bhūr, verily, is the Rig verses; *Bhuvas*, the Sāman chants; *Suvar*, the Yajus formulas; [3] *Mahas*, sacred knowledge (*brahma*). Verily, all the Vedas are made greater by sacred knowledge.

Bhūr, verily, is the in-breath (*prāṇa*); *Bhuvas*, the out-breath (*apāna*); *Suvar*, the diffused breath (*vyāna*); *Mahas*, food (*anna*). Verily, all the vital breaths (*prāṇa*) are made greater by food.

Verily, these four are fourfold. The Utterances are four and four. He who knows these, knows Brahma; to him all the gods bring strength.

Sixth Anuvāka

A departing person's attainment with the four Utterances

1. This space that is within the heart—therein is the person, consisting of mind (*mano-maya*), immortal, resplendent. That which hangs down between the palates like a nipple—that is Indra's[1] place of exit.

[1] A name for the individual soul, as in Ait. 1. 3. 12, 14.

Piercing the head at the point where is the edge of the hair, with the word *Bhūr* he stands upon Agni (Fire); with the word *Bhuvas*, upon Vāyu (Wind); [2] with the word *Suvar*, upon Āditya (the Sun); with the word *Mahas*, upon Brahma. He obtains self-rule (*svā-rājya*). He obtains the lord of the mind, lord of the voice, lord of the eye, lord of the ear, lord of the understanding—this and more he becomes, even Brahma, whose body is space (*ākāśa-śarīra*), whose soul is the real (*satyātman*), whose pleasure-ground is the breathing spirit, whose mind is bliss (*mana-ānanda*), abounding in tranquillity (*śānti-samṛddha*), immortal.—Thus, O Prācīnayogya (Man of the Ancient Yoga), worship.[1]

Seventh Anuvāka

The fivefoldness of the world and of the individual

Earth,	atmosphere,	heaven,	quarters	intermediate quarters;
			of heaven,	
fire,	wind,	sun,	moon,	stars;
water,	plants,	trees,	space,	one's body.

—Thus with regard to material existence (*adhi-bhūta*).

Now with regard to oneself (*adhy-ātma*).—

Prāṇa breath,	Vyāna breath,	Apāna breath,	Udāna breath,	Samāna breath;
sight,	hearing,	mind,	speech,	touch;
skin,	flesh,	muscle,	bone,	marrow.

Having analyzed in this manner, a seer has said: 'Fivefold, verily, is this whole world. With the fivefold, indeed, one wins the fivefold.'[2]

Eighth Anuvāka

Glorification of the sacred word 'Om'

Om is *brahma*.

Om is the whole world.

[1] That is, the conditioned (*sa-guṇa*) Brahma, who may be worshiped. The absolute, unconditioned Brahma is the object of intellectual appreciation, i. e. of knowledge, not of worship.

[2] A similar theory is expressed at Bṛih. 1. 4. 17.

[3] Perhaps with a double meaning: both 'sacred word' and the philosophical 'Brahma.'

Om—that is compliance. As also, verily, it is well known—upon the words 'O! Call forth!'[1] they call forth.

With '*Om*' they sing the Sāman chants.

With '*Om! Śom!*' they recite the Invocations of Praise (*śāstra*).

With '*Om*' the Adhvaryu priest utters the Response.

With '*Om*' the Brahman priest (*brahma*) utters the Introductory Eulogy (*pra* + √*stu*).

With '*Om*' one[2] assents to the Agni-oblation (*agnihotra*).

'*Om*,' says a Brahman (*brāhmaṇa*) about to recite, 'may I get the sacred word (*brahma*)!' He does get the sacred word.[3]

NINTH ANUVĀKA

Study of the sacred word the most important of all duties

The right (*ṛta*), and also study and teaching.[4]
The true (*satya*), and also study and teaching.
Austerity (*tapas*), and also study and teaching.
Self-control (*dama*), and also study and teaching.
Tranquillity (*śama*), and also study and teaching.
The [sacrificial] fires, and also study and teaching.
The Agnihotra sacrifice, and also study and teaching.
Guests, and also study and teaching.
Humanity (*mānuṣa*), and also study and teaching.
Offspring, and also study and teaching.
Begetting, and also study and teaching.
Procreation, and also study and teaching.

'The true!'—says Satyavacas ('Truthful') Rathītara.

'Austerity!'—says Taponitya ('Devoted-to-austerity') Pauruśishti.

'Just study and teaching!'—says Nāka ('Painless') Maudgalya, 'for that is austerity—for that is austerity.'

[1] In the ritual, the signal from the Adhvaryu priest for a response from the sacrificer.

[2] That is, the person instituting the sacrifice.

[3] That is, the Veda.—Com.

[4] That is, of the Veda.—Com.

TENTH ANUVAKA

The excellence of Veda-knowledge—a meditation

I am the mover[1] of the tree!
My fame is like a mountain's peak!
Exaltedly pure, like the excellent nectar in the sun,[2]
I am a shining treasure,
Wise, immortal, indestructible[3]!
This is Triśaṅku's recitation on Veda-knowledge.[4]

ELEVENTH ANUVĀKA

Practical precepts to a student

1. Having taught the Veda, a teacher further instructs a pupil:—

Speak the truth.
Practise virtue (*dharma*).
Neglect not study [of the Vedas].
Having brought an acceptable gift to the teacher, cut not off the line of progeny.
One should not be negligent of truth.
One should not be negligent of virtue.
One should not be negligent of welfare.
One should not be negligent of prosperity.
One should not be negligent of study and teaching.

2. One should not be negligent of duties to the gods and to the fathers.

Be one to whom a mother is as a god.
Be one to whom a father is as a god.

[1] That is, 'I am the feller of the tree of world-delusion (*saṁsāra*)' according to Śaṅkara. He also proposes, as a synonym for 'mover,' *antaryāmin*, 'inner controller'—which suggests to Deussen the (less likely) interpretation: 'I am the moving (or, animating) spirit of the tree of life.'

[2] Literally 'courser'; a reference here perhaps to the 'honey in the sun' of Chānd. 3. 1.—So Śaṅkara divides the words, *vājinī 'va sv-amṛtaṁ*. But if *vājinīvasv amṛtaṁ*, as *BR*. suggest, then 'the Immortal, possessing [possibly, 'bestowing'—according to *BR*.] power.'

[3] *amṛto 'kṣitaḥ*. If *amṛtokṣitaḥ*, then 'sprinkled with immortality (or, with nectar).'

[4] Or, 'Veda-repetition' (*veda-anuvacana*). The whole paragraph is an obscure, mystical meditation, either a preparatory invocation for the study of the Vedas or a summary praise of its exalting and enlightening effect.

Be one to whom a teacher is as a god.
Be one to whom a guest is as a god.

Those acts which are irreproachable should be practised, and no others.

Those things which among us are good deeds should be revered by you, [3] and no others.

Whatever Brahmans (*brāhmaṇa*) are superior to us, for them refreshment should be procured by you with a seat.[1]

One should give with faith (*śraddhā*).
One should not give without faith.
One should give with plenty (*śrī*).[2]
One should give with modesty.
One should give with fear.
One should give with sympathy (*sam-vid*).[3]

Now, if you should have doubt concerning an act, or doubt concerning conduct, [4] if there should be there Brahmans competent to judge, apt, devoted, not harsh, lovers of virtue (*dharma*)—as they may behave themselves in such a case, so should you behave yourself in such a case.

Now, with regard to [people] spoken against, if there should be there Brahmans competent to judge, apt, devoted, not harsh, lovers of virtue—as they may behave themselves with regard to such, so should you behave yourself with regard to such.

This is the teaching. This is the admonition. This is the mystic doctrine of the Veda (*veda-upaniṣad*). This is the instruction. Thus should one worship. Thus, indeed, should one worship.

TWELFTH ANUVĀKA[4]

Invocation, adoration, and acknowledgment

Propitious unto us, Mitra! Propitious, Varuṇa!
Propitious unto us let Aryaman be!
Propitious unto us, Indra! Bṛihaspati!
Propitious unto us, Vishṇu the Wide-strider!

[1] Or, 'in their presence not a word should be breathed by you.'

[2] Or, 'according to one's plenty,' *BR*. and *MW*.; hardly 'with grace.'

[3] With these exhortations on giving compare the 'Ode on Liberality,' RV. 10. 117.

[4] Identical with the First Anuvāka, except for certain changes of tense which are appropriate here in the conclusion.

Adoration to Brahma! Adoration to thee, Vāyu!

Thou, indeed, art the perceptible Brahma. Of thee, indeed, the perceptible Brahma, have I spoken. I have spoken of the right. I have spoken of the true. That has favored me. That has favored the speaker. It has favored me. It has favored the speaker.

Om! Peace! Peace! Peace!

SECOND VALLĪ

(Brahmānanda Vallī, 'Bliss-of-Brahma Chapter')

FIRST ANUVĀKA

The all-comprehensive Brahma of the world and of the individual; knowledge thereof the supreme success

Om! He who knows Brahma, attains the highest!

As to that this [verse] has been declared:—

He who knows Brahma as the real (*satya*), as knowledge (*jñāna*), as the infinite (*ananta*),[1]
Set down in the secret place [of the heart] and in the highest heaven (*parame vyoman*),[2]
He obtains all desires,
Together with the intelligent (*vipaścit*) Brahma.

The course of evolution from the primal Ātman through the five elements to the human person

From this Soul (*Ātman*), verily, space (*ākāśa*) arose; from space, wind (*vāyu*); from wind, fire; from fire, water; from water, the earth; from the earth, herbs; from herbs, food; from food, semen; from semen, the person (*puruṣa*).

The person consisting of food

This, verily, is the person that consists of the essence of food. This, indeed, is his head; this, the right side; this, the left

[1] Deussen proposes to emend *ānanda*, 'bliss,' in order to have the customary threefold definition of Brahma as *sat-cit-ānanda*, 'being, intelligence, and bliss,' and in order to introduce the great culminating thought of the chapter.

[2] A very common Vedic phrase for the abode of the gods.

side; this, the body (*ātman*); this, the lower part, the foundation.

As to that there is also this verse:—

Second Anuvāka

Food the supporting, yet consuming, substance of all life; a phase of Brahma

From food, verily, creatures are produced
Whatsoever [creatures] dwell on the earth.
Moreover by food, in truth, they live.
Moreover into it also they finally pass.[1]
For truly, food is the chief of beings;
Therefore it is called a panacea.[2]
Verily, they obtain all food
Who worship Brahma as food.
For truly, food is the chief of beings;
Therefore it is called a panacea.
From food created things are born.
By food, when born, do they grow up.
It both is eaten and eats things.
Because of that it is called food.[3]

The person consisting of breath

Verily, other than and within that one that consists of the essence of food is the self that consists of breath. By that this is filled. This, verily, has the form of a person. According to that one's personal form is this one with the form of a person. The in-breath (*prāṇa*) is its head; the diffused breath (*vyāna*), the right wing; the out-breath (*apāna*), the left wing; space, the body (*ātman*); the earth, the lower part, the foundation.

As to that there is also this verse:—

Third Anuvāka

Breath, the life of all living beings; a phase of Brahma

The gods do breathe along with breath (*prāṇa*),
As also men and beasts.
For truly, breath is the life (*āyus*) of beings
Therefore it is called the Life-of-all (*sarvāyuṣa*).

[1] These first four lines are quoted in Maitri 6. 11.
[2] *sarvauṣadham*, literally 'consisting of all sorts of herbs.'
[3] The last four lines recur at Maitri 6. 12.

To a full life (*sarvam āyus*) go they
Who worship Brahma as breath.
For truly, breath is the life of beings;
Therefore it is called the Life-of-all.

This, indeed, is its bodily self (*śarīra-ātman*), as of the former.

The person consisting of mind

Verily, other than and within that one that consists of breath is a self that consists of mind (*mano-maya*). By that this is filled. This, verily, has the form of a person. According to that one's personal form is this one with the form of a person. The Yajur-Veda is its head; the Rig-Veda, the right side; the Sāma-Veda, the left side; teaching,[1] the body (*ātman*); the Hymns of the Atharvans and Aṅgirases, the lower part, the foundation.

As to that there is also this verse:—

FOURTH ANUVĀKA

Inexpressible, fearless bliss; a phase of Brahma

Wherefrom words turn back,
Together with the mind, not having attained—
The bliss of Brahma he who knows,
Fears not at any time at all.

This, indeed, is its bodily self (*śarīra-ātman*), as of the former.

The person consisting of understanding

Verily, other than and within that one that consists of mind is a self that consists of understanding (*vijñāna-maya*). By that this is filled. This, verily, has the form of a person. According to that one's personal form is this one with the form of a person. Faith (*śraddhā*) is its head; the right (*ṛta*), the right side; the true (*satya*), the left side; contemplation (*yoga*), the body (*ātman*); might (*mahas*), the lower part, the foundation.

As to that there is also this verse:—

[1] Possibly referring to the Brāhmaṇas, which contain 'teaching' concerning the sacrifices.

Fifth Anuvāka

Understanding, all-directing; a saving and satisfying phase of Brahma

Understanding directs the sacrifice;
And deeds also it directs.
'Tis understanding that all the gods
Do worship as Brahma, as chief.

If one knows Brahma as understanding,
And if he is not heedless thereto,
He leaves his sins (*pāpman*) in the body
And attains all desires.

This, indeed, is its bodily self, as of the former.

The person consisting of bliss

Verily, other than and within that one that consists of understanding is a self that consists of bliss (*ānanda-maya*). By that this is filled. That one, verily, has the form of a person. According to that one's personal form is this one with the form of a person. Pleasure (*priya*) is its head; delight (*moda*), the right side; great delight (*pra-moda*), the left side; bliss (*ānanda*), the body (*ātman*); Brahma, the lower part, the foundation.

As to that there is also this verse:—

Sixth Anuvāka

Assimilation either to the original or to the derivative Brahma which one knows

Non-existent (*a-sat*) himself does one become,
If he knows that Brahma is non-existent.
If one knows that Brahma exists,
Such a one people thereby know as existent.

This, indeed, is its bodily self, as of the former.

Query: Who reaches the Brahma-world of bliss?

Now next, the appurtenant questions (*anu-praśna*):—

Does any one who knows not,
On deceasing, go to yonder world?
Or is it that any one who knows,
On deceasing, attains yonder world?

All plurality and antitheses of existence developed from an original and still immanent unity

He desired: 'Would that I were many! Let me procreate myself!' He performed austerity. Having performed austerity he created this whole world, whatever there is here. Having created it, into it, indeed, he entered. Having entered it, he became both the actual (*sat*) and the yon (*tya*), both the defined (*nirukta*) and the undefined, both the based and the non-based, both the conscious (*vijñāna*) and the unconscious, both the real (*satya*) and the false (*anṛta*). As the real, he became whatever there is here. That is what they call the real.

As to that there is also this verse:—

Seventh Anuvāka

The original self-developing non-existence, the essence of existence and the sole basis of fearless bliss

In the beginning, verily, this [world] was non-existent.
Therefrom, verily, Being (*sat*) was produced.[1]
That made itself (*svayam akuruta*) a Soul (Ātman).
Therefore it is called the well-done (*su-kṛta*).[2]

Verily, what that well-done is—that, verily, is the essence (*rasa*) [of existence]. For truly, on getting the essence, one becomes blissful. For who indeed would breathe, who would live, if there were not this bliss in space! For truly, this (essence) causes bliss. For truly, when one finds fearlessness as a foundation in that which is invisible, bodiless (*an-ātmya*), undefined, non-based, then he has reached fearlessness. When, however, one makes a cavity, an interval therein, then he comes to have fear. But that indeed is the fear of one who thinks of himself as a knower.[3]

As to that there is also this verse:—

[1] This theory is controverted at Chānd. 6. 2. 1–2.

[2] Compare the saying 'A person is a thing well done,' Ait. 1. 2. 3.

[3] But who really is not a knower. If the reading should be '*manvānasya* in accordance with Śaṅkara, then '. . . the fear of one who knows, but who is unthinking.'

Eighth Anuvāka

All cosmic activity through fear of the Supreme

Through fear of Him the Wind (Vāyu) doth blow.
Through fear of Him the Sun (Sūrya) doth rise.
Through fear of Him both Agni (Fire) and Indra
And Death (Mṛityu) as fifth do speed along.[1]

The gradation of blisses up to the bliss of Brahma [2]

This is a consideration (*mīmāṁsā*) of bliss.—

Let there be a youth, a good (*sādhu*) youth, well read, very quick, very firm, very strong. Let this whole earth be full of wealth for him. That is one human bliss.

A hundred human blisses are one bliss of the human Gandharvas (genii)—also of a man who is versed in the scriptures (*śrotriya*) and who is not smitten with desire.

A hundred blisses of the human Gandharvas are one bliss of the divine Gandharvas—also of a man who is versed in the scriptures and who is not smitten with desire.

A hundred blisses of the divine Gandharvas are one bliss of the fathers in their long-enduring world—also of a man who is versed in the scriptures and who is not smitten with desire.

A hundred blisses of the fathers in their long-enduring world are one bliss of the gods who are born so by birth (*ājāna-ja*)—also of a man who is versed in the scriptures and who is not smitten with desire.

A hundred blisses of the gods who are born so by birth are one bliss of the gods who are gods by work (*karma-deva*), who go to the gods by work—also of a man who is versed in the scriptures and who is not smitten with desire.

A hundred blisses of the gods who are gods by work are one bliss of the gods—also of a man who is versed in the scriptures and who is not smitten with desire.

A hundred blisses of the gods are one bliss of Indra—also of a man who is versed in the scriptures and who is not smitten with desire.

[1] A very similar stanza is Kaṭha 6. 3.

[2] Similar hierarchies of bliss leading up to the bliss of Brahma occur at Bṛih. 4. 3. 33 K and Śat. Br. 14. 7. 1. 31–39 (= Bṛih. 4. 3. 31–39 M). Other gradations of worlds up to the world of Brahma occur at Bṛih. 3. 6. 1 and Kaush. 1. 3.

A hundred blisses of Indra are one bliss of Bṛihaspati—also of a man who is versed in the scriptures and who is not smitten with desire.

A hundred blisses of Bṛihaspati are one bliss of Prajāpati—also of a man who is versed in the scriptures and who is not smitten with desire.

A hundred blisses of Prajāpati are one bliss of Brahma—also of a man who is versed in the scriptures and who is not smitten with desire.

The knower of the unity of the human person with the personality in the world reaches the self consisting of bliss

Both he who is here in a person and he who is yonder in the sun—he is one.

He who knows this, on departing from this world, proceeds on to that self which consists of food, proceeds on to that self which consists of breath, proceeds on to that self which consists of mind, proceeds on to that self which consists of understanding, proceeds on to that self which consists of bliss.[1]

As to that there is also this verse:—

NINTH ANUVĀKA

The knower of the bliss of Brahma is saved from all fear and from all moral self-reproach

Wherefrom words turn back,
Together with the mind, not having attained—
The bliss of Brahma he who knows,
Fears not from anything at all.[2]

Such a one, verily, the thought does not torment: 'Why have I not done the good (*sādhu*)? Why have I done the evil (*pāpa*)?'[3] He who knows this, delivers (*spṛṇute*) himself (*ātmānam*) from these two [thoughts]. For truly, from both of these he delivers himself—he who knows this!

Such is the mystic doctrine (*upaniṣad*)!

[1] That is, within the self there are various selves, but the true knower must advance to the highest self.

[2] This stanza has already occurred in 2. 4, with a verbal change in the last line.

[3] Or, 'What good have I failed to do? What evil have I done?'

THIRD VALLĪ

(Bhṛigu Vallī, 'Chapter concerning Bhrigu')

Bhṛigu's progressive learning through austerity of five phases of Brahma

1. Bhṛigu Vāruṇi, verily, approached his father Varuṇa, and said: 'Declare Brahma, sir!'[1]

To him he taught that as food, as breath, as sight, as hearing, as mind, as speech.

Then he said to him: 'That, verily, whence beings here are born, that by which when born they live, that into which on deceasing they enter—that be desirous of understanding. That is Brahma.'

He performed austerity. Having performed austerity, [2]
he understood that Brahma is food. For truly, indeed, beings
here are born from food, when born they live by food, on
deceasing they enter into food.

Having understood that, he again approached his father Varuṇa, and said: 'Declare Brahma, sir!'

Then he said to him: 'Desire to understand Brahma by austerity. Brahma is austerity (*tapas*).'

He performed austerity. Having performed austerity, [3]
he understood that Brahma is breath (*prāṇa*). For truly,
indeed, beings here are born from breath, when born they live
by breath, on deceasing they enter into breath.

Having understood that, he again approached his father Varuṇa, and said: 'Declare Brahma, sir!'

Then he said to him: 'Desire to understand Brahma by austerity. Brahma is austerity!'

He performed austerity. Having performed austerity, [4]
he understood that Brahma is mind (*manas*). For truly,
indeed, beings here are born from mind, when born they live
by mind, on deceasing they enter into mind.

Having understood that, he again approached his father Varuṇa, and said: 'Declare Brahma, sir!'

[1] Another course of instruction to Bhṛigu by his father Varuṇa occurs at Śat. Br. 11. 6. 1. 1–13.

Then he said to him: 'Desire to understand Brahma by austerity. Brahma is austerity.'

He performed austerity. Having performed austerity, [5] he understood that Brahma is understanding (*vijñāna*). For truly, indeed, beings here are born from understanding, when born they live by understanding, on deceasing they enter into understanding.

Having understood that, he again approached his father Varuṇa, and said: 'Declare Brahma, sir!'

Then he said to him: 'Desire to understand Brahma by austerity. Brahma is austerity.'

He performed austerity. Having performed austerity, [6] he understood that Brahma is bliss (*ānanda*). For truly, indeed, beings here are born from bliss, when born they live by bliss, on deceasing they enter into bliss.

This is the knowledge of Bhṛigu Vāruṇi, established in the highest heaven. He who knows this, becomes established. He becomes an eater of food, possessing food. He becomes great in offspring, in cattle, in the splendor of sacred knowledge, great in fame.

7. One should not blame food. That is the rule.

The reciprocal relations of food, supporting and supported, illustrated; the importance of such knowledge

Breath (*prāṇa*), verily, is food. The body is an eater of food. The body is established on breath; breath is established on the body. So food is established on food.

He who knows that food which is established on food, becomes established. He becomes an eater of food, possessing food. He becomes great in offspring, in cattle, in the splendor of sacred knowledge, great in fame.

8. One should not despise food. That is the rule.

Water, verily, is food. Light is an eater of food. Light is established on water; water is established on light. So food is established on food.

He who knows that food which is founded on food, becomes established. He becomes an eater of food, possessing food. He becomes great in offspring, in cattle, in the splendor of sacred knowledge, great in fame.

9. One should make for himself much food. That is the rule.

The earth, verily, is food. Space is an eater of food. Space is established on the earth; the earth is established on space. So food is established on food.

He who knows that food which is established on food, becomes established. He becomes an eater of food, possessing food. He becomes great in offspring, in cattle, in the splendor of sacred knowledge, great in fame.

A giver of food is prospered accordingly

10. (1) One should not refuse anyone at one's dwelling. That is the rule.

Therefore in any way whatsoever one should obtain much food. Of such a one people say: 'Food has succeeded (*arādhi*) for him!'

This food, verily, being prepared (*rāddha*) [for the suppliant] at the beginning, for him[1] food is prepared at the beginning. This food, verily, being prepared in the middle, for him food is prepared in the middle. This food, verily, being prepared at the end, for him food is prepared at the end—(2) for him who knows this.

Manifestations of Brahma as food

As preservation (*kṣema*) in speech, acquisition and preservation (*yoga-kṣema*) in the in-breath and the off-breath (*prāṇa-apāna*), work in the hands, motion in the feet, evacuation in the anus: these are the human recognitions [of Brahma as food].

Now the divine: satisfaction in rain, strength in lightning, (3) splendor in cattle, light in the stars, procreation, immortality, and bliss in the generative organ, the all in space.

The worshiper thereof appropriates the object of his worship

One should worship It as a foundation; one [then] becomes possessed of a foundation.

One should worship It as greatness; one becomes great.

One should worship It as mind (*manas*); one becomes possessed of mindfulness.

(4) One should worship It as adoration; desires make adoration to one

[1] That is, for the giver.

One should worship It as magic formula (*brahma*); one becomes possessed of magic formula.

One should worship It as 'the dying around the magic formula' (*brahmaṇaḥ parimara*)[1]; around one die his hateful rivals, and those who are his unfriendly foes.[2]

The knower of the unity of the human person with the universal Being attains unhampered desire

Both he who is here in a person and he who is yonder in the sun—he is one.

(5) He who knows this, on departing from this world, proceeding on to that self which consists of food, proceeding on to that self which consists of breath, proceeding on to that self which consists of mind, proceeding on to that self which consists of understanding, proceeding on to that self which consists of bliss, goes up and down these worlds, eating what he desires, assuming what form he desires. He sits singing this chant (*sāman*):—

A mystical rapture of the knower of the universal unity

Oh, wonderful! Oh, wonderful! Oh, wonderful!
(6) I am food! I am food! I am food!
I am a food-eater! I am a food-eater! I am a food-eater!
I am a fame-maker (*śloka-kṛt*)! I am a fame-maker! I am a fame-maker!
I am the first-born of the world-order (*ṛta*),[3]
Earlier than the gods, in the navel of immortality!
Who gives me away, he indeed has aided me!
I, who am food, eat the eater of food!
I have overcome the whole world!

He who knows this, has a brilliantly shining light.

Such is the mystic doctrine (*upaniṣad*)!

[1] An incantation described in Ait. Br. 8. 28. A philosophical interpretation of 'dying around Brahma' occurs at Kaush. 2. 12.

[2] The word *bhrātṛvya*, 'foes,' is of sociological significance, because etymologically it means 'cousin (father's brother's son).'

[3] A phrase occurring more than once in both RV. and AV., e. g. RV. 10. 61. 19 and AV. 6. 122. 1.

AITAREYA UPANISHAD

FIRST ADHYĀYA

First Khaṇḍa

The creation of the four worlds, of the cosmic person, and of cosmic powers by the primeval Self

1. In the beginning, Ātman (Self, Soul), verily, one only, was here[1]—no other winking thing whatever. He bethought himself: 'Let me now create worlds.'

2. He created these worlds: water (*ambhas*), light-rays (*marīci*), death (*mara*), the waters (*ap*). Yon is the water, above the heaven; the heaven is its support. The light-rays are the atmosphere; death, the earth; what is underneath, the waters.

3. He bethought himself: 'Here now are worlds. Let me now create world-guardians.' Right (*eva*) from the waters he drew forth and shaped (√*mūrch*) a person.

4. Upon him he brooded (*abhi* + √*tap*).

When he had been brooded upon, his mouth was separated out, egg-like; from the mouth, speech (*vāc*); from speech, Agni (Fire).

Nostrils were separated out; from the nostrils, breath (*prāṇa*); from breath, Vāyu (Wind).

Eyes were separated out; from the eyes, sight (*cakṣus*); from sight, Āditya (the Sun).

Ears were separated out; from the ears, hearing (*śrotra*); from hearing, the quarters of heaven.

Skin was separated out; from the skin, hairs; from the hairs, plants and trees.

A heart was separated out; from the heart, mind (*manas*); from mind, the moon.

[1] Instead of meaning 'here' adverbially (as very frequently in the Brāhmaṇas and sometimes in the Upanishads), *idam* may be the neuter demonstrative with an ellipsis, thus: 'Verily, this [universe] in the beginning was Ātman (Soul), one only, ...' This sentence stands also at the beginning of Bṛih. 1. 4. 1.

A navel was separated out; from the navel, the out-breath (*apāna*); from the out-breath, death (*mṛtyu*).

A virile member was separated out; from the virile member, semen; from the semen, water (*ap*).

SECOND KHAṆḌA

The ingredience of the cosmic powers in the human person

1. These divinities, having been created, fell headlong in this great restless sea.[1] He visited it with hunger and thirst.

They [i.e. the divinities] said to him: 'Find out for us an abode wherein we may be established and may eat food.'

2. He led up a bull to them. They said: 'Verily, this is not sufficient for us.'

He led up a horse to them. They said: 'Verily, this is not sufficient for us.'

3. He led up a person to them. They said: 'Oh! well done!'—Verily, a person is a thing well done.—

He said to them: 'Enter into your respective abodes.'

4. Fire became speech, and entered the mouth.

Wind became breath, and entered the nostrils.

The sun became sight, and entered the eyes.

The quarters of heaven became hearing, and entered the ears.

Plants and trees became hairs, and entered the skin.

The moon became mind, and entered the heart.

Death became the out-breath (*apāna*), and entered the navel.

Waters became semen, and entered the virile member.

5. Hunger and thirst said to him [i.e. Ātman]: 'For us two also[2] find out [an abode].'

Unto the two he said: 'I assign you two a part among these divinities. I make you two partakers among them.' Therefore to whatever divinity an oblation is made, hunger and thirst become partakers in it.

[1] Skt. *arṇava*: etymologically 'the moving,' 'the stirring,' 'the agitated', specifically, simply 'sea,' as in Chānd. 8. 5. 3, 4.

[2] Reading *api prajanīhi*, instead of the (otherwise unquotable) compound *abhiprajanīhi*—according to Böhtlingk's emendation in his translation, p. 166. This change brings the form of the question into uniformity with the similar question in § 1.

THIRD KHAṆḌA

The creation of food of fleeting material form, and the inability of various personal functions to obtain it

1. He bethought himself: 'Here now are worlds and world-guardians. Let me create food for them.'

2. He brooded upon the waters. From them, when they had been brooded upon, a material form (*mūrti*) was produced. Verily, that material form which was produced—verily, that is food.

3. Having been created, it sought to flee away.

He sought to seize it with speech. He was not able to grasp it with speech. If indeed he had grasped it with speech, merely with uttering food one would have been satisfied.

4. He sought to grasp it with breath. He was not able to grasp it with breath. If indeed he had grasped it with breath, merely with breathing toward food one would have been satisfied.

5. He sought to grasp it with sight. He was not able to grasp it with sight. If indeed he had grasped it with sight, merely with seeing food one would have been satisfied.

6. He sought to grasp it with hearing. He was not able to grasp it with hearing. If indeed he had grasped it with hearing, merely with hearing food one would have been satisfied.

7. He sought to grasp it with the skin. He was not able to grasp it with the skin. If indeed he had grasped it with the skin, merely with touching food one would have been satisfied.

8. He sought to grasp it with the mind. He was not able to grasp it with the mind. If indeed he had grasped it with the mind, merely with thinking on food one would have been satisfied.

9. He sought to grasp it with the virile member. He was not able to grasp it with the virile member. If indeed he had grasped it with the virile member, merely with emitting food one would have been satisfied.

10. He sought to grasp it with the out-breath (*apāna*—the

digestive breath). He consumed[1] it. This grasper of food is what wind (*vāyu*) is. This one living on food (*annāyu*), verily, is what wind is.

The entrance of the Self into the body

11. He [i. e. Ātman] bethought himself: 'How now could this thing exist without me?'

He bethought himself: 'With which should I enter?'

He bethought himself: 'If with speech there is uttered, if with breath (*prāṇa*) there is breathed, if with sight there is seen, if with hearing there is heard, if with the skin there is touched, if with the mind there is thought, if with the out-breath (*apāna*) there is breathed out, if with the virile member there is emitted, then who am I?'

12. So, cleaving asunder this very[2] hair-part (*sīman*),[3] by that door he entered. This is the door named 'the cleft' (*vidṛti*). That is the delighting (*nāndana*).

He has three dwelling-places, three conditions of sleep. This is a dwelling-place. This is a dwelling-place. This is a dwelling-place.[4]

The mystic name of the sole self-existent Self

13. Having been born, he looked around on beings (*bhūta*), [thinking]: 'Of what here would one desire to speak[5] as

[1] *āvayat*, imperfect causative of √*av*; exactly like the *annam āvayat*, 'he consumed food' of RV. 10. 113. 8, and also like AV. 4. 6. 3; 5. 19. 2; VS. 21. 44; Śat. Br. 1. 6. 3. 5; 5. 5. 4. 6. Possible, but unparalleled, would be the derivation from *ā* + √*vī*, 'he overtook.' An etymologizing on *vāyu*.

[2] Probably accompanied with a deictic gesture.

[3] That is, the sagittal suture; or perhaps less specifically 'the crown.'

[4] Śaṅkara explains that the right eye is the abode during the waking state, the inner mind (*antar-manas*) during dreaming sleep, the space of the heart (*hṛdayākāśa*) during profound sleep (*suṣupti*). He offers the alternative that the three abodes are 'the body of one's father,' 'the womb of one's mother,' and 'one's own body.' Sāyaṇa and Ānandagiri understand the three abodes as 'the right eye,' 'the throat,' 'the heart.' With whatever significance, it would seem that the three demonstratives of the text must have been accompanied by explanatory pointings to certain parts of the body.

The three 'conditions of sleep' (together with a fourth) are mentioned in the Māṇḍūkya Upanishad even as they are explained by the commentators on this passage. It is in contrast with the desired condition of the metaphysically awakened self that the ordinary condition of waking is regarded as 'sleep.'

[5] Or, 'What here would desire to speak of another?' However, for this con-

another?' He saw this very person as veriest (*tatama*) Brahma. 'I have seen It (*idam adarśa*),' said he (*iti*).

14. Therefore his name is Idaṁ-dra ('It-seeing'). Idaṁ-dra, verily, is his name. Him who is Idaṁ-dra they call 'Indra' cryptically, for the gods are fond of the cryptic (*parokṣa-priya*), as it were[1]—for the gods are fond of the cryptic, as it were.

SECOND ADHYĀYA

Fourth Khaṇḍa

A self's three successive births

1. In a person (*puruṣa*), verily, this one[2] becomes at first an embryo (*garbha*). That which is semen (*retas*), is the vigor (*tejas*) come together from all the limbs. In the self, indeed, one bears a self. When he pours this in a woman, then he begets it. This is one's first birth.[3]

2. It comes into self-becoming (*ātma-bhūya*) with the woman,

struction the neuter subject and the masculine object do not seem quite congruous. Or, 'Why (or, how) here would one desire to speak of another?' Or again, *kim* may be simply the interrogative particle: 'Would one here desire to speak of another?' In addition to these uncertainties of syntax, the form of the verb causes difficulty. *Vāvadiṣat* seems to contain unmistakable elements of the intensive and of the desiderative conjugations of $\sqrt{vad}$, 'speak'; yet as it stands it is utterly anomalous. The Indian commentators furnish no help to a solution. *BR.* (vol. 6, column 650) proposes to emend to *vāvadisyat*, the future of the intensive. Böhtlingk, in his translation, pp. 169, 170, emends to *vāva diśet*, '(to see) whether anything here would point to another [than it].' And in a note there he reports Delbrück's conjecture, *vivadiṣat*, the participle of the desiderative, which would yield the translation: 'What is there here desiring to speak of another?' Deussen somehow finds a reflexive: 'What wishes to explain itself here as one different [from me]?'

In spite of the verbal difficulties, the meaning of the passage is fairly intelligible: it is a pictorial statement of a philosophical idealism (i. e. that there is naught else than spirit) bordering on solipsism (i. e. that there is naught else than the individual self).

[1] This phrase occurs verbatim in Bṛih. 4. 2. 2; Ait. Br. 3. 33 end; 7. 30 end; and almost verbatim in Śat. Br. 6. 1. 1. 2, 11.

[2] That is, the Ātman, the subject of the entire previous part of this Upanishad. Or *ayam* may denote the indefinite 'one,' as probably in the last sentence of this paragraph.

[3] The words *asya prathamaṁ janma* may denote either 'his (i. e. the Self's) first birth' or 'a self's first birth (as a particular individual).' Either interpretation is possible according to pantheistic theory.

just as a limb of her own. Therefore it injures her not. She nourishes this self of his that has come to her.

3. She, being a nourisher, should be nourished. The woman bears him as an embryo. In the beginning, indeed, he nourishes the child [and] from birth onward. While[1] he nourishes the child from birth onward, he thus nourishes his own self, for the continuation of these worlds; for thus are these worlds continued. This is one's second birth.

4. This self of one is put in one's place for pious deeds (*puṇya karman*). Then this other self of one, having done his work (*kṛta-kṛtya*), having reached his age, deceases. So, deceasing hence indeed, he is born again. This is one's third birth. As to this it has been said by a seer:—

5. Being yet in embryo, I knew well[2]
All the births of these gods!

[1] Or perhaps 'In that (*yat*) . . . .'

[2] Quoted from RV. 4. 27. 1. In the original Rig-Veda passage (as indeed in every other of the three occurrences of the same compound in the Rig-Veda, 1. 34. 2b, 1. 164. 18b, and 10. 17. 5a) the preposition *anu* seems to have served no more than to strengthen the force of the verb 'know.' As such, it is translated here by 'well' (in accordance with Grassmann's *Wörterbuch*, *BR.*, and *MW.*). Yet it would be very possible—indeed, probable—that to the author of this Upanishad, who quotes the ancient passage as scriptural corroboration of his theory of various births, that word *anu* conveyed a larger significance than it was originally intended to express. In accordance with its general meaning of 'along toward' he might understand it to intimate pregnantly that even from the embryonic stage the seer 'fore-knew,' *anu-vid*, all the births of the gods [of the various gods—be it noted —here applied to the successive births of the individual soul, *ātman*, from father to son]. As to such fine distinctions of meaning to be carefully observed in the prepositional compounds with verbs in the Upanishads, Professor Whitney (in his article on 'The Upanishads and their Latest Translation' in the *American Journal of Philology*, vol. 7, p. 15) has stated a noteworthy principle: 'It may be laid down as a rule for the prose of the Brāhmaṇas and Upanishads that every prefix to a verb has its own distinctive value as modifying the verbal idea: if we cannot feel it, our comprehension of the sense is so far imperfect; if we cannot represent it, our translation is so far defective.'

With this consideration concerning the force of *anu* and with the glaringly wresting interpretation of *śyeno* in the last line, the present instance as a whole serves well to call attention to the applicability (or non-applicability) of many of the citations in the Upanishads. Frequently passages from the Rig-Veda and from the Atharva-Veda are quoted as containing, in cryptic expressions of deep significance, early corroboration of what is really a later and very different idea. This method of the Upanishads with respect to its prior scriptures is the same method as that employed by the later Hindu commentators on the Upanishads themselves. In the course of the developments of thought this method of interpreting earlier ideas from a larger point of view is very serviceable; practically and pedagogically

A hundred iron citadels confined me,
And yet,[1] a hawk (*śyena*) with swiftness, forth I flew!

In embryo indeed thus lying (*śayāna*), Vāmadeva spoke in this wise.

6. So he, knowing this, having ascended aloft from this separation from the body (*śarīra-bheda*), obtained all desires in the heavenly world (*svarga-loka*), and became immortal—yea, became [immortal]!

THIRD ADHYĀYA

Fifth Khaṇḍa

The pantheistic Self

1. [Question:] Who is this one?[2]

[Answer:] We worship him as the Self (Ātman).

[Question:] Which one[3] is the Self?

[Answer:] [He] whereby one sees,[4] or whereby one hears,[5] or whereby one smells odors, or whereby one articulates speech, or whereby one discriminates the sweet and the unsweet; [2] that which is heart (*hṛdaya*) and mind (*manas*)—that is, consciousness (*saṁjñāna*), perception (*ājñāna*), discrimination (*vijñāna*), intelligence (*prajñāna*), wisdom (*medhas*), insight (*dṛṣṭi*), steadfastness (*dhṛti*), thought (*mati*), thoughtfulness (*manīṣā*), impulse (*jūti*), memory (*smṛti*), conception (*saṁkalpa*), purpose (*kratu*), life (*asu*), desire (*kāma*), will (*vaśa*).

it may be almost indispensable to the expounder of a philosophy or to the exhorter of a religion; yet by the scholar it is to be carefully discriminated from a historically exact exegesis of the primitive statements.

[1] Reading *adha*, as in the Rig-Veda passage and in a variant of Śaṅkara. But all editions of the text and of the commentators read *adhaḥ*, 'down.'

[2] The interpretation of *ayam* here is doubtless the same as in the opening sentence of the previous Adhyāya. See note 2 on p. 298.

All the published texts read *'yam*. But Müller and Böhtlingk emend to *yam*. With this reading and with another grouping of words the entire section might be rendered as forming consecutive queries, thus:—

'[Question:] Who is he whom we worship as the Self (Ātman)? Which one is the Self? [He] whereby one . . . . or . . . . or . . . . the unsweet?'

Then the remainder of the Adhyāya would form the answer.

[3] That is, which one of the two selves previously mentioned? the primeval, universal Self? or the individual self?

[4] Roer and the Bombay editions have here, in addition, *rūpam*, 'form.'

[5] Roer and the Bombay editions have here, in addition, *śabdam*, 'sound.'

All these, indeed, are appellations of intelligence (*prajñāna*).

3. He is Brahma; he is Indra; he is Prajāpati; [he is] all these gods; and these five gross elements (*mahā-bhūtāni*), namely earth (*pṛthivī*), wind (*vāyu*), space (*ākāśa*), water (*āpas*), light (*jyotīṁṣi*); these things and those which are mingled of the fine (*kṣudra*), as it were; origins (*bīja*)[1] of one sort and another: those born from an egg (*aṇḍa-ja*), and those born from a womb (*jāru-ja*), and those born from sweat (*sveda-ja*),[2] and those born from a sprout (*udbhij-ja*); horses, cows, persons, elephants; whatever breathing thing there is here—whether moving or flying, and what is stationary.

All this is guided by intelligence, is based on intelligence. The world is guided by intelligence. The basis is intelligence. Brahma is intelligence.

4. So he [i. e. Vāmadeva], having ascended aloft from this world with that intelligent Self (Ātman), obtained all desires in yon heavenly world, and became immortal—yea, became [immortal]!

Thus (*iti*)! *Om*!

[1] Literally, 'seeds.'

[2] This item may be a later addition to the other three, which are already similarly classified in Chānd. 6. 3. 1.

KAUSHITAKI UPANISHAD[1]

FIRST ADHYĀYA

The course of reincarnation, and its termination through metaphysical knowledge[2]

Citra and Śvetaketu concerning the path to the conclusion of reincarnation

1. Citra Gāṅgyāyani,[3] verily, being about to sacrifice, chose Āruṇi.[4] He then dispatched his son Śvetaketu, saying: 'You perform the sacrifice.' When he had arrived,[5] he asked of him: 'Son of Gautama,[6] is there a conclusion [of transmigration] in the world in which you will put me? Or is there any road? Will you put me in its world?'

Then he said: 'I know not this. However, let me ask the teacher.' Then he went to his father and asked: 'Thus and so has he asked me. How should I answer?'

Then he said: 'I too know not this. Let us pursue Veda-study (*svādhyāya*) at [his] residence, and get what our betters give. Come! Let us both go.'

Then, fuel in hand, he returned to Citra Gāṅgyāyani, and said: 'Let me come to you as a pupil.'

To him then he said: 'Worthy of sacred knowledge (*brahma*) are you, O Gautama, who have gone not unto conceit. Come! I will cause you to understand.'

[1] Throughout the notes to this Upanishad the character A designates the recension published in the Ānandāśrama Sanskrit Series, and B designates the recension published in the Bibliotheca Indica Series.

[2] Other expositions of this subject occur at Chānd. 5. 3-10 and Bṛih. 6. 2.

[3] Or Gārgyāyaṇi, according to another reading.

[4] That is, as officiating priest.—Com.

[5] So B, *abhyāgataṁ*; but A has, instead, *asīnaṁ*, 'when he was seated.'

[6] So A: *putra 'sti*; but B has the (less appropriate) reading *putro 'si*, 'You are the son of Gautama! Is there . . .'

The testing at the moon; thence either return to earth or further progress

2. Then he said: 'Those who, verily, depart from this world—to the moon, in truth, they all go. During the earlier half it thrives on their breathing spirits (*prāṇa*); with the latter half[1] it causes them to be reproduced. This, verily, is the door of the heavenly world—that is, the moon. Whoever answers it, him it lets go further. But whoever answers it not, him, having become rain, it rains down here. Either as a worm, or as a moth, or as a fish, or as a bird, or as a lion, or as a wild boar,[2] or as a snake, or as a tiger, or as a person, or as some other in this or that condition, he is born again here according to his deeds (*karman*), according to his knowledge.

When he comes thither it asks him: 'Who are you?'

He should reply:—

'From the far-shining,[3] O ye seasons, has semen been gathered,
From the fifteenfold produced,[3] from the realm of the fathers.[3]
As such send ye me in a man as an agent.
With a man as an agent in a mother infuse me.

So am I born, being born forth[4] as the twelfth or thirteenth succeeding month, by means of a twelve- or thirteen-fold father.[5] For the knowledge of this was I—for the knowledge of the opposite of this.[6] So bring ye my seasons on to

[1] Reading *aparapakṣeṇa*.

[2] In A this item is lacking, and the order of the series is different.

[3] That is, the moon.—Com.

[4] *upa-jāyamāna*: or perhaps 're-born,' a meaning which is used in the BhG. and MBh.

[5] That is, the year.—Com.

[6] 'This' = *brahma*, according to the Com. The idea is perhaps: 'A person's life is either unto knowledge of the truth, or unto ignorance.' Deussen interprets more specifically, with reference to 'the two paths' which are being expounded in this chapter, that 'this' refers to the *devayāna*, 'the path to the gods,' and 'the opposite of this' to the *pitṛyāna*, 'the path to the fathers.' Böhtlingk makes an ingenious text-emendation: *saṁ tad vide 'ham, prati tad vide 'ham*, instead of *'saṁ tadvide 'ham, pratitadvide 'ham*. But the result, 'I am conscious of this; I recollect this,' does not seem as probable as the traditional reading, although that itself does not seem altogether correct. Böhtlingk's article 'Bemerkungen zu einigen Upanishaden' contains on pp. 98-99 a rejoinder to Deussen on this same passage.

immortality. By this truth, by this austerity I am a season, I am connected with the seasons. Who am I? I am you.'

It lets him go further.

The course to the Brahma-world

3. Having entered upon this Devayāna ('Leading-to-the-gods') path, he comes to the world of Agni (Fire), then to the world of Vāyu (Wind), then to the world of Varuṇa,[1] then to the world of Indra, then to the world of Prajāpati, then to the world of Brahma. This Brahma-world, verily, has the lake Āra, the moments Yeshṭiha, the river Vijarā ('Ageless'), the tree Ilya, the city Sālajya, the abode Aparājita ('Unconquered'), the two door-keepers Indra and Prajāpati, the hall Vibhu ('Extensive'), the throne Vicakshaṇā ('Far-shining'), the couch Amitaujas ('Of Unmeasured Splendor'), and the beloved Mānasī ('Mental'), and her counterpart Cākshushī ('Visual'), both of whom, taking flowers, verily weave the worlds, and the Apsarases (Nymphs), Ambās ('Mothers') and Ambāyavīs ('Nurses'), and the rivers Ambayā ('Little Mothers'). To it comes he who knows this. To him Brahma says: 'Run ye to him! With my glory, verily, he has reached the river Vijarā ('Ageless'). He, verily, will not grow old.'

The knower's triumphal progress through the Brahma-world

4. Unto him there go forth five hundred Apsarases, one hundred with fruits in their hands, one hundred with ointments in their hands, one hundred with garlands in their hands, one hundred with vestments in their hands, one hundred with powdered aromatics in their hands. They adorn him with the adornment of Brahma. He, having been adorned with the adornment of Brahma, a knower of Brahma, unto Brahma goes on. He comes to the lake Āra. This he crosses with his mind. On coming to it, those who know only the immediate, sink. He comes to the moments Yeshṭiha. These run away from him. He comes to the river Vijarā ('Ageless'). This he crosses with his mind alone (*eva*). There he shakes off his

[1] Here A adds 'then to the world of Āditya (the Sun).'

good deeds and his evil deeds. His dear relatives succeed to the good deeds; those not dear, to the evil deeds. Then, just as one driving a chariot looks down upon the two chariot-wheels, thus he looks down upon day and night, thus upon good deeds and evil deeds, and upon all the pairs of opposites. This one, devoid of good deeds, devoid of evil deeds, a knower of Brahma, unto very Brahma goes on.

Approaching unto the very throne of Brahma

5. He comes to the tree Ilya; the fragrance of Brahma enters into him.

He comes to the city Sālajya; the flavor of Brahma enters into him.

He comes to the abode Aparājita ('Unconquered'); the brilliancy of Brahma enters into him.

He comes to the two doorkeepers, Indra and Prajāpati; these two run away from him.

He comes to the hall Vibhu ('Extensive'); the glory of Brahma enters into him.

He comes to the throne Vicakshaṇā ('Far-shining').[1] The Bṛihad and the Rathantara Sāmans are its two fore feet; the Śyaita and the Naudhasa, the two hind feet; the Vairūpa and the Vairāja, the two lengthwise pieces; the Sākvara and Raivata, the two cross ones. It is Intelligence (*prajñā*), for by intelligence one discerns.

He comes to the couch Amitaujas ('Of Unmeasured Splendor'); this is the breathing spirit (*prāṇa*). The past and the future are its two fore feet; prosperity and refreshment, the two hind feet; the Bhadra and Yajñāyajñīya [Sāmans], the two head pieces; the Bṛihad and the Rathantara, the two lengthwise pieces; the verses (*ṛc*) and the chants (*sāman*), the cords stretched lengthwise; the sacrificial formulas (*yajus*), the cross ones; the Soma-stems, the spread; the Udgītha, the bolster (*upaśrī*); prosperity, the pillow. Thereon Brahmā sits. He who knows this, ascends it with one foot only (*eva*) at first.

[1] The combined descriptions of the throne and of the couch are very similar to the description of Vrātya's seat in AV. 15. 3. 3-9, and also of Indra's throne in Ait. Br. 8. 12.

Him Brahmā asks: 'Who are you?' To him he should answer:—

Essential identity with the infinite Real

6. 'I am a season. I am connected with the seasons. From space as a womb I am produced as the semen for a wife,[1] as the brilliance of the year, as the soul (*ātman*) of every single being. You are the soul of every single being. What you are, this am I.'

To him he says: 'Who am I?'

He should say: 'The Real.'

'What is that, namely the Real (*satyam*)?'

'Whatever is other than the sense-organs (*deva*) and the vital breaths (*prāṇa*)—that is the actual (*sat*). But as for the sense-organs and the vital breaths—that is the yon (*tyam*). This is expressed by this word "*satyam*" ('the Real'). It is as extensive as this world-all. You are this world-all.'

Thus he speaks to him then. This very thing is declared by a Rig[-Veda] verse:—

Apprehension of It through the Sacred Word and through all the functions of a person; the knower's universal possession

7. Having the Yajus as his belly, having the Sāman as his head,
Having the Rig as his form, yonder Imperishable
'Is Brahma!' Thus is he to be discerned—
The great seer, consisting of the Sacred Word (*brahma-maya*).[2]

He says to him: 'Wherewith do you acquire (√*āp*) my masculine names?'

'With the vital breath (*prāṇa*, masc.),' he should answer.

'Wherewith feminine names?'[3]

'With speech (*vāc*, fem.).'

'Wherewith neuter ones?'[3]

[1] So B: *bhāryāyai retas*. A has instead *bhāyā(s) etad*, '... produced—from light; thus [I am] the brilliance...'

[2] The passage from the last sentence in the preceding section through this stanza is not found in some manuscripts, is not commented on by Śaṅkarānanda, and therefore is very probably an interpolation.

[3] Such is the order in A; but in B the items about 'feminine names' and 'neuter names' are transposed.

'With the mind (*manas*, neut.).'
'Wherewith odors?'
'With the breath (*prāṇa*[1]).'
'Wherewith forms?'
'With the eye.'
'Wherewith sounds?'
'With the ear.'
'Wherewith the flavors of food?'
'With the tongue.'
'Wherewith actions?'
'With the two hands.'
'Wherewith pleasure and pain?'
'With the body.'
'Wherewith bliss, delight, and procreation?'
'With the generative organ.'
'Wherewith goings?'
'With the two feet.'
'Wherewith thoughts, what is to be understood, and desires?'
'With intelligence (*prajñā*),' he should say.

To him he says: 'The [primeval] waters [and also: Acquisitions],[2] verily, indeed, are my world. It is yours.'

Whatever conquest is Brahma's, whatever attainment—that conquest he conquers, that attainment he attains who knows this—yea, who knows this!

SECOND ADHYĀYA

The doctrine of Prāṇa, together with certain ceremonies

Identity with Brahma; its value in service and security to oneself

1. 'The breathing spirit (*prāṇa*) is Brahma'—thus indeed was Kaushītaki wont to say.

[1] A variant in both A and B is *ghrāṇa*, 'smell.'

[2] The Com. explains *āpas* as meaning 'the primary elements.' But the word very probably has a double significance in this connection; beside its evident meaning, it refers also (though as an artificial plural of √*āp*) to the preceding questions, 'Wherewith do you acquire (√*āp*) . . .' The usual Upanishadic conclusion of such a series would very appropriately be formed if the word meant, summarily, 'acquisitions.'

Of this same breathing spirit as Brahma, verily, indeed, the mind (*manas*) is the messenger; the eye, the watchman; the ear, the announcer; speech, the handmaid.[1]

He who, verily, indeed, knows the mind as the messenger of this breathing spirit, [i.e.] of Brahma, becomes possessed of a messenger; he who knows the eye as the watchman, becomes possessed of a watchman; he who knows the ear as the announcer, becomes possessed of an announcer; he who knows speech as the handmaid, becomes possessed of a handmaid.[2]

To this same breathing spirit as Brahma, verily, all these divinities without his begging bring offering. Likewise, indeed, to this same breathing spirit all beings without his begging bring offering.

Of him who knows this, the doctrine (*upaniṣad*) is: 'One should not beg.' It is as if, having begged of a village and not having received, one were to sit down,[3] saying: 'I would not eat anything given from here!' and then those very ones who formerly refused him invite him, saying: 'Let us give to you!' Such is the virtue (*dharma*) of the non-beggar.[4] Charitable people, however, address him, saying: 'Let us give to you!'

2. 'The breathing spirit (*prāṇa*) is Brahma'—thus, indeed, was Paiṅgya wont to say.

Of this same breathing spirit as Brahma, verily, off behind the speech the eye is enclosed; off behind the eye the ear is enclosed; off behind the ear the mind is enclosed; off behind the mind the breathing spirit is enclosed.

To this same breathing spirit as Brahma, verily, all these

[1] In A this item about 'speech' comes directly after 'mind.'

[2] This paragraph is lacking in A.

[3] Or, 'fast upon [the village].' For the practice of 'suicide by starvation' see the article by Prof. Hopkins in *JAOS*. 21. 146–159, especially p. 159, where this very passage is discussed.

[4] The idea would seem to be: 'Such (i. e. the same) is true of the non-beggar who knows. Without his begging, however, he too receives.' But, instead of the *ayācatas* of B, A has *yācitas*, i. e. 'of the beggar.' Then the idea would seem to be: 'Such (i. e. as has been described) is the virtue of the beggar. He finally receives. He who knows, however—he, too, finally receives without begging solely because of his knowing.' With either reading the meaning is not altogether explicit.

divinities without his begging bring offering. Likewise, indeed, to him all beings without his begging bring offering.

Of him who knows this, the doctrine (*upaniṣad*) is: 'One should not beg.' It is as if, having begged of a village and not having received, one were to sit down, saying: 'I would not eat anything given from here!' and then those very ones who formerly refused him invite him, saying: 'Let us give to you!' Such is the virtue of the non-beggar.[1] Charitable people, however, address him, saying: 'Let us give to you!'

3 (2). Now next, the procuring of a special prize.—

In case one should covet a special prize—either on the night of a full moon or on the night of a new moon, or during the bright half of the moon under an auspicious constellation—at one of these points of time,[2] having built up a fire, having swept around, having sprinkled around, having purified,[3] having bent the right knee, with a spoon (*sruva*) or with a wooden bowl (*camasa*) or with a metal cup (*kaṁsa*),[4] he offers these oblations of melted butter:—

'The divinity named Speech is a procurer. May it procure this thing for me from so-and-so! To it, hail (*svāhā*)!

The divinity named Breath (*prāṇa*) is a procurer. May it procure this thing for me from so-and-so! To it, hail!

The divinity named Eye is a procurer. May it procure this thing for me from so-and-so! To it, hail!

The divinity named Ear is a procurer. May it procure this thing for me from so-and-so! To it, hail!

The divinity named Mind is a procurer. May it procure this thing for me from so-and-so! To it, hail!

The divinity named Intelligence is a procurer. May it procure this thing for me from so-and-so! To it, hail!'

Then having sniffed the smell of the smoke, having rubbed his limbs over with a smearing of the melted butter, silently he should go forth[5] and declare his object, or despatch a messenger. He obtains indeed.

[1] See note 4 on p. 308.
[2] This phrase is lacking in A.
[3] This word is lacking in B.
[4] The two last alternatives are lacking in B.
[5] From the place of the oblations to the house of the possessor of the object. Com.

To win another's affection

4 (3). Now next, longing in connection with the divine powers[1] (*daiva smara*).—

If one should desire to become beloved of a man, or of a woman, or of men, or of women—at one of these same [aforementioned] points of time, having built up a fire,[2] he in the same manner offers these oblations of melted butter:—

'Your Speech I sacrifice in me, you so-and-so! Hail!
Your Breath I sacrifice in me, you so-and-so! Hail!
Your Eye I sacrifice in me, you so-and-so! Hail!
Your Ear I sacrifice in me, you so-and-so! Hail!
Your Mind I sacrifice in me, you so-and-so! Hail!
Your Intelligence I sacrifice in me, you so-and-so! Hail!'

Then, having sniffed the smell of the smoke, having rubbed his limbs over with a smearing of the melted butter, silently he should go forth and desire to approach and touch, or he may simply stand and converse from windward. He becomes beloved indeed. They long for him indeed.

The perpetual sacrifice of self

5 (4). Now next, the matter of self-restraint (*sāṁyamana*) according to Pratardana, or the 'Inner Agnihotra Sacrifice,' as they call it.—

As long, verily, as a person is speaking, he is not able to breathe. Then he is sacrificing breath (*prāṇa*) in speech.

As long, verily, as a person is breathing, he is not able to speak. Then he is sacrificing speech (*vāc*) in breath.

These two are unending, immortal oblations; whether waking or sleeping, one is sacrificing continuously, uninterruptedly.[3] Now, whatever other oblations there are, they are limited, for they consist of works (*karma-maya*). Knowing this very thing, verily, indeed, the ancients did not sacrifice the Agnihotra sacrifice.

[1] Namely Speech, Breath, Eye, Ear, Mind, and Intelligence—enumerated in the previous section.

[2] This phrase is lacking in B.

[3] This word is lacking in B.

Glorification of the Uktha[1]

6. 'The Uktha (Recitation) is *brahma* (sacred word)'—thus indeed was Śushkabṛiṅgāra wont to say.

One should reverence it as the Rig (Hymn of Praise); unto such a one indeed all beings sing praise (*ṛc*) for his supremacy.

One should reverence it as the Yajus (Sacrificial Formula); unto such a one indeed all beings are united (*yujyante*) for his supremacy.

One should reverence it as the Sāman (Chant); unto such a one indeed all beings bow down (*saṁnamante*) for his supremacy.

One should reverence it as beauty (*śrī*).

One should reverence it as glory (*yaśas*).

One should reverence it as brilliancy (*tejas*).

As this [i.e. the Uktha] is the most beautiful, the most glorious, the most brilliant among the Śastras (Invocations of Praise)—even so is he who knows this, the most beautiful, the most glorious, the most brilliant among all beings.

So the Adhvaryu priest prepares (*saṁskaroti*) this soul (*ātman*) that is related to the sacrifice,[2] that consists of works. On it he weaves what consists of the Yajus. On what consists of the Yajus the Hotṛi priest weaves what consists of the Rig. On what consists of the Rig the Udgātṛi priest weaves what consists of the Sāman. This is the soul of all the threefold knowledge. And thus he who knows this, becomes the soul of Indra.[3]

Daily adoration of the sun for the removal of sin

7 (5). Now next are the all-conquering Kaushītaki's three adorations.—

The all-conquering Kaushītaki indeed was wont to[4] worship the rising sun—having performed the investiture with the sacred

[1] Compare the identification of the Uktha with *Prāṇa* at Bṛih. 5. 13. 1.

[2] So B, *aiṣṭikam*; A has instead, *aiṣṭakam*, 'that is related to the sacrificial bricks.'

[3] So B. Instead of this sentence, A has: 'And this is the soul of a person. Thus he becomes a soul who knows this.'

[4] The preceding words of this sentence are lacking in A. That has simply 'He would worship ...'

thread (*yajñopavītaṁ*),[1] having sipped[2] water, thrice having sprinkled the water-vessel—saying: 'Thou art a snatcher! Snatch my sin (*pāpman*)!'

In the same manner [he was wont to worship the sun] when it was in the mid-heaven: 'Thou art a snatcher-up! Snatch up my sin!'

In the same manner [he was wont to worship the sun] when it was setting: 'Thou art a snatcher-away! Snatch away my sin!'

Whatever evil (*pāpa*) he committed by day or night, it snatches away.[3]

Likewise also he who knows this, worships the sun in the same manner.[3] Whatever evil one commits by day or night, it snatches away.

Regular adoration of the new moon for prosperity

8. Now, month by month on the night of the new moon when it comes around[4] one should, in the same manner, worship the moon as it appears in the west; or he casts two blades of green grass[5] toward it, saying:—

'That heart of mine of contour fair (*susīma*)
Which in the moon in heaven rests—
I ween myself aware of that!
May I not weep for children's ill!'[6]

[1] This probably is the earliest reference to the Indian religious custom of investing the twice-born with a sacred thread to be worn over the left shoulder. —Max Müller (*SBE.* 1. 285, note 1).

[2] Thus **A**: *ācamya*; **B**, instead, has *ānīya*, 'having fetched.'

[3] The preceding sentence is lacking in **A**.

[4] This word, *vṛttāyām*, is lacking in **A**.

[5] Instead of this phrase *harita-tṛṇe vā praty-asyati*, **A** has *harita-tṛṇābhyāṁ vāk praty-asyati* . . . , 'with two blades of green grass speech casts toward . . .'

[6] So in **B**; but in **A** this stanza reads:—

'That heart of thine of contour fair
Which rests up in the moon—with that,
O queen of immortality,
May I not weep for children's ill!'

The meaning of '*su-sīmaṁ*' in the first line is uncertain. *sīman*, the base of this compound, is used (according to the references in *BR.*) to mean either the line of the hair-part or the line of a boundary, i. e. out-line. In the case-form in which the compound occurs in this passage it must needs, apparently, agree with 'heart'; and its meaning would involve the second-mentioned meaning of the base. Accordingly, in this poetical passage, it is rendered 'of contour fair.' This stanza

In advance of such a one, indeed, his progeny decease not. —Thus in the case of one to whom a son has been born. Now in the case of one to whom a son has not been born.—

'Be thou swelled forth. Let enter thee . . .'[1]
'In thee let juices, powers also gather . . .'[2]
'The stalk that the Ādityas cause to swell forth . . .'[3]

Having muttered these three sacred verses (*ṛc*), he says: 'Cause not thyself to swell forth with our vital breath, progeny, cattle! He who hates us and him whom we hate—cause thyself to swell forth with his vital breath, progeny, cattle![4]

Thereupon I turn myself with Indra's turn[5]; I turn myself along with the turn of the sun.'

Thereupon he turns himself toward the right arm.

9 (6). Now, on the night of the full moon one should, in the same manner, worship the moon as it appears in the east, saying:—

'Thou art King Soma. Thou art the Far-shining, the Five-mouthed, Prajāpati (Lord of Creation).

The Brahman (*brāhmaṇa*) is one mouth of thee. With that mouth thou eatest the kings. With that mouth make me an eater of food.

The king (*rājan*) is one mouth of thee. With that mouth

recurs later, though in changed form, at 2. 10—there, as well as here, with variations in **A** and **B**. The form in 2. 8 **B** seems to be quoted (though incompletely and with additional lines) at Pār. Gṛihya-Sūtra 1. 11. 9; and the form in 2. 10 **A**, similarly, at Āśv. Gṛihya-Sūtra 1. 13. 7. In all those three other instances the person addressed is different, it being there a wife addressed by her husband, while here the moon by a worshiper. And in the adapted form of the stanza as a whole this particular word also is different: *susīme*, vocative singular feminine. Its meaning there, accordingly, would seem quite evidently to be 'O thou (fem.) with fair-parted hair.' Perhaps for the sake of uniformity with these three other occurrences of the same (adapted) stanza, *BR.* and *BWb.* propose to emend here likewise to *susīme*; and Deussen is inclined to favor this. It is a plausible, but not a necessary, emendation; a derivative compound may possess a double meaning as well as its base, and may be accordant therewith.

[1] = RV. 1. 91. 16 a and 9. 31. 4 a. [2] = RV. 1. 91. 18 a.

[3] = AV. 7. 81. 6 a with the exception of *ādityās* for *devās*; found also in TS. 2. 4. 14. 1 and MS. 4. 9. 27; 4. 12. 2.

[4] The AV. chapter, a line of which was quoted just above, contains also (7. 81. 5) a petition similar to this one.

[5] That is, toward the east, which is the special region of Indra. **A** instead has *daivīm*, 'of the gods,' here as well as in the parallel passage later, 2. 9.

thou eatest the people (*viś*). With that mouth make me an eater of food.

The hawk is one mouth of thee. With that mouth thou eatest the birds. With that mouth make me an eater of food.

Fire is one mouth of thee. With that mouth thou eatest the world. With that mouth make me an eater of food.

In thee is a fifth mouth. With that mouth thou eatest all beings. With that mouth make me an eater of food.

Waste not thou away with our vital breath, progeny, cattle! He who hates us and him whom we hate—waste thou away with his vital breath, progeny, cattle!

Thereupon I turn myself with the turn of the gods[1]; I turn myself along with the turn of the sun.'

Thereupon he turns himself toward the right arm.

A prayer in connection with wife and children

10. Now, when about to lie down with a wife, one should touch her heart, and say:—

'That which in thy heart, O [dame] with fair-parted hair,
Is placed—within Prajāpati[2]—
Therewith, O Queen of immortality,
May you not come on children's ill!'[3]

In advance of such a one indeed her[4] children decease not.

[1] Deussen understands this word to refer to Varuṇa and Indra, regents of the western and the eastern quarters respectively; and therefore supposes that in this ceremony the worshiper makes a complete turn around from east to west to east, as compared with the half turn from west to east in the previous paragraph. But there A has 'of the gods' instead of 'of Indra,' and other specifications the same as here. The necessary data for determining are insufficient; the conjecture may be possible for B, but not for A.

[2] This stanza is adapted from 2. 8. Between the moon, which was addressed there, and the wife, who is addressed here and who as the bearer of progeny is pantheistically associated with Prajāpati, the Lord of Progeny, an intermediate connection is made at 2. 9 through the identification of the moon with Prajāpati. For variations in the two forms of the stanza consult page 312, note 6.

[3] Instead of these last two verses according to B, A has

'—I ween myself aware of it.
May I not weep for children's ill!'

[4] A has, instead, the masculine form of the pronoun.

A returning father's affectionate greeting to his son[1]

11 (7). Now, when one has been away, on coming back he should kiss[2] his son's head and say:—

'From every limb of mine you come!
Right from my heart you are born forth!
You are myself (*ātman*), indeed, my son![3]
So live a hundred autumns long!

So-and-so![4]'—He takes his name.

'Become a stone! Become an ax!
Become unconquerable gold!
A brilliance (*tejas*), son, indeed you are![5]
So live a hundred autumns long![6]

So-and-so![7]'—He takes his name.

Then he embraces him,[8] saying: 'Wherewith Prajāpati embraced his creatures for their security, therewith I embrace you, So-and-so!'—He takes his name.[9]

Then he mutters in his right ear:—

'Confer on him,[10] O generous one (*maghavan*), onrusning . . .'

and in the left [ear]:—

'O Indra, grant most excellent possessions!'[11]

[1] These directions are incorporated in the Gṛihya-Sūtras: Āśvalāyana 1. 15. 3, 9; Pāraskara 1. 16. 18; Khādira 2. 3. 13; Gobhila 2. 8. 21, 22; Āpastamba 6. 15. 12.

[2] So B, *abhi-jighret*; A has, instead, *abhi-mṛśet*, 'touch. On the 'sniff-kiss' see the article by Prof. Hopkins, *JAOS*. 28. 120–134.

[3] So B: *putra nāma*. Possibly, however, *putranāma*; if so, then

'You are myself, by name my son!'

A has, instead, *putra mā vitha*:

'You are myself! You've saved me, son!'

This conception accords with the later etymology of son as 'savior from hell,' *put-tra*, Mānava-Dharma-Śāstra 9. 138.

[4] This word (*asau*) is lacking in B.

[5] Or, 'A Brilliance, son, by name you are!'

[6] This stanza, with *ātmā* instead of *tejas* in the third line, occurs in the *Mādhyaṁdina* recension of Bṛih. at 6. 4. 26 (= Śat. Br. 14. 9. 4. 26) and in Pār. Gṛihya-Sūtra 1. 16. 18; with *vedas* instead of the *tejas*, it occurs, along with the two following Rig-Veda quotations, in Āśv. Gṛihya-Sūtra 1. 15. 3.

[7] This word (*asau*) is lacking in B.

[8] This phrase is lacking in A.

[9] This sentence is lacking in B.

[10] This line = RV. 3. 36. 10 a with *asme*, 'us,' adapted to *asmai*, 'him.'

[11] = RV. 2. 21. 6 a.

[and says:] 'Be not cut off![1] Be not perturbed.[2] Live a hundred autumns of life. Son, I kiss your head with your name, So-and-so!'—Thrice he should kiss his head.

'I make a lowing over you with the lowing of cows.'—Thrice he should make a lowing over his head.

The manifestation of the permanent Brahma in evanescent phenomena

(a) Cosmical powers revertible into wind

12 (8). Now next, the dying around of the gods (*daiva parimara*).[3]—

This Brahma, verily, shines when fire blazes; likewise this dies when it blazes not. Its brilliance (*tejas*) goes to the sun; its vital breath (*prāṇa*), into the wind (*vāyu*).

This Brahma, verily, shines when the sun is seen; likewise this dies when it is not seen. Its brilliance goes to the moon; its vital breath, to the wind.

This Brahma, verily, shines when the moon is seen; likewise this dies when it is not seen. Its brilliance goes to lightning; its vital breath, to the wind.

This Brahma, verily, shines when the lightning lightens; likewise this dies when it lightens not. Its brilliance goes to the wind[4]; its vital breath, to the wind.

All these divinities, verily, having entered into wind, perish not when they die in the wind; therefrom indeed they come forth again.

—Thus with reference to the divinities.

(b) An individual's powers revertible into breath

Now with reference to oneself.—

13. This Brahma, verily, shines when one speaks with

[1] *mā chitthā(s)* [—A; *chetthā(s)*—B]. Compare, in the prayer 'For some one's continued life' at AV. 8. 1. 4, *mā chitthā(s) asmāl lokād* . . .

'Be not cut off from this world,
From the sight of Agni and of the Sun!'

[2] *mā vyathiṣṭhā(s)*. Occurs in BhG. 11. 34.

[3] Compare a somewhat similar passage in Ait. Br. 8. 28 entitled 'The Dying around Brahma,' where also the wind is the ultimate in the regression of these same five phenomena (though in inverse order).

[4] So A. B has the less appropriate *diśas*, 'regions of heaven.'

speech; likewise this dies when one speaks not. Its brilliance goes to the eye; its vital breath, to the vital breath.

This Brahma, verily, shines when one sees with the eye; likewise this dies when one sees not. Its brilliance goes to the ear; its vital breath, to the vital breath.

This Brahma, verily, shines when one hears with the ear; likewise this dies when one hears not. Its brilliance goes to the mind; its vital breath, to the vital breath.

This Brahma, verily, shines when one thinks with the mind; likewise this dies when one thinks not. Its brilliance goes to the vital breath; its vital breath, to the vital breath.

All these divinities, verily, having entered into the vital breath, perish not when they die in the vital breath; therefrom indeed they come forth again.

So verily, indeed, if upon one who knows this both mountains should roll themselves forth—both the southern and the northern[1]—desiring to lay him low, indeed they would not lay him low. But those who hate him and those whom he himself (*svayaṁ*) hates—these all die around him.

The contest of the bodily powers for supremacy; the ultimate goal

14 (9). Now next, the assumption of superior excellence (*niḥśreyasādāna*).[2]—

All these divinities, verily, indeed, when disputing among themselves in the matter of self-superiority, went forth from this body. It lay, not breathing, dry,[3] become like a piece of wood.

Then speech entered into it. It just lay, speaking with speech.

Then the eye entered into it. It just lay, speaking with speech, seeing with the eye.

Then the ear entered into it. It just lay, speaking with speech, seeing with the eye, hearing with the ear.

Then the mind entered into it. It just lay, speaking with

[1] That is, the Vindhyas and the Himālayas respectively.

[2] Other accounts of the same allegory occur in Bṛih. 6. 1. 1-14; Chānd. 5. 1; and Kaush. 3. 3.

[3] The words 'not breathing, dry' are lacking in A.

speech, seeing with the eye, hearing with the ear, thinking with the mind.

Then the vital breath (*prāṇa*) entered into it. Thereupon indeed it arose.

All those divinities, verily, having recognized the superior excellence in the vital breath, and having passed into the vital breath, even the intelligential self (*prajñātman*), went forth from this body[1]—all these together. They, having entered into the wind,[2] having the nature of space (*ākāśātman*), went to heaven (*svar*).

Likewise also, indeed, he who knows this, having recognized the superior excellence in the vital breath,[3] having passed into the vital breath, even the intelligential self, of all beings,[4] goes forth from this body along with all these. He, having entered into the wind,[2] having the nature of space, goes to heaven. He goes to that [place] where these gods are. Having reached that, he becomes immortal as the gods are immortal—he who knows this.[3]

A dying father's bequest of his various powers to his son[5]

15 (10). Now next, the Father-and-son Ceremony, or the Transmission, as they call it.—

A father, when about to decease, summons his son. Having strewn the house with new grass, having built up the fire, having set down near it a vessel of water together with a dish, the father, wrapped around with a fresh garment, remains lying.[6] The son,[7] having come, lies down on top, touching

[1] A has, instead, *lokād*, 'world.'

[2] So B: *vāyu-praviṣṭa*; but A has, instead, *vāyu-pratiṣṭha*, 'established on the wind.'

[3] The previous phrase is lacking in A.

[4] The words 'of all beings' are lacking in B.

[5] Another account of a 'father-to-son transmission' is found in Bṛih. 1. 5. 17–20.

[6] So B: *pitā śete*. But A has, instead, *svayaṁ śyete*. According to this reading, what was in the other reading a main verb is lost; and the sentences must be reconstructed: 'A father . . . summons his son, having strewn . . ., having built . . ., having set down . . . dish, wrapped . . . garment, himself in white. The son, . . .'

[7] If the elision is of a locative, *putre*, instead of a nominative, *putras*, then without a grammatical impossibility (though with less probability as being an exceptional usage) the sentence might mean: 'Upon the son when he comes (or, Upon the son's coming) he lies . . .'

organs with organs. Or he may, even, transmit to him seated face to face.[1] Then he delivers over to him [thus]:—

Father: 'My speech in you I would place!'

Son: 'Your speech in me I take.'

Father: 'My breath (*prāṇa*[2]) in you I would place!'

Son: 'Your breath in me I take.'

Father: 'My eye in you I would place!'

Son: 'Your eye in me I take.'

Father: 'My ear in you I would place!'

Son: 'Your ear in me I take.'

Father: 'My tastes in you I would place!'

Son: 'Your tastes in me I take.'

Father: 'My deeds (*karman*) in you I would place!'

Son: 'Your deeds in me I take.'

Father: 'My pleasure and pain in you I would place!'

Son: 'Your pleasure and pain in me I take.'

Father: 'My bliss, delight, and procreation in you I would place!'

Son: 'Your bliss, delight, and procreation in me I take.'

Father: 'My goings in you I would place!'

Son: 'Your goings in me I take.'

Father: 'My mind[3] in you I would place!'

Son: 'Your mind in me I take.'

Father: 'My intelligence (*prajñā*)[4] in you I would place!'

Son: 'Your intelligence[4] in me I take.'

If, however, he should be unable to speak much, let the father say summarily: 'My vital breaths (*prāṇa*) in you I would place!' [and] the son [reply]: 'Your vital breaths in me I take.'[5]

Then, turning to the right, he goes forth toward the east.[6]

The father calls out after him: 'May glory (*yaśas*), sacred luster (*brahma-varcasa*),[7] and fame delight in you!'

[1] So B; but A has, instead, '. . . sit in front of him.'

[2] This word here designates 'breath' as 'the function of smell,' rather than as 'the breath of life.'

[3] This item of the series is lacking in A; but see next note.

[4] So B; A has, instead, *dhiyo vijñātavyaṁ kāmān*, 'thoughts, what is to be understood, and desires'—items which occur in a partially similar series in 1. 7.

[5] This whole sentence is lacking in A.

[6] This word, *prāṅ*, is lacking in B.

[7] Here A has, in addition, 'food to eat.'

Then the other looks over his left shoulder. Having hid [his face] with his hand, or having covered [it] with the edge of his garment, he says: 'Heavenly (*svarga*) worlds and desires do you obtain!'

If he should become well, the father should dwell under the lordship of his son, or he should wander around as a religious mendicant.[1] If, however, he should decease, so let them furnish[2] him as he ought to be furnished—as he ought to be furnished.

THIRD ADHYĀYA

Doctrine of Prāṇa (the Breathing Spirit)

Knowledge of Indra, the greatest possible boon to men

1. Pratardana Daivodāsi by fighting and virility arrived at the beloved abode of Indra.

To him then Indra said: 'Pratardana, choose a boon (*vara*)!'[3]

Then said Pratardana: 'Do you yourself choose for me the one which you deem most beneficent to mankind.'

To him then Indra said: 'A superior (*vara*), verily, chooses not for an inferior (*avara*). Do you yourself choose.'

'No boon (*a-vara*), verily, then, is it to me!' said Pratardana.

But Indra departed not from the truth, for Indra is truth.

To him then Indra said: 'Understand me, myself. This indeed I deem most beneficent to man—namely, that one should understand me. I slew the three-headed son of Tvashṭṛi.[4]

[1] *pari* + √*vraj*.

[2] That is, with obsequies. Understood thus, the subject of the verb is indefinite; and the object is 'the deceased father.' Possibly (though less probably, it would seem), 'the *prāṇas* of the father' are intended as the subject; and the son is intended as the object—Deussen's interpretation. The reading of A gives yet another meaning: 'According as he [i. e. the father] furnishes him [i. e. the son], so ought he to be furnished—so ought he to be furnished.'

[3] A has, instead, 'A boon I would give you.'

[4] This exploit of Indra's is referred to at RV. 10. 8. 8, 9; 10. 99. 6; Śat. Br. 1. 2. 3. 2; 12. 7. 1. 1. Further accounts of this conflict between Indra and Viśvarūpa, as the son of Tvashṭṛi is called, occur at Tait. Saṁhitā 2. 5. 1. 1 ff.; Śat. Br. 1. 6. 3. 1, 2; 5. 5. 4. 2, 3; and Kāṭhaka 12. 10 (cited in Weber's *Indische Studien*, 3. 464).

I delivered the Arunmukhas, ascetics, to the wild dogs.[1] Transgressing many compacts, I transfixed the people of Prahlāda[2] in the sky, the Paulomas[3] in the atmosphere, the Kālakāñjas[4] on earth.[5] Of me, such a one as I was then (*tasya me tatra*), not a single hair was injured!

So he who understands me—by no deed whatsoever of his is his world injured, not by stealing, not by killing an embryo, not by the murder of his mother, not by the murder of his father; if he has done any[6] evil (*pāpa*), the dark color departs not[7] from his face.[8]'

His identity with life and immortality

2. Then he said: 'I am the breathing spirit (*prāṇa*), the intelligential self (*prajñātman*). As such (*tam*[9]), reverence me as life (*āyus*), as immortality. Life is the breathing spirit. The breathing spirit, verily, is life. The breathing spirit, indeed, is immortality.[10] For, as long as the breathing spirit remains in this body, so long is there life. For indeed, with the breathing spirit in this[11] world one obtains immortality; with intelligence, true conception (*saṁkalpa*).

So he who reverences me as life, as immortality, reaches the full term of life in this world; he obtains immortality, indestructibility (*akṣiti*) in the heavenly world (*svarga-loka*).'

[1] The foregoing exploits of Indra are mentioned at Ait. Br. 7. 28.

[2] Or, *Prahrāda*, a chief of the Asuras.

[3] A troop of demons. [4] A tribe of Asuras.

[5] Weber has an extensive discussion concerning the meaning of the foregoing names and the identity of the personages, together with numerous relevant literary references, in his *Indische Studien*, 1. 410–418.

[6] This word, *cana*, is lacking in B.

[7] That is, 'he does not become pale.'

[8] Professor Deussen's note on this sentence (*Sechzig Upanishad's*, p. 44, note 1) is an acute and concise interpretation of the general Upanishadic theory: 'Whoever has attained the knowledge of the Ātman and his unity with it, and thereby has been delivered from the illusion of individual existence, his good and evil deeds come to nought; they are no longer his deeds, simply because he is no longer an individual.'

[9] So A. But B has, instead, *prajñātmanam*; accordingly the sentences must be reconstructed thus: 'I am the breathing spirit (*prāṇa*). Reverence me as the intelligential self, as life, . . .'

[10] This sentence is lacking in B.

[11] So B; but A has, instead, 'yonder.'

The unity of an individual's functions or special prāṇas

Now on this point some say: 'The vital breaths (*prāṇa*), verily, go into a unity, for'—so they say (*iti*)—' [otherwise] no one would be able at once to cause to know a name with speech, a form with the eye, a sound with the ear, a thought with the mind. As a unity, verily, the vital breaths, every single one, cause to know all things here.

All the vital breaths speak along with speech when it speaks.
All the vital breaths see along with the eye when it sees.
All the vital breaths hear along with the ear when it hears.
All the vital breaths think along with the mind when it thinks.
All the vital breaths breathe along with breath (*prāṇa*) when it breathes.'

'That is indeed so,' said Indra. 'There is, however,' he continued (*iti*), 'a superior excellence among the vital breaths.

The really vitalizing and unifying 'vital breath,' the breathing spirit or conscious self

3. One lives with speech gone, for we see the dumb;
one lives with eye gone, for we see the blind;
one lives with ear gone, for we see the deaf;
one lives with mind gone, for we see the childish;
one lives with arms cut off, one lives with legs cut off, for thus we see.

But now it is the breathing spirit (*prāṇa*), even the intelligential self (*prajñātman*), that seizes hold of and animates (*ut-thā*) this body. This, therefore, one should reverence as the Uktha.[1]

This is the All-obtaining (*sarvāpti*)[2] in the breathing spirit (*prāṇa*).[3]

As for the breathing spirit—verily, that is the intelligential

[1] 'The Recitation of Praise' in the ritual. The same identification occurs also at Bṛih. 5. 13. 1.

[2] That is, 'it is in (the individual) conscious spirit that all facts are obtained.' This compact expression might possibly be understood to summarize the earlier practical teaching that 'in Prāṇa a knower thereof obtains all things'; and also, pregnantly, the teaching (both earlier and later in this Upanishad) that 'in the conscious Self all things do obtain [both ontologically and ethically—' obtain' being used in its intransitive meaning].'

[3] This sentence is lacking in B.

self! As for the intelligential self—verily, that is the breathing spirit. For truly, these two dwell in this body; together the two depart.'

This is the view (*dṛṣṭi*) thereof, this the understanding (*vijñāna*):—

When a person is so asleep that he sees no dream whatever, then he becomes unitary in this breathing spirit. Then

speech together with all names goes to it;
the eye together with all forms goes to it;
the ear together with all sounds goes to it;
the mind together with all thoughts goes to it.

When he awakens—as from a blazing fire sparks would disperse in all directions, even so from this self (*ātman*) the vital breaths (*prāṇa*) disperse to their respective stations; from the vital breaths the sense-powers (*deva*); from the sense-powers, the worlds.

This selfsame breathing spirit as the intelligential self seizes hold of and animates (*ut-thā*) this body. This therefore one should reverence as the Uktha.

This is the All-obtaining in the breathing spirit.

As for the breathing spirit—verily, that is the intelligential self. As for the intelligential self—verily, that is the breathing spirit.[1]

This is the proof (*siddhi*) thereof, this the understanding:—

When a sick person about to die comes to such weakness that he comes to a stupor (*sammoha*), then they say of him: 'His thought (*citta*) has departed. He hears not. He sees not. He speaks not with speech. He thinks not.' Then he becomes unitary in this breathing spirit (*prāṇa*). Then

speech together with all names goes to it;
the eye together with all forms goes to it;
the ear together with all sounds goes to it;
the mind together with all thoughts goes to it.[2]

[1] The preceding three paragraphs (which have already occurred in this section) are lacking in **A**.

[2] **A** has here in addition: 'When he awakens—as from a blazing fire sparks would disperse in all directions, even so from this self the vital breaths disperse to their respective stations; from the vital breaths, the sense-powers; from the sense-powers, the worlds.' But in the present context this sentence seems to be an inapt refrain from the previous paragraph.

(4) When he departs from this body, he departs together with all these.

The 'All-obtaining' in Prāṇa through the vital breaths

4. Speech pours[1] all names in it[2]; with speech it obtains all names.

Breath (*prāṇa*) pours all odors in it; with breath it obtains all odors.

The eye pours all forms in it; with the eye it obtains all forms.

The ear pours all sounds in it; with the ear it obtains all sounds.

The mind pours all thoughts in it; with the mind it obtains all thoughts.

This is the All-obtaining (*sarvāpti*)[3] in the breathing spirit.

As for the breathing spirit (*prāṇa*)—verily, that is the intelligence (*prajñā*); as for the intelligence—verily, that is the breathing spirit,[4] for together these two dwell in this body, together the two depart.

The correlation of the individual's functions with the facts of existence

Now then, we will explain how all beings (*bhūta*) become one with this intelligence.—

5. Speech is one portion thereof taken out. Name is its externally correlated (*parastāt prati-vi-hita*) existential element (*bhūta-mātrā*).

Breath (*prāṇa*) is one portion thereof taken out. Odor is its externally correlated existential element.

The eye is one portion thereof taken out. Form (*rūpa*) is its externally correlated existential element.

The ear is one portion thereof taken out. Sound is its externally correlated existential element.

The tongue is one portion thereof taken out. Taste is its externally correlated existential element.

[1] So A: *abhivisṛjate*. [2] So B: *asmin*.
[3] On this word see p. 322, n. 2, above.
[4] The previous sentence is lacking in B.

The two hands are one portion thereof taken out. Work (*karman*) is their externally correlated existential element.

The body is one portion thereof taken out. Pleasure and pain are its externally correlated existential element.

The generative organ is one portion thereof taken out. Bliss, delight, and procreation are its externally correlated existential element.

The two feet are one portion thereof taken out. Goings are their externally correlated existential element.

The mind (*manas*[1]) is one portion thereof taken out. Thoughts[2] and desires are its externally correlated existential element.

The supremacy of consciousness in all the functions and facts of existence

6. With intelligence (*prajñā*) having mounted on speech, with speech one obtains all names.

With intelligence having mounted on breath (*prāṇa*), with breath one obtains all odors.

With intelligence having mounted on the eye, with the eye one obtains all forms.

With intelligence having mounted on the ear, with the ear one obtains all sounds.

With intelligence having mounted on the tongue, with the tongue one obtains all tastes.

With intelligence having mounted on the two hands, with the two hands one obtains all works.

With intelligence having mounted on the body, with the body one obtains pleasure and pain.

With intelligence having mounted on the generative organ, with the generative organ one obtains bliss, delight, and procreation.

With intelligence having mounted on the two feet, with the two feet one obtains all goings.

With intelligence having mounted on the mind (*manas*),[3] with the mind one obtains all thoughts.[4]

[1] A has here, instead, 'intelligence (*prajñā*).'
[2] A has here, in addition, 'what is to be understood (*vijñātavyam*).'
[3] A has here, instead, *dhī*, 'thought.'
[4] A has here, in addition, 'what is to be understood and desired.'

The indispensableness of consciousness for all facts and experience

7. For truly, apart from intelligence (*prajñā*) speech would not make cognizant (*pra* + √*jñā*) of any name whatsoever. 'My mind was elsewhere,' one says; 'I did not cognize that name.'

For truly, apart from intelligence breath would not make cognizant of any odor whatsoever. 'My mind was elsewhere,' one says; 'I did not cognize that odor.'

For truly, apart from intelligence the eye would not make cognizant of any form whatsoever. 'My mind was elsewhere,' one says; 'I did not cognize that form.'

For truly, apart from intelligence the ear would not make cognizant of any sound whatsoever. 'My mind was elsewhere,' one says; 'I did not cognize that sound.'

For truly, apart from intelligence the tongue would not make cognizant of any taste whatsoever. 'My mind was elsewhere,' one says; 'I did not cognize that taste.'

For truly, apart from intelligence the two hands would not make cognizant of any action whatsoever. 'My (*me*) mind was elsewhere,' one says (*āha*); 'I (*aham*) did not cognize (*prājñāsiṣam*)[1] that action.'

For truly, apart from intelligence the body would not make cognizant of any pleasure or pain whatsoever. 'My mind was elsewhere,' one says; 'I did not cognize that pleasure or pain.'

For truly, apart from intelligence the generative organ would not make cognizant of any bliss, delight, and procreation whatsoever. 'My mind was elsewhere,' one says; 'I did not cognize that bliss, delight, and procreation.'

For truly, apart from intelligence the two feet would not make cognizant of any going whatsoever. 'My mind was elsewhere,' one says; 'I did not cognize that going.'

For truly, apart from intelligence no thought (*dhī*) whatsoever would be effected; nothing cognizable would be cognized.

[1] These singular forms of A seem preferable to the dual forms of the readings in B; similarly in the third sentence following, about 'feet.' Accordingly, the speaker in all these direct quotations is to be understood as indefinite rather than as the particular organ mentioned.

The subject of all knowledge, the paramount object of knowledge

8. Speech is not what one should desire to understand. One should know the speaker.

Smell is not what one should desire to understand. One should know the smeller.

Form is not what one should desire to understand. One should know the seer.[1]

Sound is not what one should desire to understand. One should know the hearer.

Taste is not what one should desire to understand. One should know the discerner of taste.

The deed is not what one should desire to understand. One should know the doer.

Pleasure and pain are not what one should desire to understand. One should know the discerner of pleasure and pain.

Bliss, delight, and procreation are not what one should desire to understand. One should know the discerner of bliss, delight, and procreation.

Going is not what one should desire to understand. One should know the goer.

Mind (*manas*) is not what one should desire to understand. One should know the thinker (*mantṛ*).

The absolute correlativity of knowing and being

These ten existential elements (*bhūta-mātrā*), verily, are with reference to intelligence (*adhi-prajña*). The ten intelligential elements (*prajñā-mātrā*) are with reference to existence (*adhi-bhūta*). For truly, if there were no elements of being, there would be no elements of intelligence. Verily, if there were no elements of intelligence, there would be no elements of being. (9) For truly, from either alone no appearance (*rūpa*) whatsoever would be effected.

Their unity in the conscious self

And this is not a diversity. But as of a chariot the felly is fixed on the spokes and the spokes are fixed on the hub,

[1] So **B**; but **A** has, instead, 'the knower of form.'

even so these elements of being (*bhūta-mātrā*) are fixed on the elements of intelligence (*prajñā-mātrā*), and the elements of intelligence are fixed on the breathing spirit (*prāṇa*).

This same breathing spirit, in truth, is the intelligential self (*prajñātman*); [it is] bliss, ageless, immortal.

A person's ethical irresponsibility, his very self being identical with the world-all

He does not become greater (*bhūyas*) with good action, nor indeed lesser (*kanīyas*) with bad action.

This one, truly, indeed, causes him whom he wishes to lead up from these worlds, to perform good action. This one, also, indeed, causes him whom he wishes to lead downward, to perform bad action.

He is the world-protector (*loka-pāla*). He is the world-sovereign (*lokādhipati*). He is the lord of all.[1]

'He is my self (*ātman*)'—this one should know. 'He is my self'—this one should know.

FOURTH ADHYĀYA

A progressive definition of Brahma[2]

Bālāki's offer of instruction concerning Brahma

1. Now then, verily, there was Gārgya Bālāki, famed as learned in the scriptures (*anūcāna*). He dwelt among the Uśīnaras, among the Satvans and the Matsyas,[3] among the Kurus and the Pañcālas, among the Kāśis and the Videhas.

He, then, coming to Ajātaśatru, [king] of Kāśi,[4] said: 'Let me declare Brahma to you.'

To him then Ajātaśatru said: 'A thousand [cows] we give to you! At such a word as this, verily, indeed, people would run together, crying, "A Janaka![5] A Janaka!"'

[1] So A: *sarveśa*; but B has, instead, *lokeśa*, 'world-lord.'

[2] Another narration of the same dialogue occurs at Bṛih. 2. 1.

[3] Adopting the reading *satvan-matsyeṣu* in agreement with *BR*. s.v., Weber (*Indische Studien*, 1. 419), and Deussen.

[4] The modern Benares.

[5] A king famed for his great knowledge.

Clue-words of the subsequent conversation

2.[1] In the sun—the Great,
in the moon—Food,
in lightning—Truth,
in thunder—Sound,
in wind—Indra Vaikuṇṭha,
in space—the Plenum,
in fire—the Vanquisher,
in water—Brilliance (*tejas*).

—Thus with reference to the divinities (*adhi-daivata*). Now with reference to the self (*adhy-ātma*).—

In the mirror—the Counterpart,
in the shadow—the Double,
in the echo—Life (*asu*),
in sound—Death,
in sleep—Yama [Lord of the dead],
in the body—Prajāpati [Lord of Creation],
in the right eye—Speech,
in the left eye—Truth.

Bālāki's and Ajātaśatru's progressive determination of Brahma

(a) In various cosmic phenomena

3. Then said Bālāki: 'Him who is this person in the sun—him indeed I reverence.'

To him then Ajātaśatru said: 'Make me not to converse on him! As the Great, the White-robed, the Pre-eminent (*atiṣṭhā*), the Head of all beings—thus, verily, I reverence him.'

He then who reverences him thus, becomes pre-eminent, the head of all beings.

4. Then said Bālāki: 'Him who is this person in the moon—him indeed I reverence.'

To him then Ajātaśatru said: 'Make me not to converse on him! As King Soma,[2] as the soul (*ātman*) of Food—thus, verily, I reverence him.'

He then who reverences him thus, becomes the soul of food.

[1] This entire paragraph is lacking in some manuscripts. It is merely a list of clue-words summarizing the following conversation.

[2] The phrase is lacking in B.

5. Then said Bālāki: 'Him who is this person in the lightning—him indeed I reverence.'

To him then Ajātaśatru said: 'Make me not to converse on him! As the soul of Truth[1]—thus, verily, I reverence him.'

He then who reverences him thus, becomes the soul of truth.[1]

6. Then said Bālāki: 'Him who is this person in thunder—him indeed I reverence.'

To him then Ajātaśatru said: 'Make me not to converse on him! As the soul of Sound—thus, verily, I reverence him.'

He then who reverences him thus, becomes the soul of sound.

7 (8).[2] Then said Bālāki: 'Him who is this person in wind—him indeed I reverence.'

To him then Ajātaśatru said: 'Make me not to converse on him! As Indra Vaikuṇṭha, the unconquered hero—thus, verily, I reverence him.'

He then who reverences him thus, becomes indeed triumphant, unconquerable, a conqueror of adversaries.

8 (7).[2] Then said Bālāki: 'Him who is this person in space—him indeed I reverence.'

To him then Ajātaśatru said: 'Make me not to converse on him! As the Plenum (*pūrṇa*), the non-active (*a-pravartin*) Brahma—thus, verily, I reverence him.'

He then who reverences him thus, becomes filled (*pūryate*) with offspring, cattle,[3] splendor (*yaśas*), the luster of sanctity (*brahma-varcasa*), and the heavenly world (*svarga-loka*); he reaches the full term of life.

9. Then said Bālāki: 'Him who is this person in fire—him indeed I reverence.'

To him then Ajātaśatru said: 'Make me not to converse on him! As the Vanquisher—thus, verily, I reverence him.'

He then who reverences him thus, becomes verily a vanquisher amid others.[4]

[1] A has here, instead, 'of brilliance.'

[2] A inverts the order of sections from B.

[3] Instead of the following portion of this paragraph, A has: 'Neither he nor his offspring moves on (*pra-vartate*) before the time.'

[4] So B: *vā' anyeṣu*; but A has, instead, *evā 'nv eṣa*, '. . . , such a one in consequence becomes a vanquisher indeed.'

10. Then said Bālāki: 'Him who is this person in water—him indeed I reverence.'

To him then Ajātaśatru said: 'Make me not to converse on him! As the soul (*ātman*) of Brilliance [1]—thus, verily, I reverence him.'

He then who reverences him thus, becomes the soul of brilliance.[1]

—Thus with reference to the divinities.

(b) In the self

Now with reference to the self.—

11. Then said Bālāki: 'Him who is this person in the mirror—him indeed I reverence.'

To him then Ajātaśatru said: 'Make me not to converse on him! As the Counterpart—thus, verily, I reverence him.'

He then who reverences him thus—a very counterpart of him is born in his offspring, not an unlikeness.

12. Then said Bālāki: 'Him who is this person in the shadow [2]—him indeed I reverence.'

To him then Ajātaśatru said: 'Make me not to converse on him! As the inseparable Double—thus, verily, I reverence him.'

He then who reverences him thus, obtains from his double [3]; he becomes possessed of his double.[4]

13. Then said Bālāki: 'Him who is this person in the echo[5]—him indeed I reverence.'

To him then Ajātaśatru said: 'Make me not to converse on him! As Life (*asu*) [6]—thus, verily, I reverence him.'

He then who reverences him thus,[7] passes not into unconsciousness (*saṁmoha*) before the time.

[1] So B: *tejasas*; but A has, instead, 'of name.'

[2] Instead of this word, A has 'the echo.'

[3] That is, his wife.

[4] In offspring.—Com.

[5] Instead of this phrase, A has: 'The sound that follows a person—that indeed . . .'

[6] Strictly 'the breath of life'; but A has, instead, *āyu*, 'life,' strictly 'the duration of life.' In either recension the conception of life seems to imply an active response to, and correspondence with, environment.

[7] A has here, in addition, 'neither he nor his offspring.'

14. Then said Bālāki: 'Him who is this person in sound[1]—him indeed I reverence.'

To him then Ajātaśatru said: 'Make me not to converse on him! As Death—thus, verily, I reverence him.'

He then who reverences him thus,[2] deceases not before the time.

15 (16).[3] Then said Bālāki: 'The person here who, asleep,[4] moves about in a dream—him indeed I reverence.'

To him then Ajātaśatru said: 'Make me not to converse on him! As King Yama—thus, verily, I reverence him.'

He then who reverences him thus—everything here is subdued (√ *yam*) to his supremacy.

16 (15).[3] Then said Bālāki: 'Him who is this person in the body—him indeed I reverence.'

To him then Ajātaśatru said: 'Make me not to converse on him! As Prajāpati (Lord of Creation)—thus, verily, I reverence him.'

He then who reverences him thus, becomes procreated (*prajāyate*) with offspring, cattle,[5] splendor, the luster of sanctity, the heavenly world; he reaches the full term of life (*āyu*).

17. Then said Bālāki: 'Him who is this person in the right eye—him indeed I reverence.'

To him then Ajātaśatru said: 'Make me not to converse on him! As the soul (*ātman*) of Speech,[6] the soul of fire, the soul of light—thus, verily, I reverence him.'

He then who reverences him thus, becomes the soul of all these.

18. Then said Bālāki: 'Him who is this person in the left eye—him indeed I reverence.'

To him then Ajātaśatru said: 'Make me not to converse on him! As the soul of Truth, the soul of lightning, the soul of brightness—thus, verily, I reverence him.'

[1] Instead of this phrase, A has: 'Him who is this shadow-person—.'
[2] A has here, in addition, 'neither he nor his offspring.'
[3] A inverts the order from B.
[4] A has here, instead, 'This intelligent self whereby a person here, asleep . . .'
[5] The following part of this sentence is lacking in A.
[6] A has here, instead, 'name.'

He then who reverences him thus, becomes the soul of all these.

The universal creator in the covert of the heart

19. Thereupon Bālāki was silent. To him then Ajātaśatru said: 'So much only, Bālāki?'

'So much only,' said Bālāki.

To him then Ajātaśatru said: 'In vain, verily, indeed, did you make me to converse, saying, "Let me declare Brahma to you." He, verily, O Bālāki, who is the maker of these persons [whom you have mentioned in succession], of whom, verily, this is the work—he, verily, should be known.'

Thereupon Bālāki, fuel in hand,[1] approached, saying: 'Receive me as a pupil.'

To him then Ajātaśatru said: 'This I deem [2] an appearance (*rūpa*) contrary to nature [3]—that a Kshatriya should receive a Brahman as pupil. But come! I will cause you to understand.' Then, taking him by the hand, he went forth. The two then came upon a person asleep. Him then Ajātaśatru addressed: 'O great, white-robed King Soma!' But he just lay silent.[4] Thereupon he threw at him with a stick. Thereupon he arose.

To him then Ajātaśatru said: 'Where in this case, O Bālāki, has this person lain? What has become of him here? Whence has he returned here?'

Thereupon Bālāki understood not.

To him then Ajātaśatru said: 'Where in this case, O Bālāki, this person has lain, what has become of him here, whence he has returned here—as I asked (*iti*)—is, the channels of a person [5] called *hitā* ('the Beneficent'). From the heart they spread forth to the pericardium. Now, they are as minute as a hair subdivided a thousandfold. They consist of a minute essence, reddish-brown, white, black, yellow, and red. In these one remains while, asleep, he sees no dream whatsoever.

[1] The sign of suppliant pupilship.

[2] So B: *manye*; but A has, instead, *syāt*, 'would be.'

[3] *prati-loma*, literally 'against the hair.'

[4] This last word is lacking in B.

[5] A has, instead, 'of the heart.'

The ultimate unity in the self—creative, pervasive, supreme, universal

20. Then he becomes unitary in this Prāṇa.
Then speech together with all names goes to it;
the eye together with all forms goes to it;
the ear together with all sounds goes to it;
the mind (*manas*) together with all thoughts goes to it.

When he awakens—as from a blazing fire sparks would disperse in all directions, even so from this self (*ātman*) the vital breaths (*prāṇa*) disperse to their respective stations; from the vital breaths, the sense-powers (*deva*); from the sense-powers, the worlds.

This selfsame breathing spirit (*prāṇa*), even the intelligential self (*prajñātman*), has entered this bodily self (*śarīra-ātman*) up to the hair and fingernail tips.[1] (20) Just as a razor might be hidden in a razor-case, or fire[2] in a fire-receptacle, even thus this intelligential self has entered this bodily self up to the hair and the fingernail tips. Upon that self these selves depend, as upon a chief his own [men]. Just as a chief enjoys his own [men], or as his own [men] are of service to a chief, even thus this intelligential self enjoys these selves; even thus these selves are of service to that self.

Verily, as long as Indra understood not this self, so long the Asuras (demons) overcame him. When he understood, then, striking down and conquering the Asuras, he compassed (*pari* + $\sqrt{}$*i*) the supremacy (*śraiṣṭhya*), independent sovereignty (*svārājya*), and overlordship (*ādhipatya*) of all gods and of all beings.

Likewise also, he who knows this, striking off all evils (*pāpman*), compasses the supremacy, independent sovereignty, and overlordship of all beings—he who knows this, yea, he who knows this!

[1] In **A** the previous sentence is lacking, and § 20 begins at this point.

[2] For a discussion of the exact meaning of this phrase consult the footnote to the parallel passage in Bṛih. 1. 4. 7.

KÉNA UPANISHAD[1]

(FIRST KHAṆḌA)

Query: The real agent in the individual?

[Question:]

1. By whom impelled soars forth the mind projected?
By whom enjoined goes forth the earliest breathing?
By whom impelled this speech do people utter?
The eye, the ear—what god, pray, them enjoineth?

The all-conditioning, yet inscrutable agent, Brahma

[Answer:]

2. That which is the hearing of the ear, the thought of the mind,
The voice of speech, as also the breathing of the breath,
And the sight of the eye![2] Past these escaping, the wise,
On departing from this world, become immortal.

3. There the eye goes not;
Speech goes not, nor the mind.
We know not, we understand not
How one would teach It.
Other, indeed, is It than the known,
And moreover above the unknown.
—Thus have we heard of the ancients (*pūrva*)
Who to us have explained It.[3]

[1] This name of the Upanishad is taken from its first word *kena*, 'by whom.' It is also known as the *Talavakāra*, the name of the Brāhmaṇa of the Sāma-Veda to which the Upanishad in one of its recensions belongs.

[2] The first two and a half lines of this second stanza seem to form a direct answer to the query of the first stanza. But their metrical structure is irregular; that would be improved by the omission of *sa u*, 'as also.' And—more seriously—the grammatical structure of the phrases is apparently impossible; one phrase is certainly in the nominative, one certainly in the accusative, the other three might be construed as either. Moreover, in each of the five phrases it is the same word that is repeated (as in a similar passage at Bṛih. 4. 4. 18); accordingly, a strictly literal rendering of them would be, 'the ear of the ear, the mind of the mind, the speech of speech, the breath of breath, the eye of the eye.' However, very frequently in the Upanishads these words for the five 'vital breaths' are used either for the abstract function or for the concrete instrument of the function. Here, more evidently than in many places, the connotation seems to be double. But at Chānd. 8. 12. 4 and Ait. 2. 4 the distinction between the function and its sense organ is clearly conceived.

[3] 3g and h recur, with slight variation, as Īśā 10c and d, and Īśā 13c and d.

4. That which is unexpressed with speech (*vāc*, voice),
That with which speech is expressed—
That indeed know as Brahma,
Not this that people worship as this.

5. That which one thinks not with thought (*manas*, mind),
[or, That which thinks not with a mind,][1]
That with which they say thought (*manas*, mind) is thought—
That indeed know as Brahma,
Not this that people worship as this.

6. That which one sees not with sight (*cakṣus*, eye),
[or, That which sees not with an eye,][1]
That with which one sees sights (*cakṣūṁṣi*)[2]—
That indeed know as Brahma,
Not this that people worship as this.

7. That which one hears not with hearing (*śrotra*, ear),
[or, That which hears not with an ear,][1]
That with which hearing here is heard—
That indeed know as Brahma,
Not this that people worship as this.

8. That which one breathes (*prāṇiti*) not with breathing (*prāṇa*, breath),
[or, That which breathes not with breath,][1]
That with which breathing (*prāṇa*) is conducted (*praṇīyate*)—
That indeed know as Brahma,
Not this that people worship as this.

(SECOND KHAṆḌA)

The paradox of Its inscrutability

9 (1). [Teacher:] If you think 'I know well,' only very slightly now do you know!—a form of Brahma!—what thereof is yourself, and what thereof is among the gods! So then it is to be pondered upon (*mīmāṁsyam*) indeed by you.

[Pupil:] I think it is known.[3]

[1] Both renderings of the verse are permissible, and both are in harmony with the theory which is being expounded.

[2] Or, 'That with which one sees the eyes.'

[3] What has been translated as two sentences might also be construed as one sentence, still a part of the teacher's reproof to the undiscerning pupil :—'So then I think that what is "known" by you is [still] to be pondered upon indeed.'

10 (2). I think not 'I know well';
Yet I know not 'I know not'!
He of us who knows It, knows It;
Yet he knows not 'I know not.'

11 (3). [Teacher:]

It is conceived of by him by whom It is not conceived of.
He by whom It is conceived of, knows It not.
It is not understood by those who [say they] understand It.
It is understood by those who [say they] understand It not.

The value of knowledge of It

12 (4). When known by an awakening, It is conceived of;
Truly it is immortality one finds.
With the Soul (Ātman) one finds power[1];
With knowledge one finds the immortal.

13 (5). If one have known [It] here, then there is truth.
If one have known [It] not here, great is the destruction
(*vinaṣṭi*).[2]
Discerning [It] in every single being, the wise,
On departing from this world, become immortal.

(THIRD KHAṆḌA)[3]

Allegory of the Vedic gods' ignorance of Brahma

14 (1). Now, Brahma won a victory for the gods. Now, in the victory of this Brahma the gods were exulting. They bethought themselves: 'Ours indeed is this victory![4] Ours indeed is this greatness!'

15 (2). Now, It understood this of them. It appeared to them. They did not understand It. 'What wonderful being (*yakṣa*) is this?' they said.

[1] Perhaps 'power [to know]; and with the knowledge [thus gained] one finds . . .'

[2] With a slight variation this line is found also at Bṛih. 4. 4. 14 b.

[3] The Kena Upanishad consists of two quite distinct parts. The prose portion, §§ 14–34, is evidently the simpler and earlier. The portion §§ 1–13 (all in verse, except § 9) contains much more elaborated doctrine and would seem to be later in date of composition.

[4] An account of the victory of the gods over the demons (Asuras) occurs at Bṛih. 1. 3. 1–7.

16 (3). They said to Agni (Fire): 'Jātavedas,[1] find out this—what this wonderful being is.'

'So be it.'

17 (4). He ran unto It.

Unto him It spoke: 'Who are you?'

'Verily, I am Agni,' he said. 'Verily, I am Jātavedas.'[1]

18 (5). 'In such as you what power is there?'

'Indeed, I might burn everything here, whatever there is here in the earth!'

19 (6). It put down a straw before him. 'Burn that!'

He went forth at it with all speed. He was not able to burn it. Thereupon indeed he returned, saying: 'I have not been able to find out this—what this wonderful being is.'

20 (7). Then they said to Vāyu (Wind): 'Vāyu, find out this—what this wonderful being is.'

'So be it.'

21 (8). He ran unto It.

Unto him It spoke: 'Who are you?'

'Verily, I am Vāyu,' he said. 'Verily, I am Mātariśvan.'

22 (9). 'In such as you what power is there?'

'Indeed, I might carry off everything here, whatever there is here in the earth.'

23 (10). It put down a straw before him. 'Carry that off!'

He went at it with all speed. He was not able to carry it off. Thereupon indeed he returned, saying: 'I have not been able to find out this—what this wonderful being is.'

24 (11). Then they said to Indra: 'Maghavan ('Liberal'), find out this—what this wonderful being is.'

'So be it.'

He ran unto It. It disappeared from him.

25 (12). In that very space he came upon a woman exceedingly beautiful, Umā,[2] daughter of the Snowy Mountain (*Himavat*).

To her he said: 'What is this wonderful being?'

[1] Meaning either 'All-knower or 'All-possessor.'

[2] Com. allegorizes her as 'Knowledge,' who dispels Indra's ignorance. In later mythology Umā is an epithet, along with Durgā, Kālī, and Pārvatī, for the wife of Śiva; and she is represented as living with him in the Himālayas. Weber, *Indische Studien*, 2. 186–190, has an extended discussion of the identity of this

(FOURTH KHAṆḌA)

Knowledge of Brahma, the ground of superiority

26 (1). 'It is Brahma,' she said. 'In that victory of Brahma, verily, exult ye.'

Thereupon he knew it was Brahma.

27 (2). Therefore, verily, these gods, namely Agni, Vāyu, and Indra, are above the other gods, as it were; for these touched It nearest, for these and [especially] he [i.e. Indra] first knew It was Brahma.

28 (3). Therefore, verily, Indra is above the other gods, as it were; for he touched It nearest, for he first knew It was Brahma.

Brahma in cosmic and in individual phenomena

29 (4). Of It there is this teaching.—

That in the lightning which flashes forth, which makes one blink, and say 'Ah!'—that 'Ah!' refers to divinity.

30 (5). Now with regard to oneself.—

That which comes, as it were, to the mind, by which one repeatedly [1] remembers—that conception (*saṁkalpa*) [is It]!

Brahma, the great object of desire

31 (6). It is called *Tad-vana* ('It-is-the-desire'). [2] As 'It-is-the-desire' (*Tad-vana*) It should be worshiped. For him who knows it thus, all beings together yearn.

Concluding practical instruction and benefits

32 (7). 'Sir, tell me the mystic doctrine (*upaniṣad*)!'

'The mystic doctrine has been declared to you. Verily, we have told you the mystic doctrine of Brahma (*brāhmī upaniṣad*).'

personage and of the divinities in this passage in their significance for later mythological and sectarian developments.

[1] Deussen translates the word *abhīkṣṇaṁ* differently, and consequently interprets this section and the preceding far differently.

[2] A mystical designation. Compare a similar compound at Chānd. 3. 14. 1, *taj-ja-lan*.

33 (8). Austerity (*tapas*), restraint (*dama*), and work (*karman*) are the foundation of it [i.e. the mystic doctrine]. The Vedas are all its limbs. Truth is its abode.

34 (9). He, verily, who knows it [i.e. the mystic doctrine] thus, striking off evil (*pāpman*), becomes established in the most excellent,[1] endless, heavenly world—yea, he becomes established!

[1] So the Com. interprets *jyeye*. Max Müller and Deussen would emend to *ajyeye*, 'unconquerable.'

KAṬHA UPANISHAD

FIRST VALLĪ[1]

Prologue: Naciketas devoted to Death

1. Now verily, with zeal did Vājasravasa give his whole possession [as a religious gift]. He had a son, Naciketas by name.

2. Into him, boy as he was, while the sacrificial gifts were being led up, faith (*śraddhā*) entered. He thought to himself:

3. 'Their water drunk, their grass eaten,
Their milk milked, barren!—
Joyless (*a-nanda*) certainly are those worlds[2]
He goes to, who gives such [cows]!'

4. Then he said to his father: 'Papa, to whom will you give me?'[3]—a second time—a third time.

To him then he said: 'To Death I give you!'

Naciketas in the house of Death

[Naciketas reflects:]

5. Of many I go as the first.
Of many I go as an intermediate.
What, pray, has Yama (Death) to be done
That he will do with me today?

[1] The narrative and dialogue at the opening of this Upanishad seem to be taken —with some variation, but with some identical language—from the earlier Taittirīya Brāhmaṇa, 3. 11. 8. 1–6. The old tradition of Naciketas in the realm of Death being in a position to return to earth with knowledge of the secret of life after death, is here used to furnish a dramatic setting for the exposition which forms the body of the Upanishad.

[2] This line is found at Bṛih. 4. 4. 11 a K verbatim; with variant in the first word, at Īśā 3 a and Bṛih. 4. 4. 11 a M.

[3] That is, Naciketas voluntarily offers himself in order to fulfil the vow which his father was paying so grudgingly. Thereupon the father, in anger at the veiled reproof, exclaims: 'Oh! go to Hades!'

6. Look forward, how [fared] the former ones.
Look backward; so [will] the after ones.
Like grain a mortal ripens!
Like grain he is born hither (*ā-jāyate*) again!

Warning on the neglect of a Brahman guest

[Voice:[1]]

7. As fire, enters
A Brahman (*brāhmaṇa*) guest into houses.
They make this the quieting thereof[2]:—
Fetch water, Vaivasvata![3]

8. Hope and expectation, intercourse and pleasantness,[4]
Sacrifices and meritorious deeds,[5] sons and cattle, all—
This he snatches away from the man of little understanding
In whose home a Brahman remains without eating.

Three boons offered to Naciketas

[Death (Yama), returning from a three days' absence and finding that Naciketas has not received the hospitality which is due to a Brahman, says:]

9. Since for three nights thou hast abode in my house
Without eating, O Brahman (*brahman*), a guest to be reverenced,
Reverence be to thee, O Brahman! Well-being (*svasti*) be to me!
Therefore in return choose three boons!

Naciketas's first wish: return to an appeased father on earth

[Naciketas:]

10. With intent appeased, well-minded, with passion departed,
That Gautama toward me may be, O Death;
That cheerfully he may greet me, when from thee dismissed—
This of the three as boon the first I choose!

1 As in the Taittirīya Brāhmaṇa narrative.

2 *śāntiṁ tasya*; both words probably with a double significance, 'extinguishment of fire' and 'appeasement of the Brahman' by bringing water.

3 A Vedic epithet of Yama (Death).

4 *sūnṛtām*, according to a strict etymology, might mean 'good fellowship.'

5 If derived from √*iṣ* (instead of from √*yaj*), *iṣṭāpūrte* might possibly (though less probably) mean 'wishes and fulfilment.'

[Death:]

11. Cheerful as formerly will he be—
Auddālaki Āruṇi, from me dismissed.[1]
Happily will he sleep o' nights, with passion departed,
When he has seen thee from the mouth of Death released.

Naciketas's second wish: an understanding of the Naciketas sacrificial fire that leads to heaven

[Naciketas:]

12. In the heavenly world is no fear whatsoever.
Not there art thou. Not from old age does one fear.
Over both[2] having crossed—hunger, and thirst too—
Gone beyond sorrow, one rejoices in the heaven-world.

13. Thyself, O Death, understandest the heavenly fire.
Declare it to me who have faith (*śraddadhāna*).
Heaven-world people partake of immortality.
This I choose with boon the second.

[Death:]

14. To thee I do declare, and do thou learn it of me—
Understanding about the heavenly fire, O Naciketas!
The attainment of the infinite world, likewise too its establishment—
Know thou that as set down in the secret place [of the heart].

[Narrative:]

15. He told him of that fire as the beginning of the world,
What bricks, and how many, and how [built].
And he too repeated that, as it was told.
Then, pleased with him, Death said again—

16. Delighting, the great soul (*mahātman*) said to him:—

[1] As it stands, *prasṛṣṭaḥ* is nominative and must agree with the subject, 'Auddālaki Āruṇi.' But in such a connection it is hardly applicable; and in the previous stanza it was used with reference to Naciketas. To relieve the difficulty Böhtlingk (in his translation of the Kaṭha, Aitareya, and Praśna Upanishads, *Berichte über die Verhandlungen der Königlich Sächsischen Gesellschaft der Wissenschaften zu Leipzig, philologisch-historische Classe*, 1890, pp. 127–197), p. 132, emends to *prasṛṣṭe*, i.e. 'toward one from me dismissed'; and Whitney (in his 'Translation of the Kaṭha Upanishad' in the *Transactions of the American Philological Association*, 21. 88–112), p. 94, emends to *prasṛṣṭaṁ*, and translates: 'be cheerful [toward thee], sent forth by me.' Śaṅkara solves the difficulty by giving the word a sense, 'authorized,' which is quite different from what it evidently has in the previous stanza.

[2] That is, both death and old age.

[Death resumes:]

A further boon I give thee here today.
By thy name indeed shall this fire be [known].
This multifold garland (*sṛṅkā*), too, accept.

17. Having kindled a triple Naciketas-fire, having attained union with the three,[1]
Performing the triple work,[2] one crosses over birth and death.
By knowing the knower of what is born from Brahma,[3] the god to be praised,[4]
[And] by revering[5] [him], one goes for ever to this peace (*śānti*).[6]

18.[7] Having kindled a triple Naciketas-fire, having known this triad,
He who knowing thus, builds up the Naciketas-fire—
He, having cast off in advance the bonds of death,
With sorrow overpassed, rejoices in the heaven-world.

19. This, O Naciketas, is thy heavenly fire,
Which thou didst choose with the second boon.
As thine, indeed, will folks proclaim this fire,
The third boon, Naciketas, choose!

Naciketas's third wish: knowledge concerning the effect of dying

[Naciketas:]

20. This doubt that there is in regard to a man deceased:
'He exists,' say some; 'He exists not,' say others—
This would I know, instructed by thee!
Of the boons this is boon the third.

[Death:]

21. Even the gods had doubt as to this of yore,
For truly, it is not easily to be understood. Subtile is this matter (*dharma*).
Another boon, O Naciketas, choose!
Press me not! Give up this one for me!

[1] Śaṅkara explains these as 'father, mother, and teacher.'

[2] Namely, 'sacrifice, study of the scriptures, and alms-giving.'

[3] *brahma-ja-jña* perhaps is a synonym of *jāta-vedas*, 'the All-knower,' a common epithet of Agni (Fire, here specialized as the Naciketas sacrifice-fire).

[4] *īdya*, a very common Vedic epithet of Agni (Fire).

[5] *nicāyya* may carry a double meaning here, i.e. also 'by building [it, i.e. the Naciketas-fire].'

[6] Half of the third line and the fourth line recur at Śvet. 4. 11.

[7] Stanzas 16–18 are not quite apt here. They may be an irrelevant interpolation —as previous translators have suggested.

This knowledge preferable to the greatest earthly pleasures

[Naciketas:]

22. Even the gods had doubt, indeed, as to this,
And thou, O Death, sayest that it is not easily to be understood
And another declarer of it the like of thee is not to be obtained.
No other boon the equal of it is there at all.

[Death:]

23. Choose centenarian sons and grandsons,
Many cattle, elephants, gold, and horses.
Choose a great abode of earth.
And thyself live as many autumns as thou desirest.

24. This, if thou thinkest an equal boon,
Choose—wealth and long life!
A great one on earth, O Naciketas, be thou.
The enjoyer of thy desires I make thee.

25. Whate'er desires are hard to get in the mortal world—
For all desires at pleasure make request.
These lovely maidens with chariots, with lyres—
Such [maidens], indeed, are not obtainable by men—
By these, from me bestowed, be waited on!
O Naciketas, question me not regarding dying (*maraṇa*)!

[Naciketas:]

26. Ephemeral things! That which is a mortal's, O End-maker,
Even the vigor (*tejas*) of all the powers, they wear away.
Even a whole life is slight indeed.
Thine be the vehicles (*vāha*)! Thine be the dance and song!

27. Not with wealth is a man to be satisfied.
Shall we take wealth, if we have seen thee?
Shall we live so long as thou shalt rule?
—This, in truth, is the boon to be chosen by me.

28. When one has come into the presence of undecaying immortals,
What decaying mortal, here below, that understands,
That meditates upon the pleasures of beauty and delight,
Would delight in a life over-long?

29. This thing whereon they doubt, O Death:
What there is in the great passing-on—tell us that!
This boon, that has entered into the hidden—
No other than that does Naciketas choose.

SECOND VALLĪ

The failure of pleasure and of ignorance; the wisdom of the better knowledge

[Death:]

1. The better (*śreyas*) is one thing, and the pleasanter (*preyas*) quite another.
Both these, of different aim, bind a person.
Of these two, well is it for him who takes the better;
He fails of his aim who chooses the pleasanter.

2. Both the better and the pleasanter come to a man.
Going all around the two, the wise man discriminates.
The wise man chooses the better, indeed, rather than the pleasanter.
The stupid man, from getting-and-keeping (*yoga-kṣema*), chooses the pleasanter.

3. Thou indeed, upon the pleasant and pleasantly appearing desires
Meditating, hast let them go, O Naciketas.
Thou art not one who has taken that garland[1] of wealth
In which many men sink down.

4. Widely opposite and asunder are these two:
Ignorance (*avidyā*) and what is known as 'knowledge' (*vidyā*).
I think Naciketas desirous of obtaining knowledge!
Many desires rend thee not.[2]

5. Those abiding in the midst of ignorance,
Self-wise, thinking themselves learned,
Running hither and thither, go around deluded,
Like blind men led by one who is himself blind.[3]

Heedlessness the cause of rebirth

6. The passing-on[4] is not clear to him who is childish,
Heedless, deluded with the delusion of wealth.
Thinking 'This is the world! There is no other!'—
Again and again he comes under my control.

[1] The word *sṛṅkā* occurs nowhere else in the language—so far as has been reported—than in 1. 16 and here. Its meaning is obscure and only conjectural Śaṅkara glosses it differently in the two places, here as 'way.'

[2] This stanza recurs with unimportant variants in Maitri 7. 9.

[3] With a variation, this stanza recurs in Muṇḍ. 1. 2. 8; similarly in Maitri 7. 9.

[4] That is, death, the great transition, mentioned at 1. 29.

The need for a competent teacher of the soul

7. He who by many is not obtainable even to hear of,
He whom many, even when hearing, know not—
Wonderful is the declarer, proficient the obtainer of Him!
Wonderful the knower, proficiently taught!

8. Not, when proclaimed by an inferior man, is He[1]
To be well understood, [though] being manifoldly considered.[2]
Unless declared by another,[3] there is no going thither;
For He is inconceivably more subtile than what is of subtile measure.

9. Not by reasoning (*tarka*) is this thought (*mati*) to be attained.
Proclaimed by another, indeed, it is for easy understanding, dearest friend (*preṣṭha*)!—
This which thou hast attained! Ah, thou art of true steadfastness!
May there be for us a questioner (*praṣṭā*) the like of thee, O Naciketas!

Steadfast renunciation and self-meditation required

[Naciketas:]

10. I know that what is known as treasure is something inconstant.
For truly, that which is steadfast is not obtained by those who are unsteadfast.
Therefore the Naciketas-fire has been built up by me,
And with means which are inconstant I have obtained that which is constant.

[Death:]

11. The obtainment of desire, the foundation of the world (*jagat*),
The endlessness of will,[4] the safe shore of fearlessness,

[1] With different grouping of words the first two lines may also mean:
(1) 'Not by an inferior man is He, [even] when proclaimed,
To be well understood, [though] being often meditated upon.'
That is, the Ātman is to be obtained only by a superior person, as is stated in Muṇḍ. 3. 2. 4.
Or, (2) 'Not by an inferior man is He proclaimed.
[But] He is easily to be understood when repeatedly meditated upon.'

[2] Or perhaps, '. . . [because] being considered manifoldly,' i. e. by the inferior man, the Ātman is falsely 'conceived of as a plurality,' while in reality He is absolute unity.

[3] Either (1) by another than an inferior man, i. e. by a proficient understander, or (2) by another than oneself, i.e. by some teacher.

[4] Or perhaps 'work.'

The greatness of praise, the wide extent, the foundation
(having seen [1]),
Thou, O Naciketas, a wise one, hast with steadfastness let
[these] go!

12. Him who is hard to see, entered into the hidden,
Set in the secret place [of the heart], dwelling in the depth,
primeval—
By considering him as God, through the Yoga-study of what
pertains to self,
The wise man leaves joy and sorrow behind.

The absolutely unqualified Soul

13. When a mortal has heard this and fully comprehended,
Has torn off what is concerned with the right (*dharmya*),[2] and
has taken Him as the subtile,
Then he rejoices, for indeed he has obtained what is to be
rejoiced in.
I regard Naciketas a dwelling open [for Ātman [3]].

14. Apart from the right (*dharma*) and apart from the unright
(*a-dharma*),
Apart from both what has been done and what has not been
done here,
Apart from what has been and what is to be—
What thou seest as that, speak that!

[Naciketas being unable to mention that absolutely unqualified object, Death continues to explain:] [4]

The mystic syllable 'Om' as an aid

15. The word [5] which all the Vedas rehearse,
And which all austerities proclaim,

[1] The word *dṛṣṭvā* is superfluous both logically and metrically.

[2] Here, in contrast with the latter half of the line, the idea of *dharma* may be philosophical: i.e. 'the qualified.' In the next stanza it is certainly ethical.

[3] Compare Muṇḍ. 3. 2. 4 d: 'Into his Brahma-abode [i.e. that of a person qualified to receive Him] this Ātman enters.' See also Chānd. 8. 1. 1.

[4] Śaṅkara and all translators except Deussen regard the previous section as an utterance by Naciketas. Instead of assigning so pregnant an inquiry to a pupil still being instructed, the present distribution of the parts of this dialogue interprets it (in agreement with Deussen) as continued exposition, rhetorically put in the form of an interrogation by the teacher himself.

[5] The word *pada* here doubtless is pregnant with some other of its meanings (twenty-two in all enumerated by Apte in his *Sanskrit-English Dictionary*), particularly 'way,' 'place,' 'goal,' or 'abode.'

Desiring which men live the life of religious studentship
(*brahmacarya*)—
That word to thee I briefly declare.[1]
That is *Om*!

16. That syllable,[2] truly, indeed, is Brahma![3]
That syllable indeed is the supreme!
Knowing that syllable, truly, indeed,
Whatever one desires is his![4]

17. That is the best support.
That is the supreme support.
Knowing that support,
One becomes happy in the Brahma-world.

The eternal indestructible soul

18. The wise one [i.e. the soul, the *ātman*, the self] is not born,
nor dies.
This one has not come from anywhere, has not become anyone.
Unborn, constant, eternal, primeval, this one
Is not slain when the body is slain.[5]

19. If the slayer think to slay,
If the slain think himself slain,
Both these understand not.
This one slays not, nor is slain.[6]

The Soul revealed to the unstriving elect

20. More minute than the minute, greater than the great,
Is the Soul (Ātman) that is set in the heart of a creature here.
One who is without the active will (*a-kratu*) beholds Him,
and becomes freed from sorrow—

[1] The ideas and some of the language of this stanza recur in BhG. 8. 11.

[2] The word *akṣaram* here may also be pregnant with the meaning 'imperishable' (Apte gives fourteen meanings in all). Thus:—

'That, truly, indeed, is the imperishable Brahma!
That indeed is the supreme imperishable!
Knowing that imperishable, truly, indeed, . . .'

[3] The word *brahma*(*n*) here may contain some of its liturgical meaning, 'sacred word,' as well as the philosophical meaning 'Brahma.' Thus:—

'That syllable, truly, indeed, is sacred word!'
or 'That, truly, indeed, is imperishable sacred word!'

[4] This stanza recurs with slight verbal variation in Maitri 6. 4.

[5] Substantially this stanza is identical with BhG. 2. 20.

[6] Substantially this stanza is identical with BhG. 2. 19.

When through the grace (*prasāda*)[1] of the Creator (*dhātṛ*) he
beholds the greatness of the Soul (Ātman).

His opposite characteristics

21. Sitting, he proceeds afar;
Lying, he goes everywhere.
Who else than I (*mad*) is able to know
The god (*deva*) who rejoices and rejoices not (*madāmada*)?

22. Him who is the bodiless among bodies,
Stable among the unstable,
The great, all-pervading Soul (Ātman)—
On recognizing Him, the wise man sorrows not.

The conditions of knowing Him

23. This Soul (Ātman) is not to be obtained by instruction,
Nor by intellect, nor by much learning.
He is to be obtained only by the one whom he chooses;
To such a one that Soul (Ātman) reveals his own person
(*tanūm svām*).[2]

24. Not he who has not ceased from bad conduct,
Not he who is not tranquil, not he who is not composed,
Not he who is not of peaceful mind
Can obtain Him by intelligence (*prajñā*).

[1] This is an important passage, as being the first explicit statement of the doctrine of Grace (*prasāda*). The idea is found earlier in the celebrated Hymn of the Word (Vāc), RV. 10. 125. 5 c, d, and again in Muṇḍ. 3. 2. 3 c, d. This same stanza occurs with slight verbal variation at Śvet. 3. 20 and Mahānārāyaṇa Upanishad 8. 3 (= Taittirīya Āraṇyaka 10. 10. 1).

Inasmuch as this method of salvation 'through the grace of the Creator' is directly opposed to the general Upanishadic doctrine of salvation 'through knowledge,' Śaṅkara interprets *dhātuḥ prasādāt* as *dhātu-samprasādāt*, 'through the tranquillity of the senses,' according to the practice of the Yoga-method. There is this possibility of different interpretation of the word *prasāda*; for it occurs unquestionably in the sense of 'tranquillity' at Maitri 6. 20 and 6. 34; compare also the compounds *jñāna-prasāda*, 'the peace of knowledge,' at Muṇḍ. 3. 1. 8, and *varṇa-prasāda*, 'clearness of complexion,' at Śvet. 2. 13. In the Bhagavad-Gītā there is the same double use:—'peace' or 'tranquillity,' at 2. 64; 2. 65; 18. 37; and 'the grace of Kṛishṇa,' at 18. 56; 18. 58; 18. 62; 18. 73; and 'the grace of Vyāsa,' at 18. 75.

The development of the doctrine of 'salvation by grace' by the Vishnuites proceeds through the Epic, culminating in the sharp controversy against this 'Cat-doctrine' by the 'Monkey-doctrine' of 'salvation by works.' Compare Hopkins, *Religions of India*, pp. 500, 501.

[2] This stanza = Muṇḍ. 3. 2. 3.

The all-comprehending incomprehensible

25. He for whom the priesthood (*brahman*) and the nobility (*kṣatra*)
Both are as food,
And death is as a sauce—
Who really knows where He is?

THIRD VALLĪ

The universal and the individual soul

1. There are two that drink of righteousness (*ṛta*) in the world of good deeds;
Both are entered into the secret place [of the heart], and in the highest upper sphere.
Brahma-knowers speak of them as 'light' and 'shade,'
And so do householders who maintain the five sacrificial fires, and those too who perform the triple Naciketas-fire.

The Naciketas sacrificial fire as an aid

2. This which is the bridge for those who sacrifice,
And which is the highest imperishable Brahma
For those who seek to cross over to the fearless farther shore—
The Naciketas-fire may we master!

Parable of the individual soul in a chariot

3. Know thou the soul (*ātman*, self) as riding in a chariot,
The body as the chariot.
Know thou the intellect (*buddhi*) as the chariot-driver,
And the mind (*manas*) as the reins.

4. The senses (*indriya*), they say, are the horses;
The objects of sense, what they range over.
The self combined with senses and mind
Wise men call 'the enjoyer' (*bhoktṛ*).

5. He who has not understanding (*a-vijñāna*),
Whose mind is not constantly held firm—
His senses are uncontrolled,
Like the vicious horses of a chariot-driver.

6. He, however, who has understanding,
Whose mind is constantly held firm—
His senses are under control,
Like the good horses of a chariot-driver.

Intelligent control of the soul's chariot needed to arrive beyond reincarnation

7. He, however, who has not understanding,
Who is unmindful and ever impure,
Reaches not the goal,
But goes on to reincarnation (*saṁsāra*).

8. He, however, who has understanding,
Who is mindful and ever pure,
Reaches the goal
From which he is born no more.

9. He, however, who has the understanding of a chariot-driver,
A man who reins in his mind—
He reaches the end of his journey,
That highest place of Vishṇu.[1]

The order of progression to the supreme Person

10. Higher than the senses are the objects of sense.
Higher than the objects of sense is the mind (*manas*);
And higher than the mind is the intellect (*buddhi*).
Higher than the intellect is the Great Self (Ātman).

11. Higher than the Great is the Unmanifest (*avyakta*).
Higher than the Unmanifest is the Person.
Higher than the Person there is nothing at all.
That is the goal. That is the highest course.

The subtle perception of the all-pervading Soul

12. Though He is hidden in all things,
That Soul (Ātman, Self) shines not forth.
But he is seen by subtle seers
With superior, subtle intellect.

The Yoga method—of suppression

13. An intelligent man should suppress his speech and his mind.
The latter he should suppress in the Understanding-Self
(*jñāna ātman*).

[1] The last line of this stanza = RV. 1. 22. 20 a, and also, with a slight change, RV. 1. 154. 5 d.

The understanding he should suppress in the Great Self
[= *buddhi*, intellect].
That he should suppress in the Tranquil Self (*śānta ātman*).

Exhortation to the way of liberation from death

14. Arise ye! Awake ye!
Obtain your boons[1] and understand them!
A sharpened edge of a razor, hard to traverse,
A difficult path is this—poets (*kavi*) declare!

15. What is soundless, touchless, formless, imperishable,
Likewise tasteless, constant, odorless,
Without beginning, without end, higher than the great, stable—
By discerning That, one is liberated from the mouth of death.

The immortal value of this teaching

16. The Naciketas tale,
Death's immemorial teaching—
By declaring and hearing this, a wise man
Is magnified in the Brahma-world.

17. If one recites this supreme secret
In an assembly of Brahmans,
Or at a time of the ceremony for the dead, devoutly—
That makes for immortality!
—That makes for immortality!

FOURTH VALLĪ

The immortal Soul not to be sought through outward senses

1. The Self-existent (*svayambhū*) pierced the openings [of the senses] outward;
Therefore one looks outward, not within himself (*antarātman*).
A certain wise man, while seeking immortality,
Introspectively beheld the Soul (Ātman) face to face.

2. The childish go after outward pleasures;
They walk into the net of widespread death.
But the wise, knowing immortality,
Seek not the stable among things which are unstable here.

[1] The commentators interpret 'boons' as referring to 'teachers.' But the word may imply 'answers to your questions.'

Yet the agent in all the senses, in sleeping and in waking

3. That by which [one discerns] form, taste, smell,
Sound, and mutual touches—
It is with That indeed that one discerns.
What is there left over here!

This, verily, is That!

4. By recognizing as the great pervading Soul (Ātman)
That whereby one perceives both
The sleeping state and the waking state,
The wise man sorrows not.

The universal Soul (Ātman), identical with the individual and with all creation

5. He who knows this experiencer [1]
As the living Soul (Ātman) near at hand,
Lord of what has been and of what is to be—
He does not shrink away from Him.

This, verily, is That!

6. He who was born of old from austerity (*tapas*),
Was born of old from the waters,
Who stands entered into the secret place [of the heart],
Who looked forth through beings—[2]

This, verily, is That!

7. She [3] who arises with life (*prāṇa*),
Aditi (Infinity), maker of divinity,
Who stands entered into the secret place [of the heart],
Who was born forth through beings—

This, verily, is That!

8. Fire (Agni), the all-knower (*jātavedas*), hidden away in the two fire-sticks
Like the embryo well borne by pregnant women,
Worthy to be worshiped day by day
By watchful men with oblations—[4]

This, verily, is That!

[1] *madhv-ad,* literally 'honey-eater,' i. e. the empirical self.

[2] This stanza contains an ungrammatical form and impossible constructions. The text here, as also in § 7, is probably corrupt. The reference here is probably to the Sāṁkhyan Purusha, Person.

[3] Traditionally interpreted as Prakṛiti, Nature.

[4] This stanza = SV. 1. 2. 3. 7, and also, with slight variation, RV. 3. 29. 2.

9. Whence the sun rises,
And where it goes to rest—
On Him all the gods are founded;
And no one ever goes beyond it.[1]

This, verily, is That!

Failure to comprehend the essential unity of being regarded as the cause of reincarnation

10. Whatever is here, that is there.
What is there, that again is here.
He obtains death after death
Who seems to see a difference here.[2]

11. By the mind, indeed, is this [realization] to be attained:—
There is no difference here at all![3]
He goes from death to death
Who seems to see a difference here.

The eternal Lord abiding in one's self

12. A Person of the measure of a thumb
Stands in the midst of one's self (*ātman*),
Lord of what has been and of what is to be.
One does not shrink away from Him.

This, verily, is That!

13. A Person of the measure of a thumb,
Like a light without smoke,
Lord of what has been and what is to be.
He alone is today, and tomorrow too.

The result of seeing multiplicity or else pure unity

14. As water rained upon rough ground
Runs to waste among the hills,
So he who sees qualities (*dharma*) separately,
Runs to waste after them.

15. As pure water poured forth into pure
Becomes the very same,
So becomes the soul (*ātman*), O Gautama,
Of the seer (*muni*) who has understanding.

[1] With slight variation in line c this stanza = Bṛih. 1. 5. 23. Lines a and b also = AV. 10. 18. 16 a, b.

[2] Lines c and d = Bṛih. 4. 4. 19 c, d.

[3] Lines a and b = Bṛih. 4. 4. 19 a, b with a verbal variation.

FIFTH VALLI

The real soul of the individual and of the world

1. By ruling over the eleven-gated citadel[1]
Of the Unborn, the Un-crooked-minded one,
One sorrows not.
But when liberated [from the body], he is liberated indeed.

This, verily, is That!

2. The swan [i.e. sun] in the clear, the Vasu in the atmosphere,
The priest by the altar, the guest in the house,
In man, in broad space, in the right (*ṛta*), in the sky,
Born in water, born in cattle, born in the right, born in rock,
is the Right, the Great![2]

3. Upwards the out-breath (*prāṇa*) he leadeth.
The in-breath (*apāna*) inwards he casts.
The dwarf who is seated in the middle[3]
All the gods (*deva*) reverence!

4. When this incorporate one that stands in the body
Is dissolved,
And is released from the body,
What is there left over here?[4]

This, verily, is That!

5. Not by the out-breath (*prāṇa*) and the in-breath (*apāna*)[5]
Doth any mortal whatsoever live.
But by another do men live—
Even That whereon both these depend.

The appropriate embodiment of the reincarnating soul

6. Come! I will declare this to you:
The hidden, eternal Brahma;
And how, after it reaches death,
The soul (*ātman*) fares, O Gautama!

[1] That is, the body, with its eleven orifices: two eyes, two ears, two nostrils, mouth, the two lower orifices, the navel, and the sagittal suture (*vidṛti*—Ait. 3. 12). By the omission of the last two, the body is conceived of as a nine-gated city at Śvet. 3. 18 and BhG. 5. 13.

[2] With the omission of the last word this stanza = RV. 4. 40. 5; exactly as here it = VS. 10. 24; 12. 14; TS. 3. 2. 10. 1; Śat. Br. 6. 7. 3. 11.

[3] That is, in the middle of the body, and the *devās* are the bodily powers (or 'senses,' as not infrequently), according to Śaṅkara's interpretation.

[4] Line d = 4. 3 d.

[5] As in 5. 3 a, b.

7. Some go into a womb
For the embodiment of a corporeal being.
Others go into a stationary thing
According to their deeds (*karman*), according to their knowledge.

One's real person, the same as the world-ground

8. He who is awake in those that sleep,
The Person who fashions desire after desire—
That indeed is the Pure. That is Brahma.
That indeed is called the Immortal.
On it all the worlds do rest;
And no one soever goes beyond it.[1]

This, verily, is That!

The unitary world-soul, immanent yet transcendent

9. As the one fire has entered the world
And becomes corresponding in form to every form,
So the one Inner Soul (*antarātman*) of all things
Is corresponding in form to every form, and yet is outside.

10. As the one wind has entered the world
And becomes corresponding in form to every form,
So the one Inner Soul of all things
Is corresponding in form to every form, and yet is outside.

11. As the sun, the eye of the whole world,
Is not sullied by the external faults of the eyes,
So the one Inner Soul of all things
Is not sullied by the evil in the world, being external to it.

The indescribable bliss of recognizing the world-soul in one's own soul

12. The Inner Soul (*antarātman*) of all things, the One Controller,
Who makes his one form manifold—
The wise who perceive Him as standing in oneself,
They, and no others, have eternal happiness!

13. Him who is the Constant among the inconstant, the Intelligent among intelligences,
The One among many, who grants desires—

[1] The last four lines recur again as 6. 1 c–f.

The wise who perceive Him as standing in oneself,
They, and no others, have eternal peace!

14. 'This is it!'—thus they recognize
The highest, indescribable happiness.
How, now, shall I understand 'this'?
Does it shine [of itself] or does it shine in reflection?

The self-luminous light of the world

15. The sun shines not there, nor the moon and stars,
These lightnings shine not, much less this (earthly) fire!
After Him, as He shines, doth everything shine,
This whole world is illumined with His light.[1]

SIXTH VALLĪ

The world-tree rooted in Brahma

1. Its root is above, its branches below—
This eternal fig-tree![2]
That (root) indeed is the Pure. That is Brahma.
That indeed is called the Immortal.
On it all the worlds do rest,
And no one soever goes beyond it.[3]

This, verily, is That!

The great fear

2. This whole world, whatever there is,
Was created from and moves in Life (*prāṇa*).
The great fear, the upraised thunderbolt—
They who know That, become immortal.

3. From fear of Him fire (Agni) doth burn.
From fear the sun (Sūrya) gives forth heat.
From fear both Indra and Wind (Vāyu),
And Death (Mṛityu) as fifth, do speed along.[4]

[1] This stanza = Muṇḍ. 2. 2. 10 and Śvet. 6. 14.
[2] This same simile of the world as an eternal fig-tree growing out of Brahma is further elaborated in BhG. 15. 1–3.
[3] These last four lines = 5. 8 c–f.
[4] A very similar stanza is found in Tait. 2. 8.

Degrees of perception of the Soul (Ātman).

4. If one has been able to perceive [Him] here on earth
Before the dissolution of the body,
According to that [knowledge] he becomes fitted
For embodiment in the world-creations.[1]

5. As in a mirror, so is it seen in the body (*ātman*);
As in a dream, so in the world of the fathers;
As if in water, so in the world of the Gandharvas (genii);
As if in light and shade, so in the world of Brahma.

The gradation up to the supersensible Person

6. The separate nature of the senses,
And that their arising and setting
Is of things that come into being apart [from himself],
The wise man recognizes, and sorrows not.

7. Higher than the senses (*indriya*) is the mind (*manas*);
Above the mind is the true being (*sattva*).
Over the true being is the Great Self [i.e. *buddhi*, intellect];
Above the Great is the Unmanifest (*avyakta*).

8. Higher than the Unmanifest, however, is the Person (Purusha),
All-pervading and without any mark (*a-liṅga*) whatever.
Knowing which, a man is liberated
And goes to immortality.

9. His form (*rūpa*) is not to be beheld.
No one soever sees Him with the eye.[2]
He is framed by the heart, by the thought, by the mind.
They who know That become immortal.[3]

The method of Yoga, suppressive of the lower activity

10. When cease the five
[Sense-]knowledges, together with the mind (*manas*),

[1] The reading *svargeṣu* instead of *sargeṣu* would yield the more suitable meaning 'in the heavenly worlds.' At best, the stanza contradicts the general theory that perception of the Ātman produces release from reincarnation immediately after death. Consequently Śaṅkara supplies an ellipsis which changes the meaning entirely, and Max Müller hesitatingly inserts a 'not' in the first line. The present translation interprets the meaning that the degree of perception of the Ātman in the present world determines one's reincarnate status.

[2] These two lines recur at Śvet. 4. 20 a, b.

[3] These two lines recur at Śvet. 3. 13 c, d and 4. 17 c, d.

And the intellect (*buddhi*) stirs not—
That, they say, is the highest course.[1]

11. This they consider as Yoga[2]—
The firm holding back of the senses.
Then one becomes undistracted.[3]
Yoga, truly, is the origin and the end.[4]

The Soul incomprehensible except as existent

12. Not by speech, not by mind,
Not by sight can He be apprehended.
How can He be comprehended
Otherwise than by one's saying 'He is'?[5]

13. He can indeed be comprehended by the thought 'He is' (*asti*)
And by [admitting] the real nature of both [his comprehensibility and his incomprehensibility].[6]
When he has been comprehended by the thought 'He is'
His real nature manifests itself.

A renunciation of all desires and attachments the condition of immortality

14. When are liberated all
The desires that lodge in one's heart,
Then a mortal becomes immortal!
Therein he reaches Brahma![7]

15. When are cut all
The knots of the heart here on earth,

[1] Quoted in Maitri 6. 30.

[2] Literally 'yoking'; both a 'yoking,' i. e. subduing, of the senses; and also a 'yoking,' i. e. a 'joining' or 'union,' with the Supreme Spirit.

[3] *apramatta*, a technical Yoga term.

[4] Perhaps, of 'the world' of beings and experiences—here too, as in Māṇḍ. 6, where the phrase occurs. That is: 'the world' becomes created for the person when he emerges from the Yoga state, and passes away when he enters into it. Or perhaps the translation should be 'an arising and a passing away': i. e. is transitory—according to Śaṅkara.

[5] The same thought of the incomprehensibility of the ultimate occurs at Kena 3 a, b, and Muṇḍ. 3. 1. 8 a, b.

[6] That is, both the affirmable, 'He is' and the absolutely non-affirmable 'No! No!' *neti, neti* of Bṛih. 2. 3. 6; both 'being' (*sad*) and 'non-being' (*asad*) of Muṇḍ. 2. 2. 1 d and Praśna 2. 5 d. Śaṅkara interprets 'both' as referring to the 'conditioned' and the 'unconditioned' Brahma.

[7] This stanza is found also at Bṛih. 4. 4. 7 a.

Then a mortal becomes immortal!
—Thus far is the instruction.

The passage of the soul from the body to immortality—or elsewhere

16. There are a hundred and one channels of the heart.
One of these passes up to the crown of the head.
Going up by it, one goes to immortality.
The others are for departing in various directions.[1]

17. A Person of the measure of a thumb is the inner soul (*antarātman*),
Ever seated in the heart of creatures.
Him one should draw out from one's own body
Like an arrow-shaft out from a reed, with firmness.
Him one should know as the Pure, the Immortal—
Yea, Him one should know as the Pure, the Immortal.

This teaching, the means of attaining Brahma and immortality

18. Then Naciketas, having received this knowledge
Declared by Death, and the entire rule of Yoga,
Attained Brahma and became free from passion, free from death
And so may any other who knows this in regard to the Soul (Ātman).

[1] This stanza is found also at Chānd. 8. 6. 6. Cf. also Kaush. 4. 19 and Brih. 4. 2. 3.

ĪŚĀ UPANISHAD[1]

Recognition of the unity underlying the diversity of the world

1. By the Lord (*īśā*) enveloped must this all be—
Whatever moving thing there is in the moving world.
With this renounced, thou mayest enjoy.
Covet not the wealth of anyone at all.

Non-attachment of deeds on the person of a renouncer

2. Even while doing deeds here,
One may desire to live a hundred years.
Thus on thee—not otherwise than this is it—
The deed (*karman*) adheres not on the man.

The forbidding future for slayers of the Self

3. Devilish (*asurya*[2]) are those worlds called,[3]
With blind darkness (*tamas*) covered o'er!
Unto them, on deceasing, go
Whatever folk are slayers[4] of the Self.[5]

The all-surpassing, paradoxical world-being

4. Unmoving, the One (*ekam*) is swifter than the mind.
The sense-powers (*deva*) reached not It, speeding on before.
Past others running, This goes standing.
In It Mātariśvan places action.[6]

[1] So called from its first word; or sometimes 'Īśāvāsyam' from its first two words; or sometimes the 'Vājasaneyi-Saṁhitā Upanishad' from the name of the recension of the White Yajur-Veda of which this Upanishad forms the final, the fortieth, chapter.

[2] Compare the persons called 'devilish,' *āsura*, at Chānd. 8. 8. 5. A variant reading here (accordant with a literalism interpreted in the following line) is *a-sūrya*, 'sunless.'

[3] The word *nāma* here might mean 'certainly' instead of 'called.'

[4] This idea is in apparent contrast with the doctrine of Kaṭha 2. 19 d (and BhG. 2. 19), where it is stated that 'he [i. e. the Self] slays not, is not slain.' The word *ātma-han* here, of course, is metaphorical, like 'smother,' 'stifle,' 'completely suppress.'

[5] The whole stanza is a variation of Bṛih. 4. 4. 11.

[6] So Com. But *apas* may refer, cosmogonically, to 'the [primeval] waters.'

5. It moves. It moves not.
It is far, and It is near.
It is within all this,
And It is outside of all this.[1]

6. Now, he who on all beings
Looks as just (*eva*) in the Self (Ātman),
And on the Self as in all beings—[2]
He does not shrink away from Him.[3]

7. In whom all beings
Have become just (*eva*) the Self of the discerner—
Then what delusion (*moha*), what sorrow (*śoka*) is there
Of him who perceives the unity!

Characteristics of the world-ruler

8. He has environed. The bright, the bodiless, the scatheless,
The sinewless, the pure (*śuddha*), unpierced by evil (*a-pāpa-viddha*)!
Wise (*kavi*), intelligent (*manīṣin*), encompassing (*paribhū*), self-existent (*svayambhū*),
Appropriately he distributed objects (*artha*) through the eternal years.

Transcending, while involving, the antithesis of knowing

9. Into blind darkness enter they
That worship ignorance;
Into darkness greater than that, as it were, they
That delight in knowledge.[4]

10. Other, indeed, they say, than knowledge!
Other, they say, than non-knowledge![5]
—Thus we have heard from the wise (*dhīra*)
Who to us have explained It.[6]

1 The very same ideas as in this stanza, though not all the same words, recur at BhG. 13. 15 a, b, d.

2 This universal presence is claimed by Kṛishṇa for himself at BhG. 6. 30 a, b.

3 The indefinite word *tatas* may mean 'from these beings,' or 'from this Self,' or 'from this time on,' or pregnantly all these.—The whole line recurs at Bṛih. 4. 4. 15 d; Kaṭha 4. 5 d; 4. 12 d.

4 This stanza is identical with Bṛih. 4. 4. 10.

5 The point here made is that both knowledge and lack of knowledge are inadequate for apprehending the Ultimate.

6 A somewhat more concrete, and perhaps earlier, form of this stanza occurs as Kena 3 e–h.

11. Knowledge and non-knowledge—
He who this pair conjointly (*saha*) knows,
With non-knowledge passing over death,
With knowledge wins the immortal.[1]

The inadequacy of any antithesis of being

12. Into blind darkness enter they
Who worship non-becoming (*a-sambhūti*);
Into darkness greater than that, as it were, they
Who delight in becoming (*sambhūti*).

13. Other, indeed—they say—than origin (*sambhava*)!
Other—they say—than non-origin (*a-sambhava*)!
—Thus have we heard from the wise
Who to us have explained It.

Becoming and destruction a fundamental duality

14. Becoming (*sambhūti*) and destruction (*vināśa*)—
He who this pair conjointly (*saha*) knows,
With destruction passing over death,
With becoming wins the immortal.

A dying person's prayer

15. With a golden vessel[2]
The Real's face is covered o'er.
That do thou, O Pūshan, uncover
For one whose law is the Real[3] to see.[4]

16. O Nourisher (*pūṣan*), the sole Seer (*ekarṣi*), O Controller (*yama*), O Sun (*sūrya*), offspring of Prajāpati, spread forth thy rays! Gather thy brilliance (*tejas*)![5] What is thy

[1] This stanza occurs again in Maitri 7. 9.

[2] The sun.

[3] For the petitioner (who calls himself '*satya-dharma*') to see through; or 'For Him whose law is Truth (or, true) to be seen,' [as, e. g., for Savitṛi in RV. 10. 34. 8; 10. 139. 3; or the Unknown Creator, RV. 10. 121. 9; VS. 10. 103; or Agni, RV. 1. 12. 7]; or, 'For that [neuter] which has the Real as its nature [or, essence; or, law] to be seen.'

[4] These lines occur with slight variations at Maitri 6. 35 and Bṛih. 5. 15. 1.

[5] According to this translation the idea is entirely honorific of the effulgence of the sun. Or, with a different grouping of words, the meaning might possibly be the petition: 'Spread apart thy rays [that I may enter through the sun (as well as see through—according to the previous petition) into the Real; then] gather [thy rays together again, as normal]. The brilliance which is thy fairest form, . . .' At best the passage is of obscure mystical significance.

fairest form—that of thee I see. He who is yonder, yonder Person (*puruṣa*)—I myself am he!

17. [My] breath (*vāyu*) to the immortal wind (*anila*)![1] This body then ends in ashes! *Om*!

> O Purpose (*kratu*[2]), remember! The deed (*kṛta*) remember!
> O Purpose, remember! The deed remember!

General prayer of petition and adoration

18. O Agni, by a goodly path to prosperity (*rai*) lead us,
Thou god who knowest all the ways!
Keep far from us crooked-going sin (*enas*)![3]
Most ample expression of adoration to thee would we render![4]

[1] This formula recurs at Bṛih. 5. 15. The idea that at death the several parts of microcosmic man revert to the corresponding elements of the macrocosm is expressed several times in Sanskrit literature. With the specific mention here, compare 'his spirit (*ātman*) to the wind (*vāta*)' in the Cremation Hymn, RV. 10. 16. 3 a; 'with his breath (*prāṇa*) to wind (*vāyu*),' Śat. Br. 10. 3. 3. 8; 'his breath (*prāṇa*) to wind (*vāta*),' Bṛih. 3. 2. 13; and even of the sacrificial animal, 'its breath (*prāṇa*) to wind (*vāta*),' Ait. Br. 2. 6.

[2] Compare the statement in Chānd. 3. 14. 1, 'Now, verily, a person consists of purpose (*kratu-maya*).'

[3] Other prayers for freedom from sin (*enas*, compare also *āgas*) are at RV. 1. 24. 9 d; 3. 7. 10 d; 7. 86. 3 a, 4 d; 7. 88. 6 c; 7. 89. 5 c, d; 7. 93. 7 c, d; 8. 67 (56). 17; 10. 35. 3 a, c; 10. 37. 12; AV. 6. 97. 2 d; 6. 115. 1, 2, 3; 6. 116. 2, 3; 6. 117; 6. 118; 6. 119; 6. 120.

[4] This stanza is identical with RV. 1. 189. 1, and the second line also with AV. 4. 39. 10 b.

MUṆḌAKA UPANISHAD

FIRST MUṆḌAKA

Preparation for the knowledge of Brahma

FIRST KHAṆḌA

The line of tradition of this knowledge from Brahmā himself

1. Brahmā arose as the first of the gods—
The maker of all, the protector of the world.
He told the knowledge of Brahma (*brahma-vidyā*), the foundation of all knowledge,
To Atharva[n], his eldest son.

2. What Brahmā taught to Atharvan,
Even that knowledge of Brahma, Atharvan told in ancient time to Aṅgir.
He told it to Bhāradvāja Satyavāha;
Bhāradvāja, to Aṅgiras—both the higher and the lower [knowledge].

Śaunaka's quest for the clue to an understanding of the world

3. Śaunaka, verily, indeed, a great householder, approached Aṅgiras according to rule, and asked: 'Through understanding of what, pray, does all this world become understood, sir?'[1]

Two kinds of knowledge: the traditions of religion, and the knowledge of the eternal

4. To him then he said: 'There are two knowledges to be known—as indeed the knowers of Brahma are wont to say[2]: a higher (*para*) and also a lower (*apara*).

[1] The very same knowledge which Yājñavalkya declared to Maitreyī, Bṛih. 2. 4. 5 (end).

[2] Cf. Maitri 6. 22.

5. Of these, the lower is the Rig-Veda, the Yajur-Veda, the Sāma-Veda, the Atharva-Veda,

Pronunciation (*śikṣā*), Ritual (*kalpa*), Grammar (*vyākaraṇa*), Definition (*nirukta*), Metrics (*chandas*), and Astrology (*jyotiṣa*).[1]

Now, the higher is that whereby that Imperishable (*akṣara*) is apprehended.

The imperishable source of all things

6. That which is invisible, ungraspable, without family, without caste (*a-varṇa*)—
Without sight or hearing is It, without hand or foot,
Eternal, all-pervading, omnipresent, exceedingly subtile;
That is the Imperishable, which the wise perceive as the source of beings.

7. As a spider emits and draws in [its thread],
As herbs arise on the earth,
As the hairs of the head and body from a living person,
So from the Imperishable arises everything here.

8. By austerity (*tapas*) Brahma becomes built up.
From that, food is produced;
From food—life-breath, mind, truth,
The worlds, immortality too in works.

9. He who is all-knowing, all-wise,
Whose austerity consists of knowledge—
From Him are produced the Brahma here,
[Namely] name and form,[2] and food.

SECOND KHAṆḌA

All the ceremonies of religion scrupulously to be practised

1. This is the truth:—

The works which the sages (*kavi*) saw in the sacred sayings (*mantra*, i.e. Vedic hymns)
Are manifoldly spread forth in the triad [of the Vedas].
Follow them (*ācaratha*) constantly, ye lovers of truth (*satya-kāma*)!
This is your path to the world of good deeds.

[1] The six subsidiary Vedāṅgas, 'Limbs-of-the-Vedas,' later elaborated as explanatory of the Vedas.

[2] A Sanskrit idiom for the modern term 'individuality.'

2. When the flame flickers,
After the oblation fire has been kindled,
Then, between the two portions of melted butter, his oblations
One should throw—an offering made with faith (*śraddhā*).

3. If one's Agnihotra sacrifice is not followed by the sacrifice of the new moon and of the full moon, by the four-months sacrifice, by the harvest sacrifice, if it is unattended by guests, or not offered at all, or without the ceremony to all the gods, or not according to rule, it destroys his seven worlds.

4. The Black (*kālī*), and the Terrible, and the Swift-as-Thought,
The Very-red, and the Very-smoky-colored,
The Scintillating, and the All-formed,[1] divine one,
Are the seven so-called flickering tongues [of flame].[2]

Rewards of ceremonial observances

5. If one performs sacrifices when these are shining,
Offering the oblations at the proper time, too,
These (flames) as rays of the sun lead him
To where is resident the one lord (*pati*) of the gods.

6. Saying to him "Come! Come!" the splendid offerings
Carry the sacrificer with the rays of the sun,
Addressing pleasant speech, praising, and saying:
"This is your meritorious (*puṇya*) Brahma-world, gained by good works."

Sacrificial forms ineffective against rebirth

7. Unsafe boats, however, are these sacrificial forms,
The eighteen,[3] in which is expressed the lower work.
The fools who approve that as the better,
Go again to old age and death.

The consequences of ignorance

8. Those abiding in the midst of ignorance,
Self-wise, thinking themselves learned,
Hard smitten, go around deluded,
Like blind men led by one who is himself blind.[4]

[1] A variant reading is *viśva-rucī*, 'All-gleaming.'

[2] Cf. 'the seven-rayed Fire' in RV. 1. 146. 1. Seven was an early sacrosanct number.

[3] That is, the four Vedas, each including Saṁhitā, Brāhmaṇa, and Sūtra, and in addition the six Vedāṅgas which are enumerated at Muṇḍ. 1. 1. 5.

[4] With slight variation = Kaṭha 2. 5 and Maitri 7. 9.

9. Manifoldly living in ignorance,
They think to themselves, childishly: "We have accomplished our aim!"
Since doers of deeds (*karmin*) do not understand, because of passion (*rāga*),
Therefore, when their worlds are exhausted, they sink down wretched.

10. Thinking sacrifice and merit is the chiefest thing,
Naught better do they know—deluded!
Having had enjoyment on the top of the heaven won by good works,
They re-enter this world, or a lower.

But unstriving, retiring knowers, without sacrifice, reach the eternal Person

11. They who practise austerity (*tapas*) and faith (*śraddhā*) in the forest,
The peaceful (*śānta*) knowers who live on alms,
Depart passionless (*vi-rāga*) through the door of the sun,
To where is that immortal Person (Purusha), e'en the imperishable Spirit (Ātman).

This knowledge of Brahma to be sought properly from a qualified teacher

12. Having scrutinized the worlds that are built up by work, a Brahman
Should arrive at indifference. The [world] that was not made[1] is not [won] by what is done.
For the sake of this knowledge let him go, fuel in hand,[2]
To a spiritual teacher (*guru*) who is learned in the scriptures and established on Brahma.

13. Such a knowing [teacher], unto one who has approached properly,
Whose thought is tranquilized, who has reached peace,
Teaches in its very truth that knowledge of Brahma
Whereby one knows the Imperishable, the Person, the True.

[1] Cf. 'the uncreated Brahma-world,' Chānd. 8. 13.
[2] The token of pupilship.

SECOND MUṆḌAKA

The Doctrine of Brahma-Ātman

First Khaṇḍa

The Imperishable, the source and the goal of all beings

1. This is the truth :—

As, from a well-blazing fire, sparks
By the thousand issue forth of like form,
So from the Imperishable, my friend, beings manifold
Are produced, and thither also go.

The supreme Person

2. Heavenly (*divya*), formless (*a-mūrtta*) is the Person (Purusha).
He is without and within, unborn,
Breathless (*a-prāṇa*), mindless (*a-manas*), pure (*śubhra*),
Higher than the high Imperishable.

The source of the human person and of the cosmic elements

3. From Him is produced breath (*prāṇa*),
Mind (*manas*), and all the senses (*indriya*),
Space (*kha*), wind, light, water,
And earth, the supporter of all.

The macrocosmic Person

4. Fire is His head ; His eyes, the moon and sun ;
The regions of space, His ears ; His voice, the revealed Vedas ;
Wind, His breath (*prāṇa*) ; His heart, the whole world. Out of His feet,
The earth. Truly, He is the Inner Soul (Ātman) of all.

The source of the world and of the individual

5. From Him [proceeds] fire, whose fuel is the sun ;
From the moon (Soma), rain ; herbs, on the earth.
The male pours seed in the female.
Many creatures are produced from the Person (Purusha).

The source of all religious rites

6. From Him the Rig Verses, the Sāman Chant, the sacrificial formulas (*yajus*), the initiation rite (*dīkṣā*).

And all the sacrifices, ceremonies, and sacrificial gifts (*dakṣiṇā*),
The year too, and the sacrificer, the worlds
Where the moon (Soma) shines brightly, and where the sun.[1]

The source of all forms of existence

7. From Him, too, gods are manifoldly produced,
The celestials (Sādhyas), men, cattle, birds,
The in-breath and the out-breath (*prāṇāpanau*), rice and barley, austerity (*tapas*),
Faith (*śraddhā*), truth, chastity, and the law (*vidhi*).

The source of the activity of the senses

8. From Him come forth the seven life-breaths (*prāṇa*),[2]
The seven flames, their fuel, the seven oblations,
These seven worlds, wherein do move
The life-breaths that dwell in the secret place [of the heart] placed seven and seven.

The source of the world—the immanent Soul of things

9. From Him, the seas and the mountains all.
From Him roll rivers of every kind.
And from Him all herbs, the essence, too,
Whereby that Inner Soul (*antarātman*) dwells in beings.

The supreme Person found in the heart

10. The Person (Purusha) himself is everything here:
Work (*karman*) and austerity (*tapas*) and Brahma, beyond death.
He who knows That, set in the secret place [of the heart]—
He here on earth, my friend, rends asunder the knot of ignorance.

[1] That is, the world of the fathers, and the world of the gods, respectively; described in Chānd. 5. 10.

[2] Śaṅkara explains these seven *prāṇa* as the seven organs of sense in the head (i.e. two eyes, two ears, two nostrils, and the mouth). They are compared to seven different sacrificial oblations. The enlightenments produced by their activity are the flames of the sacrifice; the objects which supply their action, the fuel. Each sense moves in an appropriate world of its own; but they are all co-ordinated by the mind (*manas*), which is located in the heart. These same seven flames are probably referred to in Praśna 3. 5, end. Compare the seven flames of the regular sacrifices named at Muṇḍ. 1. 2. 4.

Second Khaṇḍa

The all-inclusive Brahma

1. Manifest, [yet] hidden; called 'Moving-in-secret';
The great abode! Therein is placed that
Which moves and breathes and winks.[1]
What that is, know as Being (*sad*) and Non-being (*a-sad*),
As the object of desire, higher than understanding,
As what is the best of creatures!

2. That which is flaming, which is subtler than the subtle,
On which the worlds are set, and their inhabitants—
That is the imperishable Brahma.
It is life (*prāṇa*), and It is speech and mind.
That is the real. It is immortal.
It is [a mark] to be penetrated. Penetrate It, my friend!

A target to be penetrated by meditation on 'Om'

3. Taking as a bow the great weapon of the Upanishad,
One should put upon it an arrow sharpened by meditation.
Stretching it with a thought directed to the essence of That,
Penetrate[2] that Imperishable as the mark, my friend.

4. The mystic syllable *Om* (*praṇava*) is the bow. The arrow is the soul (*ātman*).
Brahma is said to be the mark (*lakṣya*).
By the undistracted man is It to be penetrated.
One should come to be in It, as the arrow [in the mark].

The immortal Soul, the one warp of the world and of the individual

5. He on whom the sky, the earth, and the atmosphere
Are woven, and the mind, together with all the life-breaths (*prāṇa*),
Him alone know as the one Soul (Ātman). Other
Words dismiss. He is the bridge to immortality.

[1] The first three lines of this stanza = AV. 10. 8. 6.

[2] With a double meaning, doubtless, in accordance with the great thought of metaphysical knowledge which is here being expounded. Besides being derivable from √ *vyadh*, 'to penetrate,' *viddhi* means also 'know.'

The great Soul to be found in the heart

6. Where the channels are brought together
Like the spokes in the hub of a wheel—
Therein he moves about,
Becoming manifold.
Om!—Thus meditate upon the Soul (Ātman).
Success to you in crossing to the farther shore beyond darkness!

7. He who is all-knowing, all-wise,
Whose is this greatness on the earth—
He is in the divine Brahma city[1]
And in the heaven established! The Soul (Ātman)!
Consisting of mind, leader of the life-breaths and of the body,
He is established on food, controlling[2] the heart.
By this knowledge the wise perceive
The blissful Immortal that gleams forth.

Deliverance gained through vision of Him

8. The knot of the heart is loosened,
All doubts are cut off,
And one's deeds (*karman*) cease
When He is seen—both the higher and the lower.

The self-luminous light of the world

9. In the highest golden sheath
Is Brahma, without stain, without parts.
Brilliant is It, the light of lights—
That which knowers of the Soul (Ātman) do know!

10. The sun shines not there, nor the moon and stars;
These lightnings shine not, much less this [earthly] fire!
After Him, as He shines, doth everything shine.
This whole world is illumined with His light.[3]

The omnipresent Brahma

11. Brahma, indeed, is this immortal. Brahma before,
Brahma behind, to right and to left.
Stretched forth below and above,
Brahma, indeed, is this whole world, this widest extent.

[1] That is, 'in the body,' as in Chānd. 8. 1. 1.
[2] From *saṁ-ni-√dhā*, with the same meaning as in Praśna 3. 4.
[3] This stanza = Kaṭha 5. 15 and Śvet. 6. 14.

THIRD MUNDAKA

The Way to Brahma

FIRST KHAṆḌA

Recognition of the Great Companion, the supreme salvation

1. Two birds, fast bound companions,
Clasp close the self-same tree.
Of these two, the one eats sweet fruit;
The other looks on without eating.[1]

2. On the self-same tree a person, sunken,
Grieves for his impotence, deluded;
When he sees the other, the Lord (*īś*), contented,
And his greatness, he becomes freed from sorrow.[2]

3. When a seer sees the brilliant
Maker, Lord, Person, the Brahma-source,
Then, being a knower, shaking off good and evil,[3]
Stainless, he attains supreme identity (*sāmya*) [with Him].

Delight in the Soul, the life of all things

4. Truly, it is Life (*prāṇa*) that shines forth in all things!
Understanding this, one becomes a knower. There is no superior speaker.
Having delight in the Soul (Ātman), having pleasure in the Soul,[4] doing the rites,
Such a one is the best of Brahma-knowers.

The pure Soul obtainable by true methods

5. This Soul (Ātman) is obtainable by truth, by austerity (*tapas*),
By proper knowledge (*jñāna*), by the student's life of chastity (*brahmacarya*) constantly [practised].
Within the body, consisting of light, pure is He
Whom the ascetics (*yati*), with imperfections done away, behold.

[1] This stanza is quoted from RV. 1. 164. 20; repeated at Śvet. 4. 6. Compare also Kaṭha 3. 1.

[2] Repeated at Śvet. 4. 7.

[3] The first three lines of this stanza are quoted at Maitri 6. 18.

[4] As in Chānd. 7. 25. 2.

6. Truth alone conquers, not falsehood.
By truth is laid out the path leading to the gods (*devayāna*)
By which the sages whose desire is satisfied ascend
To where is the highest repository of truth.

The universal inner Soul

7. Vast, heavenly, of unthinkable form,
And more minute than the minute, It shines forth.
It is farther than the far, yet here near at hand,
Set down in the secret place [of the heart], even here among those who behold [It].

Obtainable by contemplation, purified from sense

8. Not by sight is It grasped, not even by speech,
Not by any other sense-organs (*deva*), austerity, or work.
By the peace of knowledge (*jñāna-prasāda*), one's nature purified—
In that way, however, by meditating, one does behold Him who is without parts.

9. That subtile Soul (Ātman) is to be known by thought (*cetas*)
Wherein the senses (*prāṇa*) fivefoldly have entered.
The whole of men's thinking is interwoven with the senses.
When that is purified, the Soul (Ātman) shines forth.

The acquiring power of thought

10. Whatever world a man of purified nature makes clear in mind,
And whatever desires he desires for himself—
That world he wins, those desires too.
Therefore he who is desirous of welfare should praise the knower of the Soul (Ātman).

SECOND KHAṆḌA

Desires as the cause of rebirth

1. He knows that Supreme Brahma-abode,
Founded on which the whole world shines radiantly.
They who, being without desire, worship the Person (Purusha)
And are wise, pass beyond the seed (*śukra*) [of rebirth] here.

2. He who in fancy forms desires,
Because of his desires is born [again] here and there.
But of him whose desire is satisfied, who is a perfected soul (*kṛtātman*),
All desires even here on earth vanish away.

The Soul (Ātman) known only by revelation to His own elect

3. This Soul (Ātman) is not to be obtained by instruction,
Nor by intellect, nor by much learning.
He is to be obtained only by the one whom He chooses;
To such a one that Soul (Ātman) reveals His own person (*tanūm svām*).[1]

Certain indispensable conditions, pre-eminently knowledge

4. This Soul (Ātman) is not to be obtained by one destitute of fortitude,
Nor through heedlessness, nor through a false notion of austerity (*tapas*).
But he who strives by these means, provided he knows—
Into his Brahma-abode this Soul (Ātman) enters.

In tranquil union with the Soul of all is liberation from death and from all distinctions of individuality

5. Attaining Him, the seers (*ṛṣi*) who are satisfied with knowledge,
Who are perfected souls (*kṛtātman*), from passion free (*vīta-rāga*), tranquil—
Attaining Him who is the universally omnipresent, those wise,
Devout souls (*yuktātman*) into the All itself do enter.

6. They who have ascertained the meaning of the Vedānta-knowledge,
Ascetics (*yati*) with natures purified through the application of renunciation (*saṁnyāsa-yoga*)—
They in the Brahma-worlds at the end of time
Are all liberated beyond death.

7 Gone are the fifteen parts[2] according to their station,
Even all the sense-organs (*deva*) in their corresponding divinities!
One's deeds (*karman*) and the self that consists of understanding (*vijñāna-maya ātman*)—
All become unified in the supreme Imperishable.

8. As the flowing rivers in the ocean
Disappear, quitting name and form,[3]
So the knower, being liberated from name and form,
Goes unto the Heavenly Person, higher than the high.

[1] This stanza recurs at Kaṭha 2. 23.

[2] That is, of the microcosm back into the macrocosm. Cf. Praśna 6. 5.

[3] The Sanskrit idiom for 'individuality.'

The rewards and the requisite conditions of this knowledge of Brahma

9. He, verily, who knows that supreme Brahma, becomes very Brahma.[1] In his family no one ignorant of Brahma arises. He crosses over sorrow. He crosses over sin (*pāpman*). Liberated from the knots of the heart, he becomes immortal.

10. This very [doctrine] has been declared in the verse:—

They who do the rites, who are learned in the Vedas, who are intent on Brahma,
They who, possessing faith (*śraddhayan*), make oblation of themselves, even of the one seer[2]—
To them indeed one may declare this knowledge of Brahma,
When, however, the Muṇḍaka-vow[3] has been performed by them according to rule.'

11. This is the truth. The seer (*ṛṣi*) Aṅgiras declared it in ancient time. One who has not performed the vow does not read this.

Adoration to the highest seers!
Adoration to the highest seers!

[1] In the title to his Latin translation, 'Oupnekhat,' Anquetil Duperron set this sentence evidently as the summary of the contents of the Upanishads: 'Quisquis Deum intelligit, Deus fit,' 'whoever knows God, becomes God.'

[2] Identified with Prāṇa, 'Life,' in Praśna 2. 11. The reference, then, is probably to the mystical Prāṇāgnihotra sacrifice, in which 'breath' is symbolically sacrificed for an Agnihotra ceremony.

[3] Śaṅkara explains this as 'carrying fire on the head—a well-known Vedic vow among followers of the Atharva-Veda.' But it is more likely to be 'shaving the head,' as Buddhist monks did later. This preliminary requisite to the study of the Upanishad doubtless gave it the title 'The Shaveling Upanishad,' or 'The Upanishad of the Tonsured.'

PRAŚNA UPANISHAD[1]

FIRST PRAŚNA

Six questioners seek the highest Brahma from a teacher

1. Sukeśan Bhāradvāja, and Śaibya Satyakāma, and Sauryāyaṇin Gārgya, and Kauśalya Āśvalāyana, and Bhārgava Vaidarbhi, and Kabandhin Kātyāyana—these, indeed, were devoted to Brahma, intent upon Brahma, in search of the highest Brahma. Thinking 'He, verily, will tell it all,' with fuel in hand[2] they approached the honorable Pippalāda.

2. To them then that seer (*ṛṣi*) said: 'Dwell with me (*samvatsyatha*) a year (*samvatsara*) more, with austerity (*tapas*), chastity (*brahmacarya*), and faith (*śraddhā*). Then ask what questions you will. If we know, we will tell you all.'

Question: Concerning the source of creatures on earth

3. Then Kabandhin Kātyāyana came up and asked: 'Sir, whence, verily, are creatures here born?'

The Lord of Creation created matter and life for dual parentage of creatures

4. To him then he said: 'The Lord of Creation (Prajāpati), verily, was desirous of creatures (offspring, *prajā*). He performed austerity. Having performed austerity, he produces a pair, matter (*rayi*, fem.) and life (*prāṇa*, masc.), thinking "These two will make creatures for me in manifold ways."

The sun and moon, such a pair

5. The sun, verily, is life; matter, indeed, is the moon.

Matter identified with every form of existence

Matter, verily, is everything here, both what is formed and what is formless. Therefore material form (*mūrti*) indeed is matter.

[1] That is, Question Upanishad.

[2] The ancient token with which a person presented himself as a pupil unto a teacher whose instruction he desired.

The sun, identified with the life of creatures

6. Now the sun, when it rises, enters the eastern quarter. Thereby it collects the living beings (*prāṇa*) of the east in its rays. When it illumines the southern, the western, the northern, the lower, the upper, the intervening quarters, when it illumines everything—thereby it collects all living beings in its rays.

7. That fire rises as the universal, all-formed life. This very [doctrine] has been declared in the verse:—

8. [. . . Him] who has all forms, the golden one, all-knowing,[1]
The final goal, the only light, heat-giving.
The thousand-rayed, the hundredfold revolving,
Yon sun arises as the life of creatures.[2]

The year identified with the Lord of Creation; the two paths: of reincarnation and of non-reincarnation

9. The year, verily, is Lord of Creation (Prajāpati). This has two paths, the Southern and the Northern.[3]

Now, those, verily, indeed, who worship, thinking "Sacrifice and merit are our work (*kṛta*)!"— they win only the lunar world. They, indeed, return hither again.[4] Therefore those seers (*ṛṣi*) who are desirous of offspring go the Southern course. This matter (*rayi*) verily it is, that leads to the fathers (*pitṛyāṇa*).

10. But they who seek the Soul (Ātman) by austerity, chastity, faith, and knowledge—they by the Northern course win the sun. That, verily, is the support of life-breaths. That is the immortal, the fearless. That is the final goal. From that they do not return—as they say (*iti*). That is the stopping [of rebirth]. As to that there is this verse (*śloka*):—

[1] Or, according to a different exegesis, the word *jātavedasam* may mean 'all-finding.'

[2] This stanza occurs again in Maitri 6. 8, as the conclusion of a section which expounds the unity of Prāṇa (life) and Āditya (the sun).

[3] Elaborated in Bṛih. 6. 2. 15–16; Chānd. 4. 15. 5; Chānd. 5. 10; and BhG. 8. 24–26 as the half-year of the sun's southward course and as the half-year of the sun's northward course, respectively.

[4] This belief in rebirth is already expressed in AV. 12. 2. 52 b.

Two old Vedic interpretations of the year

11. They speak of a father, five-footed, twelve-formed,[1]
Rich in moisture, as in the higher half of heaven.
But others here speak of a sage[2] in the lower half,
Set in a seven-wheeled, six-spoked[3] [chariot].[4]

The twofold month, identified with the Lord of Creation; to be properly observed in sacrifice

12. The month, verily, is the Lord of Creation (Prajāpati). Its dark half, indeed, is matter; its bright half, life. Therefore these seers (*ṛṣi*) perform sacrifice in the bright half; other people, in the other half.

Day and night, identified with the Lord of Creation; to be properly observed in procreation

13. Day and night, verily, are the Lord of Creation (Prajāpati). Of this, day indeed is life; the night, matter. Verily, they waste their life who join in sexual enjoyment by day; it is chastity that they join in sexual enjoyment by night.

Food, the direct source of creatures

14. Food, verily, is the Lord of Creation (Prajāpati). From this, verily, is semen. From this creatures here are born.

Concluding assurance

15. Now, they who practise this rule of Prajāpati[5] produce a pair.[6]

They indeed possess that Brahma-world,
Who possess austerity (*tapas*) and chastity (*brahmacarya*),
In whom the truth is established.

16. To them belongs yon stainless Brahma-world,
In whom there is no crookedness and falsehood, nor trickery (*māyā*).'

[1] Both Śaṅkara here and Sāyaṇa on the Rig-Veda passage explain this as 'the year,' 'with five seasons,' and 'with twelve months.'
[2] Or 'one far-shining,' *vicakṣaṇa*.
[3] 'With seven steeds, and with six seasons.'—Com.
[4] This stanza = RV 1. 164. 12.
[5] As stated above in § 13.
[6] That is, offspring, like Prajāpati himself according to § 4.

SECOND PRAŚNA

Concerning the several personal powers and their chiefest

1. Then Bhārgava Vaidarbhi asked him [i. e. Pippalāda]:—
[a] 'Sir, how many powers (*deva*) support a creature?
[b] How many illumine this [body]?
[c] Which one again is the chiefest of them?'

[a and b] **The supporting and illumining powers**

2. To him then he said: 'Space (*ākāśa*), verily, is such a power (*deva*)—wind, fire, water, earth, speech, mind, sight, and hearing, too.[1] These, having illumined it, declare: "We uphold and support this trunk (*bāṇa*)!"

[c] **Life, the essential and chiefest**

3. To them Life (*prāṇa*, the life-breath), the chiefest, said: "Fall not into delusion! I indeed, dividing myself (*ātmānam*) fivefold, support and sustain this body!"

4. They were incredulous. He, from pride, as it were, rises up aloft. Now when he rises up, then all the others also rise up; and when he settles down, they all settle down with him.

Now, as all the bees rise up after the king bee when he rises up, and all settle down when he settles down, even so speech, mind, sight, and hearing. They, being satisfied, praise Life (*prāṇa*, the life-breath).

The universal Life

5. As fire (Agni), he warms. He is the sun (Sūrya).
He is the bountiful[2] rain (Parjanya). He is the wind (Vāyu).
He is the earth, matter (*rayi*), God (*deva*),
Being (*sat*) and Non-being (*asat*), and what is immortal.

6. Like the spokes on the hub of a wheel,
Everything is established on Life (*prāṇa*):—
The Rig verses, the Yajus formulas, the Sāman chants,
The sacrifice, the nobility (*kṣatra*), and the priesthood (*brahman*)!

[1] That is, the five cosmic elements, and with *prāṇa* (life-breath) the five personal functions.

[2] The reference may be to 'Indra,' for whom *maghavan* is a very common Vedic epithet.

7. As the Lord of Creation (Prajāpati), thou movest in the womb.
'Tis thou thyself that art born again.
To thee, O Life, creatures here bring tribute—[1]
Thou, who dwellest with living beings!

8. Thou art the chief bearer [of oblations] to the gods!
Thou art the first offering to the fathers!
Thou art the true practice of the seers,
Descendants of Atharvan and Aṅgiras

9. Indra art thou, O Life, with thy brilliance!
Rudra art thou as a protector!
Thou movest in the atmosphere
As the sun (Sūrya), thou Lord of lights!

10. When thou rainest upon them,
Then these creatures of thine, O Life,
Are blissful, thinking:
"There will be food for all desire!"

11. A Vrātya[2] art thou, O Life, the only seer,
An eater, the real lord of all!
We are the givers of thy food!
Thou art the father of the wind (Mātariśvan).

12. That form of thine which abides in speech,
Which abides in hearing, which abides in sight,
And which is extended in the mind,
Make propitious! Go not away!

13. This whole world is in the control of Life—
E'en what is established in the third heaven!
As a mother her son, do thou protect [us]!
Grant to us prosperity (*śrī*) and wisdom (*prajñā*)!'

[1] This line is a reminiscence of AV. 11. 4. 19 a, b, a hymn to Prāṇa, of which there are other reminiscences in this Praśna Upanishad.

[2] Śaṅkara explains this word as meaning 'uninitiated' because of his being the first born, and there being no one else to initiate him; therefore 'pure by nature.' This is a noteworthy characterization; for later a Vrātya is either a despised, non-Brahmanical low-caste man, or else a man who has lost caste through the non-observance of proper ceremonies! Yet compare the glorification of the Vrātya in AV. 15.

THIRD PRAŚNA

Six questions concerning a person's life

1. Then Kausalya Āśvalāyana asked him [i. e. Pippalāda]:

[a] 'Whence, sir, is this life (*prāṇa*) born?

[b] How does it come into this body?

[c] And how does it distribute itself (*ātmānam*), and establish itself?

[d] Through what does it depart?

[e] How does it relate itself to the external?

[f] How with reference to the self?'

2. To him then he said: 'You are asking questions excessively. But you are pre-eminently a Brahman[1]—methinks (*iti*). Therefore I tell you.

[a] The source of a person's life

3. This life (*prāṇa*) is born from the Spirit (Ātman, Self).

[b] Its embodiment

As in the case of a person there is this shadow extended, so it is in this case. By the action of the mind [in one's previous existence[2]] it comes into this body.

[c] Its establishment and distribution in the body

4. As an overlord commands his overseers, saying: "Superintend such and such villages," even so this life (*prāṇa*) controls the other life-breaths one by one.

5. The out-breath (*apāna*) is in the organs of excretion and generation. The life-breath (*prāṇa*) as such (*svayam*) establishes itself in the eye and ear, together with the mouth and nose. While in the middle is the equalizing breath (*samāna*),

[1] Or, 'most devoted to Brahma,' *brahmiṣṭha*.

[2] Such seems to be the implication of the important preceding word *manokṛtena*, in accordance with the theory of rebirth which is assumed later in this same Upanishad. That is: a person's life in this body is the sure and appropriate result of his thoughts in a previous existence, even as a shadow is the similitude unavoidably cast from a person's body. A different, but not contradictory, interpretation is possible from the reading *mano'kṛtena*, 'without action of the mind (which Deussen proposes): i. e. that a person's life in this body is an involuntary shadow cast from the great Self.

for it is this [breath] that equalizes [in distribution] whatever has been offered as food.[1] From this arise the seven flames.[2]

6. In the heart, truly, is the self (*ātman*). Here there are those hundred and one channels.[3] To each one of these belong a hundred smaller channels. To each of these belong seventy-two thousand[4] branching channels (*hitā*). Within them moves the diffused breath (*vyāna*).

[d] Its departure

7. Now, rising upward through one of these [channels],[5] the up-breath (*udāna*) leads in consequence of good [work] (*puṇya*) to the good world; in consequence of evil (*pāpa*), to the evil world; in consequence of both, to the world of men.

[e and f] Its cosmic and personal relations[6]

8. The sun, verily, rises externally as life[7]; for it is that which helps the life-breath in the eye. The divinity which is in the earth supports a person's out-breath (*apāna*). What is between [the sun and the earth], namely space (*ākāśa*), is the equalizing breath (*samāna*). The wind (Vāyu) is the diffused breath (*vyāna*).

9. Heat (*tejas*), verily, is the up-breath (*udāna*). Therefore one whose heat has ceased goes to rebirth, with his senses (*indriya*) sunk in mind (*manas*).

One's thinking determines life and destiny

10. Whatever is one's thinking (*citta*), therewith he enters into life (*prāṇa*). His life joined with his heat, together with the self (*ātman*), leads to whatever world has been fashioned [in thought].[8]

[1] Or possibly, as rendered by Deussen, '. . . it is this [breath] that brings to sameness [i. e. assimilates, digests] this offered food.' But cf. Praśna 4. 4.

[2] Compare Muṇḍ. 2. 1. 8.

[3] Mentioned in Chānd. 8. 6. 6.

[4] Mentioned in Bṛih. 2. 1. 19.

[5] Called the *suṣumnā*. Cf. Maitri 6. 21.

[6] The idea expounded is that the five bodily life functions are correlated with five cosmic powers.

[7] As already identified in 1. 5.

[8] The destiny-making power of thought, especially as instanced in a person's last thoughts, is similarly expressed in BhG. 8. 6.

Recapitulation

11. The knower who knows life (*prāṇa*) thus—his offspring truly is not lost; he becomes immortal. As to this there is this verse (*śloka*):—

12. The source, the entrance, the location,
The fivefold extension,
And the relation to self (*adhyātma*) of the life (*prāṇa*)—
By knowing these one obtains immortality!
By knowing these one obtains immortality!'

FOURTH PRAŚNA

Concerning sleep and the ultimate basis of things

1. Then Sauryāyaṇin Gārgya asked him [i. e. Pippalāda]:—
[a] 'Sir, what are they that sleep in a person here?
[b] What are they that remain awake in him?
[c] Which is the god (*deva*) that sees the dreams?
[d] Whose is the happiness?
[e] In whom, pray, are all things established?'

[a] All sense-functions unified in the mind during sleep

2. To him then he said: 'O Gārgya, as the rays of the setting sun all become one in an orb of brilliance and go forth again and again when it rises, even so, verily, everything here becomes one in mind (*manas*), the highest god.

Therefore in that condition (*tarhi*) the person hears not, sees not, smells not, tastes not, touches not, speaks not, takes not, enjoys not, emits not, moves not about. "He sleeps!" they say.

[b] The five life-functions, like sacrificial fires, slumber not

3. Life's fires, in truth, remain awake in this city.

The out-breath (*apāna*) is the Gārhapatya (Householder's) fire. The diffused breath (*vyāna*) is the Anvāhāryapacana (Southern Sacrificial) fire. The in-breath (*prāṇa*) is the Āhavanīya (Oblation) fire, from "being taken" (*praṇayana*), since it is taken (*praṇīyate*) from the Gārhapatya fire.[1]

[1] Life itself being conceived of as a sacrifice, these three life-breaths are symbolically identified with the three fires which are used in the Vedic sacrificial rites. Compare the identification of the sacrificer's priest, wife, and son with these same three altar fires at Ait. Br. 8. 24.

4. The equalizing breath (*samāna*) is so called because it "equalizes" (*samaṁ nayati*) the two oblations: the in-breathing and the out-breathing (*ucchvāsa-niḥśvāsa*). The mind, verily, indeed, is the sacrificer. The fruit of the sacrifice is the up-breath (*udāna*). It leads the sacrificer to Brahma day by day.

[c] The universal mind, the beholder of dreams

5. There, in sleep, that god experiences greatness. Whatever object has been seen, he sees again; whatever has been heard, he hears again. That which has been severally experienced in different places and regions, he severally experiences again and again. Both what has been seen and what has not been seen, both what has been heard and what has not been heard, both what has been experienced and what has not been experienced, both the real (*sat*) and the unreal (*a-sat*)—he sees all. He sees it, himself being all.

[d] The brilliant happiness of dreamless sleep, in the mind's non-action

6. When he is overcome with brilliance (*tejas*), then that god sees no dreams; then here in this body arises this happiness (*sukha*).

[e] The Supreme Soul the ultimate basis of the manifold world and of the individual

7. As birds resort to a tree for a resting-place, even so, O friend, it is to the supreme Soul (Ātman) that everything here resorts[1]:—

8. Earth and the elements (*mātra*) of earth, water and the elements of water, heat (*tejas*) and the elements of heat, wind and the elements of wind, space and the elements of space, sight and what can be seen, hearing and what can be heard, smell and what can be smelled, taste and what can be tasted, the skin and what can be touched, speech and what can be spoken, the hands and what can be taken, the organ of genera-

[1] The following is a noteworthy Sāṁkhya enumeration, including the five cosmic elements, the ten organs (*indriya*), and *manas*, *buddhi*, *ahaṁkāra*, *citta*, together with light and life. Cf. p. 391, note 4.

tion and what can be enjoyed, the anus and what can be excreted, the feet and what can be walked, mind (*manas*) and what can be perceived, intellect (*buddhi*) and what can be conceived, egoism (*ahaṁkāra*) and what can be connected with "me," thought (*citta*) and what can be thought, brilliance (*tejas*) and what can be illumined, life-breath (*prāṇa*) and what can be supported.

9. Truly, this seer, toucher, hearer, smeller, taster, thinker (*mantṛ*), conceiver (*boddhṛ*), doer, the conscious self (*vijñānātman*), the person—his resort is in the supreme imperishable Soul (Ātman, Self).

Knowing, and reaching, the world-ground

10. Verily, O friend! he who recognizes that shadowless, bodiless, bloodless, pure Imperishable, arrives at the Imperishable itself. He, knowing all, becomes the All. On this there is the verse (*śloka*):—

> 11. O friend! he who recognizes as the Imperishable
> That whereon the conscious self, with all its powers (*deva*),
> And the life-breaths (*prāṇa*) and the elements (*bhūta*) do rest—
> He, knowing all, into the All has entered.'

FIFTH PRAŚNA

Concerning the value of meditation on 'Om'

1. Then Śaibya Satyakāma asked him [i. e. Pippalāda]: 'Verily, sir, if some one among men here should meditate on the syllable *Om* until the end of his life, which world, verily, does he win thereby?'

Partial or complete comprehension of 'Om' and of Brahma affords temporary or final cessation of rebirth

2. To him then he said: 'Verily, O Satyakāma, that which is the syllable *Om* is both the higher and the lower Brahma.[1]

[1] Compare Muṇḍ. 1. 1. 4 for the two kinds of sacred knowledge. So here probably *brahma* may be used in the sense of 'sacred knowledge' as well as in a strictly metaphysical sense referring to the *nir-guṇa*, 'un-qualified,' and the *sa-guṇa*, 'qualified,' Brahma respectively.

Therefore with this support, in truth, a knower reaches one or the other.

3. If he meditates on one element [namely *a*], having been instructed by that alone he quickly comes into the earth [after death]. The Rig verses lead him to the world of men. There, united with austerity, chastity, and faith, he experiences greatness.

4. Now, if he is united in mind with two elements [namely *a* + *u*], he is led by the Yajus formulas to the intermediate space, to the world of the moon. Having experienced greatness in the world of the moon, he returns hither again.

5. Again, he who meditates on the highest Person (Purusha) with the three elements of the syllable *Om* [namely *a* + *u* + *m*] is united with brilliance (*tejas*) in the sun. As a snake is freed from its skin, even so, verily, is he freed from sin (*pāpman*) He is led by the Sāman chants to the world of Brahma. He beholds the Person that dwells in the body and that is higher than the highest living complex. As to this there are these two verses (*śloka*):—

6. The three elements are deadly when employed
One after the other, separately.
In actions external, internal, or intermediate
When they are properly employed, the knower trembles not.

7. With the Rig verses, to this world; with the Sāman chants, to the intermediate space;
With the Yajus formulas, to that which sages (*kavi*) recognize;
With the syllable *Om* in truth as a support, the knower reaches That
Which is peaceful, unaging, immortal, fearless, and supreme!'

SIXTH PRAŚNA

Concerning the Person with sixteen parts [1]

1. Then Sukeśan Bhāradvāja asked him [i. e. Pippalāda]: 'Sir, Hiraṇyanābha, a prince of the Kośalas, came to me and

[1] In VS. 8. 36 Prajāpati, 'Lord of Creation,' is addressed as *ṣoḍaśin*, 'with sixteen parts.' In Bṛih. 1 5. 14 the year is identified with Prajāpati and explained

asked this question: "Bhāradvāja, do you know the Person with the sixteen parts?" I said to the youth: "I know him not. If I had known him, would I not have told you? Verily, he dries up even to the roots, who speaks untruth. Therefore it is not proper that I should speak untruth." In silence he mounted his chariot and departed.

I ask it of you: "Where is that Person?"'

2. To him he then said: 'Even here within the body, O friend, is that Person in whom they say the sixteen parts arise.

3. He [i. e. the Person] thought to himself: "In whose departure shall I be departing? In whose resting firm, verily, shall I be resting firm?"

4. He created life (*prāṇa*); from life, faith (*śraddhā*), space (*kha*), wind, light, water, earth, sense-faculty (*indriya*), mind, food; from food, virility, austerity, sacred sayings (*mantra*), sacrifice, the worlds; and in the worlds, name [i. e. the individual].

5. As these flowing rivers that tend toward the ocean, on reaching the ocean, disappear, their name and form (*nāma-rūpa*) are destroyed, and it is called simply "the ocean"—even so of this spectator these sixteen parts that tend toward the Person, on reaching the Person, disappear, their name and form are destroyed, and it is called simply "the Person." That one continues without parts, immortal! As to that there is this verse:—

as having sixteen parts because its component half-months each consist of fifteen days and a turning-point. According to Bṛih. 1. 5. 15 the human person who understands this fact becomes similarly characterized. A practical proof of a person's sixteenfoldness is adduced at Chānd. 6. 7, and an etymological proof at Śat. Br. 10. 4. 1. 17.

These old conceptions, namely that the 'Lord of Creation' is sixteenfold and that a human person also is sixteenfold, are here philosophically interpreted in accordance with the general monism of the Upanishads.

Analysis: §§ 2, 3, the cosmic Person is immanent in the human person, which is His most distinctive manifestation; § 4, the human person is the culmination and recapitulation of the sixteenfold evolution of the thought of the creative Person; § 5, the sixteenfold human person tends to return to, and merge into, the immortal Person, and therein to lose his finite individuality; § 6, an appreciation of the unitary basis of the manifold world as being a knowable Person removes the fear of death.

6. Whereon the parts rest firm
Like the spokes on the hub of a wheel—
Him I know as the Person to be known!
So let death disturb you not!'

Conclusion of the instruction

7. To them then he [i. e. Pippalāda] said: 'Thus far, in truth, I know that supreme Brahma. There is naught higher than It.'

8. They praised him and said: 'You truly are our father—you who lead us across to the shore beyond ignorance.'

Adoration to the supreme seers!

Adoration to the supreme seers!

MĀṆḌŪKYA UPANISHAD

The mystic symbolism of the word 'Om':
(a) identified with the fourfold, monistic time-Brahma

1. *Om*!—This syllable[1] is this whole world.

Its further explanation is:—

The past, the present, the future—everything is just the word *Om*.

And whatever else that transcends threefold time[2]—that, too, is just the word *Om*.

2. For truly, everything here is Brahma; this self (*ātman*) is Brahma. This same self has four fourths.

(b) representing in its phonetic elements the four states of the Self

3. The waking state (*jāgarita-sthāna*), outwardly cognitive, having seven limbs,[3] having nineteen mouths,[4] enjoying the gross (*sthūla-bhuj*), the Common-to-all-men (*vaiśvānara*), is the first fourth.

4. The dreaming state (*svapna-sthāna*), inwardly cognitive, having seven limbs, having nineteen mouths, enjoying the exquisite (*pravivikta-bhuj*), the Brilliant (*taijasa*), is the second fourth.

[1] Inasmuch as *akṣaraṁ* means also 'imperishable,' the word may in this connection be used with a double significance, namely, 'This imperishable syllable...'

[2] A similar phrase occurs at Śvet. 6. 5 b.

[3] Śaṅkara refers to the enumeration of the several parts of the universal (*vaiśvānara*) Self at Chānd. 5. 18. 2; there, however, the list is longer than seven. The exact significance of the number here is uncertain.

[4] Śaṅkara explains this to mean: the five organs of sense (*buddhīndriya*), namely those of hearing, touch, sight, taste, and smell, the five organs of action (*karmendriya*), namely those of speech, handling, locomotion, generation, and excretion, the five vital breaths (*prāṇa*), the sensorium (*manas*), the intellect (*buddhi*), egoism (*ahaṁkāra*), and thinking (*citta*).

5. If one asleep desires no desire whatsoever, sees no dream whatsoever,[1] that is deep sleep (*suṣupta*).

The deep-sleep state (*suṣupta-sthāna*), unified (*ekī-bhūta*),[2] just (*eva*) a cognition-mass (*prajñāna-ghana*),[3] consisting of bliss (*ānanda-maya*),[4] enjoying bliss (*ānanda-bhuj*), whose mouth is thought (*cetas-*), the Cognitional (*prājña*), is the third fourth.

6. This is the lord of all (*sarveśvara*).[5] This is the all-knowing (*sarva-jña*).[6] This is the inner controller (*antar-yāmin*).[7] This is the source (*yoni*)[8] of all, for this is the origin and the end (*prabhavāpyayau*)[9] of beings.

7. Not inwardly cognitive (*antaḥ-prajña*), not outwardly cognitive (*bahiḥ-prajña*), not both-wise cognitive (*ubhayataḥ-prajña*), not a cognition-mass (*prajñāna-ghana*), not cognitive (*prajña*), not non-cognitive (*a-prajña*), unseen (*a-dṛṣṭa*), with which there can be no dealing (*a-vyavahārya*), ungraspable (*a-grāhya*), having no distinctive mark (*a-lakṣaṇa*), non-thinkable (*a-cintya*), that cannot be designated (*a-vyapadeśya*), the essence of the assurance of which is the state of being one with the Self[10] (*ekātmya-pratyaya-sāra*), the cessation of development (*prapañcopaśama*), tranquil (*śānta*), benign (*śiva*), without a second (*a-dvaita*)—[such] they think is the fourth.[11] He is the Self (Ātman). He should be discerned.

8. This is the Self with regard to the word *Om*, with regard to its elements. The elements (*mātra*) are the fourths;

[1] The part of the sentence up to this point has occurred already in Bṛih. 4. 3. 19.

[2] A detailed description of the condition of being 'unified' occurs at Bṛih. 4. 4. 2.

[3] This compound has already occurred in Bṛih. 4. 5. 13.

[4] A description of the self 'consisting of bliss' occurs in Tait. 2. 5. It is declared to be the acme of attainment over every other form of self at Tait. 2. 8. 1 and 3. 10. 5.

[5] A phrase in Bṛih. 4. 4. 22.

[6] A phrase in Muṇḍ. 1. 1. 9; 2. 2. 7.

[7] The subject of discourse in Bṛih. 3. 7.

[8] Literally, 'womb.'

[9] A phrase in Kaṭha 6. 11.

[10] Or, according to the reading *ekātma-*, 'the oneness of the Self' or 'one's own self.'

[11] The designation here used for the 'fourth,' or superconscious, state is *caturtha*, the usual and regular form of the ordinal numeral adjective. In Bṛih. (at 5. 14. 3, 4, 6, 7) it is named *turīya*, and in Maitri (at 6. 19; 7. 11. 7) *turya*—variant forms of the same ordinal. All later philosophical treatises have the form *turīya*, which came to be the accepted technical term.

the fourths, the elements: the letter *a*, the letter *u*, the letter *m*.[1]

9. The waking state, the Common-to-all-men, is the letter *a*, the first element, from *āpti* ('obtaining') or from *ādimatvā* ('being first').

He obtains, verily, indeed, all desires, he becomes first—he who knows this.

10. The sleeping state, the Brilliant, is the letter *u*, the second element, from *utkarṣa* ('exaltation') or from *ubhayatvā* ('intermediateness').

He exalts, verily, indeed, the continuity of knowledge; and he becomes equal[2] (*samāna*); no one ignorant of Brahma is born in the family of him who knows this.

11. The deep-sleep state, the Cognitional, is the letter *m*, the third element, from *miti* ('erecting') or from *apīti*[3] ('immerging').

He, verily, indeed, erects (*minoti*) this whole world,[4] and he becomes its immerging—he who knows this.

12. The fourth is without an element, with which there can be no dealing, the cessation of development, benign, without a second.

Thus *Om* is the Self (Ātman) indeed.

He who knows this, with his self enters the Self[5]—yea, he who knows this!

[1] In Sanskrit the vowel *o* is constitutionally a diphthong, contracted from *a* + *u*. *Om* therefore may be analyzed into the elements *a* + *u* + *m*.

[2] Either (1) in the sense of 'equable,' i. e. unaffected in the midst of the pairs of opposites (*dvandva*); or (2) in the sense of 'equitable,' i. e. impartial, alike, indifferent to both friend and foe; or (3) in the sense of 'equalized,' i. e. with the universe, which a knower understands exists only as his Self's consciousness; or even (4) in the very common sense of 'same,' i. e. the same as that which he knows. All these four (and more) are possible interpretations. They evidence how vague (or, how pregnant—it is urged) are some of the statements in the Upanishads, and how capable therefore of various interpretations.

Of each of sections 8–10 there are, similarly, several interpretations.

[3] Possibly as a synonym for another meaning of *miti* (derived from √*mi*, *mināti*), 'destroying' or 'perishing.'

[4] That is, out of his own consciousness—according to the philosophic theory of subjective idealism expounded in the Upanishads.

[5] This is a phrase which has previously occurred at VS. 32. 11.

ŚVETĀŚVATARA UPANISHAD

FIRST ADHYĀYA

Conjectures concerning the First Cause

1. Discoursers on Brahma (*brahma-vādin*) say:—

What is the cause? Brahma?[1] Whence are we born?
Whereby do we live? And on what are we established?
Overruled by whom, in pains and pleasures,
Do we live our various conditions, O ye theologians (*brahma-vid*)?

2. Time (*kāla*), or inherent nature (*sva-bhāva*), or necessity (*niyati*), or chance (*yadṛcchā*),
Or the elements (*bhūta*), or a [female] womb (*yoni*), or a [male] person (*puruṣa*) are to be considered [as the cause];
Not a combination of these, because of the existence of the soul (*ātman*).
The soul certainly is impotent over the cause of pleasure and pain.

3. Those who followed after meditation (*dhyāna*) and abstraction (*yoga*)
Saw the self-power (*ātma-śakti*) of God (*deva*) hidden in his own qualities (*guṇa*).
He is the One who rules over all these causes,
From 'time' to 'the soul.'

The individual soul in manifold distress

4. We understand him [as a wheel] with one felly, with a triple[2] tire,
With sixteen end-parts,[3] fifty spokes,[4] twenty counter-spokes,[5]

[1] The words *kiṁ kāraṇam brahma* might mean also 'What is the cause? Is it Brahma?' or 'What is the cause? What is Brahma?' or 'Is the cause Brahma?' or 'Is Brahma the cause?' or even 'What sort of a cause is Brahma?'

[2] That is, consisting of the Three Qualities according to the Sāṁkhya philosophy (see Introduction, p. 8): *sattvam*, *rajas*, and *tamas*—pureness, passion, and darkness.

[3] That is, the five elements (*bhūta*), the five organs of perception (*buddhīndriya*), the five organs of action (*karmendriya*), and the mind (*manas*).

[4] The fifty conditions (*bhāva*) of the Sāṁkhya philosophy (cf. Sāṁkhya-kārikā 46).

[5] The ten senses (*indriya*) and their ten corresponding objects.

With six sets of eights,[1] whose one rope[2] is manifold,
Which has three different paths,[3] whose one illusion (*moha*)[4] has two conditioning causes.[5]

5. We understand him as a river of five streams[6] from five sources,[7] impetuous and crooked,
Whose waves are the five vital breaths, whose original source is fivefold perception (*buddhi*),
With five whirlpools,[8] an impetuous flood of fivefold misery,
Divided into five distresses,[9] with five branches.

6. In this which vitalizes all things, which appears in all things, the Great—
In this Brahma-wheel the soul (*haṁsa*) flutters about,
Thinking that itself (*ātmānam*) and the Actuator are different.
When favored by Him, it attains immortality.

The saving knowledge of the one inclusive Brahma

7. This has been sung as the supreme Brahma.
In it there is a triad.[10] It is the firm support, the Imperishable.
By knowing what is therein, Brahma-knowers
Become merged in Brahma, intent thereon, liberated from the womb [i. e. from rebirth].

8. That which is joined together as perishable and imperishable,
As manifest and unmanifest—the Lord (*īśa*, Potentate) supports it all.
Now, without the Lord the soul (*ātman*) is bound, because of being an enjoyer;
By knowing God (*deva*) one is released from all fetters.

9. There are two unborn ones: the knowing [Lord] and the unknowing [individual soul], the Omnipotent and the impotent.

[1] That is, (1) eight producing causes of Prakṛiti, namely the five elements, mind (*manas*), intellect (*buddhi*), and self-consciousness (*ahaṁkāra*); (2) eight constituents of the body (*dhātu*); (3) eight forms of superhuman power; (4) eight conditions (*bhāva*); (5) eight gods; (6) eight virtues.

[2] That is, desire.

[3] Namely religiousness (*dharma*), irreligiousness (*a-dharma*), and knowledge (*jñāna*).

[4] That is, the illusion of self-consciousness.

[5] Namely the consequences of good and of evil deeds.

[6] The five senses. [7] The five elements.

[8] The five objects of sense.

[9] According to Śaṅkara's reading. The traditional text has 'divided fiftyfold.'

[10] The world, the individual soul, and the cosmic Soul.

She [i.e. Nature, Prakṛiti], too, is unborn, who is connected with the enjoyer and objects of enjoyment.
Now, the soul (*ātman*) is infinite, universal, inactive.
When one finds out this triad, that is Brahma.

10. What is perishable, is Primary Matter (*pradhāna*). What is immortal and imperishable, is Hara (the 'Bearer,' the soul).
Over both the perishable and the soul the One God (*deva*) rules.
By meditation upon Him, by union with Him, and by entering into His being
More and more, there is finally cessation from every illusion (*māyā-nivṛtti*).

11. By knowing God (*deva*) there is a falling off of all fetters;
With distresses destroyed, there is cessation of birth and death.
By meditating upon Him there is a third stage at the dissolution of the body,
Even universal lordship; being absolute (*kevala*), his desire is satisfied.

12. That Eternal should be known as present in the self (*ātmasaṁstha*).
Truly there is nothing higher than that to be known.
When one recognizes the enjoyer, the object of enjoyment, and the universal Actuator,
All has been said. This is the threefold Brahma.

Made manifest like latent fire, by the exercise of meditation

13. As the material form (*mūrti*) of fire when latent in its source [i. e. the fire-wood]
Is not perceived—and yet there is no evanishment of its subtile form (*liṅga*)—
But may be caught again by means of the drill in its source,
So, verily, both [the universal and the individual Brahma] are [to be found] in the body by the use of *Om*.

14. By making one's own body the lower friction-stick
And the syllable *Om* the upper friction-stick,
By practising the friction of meditation (*dhyāna*),
One may see the God (*deva*) who is hidden, as it were.

The all-pervading Soul

15. As oil in sesame seeds, as butter in cream,
As water in river-beds, and as fire in the friction-sticks,
So is the Soul (Ātman) apprehended in one's own soul,
If one looks for Him with true austerity (*tapas*).

16. The Soul (Ātman), which pervades all things
As butter is contained in cream,
Which is rooted in self-knowledge and austerity—
This is Brahma, the highest mystic doctrine (*upaniṣad*)![1]
This is Brahma, the highest mystic doctrine!

SECOND ADHYĀYA

Invocation to the god of inspiration for inspiration and self-control[2]

1. Savitṛi (the Inspirer), first controlling mind
And thought for truth,
Discerned the light of Agni (Fire)
And brought it out of the earth.[3]

2. With mind controlled, we are
In the inspiration of the god Savitṛi,
For heaven and strength.

3. With mind having controlled the powers
That unto bright heaven through thought do go,
May Savitṛi inspire them,
That they may make a mighty light!

4. The sages of the great wise sage
Control their mind, and control their thoughts.
The One who knows the rules has arranged the priestly functions.
Mighty is the chorus-praise of the god Savitṛi.[4]

5. I join your ancient prayer (*brahma pūrvyam*) with adorations!
My verses go forth like suns upon their course.
All the sons of the immortal listen,
Even those who ascended to heavenly stations![5]

[1] Or 'This is the highest mystic doctrine concerning Brahma (*brahmopaniṣad*)!'

[2] These five stanzas = TS. 4. 1. 1. 1–5 and with variation also = VS. 11. 1–5, from which again they are cited and applied liturgically at Śat. Br. 6. 3. 1. 12–17.

[3] Or possibly dative, 'to the earth.'

[4] In addition to the references cited in note 2, above, this stanza also = RV. 5. 81. 1; VS. 5. 14 and 11. 4. It is quoted in Śat. Br. 3. 5. 3. 11, 12.

[5] This stanza also = RV. 10. 13. 1; VS. 11. 5. Lines a, b, c with slight variants = AV. 18. 3. 39 b, c, d.

Spiritual significance of the sacrificial worship

6. Where the fire is being kindled,
Where the wind is applied thereto,
Where the Soma overflows,
There is inspiration (*manas*) born.

7. With Savitṛi as the inspirer
One should delight in the ancient prayer (*brahma pūrvyam*).
If there thou make thy source,
The former [work] besmears thee not.[1]

Rules and results of Yoga

8. Holding his body steady with the three [upper parts [2]] erect,
And causing the senses with the mind to enter into the heart,
A wise man with the Brahma-boat should cross over
All the fear-bringing streams.

9. Having repressed his breathings here in the body, and having his movements checked,
One should breathe through his nostrils with diminished breath.
Like that chariot yoked with vicious horses,[3]
His mind the wise man should restrain undistractedly.

10. In a clean level spot, free from pebbles, fire, and gravel,
By the sound of water and other propinquities
Favorable to thought, not offensive to the eye,
In a hidden retreat protected from the wind, one should practise Yoga.

11. Fog, smoke, sun, fire, wind,
Fire-flies, lightning, a crystal, a moon—
These are the preliminary appearances,
Which produce the manifestation of Brahma in Yoga.

12. When the fivefold quality of Yoga has been produced,
Arising from earth, water, fire, air, and space,[4]
No sickness, no old age, no death has he
Who has obtained a body made out of the fire of Yoga.

13. Lightness, healthiness, steadiness,[5]
Clearness of countenance and pleasantness of voice,
Sweetness of odor, and scanty excretions—
These, they say, are the first stage in the progress of Yoga.

[1] Such is the traditional interpretation of a line which, even in its original source (RV. 6. 16. 18a with a very slight alteration), is of doubtful meaning.
[2] Head, chest, and neck—so prescribed at BhG. 6. 13.
[3] Described at Kaṭha 3. 4.
[4] That is, the five cosmic elements.
[5] Or, with another reading, *alolubhatvam*, 'freedom from desires.'

The vision of God

14. Even as a mirror stained by dust
Shines brilliantly when it has been cleansed,
So the embodied one, on seeing the nature of the Soul (Ātman),
Becomes unitary, his end attained, from sorrow freed.

15. When with the nature of the self, as with a lamp,
A practiser of Yoga beholds here the nature of Brahma,
Unborn, steadfast, from every nature free—
By knowing God (*deva*) one is released from all fetters!

The immanent God

16. That God faces all the quarters of heaven.
Aforetime was he born, and he it is within the womb.
He has been born forth. He will be born.
He stands opposite creatures, having his face in all directions.[1]

17. The God who is in fire, who is in water, who has entered into the whole world, who is in plants, who is in trees—to that God be adoration!—yea, be adoration!

THIRD ADHYĀYA

The One God identified with Rudra

1. The One spreader of the net, who rules with his ruling powers,
Who rules all the worlds with his ruling powers,
The one who alone stands in their arising and in their continued existence—
They who know That, become immortal.

2. For truly, Rudra (the Terrible) is the One—they stand not for a second—
Who rules all the worlds with his ruling powers.
He stands opposite creatures. He, the Protector,
After creating all beings, merges them together at the end of time.

[1] This stanza = VS. 32. 4.

3. Having an eye on every side and a face on every side,
Having an arm on every side and a foot on every side,
The One God forges[1] together with hands, with wings,
Creating the heaven and the earth.[2]

4. He who is the source and origin of the gods,
The ruler of all, Rudra, the great seer,
Who of old created the Golden Germ (Hiraṇyagarbha)—
May He endow us with clear intellect![3]

Prayers from the Scriptures unto Rudra for favor[4]

5. The form of thine, O Rudra, which is kindly (*śiva*),
Unterrifying, revealing no evil—
With that most benign form to us
Appear, O dweller among the mountains!

6. O dweller among the mountains, the arrow
Which thou holdest in thy hand to throw
Make kindly (*śiva*), O mountain-protector!
Injure not man or beast!

Knowing the One Supreme Person overcomes death

7. Higher than this[5] is Brahma. The Supreme, the Great,
Hidden in all things, body by body,
The One embracer of the universe—
By knowing Him as Lord (*īś*) men become immortal.

8. I know this mighty Person (Purusha)
Of the color of the sun, beyond darkness.
Only by knowing Him does one pass over death.
There is no other path for going there.[6]

9. Than whom there is naught else higher,
Than whom there is naught smaller, naught greater,
The One stands like a tree established in heaven.[7]
By Him, the Person, this whole world is filled.[8]

[1] Compare RV. 10. 72. 2, where Brahmaṇaspati 'forged together' (*sam-adhamat*) all things here.

[2] With variants this stanza = RV. 10. 81. 3; VS. 17. 19; AV. 13. 2. 26; TS. 4. 6. 2. 4; TA. 10. 1. 3; MS. 2. 10. 2.

[3] With variants this stanza = 4. 12 and Mahānār. 10. 19.

[4] These two stanzas = VS. 16. 2–3.

[5] Either 'higher than this [Terrible, Vedic god Rudra],' or higher than this [world].'

[6] This stanza = VS. 31. 18.

[7] Compare 'the eternal fig-tree rooted in heaven,' described at Kaṭha 6. 1.

[8] This stanza = Mahānār. 10. 20.

10. That which is beyond this world
Is without form and without ill.
They who know That, become immortal;
But others go only to sorrow.[1]

The cosmic Person with human and superhuman powers

11. Who is the face, the head, the neck of all,
Who dwells in the heart of all things,
All-pervading is He, and bountiful (*maghavan*);[2]
Therefore omnipresent, and kindly (*śiva*).

12. A mighty lord (*prabhu*) is the Person,
The instigator of the highest being (*sattva*)[3]
Unto the purest attainment,
The ruler, a light imperishable!

13. A Person of the measure of a thumb is the inner soul (*antar-ātman*),
Ever seated in the heart of creatures.
He is framed by the heart, by the thought, by the mind.
They who know That, become immortal.[4]

14. The Person has a thousand heads,
A thousand eyes, a thousand feet;
He surrounds the earth on all sides,
And stands ten fingers' breadth beyond.[5]

15. The Person, in truth, this whole world is,
Whate'er has been and whate'er will be;
Also ruler of immortality,
[And] whatever grows up by food.[6]

16. It has a hand and foot on every side,
On every side an eye and head and face,
It has an ear everywhere in the world.
It stands encompassing all.[7]

[1] The last two lines = Bṛih. 4. 4. 14 c, d.

[2] The first three lines are reminiscent of RV. 10. 81. 3 and 10. 90. 1. Cf. also 3. 3 above.

[3] Cf. Kaṭha 6. 7.

[4] Line a = Kaṭha 6, 17 a. The first part of it also = Kaṭha 4. 12 a; 4. 13 a. Lines c and d = Kaṭha 6. 9 c, d. Lines b, c, d recur at Śvet. 4. 17 b, c, d.

[5] This stanza = RV. 10. 90. 1; VS. 31. 1; SV. 1. 618; TA. 3. 12. 1; AV. 19. 6. 1.

[6] This stanza = RV. 10. 90. 2; VS. 31. 2; SV. 1. 620; AV. 19. 6. 4; TA. 3. 12. 1, with variants.

[7] This stanza = BhG. 13. 13.

17. Seeming to possess the quality (*guṇa*) of all the senses,
It is devoid of all the senses![1]
The lord (*prabhu*), the ruler of all,
The great shelter of all—

18. Though in the nine-gated city[2] embodied,
Back and forth to the external hovers the soul (*haṁsa*),
The Controller of the whole world,
Both the stationary and the moving.

19. Without foot or hand, he is swift and a seizer!
He sees without eye; he hears without ear!
He knows whate'er is to be known; him there is none who knows!
Men call him the Great Primeval Person.

20. More minute than the minute, greater than the great,
Is the Soul (Ātman) that is set in the heart of a creature here.
One beholds Him as being without the active will, and becomes freed from sorrow—
When through the grace (*prasāda*) of the Creator he sees the Lord (*īś*) and his greatness.[3]

21. I know this undecaying, primeval
Soul of all, present in everything through immanence,
Of whose exemption from birth they speak—
For the expounders of Brahma (*brahma-vādin*) speak of Him as eternal.

FOURTH ADHYĀYA

The One God of the manifold world

The One who, himself without color, by the manifold application of his power (*śakti-yoga*)
Distributes many colors in his hidden purpose,
And into whom, its end and its beginning, the whole world dissolves—He is God (*deva*)!
May He endow us with clear intellect!

[1] The first two lines occur at BhG. 13. 14 a, b.

[2] That is, in the body, cf. Kaṭha 5. 1 and BhG. 5. 13.

[3] This stanza = TA. 10. 10. 1 (= Mahānār. 10. 1, or in the Atharva Recension, 8. 3), and also, with slight variation, Kaṭha 2. 20.

The One God described as immanent

2. That surely is Agni (fire). That is Āditya (the sun).
That is Vāyu (the wind), and That is the moon.
That surely is the pure. That is Brahma.
That is the waters. That is Prajāpati (Lord of Creation).[1]

3. Thou art woman. Thou art man.
Thou art the youth and the maiden too.
Thou as an old man totterest with a staff.
Being born, thou becomest facing in every direction.[2]

4. Thou art the dark-blue bird and the green [parrot] with red eyes
Thou hast the lightning as thy child. Thou art the seasons and the seas.
Having no beginning, thou dost abide with immanence,
Wherefrom all beings are born.

The universal and the individual soul

5. With the one unborn female, red, white, and black,[3]
Who produces many creatures like herself,
There lies the one unborn male[4] taking his delight.
Another unborn male[5] leaves her with whom he has had his delight.

6. Two birds, fast-bound companions,
Clasp close the self-same tree.
Of these two, the one[6] eats sweet fruit;
The other[7] looks on without eating.[8]

7. On the self-same tree a person, sunken,
Grieves for his impotence, deluded;
When he sees the other, the Lord (*īś*), contented,
And his greatness, he becomes freed from sorrow.[9]

The ignorant soul in the illusion of a manifold universe

8. That syllable of the sacred hymn (*ṛc*, Rig-Veda) whereon, in highest heaven,
All the gods are seated—

[1] This stanza = VS. 32. 1.

[2] This stanza = AV. 10. 8. 27.

[3] That is, Nature, Prakṛiti, with three constituent Qualities (*guṇa*), namely Pureness (*sattva*), Passion (*rajas*), and Darkness (*tamas*).

[4] The cosmic Person, father of all being.

[5] The individual soul, or experiencer.

[6] That is, the individual person.

[7] That is, the universal Brahma.

[8] This stanza = RV. 1. 164. 20 and Muṇḍ. 3. 1. 1.

[9] This stanza = Muṇḍ. 3. 1. 2.

Of what avail is the sacred hymn (*ṛc*, Rig-Veda) to him who knows not That?
They, indeed, who know That, are here assembled.[1]

9. Sacred poetry (*chandas*), the sacrifices, the ceremonies, the ordinances,
The past, the future, and what the Vedas declare—
This whole world the illusion-maker (*māyin*) projects out of this [Brahma].
And in it by illusion (*māyā*) the other[2] is confined.

10. Now, one should know that Nature (Prakṛiti) is illusion (*māyā*),
And that the Mighty Lord (*maheśvara*) is the illusion-maker (*māyin*).
This whole world is pervaded
With beings that are parts of Him.

The saving knowledge of the one, kindly, immanent supreme God of the universe

11. The One who rules over every single source,
In whom this whole world comes together and dissolves,
The Lord (*īśāna*), the blessing-giver, God (*deva*) adorable—
By revering Him one goes for ever to this peace (*śānti*).

12. He who is the source and origin of the gods,
The ruler of all, Rudra (the Terrible), the great seer,
Who beheld the Golden Germ (Hiraṇyagarbha) when he was born—
May He endow us with clear intellect![3]

13. Who is the overlord of the gods,
On whom the worlds do rest,
Who is lord of biped and quadruped here—
To what god will we give reverence with oblations?[4]

14. More minute than the minute, in the midst of confusion
The Creator of all, of manifold forms,
The One embracer of the universe—[5]
By knowing Him as kindly (*śiva*) one attains peace forever.

[1] This stanza = RV. 1. 164. 39.
[2] That is, the individual soul.
[3] This stanza = 3. 4 and Mahānār. 10. 19 with variants.
[4] The last two lines = RV. 10. 121. 3 c, d.
[5] The third line = 3. 7 c and 4. 16 c. The whole stanza recurs, with modifications, as 5. 13.

15. He indeed is the protector of the world in time,
The overlord of all, hidden in all things,
With whom the seers of Brahma and the divinities are joined in union.
By knowing Him thus, one cuts the cords of death.

16. By knowing as kindly (*śiva*) Him who is hidden in all things,
Exceedingly fine, like the cream that is finer than butter,
The One embracer of the universe—
By knowing God (*deva*) one is released from all fetters.

17. That God, the All-worker, the Great Soul (*mahātman*),
Ever seated in the heart of creatures,
Is framed by the heart, by the thought, by the mind—
They who know That, become immortal.[1]

18. When there is no darkness,[2] then there is no day or night,
Nor being, nor non-being, only the Kindly One (*śiva*) alone.
That is the Imperishable. 'That [is the] choicest [splendor] of Savitṛi (the Sun).'[3]
And from that was primeval Intelligence (*prajñā*) created.

19. Not above, not across,
Nor in the middle has one grasped Him.
There is no likeness of Him
Whose name is Great Glory (*mahad yaśas*).[4]

20. His form is not to be beheld.
No one soever sees Him with the eye.
They who thus know Him with heart and mind
As abiding in the heart, become immortal.[5]

Supplications to Rudra for favor

21. With the thought 'He is eternal!'
A certain one in fear approaches.
O Rudra, that face of thine which is propitious—
With that do thou protect me ever!

[1] Lines b, c, d = 3. 3 b, c, d. Lines c and d also = Kaṭha 6. 9 c, d.

[2] *tamas*, perhaps metaphorically as well as literally. That is: when the darkness of ignorance and illusion has been removed, then all fluctuations and distinctions are also overpassed. Undifferenced bliss only remains. Compare the similar descriptions at Chānd. 3. 11. 3 and 8. 4. 1–2.

[3] The first phrase of the famous Gāyatrī Prayer, RV. 3. 62. 10.

[4] This stanza = VS. 32. 2 c, d + 32. 3 a, b; TA. 10. 1. 2; Mahānār. 1. 10.

[5] This stanza = Kaṭha 6. 9 and Mahānār. 1. 11 with slight variation.

22. Injure us not in child or grandchild, nor in life!
Injure us not in cattle! Injure us not in horses!
Slay not our strong men in anger, O Rudra!
With oblations ever we call upon thee.[1]

FIFTH ADHYĀYA

Brahma, the One God of the manifold world

1. In the imperishable, infinite, supreme Brahma are two things;
For therein are knowledge and ignorance placed hidden.
Now ignorance is a thing perishable, but knowledge is a thing immortal.
And He who rules the ignorance and the knowledge is another,

2. [Even] the One who rules over every single source,
All forms and all sources;
Who bears in his thoughts, and beholds when born,
That red (*kapila*[2]) seer who was engendered in the beginning.

3. That God spreads out each single net [of illusion] manifoldly,
And draws it together here in the world.[3]
Thus again, having created his Yatis,[4] the Lord (*īśa*),
The Great Soul (*mahātman*), exercises universal overlordship.

4. As the illumining sun shines upon
All regions, above, below, and across,
So that One God, glorious, adorable,
Rules over whatever creatures are born from a womb.

5. The source of all, who develops his own nature,
Who brings to maturity whatever can be ripened,
And who distributes all qualities (*guṇa*)—
Over this whole world rules the One.

6. That which is hidden in the secret of the Vedas, even the Mystic Doctrines (*upaniṣad*)—
Brahmā knows That as the source of the sacred word (*brahman*).
The gods and seers of old who knew That,
They, [coming to be] of Its nature, verily, have become immortal.

[1] This stanza = RV. 1. 114. 8; TS. 4. 5. 10. 3; and VS. 16. 16 with variations.

[2] The reference may be to 'the sage Kapila,' the founder of the Sāṁkhya philosophy. But in the similar stanza 4. 12 (compare also 3. 4) the reference is clearly to the Demiurge Hiraṇyagarbha, 'The Golden Germ.'

[3] Literally, 'in this field.'

[4] 'Marshals'; literally, 'Exercisers.' According to RV. 10. 72. 7 they were Demiurges who assisted in the creation of the world.

The reincarnating individual soul

7. Whoever has qualities (*guṇa*, distinctions) is the doer of deeds
 that bring recompense;
And of such action surely he experiences the consequence.
Undergoing all forms, characterized by the three Qualities,[1]
 treading the three paths,[2]
The individual self[3] roams about[4] according to its deeds (*karman*).

8. He is of the measure of a thumb, of sun-like appearance,
When coupled with conception (*saṁkalpa*) and egoism (*ahaṁkāra*).
But with only the qualities of intellect and of self,
The lower [self] appears of the size of the point of an awl.

9. This living [self] is to be known as a part
Of the hundredth part of the point of a hair
Subdivided a hundredfold;
And yet it partakes of infinity.

10. Not female, nor yet male is it;
Nor yet is this neuter.
Whatever body he takes to himself,
With that he becomes connected.

11. By the delusions (*moha*) of imagination, touch, and sight,
And by eating, drinking, and impregnation there is a birth
 and development of the self (*ātman*).
According unto his deeds (*karman*) the embodied one successively
Assumes forms in various conditions.

12. Coarse and fine, many in number,
The embodied one chooses forms according to his own qualities.
[Each] subsequent cause of his union with them is seen to be
Because of the quality of his acts and of himself.

Liberation through knowledge of the One God

13. Him who is without beginning and without end, in the midst
 of confusion,
The Creator of all, of manifold form,
The One embracer of the universe[5]—
By knowing God (*deva*) one is released from all fetters.[6]

[1] Namely, pureness (*sattva*), passion (*rajas*), and darkness (*tamas*).

[2] Namely, religiousness (*dharma*), irreligiousness (*adharma*), and knowledge (*jñāna*). Cf. Śvet. 1. 4 d.

[3] Literally 'ruler of the vital breaths' (*prāṇādhipa*).

[4] In reincarnation.

[5] This third line = 3. 7 c; 4. 14 c; 4. 16 c.

[6] The fourth line of this stanza = 1. 8 d; 2. 15 d; 4. 16 d; 6. 13 d.

14. Him who is to be apprehended in existence, who is called 'incorporeal,'
The maker of existence (*bhāva*) and non-existence, the kindly one (*śiva*),
God (*deva*), the maker of the creation and its parts—
They who know Him, have left the body behind.

SIXTH ADHYĀYA

The One God, Creator and Lord, in and over the world

1. Some sages discourse of inherent nature (*sva-bhāva*);
Others likewise, of time.[1] Deluded men!
It is the greatness of God in the world
By which this Brahma-wheel is caused to revolve.
2. He by whom this whole world is constantly enveloped
Is intelligent, the author of time, possessor of qualities (*guṇin*), omniscient.
Ruled o'er by Him, [his] work (*karman*)[2] revolves—
This which is regarded as earth, water, fire, air, and space![3]
3. He creates this work, and rests again.
Having entered into union (*yoga*) with principle (*tattva*) after principle,
With one, with two, with three, or with eight,[4]
With time, too, and the subtile qualities of a self—
4. He begins with works which are connected with qualities (*guṇa*),
And distributes all existences (*bhāva*).[5]
In the absence of these [qualities] there is a disappearance of the work that has been done.
[Yet] in the destruction of the work he continues essentially other [than it].

[1] As the First Cause—as in 1. 2. See Introduction, p. 8.

[2] That is, the world.

[3] The same list of five cosmic elements as in 2. 12 b.

[4] That is, the principles as arranged in groups by systematized Sāṁkhya philosophy: the sole principle—the Person (Purusha); dual principles—the Unmanifest (*avyakta*) and the Manifest (*vyakta*); triple principles—the three Qualities (*guṇa*), i. e. Pureness (*sattva*), Passion (*rajas*), and Darkness (*tamas*); eight principles—the five cosmic elements together with mind, intellect, and self-consciousness (so enumerated, e. g., at BhG. 7. 4.)

[5] Compare the similar line 5. 5 c.

5. The beginning, the efficient cause of combinations,
He is to be seen as beyond the three times (*kāla*),[1] without parts (*a-kala*) too!
Worship Him as the manifold, the origin of all being,
The adorable God who abides in one's own thoughts, the primeval.

6. Higher and other than the world-tree,[2] time, and forms
Is He from whom this expanse proceeds.
The bringer of right (*dharma*), the remover of evil (*pāpa*), the lord of prosperity—
Know Him as in one's own self (*ātma-stha*), as the immortal abode of all.

7. Him who is the supreme Mighty Lord (*maheśvara*) of lords,
The supreme Divinity of divinities,
The supreme Ruler of rulers, paramount,
Him let us know as the adorable God, the Lord (*īś*) of the world.

8. No action or organ of his is found;
There is not seen his equal, nor a superior.
His high power (*śakti*) is revealed to be various indeed;
And innate is the working of his intelligence and strength.

9. Of Him there is no ruler in the world,
Nor lord; nor is there any mark (*liṅga*) of Him.
He is the Cause (*kāraṇa*), lord of the lords of sense-organs.
Of Him there is no progenitor, nor lord.

10. The one God who covers himself,
Like a spider, with threads
Produced from Primary Matter (*pradhāna*), according to his own nature (*svabhāvatas*)—
May He grant us entrance in Brahma!

11. The one God, hidden in all things,
All-pervading, the Inner Soul of all things,
The overseer of deeds (*karman*), in all things abiding,
The witness, the sole thinker,[3] devoid of qualities (*nir-guṇa*),

12. The one controller of the inactive many,
Who makes the one seed manifold—
The wise who perceive Him as standing in one's self—
They, and no others, have eternal happiness.[4]

[1] That is, without past, present, or future—as in Māṇḍ. 1.
[2] Which is described in Kaṭha 6. 1.
[3] Reading *cettā* instead of the tautologous *cetā*, 'observer.'
[4] This stanza = Kaṭha 5. 12 with slight variation in a and b.

13. Him who is the constant among the inconstant, the intelligent among intelligences,
The One among many, who grants desires,[1]
That Cause, attainable by discrimination and abstraction (*sāṁkhya-yoga*)—
By knowing God, one is released from all fetters![2]

14. The sun shines not there, nor the moon and stars;
These lightnings shine not, much less this [earthly] fire!
After Him, as He shines, doth everything shine.
This whole world is illumined with his light.[3]

15. The one soul (*haṁsa*) in the midst of this world—
This indeed is the fire which has entered into the ocean.
Only by knowing Him does one pass over death.
There is no other path for going there.[4]

16. He who is the maker of all, the all-knower, self-sourced,
Intelligent, the author of time, possessor of qualities, omniscient,[5]
Is the ruler of Primary Matter (*pradhāna*) and of the spirit (*kṣetra-jña*), the lord of qualities (*guṇa*),
The cause of reincarnation (*saṁsāra*) and of liberation (*mokṣa*), of continuance and of bondage.

17. Consisting of That, immortal, existing as the Lord,
Intelligent, omnipresent, the guardian of this world,
Is He who constantly rules this world.
There is no other cause found for the ruling.

18. To Him who of old creates Brahmā,
And who, verily, delivers to him the Vedas—
To that God, who is lighted by his own intellect,[6]
Do I, being desirous of liberation, resort as a shelter—

19. To Him who is without parts, without activity, tranquil (*śānta*),
Irreproachable, spotless,
The highest bridge of immortality,
Like a fire with fuel burned.[7]

1 These first two lines = Kaṭha 5. 13 a and b.
2 The last line of the stanza is repeated at 5. 13 d, etc.
3 This stanza = Kaṭha 5. 15 and Muṇḍ. 2. 2. 10.
4 The last two lines = 3. 8. c, d and VS. 31. 18 c, d.
5 This line = 6. 2 b.
6 Or, 'who is the light of self-knowledge'; or, according to the variant reading *ātma-buddhi-prasādam*, 'who through his own grace lets himself be known.'
7 Cf. Kaṭha 4. 13 b, 'Like a light without smoke.'

20. When men shall roll up space
As it were a piece of leather,[1]
Then will there be an end of evil
Apart from knowing God!

Epilogue

21. By the efficacy of his austerity and by the grace of God (*deva-prasāda*)
The wise Śvetāśvatara in proper manner declared Brahma
Unto the ascetics of the most advanced stage as the supreme means of purification—
This which is well-pleasing to the company of seers.

The conditions for receiving this knowledge

22. The supreme mystery in the Veda's End (Vedānta),
Which has been declared in former time,
Should not be given to one not tranquil,
Nor again to one who is not a son or a pupil.[2]

23. To one who has the highest devotion (*bhakti*) for God,
And for his spiritual teacher (*guru*) even as for God,
To him these matters which have been declared
Become manifest [if he be] a great soul (*mahātman*)—
Yea, become manifest [if he be] a great soul!

[1] That is, when the impossible becomes possible.
[2] Similar restrictions are imposed at Bṛih. 6. 3. 12 and Maitri 6. 29.

MAITRI UPANISHAD

FIRST PRAPĀṬHAKA

Meditation upon the Soul (Ātman), the essence and the true completion of religious sacrifice

1. That which for the ancients was [merely] a building up [of sacrificial fires] was, verily, a sacrifice to Brahma.[1] Therefore with the building of these sacrificial fires the sacrificer should meditate upon the Soul (Ātman). So, verily, indeed, does the sacrifice become really complete and indeficient.

Who is he that is to be meditated upon?

He who is called Life (*prāṇa*)!

A tale thereof:—

The ascetic king Bṛihadratha, being offered a boon, chooses knowledge of the Soul (Ātman)

2. Verily, a king, Bṛihadratha by name, after having established his son in the kingdom, reflecting that this body is non-eternal, reached the state of indifference towards the world (*vairāgya*), and went forth into the forest. There he stood, performing extreme austerity, keeping his arms erect, looking up at the sun.

At the end of a thousand [days][2] there came into the presence of the ascetic, the honorable knower of the Soul (Ātman), Śākāyanya, like a smokeless fire, burning as it were with glow. 'Arise! Arise! Choose a boon!' said he to the king.

He did obeisance to him and said: 'Sir, I am no knower of the Soul (Ātman). You are one who knows its true nature, we have heard. So, do you tell us.'

'Such things used to occur! Very difficult [to answer] is

[1] Or the meaning may be: 'The building up of the previous [sacrificial fires, described in the antecedent Maitrāyaṇī Saṁhitā,] was verily a sacrifice to Brahma.'

[2] The commentator Rāmatīrtha supplies 'years.'

this question! Aikshvāka, choose other desires!' said Śākāyanya.

With his head touching that one's feet, the king uttered this speech:—

Pessimistically he rejects evanescent earthly desires, and craves only liberation from reincarnate existence

3. 'Sir, in this ill-smelling, unsubstantial body, which is a conglomerate of bone, skin, muscle, marrow, flesh, semen, blood, mucus, tears, rheum, feces, urine, wind, bile, and phlegm, what is the good of enjoyment of desires? In this body, which is afflicted with desire, anger, covetousness, delusion, fear, despondency, envy, separation from the desirable, union with the undesirable, hunger, thirst, senility, death, disease, sorrow, and the like, what is the good of enjoyment of desires?

4. And we see that this whole world is decaying, as these gnats, mosquitoes, and the like, the grass, and the trees that arise and perish.

But, indeed, what of these? There are others superior, great warriors, some world-rulers, Sudyumna, Bhūridyumna, Indradyumna, Kuvalayāśva, Yauvanāśva, Vadhryaśva, Aśvapati, Śaśabindu, Hariścandra, Ambarīsha, Nahusha, Śaryāti, Yayāti, Anaraṇya, Ukshasena, and the rest; kings, too, such as Marutta, Bharata, and others. With a crowd of relatives looking on, they renounced great wealth and went forth from this world into that.

But, indeed, what of these? There are others superior. We see the destruction of Gandharvas (demigods), Asuras (demons), Yakshas (sprites), Rākshasas (ogres), Bhūtas (ghosts), spirit-bands, goblins, serpents, vampires, and the like.

But, indeed, what of these? Among other things, there is the drying up of great oceans, the falling away of mountain peaks, the deviation of the fixed pole-star, the cutting of the wind-cords [of the stars], the submergence of the earth, the retreat of the celestials from their station.

In this sort of cycle of existence (*saṁsāra*) what is the good of enjoyment of desires, when after a man has fed on them there is seen repeatedly his return here to earth?

Be pleased to deliver me. In this cycle of existence I am like a frog in a waterless well. Sir, you are our way of escape—yea, you are our way of escape!'

SECOND PRAPĀṬHAKA

Sakayanya's instruction concerning the Soul (Ātman)[1]

1. Then the honorable Śākāyanya, well pleased, said to the king: 'Great king Bṛihadratha, banner of the family of Ikshvāku, speedily will you who are renowned as "Swift Wind" (Marut) attain your purpose and become a knower of the Soul (Ātman)!

This one, assuredly, indeed, is your own self (*ātman*).'

'Which one is it, sir?'

Then he said to him:—

The Soul—a self-luminous, soaring being, separable from the body, identical with Brahma

2. 'Now, he who, without stopping the respiration, goes aloft and who, moving about, yet unmoving, dispels darkness—he is the Soul (Ātman). Thus said the honorable Maitri. For thus has it been said[2]: "Now, that serene one who, rising up out of this body, reaches the highest light and appears with his own form—he is the Soul (Ātman)," said he. "That is the immortal, the fearless. That is Brahma."

The unqualified Soul, the driver of the unintelligent bodily vehicle

3. Now, indeed, O king, this is the Brahma-knowledge, even the knowledge contained in all the Upanishads, as declared to us by the honorable Maitri. I will narrate it to you.

Now, the Vālakhilyas are reputed as free from evil, of resplendent glory, living in chastity. Now, they said to Kratu Prajāpati[3]: "Sir, this body is like a cart without intelligence (*a-cetana*). To what supersensuous being, forsooth, belongs such power whereby this sort of thing is set up in the

[1] The particular course of instruction here begun continues through 6. 28.

[2] Chānd. 8. 3. 4.

[3] Śākāyanya's report of this conversation between the Vālakhilyas and Prajāpati continues to the end of 4. 6.

possession of this sort of intelligence? Or, in other words, who is its driver? Sir, tell us what you know!"

Then he said to them:—

4. "He, assuredly, indeed, who is reputed as standing aloof, like those who, among qualities, abstain from intercourse with them—He, verily, is pure, clean, void, tranquil, breathless, selfless, endless, undecaying, steadfast, eternal, unborn, independent. He abides in his own greatness. By him this body is set up in possession of intelligence; or, in other words, this very one, verily, is its driver."

Then they said: "Sir, how by this kind of indifferent being is this sort of thing set up in possession of intelligence? Or, in other words, how is this one its driver?"

Then he said to them:—

Every intelligent person a partial individuation of the supersensuous, self-limiting Person

5. "Verily, that subtile, ungraspable, invisible one, called the Person, turns in here [in the body] with a part [of himself] without there being any previous awareness, even as the awakening of a sleeper takes place without there being any previous awareness.

Now, assuredly, indeed, that part of Him is what the intelligence-mass here in every person is—the spirit (*kṣetra-jña*, 'knower-of-the-body') which has the marks of conception, determination, and self-conceit (*abhimāna*), Prajāpati (Lord of Creation) under the name of individuality.[1]

By Him, as intelligence, this body is set up in possession of intelligence; or, in other words, this very one is its driver."

Then they said: "Sir, if by this kind of indifferent being this kind of body is set up in possession of intelligence, still how, in other words, is this one its driver?"

Then he said to them:—

The primeval Person progressively differentiated himself into [a] inanimate beings, [b] the five physiological functions, [c] the human person, [d] a person's functions

6. "Verily, in the beginning Prajāpati stood alone. He had

[1] The Sanskrit word *viśva*, the ordinary word for 'everyone,' is doubtless used here in its individual, as well as in its collective, reference.

no enjoyment, being alone. He then, by meditating upon himself (*ātmānam*), created numerous offspring.

[a] He saw them inanimate and lifeless, like a stone, standing like a post. He had no enjoyment. He then thought to himself: 'Let me enter within, in order to animate them.'

[b] He made himself like wind and sought to enter within. As one, he was unable. So he divided himself fivefold—he who is spoken of as the Prāṇa breath, the Apāna breath, the Samāna breath, the Udāna breath, the Vyāna breath.

Now, that breath which passes up—that, assuredly, is the Prāṇa breath. Now, that which passes down—that, assuredly, is the Apāna breath. Now, that, verily, by which these two are supported—that, assuredly, is the Vyāna breath. Now, that which conducts into the Apāna breath [what is] the coarsest element of food and distributes (*sam-ā-nayati*) in each limb [what is] the most subtile—that, assuredly, is named the Samāna breath. It is a higher form of the Vyāna breath, and between them is the production of the Udāna breath. Now, that which 'belches forth and swallows down what has been drunk and eaten'—that, assuredly, is the Udāna breath.

[c] Now, the Upāṁśu vessel is over against the Antaryāma vessel, and the Antaryāma vessel over against the Upāṁśu vessel. Between these two, God (*deva*) generated heat. The heat is a person,[1] and a person is the universal fire (Agni Vaiśvānara). It has elsewhere[2] been said: 'This is the universal fire, namely that which is here within a person, by means of which the food that is eaten is cooked. It is the noise thereof that one hears on covering the ears thus.[3] When he [i. e. a person] is about to depart, one hears not this sound.'

'He, verily, having divided himself fivefold, is hidden away in secret—He who consists of mind, whose body is life (*prāṇa*), whose form is light, whose conception is truth, whose soul is space.'[4]

[1] According to the commentator, the Prāṇa and Apāna breaths are here compared to the two vessels, Upāṁśu and Antaryāma, which stand on either side of the central altar at the Soma sacrifice; and a person is compared to the heat produced between the two.

[2] Bṛih. 5. 9. A similar idea is found in Chānd. 3. 13. 8.

[3] Deictically.

[4] Repeated from Chānd. 3. 14. 2.

[d] Verily, not having attained his purpose, He thought to himself from within the heart here: 'Let me enjoy objects.' Thence, having pierced these openings, He goes forth and 'enjoys objects with five reins.' These reins of his are the organs of perception. His steeds are the organs of action. The body is the chariot. The charioteer is the mind. The whip is made of one's character (*prakṛti-maya*). By Him forsooth driven, this body goes around and around, like the wheel [driven] by the potter. So, this body is set up in possession of consciousness; or, in other words, this very one is its driver.

But the Soul itself is non-active, unqualified, abiding

7. Verily, this Soul (Ātman)—poets declare—wanders here on earth from body to body, unovercome, as it seems, by the bright or the dark fruits of action. He who on account of his unmanifestness, subtility, imperceptibility, incomprehensibility, and selflessness is [apparently] unabiding and a doer in the unreal—he, truly, is not a doer, and he is abiding. Verily, he is pure, steadfast and unswerving, stainless, unagitated, desireless, fixed like a spectator, and self-abiding. As an enjoyer of righteousness, he covers himself (*ātmānam*) with a veil made of qualities; [but] he remains fixed—yea, he remains fixed!"

THIRD PRAPĀṬHAKA

The great Soul,
and the individual, suffering, reincarnating soul

1. Then they said: "Sir, if thus you describe the greatness of this Soul (Ātman), there is still another, different one. Who is he, called soul (*ātman*), who, being overcome by the bright or the dark fruits of action (*karman*), enters a good or an evil womb, so that his course is downward or upward and he wanders around, overcome by the pairs of opposites (*dvandva*)?"

The soul that is subject to elements and qualities,
confused and self-conceited, suffers and reincarnates

2. [Then he said:] "There is indeed another, different soul, called 'the elemental soul' (*bhūtātman*)—he who, being over-

come by the bright or the dark fruits of action, enters a good or an evil womb, so that his course is downward or upward and he wanders around, overcome by the pairs of opposites.

The further explanation of this is:—

The five subtile substances (*tan-mātra*) [1] are spoken of by the word 'element' (*bhūta*). Likewise, the five gross elements (*mahā-bhūta*) are spoken of by the word 'element.' Now, the combination of these is said to be 'the body' (*śarīra*). Now, he, assuredly, indeed, who is said to be in 'the body' is said to be 'the elemental soul.' Now, its immortal soul (*ātman*) is like 'the drop of water on the lotus leaf.' [2]

This [elemental soul], verily, is overcome by Nature's (*prakṛti*) qualities (*guṇa*).

Now, because of being overcome, he goes on to confusedness; because of confusedness, he sees not the blessed Lord (*prabhu*), the causer of action, who stands within oneself (*ātma-stha*). Borne along and defiled by the stream of Qualities (*guṇa*), unsteady, wavering, bewildered, full of desire, distracted, this one goes on to the state of self-conceit (*abhimānatva*). In thinking 'This is I' and 'That is mine,' he binds himself with his self, as does a bird with a snare.

Consequently (*anu*) 'being overcome by the fruits of his action, he enters a good or an evil womb, so that his course is downward or upward and he wanders around, overcome by the pairs of opposites.'"

"Which one is this?"

Then he said to them:—

The inner Person remains unaffected in the elemental soul's transformations

3. "Now, it has elsewhere been said [3]: 'Verily, he who is the doer is the elemental soul. The causer of action through the organs is the inner Person. Now, verily, as a lump of iron, overcome by fire and beaten by workmen, passes over into a different form—so, assuredly, indeed, the elemental soul,

[1] This is probably the earliest occurrence of the word in Sanskrit literature. For an exposition of the doctrine, consult Garbe's *Die Samkhya-Philosophie*, pp. 236–239.

[2] That is, it is unaffected; for the simile see Chānd. 4. 14. 3.

[3] So again in Mānava-Dharma-Śāstra 12. 12.

overcome by the inner Person and beaten by Qualities, passes over into a different form. The mode of that different form, verily, has a fourfold covering,[1] is fourteenfold,[2] is transformed in eighty-four[3] different ways, is a host of beings. These varieties, verily, are driven by the Person, like "the wheel by the potter." Now, as, when a lump of iron is being hammered, the fire [in it] is not overcome, so that Person is not overcome. This elemental soul (*bhūtātman*) is overcome (*abhibhūta*) because of its attachment [to Qualities].'

The body a loathsome conglomerate

4. Now, it has elsewhere been said: 'This body arises from sexual intercourse. It passes to development in hell[-darkness] (*niraya*).[4] Then it comes forth through the urinary opening. It is built up with bones; smeared over with flesh; covered with skin; filled full with feces, urine, bile, phlegm, marrow, fat, grease, and also with many diseases, like a treasure-house with wealth.'

The overcoming and transforming effects of the dark and of the passionate qualities

5. Now, it has elsewhere been said: 'The characteristics of the Dark Quality (*tamas*) are delusion, fear, despondency, sleepiness, weariness, heedlessness, old age, sorrow, hunger, thirst, wretchedness, anger, atheism (*nāstikya*), ignorance, jealousy, cruelty, stupidity, shamelessness, religious neglect, pride, unequableness.

The characteristics of the Passionate Quality (*rajas*), on the other hand, are inner thirst, affection, emotion, covetousness, maliciousness, lust, hatred, secretiveness, envy, insatiability, unsteadfastness, fickleness, distractedness, ambitiousness, acquisitiveness, favoritism towards friends, dependence upon

[1] Referring either, as in 6. 28 and again in 6. 38, to the doctrine of the four sheaths (*kośa*), namely food, breath, mind, and knowledge (the same characteristics of four different selves are mentioned in Tait. 2. 1-4), or, according to the Scholiast, to the four forms of animal life, characterized as born alive, born from an egg, born from moisture, born from a germ (Ait. 5. 3).

[2] Referring to the fourteen classes of beings, Sāṁkhya-kārikā 53, or to the fourteen worlds of Vedāntasāra 129—so Deussen interprets.

[3] Meaning probably merely 'very many.'

[4] That is, in the womb.

surroundings, hatred in regard to unpleasant objects of sense, overfondness in regard to pleasant objects, sourness of utterance, gluttonousness. With these this elemental soul (*bhūtātman*) is filled full; with these it is "overcome" (*abhibhūta*). Therefore it undergoes different forms—yea, it undergoes different forms!'"

FOURTH PRAPĀṬHAKA

The rule for the elemental soul's complete union with the Soul at death

1. Then, indeed, assuredly, those chaste [Vālakhilyas], exceedingly amazed, united and said: "Sir, adoration be to you! Instruct us further. You are our way [of escape]. There is no other.

What is the rule (*vidhi*) for this elemental soul, whereby, on quitting this body, it may come to complete union (*sāyujya*) with the Soul (Ātman)?"

Then he said to them:—

The miserable condition of the individual Soul

2. "Now, it has elsewhere been said: 'Like the waves in great rivers, there is no turning back of that which has previously been done. Like the ocean tide, hard to keep back is the approach of one's death. Like a lame man—bound with the fetters made of the fruit of good and evil (*sad-asad*); like the condition of one in prison—lacking independence; like the condition of one in the realm of death—in a condition of great fear; like one intoxicated with liquor—intoxicated with delusion (*moha*); like one seized by an evil being—rushing hither and thither; like one bitten by a great snake—bitten by objects of sense; like gross darkness—the darkness of passion; like jugglery (*indrajāla*)—consisting of illusion (*māyā-maya*); like a dream—falsely apparent; like the pith of a banana-tree—unsubstantial; like an actor—in temporary dress; like a painted scene—falsely delighting the mind.'

Moreover it has been said:—

Objects of sound and touch and sense
Are worthless objects in a man.
Yet the elemental soul through attachment to them
Remembers not the highest place.

The antidote: study of the Veda, performance of one's own duty, and austerity

3. The antidote, assuredly, indeed, for this elemental soul (*bhūtātman*) is this: study of the knowledge of the Veda, and pursuit of one's regular duty. Pursuit of one's regular duty, in one's own stage of the religious life—that, verily, is the rule! Other rules are like a bunch of grass. With this, one tends upwards; otherwise, downwards. That is one's regular duty, which is set forth in the Vedas. Not by transgressing one's regular duty does one come into a stage of the religious life. Some one says: 'He is not in any of the stages of the religious life! Verily, he is one who practises austerity!' That is not proper. [However], if one does not practise austerity, there is no success in the knowledge of the Soul (Ātman) nor perfection of works. For thus has it been said:—

'Tis goodness (*sattva*) from austerity (*tapas*),
And mind from goodness, that is won;
And from the mind the Soul is won;
On winning whom, no one returns.

Knowledge of Brahma, austerity, and meditation: the means of union with the Soul

4. 'Brahma is!' says he who knows the Brahma-knowledge. 'This is the door to Brahma!' says he who becomes free of evil by austerity.

'*Om* is the greatness of Brahma!' says he who, completely absorbed, meditates continually.

Therefore, by knowledge (*vidyā*), by austerity (*tapas*), and by meditation (*cintā*) Brahma is apprehended.

He becomes one who goes beyond [the lower] Brahma, even to the state of supreme divinity above the gods; he obtains a happiness undecaying, unmeasured, free from sickness—he who, knowing this, reverences Brahma with this triad [i. e. knowledge, austerity, and meditation].

So when this chariot-rider[1] is liberated from those things wherewith he was filled full and overcome, then he attains complete union (*sāyujya*) with the Ātman (Soul)."

Worship of the various popular gods is permissible and rewarding, but temporary and inferior

5. Then they said: "Sir, you are the explainer! You are the explainer![2] What has been said has been duly fixed in mind by us.—Now, answer a further question.

Agni (Fire), Vāyu (Wind), and Āditya (Sun); time—whatever it is—, breath, and food; Brahmā, Rudra, and Vishṇu[3]—some meditate upon one, some upon another. Tell us which one is the best?"

Then he said to them:—

6. "These are, assuredly, the foremost forms of the supreme, the immortal, the bodiless Brahma. To whichever one each man is attached here, in its world he rejoices indeed. For thus has it been said[4]: 'Verily, this whole world is Brahma.'

Verily, these, which are its foremost forms, one should meditate upon, and praise, but then deny. For with these one moves higher and higher in the worlds. But in the universal dissolution he attains the unity of the Person—yea, of the Person!"'[5]

FIFTH PRAPĀṬHAKA

Hymn to the immanent Soul

1. Now, then, this is Kutsāyana's Hymn of Praise.—

[1] For the same metaphor of the individual soul riding in the body as in a vehicle see above, 2. 3. and 2. 6; also Kaṭha 3. 3.

[2] If instead of *abhivādī* the reading should be *ativādī*, as in Chānd. 7. 15. 4 and Muṇḍ. 3. 1. 4, then the translation would be: 'You are a superior speaker! You are a superior speaker!'

[3] Note the three triads: an old Vedic trinity, three principles speculated about as philosophic causes, and the famous Brahmanic trinity.

[4] Chānd. 3. 14. 1.

[5] This evidently is the end of the conversation, begun in 2. 3, between the Vālakhilyas and Prajāpati, as derived by tradition from Maitri and narrated by Śākāyanya to King Bṛihadratha. The remainder of the Upanishad up to 6. 29 is supposedly a continuation of Śākāyanya's long discourse; but without a doubt it consists of several supplements, as even the commentator explains with regard to the Sixth and Seventh Prapāṭhakas.

Thou art Brahmā, and verily thou art Vishṇu.
Thou art Rudra. Thou art Prajāpati.
Thou art Agni, Varuna, and Vāyu.
Thou art Indra. Thou art the Moon.
Thou art food. Thou art Yama. Thou art the Earth.
Thou art All. Yea, thou art the unshaken one!

For Nature's sake and for its own
Is existence manifold in thee.
O Lord of all, hail unto thee!
The Soul of all, causing all acts,
Enjoying all, all life art thou!
Lord (*prabhu*) of all pleasure and delight!

Hail unto thee, O Tranquil Soul (*śāntātman*).
Yea, hail to thee, most hidden one,
Unthinkable, unlimited,
Beginningless and endless, too!

The progressive differentiation of the Supreme Soul

2. Verily, in the beginning this world was Darkness (*tamas*) alone. That, of course, would be in the Supreme. When impelled by the Supreme, that goes on to differentiation. That form, verily, is Passion (*rajas*). That Passion, in turn, when impelled, goes on to differentiation. That, verily, is the form of Purity (*sattva*).

That Purity, when impelled, flowed forth as Essence (*rasa*). That part is what the intelligence-mass here in every person is—the spirit which has the marks of conception, determination, and self-conceit, Prajāpati (Lord of Creation) under the name individuality.[1] These forms of Him have previously been mentioned.[2]

Now then, assuredly, indeed, the part of Him which is characterized by Darkness (*tamas*)—that, O ye students of sacred knowledge, is this Rudra. Now then, assuredly, indeed, the part of Him which is characterized by Passion (*rajas*)—that, O ye students of sacred knowledge, is this Brahmā. Now then, assuredly, indeed, the part of Him which is

[1] 'Individuality' is the precise modern technical philosophical term for the indefinite word *viśva*, which means simply 'everyone.'

[2] In 2. 5.

characterized by Purity (*sattva*)—that, O ye students of sacred knowledge, is this Vishṇu.

Verily, that One became threefold. He developed forth eightfold, elevenfold, twelvefold, into an infinite number of parts. Because of having developed forth, He is a created being (*bhūta*), has entered into and moves among created beings; He became the overlord of created beings. That is the Soul (Ātman) within and without—yea, within and without!

SIXTH PRAPĀṬHAKA

Two correlated manifestations of the Soul: inwardly the breathing spirit, and outwardly the sun

1. He [i. e. the Soul, Ātman] bears himself (*ātmānam*) twofold: as the breathing spirit (*prāṇa*) here, and as yon sun (*āditya*).

Likewise, two in number, verily, are these his paths: an inner and an outer. Both these return upon themselves with a day and a night.

Yon sun, verily, is the outer Soul (Ātman). The inner Soul (Ātman) is the breathing spirit.

Hence the course of the inner Soul (Ātman) is measured by the course of the outer Soul (Ātman).[1] For thus has it been said: 'Now, whoever is a knower, freed from evil, an overseer of his senses, pure-minded, established on That, introspective, is even He [i. e. the Soul, the Ātman].'

And the course of the outer Soul (*bahir-ātman*) is measured by the course of the inner Soul (*antar-ātman*). For thus has it been said: 'Now, that golden Person who is within the sun,[2] who looks down upon this earth from his golden place, is even He who dwells within the lotus of the heart and eats food.'

The inner Soul identified with the Soul in space, which is localized in the sun

2. Now, He who dwells within the lotus of the heart and eats food is the same as that solar fire which dwells in the sky, called Time, the invisible, which eats all things as his food.

[1] That is to say, waking and sleeping are correlated with day and night.

[2] Thus far the quotation may be found in Chānd. 1. 6. 6.

What is the lotus and of what does it consist?

This lotus, assuredly, is the same as space. These four quarters of heaven and the four intermediate quarters are the form of its leaves.

These two, the breathing spirit and the sun, go forth toward each other.

One should reverence them with the syllable *Om* [§ 3-5], with the Mystic Utterances (*vyāhṛti*)[1] [§ 6], and with the Sāvitrī Prayer [§ 7].

The light of the sun, as a form of Brahma, represented by the mystic syllable 'Om'

3. There are, assuredly, two forms of Brahma: the formed and the formless.[2] Now, that which is the formed is unreal; that which is the formless is real, is Brahma, is light.

That light is the same as the sun.

Verily, that came to have *Om* as its soul (*ātman*). He divided himself (*ātmānam*) threefold.[3] *Om* is three prosodial units ($a+u+m$). By means of these 'the whole world is woven, warp and woof, across Him.'[4]

For thus has it been said: 'One should absorb himself, meditating that the sun is *Om*.'

4. Now it has elsewhere[5] been said: 'Now, then, the Udgītha is *Om*; *Om* is the Udgītha. And so, verily, the Udgītha is yonder sun, and it is *Om*.'

For thus has it been said: '... the Udgītha, which is called *Om*, a leader, brilliant, sleepless, ageless, deathless, three-footed,[6] three-syllabled,[7] also to be known as fivefold,[8] hidden in the secret place [of the heart].'

For thus has it been said[9]: 'The three-quartered Brahma

[1] Namely, *bhūr*, *bhuvas*, and *svar*.

[2] A repeated phrase, Bṛih. 2. 3. 1.

[3] A statement regarding primeval being occurring in Bṛih. 1. 2. 3.

[4] 'Across Him,' i. e. reading *asminn iti* instead of *asmīti*. The main statement is a stereotyped formula, used repeatedly in Bṛih. 3. 6.

[5] Quoted from Chānd. 1. 5. 1.

[6] According to the commentator, referring to the three conditions of waking dreaming, and profound slumber.

[7] That is, $a+u+m$.

[8] Embracing the five breaths, Prāṇa, Apāna, Vyāna, Samāna, Udāna.

[9] RV. 10. 90. 3-4.

has its root above.[1] Its branches are space, wind, fire, water, earth, and the like. This Brahma has the name of 'the Lone Fig-tree.' Belonging to It is the splendor which is yon sun, and the splendor too of the syllable *Om*. Therefore one should worship it with *Om* continually. He is the only enlightener of a man.'

For thus has it been said:—

> That syllable, indeed, is holy (*puṇya*).
> That syllable, indeed, is supreme.
> By knowing that syllable, indeed,
> Whatever one desires, is his![2]

Various triads of the forms of the Soul, worshiped by the use of the threefold 'Om'

5. Now, it has elsewhere been said: 'This, namely, *a*, *u*, and *m* [=*Om*], is the sound-form of this [Ātman, Soul].'

Feminine, masculine, and neuter: this is the sex-form.

Fire, wind, and sun: this is the light-form.

Brahmā, Rudra, and Vishṇu: this is the lordship-form.

The Gārhapatya sacrificial fire, the Dakshiṇāgni sacrificial fire, and the Āhavanīya sacrificial fire: this is the mouth-form.

The Rig-Veda, the Yajur-Veda, and the Sāma-Veda: this is the understanding-form.

Earth (*bhūr*), atmosphere (*bhuvas*), and sky (*svar*): this is the world-form.

Past, present, and future: this is the time-form.

Breath, fire, and sun: this is the heat-form.

Food, water, and moon: this is the swelling-form.

Intellect (*buddhi*), mind (*manas*), and egoism (*ahaṁkāra*): this is the intelligence-form.

The Prāṇa breath, the Apāna breath, and the Vyāna breath: this is the breath-form.

Hence these are praised, honored, and included by saying *Om*. For thus has it been said[3]: 'This syllable *Om*, verily, O Satyakāma, is both the higher and the lower Brahma.'

[1] Cf. Kaṭha 6. 1 for the eternal fig-tree with its root above and its branches below.

[2] This stanza is quoted from Kaṭha 2. 16 with certain verbal changes.

[3] In Praśna 5. 2.

Worship of the world and the Soul by the use of the original three world-creating Utterances

6. Now [in the beginning], verily, this world was unuttered. When he [the Soul, Ātman], who is the Real (*satya*), who is Prajāpati (Lord of Creation), had performed austerity, he uttered *bhūr* (earth), *bhuvas* (atmosphere), and *svar* (sky).

This, indeed, is Prajāpati's coarsest form, this 'world-form.' Its head is the sky (*svar*). The atmosphere (*bhuvas*) is the navel. The feet are the earth (*bhūr*). The eye is the sun (*āditya*), for a person's great material world (*mātrā*) depends upon the eye, for with the eye he surveys material things. Verily, the eye is the Real; for stationed in the eye a person moves about among all objects.

Therefore one should reverence *bhūr* (earth), *bhuvas* (atmosphere), and *svar* (sky); for thereby Prajāpati, the Soul of all, the eye of all, becomes reverenced, as it were.

For thus has it been said: 'Verily, this is the all-supporting form of Prajāpati. This whole world is hidden in it, and it is hidden in this whole world. Therefore this [is what] one should worship.'

Worship of the Soul (Ātman) in the form of the sun by the use of the Sāvitrī Prayer[1]

7. *tat savitur vareṇyaṁ*
That desirable [splendor] of Savitṛi—

Yonder sun, verily, is Savitṛi. He, verily, is to be sought thus by one desirous of the Soul (Ātman)—say the expounders of Brahma (*brahma-vādin*).

bhargo devasya dhīmahi[2]
May we meditate upon [that] splendor of the god!

Savitṛi, verily, is God. Hence upon that which is called his splendor do I meditate—say the expounders of Brahma.

[1] RV. 3. 62. 10.
[2] The original meaning of *dhīmahi* is more likely to have been 'obtain,' from √*dhā*, although it is possible to derive the form from √*dhī*, 'to meditate upon,' as here interpreted.

dhiyo yo naḥ pracodayāt
And may he inspire our thoughts!

Thoughts, verily, are meditations. And may he inspire these for us—say the expounders of Brahma.

Etymological significance of the names of the cosmic manifestations of the Soul

Now, 'splendor' (*bharga*).—

Verily, he who is hidden in yonder sun is called 'splendor,' and the pupil in the eye, too! He is called '*bhar-ga*' because with the light-rays (*bhā*) is his course (*gati*).

Or, Rudra (the Terrible) is called '*bharga*' because he causes to dry up (*bharjayati*)—say the expounders of Brahma.

Now *bha* means that he illumines (*bhāsayati*) these worlds. *ra* means that he gladdens (*rañjayati*) beings here. *ga* means that creatures here go (*gacchanti*) into him and come out of him. Therefore, because of being *bha-ra-ga*, he is '*bharga*.'

Sūrya (the sun) is [so named] because of the continual pressing out (*sūyamāna*).[1] *Savitṛi* (the sun) is [so named] because of its stimulating (*savana*). *Āditya* (the sun) is [so named] because of its taking up unto itself (*ādāna*). *Pāvana* (fire) is [so named] because of its purifying (*pavana*). Moreover, *Āpas* (water) is [so named] because of its causing to swell (*āpyāyana*).

The Soul (Ātman) the agent in a person's various functions

For thus has it been said[2]: 'Assuredly, the Soul (Ātman) of one's soul is called the Immortal Leader. As perceiver, thinker, goer, evacuator, begetter, doer, speaker, taster, smeller, seer, hearer—and he touches—the All-pervader [i.e. the Soul, the Ātman] has entered the body.'

The Soul (Ātman), the subject in all objective knowledge; but itself, as unitary, never an object of knowledge

For thus has it been said[3]: 'Now, where knowledge is of a dual nature,[4] there, indeed, one hears, sees, smells, tastes, and

[1] Of the Soma juice in the sacrifices to the sun.
[2] Cf. Praśna 4. 9 for a similar list.
[3] Cf. Bṛih. 2. 4. 14 for this same theory of knowledge.
[4] That is, implying both a subject which knows and an object which is known.

also touches; the soul knows everything. Where knowledge is not of a dual nature, being devoid of action, cause, or effect, unspeakable, incomparable, indescribable—what is that? It is impossible to say!'

The Soul (Ātman) identical with various gods and powers

8. This Soul (Ātman), assuredly, indeed, is Īśāna (Lord), Śambhu (the Beneficent), Bhava (the Existent), Rudra (the Terrible), Prajāpati (Lord of Creation), Viśvasṛij (Creator of All), Hiraṇyagarbha (Golden Germ), Truth (*satya*), Life (*prāṇa*), Spirit (*haṁsa*), Śāstṛi (Punisher, or Commander, or Teacher), Vishṇu (Pervader), Nārāyaṇa (Son of Man),[1] Arka (the Shining), Savitṛi (Vivifier, the sun), Dhātṛi (Creator), Vidhātṛi (Ordainer), Samrāj (Sovereign), Indra, Indu (the moon). He it is who gives forth heat, who is covered with a thousand-eyed, golden ball, like a fire [covered] with a fire. Him, assuredly, one should desire to know. He should be searched for.

To be perceived by the meditative hermit

Having bidden peace to all creatures, and having gone to the forest, then having put aside objects of sense, from out of one's own body one should perceive Him,

> Who has all forms, the golden one, all-knowing,[2]
> The final goal, the only light, heat-giving.
> The thousand-rayed, the hundredfold revolving,
> Yon sun arises as the life of creatures.[3]

The liturgy for making the eating of food an oblation unto the Soul in one's own breath

9. Therefore, verily, he who knows this has both these [i.e. breath and the sun] as his soul (*ātman*, self); he (Ātman), meditates only in himself, he sacrifices only in himself. Such meditation and a mind devoted to such practice—that is a thing praised by the wise.

One should purify the impurity of his mind with [the

[1] The paragraph up to this point recurs later in 7. 7.

[2] Or, according to a different exegesis, *jātavedasam* may mean 'all-finding.'

[3] This stanza = Praśna 1. 8.

formula] 'What has been touched by leavings.' He repeats the formula (*mantra*):—

'Leavings and what has been touched by leavings,
And what has been given by a bad man, or [what is impure]
because of a still-birth—
Let the cleansing power of Vasu, Agni, and the rays of Savitṛi
Purify my food and any other thing that may be evil!'

First [i.e. before eating] he swathes [his breath] with water.[1] 'Hail to the Prāṇa breath! Hail to the Apāna breath! Hail to the Vyāna breath! Hail to the Samāna breath! Hail to the Udāna breath!'—with these five Hails he offers the oblation.

Then, with voice restrained, he eats the remainder.

Then, afterwards, he again swathes with water.

So, having sipped, having made the sacrifice to the Soul, he should meditate upon the Soul with the two [formulas] 'As breath and fire' and 'Thou'rt all':—

'As breath and fire, the highest Soul (Ātman)
Has entered in with the five winds.
May He, when pleased himself, please all—
The all-enjoyer!'

'Thou'rt all, the Universal art!
By thee is everything that's born supported;
And into thee let all oblations enter!
There creatures live, where thou art, All-immortal!'

So he who eats by this rule, indeed, comes not again into the condition of food.[2]

Applications of the principle of food (according to the Sāṁkhya doctrine)

10. Now, there is something else to be known. There is a higher development of this Ātman-sacrifice, namely as concerns food and the eater. The further explanation of this [is as follows].

The conscious person stands in the midst of Matter (*pradhāna*). He is an enjoyer, for he enjoys the food of Nature (*prakṛti*). Even this elemental soul (*bhūtātman*) is food for

[1] By taking a sip into the mouth. On the whole procedure of this ritual cf. Chānd. 5. 2. 2–5 and 5. 19–24.

[2] That is, is not reborn, and is not eaten again by others.

him; its maker is Matter. Therefore that which is to be enjoyed consists of the three Qualities (*guṇa*), and the enjoyer is the person who stands in the midst.

Here observation is clearly proof. Since animals spring from a source, therefore what is to be enjoyed is the source. Thereby is explained the fact that Matter is what is to be enjoyed. Therefore the person is an enjoyer, and Nature is what is to be enjoyed. Being therein, he enjoys.

The food derived from Nature through the transformation in the partition of the three Qualities becomes the subtile body (*liṅga*), which includes from intellect up to the separate elements (*viśeṣa*). Thereby an explanation is made of the fourteenfold course.[1]

> Called pleasure, pain, and delusion (*moha*),
> Truly, this whole world exists as food!

There is no apprehension of the sweetness of the source, so long as there has been no production.

It [i.e. Nature] also comes to have the condition of food in these three conditions: childhood, youth, and old age. The condition of food is because of the transformation.

Thus, as Matter passes on to the state of being manifest, there arises the perception of it. And therein, [namely] in [the tasting of] sweetness, there arise intellect and the like, even determination, conception, and self-conceit. So, in respect to objects of sense, the five [organs of sense] arise in [the tasting of] sweetness. Thus arise all actions of organs and actions of senses.[2]

Thus the Manifest is food, and the Unmanifest is food.

The enjoyer thereof is without qualities. [But] from the fact of his enjoying it is evident that he possesses consciousness (*caitanya*).

As Agni (Fire), verily, is the eater of food among the gods and Soma is the food,[3] so he who knows this eats food with Fire.[4]

[1] Of nature through intellect, mind, thought, self-consciousness, the five organs of sense-perception, and the five organs of action.

[2] That is, in interaction with the correlated objects in Nature.

[3] So intimated in Bṛih. 1. 4. 6.

[4] By knowing this fact about fire he becomes identified with fire and so, like fire, is not defiled by the impurities of the food eaten.

The elemental soul (*bhūtātman*) is called Soma. He who has the Unmanifest as his mouth is called Agni (Fire), because of the saying: 'The person, truly, with the Unmanifest as his mouth, enjoys the three Qualities.'

The renouncer of objects of sense the true ascetic

He indeed who knows this is an ascetic (*saṁnyāsin*) and a devotee (*yogin*) and a 'performer of the sacrifice to the Soul (Ātman).' Now, as there is no one to touch harlots who have entered into a vacant house, so he who does not touch objects of sense that enter into him is an ascetic and a devotee and a 'performer of the sacrifice to the Soul (Ātman).'

Food, as the life, source, goal, and desire of all, to be reverenced as the highest form of the Soul (Ātman)

11. This, verily, is the highest form of the Soul (Ātman), namely food; for truly, this life (*prāṇa*, breath) consists of food. For thus has it been said[1]: 'If one does not eat, he becomes a non-thinker, a non-hearer, a non-toucher, a non-seer, a non-speaker, a non-smeller, a non-taster, and he lets go his vital breaths.' [And furthermore:] 'If, indeed, one eats, he becomes well supplied with life; he becomes a thinker; he becomes a hearer; he becomes a toucher; he becomes a speaker; he becomes a taster; he becomes a smeller; he becomes a seer.' For thus has it been said[2]:—

> From food, verily, creatures are produced,
> Whatsoever [creatures] dwell on the earth.
> Moreover by food, in truth, they live.
> Moreover into it also they finally pass.

12. Now, it has elsewhere been said: 'Verily, all things here fly forth, day by day, desiring to get food. The sun takes food to himself by his rays. Thereby he gives forth heat. When supplied with food, living beings here digest.[3] Fire, verily, blazes up with food.' This world was fashioned by

[1] The quotation is made loosely from Chānd. 7. 9. 1.
[2] In Tait. 2. 2.
[3] Literally: 'When sprinkled with food, living beings here cook [it].

Brahma with a desire for food. Hence, one should reverence food as the Soul (Ātman). For thus has it been said[1]:—

From food created things are born.
By food, when born, do they grow up.
It both is eaten and eats things.
Because of that it is called food.

The theory of food

13. Now, it has elsewhere been said: 'That form of the blessed Vishṇu which is called the All-supporting—that, verily, is the same as food. Verily, life (*prāṇa*) is the essence of food; mind, of life; understanding (*vijñāna*), of mind; bliss, of understanding.' He becomes possessed of food, life, mind, understanding, and bliss who knows this. Verily, in as many things here on earth as do eat food does he eat food who knows this.

Food does, indeed, prevent decay,
Food is allaying, 'tis declared.
Food is the life of animals,
Is foremost, healing, 'tis declared.

The theory of time

14. Now, it has elsewhere been said: 'Food, verily, is the source of this whole world; and time, of food. The sun is the source of time.'

The form thereof is the year, which is composed of the moments and other durations of time, and which consists of twelve [months]. Half of it is sacred to Agni: half, to Varuṇa. From the asterism Maghā (the Sickle) to half of Śravishṭhā (the Drum)[2] in the [sun's southward] course is sacred to Agni. In its northward course, from Sarpa (the Serpent) to half of Śravishṭhā is sacred to Soma. Among these [asterisms] each month of Ātman [viewed as the year] includes nine quarters[3] according to the corresponding course [of the sun through the asterisms]. On account of the subtilty [of time] this [course of

[1] In Tait. 2. 2.
[2] That is, from June up to December.
[3] A twelfth part of the twenty-seven asterisms through which the sun moves in the course of the year is two and a quarter, or nine quarters.

the sun] is the proof, for only in this way is time proved. Apart from proof there is no ascertaining of the thing to be proved. However, the thing to be proved [e.g. time] may come to be proved from the fact of its containing parts [e.g. moments, etc.], to the cognizance of the thing itself. For thus has it been said:—

> However many parts of time—
> Through all of them runs yonder [sun]!

Whoever reverences Time as Brahma, from him time withdraws afar. For thus has it been said:—

> From Time flow forth created things.
> From Time, too, they advance to growth.
> In Time, too, they do disappear.
> Time is a form and formless too.

15. There are, assuredly, two forms of Brahma: Time and the Timeless. That which is prior to the sun is the Timeless (*a-kāla*), without parts (*a-kala*). But that which begins with the sun is Time, which has parts. Verily, the form of that which has parts is the year. From the year, in truth, are these creatures produced. Through the year, verily, after having been produced, do they grow. In the year they disappear. Therefore the year, verily, is Prajāpati, is Time, is food, is the Brahma-abode, and is Ātman. For thus has it been said:—

> 'Tis Time that cooks created things,
> All things, indeed, in the Great Soul (*mahātman*).
> In what, however, Time is cooked—
> Who knows that, he the Veda knows!

16. This embodied Time is the great ocean of creatures. In it abides he who is called Savitṛi,[1] from whom, indeed, are begotten moon, stars, planets, the year, and these other things. And from them comes this whole world here, and whatever thing, good or evil, may be seen in the world. Therefore Brahma is the soul (*ātman*) of the sun. So, one should reverence the sun as a name of Time. Some say[2]: 'Brahma is the sun.' Moreover it has been said:—

[1] The sun: etymologically, the Begetter.
[2] Quoted from Chānd. 3. 19. 1.

The offerer, the enjoyer, the oblation, the sacrificial formula (*mantra*),
The sacrifice, Vishṇu, Prajāpati—
Everyone whatsoever is the Lord (*prabhu*), the Witness,
Who shines in yonder orb.

The infinite Brahma—the eternal, unitary Soul (Ātman) of the world and of the individual

17. Verily, in the beginning this world was Brahma, the limitless One—limitless to the east, limitless to the south, limitless to the west, limitless to the north, and above and below, limitless in every direction. Truly, for him east and the other directions exist not, nor across, nor below, nor above.

Incomprehensible is that supreme Soul (Ātman), unlimited, unborn, not to be reasoned about, unthinkable—He whose soul is space (*ākāśātman*)[1]! In the dissolution of the world He alone remains awake. From that space He, assuredly, awakes this world, which is a mass of thought. It is thought by Him, and in Him it disappears.

His is that shining form which gives heat in yonder sun and which is the brilliant light in a smokeless fire, as also the fire in the stomach which cooks food. For thus has it been said: 'He who is in the fire, and he who is here in the heart, and he who is yonder in the sun—he is one.'

To the unity of the One goes he who knows this.

The Yoga method for attaining this pure unity

18. The precept for effecting this [unity] is this: restraint of the breath (*prāṇāyāma*), withdrawal of the senses (*pratyāhāra*), meditation (*dhyāna*), concentration (*dhāraṇā*), contemplation (*tarka*), absorption (*samādhi*). Such is said to be the sixfold Yoga. By this means

When a seer sees the brilliant
Maker, Lord, Person, the Brahma-source,
Then, being a knower, shaking off good and evil,[2]
He reduces everything to unity in the supreme Imperishable.

[1] A phrase from Chānd. 3. 14. 2 and Kaush. 2. 14.
[2] The first three lines of this stanza = Muṇḍ. 3. 1. 3 a, b, c.

For thus has it been said:—

As to a mountain that's enflamed
Deer and birds do not resort—
So, with the Brahma-knowers, faults
Do never any shelter find.

Withdrawal from sense-objects into absence of all thought

19. Now, it has elsewhere been said: 'Verily, when a knower has restrained his mind from the external, and the breathing spirit (*prāṇa*) has put to rest objects of sense, thereupon let him continue void of conceptions. Since the living individual (*jīva*) who is named "breathing spirit" has arisen here from what is not breathing spirit, therefore, verily, let the breathing spirit restrain his breathing spirit in what is called the fourth condition (*turya*).'[1] For thus has it been said:—

That which is non-thought, [yet] which stands in the midst of thought,
The unthinkable, supreme mystery!—
Thereon let one concentrate his thought
And the subtile body (*liṅga*), too, without support.

The selfless, liberated, joyous vision of the Self (Ātman)

20. Now, it has elsewhere been said: 'One may have a higher concentration than this. By pressing the tip of his tongue against the palate, by restraining voice, mind, and breath, one sees Brahma through contemplation.' When through self, by the suppressing of the mind, one sees the brilliant Self which is more subtile than the subtile, then having seen the Self through one's self, one becomes self-less (*nir-ātman*). Because of being selfless, he is to be regarded as incalculable (*a-saṁkhya*), without origin—the mark of liberation (*mokṣa*). This is the supreme secret doctrine (*rahasya*). For thus has it been said:—

For by tranquillity (*prasāda*) of thought
Deeds (*karman*), good and evil, one destroys!
With soul (*ātman*) serene, stayed on the Soul (Ātman),
Delight eternal one enjoys!

[1] Described in Māṇḍ. 7. On the term *turya* see p. 392, note 11.

The Yoga method of attaining to non-experiencing selflessness and to ultimate unity

21. Now, it has elsewhere been said: 'There is a channel called the Sushumnā,[1] leading upward, conveying the breath, piercing through the palate. Through it, by joining (√*yuj*) the breath, the syllable *Om*, and the mind, one may go aloft. By causing the tip of the tongue to turn back against the palate and by binding together (*saṁ-yojya*) the senses, one may, as greatness, perceive greatness.' Thence he goes to selflessness. Because of selflessness, one becomes a non-experiencer of pleasure and pain; he obtains the absolute unity (*kevalatva*). For thus has it been said:—

> After having first caused to stand still
> The breath that has been restrained, then,
> Having crossed beyond the limited, with the unlimited
> One may at last have union in the head.

Reaching the higher, non-sound Brahma by meditation on the sound 'Om'

22. Now, it has elsewhere been said: 'Verily, there are two Brahmas to be meditated upon: sound and non-sound. Now, non-sound is revealed only by sound.' Now, in this case the sound-Brahma is *Om*. Ascending by it, one comes to an end in the non-sound. So one says: 'This, indeed, is the way. This is immortality. This is complete union (*sāyujyatva*) and also peacefulness (*nirvṛtatva*).'

Now, as a spider mounting up by means of his thread (*tantu*) obtains free space, thus, assuredly, indeed, does that meditator, mounting up by means of *Om*, obtain independence (*svātantrya*).

Others expound the sound[-Brahma] in a different way. By closing the ears with the thumbs they hear the sound of the space within the heart. Of it there is this sevenfold comparison: like rivers, a bell, a brazen vessel, a wheel, the croaking of frogs, rain, as when one speaks in a sheltered place.

Passing beyond this variously characterized [sound-Brahma],

[1] So described, but not so designated, in Chānd. 8. 6. 6 and Kaṭha 6. 16. Hinted at also in Tait. 1. 6 and Praśna 3. 7. See the Appendix, p. 521.

men disappear in the supreme, the non-sound, the unmanifest Brahma. There they are unqualified, indistinguishable, like the various juices which have reached the condition of honey.[1] For thus has it been said :—

There are two Brahmas to be known:
Sound-Brahma, and what higher is.
Those people who sound-Brahma know,
Unto the higher Brahma go.

23. Now, it has elsewhere been said: 'The sound-Brahma is the syllable *Om*. That which is its acme is tranquil, soundless, fearless, sorrowless, blissful, satisfied, steadfast, immovable, immortal, unshaken, enduring, named Vishṇu (the Pervader). So for paramountcy one should reverence both these. For thus has it been said :—

Who is both higher and lower,
That god, known by the name of *Om*,
Soundless and void of being, too—
Thereon concentrate in the head!

Piercing, in spiritual meditation, through darkness to the shining, immortal, Brahma

24. Now, it has elsewhere been said: 'The body is a bow.[2] The arrow is *Om*. The mind is its point. Darkness is the mark. Having pierced through the darkness, one goes to what is not enveloped in darkness. Then, having pierced through what is thus enveloped, one sees Him who sparkles like a wheel of fire, of the color of the sun, mightful, the Brahma that is beyond darkness, that shines in yonder sun, also in the moon, in fire, in lightning. Now, assuredly, when one has seen Him, one goes to immortality.' For thus has it been said :—

The meditation that is on the highest principle within
Is also directed upon outer objects.
Hence the unqualified understanding
Comes into qualifiedness.

[1] Cf. Chānd. 6. 9. 1–2.

[2] For another parable of a bow and arrow in mystical meditation see Muṇḍ. 2. 2. 3–4.

But when the mind has been dissolved,
And there is the joy whose only witness is the self—
That is Brahma, the immortal, the pure!
That is the way! That indeed is the world!

The vision of the brilliant Soul in the perfect unity of Yoga

25. Now, it has elsewhere been said: 'He who, with senses indrawn as in sleep, with thoughts perfectly pure as in slumber, being in the pit of senses yet not under their control, perceives Him who is called *Om*, a leader, brilliant, sleepless, ageless, deathless,[1] sorrowless—he himself becomes called *Om*, a leader, brilliant, sleepless, ageless, deathless, sorrowless.' For thus has it been said:—

Whereas one thus joins breath and the syllable *Om*
And all the manifold world—
Or perhaps they are joined!—
Therefore it has been declared (*smṛta*) to be Yoga ('Joining').
The oneness of the breath and mind,
And likewise of the senses,
And the relinquishment of all conditions of existence—
This is designated as Yoga.

In the sacrifice of suppressed breath in Yoga the light of the world-source becomes visible

26. Now, it has elsewhere been said: 'Verily, as the huntsman draws in fish with his net and sacrifices them in the fire of his stomach, thus, assuredly, indeed, does one draw in these breaths with *Om* and sacrifice them in the fire that is free from ill.[2]

Furthermore, it is like a heated caldron. Now, as ghee in a heated caldron lights up by contact with [lighted] grass or wood, thus, assuredly, indeed, does he who is called non-breath light up by contact with the breaths.

Now, that which lights up is a form of Brahma, and that is the highest place of Vishṇu, and that is the Rudra-hood of

[1] 'Called *Om* . . . deathless' is a stereotyped expression from 6. 4.

[2] That is, Brahma-Ātman, which is designated by this same epithet at Śvet. 3. 10.

Rudra. That, having divided itself (*ātmānam*) thus unmeasured times, fills these worlds. For thus has it been said:—

> And as, indeed, from fire the sparks do issue,
> And likewise, too, from out the sun its light-rays,
> From It repeatedly all breathing creatures
> Come forth into this world, each in its order.

The light of the Brahma hidden in the body, made fully manifest and entered into in Yoga

27. Now, it has elsewhere been said: 'Assuredly, this is the heat of Brahma, the supreme, the immortal, the bodiless—even the warmth of the body.'

For that [heat] this [body] is the melted butter (ghee).[1]

Now, although it [i.e. the heat] is manifest, verily it is hidden[2] in the ether (*nabhas*) [of the heart]. Therefore by intense concentration they so disperse the space in the heart that the light, as it were, of that [heat] appears.

Thereupon one passes speedily into the same condition [of light], as a lump of iron that is hidden in the earth passes speedily into the condition of earthiness. As fire, iron-workers, and the like do not overcome a lump of iron that is in the condition of clay, so [in Yoga] thought together with its support vanishes away.[3] For thus has it been said:—

> The ether-storehouse of the heart
> Is bliss, is the supreme abode!
> This is ourself, our Yoga too;
> And this, the heat of fire and sun.

Entrance into the hall of Brahma after slaying the door-keeper, self-consciousness

28. Now, it has elsewhere been said: 'Having passed beyond the elements (*bhūta*), the senses, and objects of sense; thereupon having seized the bow whose string is the life of a religious mendicant (*pravrajyā*) and whose stick is steadfastness; and with the arrow which consists of freedom from self-conceit (*an-abhimāna*) having struck down the first warder of

[1] That is, because it manifests the presence of heat.
[2] As in Muṇḍ. 2. 2. 1 a: 'manifest, [yet] hidden.'
[3] —and is not overcome.

the door to Brahma [i.e. egoism, *ahaṁkāra*]—he who has confusion (*sammoha*) as his crown, covetousness and envy as his ear-rings, lassitude, drunkenness, and impurity (*agha*) as his staff, lord of self-conceit, who seizes the bow whose string is anger and whose stick is lust, and who slays beings here with the arrow of desire—having slain him, having crossed over with the raft of the syllable *Om* to the other side of the space in the heart, in the inner space which gradually becomes manifest one should enter the hall of Brahma, as the miner seeking minerals enters into the mine. Then let him disperse the fourfold[1] sheath of Brahma by the instruction of a spiritual teacher (*guru*).

The unhampered soul—the perfect Yogī

Henceforth being pure, clean, void, tranquil, breathless, selfless, endless, undecaying, steadfast, eternal, unborn, independent, he abides in his own greatness.[2]

Henceforth, having seen [the soul] which abides in his own greatness, he looks down upon the wheel of transmigrating existence (*saṁsāra*) as upon a rolling chariot-wheel.'

For thus has it been said:—

If a man practises Yoga for six months,
And is constantly freed [from the senses],
The infinite, supreme, mysterious
Yoga is perfectly produced.

But if a man is afflicted with Passion (*rajas*) and Darkness (*tamas*),
Enlightened as he may be—
If to son and wife and family
He is attached—for such a one, no, never at all!

Conclusion of the instruction on Brahma-knowledge and on Yoga

29. Having spoken thus, absorbed in thought, Śākāyanya did obeisance to him[3] and said: 'By this Brahma-knowledge,

[1] Consisting, according to the commentator, of food, breath, mind, and understanding, as in Tait. 2. 1–4. The same exhortation recurs below in 6. 38.

[2] The words 'pure, clean . . . greatness' are repeated from 2. 4.

[3] That is, to Bṛihadratha, concluding the conversation begun at 1. 2 and the course of instruction begun at 2. 1.

O king, did the sons of Prajāpati[1] ascend the path of Brahma.

By the practice of Yoga one gains contentment, endurance of the pairs of opposites (*dvandva*), and tranquillity (*śāntatva*).

This profoundest mystery one should not mention[2] to anyone who is not a son, or who is not a pupil, or who is not tranquil. However, to one who is devoted to none other [than to his teacher] or to one who is supplied with all the qualifications (*guṇa*), one may give it.

Liberation into the real Brahma by relinquishment of all desires, mental activity, and self-consciousness

30. *Om*! One should be in a pure place, himself pure (*śuci*), abiding in pureness (*sattva*), studying the Real (*sat*), speaking of the Real, meditating upon the Real, sacrificing to the Real.[3] Henceforth, in the real Brahma which longs for the Real, he becomes completely other. So he has the reward (*phala*) of having his fetters cut; becomes void of expectation, freed from fear in regard to others [as fully] as in regard to himself, void of desire. He attains to imperishable, immeasurable happiness, and continues [therein].

Verily, freedom from desire (*niṣkāmatva*) is like the choicest extract from the choicest treasure. For, a person who is made up of all desires, who has the marks of determination, conception, and self-conceit, is bound. Hence, in being the opposite of that, he is liberated.

On this point some say: "It is a quality (*guṇa*) which by force of the developing differentiation of Nature (*prakṛti*) comes to bind the self with determination [and the like], and that liberation results from the destruction of the fault of determination [and the like]."

[But] it is with the mind, truly, that one sees. It is with the mind that one hears. Desire, conception, doubt, faith, lack of

[1] The Vālakhilyas (according to the commentator Rāmatīrtha), who at 2. 3 are described as having come to Prajāpati for this knowledge.

[2] This same prohibition is imposed near the end of two previous Upanishads, namely at Bṛih. 6. 3. 12 and at Śvet. 6. 22.

[3] As directed at 6. 9.

faith, steadfastness, lack of steadfastness, shame, meditation, fear—all this is truly mind.[1]

Borne along and defiled by the stream of Qualities, unsteady, wavering, bewildered, full of desire, distracted, one goes on into the state of self-conceit. In thinking "This is I" and "That is mine" one binds himself with himself, as does a bird with a snare![2] Hence a person who has the marks of determination, conception, and self-conceit is bound. Hence, in being the opposite of that, he is liberated.[3] Therefore one should stand free from determination, free from conception, free from self-conceit. This is the mark of liberation (*mokṣa*). This is the pathway to Brahma here in this world. This is the opening of the door here in this world. By it one will go to the farther shore of this darkness, for therein all desires are contained.[4] On this point they quote[5]:–

> When cease the five
> [Sense-]knowledges, together with the mind,
> And the intellect stirs not—
> That, they say, is the highest course.'[6]

Śākāyanya's final course upward through the sun to Brahma

Having spoken thus, Śākāyanya became absorbed in thought.

Marut, having done obeisance and shown proper honor to him, having attained his end, departed by the northern course of the sun, for there is no approach by a side-path here in the world. This is the path to Brahma here in the world. Piercing through the door of the sun, he departed aloft. On this point they quote[7]:—

> Unending are the rays of him
> Who like a lamp dwells in the heart.
> They're white and black and brown and blue;
> They're tawny and of pale red hue.

1 This paragraph has already occurred in Bṛih. 1. 5. 3.
2 The paragraph up to this point has already occurred above at 3. 2.
3 These two sentences have already occurred in this same section.
4 The last clause of this sentence has already occurred in Chānd. 8. 1. 5.
5 Kaṭha 6. 10.
6 The last line of this stanza recurs at BhG. 8. 21 b.
7 Compare Chānd. 8. 6. 6.

Aloft arises one of these,
Which, piercing through the sun's round disk,
On to the Brahma-world extends.
Thereby men go the highest course.

What are its other hundred rays,
Are similarly upwards ranged;
Thereby unto the various gods'
Abiding-places one arrives.

But by its feebly shining rays
Which manifoldly downward lead
One roams about here helplessly
For the consuming of his deeds.

Therefore yonder blessed sun is the cause of creation (*sarga*), of heaven (*svarga*), and of final emancipation (*apavarga*).[1]

The evidences of the Soul in the senses and in the mind

31. Of what nature, verily, are these senses that range forth? And who is the one here who goes forth and restrains them?—Thus has it been said.

The answer is: 'They are of the nature of soul (*ātmaka*), for the soul is he who goes forth and restrains them. There are enticing objects of sense (*apsaras*), and there are so-called luminous rays. With his five rays he feeds upon objects (*viṣaya*).'

'Which soul?'

'He who has been described[2] as "pure, clean, void, tranquil, and of other marks." He is to be apprehended by his own peculiar marks.

Some say[3] that the mark of Him who is without any mark is what heat and [anything] pervaded by it is to fire, and what a most agreeable taste is to water.

Now others say[4] it is speech, hearing, sight, mind, breath; now others[5] that it is intellect, steadfastness, memory,

[1] Rāmatīrtha, the commentator, explains this as:—of re-creation for the man who does not worship the sun; of heaven [with temporary enjoyment] for the man who worships the sun as a divinity; of final cessation of rebirth for the man who worships the sun as Brahma-Ātman.

[2] As in 2. 4 and in 6. 28.

[3] As in 6. 27.

[4] As in Bṛih. 4. 4. 18 and Kena 2.

[5] As in Ait. 5. 2.

intelligence. Now, verily, these are the marks of Him, even as sprouts here are the mark of a seed, as smoke, light, and sparks are the marks of a fire. On this point they quote[1]:—

The Soul, the source of all

And as, indeed, from fire the sparks do issue,
And likewise, too, from out the sun its light-rays,
From It repeatedly all breathing creatures
Come forth into this world, each in its order.

32. From Him, indeed, [who is] in the soul (*ātman*) come forth all breathing creatures, all worlds, all the Vedas, all gods, all beings. The mystic meaning (*upaniṣad*) thereof is: The Real of the real.[2]

Now, as from a fire, laid with damp fuel, clouds of smoke separately issue forth; so, lo verily, from this great Being (*bhūta*) has been breathed forth that which is Rig-Veda, Yajur-Veda, Sāma-Veda, [Hymns of] the Atharvans and Aṅgirases, Legend (*itihāsa*), Ancient Lore (*purāṇa*), Sciences (*vidyā*), Mystic Doctrines (*upaniṣad*), Verses (*śloka*), Aphorisms (*sūtra*), Explanations (*anuvyākhyāna*), and Commentaries (*vyākhyāna*). From It, indeed, all beings here [were breathed forth].'[3]

The mystical significance of the three fires in the religious sacrifice[4]

33. Verily, this [Gārhapatya] sacrificial fire with its five bricks is the year. For that [fire] the bricks are these: spring, summer, the rains, autumn, winter. So it has a head, two wings, a back, and a tail. In the case of one who knows the Person this sacrificial fire is the earth, Prajāpati's first sacrificial pile. With its hands it raises the sacrificer up to the atmosphere and offers him to Vāyu (the Wind). Verily, the wind is breath.

Verily, breath (*prāṇa*) is a sacrificial fire [i. e. the second, the

[1] Already quoted in 6. 26.

[2] Most of this paragraph is repeated from Bṛih. 2. 1. 20 with the addition of the words 'all the Vedas.'

[3] This paragraph is repeated from Bṛih. 2. 4. 10 with slight variation.

[4] The three fires which are used in the religious sacrifice are interpreted to represent the three successive sacrificial piles which were erected by the Lord of Creation in the cosmos, namely the earth, the atmosphere, and the sky. The power which rules in each of these world-regions, namely the year, the wind, and the sun, successively elevates the sacrificer to the next superior, finally to the supreme Brahma.

Dakshiṇa fire]. For that the bricks are these: the Prāṇa breath, the Vyāna breath, the Apāna breath, the Samāna breath, the Udāna breath. So it has a head, two wings, a back, and a tail. In the case of one who knows the Person this sacrificial fire is the atmosphere, Prajāpati's second sacrificial pile. With its hands it raises the sacrificer up to the sky, and offers him to Indra. Verily, Indra is yonder sun.

He [Indra] is this [third, the Āhavanīya] fire. For that the bricks are these: the Rig-Veda, the Yajur-Veda, the Sāma-Veda, [the Hymns of] the Atharvans and Aṅgirases [i.e. the Atharva-Veda], Legend (*itihāsa*), and Ancient Lore (*purāṇa*). So it has a head, two wings, a back, and a tail. In the case of one who knows the Person this sacrificial fire is that sky, Prajāpati's third sacrificial pile. With its hands it makes a present of the sacrificer to the Knower of Ātman (the Soul).[1] Then the Knower of Ātman raises him up and offers him to Brahma. There he becomes blissful, joyful.

One's own digestion to be attended to, as a compend of cosmic sacrificial fires

34. The Gārhapatya fire is the earth. The Dakshiṇa fire is the atmosphere. The Āhavanīya fire is the sky. Hence they are [called] 'Purifying' (*pavamāna*), 'Purifier' (*pāvaka*), and 'Pure' (*śuci*).[2] Thereby one's sacrifice is made manifest.

Since the digestive fire also is a combination of 'Purifying,' 'Purifier,' and 'Pure,' therefore this fire should be worshiped with oblations, should be built up, should be praised, should be meditated upon.

The Self intended in religious sacrifices and verses

The sacrificer, when he takes the sacrificial butter, seeks meditation upon divinity thus:—

> 'Who is the bird of golden hue,
> Who dwells in both the heart and sun,
> Swan, diver-bird, surpassing bright—
> Him let us worship in this fire!'

[1] That is, to Prajāpati.

[2] Epithets of three oblations offered in the fire at a sacrifice; so by transference, applied, as epithets, to the fire itself.

And thus too one discerns the meaning of the sacred verse (*mantra*).[1] 'That desirable splendor of Savitri' should be meditated upon as [the desirable splendor] of Him who is the meditator abiding in the intellect. Here in the world one reaches the place of tranquillity for the mind; he places it in the Self (Ātman) indeed.

Liberation in the control of one's thoughts

On this point there are these verses:—

As fire, of fuel destitute,
Becomes extinct in its own source,
So thought by loss of activeness
Becomes extinct in its own source.

Becomes extinct in its own source,
Because the mind the Real seeks!
For one confused by things of sense,
There follow action's false controls.

Saṁsāra is just one's own thought;
With effort he should cleanse it, then.
What is one's thought, that he becomes;
This is the eternal mystery.[2]

For by tranquillity (*prasāda*) of thought,
Deeds (*karman*), good and evil, one destroys.
With soul serene, stayed on the Soul,
Delight eternal one enjoys![3]

As firmly as the thought of man
Is fixed within the realm of sense—
If thus on Brahma it were fixed,
Who would not be released from bond?

The mind is said to be twofold:
The pure and also the impure;
Impure—by union with desire;
Pure—from desire completely free!

By making mind all motionless,
From sloth and from distraction freed,
When unto mindlessness one comes,
Then that is the supreme estate!

[1] In RV. 3. 62. 10.
[2] This same great truth, of the character-making power of thought, is expressed also in the Buddhist scripture, Dhammapada 1. 1, 2.
[3] This quatrain has already occurred in 6. 20.

So long the mind should be confined,
Till in the heart it meets its end.
That is both knowledge and release!
All else is but a string of words![1]

With mind's stains washed away by concentration,
What may his joy be who has entered Ātman—
Impossible to picture then in language!
Oneself must grasp it with the inner organ.

In water, water; fire in fire;
In air, air one could not discern.
So he whose mind has entered in—
Released is he from everything!

The mind, in truth, is for mankind
The means of bondage and release:
For bondage, if to objects bound;
From objects free—that's called release!

Both sacrifice and meditative knowledge needed

Hence, for those who do not perform the Agnihotra sacrifice, who do not build up the fire, who do not know, who do not meditate, the recollection of the heavenly abode of Brahma is obstructed. Therefore, the fire should be worshiped with oblations, should be built up, should be praised, should be meditated upon.

Brahma, transcending all fragmentary manifestations, the supreme object of worship

35. Adoration to Agni (Fire), who dwells in the earth, who remembers the world![2] Bestow the world upon this worshiper!

Adoration to Vāyu (Wind), who dwells in the atmosphere, who remembers the world! Bestow the world upon this worshiper!

Adoration to Āditya (Sun), who dwells in heaven, who remembers the world! Bestow the world upon this worshiper![3]

[1] Or perhaps 'an extension of the knots [that bind the soul].'

[2] According to the reading of the text, *lokasmṛte*. Or, with the reading *lokaspṛte* of TS. 7. 5. 24. 1, 'who protects the world.'

[3] These same three invocations occur, with the variation 'who protects the world,' in TS. 7. 5. 24. 1.

Adoration to Brahma, who dwells in all, who remembers all! Bestow all upon this worshiper!

> With a golden vessel
> The Real's face is covered o'er.
> That do thou, O Pūshan, uncover
> Unto the Eternal Real (*satya-dharma*), the Pervader (Vishṇu).[1]

He who is yonder, yonder Person in the sun—I myself am he.

Verily, that which is the sunhood of the sun is the Eternal Real. That is the pure, the personal, the sexless (*a-liṅga*).

Of the bright power that pervades the sky (*nabhas*) it is only a portion which is, as it were, in the midst of the sun, in the eye, and in fire. That is Brahma. That is the Immortal. That is Splendor. That is the Eternal Real.

Of the bright power that pervades the sky it is only a portion which is the nectar in the midst of the sun, of which, too, the moon (Soma) and breathing spirits (*prāṇa*) are only sprouts. That is Brahma. That is the Immortal. That is Splendor. That is the Eternal Real.

Of the bright power that pervades the sky it is only a portion which shines as the Yajur-Veda[2] in the midst of the sun. That is *Om*, water, light, essence—the immortal Brahma! *Bhūr*! *Bhuvas*! *Svar*! *Om*!

> Eight-footed, undefiled, a swan,
> Three-stringed, minute, immutable,
> To good, bad blinded, lustrous bright—
> On seeing Him, one sees the all.

Of the bright power that pervades the sky it is only a portion which, rising in the midst of the sun, becomes the two light-rays. That is the knower of unity, the Eternal Real. That is the Yajur-Veda. That is heat. That is fire. That is wind. That is breath. That is water. That is the moon. That is the bright. That is the immortal. That is the realm of Brahma. That is the ocean of light. In It, indeed,

[1] These lines and the following phrase occur with slight variations in Īśā 15, 16 and Bṛih. 5. 15. 1.

[2] Regarded as the highest of the Vedas, for it is the one to which this Maitri Upanishad is attached.

worshipers become dissolved like the lump of salt.[1] That, verily, is the Brahma-unity, for therein all desires are contained.[2] On this point they quote:—

Transitory worshipers of the gods, and terminating knowers of real unity

E'en as a lamp stirred by a gentle zephyr,
So flares up he who moves among the celestial gods.
But he who knows this—he is a knower of unity, he is a knower of duality!
He will go to the Sole Abode and become partaker of its nature!
They who rise forth perpetually like the spray-drops,
Like the lightning that is hid in the highest heaven—
They, verily, by force of their source of glorious light
Correspond unto the fire [only] like its twisting flames.

Sacrifice of the two forms of Brahma, in space and in one's own self

36. Assuredly, indeed, of the light-Brahma there are these two forms: one, the Tranquil (*śānta*); and the other, the Abounding.

Now, of that which is the Tranquil, space (*kha*) is the support. And of that which is the Abounding, food here is the support.

Therefore one should offer sacrifice in the sacrificial space (*vedi*) with sacred verses (*mantra*), herbs, ghee, flesh, sacrificial cakes, boiled rice, and the like, and also—regarding the mouth as the Āhavanīya fire—with food and drink cast (*avasṛṣṭa*) in the mouth, for the sake of an abundance of vigor, for the winning of the holy (*puṇya*) world, and for immortality.

On this point they quote: 'One who is desirous of heaven (*svarga*) should offer the Agnihotra sacrifice. One wins the realm of Yama with the Agnishṭoma sacrifice, the realm of the moon (Soma) with the Uktha, the realm of the sun (*sūrya*) with the Shodaśin (the sixteen-day sacrifice), an independent realm

[1] For the simile see Bṛih. 2. 4. 12

[2] The last clause has already occurred in Chānd. 8. 1. 5 and Maitri 6. 30, and recurs again in 6. 38.

with the Atirātra sacrifice, that of the Lord of Creation (Prajāpati) with the sacrifice which continues to the end of a thousand years.'

The Inner Soul in the material world furnishes the individual's and the sun's existence

As the existence of a lamp
Is because of combination of wick, support, and oil,
So these two, the self and the bright (sun),
Exist because of the combination of the Inner One and the world-egg.

The offering of food passes through fire to the sun and back into life

37. Therefore, one should reverence with *Om* that unlimited bright power. This has been manifested in threefold wise: in fire, in the sun, and in the breath of life.

Now, the channel [which is between them] causes the abundance of food that has been offered in this fire to go unto the sun. The moisture which flows therefrom rains down like a chant (Udgītha). Thereby living creatures here exist. From living creatures come offspring.

On this point they quote: 'The oblation which has been offered in the fire it causes to go unto the sun. The sun rains that down with its rays. Thereby arises food; from food, the production of beings.'

For thus has it been said:—

The offering fitly cast in fire
Arises up unto the sun.
From out the sun, rain is produced;
From rain, food; living creatures thence.[1]

The course to the ultimate Brahma even here in the body

38. He who performs the Agnihotra sacrifice rends the net of eager desire (*lobha*).

Thence, having cut off confusion (*sammoha*), he no longer approves of anger.

[1] This same stanza occurs also in Mānava-Dharma-Śāstra 3. 76.

Meditating upon desire, he then cuts through the fourfold sheath [1] of Brahma.

Thence he goes to the highest ether. There, truly, having cut through the spheres of the sun, of the moon, of fire, and of Pure Being, himself being purified (*śuddha*), he sees the Intelligence (*caitanya*) which abides within Pure Being (*sattva*), immovable, immortal, unshaken, enduring, named Vishṇu,[2] the ultimate abode, endowed with true desires and with omniscience, independent, which stands in its own greatness. On this point they quote:—

In the midst of the sun stands the moon (Soma);
In the midst of the moon, fire.
In the midst of fire stands Pure Being (*sattva*).
In the midst of Pure Being stands the Unshaken One.

Having meditated upon him who is of the measure of a thumb or of a span within the body, more subtile than the subtile, then one goes to the supreme condition; for therein all desires are contained.[3] On this point they quote:—

Of size of thumb or span within the body,
A light of twofold or of threefold brightness,
This Brahma who is being praised,
The great god—He has entered in all beings!

Om! Adoration to Brahma! yea, adoration!

SEVENTH PRAPĀṬHAKA

The Soul (Ātman) as the world-sun, and its rays [4]

1. Agni, the Gāyatrī meter, the Trivṛit hymn, the Rathantara chant, the spring season, the Prāṇa breath, the stars, the Vasu gods, issue forth to the east; they shine, they rain, they praise, they enter again within and peer through an opening.

[1] Composed of food, breath, mind, and understanding—according to Tait. 2. 1–4. This same exhortation has occurred in 6. 28.

[2] The words 'immovable . . . Vishṇu' are repeated from 6. 23.

[3] The last clause is repeated from 6. 30 and 6. 35.

[4] An analytic and philosophic statement of the contents of this section, 1–6, would be:—

The various divinities, meters, hymns, chants, seasons, breaths, heavenly bodies, celestial gods, and earthly beings are transient emanations in the six different directions, returning again into the one unlimited Soul (Ātman) of the whole world.

He is unthinkable, formless, unfathomable, concealed, unimpeachable, compact, impenetrable, devoid of Qualities, pure, brilliant, enjoying Qualities (*guṇa*), fearful, unproduced, a master Yogī, omniscient, munificent, immeasurable, without beginning or end, illustrious, unborn, intelligent, indescribable, the creator of all, the soul (*ātman*) of all, the enjoyer of all, the lord of all, the inmost being of everything.

2. Indra, the Trishṭubh meter, the Pañcadaśa hymn, the Bṛihad chant, the summer season, the Vyāna breath, the moon, the Rudra gods, issue forth to the south. They shine, they rain, they praise, they enter again within and peer through an opening.

He is without beginning or end, unmeasured, unlimited, not to be moved by another, independent, devoid of marks, formless, of endless power, the creator, the enlightener.

3. The Maruts, the Jagatī meter, the Saptadaśa hymn, the Vairūpa chant, the rainy season, the Apāna breath, the planet Venus, the Āditya gods, issue forth to the west. They shine, they rain, they praise, they enter again within and peer through an opening.

That is tranquil, soundless, fearless, sorrowless, blissful, satisfied, steadfast, immovable, immortal, enduring, named Vishṇu (the Pervader),[1] the ultimate abode.

4. The Viśvadevas, the Anushṭubh meter, the Ekaviṁśa hymn, the Vairāja chant, the autumn season, the Samāna breath, Varuṇa, the Sādhya gods, issue forth to the north. They shine, they rain, they praise, they enter again within and peer through an opening.

He is pure within, clean, void, tranquil, breathless, selfless, endless.

5. Mitra and Varuṇa, the Paṅkti meter, the Triṇava and Trayastriṁśa hymns, the Śākvara and Raivata chants, the winter and the dewy seasons,[2] the Udāna breath, the Aṅgirases, the moon, issue forth above. They shine, they rain, they praise, they enter again within and peer through an opening.

[1] The sentence up to this point is repeated from 6. 23.

[2] The winter season (*hemanta*) in India is reckoned to last about two months, from the middle of November to the middle of January; the dewy season (*śiśira*) about two months, from the middle of January to the middle of March.

. . . Him who is called *Om*, a leader, brilliant, sleepless, ageless, deathless, sorrowless.[1]

6. Śani (Saturn), Rāhu (the Dragon's Head), Ketu (the Dragon's Tail), serpents, the Rākshasas (ogres), the Yakshas (sprites), men, birds, deer, elephants, and the like issue forth below. They shine, they rain, they praise, they enter again within and peer through an opening.

. . . . He who is intelligent, the avenger, within all, imperishable, pure, clean, shining, patient, tranquil.

The one unlimited Soul (Ātman) of the whole world

7. He, truly, indeed, is the Self (Atman) within the heart, very subtile, kindled like fire, assuming all forms. This whole world is his food. On Him creatures here are woven.[2]

He is the Self which is free from evil, ageless, deathless, sorrowless, free from uncertainty, free from fetters,[3] whose conception is the Real, whose desire is the Real. He is the supreme Lord. He is the ruler of beings. He is the protector of beings. He is the separating bridge [or dam] (*setu*).[4]

This Soul (Ātman), assuredly, indeed, is Īśāna (Lord), Śambhu (the Beneficent), Bhava (the Existent), Rudra (the Terrible), Prajāpati (Lord of Creation), Viśvasṛij (Creator of All), Hiraṇyagarbha (Golden Germ), Truth (*satya*), Life (*prāṇa*), Spirit (*haṁsa*), Śāstṛi (Punisher, or Commander, or Teacher), the Unshaken, Vishṇu (Pervader), Nārāyaṇa (Son of Man).[5]

He who is in the fire, and he who is here in the heart, and he who is yonder in the sun—he is one.[6]

To Thee who art this, the all-formed, hidden in the real ether, be adoration!

[1] A description repeated from 6. 4 and also 6. 25.

[2] For the same metaphor of warp and woof see Bṛih. 3. 6 and 3. 8.

[3] Reading *vipāśaḥ*.

[4] This same metaphor occurs at Bṛih. 4. 4. 22 and Chānd. 8. 4. 1.

[5] This entire paragraph is repeated from 6. 8 with the addition of the epithet 'the Unshaken.'

[6] The sentence is repeated from 6. 17.

Warnings against the disorderly and against false teachers

8. Now then, the hindrances to knowledge, O king.

Verily, the source of the net of delusion (*moha*) is the fact of the association of one who is worthy of heaven with those who are not worthy of heaven. That is it. Although a grove is said to be before them, they cling to a low shrub.

Now, there are some who are continually hilarious, continually abroad, continually begging, continually living upon handicraft.

And moreover, there are others who are town-beggars, who perform the sacrifice for the unworthy, who are disciples of Śūdras, and who, though Śūdras, know the Scriptures (*śāstra*).

And moreover, there are others, who are rogues, who wear their hair in a twisted knot, who are dancers, mercenaries, religious mendicants, actors, renegades in the royal service, and the like.

And moreover, there are others who say 'For a price we allay [the evil influences] of Yakshas (sprites), Rākshasas (ogres), Bhūtas (ghosts), spirit-bands, goblins, serpents, vampires, and the like.'

And moreover, there are others who falsely wear the red robe, ear-rings, and skulls.

And moreover, there are others who love to be a stumbling-block among believers in the Vedas by the stratagem of deceptive arguments in a circle, and false and illogical examples.

With these one should not associate. Verily, these creatures are evidently robbers, unfit for heaven. For thus has it been said:—

> By the jugglery of a doctrine that denies the Soul,
> By false comparisons and proofs
> Disturbed, the world does not discern
> What is the difference between knowledge and ignorance.[1]

Warning against ignorance and perverted doctrine

9. Verily, Bṛihaspati [the teacher of the gods] became Śukra [the teacher of the Asuras], and for the security of

[1] Reading *vedāvidyāntaram.*

Indra created this ignorance (*avidyā*) for the destruction of the Asuras (devils).[1]

By this [ignorance] men declare that the inauspicious is auspicious, and that the auspicious is inauspicious. They say that there should be attention to law (*dharma*) which is destructive of the Veda and of other Scriptures (*śāstra*). Hence, one should not attend to this [teaching]. It is false. It is like a barren woman. Mere pleasure is the fruit thereof, as also of one who deviates from the proper course. It should not be entered upon. For thus has it been said[2]:—

Widely opposite and asunder are these two:
Ignorance (*avidyā*), and what is known as 'knowledge.'
I think Naciketas desirous of obtaining knowledge!
Many desires rend thee not.

Knowledge and non-knowledge—
He who this pair conjointly (*saha*) knows,
With non-knowledge passing over death,
With knowledge wins the immortal.[3]

Those abiding in the midst of ignorance,
Self-wise, thinking themselves learned,
Hard smitten, go around deluded,
Like blind men led by one who is himself blind.[4]

Warning against devilish, false, non-Vedic doctrine

10. Verily, the gods and the devils (Asuras), being desirous of the Self (Ātman), came into the presence of Brahma. They did obeisance to him and said: 'Sir, we are desirous of the Self (Ātman). So, do you tell us.'

Then, meditating long, he thought to himself: 'Verily, these devils are desirous of a Self (Ātman) different [from the true one].' Therefore a very different doctrine was told to them.

Upon that fools here live their life with intense attachment, destroying the saving raft and praising what is false. They see the false as if it were true, as in jugglery.

Hence, what is set forth in the Vedas—that is true! Upon what is told in the Vedas—upon that wise men live their life.

[1] Compare the instruction of Indra, the representative of the gods, and Virocana, the representative of the devils, by Prajāpati in Chānd. 8. 7 ff.

[2] In Kaṭha 2. 4.

[3] This quatrain = Īśā 11.

[4] This stanza is repeated from Katha 2. 5 and Muṇḍ. 1. 2. 8 with slight variation.

Therefore a Brahman (*brāhmaṇa*) should not study what is non-Vedic. This should be the purpose.

The bright Brahma in the heart, stirred into all-pervading manifestation by meditation on 'Om'

11. Assuredly, the nature of the ether within the space [of the heart] is the same as the supreme bright power. This has been manifested in threefold wise: in fire, in the sun, and in the breath of life.[1]

Verily, the nature of the ether within the space [of the heart] is the same as the syllable *Om*.

With this [syllable], indeed, that [bright power] is raised up from the depths, goes upwards, and is breathed forth. Verily, therein is a perpetual support for meditation upon Brahma.

In the stirring up, that [bright power] has its place in the heat that casts forth light. In the stirring up, that is like [the action] of smoke; it rises up into a great tree in the sky, issuing forth into one branch after another.

That is like the casting forth of salt into water, like the heat in melted butter, like the range [of the thought] of a meditator [i.e. all-pervading].

On this point they quote: 'Now, wherefore is it said to be like lightning? Because in the very moment of going forth it lights up the whole body.'

Therefore, one should reverence with *Om* that unlimited bright power.[2]

The persons in the eyes, and their abode in the heart

(1) This Person who is in the eye,
Who has his place in the right eye—
This one is Indra; this, his wife,
Who has her place in the left eye.

(2) The meeting-place of these two is
Within the hollow of the heart.
The lump of blood which is therein
Is the life-vigor of these two.[3]

[1] The words 'bright power . . . breath of life' are repeated from 6. 37.

[2] This sentence is repeated from 6. 37.

[3] For this same thought see Bṛih. 4. 2. 3.

(3) Extended from the heart up to
The eye and firmly fastened there,
That channel serveth both of them
By being double, though but one.

The utterance of the various sounds of the alphabet, produced by breath started from the mind

(4) The mind stirs up the body's fire[1];
The fire then sets in motion wind;
The wind then, moving through the chest,
Produces pleasurable sound.

(5) As stirred in heart by means of fire of friction,
Less is it than the least; in throat, is doubled;
And know that on the tongue-tip it is trebled;
Come forth, it is the alphabet!—They say thus.

The true seer of the All beyond all evil

(6) The seer sees not death,
Nor sickness, nor any distress.
The seer sees only the All,
Obtains the All entirely.[2]

The larger self found in the superconscious; but a purposeful duality in the Self

(7) He who sees with the eye, and he who moves in dreams,
He who is deep asleep, and he who is beyond the deep sleeper—
These are a person's four distinct conditions.
Of these the fourth (*turya*) is greater [than the rest].

(8) In the three a quarter Brahma moves;
A three-quarter, in the last.[3]
For the sake of experiencing the true and the false,
The Great Ātman (Soul, Self) has a dual nature!
—Yea, the Great Ātman has a dual nature!

[1] The well-known *uṣman*.

[2] This stanza is repeated with slight verbal variation from Chānd. 7. 26. 2.

[3] A re-assertion in somewhat different form of the thought of RV. 10. 90. 3, 4, namely, that one quarter of Brahma exists in the actual and that three quarters constitute the eternal part of existence.

The four conditions have already been enumerated in the Māṇḍūkya Upanishad.

A BIBLIOGRAPHY OF THE UPANISHADS

SELECTED, CLASSIFIED, AND ANNOTATED

NATURE AND SCOPE OF THE BIBLIOGRAPHY

SPECIAL attention is called to the three words in which the nature and scope of this bibliography are indicated.

It is a *selected* bibliography. In general, only those titles have been included which are likely to prove in some way useful, or which have a special interest, historic or other. Many of the works listed have been consulted in the preparation of the translation presented in this volume.

It is a *classified* bibliography. The titles have been grouped in nine sections, as indicated on the following page, in order to secure a more helpful collocation than would be afforded by one continuous alphabetic or chronological sequence.

It is an *annotated* bibliography. The titles have been supplemented, in many cases, by descriptions, estimates, and quotations, with a view to indicating more precisely the nature and value of the publications recorded.

In the compilation of this list of titles purely bibliographical considerations have everywhere been subordinated to those of practical usefulness. It seemed better to devote the available space to annotations than to unimportant titles and a barren record of editions and reprints. Certain general works in division 9 are thus cited only in their English translations.

Titles in Sanskrit and in Indian vernaculars are given in condensed English paraphrase, rather than in a transliteration of their native wording, so that the contents of the publications may be readily discernible.

ARRANGEMENT OF THE BIBLIOGRAPHY

The titles here brought together are grouped in nine sections as follows:—

1. Translations of Collected Upanishads.
2. Translations of Single Upanishads.
3. Translations of Selections from the Upanishads.
4. Translations, with Text, of Collected Upanishads.
5. Translations, with Text, of Single Upanishads.
6. Text-Editions of Collected Upanishads.
7. Text-Editions of Single Upanishads.
8. Treatises, chiefly Linguistic.
9. Treatises, chiefly Expository.

Within each of these nine main sections the entries are arranged in chronological sequence, except in the case of reprints or translations of works listed, which immediately follow the main entry.

The order of the individual Upanishads (in Sections 2, 5, and 7) is the same as that followed in the Translation, namely: Bṛihad-Āraṇyaka, Chāndogya. Taittirīya, Aitareya, Kaushītaki, Kena, Kaṭha, Īśā, Muṇḍaka, Praśna, Māṇḍūkya, Śvetāśvatara, Maitri.

For the few abbreviations that have been used, consult pages xv–xvi.

1. TRANSLATIONS OF COLLECTED UPANISHADS

Duperron, Anquetil. Oupnek'hat [i. e. Upanishad], 2 vols. Strassburg, Levrault, 1801–1802. 735 and 916 pages.

A translation into *Latin* of a translation into *Persian* of the original Sanskrit of fifty of the Upanishads. The primary translation was made at Delhi 1656–1657 by pandits who had been brought from Benares for this purpose by the Muhammadan Prince Dārā Shukōh, son of the Moghul Emperor Shāh Jahān. This secondary translation was made by the very first European who went to India for the purpose of studying Oriental religions. At second remove from the original Sanskrit text, this translation is, nevertheless, of prime historical importance, because it was the first book which brought a knowledge of the Upanishads to the West.

It was with reference to this indirect Latin translation of the Upanishads through a medieval Persian translation that the German philosopher Schopenhauer expressed an appreciation which has been oft quoted in India: 'It has been the most rewarding and the most elevating reading which (with the exception of the original text) there can possibly be in the world. It has been the solace of my life, and will be of my death.' See *Parerga*, 2, § 185 (*Werke*, 6. 427).

The foregoing translated into *German*:

—— Das Oupnek'hat. In das Deutsche übertragen von Franz Mischel. Dresden, Heinrich, 1882. 618 pages.

This work exhibits in a unique degree the continued fascination and the far-distant influence which the Upanishads have exercised. Perhaps never before, or since, has the linguistic work of translating an important religious document been carried so far as to the third remove from the original language, as has been done in this particular case of translating the Upanishads, namely from the Sanskrit into Persian, thence into Latin, and thence into German.

Roy, Rammohun. Collected works. 2 vols. 2d ed., London, Parbury, Allen & Co., 1832.

Volume 2, entitled 'Translation of Several Principal Books, Passages and Texts of the Veds and of Some Controversial Works in Brahmunical Theology' (282 pp.), contains (at pp. 23–105) translations of Muṇḍ., Kena, Kaṭha, and Īśā, which had previously appeared separately.

The very first translation of collected Upanishads to be published in England.

The translator, with a high but not unqualified estimate of the value of the Upanishads, had been the leader of that remarkable reform movement in India at the beginning of the nineteenth century, the Brāhma Samāj. Indeed, he had gained his success as a theistic reformer partly by appealing to, and actually disseminating, the ancient sacred Upanishads. But these translations were executed as a part of the great reformer's religious studies and propaganda, not with a distinctively scholarly purpose nor with scientific method; the result is manifestly lacking in philological accuracy.

The foregoing reprinted:

—— The English works of Raja Rammohun Roy, edited by Jogendra Chunder Ghose. 2 vols. Calcutta, Bhowanipore Oriental Press, 1885–1887.

Translation of Muṇḍ., Kena, Kaṭha, and Īśā are contained in vol. 1, at pages 21–92.

The original second volume (of 1832) reprinted:

—— Calcutta, Society for the Resuscitation of Indian Literature, 1903. 335 pages.

Röer, E. Nine Upanishads [viz. Tait., Ait., Śvet., Kena, Īśā, Kaṭha, Praśna, Muṇḍ., and Māṇḍ.], translated. Calcutta, 1853. 170 pages. (Bibliotheca Indica.)

Müller, F. Max. The Upanishads. 2 vols. Oxford, Clarendon Press, 1879, 1884. (Sacred Books of the East, vols. 1 and 15.)

At the time of its publication this was the best and most extensive translation into English. But it is padded with considerable extraneous matter, which was added by the translator for the sake of greater intelligibility, yet which contrary to modern rules of scholarly procedure is left undifferentiated from the actual text.

In this very work the translator has declared the inherent difficulties of translating certain passages, e.g. 'These it is impossible to render in any translation; nay, they hardly deserve being translated.' (Vol. 1, p. 132.)

This translation by Max Müller has been severely criticized by other scholars, e.g. W. D. Whitney in his extensive and searching review of the work in *AJP*. 1886, pages 1–26, especially on pages 4, 6, 7, 9, 25, 26; by C. R. Lanman in his *Beginnings of Hindu Pantheism*, page 12, footnote; and by H. C. Tolman in his *Art of Translating*, page 37.

The foregoing reprinted:

—— 2 volumes bound in one. New York, Christian Literature Society [= Scribners], 1897. (Sacred Books of the East, American edition, vol. 1.)

Contains vols. 1 and 15 of the original Oxford edition, with a seven-page preface by F. Max Müller.

The twelve principal Upanishads: An English translation, with notes from the Commentaries of Sankaráchárya and the Gloss of Ánandagiri. Bombay, Tookaram Tatya, 'for the Bombay Theosophical Publication Fund,' 1891. 710 pages.

Merely a combined reprint of the translations of the Upanishads which had appeared in the Bibliotheca Indica, viz. of Chāndogya by Mitra, of Kaushītaki by Cowell, and of the following ten by Röer: Ait., Bṛih., Śvet., Kaṭha, Tait., Īśā, Muṇḍ., Kena, Praśna, and Mānḍ.

This list is the same as is contained in Max Müller's Translation, except that this collection omits Maitri and adds Māṇḍūkya.

The foregoing reprinted:

—— Bombay, Rajaram Tukaram Press, 1907. 719 pages.

Johnston, Charles. From the Upanishads. Dublin, Whaley, 1896. 66 pages.

Contains excellent translations of Kaṭha, of Praśna, and of Chāndogya 6.

'I have found them wise, beyond all others; and, beyond all others, filled with that very light which makes all things new . . . That glowing heart within us, we are beginning to guess, is the heart of all things, the everlasting foundation of the world . . . That teaching of oneness, of our hearts and the heart eternal as eternally one . . . You will find in these passages from the book of Wisdom, besides high intuition, a quaint and delightful flavour, a charm of childlike simplicity; yet of a child who is older than all age, a child of the eternal and the infinite, whose simplicity is better than the wisdom of the wise.' (Page x, Dedicatory Preface.)

The foregoing reprinted:

—— Portland, Maine, Thomas B. Mosher, 1897. 81 pages. (Smaller edition, 1913, 90 pages.)

Mead, G. R. S., and Jagadîsha Chandra Chaṭṭopâdhyâya (Roy Choudhuri). The Upaniṣhads. 2 vols. London. Theosophical Publishing Society, 1896.

Vol. 1 contains Īśā, Kena, Kaṭha, Praśna, Muṇḍ., and Mānḍ. Vol. 2 contains Tait., Ait., and Śvet.

'The present translation is an attempt to place the sublime teachings of the Upaniṣhads within the reach of every man and woman who can read the English tongue. Its price is purely nominal. The Upaniṣhads, we believe, should be allowed to speak for themselves, and not left to the mercy of artificial commentaries. They are grand outpourings of religious enthusiasm, raising the mind out of the chaos of ceremony and the

metaphysical and philological word-spinning of the schools . . . world-scripture, that is to say, a scripture appealing to the lovers of religion and truth in all races and at all times, without distinction.' (Preamble, vol. 1, pp. 4-5.)

The foregoing translated into French:

—— Neuf Upanishads, tr. E. Marcault. Paris, Libr. de l'Art Indépendant, 1905. 192 pages.

The same translated into Dutch:

—— Tr. Clara Streubel. Amsterdam, Theosophical Society, 2 vols., 1908.

Deussen, Paul. Sechzig Upanishad's des Veda. Leipzig, Brockhaus, 1897. 946 pages. (Second edition, 1905; reprint, 1921.)

Contains the classical Upanishads, all the fifty included in Duperron's *Oupnek'hat*, together with the more important of the later Atharvan Upanishads.

The most scholarly translation of the Upanishads which has hitherto been made. Brings to bear an extensive, intimate, and appreciative knowledge of European, as well as of Indian, philosophy. Contains informing and interpretative introductions to each separate section of each Upanishad, as well as to each Upanishad as a whole, also cross-references and explanatory notes. This translation is virtually indispensable to any thoroughly scholarly attempt to translate the Upanishads.

Thirty minor Upanishaḍs, translated by K. Nārāyaṇasvāmi Aiyar. Madras, 1914. 296 pages.

Srisa Chandra Vidyarnava. Studies in the first six Upanisads, and the Isa and Kena Upanisads, with Commentaries of Sankara, translated. Allahabad, Panini Office, 1919. 152 pages. (Sacred Books of the Hindus, vol. 22, part 1.)

Deals with Īśā, Kena, Kaṭha, Praśna, Muṇḍaka, and Māṇḍūkya. Contains complete translations only of Īśā and Kena, with various interpretations and studies.

Paramananda, Swami. The Upanishads: translated and commentated from the original Sanskrit text. Volume 1. Boston, Vedanta Centre, 1919. 116 pages.

Contains a translation of Īśā, Kaṭha, and Kena, paragraph by paragraph, with comments on some of the paragraphs.

The Upanishads complete: The doctrine of Brahma. [In Japanese.] 9 vols. Tokyo, Sekai Bunko Kanko-kwai, 1922–1924.

Contains a translation into Japanese of 116 Upanishads by 27 translators, adding also a translation of the 10 Upanishads from Duperron's version that are given by Deussen on pages 827-879.

2. TRANSLATIONS OF SINGLE UPANISHADS

Bṛihad-Āraṇyaka Upanishad

Poley, L. H. Th. Colebrooke's Abhandlung über die heiligen Schriften der Indier, aus dem Englischen übersetzt, nebst Fragmenten der ältesten religiösen Dichtungen der Indier. Leipzig, Teubner, 1847. 182 pages.

In his German translation of Colebrooke's 'Essay' Poley has added at pages 130-176, among other translations from the Upanishads, this original German translation of Bṛih. 1. 1 – 3. 2.

Röer, E. The Brihad Aranyaka Upanishad, and the Commentary of Sankara Acharya on its first chapter, translated from the original Sanskrit. Calcutta, 1856. 279 pages. (Bibliotheca Indica.)

The foregoing reprinted:

—— Published by the Society for the Resuscitation of Indian Literature. Calcutta, Elysium Press, 1908. 295 pages.

Herold, A.-F. L'Upanishad du Grand Aranyaka, Brihadaranyakopanishad traduite pour la première fois du Sanskrit en francais. Paris, Saint-Amand, 1894. 159 pages.

According to the Mādhyaṁdina recension.

Böhtlingk, Otto. Bṛhadaranjakopanishad in der Mâdhjaṁdina-Recension, übersetzt. St. Petersburg, Kaiserliche Akademie der Wissenschaften, 1889. 100 pages.

This German translation has also been printed along with the Sanskrit text.

Johnston, Charles. The Song of Life. Flushing, New York, published by the author, 1901. 69 pages.

A rather free rendering of Bṛih. 4. 3–4.

The foregoing translated into German:

—— Das Lied des Lebens. Berlin, P. Raatz, no date (but not later than 1906). 66 pages.

CHĀNDOGYA UPANISHAD

Mitra, Rajendralala. Chāndogya Upanishad of the Sāma Veda, with extracts from the Commentary of Sankara Āchārya, translated. Calcutta, 1862. 144 pages. (Bibliotheca Indica.)

AITAREYA UPANISHAD

Colebrooke, Henry Thomas. A translation of the Aitareya Upanishad is contained in the essay 'On the Vedas or the sacred writings of the Hindus,' first published and reprinted as follows:

Asiatic Researches, vol. 8, Calcutta, 1805, pages 421–425;

Miscellaneous Essays, vol. 1, London, Williams & Norgate, 1837 (new edition, 1858), pages 47–53;

Life and Essays, vol. 2, London, Trübner, 1873, pages 42–47.

Eckstein, Baron d'. Analyse du quatrième chapitre de l'Aitareya Upanishad, extrait du Rig-Véda. In *Journal Asiatique*, series 2, vol. 11, pp. 193–221, 289–317, 414–446; vol. 12, pp. 53–78; Paris, Imprimerie Royale, 1833.

Contains a French translation and discussion of the fourth chapter of the Aitareya Upanishad, based on Duperron's Latin translation in his *Oupnek'hat*, vol. 2, pp. 57–63, and on Colebrooke's English translation in *Asiatic Researches*, vol. 8, pp. 421–425

KAUSHĪTAKI UPANISHAD

Harlez, C. de. Kaushitaki-Upanishad, avec le commentaire de Çankarânanda et Sarvopanishadarthânubhûtiprakâças, chapitre viii Louvain, Lefever, 1887. 46 pages.

The rendering in some places should more properly be designated a paraphrase than a translation. And in some places, by reason of following the native commentator so closely (as did Cowell and Müller before him), this author quite misses the inherent sense. There is undesignated extraneous matter in the midst of the text, somewhat as in Max Müller's translation, though not to the same extent.

'We have followed generally the text of the Dîpaka; and for the translation, the commentary of Çankarânanda has been used with profit.' (Preamble, page 2.)

KENA UPANISHAD

Roy, Rammohun. Translation of the Céna Upanishad, one of the chapters of the Sáma Véda, according to the gloss of the celebrated Shankaráchāryu establishing the unity and the sole omnipotence of the Supreme Being, and that He alone is the object of worship. Calcutta, Philip Pereira, Hindoostanee Press, 1816. 12 pages.

Hiriyanna, M. Kenopanishad, with the commentary of Sri Sankaracharya. Srirangam, Sri Vani Vilas Press, 1912. 72 pages.

Translation of the Kena Upanishad and of Sankara's commentary, together with some additional notes by the translator.

Kaṭha Upanishad

Roy, Rammohun. Translation of the Kut'h-Oopanishud of the Ujoor-Ved, according to the gloss of the celebrated Sunkuracharyu. Calcutta, 1819.

Poley, L. Kathaka-Oupanichat; extrait du Yadjour-Véda, traduit du sanskrit en français. Paris, Dondey-Dupré, 1835. 22 pages.

Eckstein, Baron d'. Analyse du Kâthaka-Oupanischat, extrait du Yadschour-Véda. In *Journal de l'Institut Historique*, Paris, 1835, pp. 97–117.

Contains short extracts of the text in Roman transliteration, together with translations of short extracts from other Sanskrit books.

Poley, L. Kâthaka-Oupanichat, extrait du Yadjour-Véda, et Moundaka-Oupanichat, extrait de l'Atharva-Véda: traduit du sanskrit en français. Paris, Dondey-Dupré, 1837. 39 pages.

This is a revised edition, and in combined form, of the same author's previous separate French translations of the Kaṭha Upanishad in 1835 and of the Muṇḍaka Upanishad in 1836.

Poley, L. H. Th. Colebrooke's Abhandlung über die heiligen Schriften der Indier, aus dem Englischen übersetzt, nebst Fragmenten der ältesten religiösen Dichtungen der Indier. Leipzig, Teubner, 1847. 182 pages.

In his German translation of Colebrooke's famous 'Essay on the sacred writings of the Hindus,' Poley added, at pp. 113–128, among other translations, this original German translation from the Sanskrit of the Kaṭha Upanishad.

Arnold, Edwin. The Secret of Death, with some collected poems. London, Trübner, 1885; reprinted 1899.

Contains (at pages 14–45 of 1885 ed., pages 7–40 of 1899 ed.) a free metrical version of the first three Vallīs (or 'Lotus-stems') of the Katha Upanishad.

> 'The subtle thought, the far-off faith,
> The deathless spirit mocking Death,
> The close-packed sense, hard to unlock
> As diamonds from the mother-rock,
> The solemn, brief simplicity,
> The insight, fancy, mystery
> Of Hindoo scriptures—all are had
> In this divine Upanishad.' (Introduction, p. 2.)

Whitney, W. D. Translation of the Kaṭha-Upanishad. In *Transactions of the American Philological Association*, vol. 21, pp. 88–112, Boston, 1890.

This is the first English translation of an Upanishad in which the verse-portions were indicated as different from the prose-portions. A very careful translation, with an introduction, valuable exegetical and linguistic notes, and a number of proposed textual emendations.

Butenschön, Andrea. Kâthaka-Upanishad, öfversatt fr. Sanskrit. Stockholm, Norstedt, 1902. 62 pages.

A translation into Swedish.

Belloni-Filippi, Ferdinando. Kâthaka-Upanisad, tradotta in italiano e preceduta da una notizia sul panteismo indiano. Pisa, Orsolini-Prosperi, 1905. 158 pages.

A translation into Italian.

Old, W. Gorn. The Yoga of Yama: what Death said: a version of the Katopanishad, with commentary; being a system of Yoga or means of attainment. London, Rider, 1915. 64 pages.

Charpentier, Jarl. Kâṭhaka Upaniṣad: introduction, translation and notes. In *Indian Antiquary*, vol. 57 (1928), pp. 201–207, 221–228; 58 (1929), pp. 1–5.

Īśā Upanishad

Jones, Sir William. Ísávásyam; or, an Upanishad from the Yajur Veda. In his *Works*, vol. 6, pp. 423–425, London, Robinson, 1799.

A translation by no means literal, but noteworthy as having been the very first translation of any of the Upanishads into English.

Reprinted in his *Works*, London, Stockdale, 1807, vol. 13, pp. 374–377.

Roy, Rammohun. The Íshopanishad, one of the chapters of the Yajur Véda, according to the commentary of the celebrated Shankar-Ácharya, establishing the unity and incomprehensibility of the Supreme Being, and that His worship alone can lead to eternal beatitude. Calcutta, Philip Pereira, Hindoostanee Press, 1816. 36 pages.

Ramaswamier, S. The Vaja-saneya-samhitopanishad with the Bhashya of Srimat Sankaracharya. Madras, National Press, 1884. 19 pages.

A translation of the 18 stanzas of the Upanishad and also of the Commentary of the chief Indian commentator on all the classical Upanishads.

Vasu, Srisa Chandra. The Îśâvâsyopanishad, translated into English with the Commentaries of Sri Sankaracharya and Sri Anantacharya, and notes from the Tikas of Anandagiri, Uvatacharya, Sankarananda, Ramchandra Pandit and Anandabhatta. Bombay, Tookaram Tatya, for the Bombay Theosophical Publication Fund, 1896. 78 pages.

Griffith, R. T. H. The texts of the White Yajurveda, with a popular commentary. Benares, Lazarus, 1898. 364 pages.

The Īśā Upanishad, being originally the fortieth chapter of the Vāja-saneyi Saṁhitā, is here translated at pages 304–308.

Muṇḍaka Upanishad

Roy, Ram Mohun. Translation of the Moonduk-Opunishud of the Uthurvu-Ved according to the gloss of the celebrated Shunkura-Charyu. Calcutta, D. Lankpeet, Times Press, 1819. 17 pages.

'An attentive perusal of this, as well as of the remaining books of the Vedantu, will, I trust, convince every unprejudiced mind that they, with great consistency, inculcate the unity of God, instructing men at the same time in the pure mode of adoring him in spirit.' (Introduction.)

Poley, L. Moundaka-Oupanichat; extrait de l'Atharva-Véda, traduit du Sanskrit en Français. Paris, Bertrand, 1836. 15 pages.

The foregoing reprinted:

—— Kâtha-Oupanichat, extrait du Yadjour-Véda, et Moundaka-Oupanichat, extrait de l'Atharva-Véda, traduit du Sanskrit en Francais. Paris, Dondey-Dupré, 1837. 39 pages.

Poley, L. H. Th. Colebrooke's Abhandlung über die heiligen Schriften der Indier, aus dem Englischen übersetzt, nebst Fragmenten der ältesten religiösen Dichtungen der Indier. Leipzig, Teubner, 1847. 182 pages.

In his German translation of Colebrooke's famous 'Essay on the Sacred Scriptures of the Hindus,' Poley added, among other translations, this original German translation from the Sanskrit of the Muṇḍaka Upanishad.

Śvetāśvatara Upanishad

Nallaswami Pillai, J. M. The Swetaswatara Upanishad, translated and expounded. In *Madras Review*, vol. 6 (1900), pp. 369–376; vol. 7 (1901), pp. 267–279.

Māṇḍūkya Upanishad

Dvivedi, Manilal N. Mândûkyopanishad with Gaudapâda's Kârikâs and the Bhâshya of Śankara. Bombay, Tattva-Vivechaka Press, 1894. 137 pages.

The foregoing reprinted:

—— Bombay, Rajaram Tukaram, 1909.

3. TRANSLATIONS OF SELECTIONS FROM THE UPANISHADS

Poley, L. H. Th. Colebrooke's Abhandlung über die heiligen Schriften der Indier, aus dem Englischen übersetzt, nebst Fragmenten der ältesten religiösen Dichtungen der Indier. Leipzig, Teubner, 1847. 182 pages.

The German translator added at pages 110–176 original translations from the Sanskrit of Kaṭha, Īśā, and Bṛih. 1. 1–3. 2. The text-basis used for these translations was the text published by Poley himself in 1844.

Weber, Albrecht. Indische Studien. Berlin, Dümmler. Vol. 1, 1849–1850; vol. 2, 1853.

A series of articles entitled 'Analyse der in Anquetil du Perron's Uebersetzung enthaltenen Upanishad,' contains translations of important parts, together with summaries of intervening parts and also valuable elaborate discussion of Chānd., Maitri, Muṇḍ, and Īśā in vol. 1, pp. 254–301; of Kaush., Śvet., and Praśna in vol. 1, pp. 392–456; of Māṇḍ. in vol. 2, pp. 100–111; and of Kena, Kaṭha, and Tait. 2–3 in vol. 2, pp. 181–236.

Muir, John. Original Sanskrit texts on the origin and history of the people of India, their religion and institutions. London, 1858–1870. Vols. 1–3, Williams & Norgate; vols. 4–5, Trübner. Second edition, 1868–1872.

The most comprehensive treasury of excerpts, in transliteration and translation, from a wide range of Sanskrit literature. The numerous, mostly brief, translations from the Upanishads are gathered under a variety of topics, but are available from the indices.

Monier-Williams, Sir Monier. Indian wisdom; or examples of the religious, philosophical, and ethical doctrines of the Hindus. London, Luzac, 1875; 4th ed., 1893. 575 pages.

Chap. 2 on 'The Brāhmaṇas and Upanishads' contains original translations of representative selections from the Īśā, Kaṭha, Śvet., and Maitri, together with briefer extracts from Bṛih., Chānd., and Muṇḍ.

'These Upanishads are practically the only Veda of all thoughtful Hindus in the present day.' (Page 33.)

Regnaud, Paul. Matériaux pour servir à l'histoire de la philosophie de l'Inde. 2 vols. Paris, Vieweg, 1876, 1878.

This was the standard work in French on the subject until the appearance in 1907 of Oltramare's *L'Histoire*. Contains numerous extracts from the Upanishads, assembled under various topics.

Muir, John. Metrical translations from Sanskrit writers, with an introduction, many prose versions, and parallel passages from classical authors. London, Trübner, 1879. 376 pages.

Contains translations from the Bṛih., Kaṭha, and Śvet.

Scherman, Lucian. Philosophische Hymnen aus der Rig- und Atharva-Veda-Samhitâ verglichen mit den Philosophemen der älteren Upanishad's. Strassburg and London, Trübner, 1887. 96 pages.

Contains a number of extracts from the Upanishads with footnotes collecting comparative translations of the same. The 'Index der Upanishad-Citate' renders all this material easily accessible.

Müller, F. Max. Three lectures on the Vedānta philosophy. London, Longmans Green, 1894. 173 pages.

These rather general, unsystematic lectures contain, besides numerous remarks on the Upanishads, a running summary and extracts of the Kaṭha on pp. 47–53 and a brief sketch of the Maitri on pp. 55–61.

Dutt, Romesh Chandra. Lays of Ancient India: Selections from Indian poetry rendered into English verse. London, Trübner, 1894. 221 pages.

Along with selections from Vedic and Buddhist books, there are English versified translations of eight episodes from the Upanishads, viz. Chānd. 3. 14; 4. 4; Bṛih. 3. 1-8; 4. 5; Kena 3-5; Kaṭha 1; Īśā; and Kaush. 4.

Dvivedi, Manilal N. The Imitation of Śankara, being a collection of several texts bearing on the Advaita. Bombay, Tattva-Vivechaka Press, 1895. 255 pages.

Contains selections, assembled under eighteen topics, from all of the thirteen Upanishads included in the present translation, except the Maitri.

Selections from the Upanishads, translated into English, with notes from Sankara Acharya and others. Prefatory note by J. Murdoch. Madras, Christian Literature Society, 1895. 114 pages.—Forms the first part of The Sacred Books of the East described and explained: Hindu Series, volume 2, Madras, Christian Literature Society, 1898. (Reprinted 1904.)

Contains complete translations of the Kaṭha, Īśā, and Śvet. by Röer, part of Röer's Bṛih. and part of Mitra's Chānd., together with a very disparaging 'Examination of the Upanishads' by an anonymous compiler.

World's great classics, volume 7. Sacred books of the East, comprising the Vedic Hymns, Zend Avesta, Dhammapada, Upanishads, the Koran, and the Life of Buddha, with critical and biographical sketches by Epiphanius Wilson. New York, Colonial Press, 1899. (Revised edition, 1900.)

The section of the Upanishads occupies pages 153-172 and contains a two-page introduction and the first three Adhyāyas of F. Max Müller's translation of the Kaushītaki Upanishad.

Dutt, Romesh Chandra. The epics and lays of Ancient India, condensed into English verse. Calcutta, R. P. Mitra, 1903. 510 pages.

This is an abridged combined Indian reprint of three earlier publications of the same author which had appeared in England. In the third section there is a collection of six passages from the Upanishads (pages 55-82), namely, Chānd. 3. 14; 4. 4; Bṛih. 3. 1. 8; 4. 5: Kaush. 4; Kaṭha 1.

Johnston, Charles. The Kingdom of Heaven, and the Upanishads. In *Open Court*, vol. 19 (1905), pp. 705–716.

Gives original translations of eleven quotations from the Upanishads as parallels to passages from the New Testament.

Barnett, Lionel D. Some sayings from the Upanishads, done into English with notes. London, Luzac, 1905. 59 pages.

Contains translations of Chând. 6. 3. 14, Bṛih. 4. 3–5, and Kaṭha 1, 2, 5, and 6. A work of scholarly and literary merit.

Deussen, Paul. Die Geheimlehre des Veda: Ausgewählte Texte der Upanishad's, aus dem Sanskrit übersetzt. Leipzig, Brockhaus, 1907 (6th ed., 1921). 245 pages.

Consists almost entirely of German translations of selected passages from fourteen Upanishads exactly as rendered in the same author's *Sechzig Upanishad's des Veda.* Here the extracts are arranged topically under each Upanishad. The Īśā is presented complete.

The spirit of the Upanishads; or, The aphorisms of the wise: a collection of texts, sayings, proverbs, &c., from the Upanishads or sacred writings of India, compiled and adapted from over fifty authorities, expressing the cream of the Hindu philosophical thought. Chicago, Yogi Publishing Society, 1907. 85 pages.

The selections have been arranged under sixteen topics by an anonymous compiler. None of the selections are specifically documented. Only the name of the document or of the author in the original Sanskrit is mentioned. Acknowledgment is made that Manilal N. Dvivedi of Bombay was the translator of many of these aphorisms, but no other translator is acknowledged. And throughout the work there have been 'such supplementary changes and rearrangement as have seemed desirable.' (Preface, p. 8.)

Johnston, Charles. The dramatic element in the Upanishads. In *The Monist*, vol. 20 (1910), pp. 185–216.

Contains original translations of several passages, mostly dialogues, in the Bṛih., Chând., Kaṭha, Praśna, and Māṇḍ. Upanishads.

Barnett, Lionel D. Brahma-Knowledge: An outline of the philosophy of the Vedânta as set forth by the Upanishads and by Śankara. New York, Dutton, 1911. 113 pages.

Part 1 (55 pages) consists of an exposition, 'An account of the Vedânta.' Part 2 (46 pages) contains translations of fifteen important episodes from the Upanishads. A translation of high literary merit. But unfortunately there is no Index or Table of Citations to make the material readily available from the sources.

Eberhardt, Paul. Der Weisheit letzter Schluss: Die Religion der Upanishads im Sinne gefasst. Jena, Diederichs, 1912. 126 pages.

A German translation of thirty-seven passages from the Upanishads, topically arranged.

The sacred books and early literature of the East, edited by Charles F. Horne. Volume 9: India and Brahmanism. London and New York, Parke, Austin & Lipscombe, 1917.

Contains a section (pp. 67–113) which presents some selections from Max Müller's translations of 'The Upanishads, or hidden wisdom (1000–500 B.C.).'

Milburn, R. Gordon. The religious mysticism of the Upanishads: selected texts with translations and notes. Calcutta, Cambray, 1919. 214 pages.

Selections from twelve of the Upanishads are arranged under three main themes: A. The being of God and epistemology; B. Ethics, practical religion and soteriology; C. Devotional.

Salet, Pierre. Les Upanishads: morceaux choisis. Paris, Payot, 1920. 95 pages.

Hillebrandt, Alfred. Aus Brahmanas und Upanisaden: Gedanken altindischer Philosophen, übertragen und eingeleitet. Jena, Diederichs, 1921. 188 pages. (Religiöse Stimmen der Völker: Die Religion des alten Indiens, I.)

Hertel, Johannes. Die Weisheit der Upanischaden: eine Auswahl aus den ältesten Texten, aus dem Sanskrit übersetzt und erläutert. München, Beck, 1921 (2d ed., 1922). 193 pages.

Selections from seven Upanishads, the Aitareya being complete.

Geldner, K. F. Vedismus und Brahmanismus. Mohr, Tübingen, 1928. 185 pages.

This constitutes Part 9 of Alfred Bertholet's *Religionsgeschichtliches Lesebuch*, 2d enlarged edition. Contains 60 pages of selections from twelve Upanishads, topically arranged.

Hoffmann, Paul T. Upanishad. Die indischen Geheimlehren: ausgewählt, eingeleitet und erläutert. München, 1928. 88 pages. (Kunstwart-Bücherei, vol. 49.)

Mukerji, Dhan Gopal. Devotional passages from the Hindu Bible, adapted into English. New York, Dutton, 1929. 57 pages.

'Though not a scholar and a Sanskritist, I have ventured to bring the mystical utterances of India to the door of the American reader in a fanciful garb, as I have brought many another thing from the East, with the hope that it may serve him to augment his efforts in the direction of reconciling the East with the West.' (Preface.)

4. TRANSLATIONS, WITH TEXT, OF COLLECTED UPANISHADS

Pauthier, Guillaume. Mémoire sur l'origine et la propagation de la doctrine du Tao, fondée par Lao-Tseu; traduit du chinois, et accompagné d'un commentaire tiré des livres sanskrits et du Tao-te-king de Lao-Tseu; établissant la conformité de certaines opinions philosophiques de la Chine et de l'Inde; orné d'un dessein chinois; suivi de deux Oupanichads des Védas, avec le texte sanskrit et persan. Paris, 1831.

Contains a French translation of the Kena and Īśā Upanishads, together with the Sanskrit and Persian texts of the same.

The foregoing particulars are taken from a notice of the book in the *Nouveau Journal Asiatique*, vol. 7 (1831), page 465.

Poley, L. Collection des Oupanichats, extraits des Védas, traduits du Sanskrit en Français. Paris, six instalments, 1835–1837; the first four published by Dondey-Dupré; the last two by Bertrand.

The first part, with 39 consecutively numbered pages, is occupied with a French translation of the Kaṭha and Muṇḍaka Upanishads, both of which had appeared separately.

The second part, with 199 consecutively numbered pages, is occupied with the text of the preceding two Upanishads and of the Kena, followed by Śaṅkara's commentaries on these three, followed by the text of the Īśā.

This would seem to be the first edition of collected Upanishads in the Devanāgarī character published in Europe.

Pala, Mahesachandra. Nine Upanishads in the Bengali character, viz. Ait., Īśā, Kena, Śvet., Kaṭha, Tait., Māṇḍ., Muṇḍ., and Praśna, with Sankara Acharya's Commentaries, and Bengali translations. Calcutta, 1881–1889.

Böhtlingk, Otto. Drei kritisch gesichtete und übersetzte Upanishad mit erklärenden Anmerkungen. In *Berichte über die Verhandlungen der Königlich Sächsischen Gesellschaften zu Leipzig, philologisch-historische Classe*, vol. 24, pages 127–197, Leipzig, 1891.

Contains the Devanāgarī text of the Kaṭha, Aitareya, and Praśna Upanishads, together with German translation and critical notes.

'In the main I have paid very little attention to Çaṁkara's Commentary, since the man knows the older language very imperfectly, has no presentiment of philological criticism, and explains the text from his own philosophical standpoint. If any one wishes to place a deeper meaning in the often obscure expressions, let him do so at his own risk without any prepossession. I have refrained from any sort of interpretation, and have striven only to give a philologically justifiable translation.' (Translated from the preliminary explanations on page 128.)

Uddhavaji, Ranachhodaji. Four Upanishads, viz. Īśā, Kena, Muṇḍ., and Ait., with Gujarati translations and commentaries. Bombay, Sarasvati Printing Press, 1896. 103 pages.

Sastri, S. Sitarama, and **Ganganath Jha.** The Upanishads and Sri Sankara's Commentary. 5 vols. Madras, published by V. C. Sesacharri at the Press of Natesan, 1898–1901.

The contents and authorship are as follows:

Vol. 1, Īśā, Kena, and Muṇḍaka: Sastri, 1898. 174 pages.
Vol. 2, Kaṭha and Praśna: Sastri, 1898. 193 pages.
Vol. 3, Chāndogya 1–4: Jha, 1899. 311 pages.
Vol. 4, Chāndogya 5–8: Jha, 1899. 374 pages.
Vol. 5, Aitareya and Taittirīya: Sastri, 1901. 230 pages.

Tattvabhushana, Sitanatha. The Upanishads, edited with annotations and English translation. 2 vols. Calcutta, Som Brothers, 1900, 1904.

The contents are as follows:

Vol. 1, Īśā, Kena, Kaṭha, Praśna, Muṇḍ., and Māṇḍ.; 1900. 163 pages.
Vol. 2, Śvet., Ait., Tait., and Kaush.; 1904. 225 pages.

The Kaushītaki Upanishad in vol. 2 is presented in the same recension as in the Ānandāśrama edition of that Upanishad, which is designated as **A** in the footnotes of the present Translation, in distinction from the recension presented in the Bibliotheca Indica edition, which is designated as **B**.

Vasu, Sris Chandra and **A. C. Thirlwall.** Isa and Kena Upanishads with the Sanskrit text, anvaya, vritti, word-meaning, translation, notes and index. Allahabad, Indian Press, 1902. 172 pages. (Vedanta Series.)

Vasu, Sris Chandra. Isa, Kena, Kaṭha, Praśna, Muṇḍaka and Mâṇḍuka Upaniṣads. Allahabad, Panini Office, 1909 (also reprinted subsequently). 321 pages. (Sacred Books of the Hindus, vol. 1.)

Text, translation, notes, and extracts from Madhava's Commentary.

Bhagavat, Hari Raghunath. The Upanishads, vol. I [Isha, Kena, Katha, Prashna, Mundaka, Taittiriya and Aitareya]: text, translation and notes. 2d ed. Poona, Ashtekar & Co., 1924. 143 pages. (Collective Series.)

Belvalkar, S. K. 1. Four unpublished Upaniṣadic texts (Bāṣkala, Chāgaleya, Ārṣeya, and Śaunaka), tentatively edited and translated for the first time. 2. The Paryaṅka-vidyā (Kauṣītakibrāhmaṇopaniṣad, Chap. 1): an attempt to settle and interpret the text. Madras, 1925. 35 pages. (Reprinted from the *Report of the Third Oriental Conference, Madras.*)

Tattvabhushan, Sitanath. The ten Upanishads, Íśá, Kena, Katha, Praśna, Mundaka, Mándúkya, Svetásvatara, Aitareya, Taittiríya and Kaushítaki, edited with Sanskrit annotations and English translation. 2d edition, revised. Calcutta, 1925. 420 pages.

A revised reprint, in one volume, of the same editor's earlier edition.

5. TRANSLATIONS, WITH TEXT, OF SINGLE UPANISHADS

Bṛihad-Āraṇyaka Upanishad

Burnouf, Eugène. Commentaire sur le Yaçna. Paris, 1833.

At pp. clxx–clxxiii there are extracts from the Bṛih. in Devanāgari characters, together with French or Latin translations.

Böhtlingk, Otto. Bṛhadâraṇjakopanishad in der Mâdhjaṁdina-Recension, herausgegeben und übersetzt. St. Petersburg, Kaiserliche Akademie der Wissenschaften, 1889. 172 pages.

The German translation was also published without the Sanskrit text.

Pitambara, Sarma. Bṛihad-Äraṇyaka Upanishad, with a Hindi translation, a Hindi commentary founded on the works of Sankara and Anandagiri, and notes. 2 vols. Bombay, Nirnaya-Sagara Press, 1892.

Vasu, Sris Chandra. Bṛihadaraṇyaka-Upaniṣad: text and English translation, together with translations of parts of Madhava's Commentary. Allahabad, Panini Office, 1913–1916. 728 pages. (Sacred Books of the Hindus, vol. 14.)

Chāndogya Upanishad

Pala, Mahesachandra. Chāndogya Upanishad, with the Commentary of Sankara Acharya and a Bengali translation. Calcutta, 1885–1887. 674 pages.

Böhtlingk, Otto. Khandogjopanishad, kritisch herausgegeben und übersetzt. Leipzig, Haessel, 1889. 201 pages.

Along with the same author's edition of the Bṛih., which appeared in the same year, this edition of the Chāndogya is the first text-edition of any Upanishad in which the attempt has been made to differentiate the verse-portions from the prose-portions, namely by giving to the verse a wider margin in the text than to the prose, and by using, in the metrical part of the text, the modern method of arranging the verses in their metrical form.

The text is in notably distinct Devanāgarī characters.

In contrast with the customary method of printing Sanskrit prose texts without a single punctuation mark, this edition indicates clause-divisions and sentence-divisions by a simple upright bar—a method which renders the sense much more easily intelligible to a reader who is accustomed to helpful modern punctuation.

In spite of certain criticisms which may be directed against this work of thirty years ago, the total estimate of Böhtlingk's editions both of the Bṛih. and of the Chānd. must be very high.

The character of Böhtlingk's translation is explicitly defined by the translator himself in his Vorwort (p. ix): 'It is a purely philological work, in which no reference has been made—nor need be made—to the Vedāntic interpretation of Çaṁkarâkârja, since that impresses upon the Upanishad an entirely false stamp.'

Pantulu, M. B. Chāndogya Upanishad, with a Telugu translation and commentary. Madras, Sree Rajah Ram Mohan Roy Press, 1899. 674 pages.

Sarma, Sivasankara. Chāndogya Upanishad, with Hindi translation and commentary, also a Sanskrit Commentary setting forth the doctrines of the Arya Samaj. Ajmere, 1905. 1003 pages.

Vasu, Srisa Chandra. Chhandogya Upanisad, with [extracts from] the Commentary of Śrî Madhvâchârya called also Anandatîrtha, translated. Allahabad, Panini Office, 1909–1910 (reprinted 1917). 623 pages. (Sacred Books of the Hindus, vol. 3.)

TAITTIRĪYA UPANISHAD

Pantulu, M. B. Taittirīya Upanishad, with Telugu translation and commentary. Madras, Sree Rajah Ram Mohan Roy Press, 1889. 150 pages.

Sandrananda Acharya. Taittirīya Upanishad, with Bengali translation and notes. Calcutta, Sandrananda Press, 1896. 66 pages.

Venkatakrishnaiya, R. S. Taittirīya Upanishad, in the Kannada character, with Kannada translation and notes. Bangalore, 1901. 82 pages.

Sastri, A. Mahadeva. The Taittirîya Upanishad, with the Commentaries of *S*ankarâchârya, Sure*s*varâchârya and Sâya*n*a (Vidyâra*n*ya), translated into English. Mysore, G. T. A. Printing Works, 1903. 815 pages [Also contains the text.]

With its analytical headings for chapters and sections, and with the different fonts of type used to distinguish the material of the Upanishad itself and that of each of the commentaries, this translation has the best elaborated form of all that have appeared in India. And the rendering of the Sanskrit original is unusually close.

Vidyarnava, Srisa Chandra, and **Mohan Lal Sandal.** The Taitiriya Upanisat: text and translation with notes and commentaries. Allahabad, Panini Office, 1925. 68 pages. (Sacred Books of the Hindus, vol. 30, part 3.)

AITAREYA UPANISHAD

Bhagavata, Rajaram Ramkrishna. The Aitareya Upanishad: An attempt to interpret in Marathi the Eleven Upanishads, with preface, translation, and notes in English; 1st of the Series. Bombay, Nirnaya-Sagara Press, 1898. 40 pages.

Vidyarnava, Srisa Chandra, and **Mohan Lal Sandal.** Aitareya Upanisat. Allahabad, Panini Office, 1925. 186 pages. (Sacred Books of the Hindus, vol. 30, parts 1 and 2.)

Bhakkamkar, H. M. Translation of the Aitareya Upanishad, with Sankaracharya's Bhashya. Bombay, Univ. of Bombay, 1899. 95 pages.

KAUSHĪTAKI UPANISHAD

Cowell, E. B. Kaushitaki-Brahmana-Upanishad, with the Commentary of Sankarananda, edited with an English translation. Calcutta, Bibliotheca Indica, 1861. 191 pages.

The recension which is printed in this edition of the Kaushītaki is designated as B in the footnotes of the present Translation, thus being distinguished from the recension printed in the Ānandāśrama edition of the Kaushītaki, which is designated as **A**.

Vidyarnava, Srisa Chandra, and **Mohan Lal Sandal.** The Kaushitaki Upanishat with notes and commentary. Allahabad, Panini Office, 1925. 81 pages. (Sacred Books of the Hindus, vol. 30, part 1.)

KENA UPANISHAD

Oertel, Hanns. The Jaiminīya, or Talavakāra-Upaniṣad-Brāhmaṇa. In *JAOS.* 16 (1894), pp. 79–260.

In the Brāhmaṇa which is here presented with transliterated text, translation, and notes, the Kena Upanishad is imbedded at pp. 215–219.

Prasad, Durga. An English translation of the Kena Upanishat, with exposition. Lahore, Virajanand Press, 1898. 34 pages.

'The perusal of these Upanishads makes one religious. Nowhere God is so truly described as in those wonderful metaphysical books of India.' (Exposition, page 7.)

Sarma, Badaridatta. Kena or Talavakāra Upanishad, with a Hindi translation and exposition. Meerut, 1901. 32 pages.

Vasu, Sris Chandra, and **A. C. Thirlwall.** Kenopanishad with the Sanskrit text, anvaya, vritti, word-meaning, translation, notes and index. Allahabad, Indian Press, 1902. 107 pages. (Vedanta Series.)

Singh, Chhajju. Kainopanishat, translated into English, after consulting every gloss available. Lahore, Anglo-Sanskrit Press, 1891. 44 pages.

An elementary 'word-and-word translation,' intended apparently as a reading-text for beginners in the Sanskrit language and also as a religious tract.

Kaṭha Upanishad

Poley, L. Kathaka-Oupanichat, extrait du Yadjour-Véda, traduit du sanskrit en français. Paris, Dondey-Dupré, 1835. 22 pages.

Text and French translation.

Regnaud, Paul. Études védiques et post-védiques. Paris, Leroux, 1898. 217 pages.

The text of the Kaṭha Upanishad in Roman transliteration, stanza by stanza, with translation and commentary, occupies pages 57–167. The verse-portions of the original are lined in quatrain metrical form.

A thorough, scholarly piece of work.

Sarma, Badaridatta. Kaṭha Upanishad, with Hindi translation and exposition. Meerut, 1903. 96 pages.

Vasu, Sris Chandra. Kathopanishad, with the Sanskrit text, anvaya, vritti, word-meaning, translation, notes and index. Allahabad, Panini Office, 1905. 236 pages.

Pelly, R. L. Kaṭha Upaniṣad: introduction, text, translation and notes. Calcutta, Association Press, 1924. 73 pages.

Īśā Upanishad

Datta, Guru. Ishnopanishad, with Sanskrit text and English translation, to which an exposition is appended. Lahore, Virajanand Press, 1888. 34 pages.

The translation is extremely free, as may be seen from the following parallel:—

Guru Datta's translation	*The present translation*
2. Aspire, then, O man, to live by virtuous deeds for a hundred years in peace with thy neighbours.	Even while doing deeds here, One may desire to live a hundred years.
12. Miserable are they who worship atoms as the efficient cause of the world. But far more miserable are they who worship the visible things born of atoms.	Into blind darkness enter they Who worship non-becoming. Into darkness greater than that, as it were, they Who delight in becoming.
15. O Thou who givest sustenance to the world, unveil that face of the true sun which is now hidden by a veil of golden light; so that we may see the truth and know our whole duty.	With a golden vessel The Real's face is covered o'er. That do thou, O Pūshan, uncover For one whose law is the Real to see.

The foregoing reprinted in:

—— Works of the late Pandit Guru Datta, Vidyarthi. Lahore, Aryan Printing & G. Trading Co., 2d edition, 1902, at pages 107–124.

Muhammad, Satyananda. Īśā Upanishad, with a Hindi translation in verse. Lucknow, 1890. 12 pages.

Singh, Chhajju. Ishopanishat, translated into English, to which is appended The Vedic truth vindicated. Lahore, Anglo-Sanskrit Press, 1891. 40 pages.

An elementary 'word-and-word' Sanskrit-English translation.

Mozoomdar, Yadunatha. Isa Upanishad, or the last chapter of the Sukla Yajur Veda, with text, easy Sanskrit notes, English and Bengali translations. Jessore, Subhakari Press, 1893. 18 pages.

Gosvami, Sri Syamalala. Isa Upanishad, with the Bhashyas of Baladeva, Vidyabhushana, Sri Sankaracharyya, and the Tika of Anandagiri, etc., with Bengali translation and commentary, and with an English translation and commentary. Calcutta, Aghornath Datta, People's Press, 1895. 70 pages.

Prasad, Durga. The Third Vedic Reader, in the Dayanand High School Series. Lahore, Virajanand Press 2d ed., 1896. 34 pages.

Contains at pp. 8–31 the Īśā Upanishad (as the Fortieth Chapter of the Yajur-Veda) both in Devanāgarī and in Roman characters, with a 'word-and-word' Sanskrit-English translation.

Kriparama. Īśā Upanishad, with an Urdu translation and commentary based on the teachings of the Arya Samaj. Moradabad, 1899. 32 pages.

Sarma, Badaridatta. Īśā Upanishad, with Hindi translation and exposition. Meerut, 1901. 18 pages.

Vasu, Sris Chandra, and **A. C. Thirlwall.** Isavasya Upanishad, with the Sanskrit text, anvaya, vritti, word-meaning, translation, notes and index. Allahabad, Indian Press, 1902. 66 pages. (Vedanta Series.)

'This Upanishad has been the subject of several commentaries. We give the interpretation according to the three well-known schools,—Advaita (Sankara), Visista Advaita (Ramanuja), and Dvaita (Madhava).' (Introduction, page ii.)

Majumdar, Jnanendralal. Îsha Upanishat, with a new commentary by the Kaulâchâryya Sadânanda. Translated with introduction . . ., together with a foreword by Arthur Avalon. London, Luzac, 1918. 70 pages.

MUṆḌAKA UPANISHAD

Prasad, Durga, corrected by Pandit **Guru Datta,** Vidyarthi. The Mundakopanishat with English translation. Lahore, Virajanand Press, 2d ed., 1893. 13 pages.

The foregoing reprinted in:

—— The works of the late Pandit Guru Datta, Vidyarthi. Lahore, Aryan Printing Co., 2d edition, 1902, at pages 151–167.

Sen, Mohit Chandra. The Mundak-Opanishad. Calcutta, The Brotherhood, 82 Harrison Road, no date (but before 1928). 14 pages.

A rendering into blank verse. On the whole fairly accurate. Yet it omits certain parts; also adds some exegetical matter within parentheses, and also some extra exegetical matter not so indicated.

PRAŚNA UPANISHAD

Prasad, Durga. An English translation of the Prashnopanishat, containing six questions of life and death, with Sanskrit text. Lahore, Virajanand Press, 1899. 35 pages.

MĀṆḌŪKYA UPANISHAD

Datta, Guru. The Mandukyopanishat, being the Exposition of OM, the Great Sacred Name of the Supreme Being in the Vedas, translated and expounded. Chicago edition, printed and published under the auspices of the Arya Pratinidhi Sabha, Punjab. Lahore, Virajanand Press, 1893. 34 pages.

The foregoing reprinted in:

—— Works of the late Pandit Guru Datta, Vidyarthi. Lahore, Aryan Printing Co., 2d edition, 1902, on pages 125–149.

Narayana, Har. Vedic Philosophy; or, An Exposition of the sacred and mysterious Monosyllable AUM; The Mandukya Upanishad: text, with an English translation and commentary and an introduction. Bombay, Tatva-Vivechaka Press, 1895. 171 pages

'I venture to advise my readers to try to fit themselves for the study of Brahma-Vidya. I trustfully venture to say that they will thus finally attain liberation from reincarnation by the realization of Self, which is the only reality, the substratum of all appearances.' (Conclusion of the Introduction, pages xlii–xliii.)

Śvetāśvatara Upanishad

Bhagavata, Rajarama Ramkrishna. An attempt to interpret in Marathi the eleven Upanishads, with preface, translation and notes in English: The Shvetashvatara Upanishad, 2d of the series. Bombay, Nirnaya-Sagara Press, 1900. 119 pages.

A companion volume to the author's translation of the Aitareya Upanishad.

A detailed examination of the sectarian statements in the Upanishad is presented to the reader in support of the theory that 'the original and sweet Upanishad was encrusted with layers successively added by the Rudra-worshippers, the Kapilas, the Yogins and the followers of some of the schools now completely forgotten.' This explanation will 'prepare him for its unconnected and at times contradictory, though varied and therefore interesting, contents.' (Preface, page 8.)

In the Preface the author also contends that the Śaṅkarācārya to whom the received commentary on the Upanishad is ordinarily ascribed is not the same as the great Commentator of that name. This same theory, by the way, had been previously urged by Regnaud in 1876 in his *Matériaux*, vol. 1, p. 28, and also by Col. G. A. Jacob in his article on the Nṛisiṁhatāpanī Upanishad in the *Indian Antiquary* for March, 1886.

Siddhesvar Varma, Shastri. The Śvetāśvatara Upanishad, translated. Allahabad, Panini Office, 1916. 135 pages. (Sacred Books of the Hindus, vol. 18, part 1.)

Contains the text, English translation, and notes.

Hauschild, Richard. Die Śvetāśvatara-Upaniṣad. Eine kritische Ausgabe mit einer Übersetzung und einer Übersicht über ihre Lehren. Leipzig, Brockhaus, 1927. 110 pages. (Abhandlungen für die Kunde des Morgenlandes, 17. 3.)

An elaborate critical treatise, with the text in transliteration and a translation into German.

Maitri Upanishad

Cowell, E. B. The Maitri or Maitrāyaṇīya Upanishad, with the Commentary of Rāmatīrtha, edited with an English translation. London, Watts, 1870. 291 pages. (Bibliotheca Indica.)

Vidyarnava, Srisa Chandra, and **Mohan Lal Sandal.** The Maitri Upanishat, with notes and commentary. Allahabad, Panini Office, 1926. 155 pages. (Sacred Books of the Hindus, vol. 30, part 2.)

6. TEXT-EDITIONS OF COLLECTED UPANISHADS

Roy, Rammohun. Four Upanishads in the Bengali character, viz. Kaṭha, Īśā, Kena, and Muṇḍ. Calcutta, 1818. 191 pages.

The very first printed appearance of any collected text of the Upanishads.

Poley, L. Four Upanishads, viz. Kaṭha, Muṇḍ., Kena, and Īśā, with the Commentary of Śaṅkara on the first three. Paris, Dondey-Dupré, 1835. 200 pages.

Poley, L. Vrihadáranyakam, Káthakam, Iça, Kena, Mundakam; oder fünf Upanishads aus dem Yagur-, Sáma- und Atharva-Veda, nach den Handschriften der Bibliothek der Ost-Indischen Compagnie zu London. Bonn, Marcus, 1844. 124 pages.

Noteworthy as containing the first printed appearance of the Bṛihad-Āraṇyaka Upanishad. The text of the other four in this collection had already appeared, together with a French translation by the same author, in 1835.

Seven Upanishads in the Bengali character, viz. Kaṭha, Vājasaneya-saṁhitā, Talavakāra, Muṇḍ., Māṇḍ., Praśna, and Ait., with a verbal commentary for instruction in Brahmist schools. Calcutta, 1845. 127 pages.

Röer, E. Three Upanishads, viz. the Taittariya and the Aittareya Upanishads, edited with the Commentary of Sankara Acharya and the Gloss of Ananda Giri; and the Śwetaśwatara Upanishad, edited with the Commentary of Sankara Acharya. Calcutta, 1850. 378 pages. (Bibliotheca Indica.)

Röer, E. Six Upanishads, viz. Īśā, Kena, Kaṭha, Praśna, Muṇḍ., and Māṇḍ., edited with the Commentary of Sankara Acharya and the Gloss of Ananda Giri. Calcutta, 1850. 598 pages. (Bibliotheca Indica.)

Vidyasagara, Jibananda. Six Upanishads, viz. Īśā, Kena, Kaṭha, Praśna, Muṇḍ., and Māṇḍ., with the Commentary of Sankaracharya and the Gloss of Ananda Giri. Calcutta, 1873. 598 pages.

Vidyasagara, Jibananda. Three Upanishads, viz. Tait. and Ait., with the Commentary of Sankara Acharya and the Gloss of Ananda Giri ; and Śvet. with the Commentary of Sankara Acharya. Calcutta, 1874. 361 pages.

Ten Upanishads in the Telugu character, viz. Īśā, Kena, Kaṭha, Praśna, Muṇḍ., Māṇḍ., Tait., Bṛih., Chānd., and Ait., with a verbal commentary by Ramanujacharya. Madras, Viveka Kalanidhi Press, 1875. 540 pages. (Reprinted 1876 ; 298 pages.)

Sastri, Subrahmanya. Hundred and eight Upanishads. Madras, 1883. 1029 pages.

Ten Upanishads. Bombay, Venkatesvara Press, 1885. 357 pages.

Ramachandra, Venkatarau. Upanishatsangraha: A Collection of Upanishads, edited with Sanskrit glosses and Marathi paraphrases, notes, and introductions. Poona, 1885.

Harirātmaja, Keśavāla. Eleven Upanishads, viz. Īśā, Kena, Kaṭha, Praśna, Muṇḍ., Māṇḍ., Tait., Ait., Chānd., Bṛih., and Śvet., edited. Bombay, Nirnaya-Sagara Press, 1886. 242 pages.

This is perhaps the most convenient and reliable text-edition of the eleven Upanishads therein contained.

Pitambara, Sri. Eight Upanishads, viz. Īśā, Kena, Kaṭha, Tait., Ait., Muṇḍ., Praśna, and Māṇḍ., with a Commentary in Sanskrit. Bombay, 1890. 800 pages.

Twelve Upanishads, viz. Īśā, Kena, Kaṭha, Praśna, Muṇḍ., Māṇḍ., Tait., Ait., Chānd., Bṛih., Śvet., and Nṛisiṁhatāpanīya. Bombay, Venkatesvara Press, 1890. 372 pages.

Hundred and Eight Upanishads. Bombay, Tatva-Vivechaka Press, 1895. 868 pages.

Thirty-two Upanishads, with the Dipika of Narayana Sankarananda. Poona, Anandasrama Press, 1895.

Of the thirteen Upanishads contained in the present English translation this edition contains the text of only two, viz. Kaush. at pages 113–144, and Maitri at pages 345–476.

Sastri, K. Venkatakrishna, and **Munjurpattu Ramachandra Sastri.** Hundred and eight Upanishads in Grantha character. Madras, Star of India Press, 1896. 893 pages.

Tatacharya, A. Srinivasa. Ten Upanishads in Grantha and Telugu characters, viz. Iśā, Kena, Kaṭha, Praśna, Muṇḍ., Māṇḍ., Ait., Bṛih., Chānd., and Tait., with a Tamil commentary comprising word-for-word interpretations of the text, and translations of the Commentaries of Sankara and Ramanuja, together with the Karikas of Gaudapada in Sanskrit and Sankara's Commentary in Tamil. Madras, 1897–1898.

Phansikar, Vasudev Laxman Shastri. Twenty-eight Upanishads, Īśā, etc. Bombay, Nirnaya-Sagara Press, 1904, 334 pages; 1906 edition, 372 pages.

Contains all of the Upanishads which are contained in the present Translation, except Maitri.

Ten Upanishads. Benares, Tara Printing Works, 1906.

Bhagawan, Swami Achintya. Eleven Upanishads. Bombay, Nirnaya-Sagara Press, 1910. 732 pages.

Sastri, A. Mahadeva. The Yoga Upanishads, with the commentary of Sri Upanishad-Brahma-Yogin, edited. Adyar, Adyar Library, 1920. 630 pages.

Sastri, A. Mahadeva. The Śaiva-Upanishads, with the commentary of Sri Upanishad-Brahma-Yogin, edited. Adyar, Adyar Library, 1925. 266 pages. [Bound with The Śakta Upanishads.]

Sastri, A. Mahadeva. The Śakta Upanishads, with the commentary of Sri Upanishad-Brahma-Yogin, edited. Adyar, Adyar Library, 1925. 148 pages. [Bound with The Śaiva-Upanishads.]

7. TEXT-EDITIONS OF SINGLE UPANISHADS

Bṛihad-Araṇyaka Upanishad

Röer, E. Brihad Aranyaka Upanishad, with the Commentary of Sankara Acharya and the Gloss of Ananda Giri, edited. 2 parts. Calcutta, 1849. 1096 pages. (Bibliotheca Indica.)

Weber, Albrecht. The Çatapatha Brāhmaṇa. Berlin, 1855.

Contains in the Mādhyaṁdina recension as 10. 6. 4–5 and 14. 4–9 what in the Kāṇva recension is the separate Bṛihad-Āraṇyaka Upanishad.

Vidyasagara, Jibananda. Bṛihad-Āraṇyaka Upanishad, with the Commentary of Sankaracharya and the Gloss of Anandagiri. Calcutta, 1875. 1094 pages.

Bṛihad-Āraṇyaka Upanishad, with the Commentary of Sankaracharya and the Supercommentary of Anandagiri. Benares, 1885. 328 pages.

Agase, Kashinatha Shastri. Bṛihad-Āraṇyaka Upanishad, edited with the Commentary of Sankara and the Tika of Anandagiri. Poona, Anandasrama Press, 1891. 835 pages.

Agase, Kashinatha Bala Shastri. Bṛihad-Āraṇyaka Upanishad, edited with the commentary entitled Mitākshara of Nityānanda. Poona, Anandasrama Press, 1895. 271 pages.

Chāndogya Upanishad

Röer, E. Chhāndogya Upanishad, edited with the Commentary of Sankara Āchārya and the Gloss of Ānanda Giri. Calcutta, 1850. 628 pages. (Bibliotheca Indica.)

Vidyasagara, Jibananda. Chāndogya Upanishad, with the Commentary of Sankara Acharya and the Gloss of Anandagiri. Calcutta, 1873. 634 pages.

Chāndogya Upanishad, with the Commentary of Sankara Acharya and the Gloss of Anandagiri. Benares, 1884.

Agase, Kashinatha Sastri. Chāndogya Upanishad, with the Commentary of Sankara Acharya and the Gloss of Anandagiri. Poona, Anandasrama Press, 1890. 482 pages.

Chāndogya Upanishad, with the Commentary of Madhavacharya and the Gloss of Vedesha Tirtha. Kumbakonam, 1904. 524 pages.

Taittirīya Upanishad

Taittirīya Upanishad, with the Commentary of Sankara Acharya and a supercommentary corresponding in its text to that of Anandagiri, but here attributed to Jnanamrita Yati. Benares, 1884. 42 pages.

Taittirīya Upanishad, with the Commentary of Sureśvaráchárya and the Supercommentary of Ánandajñáṇa. Poona, Anandasrama Press, 1889. 219 pages.

Isalamapurakara, Vamanaśāstri. Taittirīya Upanishad with the Commentary of Sankara and the Supercommentary of Sankarananda and Vidyaranya. Poona, Anandasrama Press, 1889. 330 pages.

Sharma, Bhimasena. Taittirīya Upanishad, with a Hindi and a Sanskrit Commentary. Allahabad, Sarasvati Press, 1892. 190 pages. (Reprinted 1895.)

Isalamapurakara, Vamanaśāstri. Taittirīya Upanishad, with the Commentary of Sankara Acharya and the Supercommentary of Anandagiri, also with the Dipikas of Sankarananda and of Vidyaranya. Poona, Anandasrama Press, 1897. 163 pages.

Ramakrishna Sastri. Taittirīya Upanishad, in the Grantha character, together with selections from the Taittirīya-Brāhmaṇa and the Taittirīya-Āraṇyaka. Palghat, 1900. 78 pages.

Singh, Zalim. Taittirīya Upanishad, with Hindi glossaries. Lucknow, 1900. 127 pages.

Vaidyanatha, Mullangudi. Taittirīya Upanishad, in the Grantha character and in the Dravidian recension. Kumbakonam, 1903. 44 pages.

Sutaiya, Gorti. Taittirīya Upanishad, in the Telugu character, with the Commentary of Sayana. Madras, 1904. 319 pages.

Aitareya Upanishad

The longer recension of the text, known as the Mahaitareya, or Bahuvricha, Upanishad, i. e. Aitareya Aranyaka 2 and 3, with the Commentary of Sankara Acharya. Benares, 1884. 70 pages.

The shorter recension of the text, i. e. Aitareya Aranyaka 2. 4–7, with the Commentary of Sankara Acharya, the Supercommentary of Anandajñāna, and a Dipika of Vidyaranya. Poona, Anandasrama Press, 1889. 113 pages.

Sarma, Bhimasena. Aitareya Upanishad, with commentaries in Sanskrit and Hindi. Etawah, Saraswati Press, 1900. 104 pages.

Singh, Zalim. Aitareya Upanishad, with Hindi glossaries. Lucknow, 1900. 50 pages.

Rajarama. Aitareya Upanishad, edited . . . with Hindi interpretation and notes. Lahore, Bombay Press, 4th ed., 1924. 31 pages.

Kena Upanishad

Roy, Rammohun. Talavakāra, i. e. Kena Upanishad, with a short commentary in Bengali. Calcutta, 1816 17 pages.

Agase, Bala Sastri. Kena Upanishad, with the Commentary of Sankara and the Supercommentary of Anandagiri, together with the Dipikas of Sankarananda and Narayana. Poona, Anandasrama Press, 1888. 89 pages.

Sarma, Bhimasena. Kena Upanishad, with commentaries in Sanskrit and Hindi. Allahabad, Sarasvati Press, 1893. 56 pages.

Agase, Kashinatha Bala Sastri. Kena Upanishad, with the Commentary of Sankara and the Dipikas of Sankarananda and Narayana. Poona, Anandasrama Press, 1896. 79 pages.

Kena Upanishad, in the Telugu character, with the Commentary of Balasubrahmanya Brahmasvami in Telugu. Madras, Kalaratnakara Press, 1900. 126 pages.

Kena Upanishad, in the Grantha and also in the Tamil characters, with the Commentary of Balasubrahmanya Brahmasvami in Tamil. Madras, Kalaratnakara Press, 1900. 207 pages.

Kaṭha Upanishad

Sarma, Bhimasena. Kaṭha Upanishad, with Sanskrit and Hindi commentaries. Allahabad, Sarasvati Press, 1893. 220 pages.

Rajvade, Vaijanath Kashinath. Kaṭha Upanishad, with the Commentary of Sankara Acharya and two Supercommentaries by Anandagiri and Gopālayatindra. Poona, Anandasrama Press, 1897. 127 pages. (Reprinted 1906, 132 pages.)

Īśā Upanishad

Roy, Rammohun. Īśā Upanishad, with a commentary in Bengali. Calcutta, 1816. 37 pages.

Tarkaratna, Taracharana. Īśā Upanishad, with a commentary called Vimala. Benares, 1880. 30 pages.

Īśā Upanishad, with a Sanskrit commentary. Punganur, 1887. 8 pages.

Īśā Upanishad, with the Commentary of Sankara Acharya and seven other commentaries. Poona, Anandasrama Press, 1888. 87 pages.

Sharma, Bhimasena. Īśā Upanishad, with Sanskrit and Hindi commentaries. Allahabad, Sarasvati Press, 1892. 50 pages.

Brahmaswamy, Bala Subramania. Īśā Upanishad in Telugu and Tamil characters, with Tamil commentaries. Madras, 1899. 107 pages.

Ganda, Brahmanishta. Īśā Upanishad, with the Commentary of Sankara Acharya and Gujarati explanations. Broach, 1906. 82 pages.

Yogiraja, Swami Maharaja. Agni Chakra Pravartana Sutram. Part I. (The Isopanishad with the 'Fiery Commentary' presenting the elements of the Universal Religion.) Compilers: Swami Prem Puri and Yogiraja's disciple Maitreya. London. Thacker, [1926]. 146 pages.

Muṇḍaka Upanishad

Yamuna Sankara. Muṇḍaka Upanishad, with a commentary in Hindi founded on the Commentaries of Sankara and Anandagiri. Lucknow, 1884. 138 pages.

Sarma, Bhimasena. Muṇḍaka Upanishad, with commentaries in Sanskrit and Hindi. Allahabad, Sarasvati Press, 1894. 154 pages.

Muṇḍaka Upanishad, with the Commentary of Sankara Acharya and the Supercommentary of Anandagiri and also a Dipika by Narayana. Poona, Anandasrama Press, 1896. 61 pages.

Singh, Zalim. Muṇḍaka Upanishad, with Hindi glossaries. Lucknow, 1900. 84 pages.

Hertel, Johannes. Muṇḍaka-Upaniṣad: kritische Ausgabe mit Rodarneudruck der Erstausgabe (Text und Kommentare) und Einleitung. Leipzig, Haessel, 1924 136 pages. (Indo-Iranische Quellen und Forschungen, part 3.)

Praśna Upanishad

Yamuna Sankara. Praśna Upanishad, with a commentary in Hindi founded on the Commentaries of Sankara and Anandagiri. Lucknow, 1884. 177 pages.

Praśna Upanishad, with the Commentary of Sankara Acharya and the Supercommentary of Narayanendra Sarasvati. Benares, 1885. 40 pages.

Śarma, Bhimasena. Praśna Upanishad, with commentaries in Sanskrit and Hindi. Allahabad, Sarasvati Press, 1890. 120 pages. (Reprinted 1894, 148 pages.)

Praśna Ūpanishad, with the Commentary of Sankara Acharya, the Supercommentary of Anandagiri, and also a Dipika of Sankarananda. Poona, Anandasrama Press, 1896. 90 pages.

Singh, Zalim. Praśna Upanishad, with Hindi glossaries. Lucknow, 1900. 90 pages.

Māṇḍūkya Upanishad

Sarma, Bhimasena. Māṇḍūkya Upanishad, with Sanskrit and Hindi commentaries. Allahabad, Sarasvati Press, 1894. 62 pages.

Kathavate, Abaji Vishnu's-son. Māṇḍūkya Upanishad, with the Karika of Gaudapada, the Commentary of Sankara Acharya, the Supercommentary of Anandagiri, and a Dipika of Sankarananda. Poona, Anandasrama Press, 1900. 233 pages.

Śvetāśvatara Upanishad

Śvetāśvatara Upanishad, with the Commentary of Sankara Acharya, a Dipika of Sankarananda, a Dipika of Narayana, and a Vivarana of Vijnana Bhagavat. Poona, Anandasrama Press, 1890. 210 pages. (Reprinted 1905, 225 pages.)

Sarma, Bhimasena. Śvetāśvatara Upanishad, with Sanskrit and Hindi commentaries. Etawah, Sarasvati Press, 1897. 211 pages.

Tulsirama, Swami. Śvetāśvatara Upanishad, with Sanskrit and Hindi commentaries. Meerut, 1897. 112 pages.

Rajarama. Śvetāśvatara Upanishad, edited . . . with Hindi interpretation and notes. Lahore, Bombay Press, 3d ed., 1924. 60 pages.

Maitri Upanishad

Cowell, E. B. The Maitri or Maitrāyaṇīya Upanishad, with the Commentary of Ramatīrtha, edited. 2d edition, revised by Satis Chandra Vidyābhūṣaṇa. Calcutta, Asiatic Society. 2 parts. 1913, 1919. 192 pages. (Bibliotheca Indica, New Sanskrit Series, nos. 1368, 1425.)

A second edition, revised by Vidyābhūṣaṇa, of the Devanāgarī text which had been published along with an English translation of the Upanishad by Cowell in 1870 (see above, page 484).

8. TREATISES, CHIEFLY LINGUISTIC

Whitney, W. D. The Upanishads and their latest translation. In *AJP.* vol. 7 (1886), pp. 1–26.

Chiefly a detailed review of Max Müller's translation.

Whitney, W. D. Böhtlingk's Upanishads. In *AJP.* vol. 11 (1890), pp. 407–439.

A detailed review of Böhtlingk's editions of the text and translation of the Chāndogya and the Bṛihad-Āraṇyaka Upanishads. 'In all respects so good as to tempt to a detailed examination, in order to the correction of occasional oversights and the suggestion of differences of view which may perhaps be found worthy of notice in case of a revisal of the works' (pages 407–408). Then the reviewer proceeds to point out 518 such instances.

Böhtlingk, Otto. A series of articles in the *Berichte über die Verhandlungen der Königlich Sächsischen Gesellschaften zu Leipzig, philologisch-historische Classe*, Leipzig, Hirzel, 1890–1897:—

(1) Über eine bisher arg missverstandene Stelle in der Kaushītaki-Brāhmaṇa-Upanishad. Vol. 42 (1891), pages 198–204.

An elaborate discussion of the variant readings and translations of Kaush. 1. 2, together with a reconstructed text and accordant translation. More learned and ingenious than necessary or convincing.

(2) Zu den von mir bearbeiteten Upanishaden. Vol. 43 (1891), pages 70–90.

A reply to Whitney's reviews of Böhtlingk's editions of Chānd., Bṛih., Ait., Praśna, and Kaṭha.

(3) Über die Verwechselung von *pra-sthā* und *prati-sthā* in den Upanishaden. Vol. 43 (1891), pages 91–95.

Proposes text-emendation and new interpretation of Śvet. 1. 1–3.

(4) Versuch Kaushītaki-Brāhmaṇa-Upanishad i. 1 zu deuten. Vol. 47 (1895), pages 347–349.

Proposes the omission of the second *dhâsyasi.* This change doubtless leaves the passage easier. But, inasmuch as the received text is perfectly intelligible, the proposed change is not necessary, except in the interest of a degree of literary perfection which perhaps was not the standard of the original author.

(5) Bemerkungen zu einigen Upanishaden. Vol. 49 (1897), pages 78–100.

A review of Deussen's translation, *Sechzig Upanishad's.* Contains numerous criticisms and dissenting opinions, e.g. on 96 passages in the Chāndogya alone.

(6) Kritische Beiträge. Vol. 49 (1897), pages 127-138.

Critical notes on several important Sanskrit works, but chiefly on the translation of passages in the Upanishads.

(7) Kritische Beiträge. Vol. 50 (1898), pages 76-86.

A continuation of the preceding series of critical notes.

Jacob, George A. A concordance to the [56] principal Upanishads and the Bhagavad-Gîtâ. Bombay, Government Central Book Depot, 1891. 1083 pages.

A great and painstaking labor. An exceedingly useful implement for detailed and exhaustive study of the texts of these Upanishads and also of the BhG.

Little, Charles Edgar. A grammatical index to the Chāndogya-Upanishad. New York, American Book Co., 1900. 193 pages. (Vanderbilt Oriental Series.)

Both a dictionary and a concordance. Every occurrence of every word is recorded, and the grammatical form in which every inflected word occurs is explicitly stated.

Wecker, Otto. Der Gebrauch der Kasus in der älteren Upaniṣad-Literatur verglichen mit der Kasuslehre der indischen Grammatiker. Tübingen, Vandenhoeck & Ruprecht, 1905. 92 pages.

An exhaustive investigation and tabulation of all the varying uses of the six oblique cases in the ten Upanishads, viz. Chānd., Bṛih., Maitri, Ait. Kaush., Kena, Īśā, Tait., Kaṭha, and Śvet. One important result of the investigation is the following conjectural chronological order and grouping of the Upanishads relative to the great grammarian Pāṇini, viz. Group I, the earliest, Bṛih., Chānd., and Kaush.; Group II, also pre-Pāṇini, Ait., Tait., and Kaṭha; Group III, possibly pre-Pāṇini, Kena and Īśā; Group IV, post-Pāṇini, Śvet. and Maitri.

The foregoing was printed also in two instalments in *Beiträge z. Kunde d. indogerman. Sprachen*, vol. 30 (1906), pp. 1-61, 177-207.

Windisch, Ernst. Zu Kauṣitaki-Brāhmaṇa-Upaniṣad 1. 2. In *Berichte über die Verhandlungen der Königlich Sächsischen Gesellschaften zu Leipzig, philologisch-historische Classe*, vol. 59, pp. 111-128, Leipzig, Teubner, 1907.

Consists of critical notes, comparing Oertel's text and translation with that of others.

Deussen, Paul. Über die Chronologie der Upanishad-Texte. In *Transactions of the International Congress for the History of Religions*, vol. 2, pp. 19-24, Oxford, Clarendon Press, 1908.

Kirfel, Willibald. Beiträge zur Geschichte der Nominalkomposition in den Upaniṣads und im Epos. Bonn, Georgi, 1908. 99 pages.

An exhaustive investigation, with statistically tabulated results, of all the phenomena of compound nouns of the five classes, *dvandva*, *upapada*, *tat-puruṣa*, *bahu-vrīhi*, and *avyayībhāva*, as these occur in five of the Upanishads, viz. Kaṭha, Praśna, Bṛih., Muṇḍ., and Śvet., and also in three episodes of the MBh. and in two chapters of the Rāmāyaṇa.

Hillebrandt, Alfred. Textkritische Bemerkungen zur Kāṭhaka- und Praśna-Upaniṣad. In *ZDMG*. vol. 68 (1914), pp. 579–582.

Fürst, Alfons. Der Sprachgebrauch der älteren Upaniṣads verglichen mit dem der früheren Vedischen Perioden und dem des klassischen Sanskrit. Göttingen, Vandenhoeck & Ruprecht, 1915. 82 pages. (Dissertation.)

Frauwallner, Erich. Untersuchungen zu den älteren Upaniṣaden. In *Zeitschrift für Indologie und Iranistik*, vol. 4 (1926), pp. 1–45.

9. TREATISES, CHIEFLY EXPOSITORY

Colebrooke, Henry Thomas. On the Vedas, or sacred writings of the Hindus. In *Asiatic Researches*, vol. 8, pages 369–476, Calcutta, 1805.

This exposition of the literature of the Vedas contains at pages 408–414 an original translation of the Aitareya Upanishad entire and also of other important sections of the Upanishads, viz. Chānd. 5. 11–24; Tait. 3. 1–6; and Muṇḍ. 1.

This article is notable for showing how over a century ago, before the great advance in modern Sanskrit scholarship, the importance of the Upanishads had been recognized, and also how the Upanishads were being actually mediated to the West.

This essay was reprinted in:

Essays on religion and philosophy of the Hindus. London, Williams & Norgate, 1837; new edition, 1858; pages 1–69.

Life and essays of H. T. Colebrooke, by his son, T. E. Colebrooke. London, Trübner, 1873, vol. 2, pages 8–132.

In the latter edition the 'Essay' is provided with numerous supplementary notes by W. D. Whitney.

Rixner, Thaddäus Anselm. Versuch einer Darstellung der uralten indischen All-Eins-Lehre, oder der berühmten Sammlung

Oupnek'hat; Erstes Stück, Oupnek'hat Tschebandouk genannt. Nürnberg, Stein, 1808.

The first appreciation on the continent of Europe, through the medium of a modern language, of the ancient religio-philosophical scriptures of India. An attempt to make more generally available the contents of Duperron's extensive (two-volume) Latin translation. Includes a German translation of the first part of the *Oupnek'hat.*

Windischmann, Friedrich Heinrich Hugo, in the work of his father, CARL JOSEPH HIERONYMUS WINDISCHMANN, Die Philosophie im Fortgange der Weltgeschichte. 3 vols. Bonn, Marcus, 1827–1833.

Book II (comprising volumes 2 and 3) deals with 'Philosophy in India.' Chap. 10 in vol. 3 deals with 'The mystical contents of the Upanishads.' Contains translations of selections from Chānd., Bṛih., Kena, Kaṭha, Īśā, Muṇḍ.

Lanjuinais, J. D. Recherches sur les langues, la littérature, la religion et la philosophie des Indiens. Paris, Dondey-Dupré, 1832.

Vol. 4 (at pages 246–357) contains an Essay entitled 'La Religion des Hindous selon les Védas, ou Analyse de l'Oupnek'hat publié par Anquetil du Perron en 1802.' This was the first rendition into French of the substance of Duperron's epoch-making Latin translation of the Upanishads.

Windischmann, Friedrich Heinrich Hugo. Sancara, sive de theologumenis Vedanticorum. Bonn, Habicht, 1833. 205 pages.

An exposition of the Vedanta philosophy in Latin. One of the very earliest treatises on the subject. Noteworthy as being the first attempt to use grammatical and historical considerations for determining the age of the Upanishads.

Chap. 2 (pages 34–88) is 'On the life of Sancara and the antiquity of the Vedanta.' Chap. 3 is 'A brief exposition of the Vedantic doctrines'. Contains numerous quotations, both in the Devanāgarī characters of the original and in Latin translation, from the Sūtras as well as from the Upanishads.

Weber, Albrecht. Akademische Vorlesungen über indische Literaturgeschichte. Berlin, Dümmler, 1852, 291 pages; 2d ed., 1876–1878, 371 pages.

The same translated into English:

—— The history of Indian literature, translated by Mann and Zachariae. London, Trübner, 4th edition, 1904. 383 pages.

Contains (at pages 153–171) a section dealing with the Upanishads.

Speir, Mrs. C[harlotte]. Life in Ancient India. **London,** Smith, Elder & Co., 1856. 481 pages.

Noteworthy as one of the earliest efforts to make a knowledge of Ancient India popularly available in England. Deals with various phases of the Upanishads in Chapters 2, 8, and 9. Cites from translations of the Aitareya by Colebrooke (1805), of the Kaṭha by Ram Mohun Roy (1819), and of the Bṛihad-Āraṇyaka by Röer (1856).

Müller, F. Max. History of ancient Sanskrit literature. London, Williams & Norgate, 1859. 607 pages.

Contains at pages 316–328 an exposition of the Upanishads, together with translations of extracts.

The foregoing reprinted:

—— Allahabad, Panini Office, 1912.

[Krempelhuber, Max Karl von.] Maha-bak, das grosse Wort der Geheim-Lehre der Brahmanen, oder die Unifikation des Welt-Ganzen: Grundgedanken über das Wesen der Weltsubstanz im Allgemeinen und des Menschengeschlechtes insbesondere: Reflexionen aus dem berühmten Oupnek'hat (Auszüge aus den Veden) für gebildete denkende Leser. Munich, G. Franz, 1869. 87 pages.

An exposition of the philosophy of the Upanishads as found in Duperron's Latin translation, particularly in relation to Western philosophy.

Manning, Mrs. [Charlotte Speir]. Ancient and Mediaeval India. 2 vols. London, Allen, 1869.

Chapter 7 of vol. 1 (pp. 122–147) presents a sketch of the period of the Upanishads with extracts from the translations of Roy, Mitra, Röer, and Müller.

Regnaud, Paul. Matériaux pour servir à l'histoire de la philosophie de l'Inde. 2 vols. Paris, Vieweg, 1876–1878.

While this book has already been listed above among Translations of Selections from the Upanishads, it aims primarily to be a systematic exposition of the philosophy of the Upanishads, arranged under various outstanding categories.

Barth, Auguste. The religions of India. Authorised translation [from the French] by J. Wood. London, Trübner, 1882. 3d edition, 1891.

'We shall now [i.e. in the chapter on "Brahmanism: II. Philosophic speculations," pages 64-86] give, in a summary form, an analysis of such of the doctrines of the Upanishads as are more especially connected with the history of religion; we shall indicate at the same time the essential developments they have undergone in the systems properly so called.' (Page 68.)

A brief sketch, but thoroughly scholarly and in correct proportions. The estimates expressed are sympathetically appreciative, yet keenly discriminating, withal judicial. The presentation of the main conceptions of the Upanishads is made with a historical perspective which exhibits clearly the course of previous development as well as the subsequent action and reaction.

'India will remain at heart attached to the manner of philosophizing found in the Upanishads. To that its sects will come back again one after another; its poets, its thinkers even, will always take pleasure in this mysticism, with its modes of procedure, at once so vague and so full of contradictions.' (Page 68.)

Gough, Archibald E. The philosophy of the Upanishads and ancient Indian metaphysics. London, Trübner, 1882; 2d edition, 1891; 3d edition, 1903. 268 pages.

Six articles originally appearing in the *Calcutta Review*, rewritten and extended. Contains translations of four complete Upanishads, viz. Muṇḍ., Kaṭha, Śvet., and Māṇḍ., the larger part of Tait., and portions of Chānd., Bṛih., and Kena, together with extracts from the works of the Indian schoolmen.

The renderings in many places are really paraphrases, rather than exact versions. Indeed, in spite of a liberal use of quotation marks, the work as a whole is a popular exposition of the popular Vedānta philosophy, rather than a scientifically rigorous translation of difficult texts.

The author states explicitly his judgment on the relation of the later 'schoolmen' to these early documents: 'The teaching of Sankara himself is the natural and legitimate interpretation of the doctrines of the Upanishads' (Preface, p. viii). And again: 'The Vedānta is only a systematic exposition of the philosophy of the Upanishads.' (Page 240.)

'The Upanishads exhibit the pantheistic view of things in a naively poetical expression, and at the same time in its coarsest form.' (Preface, pp. v–vi.) The author then proceeds to quote Hegel's estimate: 'If we wish to get so-called Pantheism in its poetic, most exalted, or—if one will—most crass form, one has to look for it in the oriental poets; and the most extensive expositions are found in the Indian poets.'

'The Upanishads are an index to the intellectual peculiarities of the Indian character. The thoughts that they express are the ideas that prevail through all subsequent Indian literature, much of which will be fully comprehensible to those only who carry with them a knowledge of these ideas to its perusal. A study of the Upanishads is the starting-point in any intelligent study of Indian philosophy. As regards religion, the philosophy of the Upanishads is the ground-work of the various forms of Hinduism, and the Upanishads have been justly characterized by Goldstücker as "the basis of the enlightened faith of India."' (Preface, page vi.)

'The Upanishads are the loftiest utterances of Indian intelligence. . . . Whatever value the reader may assign to the ideas they represent, they are the highest product of the ancient Indian mind, and almost the only elements of interest in Indian literature, which is at every stage replete with them to saturation.' (Page 268.)

Oldenberg, Hermann. Buddha: his life, his doctrine, his order, translated from the original German by William Hoey. London, Williams & Norgate, 1882. 454 pages.

Chap. 2 (pages 16–60) presents 'Hindu Pantheism and Pessimism before Buddha.' Reports 'the ideas, images, and expressions which passed to Buddhism as an inheritance from Brahmanical speculation.' (Page 54.)

Contains translations of portions of the Kaṭha Upanishad at pages 54–58 and the entire conversation of Yājñavalkya with his wife Maitreyī with running exposition at pages 33–40.

'If I am correct in my surmise as to the time of the production of this [Kaṭha] Upanishad, it contains an important contribution to the history of thought preparatory to Buddhist thought: namely, we here find the Satan of the Buddhist world, Māra, the Tempter, the demon death-foe of the deliverer, in the form of Mrityu, the God of Death.' (Pages 54–55.)

Deussen, Paul. Das System des Vedânta. Leipzig, Brockhaus, 1883, 550 pages; 2d ed., 1906, 558 pages.

The standard European treatise on the Vedānta. Contains copious references to, and translated extracts from, the principal Upanishads. All the Upanishad quotations are conveniently listed.

The foregoing translated:

—— The system of the Vedânta according to Bâdarâyaṇa's Brahma-Sûtras and Çaṅkara's Commentary thereon, set forth as a compendium of the dogmatics of Brahmanism from the standpoint of Çaṅkara; authorized translation by Charles Johnston. Chicago, Open Court, 1912. 529 pages.

'The great Upanishads are the deep, still mountain tarns, fed from the pure waters of the everlasting snows, lit by clear sunshine, or by night mirroring the high serenity of the stars.' (Page v.)

Bose, Ram Chandra. Hindu philosophy, popularly explained: the orthodox systems. New York, Funk & Wagnalls, 1884. 420 pages.

The first three chapters (pages 1–95) present an extensive survey of the Upanishads, and references to these documents occur frequently elsewhere in the book. A superficial account, without keen philosophical discernment, though quite reliable so far as it goes in facts.

'The Upanishads are the sources not only of Hindu pantheism, but of Hindu philosophy in all its phases of development.' (Page 312.)

Sreeram Lala. Vichar Sagar: The metaphysics of the Upanishads, translated. Calcutta, H. Dhole, 1885. 404 pages.

This is a translation into English of a Sanskrit compendium which, the translator explains, 'has made its way in the outlying districts of the Punjab; and every Sadhu who knows how to read and write receives instructions from his Guru on this very work, so that perusing it he learns all that is worth knowing of the Upanishads.' (Page i of Translator's Preface.)

'Thanks to the late Swamy Dayanand Saraswati and other allumini [!] there is an increasing activity noticeable everywhere for a study of our Shastras and what they teach. The impulse to this novel movement received no mean help from the Theosophical Society.

'Thus then, if the present work would tend to increase the national spirituality, if it would be the means of inciting the active sympathies of our young men and old, and stimulate them to study our ancient writings and the faith they inculcate, if it would stem the tide of materialism and supplant it with the noble and high aspirations which Non-duality teaches, if it will suppress bad karma and incite the good of our fellow creatures, we would think ourselves highly gratified and amply repaid.' (Translator's Preface, page ii.)

Schroeder, Leopold von. Indiens Literatur und Cultur in historischer Entwicklung: Ein Cyklus von fünfzig Vorlesungen, zugleich als Handbuch der indischen Literaturgeschichte, nebst zahlreichen, in deutscher Übersetzung mitgetheilten Proben aus indischen Schriftwerken. Leipzig, Haessel, 1887. 793 pages.

Lectures 15 and 16 (pp. 212–240) give a sketch of the philosophy of the Upanishads with illustrative extracts from Bṛih., Chānd., Īśā, Kaṭha, etc.

Whitney, W. D. Hindu eschatology and the Kaṭha Upanishad. In *JAOS.* vol. 13 (1889), pp. ciii–cviii.

Dutt, Romesh Chunder. A history of civilization in Ancient India, based on Sanskrit literature. Calcutta, Thacker, 3 vols., 1889–1890; London, Trübner, 2 vols., 1893.

Chap. 9 of vol. 1 is devoted to 'The religious doctrines of the Upanishads,' and contains original translations from Chānd., Kena, Īśā Bṛih., and Kaṭha. Interspersed throughout this volume are also various extracts from the Upanishads illustrating the civilization of their periods.

'Who can, even in the present day, peruse these pious inquiries and fervent thoughts of a long-buried past without feeling a new emotion in his heart, without seeing a new light before his eyes?' (Vol. 1, page 302.)

Lanman, Charles Rockwell. The beginnings of Hindu pantheism. Cambridge, Mass., 1890. 25 pages.

A brief, but appreciatively discriminating treatment, with illustrative extracts from the Upanishads.

'A good critical text of all the old Upanishads, conveniently assembled in one volume, with a philologically accurate translation and various useful appendices, is still one of the pressing needs of Indology.' (Page 12, footnote.)

Dutt, Romesh Chandra. Ancient India. London, Longmans Green, 1893. 196 pages.

Assigns the date of the Upanishads to the Epic Age, 1400–1000 B.C.

'The Upanishads are among the most remarkable works in the literature of the world.' (Page 66.)

Deussen, Paul. Elements of metaphysics: A guide to truth. London, Macmillan, 1894. 337 pages.

Contains as an appendix the author's Address delivered before the Bombay Branch of the Royal Asiatic Society, in which he concluded with this peroration: 'The Vedānta in its unfalsified form is the strongest support of pure morality, is the greatest consolation in the sufferings of life and death. Indians, keep to it!' (Page 337.)

Deussen, Paul. Erinnerungen an Indien. Kiel and Leipzig, Lipsius & Tischer, 1894. 254 pages.

Contains as an appendix the author's English address referred to in the preceding entry.

Garbe, Richard. Die Sâṃkhya-Philosophie: eine Darstellung des Indischen Rationalismus nach den Quellen. Leipzig, Haessel, 1894. 353 pages. (2d ed., 1894, 424 pages.)

Contains a thorough discussion of the relation of the Upanishads to the Sāṁkhya system.

'The influence of the Sāmkhya system on Brahmanism occurs first in the time which lies between the origin of those Upanishads which belong to the three older Vedas and the composition of the Katha, Maitri, Çvetaçvatara, Praçna and similar Upanishads.' (Page 21.)

'The pre-Buddhistic Upanishads represent a time (perhaps from the eighth to the sixth centuries) in which there developed those ideas which became determinative of Indian thought in the later time.' (Page 107.)

Apte, Raghunath N. The doctrine of Māyā: its existence in the Vedāntic Sūtra, and development in the later Vedānta. Bombay, 1896.

'His conclusions are, that the doctrine of Māyā, although it had its germ in the Upanishads, does not exist in the Sūtras, and that it arose from the fourth century A. D. on a revival of Brāhmanism and vigorous speculation of Gaudapada and Śankara.' (Quoted concerning the above Essay from Frazer's *Literary History of India*, page 199, n. 1.)

The theosophy of the Upanishads. London, Theosophical Publishing Society, 1896. 203 pages.

An attempt to expound modern theosophy as being the clear and systematic teaching of the Upanishads.

Frazer, R. W. A literary history of India. London, Unwin (New York, Scribners), 1897. 470 pages.

Chapter 6, 'From Brāhmanism to Buddhism,' contains a brief account of the Upanishads, which, especially at pages 99–113, sets forth their main contents in salient outline. It is a clear and comprehensive presentation of the connection of ideas—the progress of philosophic thought from the Vedas and Brāhmaṇas, the development and interrelations of speculations within the Upanishads themselves, and the preparation for the subsequent protest of Buddhism.

Rai, Dalpat. The Upanishads: an introduction to their study. Lahore, Arobans Press, 1897. 118 pages.

Slater, T. E. Studies in the Upanishads. Madras, Christian Literature Society for India, 1897. 74 pages.

'I find in all their best and noblest thoughts a true religious ring, and a far-off presentiment of Christian truth; their finest passages having a striking parallelism to much of the teaching of the Christian Gospels and Epistles, and so supplying the Indian soil in which many seeds of true Christianity may spring.' (Page 15.)

Baynes, Herbert. Ideals of the East. London, Swan Sonnenschein, 1898. 99 pages.

Contains original verse-translations and expositions of choice quotations from Buddhism, Taoism, Hinduism, Zoroastrianism, Muhammadanism, and Christianity, classified according to four types of the ideal, viz. ethical, metaphysical, theosophical, and religious. Under the Theosophical Ideal are cited the Īśā and Māṇḍūkya Upanishads.

'Perhaps no class of metaphysical literature is likely to exercise so great an influence on future schools of thought in Europe as those mystical products of the Indian mind known as the Upanisads.' (Page 42.)

Hopkins, E. W. The religions of India. Boston, Ginn, 1898. 612 pages.

The most scholarly book in English on the large subject. Chapter 10, 'Brahmanic Pantheism—the Upanishads' (pp. 216–241), presents an able sketch of the main religious conceptions of the Upanishads with abundant first-hand citations from the texts themselves.

Deussen, Paul. Allgemeine Geschichte der Philosophie mit besonderer Berücksichtigung der Religionen. Vol. 1, part 2: *Die Philosophie der Upanishad's.* Leipzig, Brockhaus, 1899, 368 pages; 2d edition, 1907, 401 pages (including a valuable index).

The foregoing translated into English:

—— The religion and philosophy of India: the philosophy of the Upanishads. Edinburgh, Clark, 1906. 429 pages.

The most systematic and scholarly work on the subject yet produced, executed with a rare combination of linguistic and philosophic qualification for such a task.

Garbe, Richard. The philosophy of ancient India. Chicago, Open Court, 1899. 89 pages.

An excellent summary.

'In the elder Upanishads the struggle for absolute knowledge has found an expression unique in its kind. There are indeed in these Upanishads many speculations over which we shake our heads in wonder, but the meditations keep recurring to the Brahman,—the world-soul, the Absolute, or 'Ding an sich,' or however the word so full of content may be translated,—and culminate in the thought that the Atman, the inner self of man, is nothing less than the eternal and infinite Brahman. The language of the Upanishads is enlivened in such passages by a wonderful energy, which testifies to the elevated mood in which the thinkers of that time labored to proclaim the great mystery. New phrases, figures, and similes are constantly sought, in order to put into words what words are incapable of describing.' (Pages 69–70.)

Müller, F. Max. The six systems of Indian philosophy. London and New York, Longmans Green, 1899. 618 pages.

The section on pages 159–183 presents, with the help of some extended quotations, the fundamental doctrines of the Vedānta as taught in the Upanishads.

Geden, Alfred S. Studies in Eastern religions. London, Kelly, 1900. 378 pages.

The chapter on the Upanishads (pages 82–104) contains a brief, but clear and comprehensive, sketch of these documents.

'It is by the Upanishads alone that, in the ultimate resort, native Indian students whether of philosophy or of religion establish their reasonings and justify their opinions. It is from them that all attempts at religious reform from within have taken their rise in India; and to them all orthodox native reformers have turned, as representing their religion in its purest, fairest form.' (Pages 82–83.)

Griswold, Hervey D. Brahman: A study in the history of Indian philosophy. New York, Macmillan, 1900. 89 pages.

Chapter 3 (pages 43–70) presents 'The doctrine of Brahman in the Upanishads. A. Remarks on the sources. B. Doctrine. C. Consequences: I. Religious, II. Ethical, III. Eschatological, IV. Philosophical.'

A brief but compact exposition. The product of philosophical acumen as well as of thorough general scholarship on the subject. Benefited, too, by a sympathetic but discriminating appreciation, resulting from personal contacts in India and from a broad knowledge of comparative philosophy and comparative religion. For its compass, it is noteworthy as a clear, succinct introduction to the Upanishads, and as a summary of their main conceptions.

Macdonell, Arthur A. A history of Sanskrit literature. London, Heinemann (New York, Appleton), 1900. 472 pages.

Chapter 8 on 'The Brāhmaṇas' contains (at pages 218–243) an excellent general account and summary of the several important Upanishads.

Contains the very first published reproductions of metrical portions of the Upanishads in the form of English lines which are syllabically commensurate with the Sanskrit originals.

'It must not of course be supposed that the Upanishads, either as a whole or individually, offer a complete and consistent conception of the world logically developed. They are rather a mixture of half-poetical, half-philosophical fancies, of dialogues and disputations, dealing tentatively with metaphysical questions. Their speculations were only reduced to a system in the Vedānta philosophy.' (Page 226.)

Royce, Josiah. The world and the individual; vol. 1, entitled *Four historical conceptions of being.* New York, Macmillan, 1900. 588 pages.

Chapters 4 and 5 (pp. 141–222) present the mystical method of interpreting reality, which is a characteristic feature of the Upanishads.

Contains some translations of portions of the Upanishads which were made especially for this book by the author's colleague, Charles R. Lanman, Professor of Sanskrit in Harvard University.

Upanishadas, or an account of their contents and nature. Second edition. Calcutta, H. C. Dass, Elysium Press, 1900. 109 pages. (Society for the Resuscitation of Indian Literature, vol. 5.)

'In this work the compiler claims no originality. He has simply arranged the subjects culled from the writings of eminent orientalists. In this work he is particularly indebted to the publications of the Asiatic Society of Bengal (Dr. Röer's translations), Babu Sitanath Datta, the annotator of the Upanishadas, Professor Maxmuller [!], Colebrooke and other eminent orientalists. In the appendix we have given Dr. Röer's translation of two most important Upanishadas [part of the Kaṭha and the Īśā] in order to give our readers an idea of the nature of this class of work.' (Preface.)

Pillai, J. M. Nallaswami. The Svetasvatara Upanishad. In *Madras Review*, vol. 6 (1900), pp. 369–376; vol. 7 (1901), pp. 141–149, 267–279.

'The thoughts of the Vedānta became for India a permanent and characteristic spiritual atmosphere, which pervades all the products of the later literature. To every Indian Brâhman to-day the Upanishads are what the New Testament is to the Christian.' (Preface, pages vii–viii.)

'Amongst the ancient Indians, whose consciousness of human solidarity, of common needs and common interests was but slightly developed, the sense of the objective worth of moral action (that is, the worth it possesses for others) is very inferior to ours, while their estimate of its subjective worth (that is, its significance for the actor himself) was advanced to a degree from which we may learn much.' (Pages 364–365.)

Ewing, Arthur H. The Hindu conception of the function of breath: a study in early Hindu psycho-physics. Part 1, in *JAOS.* vol. 22 (1901), pp. 249–308. Part 2, Allahabad, Liddell's Printing Works, 1903, 48 pages.

A complete collation and attempted interpretation of all the data in the Vedas, Brāhmaṇas, and Upanishads concerning the various breaths (*prāṇa*).

Hopkins, E. W. Notes on the Çvetāçvatara, etc. In *JAOS.* vol. 22 (1901), pp. 380–387.

Takes issue at three points with Professor Deussen's theory concerning the authorship of this Upanishad and concerning its relation to the Sāṁkhya system of philosophy.

Ramakrishnananda. The philosophy of the Upanishads. In *Brahmavadin* (Madras), vol. 7 (1902), pp. 314–328.

Slater, T. E. The Higher Hinduism in relation to Christianity London, Elliot Stock, 1902; 2d edition, 1903. 298 pages.

Chapter 6 (pp. 69–84) deals with 'The Upanishads and Vedantism.' The quotations are taken from Max Müller's translation.

Abhedananda, Swami. Vedanta philosophy, self-knowledge. New York, Vedanta Society, 1905. 178 pages.

An attempt to present the conceptions of the Vedānta philosophy, especially as contained in the Upanishads, in terms of modern thought.

Deussen, Paul. Outline of the Vedanta system of philosophy according to Shankara, translated by J. H. Woods and C. B. Runkle. New York, Grafton Press, 1906. 45 pages.

This consists solely of a translation from the original German of Appendix I, entitled 'Kurze Übersicht der Vedantalehre,' of the author's *Das System des Vedanta*, pp. 487–517. (Translated again in Johnston's English translation of the entire book entitled *The System of the Vedanta*, on pages 453–478.)

'On the tree of Indian wisdom there is no fairer flower than the Upanishads, and no finer fruit than the Vedanta philosophy. This system grew out of the teachings of the Upanishads, and was brought to its consummate form by the great Shankara. Even to this day Shankara's system represents the common belief of nearly all thoughtful Hindus, and deserves to be widely studied in the Occident.' (Prefatory Note by the author.)

Suresvaracharya. Sambandhu-Vartika: A metrical expansion of the introductory portion of Sankara Acharya's commentary on the Brihad-Aranyaka Upanishad, translated into English. Benares, Lazarus, 1906. 167 pages.

Barnett, L. D. Brahma-knowledge: An outline of the philosophy of the Vedānta, as set forth by the Upanishads and by Śankara. London, Murray, 1907. 113 pages. (The Wisdom of the East Series.)

Besant, Annie. The wisdom of the Upaniṣhaṭs: Four lectures. Benares, Theosophical Publishing Society, 1907. 103 pages. (2d edition, Adyar, Theosophical Publishing House, 1919, 96 pages.)

Deussen, Paul. Outlines of Indian philosophy, with an Appendix on the philosophy of the Vedanta in its relation to Occidental metaphysics. Berlin, Curtius, 1907. 70 pages.

Contains (pp. 21–23) a section on 'The Philosophy of the Upanishads.' These 'Outlines' are reprinted from their original appearance in the *Indian Antiquary* in 1900 (not in 1902, which is the date stated in the book).

The Appendix contains an address originally delivered before the Bombay Branch of the Royal Asiatic Society, Feb. 23, 1893. This address appears also as an appendix in the same author's *Elements of Metaphysics*.

'The philosophy of the Indians must become, for every one who takes any interest in the investigation of philosophical truth, an object of the highest interest; for Indian Philosophy is, and will be, the only possible parallel to what so far the Europeans have considered as philosophy.' (Prefatory Remarks.)

Oltramare, Paul. L'Histoire des idées théosophiques dans l'Inde. Vol. 1: *La Théosophie brahmanique.* Paris, Leroux, 1907. 382 pages.

The second part (pages 63–131) presents a sketch of 'The formation of theosophic ideas in the Upanishads.'

This is the most important French work on the subject, superseding Regnaud's *Matériaux.*

Rumball, Edwin A. Sin in the Upanishads. In *Open Court*, vol. 21 (1907), pp. 609–614.

'The Upanishads seek a sinless ideal, like the other religious systems' (page 612). But the specific aims and methods are different.

Bloomfield, Maurice. The Religion of the Veda: The ancient religion of India, from the Rig Veda to the Upanishads. New York & London, Putnam, 1908. 300 pages.

Lecture 6 (pp. 249–289) presents 'The final philosophy of the Veda' together with quotations from the Upanishads.

Bodas, M. R. A brief survey of the Upanishads. In *Journal of the Bombay Branch of the Royal Asiatic Society*, vol. 22 (1908), pp. 67–80.

Holmes, W. H. G. The Upanishads and the Christian Gospel. Madras, Christian Literature Society, 1908. 70 pages.

Sukthankar, Vasudev Anant. The teachings of Vedānta according to Rāmānuja. Vienna, 1908. 84 pages. [Doctoral dissertation.]

More, Paul Elmer. The forest philosophy of India. A chapter in *Shelburne Essays*, vol. 6, 'Studies in religious dualism,' New York & London, Putnam, 1909, pages 1–45.

A review and criticism of the philosophy of the Upanishads, starting with a review of Geden's translation of Deussen's *The philosophy and religion of India: The philosophy of the Upanishads.*

Winternitz, M. Geschichte der indischen Literatur, vol. 1, 2d ed., pages 196–228, Leipzig, Amelang, 1909.

Shastri, Prabhu Dutt. The doctrine of Māyā in the philosophy of the Vedānta. London, Luzac, 1911. 152 pages.

Gives an excellent summary of the main doctrines of the Upanishads in the course of a detailed and comprehensive survey of the occurrences of the term *māyā* and of its general philosophic idea not only in the Upanishads themselves, but also in the chief earlier Sanskrit documents and in the chief subsequent developments of the Vedānta philosophy.

'The conception of Māyā is as old as some of the later books of the Ṛgveda. The word Māyā in the sense of "illusion" occurs later—for the first time in the Śvetāśvatara Upaniṣad 4. 10.' (Page vii.)

Bhandarkar, Sir Ramkrishna Govind. Vaiṣṇavism, Śaivism, and minor religious systems. Strassburg, Trübner, 1913. 169 pages. (Grundriss der indo-arischen Philologie und Altertumskunde.)

'It is generally believed that the Upaniṣads teach a system of Pantheism; but a closer examination will show that they teach not one, but various systems of doctrines as regards the nature of God, man and the world, and the relations between them. The religio-philosophic systems of modern times, which are mutually inconsistent, quote texts from the Upaniṣads as an authority for their special doctrines.' (Page 1.)

Geden, Alfred S. Studies in the religions of the East. London, Kelly, 1913. 904 pages.

An enlargement of the author's earlier *Studies in Eastern Religions*. Contains (on pages 255–301) a section on the Upanishads.

Milburn, R. Gordon. Christian Vedantism. In *The Indian Interpreter* (Madras), vol. 7, no. 4, January 1913, pages 153–160.

A Christian missionary, who became Vice-Principal of Bishop's College, Calcutta, makes some noteworthy proposals both in general and in specific terms.

'Christianity in India needs the Vedanta. We missionaries have not realized this with half the clearness that we should. . . . We cannot move freely and joyfully in our own religion, because we have not sufficient terms and modes of expression wherewith to express the more immanental aspects of Christianity.' (Page 155.)

'A very useful step would be the recognition of certain books or passages in the literature of the Vedanta as constituting what might be called an Ethnic Old Testament. . . . The permission of ecclesiastical authorities could then be asked for reading passages found in such a canon of the Ethnic Old Testament at divine service along with passages from the New Testament as alternatives to the Old Testament lessons.' (Pages 158–159.)

Thereupon the writer proposes the following passages from six of the Upanishads: Śvetāśvatara 3. 7–26, 6. 1–20; Muṇḍaka 3. 1; 3. 2. 1–4;

Īśā 1–6; Kena, part 2 [stanzas 9–13]; Kaṭha 2. 20–24; Bṛihad-Āraṇyaka 3. 7. 15–33, along with extracts from the Bhagavad-Gītā and from three of the Buddhist canonical documents in the Tripitaka.

Jacobi, Hermann Georg. Über die ältere Auffassung der Upaniṣad-lehren. In *Festschrift Ernst Windisch zum siebzigsten Geburtstag*, Leipzig, Harrassowitz, 1914, pp. 153–157.

Points out some of Śaṇkara's later re-interpretations of Upanishad teachings which are quite different from the original meaning, and also some of the relations of the Upanishadic doctrines with Buddhism.

Speyer, J. S. Die indische Theosophie, aus den Quellen dargestellt. Leipzig, Haessel, 1914. 344 pages.

Tagore, Rabindranath. Sādhanā, the realisation of life. New York, Macmillan, 1914. 164 pages.

'Perhaps it is well for me to explain that the subject-matter of the papers published in this book has not been philosophically treated, nor has it been approached from the scholar's point of view. The writer has been brought up in a family where texts from the Upanishads are used in daily worship . . . To me the verses of the Upanishads and the teachings of Buddha have ever been things of the spirit, and therefore endowed with boundless vital growth; and I have used them, both in my own life and in my preaching, as being instinct with individual meaning.' (Author's Preface, pages vii–viii.)

Frazer, R. W. Indian thought, past and present. London, Unwin, 1915. 339 pages.

Chap. 3 (pp. 44–72) deals with the Upanishads.

'On these early Upanishads rests almost all of the philosophic, and much of the religious, thought of India to-day.' (Page 47.)

'The answers of the Upanishads are held by orthodox thought in India not to rest solely on abstract metaphysical reasoning, but to be divine revelations. . . . Orthodox thought in India holds that the nature of God is known, and can be explained, only through the correct interpretation of texts of Vedas and Upanishads.' (Page 49.)

Macnicol, Nicol. Indian theism. London, Oxford University Press, 1915. 292 pages.

Chapter 3 (pp. 42–61) deals with 'The theism of the Upanishads.'

Oldenberg, Hermann. Die Lehre der Upanishaden und die Anfänge des Buddhismus. Göttingen, Vandenhoeck & Ruprecht, 1915. 374 pages.

Part 1 deals with the older Upanishads; Part 2, with the later

Upanishads and the beginnings of the Sāṁkhya and Yoga philosophies; Part 3, with the beginnings of Buddhism.

This book is more than an exposition of the contents of the Upanishads. It is especially valuable for its tracing of the historical connections of the Upanishads with the other systems besides the Vedānta, which of course is the system most closely related.

Pratt, James B. India and its faiths. Boston and New York, Houghton Mifflin, 1915. 483 pages.

An unusually interesting and appreciative, yet fair and discriminating, book. Discusses the Upanishads at pages 72–79 and elsewhere in the eight chapters devoted to Hinduism.

'The directness with which the Upanishads speak to the Indian heart is finely illustrated in the *Autobiography* of Devendranath Tagore (the father of the poet). He had long been seeking inner peace in vain, when one day a page of the Īśā Upanishad blew past him. He had never read any of the Upanishads before, and the effect of this one page was the transformation of his whole life and the new-directing of all his energies. The message from the ancient book came to him as a divine answer specially sent for his salvation . . . "Oh, what a blessed day that was for me!"' (Pages 77–78.)

Edgerton, Franklin. Sources of the filosofy of the Upaniṣads. In *JAOS*. vol. 36 (1916), pp. 197–204.

Lüders, Heinrich. Zu den Upaniṣads. In *Sitzungsberichte der königlich Preussischen Akademie der Wissenschaften*, 1916, pp. 278–309.

Contains a fresh translation of Chānd. 4. 1–3, and attempts to derive the origin of that *saṁvarga-vidyā* from other early literature.

Urquhart, W. S. The Upanishads and life. Calcutta, Association Press, 1916. 156 pages.

'The aim of the present volume is to examine the fundamental doctrines of Indian philosophy, as these are indicated in the Upanishads, the chief storehouse for Indian philosophical thought, and to estimate the effect which such doctrines may be expected to have upon our practical attitude to life.' (Pages 1–2.)

Ranade, R. D. Psychology in the Upanishads. A series of three articles in *The Indian Philosophical Review*, vol. 1 (1917–18).

The three subtitles are: 'Empirical and abnormal psychology'; 'Rational psychology, A'; 'Rational psychology: life after death.'

At the end of each article the main citations are given in a list of sources quoted in Sanskrit from the text of the Upanishads.

Schomerus, H. W. Indische Erlösungslehren : Ihre Bedeutung für das Verständnis des Christentums und für die Missionspredigt. Leipzig, Hinrichs, 1919. 240 pages.

On pages 8–32 the author deals particularly with the methods of salvation propounded in the Upanishads.

Stephen, Dorothea Jane. Studies in early Indian thought. London, Cambridge University Press, 1918. 176 pages.

Chapter 2 (pp. 33–79) deals with 'The divine nature in the Upanishads.' Chapter 3 (pp. 80–113) deals with 'Human nature in the Upanishads.'

Srisa Chandra Vidyarnava. Studies in the first six Upanisads, and the Isa and Kena Upanisads, with the Commentary of Sankara, translated. Allahabad, Panini Office, 1919. 156 pages. (Sacred Books of the Hindus, vol. 22, part 1.)

Urquhart, W. S. Pantheism and the value of life, with special reference to Indian philosophy. London, Epworth Press, 1919. 744 pages.

Carpenter, Edward. Pagan and Christian creeds : their origin and meaning. London, Allen & Unwin, 1920. 318 pages.

Beside numerous references to the Upanishads, there is an 'Appendix on the teachings of the Upanishads' (pp. 283–308).

This last section was reprinted with the title 'The teaching of the Upanishads, being the substance of two lectures to popular audiences: I. Rest, II. The nature of the self.' London, Allen & Unwin, 1920. 28 pages.

Langley, G. H. The conception of Universal Spirit in the Upanishads and of its identity with individual spirit. In *The Indian Philosophical Review*, vol. 3 (1920), pp. 109–128.

Radhakrishnan, S[arvapalli]. The reign of religion in contemporary philosophy. London, Macmillan, 1920. 463 pages.

The final chapter is devoted to 'Suggestions of an approach to reality based on the Upanishads.' The concluding sentence of the book declares: 'The Upanishads being the earliest form of speculative idealism in the world, all that is good and great in subsequent philosophy looks like an unconscious commentary on the Upanishadic ideal, showing how free and expansive and how capable of accommodating within itself all forms of truth that ideal is.' (Page 451.)

Radhakrishnan, S[arvapalli]. The metaphysics of the Upanishads. In *The Indian Philosophical Review*, vol. 3 (1920), pp. 213–236, 346–362.

Barua, Benimadhab. A history of pre-Buddhistic Indian philosophy. Calcutta, Univ. of Calcutta, 1921. 468 pages.

Makes constant reference to and citations from the Upanishads.

Brown, George William. The human body in the Upanishads. Jubbulpore, Christian Mission Press, 1921. 237 pages. (Dissertation, Johns Hopkins University, 1910.)

Hillebrandt, Alfred. Über die Upanischaden. In *Zeitschrift für Buddhismus*, vol. 4 (1921), pp. 39–51.

Sarkar, Mahendra. Teachings of the Upanisads. In *Journal of the Department of Letters, University of Calcutta*, vol. 7 (1921), pp. 261–274.

Deals chiefly with the Māṇḍūkya and the Īśā.

Tattvabhusan, Sitanath. Lectures on the theism of the Upanishads and other subjects. Lahore, The Trust Society, Dayal Singh College, 1921. 181 pages.

Dasgupta, Surendranath. A history of Indian philosophy. London, Cambridge University Press, vol. 1, 1922. 544 pages.

Chapter 2 (pp. 28–61) deals with 'The earlier Upaniṣads, 700–600 B. C.' 'The Upaniṣads contain various sorts of philosophical thoughts, mostly monistic or singularistic, but also some pluralistic and dualistic ones. These are not reasoned statements, but utterances of truths intuitively perceived or felt as unquestionably real and indubitable, and carrying great force, vigour and persuasiveness with them.'

Heimann, Betty. Die Tiefschlafspekulation der alten Upanisaden. München-Neubiberg, Oskar Schloss, 1922. 22 pages.

Heimann, Betty. Madhava's (Ānandatīrtha's) Kommentar zur Kāṭhaka-Upaniṣad: Sanskrit Text in Transkription nebst Übersetzung und Noten. Leipzig, Harrassowitz, 1922. 56 pages.

Urquhart, W. S. Theosophy and Christian thought. Boston, Pilgrim Press, 1922. 222 pages.

Brings some of the teachings of the Upanishads into relation with Christian thought.

Faddegon, B. De Interpretatie der Kāṭhaka-Upaniṣad. Amsterdam, *Mededeelingen der Koninklijke Akademie van Wetenschappen, Afdeeling Letterkunde*, Deel 55, Serie A, No. 1, 1923. 18 pages.

Radhakrishnan, S. Indian philosophy. 2 volumes. London (Allen & Unwin) and New York (Macmillan), 1923, 1927.

Vol. 1, pages 137–367: The philosophy of the Upaniṣads. (Reprinted as a separate volume, 1924.)

Radhakrishnan, S. The philosophy of the Upaniṣads, with a foreword by Rabindranath Tagore, and an introduction by Edmond Holmes. London (Allen & Unwin) and New York (Macmillan), 1924. 168 pages.

A reprint of the section on the Upanishads contained in the author's *Indian Philosophy*.

Heller, Friedrich. Die Mystik in den Upanishaden. München-Neubiberg, Oskar Schloss, 1925. 46 pages. [Reprint from the *Zeitschrift für Buddhismus*.]

Keith, Arthur Berriedale. The religion and philosophy of the Veda and Upanishads. 2 volumes. Cambridge, Mass., Harvard University Press, 1925. (Harvard Oriental Series, vols. 31 and 32.)

Chapter 28 (pages 489-600) deals with the philosophy of the Upanishads.

Strauss, Otto. Indische Philosophie. München, Reinhardt, 1925. 286 pages.

Chapter 3 deals with the oldest Upanishads, chapter 4 with the later Upanishads.

Ranade, R. D. A constructive survey ot Upanishadic philosophy: being a systematic introduction to Indian metaphysics. Poona, Oriental Book Agency, 1926. 438 pages.

In the section dealing with translations, the Bibliographical Note says (p. 426): 'R. E. Hume's translation of Thirteen Principal Upanishads, Oxford, 1921, is the latest, most handy, and most serviceable of all.'

Sandal, Mohan Lal. Philosophical teachings in the Upanisats. Allahabad, Panini Office, no date (perhaps 1926). 132 pages. (Sacred Books of the Hindus, extra volume 5.)

Belvalkar, S. K., and **R. D. Ranade.** History of Indian philosophy. Vol. 2. The creative period: Brāhmana and Upanishadic philosophy and post-upanishadic thought-ferment. Poona, 1927. 556 pages.

Dasgupta, S. N. Hindu mysticism. Chicago and London, Open Court, 1927. 188 pages.

Contains six lectures delivered at Northwestern University, Evanston, Illinois. Lecture 2 (pp. 33–57) deals with the 'Mysticism of the Upanishads.'

Majumdar, S. The Vedanta philosophy, in English, with original Sutras and explanatory quotations from Upanishads, Bhagavad Gita, etc., in Sanskrit, with English translations. Bankipore, 1927. 801 pages.

Radhakrishnan, S. The Hindu view of life: Upton lectures delivered at Manchester College, Oxford, 1926. London, Allen & Unwin, 1927. 133 pages.

Contains some original translations of passages from the Upanishads along with a general exposition of the philosophy of the Upanishads as underlying Hinduism.

Winternitz, M. A history of Indian literature. University of Calcutta, vol. 1, 1927. 654 pages.

This volume was translated from the original German by Mrs. S. Ketkar, and revised and enlarged by the author.

The section at pp. 225–247 deals with the 'Āraṇyakas and Upaniṣads.' The section at pp. 247–267 deals with 'The fundamental doctrines of the Upaniṣads.' Some of the citations of passages from the Upanishads are quoted from the translation by R. E. Hume.

Bhattacharjee, Umesh Chandra. The home of the Upaniṣads In *Indian Antiquary*, vol. 57 (1928), pp. 185–189.

Sharma, A. K. The relation between Buddhism and the Upanishads. In *The Monist*, vol. 38 (1928), pp. 443–477.

The article undertakes to corroborate the opinion of Max Müller (*SBE.* 15, page lii): 'The Upanishads are to my mind the germs of Buddhism, while Buddhism is in many respects the doctrine of the Upanishads carried out to its last consequences and, what is important, employed as the foundation of a new social order.'

Shastri, Prabhu Dutt. The essentials of Eastern philosophy: being two addresses delivered in the University of Toronto at the Philosophical Conference, 1922. New York, Macmillan, 1928. 114 pages.

On pp. 46–54 there is a section which deals with the Upanishads. There are also some other quotations from the Upanishads.

Urquhart, W. S. The Vedanta and modern thought. London, Oxford University Press, 1928. 272 pages.

Chapter 2 (pp. 21–49) deals with 'Anticipations of Vedantic ideas in the Upanishads,' etc.

Edgerton, Franklin. The Upaniṣads: what do they seek, and why? In *JAOS.* vol. 49 (1929), pp. 97–121.

ADDENDA

(Section 3, page 475)

Appasamy, A. J. Temple bells: readings from Hindu religious literature. With a foreword by the Right Rev. H. M. Waller. Calcutta, Association Press, 1930. 163 pages.

Contains 13 brief extracts from the Upanishads as rendered into English by R. E. Hume (in the first edition of the present work).

(Section 5, page 478)

Senart, Émile. Chāndogya Upaniṣad, traduite et annotée. Paris, Maisonneuve, 1930. 32 pages + 142 double pages. (Collection Émile Senart, vol. 1.)

The transliterated text and the French translation face each other on opposite pages.

APPENDIX

RECURRENT AND PARALLEL PASSAGES

IN THE PRINCIPAL UPANISHADS AND THE BHAGAVAD-GITĀ

WITH REFERENCES TO OTHER SANSKRIT TEXTS

By

George C. O. Haas, Ph.D.

of New York

In intensive study of those wonderful old treasuries of Hindu theosophic lore, the Upanishads and the Bhagavad-Gītā, it is naturally essential to make careful comparison of expressions of the same thought in various passages and to assimilate and combine, or on the other hand differentiate and contrast, the statements according to their nature and their context; and it is to facilitate such comparison that I have prepared the present collection of recurrences and parallels.[1]

The material here assembled falls, broadly speaking, into three categories: (1) repeated episodes and passages, long or short; (2) recurrences of the same ideas and of the same similes; (3) allusions and the like. As will be seen at a glance, this collection of repetitions and parallels differs altogether in scope and in arrangement from Col. George A. Jacob's *Concordance to the Principal Upanishads and Bhagavad-Gîtâ* (Bombay, 1891), which is invaluable for tracing a presumable quotation, studying a technical term, or investigating a special usage. The present collection of parallels, while omitting notice of the repetition of brief formulas and

[1] This collection of references was printed, substantially in its present form, in *Journal of the American Oriental Society*, vol. 42, pp. 1–43.

phrases (see a subsequent paragraph), includes similarities of thought and of imagery, which are in many cases not revealed by a concordance, as well as numerous references to other Sanskrit texts; and its sequential arrangement makes available, section by section and line by line, without the necessity of search or collation, the material gathered in relation to each Upanishad and thus renders it serviceable in connection with consecutive reading or critical examination of any portion of the text.

The material here presented covers the thirteen principal Upanishads translated in this volume, and, in addition to these, the Bhagavad-Gītā, which is included because of its close association for many centuries with the Upanishads, but is placed last, as not being nominally a text of the same class. It has seemed worth while to add also a number of references to the Mahānārāyaṇa Upanishad, which clearly belongs in the group of older Upanishadic texts. The numerous minor and later Upanishads, however, have not been included in the scope of this study; recurrent passages in them are for the most part merely quotations from the earlier treatises, and systematic inclusion of references to them would have added considerably to the length of this appendix without commensurate advantage. On the other hand numerous references to other Sanskrit texts, especially to the philosophic sections of the Mahābhārata, have been inserted because of their interest. There are included also, for the convenience of the reader, a few stray citations of important parallels in the Brāhmaṇas, though no search has been made for others of the same kind.

In order to avoid needless expansion, it has been found necessary to omit notice of the repetition of brief formulas and phrases, as well as of sentences and turns of expression recurring at intervals in a series of sections, but found nowhere else. As chief among these may be mentioned the following:—

apa punarmṛtyuṁ jayati Bṛh. 1. 2. 7; etc. [see 3].
eṣa ta ātmā sarvāntaraḥ Bṛh. 3. 4. 1; etc.
ato 'nyad ārttam Bṛh. 3. 4. 2; etc.
dugdhe — annādo bhavati Chānd. 1. 3. 7; etc.
sarvam āyur eti Chānd. 2. 11. 2; etc.
etad evāmṛtaṁ dṛṣṭvā tṛpyati Chānd. 3. 6. 3; etc.

vāg eva brahmaṇaś caturthaḥ pādaḥ Chānd. 3. 18. 3; etc.
nāsyāvarapuruṣāḥ kṣīyante Chānd. 4. 11. 2; etc.
etad amṛtam abhayam etad brahma Chānd. 4. 15. 1; etc.; Maitri 2. 2.
bhavaty asya brahmavarcasaṁ kule Chānd. 5. 12. 2; etc.
annamayaṁ hi — vāg iti Chānd. 6. 5. 4; etc.
sa ya eṣo 'ṇimaitadātmyam — śvetaketo Chānd. 6. 8. 6-7; etc.
sa yo . . . brahmety upāste — bravītv iti Chānd. 7. 1. 5; etc.
sarveṣu lokeṣu kāmacāro bhavati Chānd. 7. 25. 2; etc.
saiṣā prāṇe sarvāptir Kauṣ. 3. 3. 4.
tad eva brahma — upāsate Kena 4-8.

All the occurrences of these expressions can be found, if required, in Jacob's *Concordance.*

No attempt has been made to decide whether one parallel passage is quoted from another. In many instances there is undoubtedly distinct quotation from an older and more authoritative Upanishad; in others the passages are drawn from a common source, as in the case of citations from the Vedas and related texts; some of the minor correspondences may be fortuitous, due to the similarity of subject and point of view. On quotations from and allusions to the Kaṭha Upanishad in the Śvetāśvatara consult Deussen, *Sechzig Upanishad's des Veda*, p. 289; on correspondences of Śvet. with Kaṭha, Muṇḍ., and BhG., see R. Hauschild, *Die Śvetāśvatara Upaniṣad*, Leipzig, 1927, pp. 69–79; on quotations in the Maitri, see Deussen, pp. 312–313; for comment on special parallels see the references in **4, 125, 210**, below. For thorough discussion of parallels between the Upanishads and the Mahābhārata see Hopkins, *Great Epic of India* (New York, 1901), pp. 27–46, cf. pp. 85–190; consult also the collection of references in Holtzmann, *Das Mahābhārata* (Kiel, 1895), 4. 20–26.[1]

Before concluding these introductory paragraphs I wish to call attention briefly to a particularly interesting group of parallel passages—assembled in a Conspectus[2] on an adjoining page—relating to the elements of man's constitution

[1] The earliest collection of comparative material relating to the Upanishads, so far as I know, is that of Weber, *Indische Studien*, 1. 247–302; 380–456 (1850); 2. 1–111; 170–236 (1853); 9. 1–173 (1865).

[2] Each individual statement in the Conspectus has prefixed to it the serial number of the entry under which its parallels are recorded. Statements marked with the same number thus relate to the same phase of the subject and may profitably be compared with one another.

designated by the term *nāḍī*. Despite the suggestion of the phrase *hṛdayasya nāḍyas*, we have here no reference to arteries or veins, nor on the other hand to nerves or analogous filaments of the bodily structure; the details of the description preclude any anatomical identification. These vessels are stated to be minute as a hair divided a thousandfold; they are filled with substance of various colours; they conduct the *prāṇa*, or life energy; they have a special relation to the phenomena of sleep; one of them is the means of egress from the body at death; and so on. It is evident that, in using the term *nāḍī*, the writers of the Upanishads had in mind those same vessels that are so elaborately described, in later Hindu writings on Yoga and related subjects, as channels of variously specialized vital energy in the subtle 'etheric' vehicle that coexists as a counterpart of the gross physical body in the composite human organism. In fact, the Maitri Upanishad (at 6. 21) actually mentions the name of the principal channel, *Suṣumnā*, which is so frequently referred to in connection with the companion channels *Iḍā* and *Piṅgala* in later texts. It is necessary, therefore, to avoid the misleading translation 'artery' or 'vein' and choose as a rendering some word of less definite connotation, such as 'duct', or 'tube', or 'channel'.[1]

SPECIAL SYMBOLS USED IN THE FOLLOWING LIST

=	indicates 'recurs verbatim at'.
= (var.)	indicates 'recurs, but with one or more variants, at'.
≎	indicates 'substantially the same passage recurs at'.
cf.	indicates 'something of a similar nature is found at'.
[ ]	square brackets enclose descriptive words indicating the passage or subject matter referred to.
—	a dash replaces Sanskrit words omitted for brevity, the reference being to the entire passage from the first word printed to the last.
...	three points indicate the omission of irrelevant words.
098	heavy-face figures refer to the serial numbers of the entries in the list of recurrences and parallels.

[1] Woods, in translating Yoga-sūtra 3. 31, renders the word 'tube' (*The Yoga-system of Patañjali*, Cambridge, Mass., 1914, p. 261).

Particular attention is called to the somewhat arbitrary use of the signs = and ≂. These do not indicate that a following reference is coextensive with the passage in question. What *is* equal or similar is the *passage* referred to, *not* necessarily the section of an Upanishad indicated by the numerical designation. Thus 'Kaṭha 4. 9 a–b = Bṛh. 1. 5. 23' means (*not* that the two lines of the Kaṭha stanza constitute *all* of Bṛh. 1. 5. 23, but) that the two lines occur *in* the section of Bṛh. indicated. Where the passage *to* which reference is made is in metrical form, the citation can of course be given exactly.

CONSPECTUS OF PASSAGES RELATING TO THE 'CHANNELS OF THE HEART'

(see page 518)

Bṛh. 2. 1. 19

24 *yadā suṣupto bhavati yadā na kasyacana veda*
25 *hitā nāma nāḍyo dvāsaptatisahasrāṇi*
26 *hṛdayāt purītatam abhipratiṣṭhante*
24 *tābhiḥ pratyavasṛpya purītati śete*

Bṛh. 4. 2. 2-3

61 [Indha (Indra) and Virāj]
63 *ya eṣo 'ntar hṛdaye lohitapiṇḍo . . .*
64 *enayor eṣā sṛtiḥ saṁcaraṇī yaiṣā hṛdayād ūrdhvā nāḍy uccarati*
65 *yathā keśaḥ sahasradhā bhinna*
25 *evam asyaitā hitā nāma nāḍyo 'ntar hṛdaye pratiṣṭhitā bhavanty eva tābhir vā etad āsravad āsravati* [*tasmād eṣa praviviktāhāratara ivaiva bhavaty asmāc charīrād ātmanaḥ*]

Bṛh. 4. 3. 20

25 *tā vā asyaitā hitā nāma nāḍyo*
65 *yathā keśaḥ sahasradhā bhinnas tāvatāṇimnā tiṣṭhanti*
71 *śuklasya nīlasya piṅgalasya haritasya lohitasya pūrṇā*

Bṛh. 4. 4. 8-9

84 *aṇuḥ panthā vitataḥ purāṇo . . .*
249 *tena dhīrā api yanti brahmavidaḥ svargaṁ lokam ita ūrdhvaṁ vimuktāḥ*
71 *tasmiñ chuklam uta nīlam āhuḥ piṅgalaṁ haritaṁ lohitaṁ ca*
84 *eṣa panthā brahmaṇā hānuvittas*
249 *tenaiti brahmavit puṇyakṛt taijasaś ca*

Chānd. 8. 6. 1-3

25 *atha yā etā hṛdayasya nāḍyas*
71 *tāḥ piṅgalasyāṇimnas tiṣṭhanti śuklasya nīlasya pītasya lohitasyety . . .*
84 *tad yathā mahāpatha ātata . . . evam evaitā ādityasya raśmaya . . .*
24 *tad yatraitatsuptaḥ samastaḥ samprasannaḥ svapnaṁ na vijānāty āsu tadā nāḍīṣu sṛpto bhavati*

Chānd. 8. 6. 6 = Kaṭha 6. 16

247 *śataṁ caikā ca hṛdayasya nāḍyas* |
64 *tāsāṁ mūrdhānam abhiniḥsṛtaikā* |
249 *tayordhvam āyann amṛtatvam eti* |
250 *viṣvaṅṅ anyā utkramaṇe bhavanti* ||

Tait. 1. 6. 1

265 *sa ya eṣo 'ntar hṛdaya ākāśaḥ tasminn ayaṁ puruṣo manomayaḥ . . .*
266 *antareṇa tāluke ya eṣa stana ivāvalambate*

Kauṣ. 4. 19

25 *hitā nāma hṛdayasya nāḍyo*
26 *hṛdayāt purītatam abhipratanvanti*
65 *yathā sahasradhā keśo vipāṭitas tāvad aṇvyaḥ*
71 *piṅgalasyāṇimnā tiṣṭhante śuklasya kṛṣṇasya pītasya lohitasyeti*
24 *tāsu tadā bhavati yadā suptaḥ svapnaṁ na kaṁcana paśyaty*

Muṇḍ. 2. 2. 6

247 *arā iva rathanābhau saṁhatā yatra nāḍyaḥ*
265 *sa eṣo 'ntaś carate*

Praśna 3. 6-7

247 *atraitad ekaśataṁ nāḍīnām*
25 *tāsāṁ śataṁ śatam ekaikasyāṁ dvāsaptatir dvāsaptatiḥ pratiśākhānāḍīsahasrāṇi bhavanty*
486 *āsu vyānaś carati*
249 *athaikayordhva udānaḥ . . .*

Maitri 6. 21

64 *ūrdhvagā nāḍī suṣumnākhyā*
486 *prāṇasaṁcāriṇī*
266 *tālvantarvicchinnā*
249 *tayā . . . ūrdhvam utkramet*

Maitri 6. 30

265 . . . | *dīpavad yaḥ sthito hṛdi* |
71 *sitāsitāḥ kadrunīlāḥ* | *kapilā mṛdulohitāḥ* ||
64 *ūrdhvam ekaḥ sthitas teṣāṁ* |
249 *yo bhittvā sūryamaṇḍalam* | *brahmalokam atikramya* | *tena yānti parāṁ gatim* ||
250 *yad asyānyad raśmiśataṁ* | . . . | *tena devanikāyānāṁ* | *svadhāmāni prapadyate* ||

Maitri 7. 11

61 [Indra and Virāj]
265 *samāgamas tayor eva* | *hṛdayāntargate suṣau* |
63 *tejas tallohitasyātra* | *piṇḍa evobhayos tayoḥ* ||
64 *hṛdayād āyatā tāvac* | *cakṣusy asmin pratiṣṭhitā* | *sāraṇī sā tayor nāḍī* | *dvayor ekā dvidhā satī* ||

LIST OF RECURRENCES AND PARALLELS

Bṛhad-Āraṇyaka Upanishad

1 Bṛh. 1. 2. 3 *sa tredhā "tmānaṁ vyakuruta* = Maitri 6. 3.

2 Bṛh. 1. 2. 4 *manasā vācaṁ mithunaṁ samabhavad* cf. *mana evāsyātmā vāg jāyā* Bṛh. 1. 4. 17.

3 Bṛh. 1. 2. 7 *apa punarmṛtyuṁ jayati* (recurs thrice) an old formula; it occurs, for example, in Tait. Br. 3. 11. 8. 6 (cf. Kauṣ. Br. 25. 1). With this conquest of 'dying again and again' (in the course of *saṁsāra*, or successive life-cycles) cf. the Gospel according to St. Luke, 20. 36, *οὐδὲ γὰρ ἀποθανεῖν ἔτι δύνανται.*

4 Bṛh. 1. 3. 1-21 [contest of gods and devils] =c Chānd. 1. 2; Jaiminīya Up. Br. 1. 18. 5; cf. ibid. 2. 1. 1; 2. 4. 1 (Oertel, *JAOS.* 15. 240-245) cf. Śat. Br. 14. 4. 1; Kauṣ. Ār. 9. (According to D. p. 69, the Bṛh. version is older than that in Chānd.) On the superiority of breath see **124.**

5 Bṛh. 1. 3. 22 [*sā + ama = sāma(n)*] =c Chānd. 1. 6. 1, etc.; cf. Bṛh. 6. 4. 20. See also Chānd. 5. 2. 6. (Oertel, *JAOS.* 16. 235, in a note on Jaiminīya [Talavakāra] Up. Br. 1. 54. 6, assembles refs. to numerous similar passages, to which should be added Ait. Br. 3. 23.)

6 Bṛh. 1. 3. 23 [etymological explanation of *udgītha*] cf. Chānd. 1. 6. 7-8.

7 Bṛh. 1. 4. 1 *ātmaivedam agra āsīt* =c Bṛh. 1. 4. 17; Ait. 1. 1; cf. Maitri 2. 6, and see **10.**

8 Bṛh. 1. 4. 6 [food and the eater of food] cf. Maitri 6. 10.

9 Bṛh. 1. 4. 7 *sa eṣa iha praviṣṭa — viśvambharakulāye* =c Kauṣ. 4. 20.

10 Bṛh. 1. 4. 10-11 *brahma vā idam agra āsīt* = (var.) Maitri 6. 17; cf. **7.**

11 Bṛh. 1. 4. 15-16 [desires, etc.] cf. Chānd. 8. 1. 6 – 8. 2. 10. See also **457.**

12 Bṛh. 1. 4. 17 *ātmaivedam agra āsīd eka eva* see **7.**

13 Bṛh. 1. 4. 17 *mana evāsyātmā vāg jāyā* see **2.**

14 Bṛh. 1. 4. 17 *pāṅktam idaṁ sarvam — ya evaṁ veda* ≈ Tait. 1. 7.

15 Bṛh. 1. 5. 3 *manasā hy eva paśyati — mana eva* = Maitri 6. 30.

16 Bṛh. 1. 5. 14-15 *ṣoḍaśakalas* see **501.** On the wheel analogy in 1. 5. 15 see **434, 522.**

17 Bṛh. 1. 5. 17-20 [Transmission ceremony] see **313.**

18 Bṛh. 1. 5. 23 *yataś codeti — gacchati* [AV. 10. 18. 16 a-b] = Kaṭha 4. 9 a-b. *sa evādya sa u śva[s]* = Kaṭha 4. 13d.

19 Bṛh. 1. 6. 1 *nāma rūpaṁ karma* cf. MBh. 12. 233. 25 (C. 8535).

20 Bṛh. 2. 1. 1-19 [dialogue of Gārgya and Ajātaśatru] ≈ Kauṣ. 4. 1-19. Cf. Bṛh. 3. 9. 10-17.

21 Bṛh. 2. 1. 5 *pūrṇam apravarti* = Chānd. 3. 12. 9; Kauṣ. 4. 8.

22 Bṛh. 2. 1. 15 [Kṣatriya instructing Brahman] cf. Chānd. 5. 3. 5, 7; Kauṣ. 4. 19; and the implication in Chānd. 1. 8. 2.

23 Bṛh. 2. 1. 17 [ether within the heart] see **265.**

24 Bṛh. 2. 1. 19 *yadā suṣupto bhavati . . . tābhiḥ pratyavasṛpya* cf. Chānd. 8. 6. 3; Kauṣ. 4. 19.

25 Bṛh. 2. 1. 19 *hitā nāma nāḍyo* ≈ Bṛh. 4. 3. 20; Kauṣ. 4. 19; Praśna 3. 6; cf. Yājñavalkīya Dharma-sūtras 3. 108. See **65, 70, 247.**

26 Bṛh. 2. 1. 19 *hṛdayāt purītatam abhipratiṣṭhante* ≈ Kauṣ. 4. 19.

27 Bṛh. 2. 1. 20 [spider and thread analogy for creation] cf. Muṇḍ. 1. 1. 7 a; Śvet. 6. 10 b; Brahma Up. 1. (The simile recurs in a different connection in Maitri 6. 22; Brahma Up. 1 and 4.)

28 Bṛh. 2. 1. 20 [sparks from fire as an analogy of creation] see **421.**

29 Bṛh. 2. 1. 20 *sarve prāṇāḥ — satyasya satyam* = (var.) Maitri 6. 32.

30 Bṛh. 2. 1. 20 *prāṇā vai — eṣa satyam* = Bṛh. 2. 3. 6.

31 Bṛh. 2. 2. 4 *sarvasyāttā — ya evaṁ veda* cf. Chānd. 5. 2. 1; see also Bṛh. 6. 1. 14; Chānd. 5. 18. 1.

32 Bṛh. 2. 3. 1 *dve — rūpe mūrtaṁ caivāmūrtaṁ ca* = (var.)

Maitri 6. 3; *dve — rūpe* recurs also at Maitri 6. 15; cf. *mūrtir amūrtimān* Maitri 6. 14 end, and see **498**.

33 Bṛh. 2. 3. 3, 5 [formless Brahma] cf. Muṇḍ. 2. 1. 2 a.

34 Bṛh. 2. 3. 3 [Person in the sun] see **149**.

35 Bṛh. 2. 3. 5 [person in the right eye] see **61** and cf. **177**.

36 Bṛh. 2. 3. 6 [lightning as descriptive of the divine Person] cf. Bṛh. 5. 7; Kena 29; Maitri 7. 11.

37 Bṛh. 2. 3. 6 *neti neti* see **57**.

38 Bṛh. 2. 3. 6 *prāṇā vai — eṣa satyam* = Bṛh. 2. 1. 20.

39 Bṛh. 2. 4 [dialogue of Yājñavalkya and Maitreyī] ≈ Bṛh. 4. 5.

40 Bṛh. 2. 4. 5 end [≈ 4. 5. 6 end] *ātmano . . . vijñānenedaṁ sarvaṁ viditam* see **409**.

41 Bṛh. 2. 4. 10 [= (var.) 4. 5. 11] = (var.) Maitri 6. 32; the part *ṛgvedo — vyākhyānāny* recurs also at Bṛh. 4. 1. 2; similar lists at Chānd. 7. 1. 2, 4; 7. 2. 1; 7. 7. 1; Maitri 6. 33; cf. also Muṇḍ. 1. 1. 5.

42 Bṛh. 2. 4. 12 [simile of the solution of salt] see **210**.

43 Bṛh. 2. 4. 12 *na pretya saṁjñā 'sti* cf. MBh. 12. 219. 2 a-b (C. 7931).

44 Bṛh. 2. 4. 14 [duality involved in cognition] = Bṛh. 4. 5. 15 ≈ 4. 3. 31; cf. Maitri 6. 7.

45 Bṛh. 2. 5. 15 *yathā rathanābhau — samarpitā* ≈ Chānd. 7. 15. 1; see **434**.

46 Bṛh. 2. 5. 19 *rūpaṁ — babhūva* = Kaṭha 5. 9 b; 5. 10b. *indro — īyate* ≈ Bāṣkalamantra Up. 11 b.

47 Bṛh. 2. 6 [Line of Tradition, *vaṁśa*] ≈ Bṛh. 4. 6; cf. 6. 5. The course of doctrinal transmission is traced also at Bṛh. 6. 3. 6-12; Chānd. 3. 11. 4 ≈ 8. 15; Muṇḍ. 1. 1. 1-2; BhG. 4. 1-2. (For a discussion of the Bṛh. lists see D. pp. 376–378.)

48 Bṛh. 3. 2. 13 *puṇyo vai puṇyena pāpena* = (var.) Bṛh. 4. 4. 5.

49 Bṛh. 3. 5. 1 *putraiṣaṇāyāś ca — eṣaṇe eva bhavatas* ≈ Bṛh. 4. 4. 22.

50 Bṛh. 3. 6 *idaṁ sarvam . . . otaṁ ca protaṁ ca* = (var.) Maitri 6. 3; cf. Bṛh. 3. 8; Muṇḍ. 2. 2. 5 b; Maitri 7. 7. On water as a primal substance see **112**.

51 Bṛh. 3. 6 [gradation of worlds] cf. Kauṣ. 1. 3.

52 Bṛh. 3. 7 *eṣa — antaryāmī* cf. Māṇḍ. 6.

53 Bṛh. 3. 8. 8-9 [characterization of the Imperishable] cf. Muṇḍ. 1. 1. 6-7 and see **412**.

54 Bṛh. 3. 9. 1-9, 18, 26 end [dialogue of Yājñavalkya and Śākalya] ≃ Śat. Br. 11. 6. 3. 4-11 (cf. D. pp. 448-449); Jaiminīya Br. 2. 76-77 (Oertel, *JAOS*. 15. 238-240).

55 Bṛh. M 3. 9. 3 [Vasus] *vāsayante* cf. Chānd. 3. 16. 1.

56 Bṛh. 3. 9. 4 [Rudras] *rodayanti* cf. Chānd. 3. 16. 3.

57 Bṛh. 3. 9. 26 *sa eṣa neti nety — na riṣyati* = Bṛh. 4. 2. 4; 4. 4. 22; 4. 5. 15; *neti neti* recurs also at Bṛh. 2. 3. 6.

58 Bṛh. 3. 9. 28, stanzas 4-5 [man cut down like a tree] cf. MBh. 12. 186. 14 (C. 6896).

59 Bṛh. 4. 1. 2 [literature-list] see **41**.

60 Bṛh. 4. 2. 2 . . . *santam indra ity — devāḥ* = Ait. 3. 14 ≃ Śat. Br. 6. 1. 1. 2 (cf. 11). Cf. Ait. Br. 3. 33; 7. 30.

61 Bṛh. 4. 2. 2-3 [Indha (Indra) and Virāj] cf. Maitri 7. 11, stanzas 1-3, and the allusion in Tait. 6; the 'person in the right eye' is referred to also at Bṛh. 2. 3. 5; 5. 5. 2; Kauṣ. 4. 17; cf. **177**.

62 Bṛh. 4. 2. 3 [ether within the heart] see **265**.

63 Bṛh. 4. 2. 3 *ya eṣo 'ntar hṛdaye lohitapiṇḍo* ≃ Maitri 7. 11, stanza 2, c.

64 Bṛh. 4. 2. 3 *yaiṣā hṛdayād ūrdhvā nāḍy uccarati* cf. Chānd. 8. 6. 6 = Kaṭha 6. 16; Praśna 3. 7; Maitri 6. 21; 6. 30; 7. 11, stanza 3.

65 Bṛh. 4. 2. 3 *yathā keśaḥ sahasradhā bhinna[s]* = Bṛh. 4. 3. 20 ≃ Kauṣ. 4. 19.

66 Bṛh. 4. 2. 3 *hitā nāma nāḍyo* see **25**.

67 Bṛh. 4. 2. 4 *sa eṣa neti nety* see **57**.

67a Bṛh. 4. 3. 7 *yo 'yaṁ . . . hṛdy antar jyotiḥ puruṣaḥ* see **452**.

68 Bṛh. 4. 3. 16 *sa vā eṣa — buddhāntāyaiva* = Bṛh. 4. 3. 34.

69 Bṛh. 4. 3. 19 *yatra supto — paśyati* = Māṇḍ. 5.

70 Bṛh. 4. 3. 20 *hitā nāma nāḍyo — tiṣṭhanti* see **25**, **65**.

71 Bṛh. 4. 3. 20 *śuklasya nīlasya — pūrṇā* ≃ Bṛh. 4. 4. 9 a-b; Kauṣ. 4. 19; Maitri 6. 30.

72 Bṛh. 4. 3. 20 [dream experiences] cf. Chānd. 8. 10; Praśna 4. 5.

73 Bṛh. 4. 3. 22 [ethical distinctions superseded] cf. Kauṣ. 3. 1.

74 Bṛh. 4. 3. 31 [duality involved in cognition] see **44**.

75 Bṛh. 4. 3. 33 [gradation of blisses] ⩦ Tait. 2. 8. [⩦ Śat. Br. 14. 7. 1. 31-39 = Bṛh. **M** 4. 3. 31-39]. Cf. the gradation of worlds, **51**.

76 Bṛh. 4. 3. 34 recurs entire in Bṛh. 4. 3. 16.

77 Bṛh. 4. 4. 2 [unification of the functions at death] see **320**.

78 Bṛh. 4. 4. 2 *ātmā niṣkramati — mūrdhno vā* cf. Tait. 1. 6. 1; note also Ait. 3. 12 (*sīman*); see **249**.

79 Bṛh. 4. 4. 4 [analogy of the transformation of gold] cf. Maitri 3. 3.

80 Bṛh. 4. 4. 5 *puṇyaḥ puṇyena — pāpena* = (var.) Bṛh. 3. 2. 13.

81 Bṛh. 4. 4. 6 [he who desires and he who is free from desire] cf. Muṇḍ. 3. 2. 2.

82 Bṛh. 4. 4. 6 [acts determine one's reincarnate status] see **192**.

83 Bṛh. 4. 4. 7 *yadā sarve pramucyante* [stanza] = Kaṭha 6. 14.

84 Bṛh. 4. 4. 8-9 *aṇuḥ panthā . . . eṣa panthā* cf. Chānd. 8. 6. 2 and see **249**.

85 Bṛh. 4. 4. 9 *tasmiñ chuklam — lohitaṁ ca* see **71**.

86 Bṛh. 4. 4. 10 = Īśā 9. Bṛh. **M** 4. 4. 10 = Īśā 12.

87 Bṛh. 4. 4. 11 = (var.) Īśā 3; pāda a recurs also as Kaṭha 1. 3 c.

88 Bṛh. 4. 4. 14 b = (var.) Kena 13 b.

89 Bṛh. 4. 4. 14 c-d = Śvet. 3. 10 c-d. On pāda c see also **541**.

90 Bṛh. 4. 4. 15 c-d see **369**.

91 Bṛh. 4. 4. 16 c *jyotiṣāṁ jyotir* cf. Muṇḍ. 2. 2. 9 c.

92 Bṛh. 4. 4. 18 a-c ⩦ Kena 2 a-c; see **333**.

93 Bṛh. 4. 4. 19 = (var.) Kaṭha 4. 11 a-b; 4. 10 c-d.

94 Bṛh. 4. 4. 21 [stanza] cf. Muṇḍ. 2. 2. 5 c-d.

95 Bṛh. 4. 4. 22 [ether within the heart] see **265**.

96 Bṛh. 4. 4. 22 *sarvasyeśānaḥ sarvasyādhipatiḥ* = Bṛh. 5. 6. Cf. *viśvādhipo* Śvet. 3. 4 b, and see **98**.

97 Bṛh. 4. 4. 22 *na sādhunā — kanīyān* = Kauṣ. 3. 8. Cf. Maitri 2. 7.

98 Bṛh. 4. 4. 22 *eṣa sarveśvara — setur vidharaṇa* = (var.) Maitri 7. 7. The phrase *eṣa sarveśvara* recurs Māṇḍ. 6. *eṣa setur vidharaṇa — asambhedāya* ≃ Chānd. 8. 4. 1; cf. Muṇḍ. 2. 2. 5 d; Śvet. 6. 19 c. See **96**.

99 Bṛh. 4. 4. 22 *putraiṣaṇāyāś ca — bhavatas* ≃ Bṛh. 3. 5. 1.

100 Bṛh. 4. 4. 22 *sa eṣa neti nety* see **57**.

101 Bṛh. 4. 4. 22 end [moral self-judgment escaped by the 'knower'] cf. Tait. 2. 9; see also Chānd. 4. 14. 3. On cessation of karma see **449**.

102 Bṛh. 4. 5 [dialogue of Yājñavalkya and Maitreyī] ≃ Bṛh. 2. 4.

103 Bṛh. 4. 5. 6 end [≃ 2. 4. 5 end] *ātmani . . . vijñāta idaṁ sarvaṁ viditam* see **409**.

104 Bṛh. 4. 5. 11 [literature-list] see **41**.

105 Bṛh. 4. 5. 13 *prajñānaghana eva* = Māṇḍ. 5. On the reference to salt see **210**.

106 Bṛh. 4. 5. 15 [duality involved in cognition] = Bṛh. 2. 4. 14 ≃ 4. 3. 31; cf. Maitri 6. 7.

107 Bṛh. 4. 5. 15 *sa eṣa neti nety* see **57**.

108 Bṛh. 4. 6 [Line of Tradition, *vaṁśa*] ≃ Bṛh. 2. 6; see **47**.

109 Bṛh. 5. 1 *pūrṇam — pūrṇam evāvaśiṣyate* [stanza ≃ AV. 10. 8. 29] ≃ MBh. 5. 46. 10 (C. 1755).

109a Bṛh. 5. 2 cf. Śat. Br. 2. 4. 2. 1-6.

110 Bṛh. 5. 4 *tad vai tad* cf. *etad vai tat* Kaṭha 4. 3, 5, etc.

111 Bṛh. 5. 4 *satyaṁ brahma* cf. Chānd. 8. 3. 4.

112 Bṛh. 5. 5. 1 [creation from water] cf. Ait. 1. 1-3; Kaṭha 4. 6. On water as a primal substance cf. also Bṛh. 3. 6; Chānd. 7. 10.

113 Bṛh. 5. 5. 1 *tad etat tryakṣaraṁ satyam iti* ≃ Chānd. 8. 3. 5.

114 Bṛh. 5. 5. 2 [person in the right eye] see **60** and cf. **177**.

115 Bṛh. 5. 6 the thought and similes recur at Chānd. 3. 14. 2-3; see **165**. On *sarvasyeśānaḥ sarvasyādhipatiḥ* see **96**.

116 Bṛh. 5. 7 [Brahma as lightning] cf. Bṛh. 2. 3. 6; Kena 29; Maitri 7. 11.

117 Bṛh. 5. 9 [universal fire] = Maitri 2. 6. On the digestive fire cf. Maitri 6. 17; on the bodily heat and the sound heard on stopping the ears cf. Chānd. 3. 13. 8; Maitri 6. 22.

118 Bṛh. 5. 10 [course of the soul after death] = Śat. Br. 14. 8. 12; cf. in general **127, 128**.

119 Bṛh. 5. 13. 1 *ukthaṁ prāṇo — utthāpayaty* ≈ Kauṣ. 3. 3.

120 Bṛh. 5. 14. 1-7 [Gāyatrī meter] see **159**. On *turīya* (3, 4, 6, 7) see **519**.

121 Bṛh. 5. 14. 4-5 [Sāvitrī stanza] see **130**. The passage *cakṣur vai satyaṁ — śraddadhyāma* is found also at Śatapatha Brāhmaṇa 1. 3. 1. 27.

122 Bṛh. 5. 15 = Īśā 15-18. The stanza *hiraṇmayena pātreṇa* etc. = (var.) Maitri 6. 35. With the 'golden vessel' cf. Muṇḍ. 2. 2. 9 a.

123 Bṛh. 6. 1. 1-5 ≈ Chānd. 5. 1. 1-5.

124 Bṛh. 6. 1. 7-14 [rivalry of the functions and superiority of breath] ≈ Chānd. 5. 1. 6 – 5. 2. 2; Kauṣ. 2. 14 (9); cf. also Bṛh. 1. 3. 1-19; Chānd. 1. 2. 1-9; Kauṣ. 3. 2-3; Praśna 2. 2-4; see also MBh. 14. 23. 6-22 (C. 689–708). Cf. the somewhat similar story at Ait. 3. 1-10.

125 Bṛh. 6. 2. 1-16 [*pañcāgnividyā* and the course of the soul in incarnations] ≈ Chānd. 5. 3-10. (D. pp. 137–139 has an extended discussion and tabular comparison of these parallels, incl. also Bṛh. **M** [Śat. Br. 14. 9. 1. 12-16]; see also D. pp. 132–133.)

126 Bṛh. 6. 2. 2 [worlds reached after death] cf. Bṛh. 1. 5. 16; Muṇḍ. 2. 1. 6 c-d.

127 Bṛh. 6. 2. 15 [course to the Brahma-world] ≈ Chānd 4. 15. 5-6; 5. 10. 1-2; cf. Muṇḍ. 1. 2. 5, 6, 11; 3. 1. 6; Praśna 1. 10; Maitri 6. 30 end; BhG. 8. 24, 26. See also Bṛh. 5. 10.

128 Bṛh. 6. 2. 16 [course to the lunar world and to rebirth] ≈ Chānd. 5. 10. 3-6; cf. Praśna 1. 9; Muṇḍ. 1. 2. 7-10; BhG. 8. 25, 26. See also Bṛh. 5. 10.

129 Bṛh. 6. 3. 2 [oblations in incantation ceremony] ≈ Chānd. 5. 2. 4-9; cf. Kauṣ. 2. 3 (2).

130 Bṛh. 6. 3. 6 [Sāvitrī stanza] quoted also at Śvet. 4. 18 c; Maitri 6. 7; 6. 34. Cf. Bṛh. 5. 14. 4-5; Chānd. 3. 12.
131 Bṛh. 6. 3. 6-12 [Line of Tradition, *vaṁśa*] see **47**.
132 Bṛh. 6. 3. 12 [reviving of a dried stump] ≎ Chānd. 5. 2. 3.
133 Bṛh. 6. 3. 12 [restrictions on imparting occult knowledge] cf. Chānd. 3. 11. 5-6; Muṇḍ. 3. 2. 10-11; Śvet. 6. 22; Maitri 6. 29; BhG. 18. 67.
134 Bṛh. 6. 4. 1 *eṣāṁ vai bhūtānāṁ — oṣadhaya* = (var.) Chānd. 1. 1. 2.
135 Bṛh. 6. 4. 3 *lomāni barhiś* = Chānd. 5. 18. 2.
136 Bṛh. 6. 4. 9 *aṅgād aṅgāt — adhijāyase* [2 lines] = Kauṣ. 2. 11 (7).
137 Bṛh. 6. 4. 12 [deprivation of an offender] cf. Kaṭha 1. 8.
138 Bṛh. 6. 4. 20 [*ama* and *sā*] see **5**.
139 Bṛh. **M** 6. 4. 26 *aśmā bhava* [stanza] = (var.) Kauṣ. 2. 11 (7).
140 Bṛh. 6. 5 [Line of Tradition, *vaṁśa*] see **47**.

Chāndogya Upanishad

141 Chānd. 1. 1. 1 = Chānd. 1. 4. 1.
142 Chānd. 1. 1. 2 *eṣām bhūtānāṁ — oṣadhayo rasa* = (var.) Bṛh. 6. 4. 1.
143 Chānd. 1. 1. 8-9 [the syllable *Om*] ≎ Tait. 1. 8. Cf. **726**, **818**.
144 Chānd. 1. 2 [contest of gods and devils] see **4**.
145 Chānd. 1. 3. 3 [explanation of *vyāna*] cf. Maitri 2. 6.
146 Chānd. 1. 4. 1 = Chānd. 1. 1. 1.
147 Chānd. 1. 5. 1 *atha khalu — eṣa praṇava* = Maitri 6. 4.
148 Chānd. 1. 6. 1 [*sā* + *ama* = *sāma(n)*] see **5**.
149 Chānd. 1. 6. 6 *atha ya eṣo — puruṣo* = Maitri 6. 1; Mahānār. 13 (Ātharv. rec. 12. 2). On the 'golden Person in the sun' see also Bṛh. 2. 3. 3; Maitri 6. 35.
150 Chānd. 1. 6. 7-8 [etymological explanation of *udgītha*] cf. Bṛh. 1. 3. 23.

151 Chānd. 1. 7. 5 *ya eṣo 'ntar akṣiṇi puruṣo dṛśyate* see **177**.

152 Chānd. 1. 8. 2 *brāhmaṇayor vadator* see **22**.

153 Chānd. 2. 21. 1 [Agni, Vāyu, Āditya] cf. the similar collocation at Chānd. 3. 15. 6; Maitri 4. 5; 6. 35; note also Chānd. 2. 24. 5, 9, 14.

154 Chānd. 2. 23. 2 (3) [Prajāpati produced *bhūr, bhuvaḥ. svar*] see **180**.

155 Chānd. 3. 1. 2 [nectar in the sun] cf. Tait. 1. 10; Maitri 6. 35.

156 Chānd. 3. 11. 1-3 [perpetual illumination in the Brahma-world] cf. Chānd. 8. 4. 1–2; Śvet. 4. 18 a; Maitri 6. 24; and see **387**.

157 Chānd. 3. 11. 4 [Line of Tradition] ⩳ Chānd. 8. 15; see **47**.

158 Chānd. 3. 11. 5-6 [restrictions on imparting occult knowledge] see **133**.

159 Chānd. 3. 12 [Gāyatrī meter] cf. Bṛh. 5. 14. 1-7; see also BhG. 10. 35 b.

160 Chānd. 3. 12. 7 [space as Brahma] cf. Chānd. 3. 18. 1.

161 Chānd. 3. 12. 9 *pūrṇam apravarti* = Bṛh. 2. 1. 5.

162 Chānd. 3. 13. 8 [bodily heat; the sound heard on stopping the ears] see **117**.

163 Chānd. 3. 14. 1 *sarvaṁ khalv idaṁ brahma* = (var., Maitri 4. 6.

164 Chānd. 3. 14. 1 [purpose determines state after death] see **786**.

165 Chānd. 3. 14. 2-3 the thought and some of the words recur at Bṛh. 5. 6; cf. Maitri 7. 7 init.; Muṇḍ. 3. 1. 7 a-b; Śvet. 3. 20a-b; 4. 14a. *manomayaḥ — ākāśātmā* = Maitri 2. 6. With *manomayah prāṇaśarīro* cf. Muṇḍ. 2. 2. 7 e. On the epithet *ākāśātman* see **656**.

166 Chānd. 3. 14. 4 [all doubts cleared away] cf. Muṇḍ. 2. 2. 8 b.

167 Chānd. 3. 15. 6 [Agni, Vāyu, Āditya] see **153**.

168 Chānd. 3. 16 [analogy of man's life and the sacrifice] ⩳ Jaiminīya Up. Br. 4. 2. 1 (Oertel, *JAOS*. 15. 245–6).

169 Chānd. 3. 16. 1 [Vasus] *vāsayanti* cf. Bṛh. **M** 3. 9. 3.

170 Chānd. 3. 16. 3 [Rudras] *rodayanti* cf. Bṛh. 3. 9. 4.

171 Chānd. 3. 19. 1 *ādityo brahmety* = Maitri 6. 16.

172 Chānd. 3. 19. 1 [primordial Non-being] ≈ Chānd. 6. 2. 1; Tait. 2. 7.

173 Chānd. 3. 19. 1 [the cosmic egg] cf. Maitri 6. 36, stanza; cf. also MBh. 12. 311. 3-4 (C. 11571–2); Bāṣkalamantra Up. 9; and see Hopkins, *Great Epic of India*, p. 187.

173 a Chānd. 4. 1. 4 = 4. 1. 6 On dice cf. 4. 3. 8.

174 Chānd. 4. 3. 1-7 ≈ Jaiminīya Up. Br. 3. 1. 1-2 (Oertel, *JAOS*. 15. 249-251).

175 Chānd. 4. 4. 5 [bringing of fuel as sign of pupilship] cf. Chānd. 5. 11. 7; 8. 7. 2; etc.; Kauṣ. 1. 1; 4. 19; Muṇḍ. 1. 2. 13; Praśna 1. 1.

176 Chānd. 4. 14. 3 [evil adheres not to the 'knower'] cf. Bṛh. 4. 4. 22 end; Tait. 2. 9; Īśā 2 d; see also **449**. On the simile of water and lotus-leaf see **607**.

177 Chānd. 4. 15. 1 *ya eṣo 'kṣiṇi puruṣo — brahmeti* = Chānd. 8. 7. 4; cf. 1. 7. 5; see also **35**, **60**. The part *eṣa ātmeti — brahmeti* = Chānd. 8. 3. 4; 8. 8. 3; 8. 10. 1; 8. 11. 1; Maitri 2. 2.

178 Chānd. 4. 15. 5-6 [course to the Brahma-world] see **127**.

179 Chānd. 4. 16 [silence of the Brahman priest at the sacrifice] ≈ Jaiminīya Up. Br. 3. 4. 2 (Oertel, *JAOS*. 15. 247–248).

180 Chānd. 4. 17. 1-3 [Prajāpati produced *bhūr*, *bhuvaḥ*, *svar*] ≈ Chānd. 2. 23. 2 (3); cf. Maitri 6. 6. For a series of parallels to 4. 17 (entire) see Oertel, 'Contributions from the Jāiminīya Brāhmaṇa', *Trans. of the Connecticut Acad. of Arts and Sciences*, 15 (1909), pp. 155–162.

181 Chānd. 5. 1. 1-5 ≈ Bṛh. 6. 1. 1-5. (For discussion of this parallel see D. pp. 132–133.)

182 Chānd. 5. 1. 6 – 5. 2. 2 [rivalry of the functions] see **124**.

183 Chānd. 5. 2. 1 *na ha vā evaṁvidi — bhavatīti* see **31**.

184 Chānd. 5. 2. 2 *purastāc — adbhiḥ paridadhati* ≈ Maitri 6. 9.

185 Chānd. 5. 2. 3 [reviving of a dried stump] ⩦ Bṛh. 6. 3. 12.

186 Chānd. 5. 2. 4-9 [oblations in incantation ceremony] see **129**.

187 Chānd. 5. 2. 6 *amo nāmāsy* see **5**.

188 Chānd. 5. 3-10 [*pañcāgnividyā* and the course of the soul in incarnations] see **125**. Sections 4-10 are apparently alluded to in Muṇḍ.; see **426**.

189 Chānd. 5. 3. 5, 7 [Kṣatriya instructing Brahman] see **22**.

190 Chānd. 5. 3. 5 *yathāham eṣāṁ — nāvakṣyam* ⩦ Praśna 6. 1.

191 Chānd. 5. 10. 1-6 [course to the Brahma-world and to the lunar world] see **127**, **128**. With 5. 10. 4-6 cf. Muṇḍ. 2. 1. 5 b-d; see **426**.

192 Chānd. 5. 10. 7 [thoughts and acts determine one's reincarnate status] cf. Bṛh. 4. 4. 6; Kauṣ. 1. 2; Kaṭha 3. 7-8; 5. 7; Praśna 3. 3 [see **481**]; 3. 7; Śvet. 5. 7, 12; Maitri 3. 2; 6. 34, stanzas 3-4. Cf. also Manusmṛti 12. 55; Yājñavalkīya Dharma-sūtras 3. 207; MBh. 14. 36. 30-31 (C. 1016-7); and see in general **236**, **786**.

193 Chānd. 5. 10. 9 a-b cf. MBh. 14. 51. 18 (C. 1442).

194 Chānd. 5. 11. 1-2 cf. the similar introduction Praśna 1. 1.

195 Chānd. 5. 11. 7 [bringing of fuel] see **175**.

196 Chānd. 5. 18. 1 *sarveṣu lokeṣu — annam atti* see **31**.

197 Chānd. 5. 18. 2 *lomāni barhir* = Bṛh. 6. 4. 3.

198 Chānd. 5. 19-23 ['Hail!' to *prāṇa*, *apāna*, etc.] cf. Maitri 6. 9.

199 Chānd. 5. 24. 3 [simile of the reed laid on a fire] cf. MBh. 13. 26. 42 (C. 1800).

200 Chānd. 6. 1. 3 *yena — avijñātaṁ vijñātam* see **409**.

201 Chānd. 6. 2. 1 [primordial Non-being] ⩦ Chānd. 3. 19. 1; Tait. 2. 7.

202 Chānd. 6. 2. 3-4 *bahu syāṁ prajāyeyeti* = Tait. 2. 6. Cf. Bṛh. 1. 2. 4; 1. 4. 3.

203 Chānd. 6. 3. 1 *trīṇy eva bījāni — udbhijjam* see **298**.

204 Chānd. 6. 4. 5 cf. Muṇḍ. 1. 1. 3; see 409.

205 Chānd. 6. 5. 1 *tasya yaḥ sthaviṣṭho dhātus* cf. Maitri 2. 6.

206 Chānd. 6. 7 [a person consists of sixteen parts] see **501**.

207 Chānd. 6. 8. 6 *tad uktaṁ purastād* namely at 6. 4. 7 — 6. 5. 4.

208 Chānd. 6. 8. 6 *vāṅ manasi — devatāyām* = Chānd. 6. 15. 2; cf. Prasna 3. 9-10.

209 Chānd. 6. 9. 1 [unified condition of honey] cf. Maitri 6. 22.

210 Chānd. 6. 13 [solution of salt in water] cf. Bṛh. 2. 4. 12; Maitri 6. 35; 7. 11. (The allusion to salt in Bṛh. 4. 5. 13 is apparently a modified form of Bṛh. 2. 4. 12; see D. p. 481.)

211 Chānd. 6. 15. 1 [consciousness of a dying person] ≈ Chānd. 8. 6. 4.

212 Chānd. 6. 15. 1-2 [unification of the functions at death] see **320**.

213 Chānd. 6. 15. 2 *vāṅ manasi — devatāyām* see **208**.

214 Chānd. 7. 1. 1 *adhīhi bhagavo* cf. Tait. 3. 1.

215 Chānd. 7. 1. 2, 4 [literature-list] see **41**.

216 Chānd. 7. 1. 3 [ignorance of Ātman confessed] cf. Maitri 1. 2.

217 Chānd. 7. 1. 3 *tarati śokam ātmavid* ≈ Muṇḍ. 3. 2. 9.

218 Chānd. 7. 2. 1 = (var.) Chānd. 7. 7. 1. See also **41**.

219 Chānd. 7. 9. 1 *yady api — vijñātā bhavati* = (var.) Maitri 6. 11.

220 Chānd. 7. 10 [water as a primal substance] see **112**.

221 Chānd. 7. 15. 1 *yathā vā arā nābhau samarpitā* ≈ Bṛh. 2. 5. 15; see **434**.

222 Chānd. 7. 16-23 *vijijñāsitavya* see **638**.

223 Chānd. 7. 24. 1 *sve mahimni* see **590**.

224 Chānd. 7. 25. 1-2 cf. Muṇḍ. 2. 2. 11.

225 Chānd. 7. 25. 2 *ātmaratir ātmakrīḍa* ≈ Muṇḍ. 3. 1. 4c.

226 Chānd. 7. 26. 2 *na paśyo* [stanza] = (var.) Maitri 7. 11, stanza 6.

227 Chānd. 7. 26. 2 [the Ātman manifold] cf. Maitri 5. 2, 6. 26 end.

228 Chānd. 7. 26. 2 [a pure nature requisite for mystic attainment] cf. Muṇ. 3. 1. 8 c-d.

229 Chānd. 7. 26. 2 [liberation from all knots (of the heart)] see **396**.

230 Chānd. 7. 26. 2 *tamasas pāraṁ* see **787**.

231 Chānd. 8. 1. 1-5 [Brahma-city, abode] cf. Kaṭha 2. 13 d; Muṇḍ. 2. 2. 7 c; 3. 2. 1 a-b, 4 d; see also **543**. On the 'ether within the heart' see **265**.

232 Chānd. 8. 1. 1 *tad anveṣṭavyaṁ tad vāva vijijñāsitavyam* see **638**.

233 Chānd. 8. 1. 5 *na vadhenāsya hanyate* = Chānd. 8. 10. 2; 8. 10. 4; cf. Kaṭha 2. 18 d = BhG. 2. 20 d.

234 Chānd. 8. 1. 5 *asmin kāmāḥ samāhitā* = (var.) Maitri 6. 30, 35, 38.

235 Chānd. 8. 1. 5 *eṣa ātmā — satyasaṁkalpo* = Chānd. 8. 7. 1; 8. 7. 3; (var.) Maitri 7. 7. The epithets *vijara vimṛtyu viśoka* recur also at Maitri 6. 25; 7. 5.

236 Chānd. 8. 2 [creative power of desire] cf. Muṇḍ. 3. 1. 10. Cf. in general **81**, **786**.

237 Chānd. 8. 3. 4 *eṣa samprasādo — etad brahmeti* = Maitri 2. 2. As far as *rūpeṇābhiniṣpadyate* the passage recurs also at Chānd. 8. 12. 3. See also **177**.

238 Chānd. 8. 3. 4 *etasya brahmaṇo nāma satyam* cf. Bṛh. 5. 4.

239 Chānd. 8. 3. 5 *trīṇy akṣarāṇi satīyam iti* ≈ Bṛh. 5. 5. 1.

240 Chānd. 8. 4. 1 *sa setur vidhṛtir — asambhedāya* see **98**.

241 Chānd. 8. 4. 1-2 [endless day] see **156**.

242 Chānd. 8. 5. 3 [marvels of the Brahma-world] cf. Kauṣ. 1. 3.

243 Chānd. 8. 6. 1 *yā etā hṛdayasya nāḍyas — lohitasyeti* see **25**, **71**.

244 Chānd. 8. 6. 2 *yathā mahāpatha* cf. Bṛh. 4. 4. 8-9.

245 Chānd. 8. 6. 3 *tad yatraitatsuptaḥ — nāḍīṣu sṛpto bhavati* see **24**. *tad — svapnaṁ na vijānāty* recurs at Chānd. 8. 11. 1.

246 Chānd. 8. 6. 4 [consciousness of a dying person] ≈ Chānd. 6. 15. 1.

247 Chānd. 8. 6. 6 *śataṁ caikā ca hṛdayasya nāḍyas* = Kaṭha 6. 16 ≈ Praśna 3. 6; cf. Muṇḍ. 2. 2. 6; Maitri 6. 30 (*raśmiśatam*). See also **25**, **65**.

248 Chānd. 8. 6. 6 *tāsāṁ mūrdhānam abhiniḥsṛtaikā* see **64**.

249 Chānd. 8. 6. 6 *tayordhvam āyann amṛtatvam eti* = Kaṭha 6. 16 ; cf. Bṛh. 4. 4. 8-9 ; Praśna 3. 7 ; Maitri 6. 21 ; 6. 30 ; 7. 11, stanza 3.

250 Chānd. 8. 6. 6 *viṣvaṅṅ anyā utkramaṇe bhavanti* = Kaṭha 6. 16 ≈ Maitri 6. 30.

251 Chānd. 8. 7-8 [instruction of gods and devils] cf. Maitri 7. 10.

252 Chānd. 8. 7. 1 ; 8. 7. 3 *eṣa ātmā — satyasaṁkalpo* see **235**.

253 Chānd. 8. 7. 3 *so 'nveṣṭavyaḥ sa vijijñāsitavyaḥ* see **638**.

254 Chānd. 8. 7. 4 ; 8. 8. 3 ; 8. 10. 1 ; 8. 11. 1 *eṣa ātmeti — brahmeti* see **177**.

255 Chānd. 8. 10 [dream experiences] cf. Bṛh. 4. 3. 20 ; Praśna 4. 5.

256 Chānd. 8. 10. 2 ; 8. 10. 4 *na vadhenāsya hanyate* see **233**.

257 Chānd. 8. 11. 1 *tad — svapnaṁ na vijānāty* = Chānd. 8. 6. 3 ; see **245**.

258 Chānd. 8. 12. 3 *eṣa samprasādo — rūpeṇābhiniṣpadyate* see **237**.

259 Chānd. 8. 12. 4 [the soul as agent in the senses] see **333**.

260 Chānd. 8. 13 *vidhūya pāpaṁ* see **449**.

261 Chānd. 8. 13 *akṛtaṁ . . . brahmalokam* cf. *akṛtaḥ* [*lokaḥ*] Muṇḍ. 1. 2. 12 b.

262 Chānd. 8. 15 [Line of Tradition] ≈ Chānd. 3. 11. 4 ; see **47**.

263 Chānd. 8. 15 [conditions of attainment] **see 526.**

Taittirīya Upanishad

264 Tait. 1. 1 ≈ Tait. 1. 12.

265 Tait. 1. 6. 1 *sa ya eṣo 'ntar hṛdaya ākāśaḥ tasminn ayaṁ puruṣo manomayaḥ* cf. Muṇḍ. 2. 2. 6 ; Maitri 6. 30 ; 7. 11, stanza 2. For the 'ether within the heart' see Bṛh. 2. 1. 17 ; 4. 2. 3 ; 4. 4. 22 ; Chānd. 8. 1. 1-3 ; Maitri 6. 22, 27, 28.

266 Tait. 1. 6. 1 *antareṇa tāluke — sendrayoniḥ* cf. *tālvantarvicchinnā* Maitri 6. 21.

267 Tait. 1. 6. 1 *yatrāsau keśānto — śīrṣakapāle* see **78**.

268 Tait. 1. 7 *pāṅktam idaṁ sarvam — ya evaṁ veda* ⇌ Bṛh. 1. 4. 17.

269 Tait. 1. 8 [the syllable *Om*] ⇌ Chānd. 1. 1. 8-9. Cf. **726**, **818**.

270 Tait. 1. 10 [nectar in the sun] cf. Chānd. 3. 1. 2; Maitri 6. 35.

271 Tait. 1. 12 ⇌ Tait. 1. 1.

272 Tait. 2. 2 a-d *annād vai — antataḥ* = Maitri 6. 11. See esp. **728**.

273 Tait. 2. 2 k-n *annād bhūtāni — ucyate* = Maitri 6. 12. See esp. **728**.

274 Tait. 2. 2-5 *annarasamaya* etc. see **649**.

275 Tait. 2. 4 *yato vāco* [stanza] = (var.) Tait. 2. 9.

276 Tait. 2. 4 *ātmā vijñānamayaḥ* cf. Muṇḍ. 3. 2. 7 c; also Praśna 4. 9 (*vijñānātman*).

277 Tait. 2. 5 *ātmā "nandamayaḥ* cf. Tait. 2. 8 end; 3. 10. 5; Māṇḍ. 5.

278 Tait. 2. 6 *bahu syāṁ prajāyeyeti* see **202**.

279 Tait. 2. 7 [primordial Non-being] ⇌ Chānd. 3. 19. 1; 6. 2. 1.

280 Tait. 2. 7 *tat sukṛtam ucyate* cf. Ait. 2. 3.

281 Tait. 2. 8 *bhīṣā 'smād* [stanza] ⇌ Kaṭha 6. 3.

282 Tait. 2. 8 [gradation of blisses] see **75**.

283 Tait. 2. 8 *sa yaś cāyaṁ puruṣe — ānandamayam ātmānam upasaṁkrāmati* ⇌ Tait. 3. 10. 4-5. See also **277**.

284 Tait. 2. 9 *yato vāco* [stanza] = (var.) Tait. 2. 4.

285 Tait. 2. 9 [moral self-judgment escaped by the 'knower'] see **101**.

286 Tait. 3. 1 *adhīhi bhagavo brahma* (5 times) cf. Chānd. 7. 1. 1.

287 Tait. 3. 1 [creation and reabsorption of beings] see **532**.

288 Tait. 3. 10. 4 [*brahmaṇaḥ parimara*] ⇌ Ait. Br. 8. 28, where this incantation is described. Cf. the *daiva parimara* of Kauṣ. 2. 12 (8).

289 Tait. 3. 10. 4-5 *sa yaś cāyaṁ puruṣe* etc. see **283**.

Aitareya Upanishad

290 Ait. 1. 1 *ātmā vā idam eka evāgra* see **7.**

291 Ait. 1. 2-3 [creation from water] see **112.**

292 Ait. 2. 3 *puruṣo vāva sukṛtam* cf. Tait. 2. 7 d.

293 Ait. 3. 1-10 [efforts of various bodily functions] see **124.**

294 Ait. 3. 12 *etam eva sīmānaṁ* cf. **78.**

295 Ait. 3. 14 . . . *santam indra ity — devāḥ* see **60.**

296 Ait. 4. 6 ⟺ Ait. 5. 4.

297 Ait. 5. 2 *prajñānaṁ . . . dhṛtir . . . smṛtiḥ* cf. Maitri 6. 31.

298 Ait. 5. 3 *bījānītarāṇi — codbhijjāni* cf. Chānd. 6. 3. 1; see also Manusmṛti 1. 43-46; MBh. 12. 312. 5 (C. 11594); 14. 42. 33 (C. 1134).

Kaushītaki Upanishad [1]

299 Kauṣ. 1. 1 [bringing of fuel] see **175.**

300 Kauṣ. 1. 2 *yathākarma yathāvidyaṁ* cf. *yathākarma yathāśrutam* Kaṭha 5. 7 d. On the dependence of one's reincarnate status on past acts see **192.**

301 Kauṣ. 1. 3 [gradation of worlds] cf. Bṛh. 3. 6.

302 Kauṣ. 1. 3 [marvels of the Brahma-world] cf. Chānd. 8. 5. 3.

303 Kauṣ. 1. 4 [looking down on chariot-wheels] cf. Maitri 6. 28 end.

304 Kauṣ. 1. 7 (6) [series of terms: *prāṇa, vāc,* etc.] cf. Kauṣ. 2. 15 (10).

305 Kauṣ. 2. 1 *tasmai vā etasmai — dadāma ta iti* = Kauṣ. 2. 2 (1).

306 Kauṣ. 2. 8 (5) *yat te susīmaṁ hṛdayam* [stanza] recurs in altered form at Kauṣ. 2. 10 (6).

307 Kauṣ. 2. 11 (7) *aṅgād aṅgāt — adhijāyase* [2 lines] = Bṛh. 6. 4. 9.

308 Kauṣ. 2. 11 (7) *aśmā bhava* [stanza] = (var.) Bṛh. M 6. 4. 26.

[1] Note that a translation of this Upanishad is comprised in A. Berriedale Keith's *Śāṅkhāyana Āraṇyaka*, London, 1908, pp. 16–41 (Oriental Translation Fund, new series, vol. 18).

309 Kauṣ. 2. 11 (7) *mā vyathiṣṭhāḥ* = BhG. 11. 34.

310 Kauṣ. 2. 12 (8) *daivaḥ parimara* cf. *brahmaṇaḥ parimara* Tait. 3. 10. 4.

311 Kauṣ. 2. 14 (9) [rivalry of the functions] see **124**.

312 Kauṣ. 2. 14 (9) *ākāśātmā* see **656**.

313 Kauṣ. 2. 15 (10) [Transmission ceremony] cf. Bṛh. 1. 5. 17-20. With the series of terms (*vāc*, *prāṇa*, etc.) cf. the series in Kauṣ. 1. 7 (6).

314 Kauṣ. 3. 1 [deeds of Indra] cf. Ait. Br. 7. 28; TS. 2. 5. 1.

315 Kauṣ. 3. 1 [ethical distinctions superseded] cf. Bṛh. 4. 3. 22.

316 Kauṣ. 3. 2-3 [superiority of *prāṇa*] see **124**.

317 Kauṣ. 3. 3 the latter half of this section parallels the former (though not so clearly in the recension published in the Ānandāśrama Sanskrit Series, which has omissions and additions).

318 Kauṣ. 3. 3 *uktham prāṇo — utthāpayaty* ≈ Bṛh. 5. 13. 1.

319 Kauṣ. 3. 3 [unification of the functions in sleep] ≈ Kauṣ. 4. 20; cf. Praśna 4. 2; Māṇḍ. 5 (*ekībhūtaḥ*).

320 Kauṣ. 3. 3 [unification of the functions at death] cf. Bṛh. 4. 4. 2; Chānd. 6. 15. 1-2; see also BhG. 15. 8.

321 Kauṣ. 3. 8 [spokes fixed in the hub] see **434**.

322 Kauṣ. 3. 8 *na sādhunā — kanīyān* ≐ Bṛh. 4. 4. 22. Cf. Maitri 2. 7.

323 Kauṣ. 4. 1-19 [dialogue of Gārgya and Ajātaśatru] ≈ Bṛh. 2. 1. 1-19. Cf. Bṛh. 3. 9. 10-17.

324 Kauṣ 4. 19 [bringing of fuel as sign of pupilship] see **175**.

325 Kauṣ. 4. 19 [Kṣatriya instructing Brahman] see **22**.

326 Kauṣ. 4. 19 *hitā nāma hṛdayasya nāḍyo* see **25**.

327 Kauṣ. 4. 19 *hṛdayāt purītatam abhipratanvanti* see **26**.

328 Kauṣ. 4. 19 *yathā sahasradhā keśo vipāṭitas* see **65**.

329 Kauṣ. 4. 19 *piṅgalasyāṇimnā — lohitasyeti* see **71**.

330 Kauṣ. 4. 19 *tāsu tadā bhavati — paśyaty* see **24**.

331 Kauṣ. 4. 20 (19) [unification of the functions in sleep] see **319**.

332 Kauṣ. 4. 20 *sa eṣa iha praviṣta — viśvambharakulāye* ⊂= Bṛh. 1. 4. 7.

Kena Upanishad

333 Kena 2 a-c ⊂= Bṛh. 4. 4. 18 a-c. Cf. Chānd. 8. 12. 4; Maitri 6. 31; see also Bṛh. 2. 4. 11; Kauṣ. 3. 4. Kena 2 d = 13 d.

334 Kena 3 a-b [the Supreme not to be apprehended by the senses] see **394**.

335 Kena 3 e-h = (var.) Īśā 10; see **404**.

336 Kena 13 b = (var.) Bṛh. 4. 4. 14 b. Kena 13 d = 2 d.

337 Kena 29 [lightning as suggestive of Brahma] cf. Bṛh. 2. 3. 6; 5. 7; Maitri 7. 11.

Kaṭha Upanishad[1]

338 Kaṭha 1. 1 the same story, partly in the same words, is found in Tait. Br. 3. 11. 8.

339 Kaṭha 1. 3 c = Bṛh. 4. 4. 11 a = (var.) Īśā 3 a.

340 Kaṭha 1. 7 cf. Vāsiṣṭha Dharma-śāstra 11. 13, where the words recur.

341 Kaṭha 1. 8 [deprivation of an offender] cf. Bṛh. 6. 4. 12.

342 Kaṭha 1. 12 d = Kaṭha 1. 18 d.

343 Kaṭha 1. 17 c-d = (var.) Śvet. 4. 11 c-d.

344 Kaṭha 1. 21 b-c [question declared difficult; another choice advised] cf. Maitri 1. 2.

345 Kaṭha 1. 26 [dissatisfaction with life] see **587**.

346 Kaṭha 2. 4 = (var.) Maitri 7. 9.

347 Kaṭha 2. 5 = (var.) Muṇḍ. 1. 2. 8; Maitri 7. 9.

348 Kaṭha 2. 7 cf. BhG. 2. 29.

349 Kaṭha 2. 12 b *gūḍham anupraviṣṭaṁ guhāhitaṁ* cf. Kaṭha 3. 1 b; 4. 6 c; 4. 7 c; Muṇḍ. 2. 1. 8 d; 3. 1. 7 d; Maitri 2. 6; 6. 4; Bāṣkalamantra Up. 18.

350 Kaṭha 2. 13 d *vivṛtaṁ sadma* see **231**.

351 Kaṭha 2. 15 ⊂= BhG. 8. 11.

352 Kaṭha 2. 16 = (var.) Maitri 6. 4.

[1] On parallels between Kaṭha and MBh. see Hopkins, *Great Epic of India*, pp. 29–32).

353 Kaṭha 2. 18, 19 = (var.) BhG. 2. 20, 19. On Kaṭha 2. 18 d see **757**.

354 Kaṭha 2. 20 = (var.) Śvet. 3. 20; etc. [see **544**]. On the doctrine of *prasāda* cf. also Muṇḍ. 3. 2. 3 [see **356**]; Śvet. 6. 21; and see Hopkins, *Great Epic of India*, p. 188.

355 Kaṭha 2. 22 c-d = Kaṭha 4. 4 c-d.

356 Kaṭha 2. 23 = Muṇḍ. 3. 2. 3.

357 Kaṭha 3. 1 b *guhāṁ praviṣṭau* see **349**.

358 Kaṭha 3. 1 d *pañcāgnayo ye ca trināciketāḥ* ≈ Manusmṛti 3. 185 a; cf. MBh. 13. 90. 26 c (C. 4296 a).

359 Kaṭha 3. 3-5 [the soul riding in the chariot of the body] cf. Śvet. 2. 9 c; Maitri 2. 3-4; 2. 6 end; 4. 4; see also MBh. 3. 2. 66 (C. 112); 3. 211. 23 (C. 13942); 5. 34. 59 (C. 1153); 5. 46. 5 (C. 1745); 11. 7. 13 (C. 175); 12. 240. 11 (C. 8744); 14. 51. 3 (C. 1426); Manusmṛti 2. 88; Mārkāṇḍeya Purāṇa 1. 42 (43); Böhtlingk, *Ind. Sprüche*, 1118; Chāgaleya Up., D. pp. 846–847.

360 Kaṭha 3. 4 [the soul called 'the enjoyer'] cf. Śvet. 1. 8 c, 9 b, 12 c; and esp. Maitri 6. 10.

361 Kaṭha 3. 7-9 [rebirth or release according to one's thoughts and acts] see **192**.

362 Kaṭha 3. 9 d [RV. 1. 22. 20 a] = Maitri 6. 26; also Rāmāyaṇa G. 6. 41. 25 d.

363 Kaṭha 3. 10-12 = (var.) MBh. 12. 248. 3-5 (C. 8953-5). Kaṭha 3. 10 ≈ BhG. 3. 42; cf. MBh. 12. 297. 19 c-d (C. 10919 a-b).

364 Kaṭha 3. 15 ≈ MBh. 12. 240. 17-18 (C. 8750-1).

365 Kaṭha 4. 1 a *parāñci khani vyatṛṇat* cf. *khānīmāni bhittvā* Maitri 2. 6.

366 Kaṭha 4. 3 d = Kaṭha 5. 4 d.

367 Kaṭha 4. 3; 4. 5; etc. *etad vai tat* cf. *tad vai tat* Bṛh. 5. 4.

368 Kaṭha 4. 4 c-d = Kaṭha 2. 22 c-d.

369 Kaṭha 4. 5 c-d = Kaṭha 4. 12 c-d; Bṛh. 4. 4. 15 c-d. Pāda c recurs also as Kaṭha 4. 13 c; pāda d as Īśā 6 d.

370 Kaṭha 4. 6 *yaḥ pūrvaṁ tapaso jātam adbhyaḥ* see **112**. On *guhāṁ praviśya* (pāda c) see **349**.

371 Kaṭha 4. 9 a-b [AV. 10. 18. 16 a-b] = Bṛh. 1. 5. 23. Kaṭha 4. 9 d = 5. 8 f = 6. 1 f.

372 Kaṭha 4. 10 c-d, 11 a-b = (var.) Bṛh. 4. 4. 19 c, d, a, b.

373 Kaṭha 4. 12 a-b [person of the size of a thumb] see **541.** Kaṭha 4. 12 a, c = 4. 13 a, c. Kaṭha 4. 12 c-d = 4. 5 c-d ; see **369.**

374 Kaṭha 4. 13 b [light without smoke] see **658.**

375 Kaṭha 4. 13 d *sa evādya sa u śva*[*s*] = Bṛh. 1. 5. 23.

376 Kaṭha 5. 1 a [eleven-gated citadel, the body] see **543.**

377 Kaṭha 5. 2 [RV. 4. 40. 5] recurs at Mahānār. 10. 6 (Ātharv. rec. 9. 3).

378 Kaṭha 5. 3 c *madhye vāmanam āsīnaṁ* see **541.**

379 Kaṭha 5. 4 d = Kaṭha 4. 3 d.

380 Kaṭha 5. 6 b *guhyaṁ brahma* see **535.**

381 Kaṭha 5. 7 d *yathākarma yathāśrutam* cf. *yathākarma yathāvidyaṁ* Kauṣ. 1. 2. Regarding the dependence of one's reincarnate status on past acts see **192.**

382 Kaṭha 5. 8 c-f = Kaṭha 6. 1 c-f. Kaṭha 5. 8 f = 4. 9 d.

383 Kaṭha 5. 9 b (= 10 b) = Bṛh. 2. 5. 19.

384 Kaṭha 5. 9 c (= 10 c, 11 c), 12 a *sarvabhūtāntarātmā* cf. Muṇḍ. 2. 1. 4 d.

385 Kaṭha 5. 12 = (var.) Śvet. 6. 12. Kaṭha 5. 12 c-d = (var.) 5. 13 c-d.

386 Kaṭha 5. 13 a-b = Śvet. 6. 13 a-b.

387 Kaṭha 5. 15 = Muṇḍ. 2. 2. 10 ; Śvet. 6. 14. Cf. Maitri 6. 24 ; BhG. 15. 6, 12. Cf. *ekaḥ sūryaḥ sarvam idaṁ vibhāti* MBh. 3. 134. 8 (C. 10658).

388 Kaṭha 6. 1 [eternal fig-tree with root above] see **813.** Kaṭha 6. 1 c-f = 5. 8 c-f. Kaṭha 6. 1 f = 4. 9 d.

389 Kaṭha 6. 3 ⪤ Tait. 2. 8.

390 Kaṭha 6. 9 = (var.) Śvet. 4. 20 ; Mahānār. 1. 11 ; MBh. 5. 46. 6 (C. 1747). See esp. also **541.**

391 Kaṭha 6. 10 = Maitri 6. 30. Pāda d recurs BhG. 8. 21.

392 Kaṭha 6. 11 c *apramattas* cf. Muṇḍ. 2. 2. 4 ; 3. 2. 4 b (*pramādāt*).

393 Kaṭha 6. 11 d *prabhavāpyayau* cf. Māṇḍ. 6.

394 Kaṭha 6. 12 [the Supreme not to be apprehended by the senses] cf. Kena 3 a-b ; Muṇḍ. 3. 1. 8 a-b.

395 Kaṭha 6. 14 = Bṛh. 4. 4. 7.

396 Kaṭha 6. 15 [liberation from the knots of the heart] cf. Chānd. 7. 26. 2; Muṇḍ. 2. 2. 8 a; 3. 2. 9.

397 Kaṭha 6. 16 = Chānd. 8. 6. 6 See **247–250.**

398 Kaṭha 6. 17 a-b [person of the size of a thumb] see **541.**

Īśā Upanishad

399 Īśā 2 d *na karma lipyate nare* see **176.**

400 Īśā 3 see **87.**

401 Īśā 5 ≂ BhG. 13. 15. Cf. Muṇḍ. 2. 1. 2 b; 3. 1. 7 c.

402 Īśā 6 ≂ BhG. 6. 29; MBh. 12. 240. 21 (C. 8754); Manusmṛti 12. 91; cf. also BhG. 4. 35 c-d; MBh. 5. 46. 25 (C. 1784) [with *kiṁ śocet* cf. Īśā 7 c]; Āpastambīya Dharma-sūtras 1. 23. 1. For recurrences of pādad see **369.**

403 Īśā 9 = Bṛh. 4. 4. 10.

404 Īśā 10 = (var.) Kena 3 e-h. Īśā 10 c-d = 13 c-d.

405 Īśā 11 = Maitri 7. 9. Cf. Īśā 14.

406 Īśā 12 = Bṛh. M 4. 4. 10.

407 Īśā 15-18 = Bṛh. 5. 15. Īśā 15 = (var.) Maitri 6. 35.

Muṇḍaka Upanishad

408 Muṇḍ. 1. 1. 1-2 [Line of Tradition] see **47.**

409 Muṇḍ. 1. 1. 3 *kasmin . . . vijñāte sarvam idaṁ vijñātaṁ* cf. Bṛh. 2. 4. 5 end; 4. 5. 6 end; Chānd. 6. 1. 3. With the whole section cf. esp. also Chānd. 6. 4. 5.

410 Muṇḍ. 1. 1. 4 *parā caivāparā ca* see **498.**

411 Muṇḍ. 1. 1. 6-7 [characterization of the Imperishable] cf. Bṛh. 3. 8. 8-9.

412 Muṇḍ. 1. 1. 6 d [the Imperishable as the source of beings] cf. Māṇḍ. 6; Śvet. 5. 5 a; note also Śvet. 4. 11 a; 5. 2 a (*yoni*).

413 Muṇḍ. 1. 1. 7 [spider and thread analogy for creation] see **27.**

414 Muṇḍ. 1. 1. 9 a = Muṇḍ. 2. 2. 7 a; cf. *sarvajña* Māṇḍ. 6

415 Muṇḍ. 1. 2. 4 [the seven flames] cf. Muṇḍ. 2. 1. 8 b; Praśna 3. 5.

416 Muṇḍ. 1. 2. 5, 6, 11 [course to the Brahma-world] see **127.**

417 Muṇḍ. 1. 2. 7-10 [course to 'heaven' and to rebirth] cf. BhG. 9. 21 and see **128**.

418 Muṇḍ. 1. 2. 8 = (var.) Kaṭha 2. 5; Maitri 7. 9.

419 Muṇḍ. 1. 2. 12 b *akṛtaḥ* [*lokaḥ*] cf. *akṛtaṁ* ... *brahmalokam* Chānd. 8. 13.

420 Muṇḍ. 1. 2. 12 c [bringing of fuel as sign of pupilship] see **175**.

421 Muṇḍ. 2. 1. 1 [sparks from fire as analogy of creation] cf. Bṛh. 2. 1. 20; Maitri 6. 26, 31. On the creation and reabsorption of beings see **532**.

422 Muṇḍ. 2. 1. 2 a [the Puruṣa is formless] cf. Bṛh. 2. 3. 5.

423 Muṇḍ. 2. 1. 2 b *sa bāhyābhyantaro* cf. Īśā 5; BhG. 13. 15.

424 Muṇḍ. 2. 1. 3 ≂ Praśna 6. 4; see **503**.

425 Muṇḍ. 2. 1. 4 d *eṣa sarvabhūtāntarātmā* cf. Kaṭha 5. 9 c (= 10 c, 11 c), 12 a.

426 Muṇḍ. 2. 1. 5-6 these 2 stanzas seem to be an epitome of Chānd. 5. 4-10: fire whose fuel is the sun, 5. 4; rain from Soma, 5. 5; crops from earth, 5. 6; procreation, 5. 7-8; sacrifices, etc., 5. 10. 3; the year, 5. 10. 2; worlds of moon and sun [see **127**, **128**], 5. 10. 2-3. The course from Soma to earthly embodiment, alluded to in Muṇḍ. 2. 1. 5, appears in fuller form in Chānd. 5. 10. 4-6.

427 Muṇḍ. 2. 1. 8-9 = (var.) Mahānār. 10. 2-3 (Ātharv. rec. 8. 4–5). On the 'seven flames' (8 b) see **415**. On *guhāśayā nihitāḥ* (8 d) see **349**.

428 Muṇḍ. 2. 2. 1 a *āviḥ saṁnihitaṁ* cf. Maitri 6. 27. See **535**.

429 Muṇḍ. 2. 2. 1 d [Being and Non-being] cf. Praśna 2. 5 d, and see also Śvet. 4. 18 b. (In Praśna 4. 5 the words have a different meaning.)

430 Muṇḍ. 2. 2. 3-4 [bow and arrow analogy for Yoga] cf. Maitri 6. 24; 6. 28. The technical term *apramatta* recurs at Kaṭha 6. 11 c; cf. also Muṇḍ. 3. 2. 4 b (*pramādāt*).

431 Muṇḍ. 2. 2. 5 b *otaṁ* see **50**.

432 Muṇḍ. 2. 2. 5 c *tam evaikaṁ jānatha — vimuñca* cf. Bṛh. 4. 4. 21.

433 Muṇḍ. 2. 2. 5 d [Ātman a bridge to immortality] see **98.**

434 Muṇḍ. 2. 2. 6 *arā iva rathanābhau — nāḍyaḥ* see **247.** The spoke and hub simile recurs verbatim at Praśna 2. 6 a; 6. 6 a; and also at Bṛh. 2. 5. 15; Chānd. 7. 15. 1; Kauṣ. 3. 8. (Wheel analogies are found also at Bṛh. 1. 5. 15; Śvet. 1. 4; Bāṣkalamantra Up. 16.)

435 Muṇḍ. 2. 2. 6 *sa eṣo 'ntaś carate* see **265.**

436 Muṇḍ. 2. 2. 6 *tamasaḥ parastāt* see **787.**

437 Muṇḍ. 2. 2. 7 a = Muṇḍ. 1. 1. 9 a; cf. Māṇḍ. 6 (*sarvajña*).

438 Muṇḍ. 2. 2. 7 c [Brahma-city] see **231.**

439 Muṇḍ. 2. 2. 7 e *manomayaḥ prāṇaśarīranetā* cf. Chānd. 3. 14. 2; see **165.**

440 Muṇḍ. 2. 2. 8 a [liberation from the knot(s) of the heart] see **396.**

441 Muṇḍ. 2. 2. 8 b [all doubts cleared away] cf. Chānd. 3. 14. 4.

442 Muṇḍ. 2. 2. 8 c [cessation of karma] see **449.**

443 Muṇḍ. 2. 2. 8 d [the higher and the lower Brahma] see **498.**

444 Muṇḍ. 2. 2. 9 a [highest golden sheath] cf. Bṛh. 5. 15. See **122.**

445 Muṇḍ. 2. 2. 9 c *jyotiṣāṁ jyotis* cf. Bṛh. 4. 4. 16 c.

446 Muṇḍ. 2. 2. 10 = Kaṭha 5. 15; Śvet. 6. 14. See **387.**

447 Muṇḍ. 2. 2. 11 cf. Chānd. 7. 25. 1-2.

448 Muṇḍ. 3. 1. 1-2 = Śvet. 4. 6 [RV. 1. 164. 20]; 4. 7.

449 Muṇḍ. 3. 1. 3 a-c = (var.) Maitri 6. 18. With *puṇyapāpe vidhūya* (pāda c) cf. *vidhūya pāpaṁ* Chānd. 8. 13. For cessation of karma see also Muṇḍ. 2. 2. 8 c and cf. **176.**

450 Muṇḍ. 3. 1. 4 c *ātmakrīḍa ātmaratiḥ* ≈ Chānd. 7. 25. 2.

451 Muṇḍ. 3. 1. 5 a-b *tapasā . . . brahmacaryeṇa* cf. *brahmacaryeṇa tapasā* Bṛh. M 4. 4. 22; also Chānd. 2. 23. 1; Praśna 1. 2, 10; 5. 3.

452 Muṇḍ. 3. 1. 5 c *antaḥ śarīre jyotirmayo* cf. *yo 'yaṁ . . . hṛdy antar jyotiḥ puruṣaḥ* Bṛh. 4. 3. 7.

453 Muṇḍ. 3. 1. 6 [path to the gods (*devayāna*)] see **127.**

454 Muṇḍ. 3. 1. 7 d *nihitaṁ guhāyām* see **349**.

455 Muṇḍ. 3. 1. 8 a-b [the Supreme not to be apprehended by the senses] see **394**.

456 Muṇḍ. 3. 1. 8 c [a pure nature requisite for occult attainment] cf. Chānd. 7. 26. 2 (*sattvaśuddhiḥ*); cf. also Muṇḍ. 3. 1. 9, 10; 3. 2. 6.

457 Muṇḍ. 3. 1. 10 [creative power of desire] cf. Bṛh. 1. 4. 15 end; Chānd. 8. 2.

458 Muṇḍ. 3. 2. 1 a-b [Brahma-abode] see **231**.

459 Muṇḍ. 3. 2. 2 [he who desires and he who is free from desire] cf. Bṛh. 4. 4. 6.

460 Muṇḍ. 3. 2. 3 = Kaṭha 2. 23. Cf. **354**.

461 Muṇḍ. 3. 2. 4 b *pramādāt* cf. the technical term *apramatta* Kaṭha 6. 11 c; Muṇḍ. 2. 2. 4.

462 Muṇḍ. 3. 2. 4 d [Brahma-abode] see **231**.

463 Muṇḍ. 3. 2. 6 = (var.) Mahānār. 10. 22 (Ātharv. rec. 10. 6).

464 Muṇḍ. 3. 2. 7-8 [unification in the Supreme Imperishable] parallel in thought and simile to Praśna 6. 5; see esp. also Praśna 4. 7-11 and cf. MBh. 12. 219. 42 (C. 7972); 14. 33. 7 (C. 919). Muṇḍ. 3. 2. 7 d = (var.) Maitri 6. 18. On the 'fifteen parts' see **501**. On *vijñānamaya ātman* see Tait. 2. 4 and cf. *vijñānātman* Praśna 4. 9.

465 Muṇḍ. 3. 2. 9 *nāsyābrahmavit kule bhavati* = Māṇḍ. 10.

466 Muṇḍ. 3. 2. 9 [*brahmavit*] *tarati śokaṁ* ⊂ Chānd. 7. 1. 3.

467 Muṇḍ. 3. 2. 9 [liberation from the knots of the heart] see **396**.

468 Muṇḍ. 3. 2. 10-11 [restrictions on imparting occult knowledge] see **133**. With *ekarṣiṁ* (10 b) cf. *eka ṛṣir* Praśna 2. 11 a.

Praśna Upanishad

469 Praśna 1. 1 cf. the similar introduction at Chānd. 5. 11. 1-2.

470 Praśna 1. 1 [bringing of fuel as sign of pupilship] see **175**.

471 Praśna 1.2, 10 [*tapas, brahmacarya, śraddhā*] see **451.**

472 Praśna 1.5 *ādityo ha vai prāṇo* cf. Praśna 3.8.

473 Praśna 1.8 *viśvarūpaṁ hariṇaṁ* [stanza] = Maitri 6.8.

474 Praśna 1.9-10 [two paths, the southern and the northern] see **127, 128.**

475 Praśna 1.14 [food as the source of creatures] see **728.**

476 Praśna 2.2-4 [superiority of *prāṇa* among the bodily functions] see **124.**

477 Praśna 2.5 d [Being and Non-being] see **429.**

478 Praśna 2.6 a [spokes fixed in the hub] = Praśna 6.6 a; Muṇḍ. 2.2.6 a; see **434.**

479 Praśna 2.11 a *eka ṛṣir* cf. *ekarṣiṁ* Muṇḍ. 3.2.10 b.

480 Praśna 3.3 *ātmana eṣa prāṇo jāyate* cf. Muṇḍ. 2.1.3 a; Praśna 6.4.

481 Praśna 3.3 *mano['dhi]kṛtenāyāty asmiñ charīre* (on text and interpretation consult Hume in this volume, p. 383, n. 2) see **192.**

482 Praśna 3.5 [etymological explanation of *samāna*] cf. Praśna 4.4; Maitri 2.6. On the food-offering see Chānd. 5.19, etc.

483 Praśna 3.5 [the seven flames] cf. Muṇḍ. 1.2.4; 2.1.8 b.

484 Praśna 3.6 *atraitad ekaśataṁ nāḍīnāṁ* see **247.**

485 Praśna 3.6 *dvāsaptatiḥ — -nāḍīsahasrāṇi* see **25.**

486 Praśna 3.6 *āsu vyānaś carati* cf. Maitri 6.21 (*prāṇa-saṁcāriṇī*).

487 Praśna 3.7 *athaikayordhva udānaḥ* see **249.**

488 Praśna 3.7 [acts determine one's reincarnate status] see **192.**

489 Praśna 3.8 *ādityo — prāṇa udayaty* cf. Praśna 1.5.

490 Praśna 3.9-10 *upaśāntatejāḥ — yuktaḥ* cf. Chānd. 6.8.6; 6.15.2.

491 Praśna 3 10 [thought determines state after death] see **786.**

492 Praśna 4.2 [unification of the functions in sleep] see **319.**

493 Praśna 4.4 [etymological explanation of *samāna*] see **482.**

494 Praśna 4. 5 [dream experiences] cf. Bṛh. 4. 3. 20; Chānd. 8. 10. On *sac cāsac ca* see **429**.

495 Praśna 4. 7-11 [unification in the Supreme Imperishable] see **464**.

496 Praśna 4. 8 [Sāṁkhya enumeration] see **522**.

497 Praśna 4. 9 cf. Maitri 6. 7 end. On *vijñānātman* see **464**.

498 Praśna 5. 2 [the higher and the lower Brahma] = Maitri 6. 5; cf. Muṇḍ. 1. 1. 4; 2. 2. 8 d; Maitri 6. 22-23. See also **32**.

499 Praśna 5. 3 [*tapas, brahmacarya, śraddhā*] see **451**.

500 Praśna 5. 5 [snake freed from its slough] cf. Kauṣ. Br. 18. 7 (see also Ait. Br. 6. 1 end); MBh. 12. 219. 48 (C. 7978-9); Śat. Br. 2. 5. 2. 47; 2. 3. 1. 6. The snake-skin simile is used in another application in Bṛh. 4. 4. 7.

501 Praśna 6. 1-2 [the *puruṣa* with sixteen parts] cf. Bṛh. 1. 5. 14-15; Chānd. 6. 7. Cf. the 'fifteen parts', Muṇḍ. 3. 2. 7 a. Cf. also MBh. 12. 242. 8 a-b (C. 8811) = (var.) 14. 51. 31 a-b (C. 1455); 12. 304. 8 (C. 11324); note also 12. 210. 33 (C. 7674); and consult Hopkins, *Great Epic of India*, p. 168. (See Śat. Br. 10. 4. 1. 17; and also VS. 8. 36, where Prajāpati is called *ṣoḍaśin*.)

502 Praśna 6. 1 *nāham imaṁ veda — nāvakṣyam* ≈ Chānd. 5. 3. 5.

503 Praśna 6. 4 *sa* [*puruṣa*] *prāṇam asṛjata* see **480**.

504 Praśna 6. 4 *khaṁ vāyur — pṛthivī-* = Muṇḍ. 2. 1. 3.

505 Praśna 6. 5 [unification in the cosmic Person] see **464**.

506 Praśna 6. 6 a [spokes fixed in the hub] = Praśna 2. 6 a; Muṇḍ. 2. 2. 6 a; see **434**.

Māṇḍūkya Upanishad

507 Māṇḍ. 1 *trikālātītaṁ* cf. *paras trikālād* Śvet. 6. 5 b.

508 Māṇḍ. 3 *saptāṅga ekonaviṁśatimukhaḥ* see **522**.

509 Māṇḍ. 4 *praviviktabhuk* cf. Bṛh. 4. 2. 3 end.

510 Māṇḍ. 5 *yatra supto — paśyati* = Bṛh. 4. 3. 19.

511 Māṇḍ. 5 *ekībhūtaḥ* [unification in sleep] see **319**.

512 Māṇḍ. 5 *prajñānaghana eva* = Bṛh. 4. 5. 13.
513 Māṇḍ. 5 *ānandamayo hy ānandabhuk* see **277**.
514 Māṇḍ. 6 *eṣa sarveśvara* see **98**.
515 Māṇḍ. 6 *eṣa sarvajña* cf. Muṇḍ. 1. 1. 9 a = 2. 2. 7 a.
516 Māṇḍ. 6 *eṣo 'ntaryāmy* cf. Bṛh. 3. 7.
517 Māṇḍ. 6 *eṣa yoniḥ sarvasya* see **412**.
518 Māṇḍ. 6 *prabhavāpyayau* cf. Kaṭha 6. 11 d.
519 Māṇḍ. 7, 12 [fourth, or superconscious, state] cf. Maitri 6. 19; 7. 11, stanzas 7-8. See also the use of *turīya* at Bṛh. 5. 14. 3-7.
520 Māṇḍ. 10 *nāsyābrahmavit kule bhavati* = Muṇḍ. 3. 2. 9.

Śvetāśvatara Upanishad [1]

521 Śvet. 1. 2 *kālasvabhāvo* cf. Śvet. 6. 1 a-b.
522 Śvet. 1. 4-5 [numerical allusions to series of philosophic terms] cf. Māṇḍ. 3; Śvet. 6. 3; Maitri 3. 3 (*caturjālaṁ caturdaśavidhaṁ caturaśītidhā pariṇataṁ*); 6. 10; see also BhG. 7. 4 and the Sāṁkhya list at Praśna 4. 8. The 'three paths' are mentioned again at Śvet. 5. 7 c. On the 'fifty spokes' see Sāṁkhyakārikā 46. With the wheel analogy cf. Bṛh. 1. 5. 15; MBh. 14. 45. 1-9 (C. 1234-42), and see **602**.
523 Śvet. 1. 8 c, 9 b, 12 c [the soul called 'the enjoyer'] see **360**.
524 Śvet. 1. 8 d = Śvet. 2. 15 d; 4. 16 d; 5. 13 d; 6. 13 d.
525 Śvet. 1. 14 [Brahma is hidden] see **535**.
526 Śvet. 2. 8-15 [rules for Yoga] cf. Kaṭha 6. 10-17; Maitri 6. 18-30; and esp. BhG. 6. 10-26; 5. 27-28; see also Chānd. 8. 15. With *same śucau* Śvet. 2. 10 a cf. Maitri 6. 30 init.; Chānd. 8. 15 (*śucau deśe*). With the 'sixfold Yoga' of Maitri 6. 18 cf. Patañjali's Yoga-sūtras 2. 29.
527 Śvet. 2. 9 c [chariot yoked with vicious horses] clearly an allusion to Kaṭha 3. 3-5; see **359**.

[1] On quotations from and allusions to Kaṭha in Śvet. see D. p. 289; on parallels between Śvet. and MBh. see Hopkins, *Great Epic of India*, p. 28; on correspondences of Śvet. with Kaṭha, Muṇḍ., and BhG., see R. Hauschild, *Die Śvetāśvatara Upaniṣad*, Leipzig, 1927, pp. 69–79.

528 Śvet. 2. 12 b [earth, water, fire, air, ether] the same cpd. recurs Śvet. 6. 2 d; cf. Maitri 6. 4; BhG. 7. 4; and also MBh. 3. 210. 17 (C. 13914); 3. 211. 3 (C. 13922); 12. 311. 10 (C. 11578).

529 Śvet. 2. 15 d = Śvet. 1. 8 d; 4. 16 d; 5. 13 d; 6. 13 d.

530 Śvet. 2. 16 [VS. 32. 4] = (var.) Mahānārāyaṇa 1. 13 (Ātharv. rec. 2. 1). *pratyaṅ janās tiṣṭhati* Śvet. 2. 16 d = Śvet. 3. 2 c.

531 Śvet. 3. 1 d see **541**.

532 Śvet. 3. 2 d [creation and reabsorption of the world and of all beings] cf. Tait. 3. 1; Muṇḍ. 2. 1. 1; Śvet. 4. 1 a-c; Maitri 6. 15, 17; BhG. 8. 18-19; cf. also MBh. 5. 44. 30 (C. 1713); Manusmṛti 1. 52, 57; Kumārasambhava 2. 8.

533 Śvet. 3. 3 [RV. 10. 81. 3 (var.)] = (var.) Mahānār. 1. 14 (Ātharv. rec. 2. 2).

534 Śvet. 3. 4 = (var.) Śvet. 4. 12; Mahānārāyaṇa 10. 19 (Ātharv. rec. 10. 3). Pāda d recurs as Śvet. 4. 1 d. On *viśvādhipo* (pāda b) see **96**.

535 Śvet. 3. 7 b [Brahma hidden in all things] cf. Kaṭha 5. 6 b; Muṇḍ. 2. 2. 1 a (≈ Maitri 6. 27); Śvet. 1. 14; 6. 11.

536 Śvet. 3. 7 c see **553**.

537 Śvet. 3. 8 c-d [VS. 31. 18] = Śvet. 6. 15 c-d. Śvet. 3. 8 b = BhG. 8. 9 d; see **787**.

538 Śvet. 3. 9 = Mahānār. 10. 20 (Ātharv. rec. 10. 4). On the 'tree established in heaven' see **388**.

539 Śvet. 3. 10 b *anāmayam* the word recurs as an epithet of Brahma-Ātman at Maitri 6. 26.

540 Śvet. 3. 10 c-d = Bṛh. 4. 4. 14 c-d. On pāda c see also **541**.

541 Śvet. 3. 13 a-b [person of the size of a thumb, seated in the heart of creatures] = Kaṭha 6. 17 a-b; cf. Kaṭha 4. 12 a; 4. 13 a; 5. 3 c (*madhye vāmanam āsīnaṁ*); Śvet. 5. 8 a; Maitri 6. 38 end; cf. also MBh. 3. 297. 17 (C. 16763); 5. 46. 15, 27 (C. 1764, 1786); for *aṅguṣṭhamātraḥ puruṣaḥ* see also MBh. 12. 284. 175 a (C. 10450 a) and cf. *prādeśamātraḥ puruṣaḥ* MBh. 12. 200. 22 c (C. 7351 c). Śvet. 3. 13 b-d = 4.

17 b-d. Śvet. 3. 13 c-d = Kaṭha 6. 9 c-d [see esp. **390**]; with pāda c cf. MBh. 12. 240. 15 (C. 8748). Śvet. 3. 13 d recurs also as Bṛh. 4. 4. 14 c; Śvet. 3. 1 d; 3. 10 c; cf. 4. 20 d.

542 Śvet. 3. 16, 17 a-b = BhG. 13. 13, 14 a-b; see **805**.

543 Śvet. 3. 18 = (var.) MBh. 12. 240. 32 (C. 8765). *navadvāre pure dehī* = BhG. 5. 13; cf. *puram ekādaśadvāram* Kaṭha 5. 1 a. (For other epic parallels see Hopkins, *Great Epic of India*, p. 166 and n. 3.) See also **231**.

544 Śvet. 3. 20 [TA. 10. 10. 1] = Mahānār. 10. 1 (Ātharv. rec. 8. 3); = (var.) Kaṭha 2. 20; ⩧ MBh. 12. 240. 30 (C. 8763). The phrase *aṇor aṇīyān* (pāda a) recurs also BhG. 8. 9 b; MBh. 5. 46. 31 (C. 1790). On the doctrine of *prasāda* see **354**.

545 Śvet. 4. 1 [creation and reabsorption of the world] see **532**. Pāda d recurs Śvet. 3. 4; see **534**.

546 Śvet. 4. 5 = (var.) Mahānār. 10. 5 (Ātharv. rec. 9. 2). Cf. *ābhāti śuklam iva lohitam ivātho kṛṣṇam* MBh. 5. 44. 25 (C. 1709); also MBh. 12. 302. 46 (C. 11259).

547 Śvet. 4. 6 [RV. 1. 164. 20] = Muṇḍ. 3. 1. 1.

548 Śvet. 4. 7 = Muṇḍ. 3. 1. 2.

549 Śvet. 4. 11 a *yo yonim̐ yonim adhitiṣṭhaty eko* see **412**.

550 Śvet. 4. 11 b = Mahānār. 1. 2 a.

551 Śvet. 4. 11 c-d = (var.) Kaṭha 1. 17 c-d.

552 Śvet. 4. 12 = (var.) Śvet. 3. 4; Mahānār. 10. 19 (Ātharv. rec. 10. 3).

553 Śvet. 4. 14 = (var.) Śvet. 5. 13. Pāda c recurs also as 3. 7 c; 4. 16 c.

554 Śvet. 4. 16 d = Śvet. 1. 8 d; 2. 15 d; 5. 13 d; 6. 13 d.

555 Śvet. 4. 17 b-d see **541**.

556 Śvet. 4. 18 a [no day or night] see **156**.

557 Śvet. 4. 18 c [Sāvitrī stanza] see **130**.

558 Śvet. 4. 19 [VS. 32. 2 c-d, 3 a-b; TA. 10. 1. 2] = Mahānār. 1. 10; ⩧ MBh. 12. 240. 26 (C. 8759).

559 Śvet. 4. 20 = (var.) Kaṭha 6. 9; Mahānār. 1. 11.

560 Śvet. 5. 2 a = Śvet. 4. 11 a; see **412**. With 5. 2 c-d cf. 4. 12 c.

561 Śvet. 5. 5 a [the One as the source of all] see **412**.

562 Śvet. 5. 5 c cf. the similar line Śvet. 6. 4 b.
563 Śvet. 5. 7, 12 [acts determine one's reïncarnate status] see **192**.
564 Śvet. 5. 7 c [three paths] cf. Śvet. 1. 4 d.
565 Śvet. 5. 8 a [of the size of a thumb] see **541**.
566 Śvet. 5. 13 = (var.) Śvet. 4. 14. Pāda c recurs also as 3. 7 c; 4. 16 c. Pāda d = 1. 8 d; 2. 15 d; 4. 16 d; 6. 13 d.
567 Śvet. 6. 1 a-b *svabhāvam eke . . . kālaṁ tathānye* cf. Śvet. 1. 2 a.
568 Śvet. 6. 2 [earth, water, fire, air, ether] see **528**. Pāda b = 6. 16 b.
569 Śvet. 6. 3 c [numerical allusions to Sāṁkhya terms] see **522**.
570 Śvet. 6. 4 b cf. the similar line Śvet. 5. 5 c.
571 Śvet. 6. 5 b *paras trikālād* cf. *trikālātītaṁ* Māṇḍ. 1.
572 Śvet. 6. 6 a [the world-tree] see **388**.
573 Śvet. 6. 10 b [spider and thread analogy for creation] see **27**.
574 Śvet. 6. 11 [the one divinity hidden in all things] see **535**.
575 Śvet. 6. 12 = (var.) Kaṭha 5. 12; see also Kaṭha 5. 13 c-d.
576 Śvet. 6. 13 a-b = Kaṭha 5. 13 a-b. On Śvet. 6. 13 d see **524**.
577 Śvet. 6. 14 = Kaṭha 5. 15; Muṇḍ. 2. 2. 10. See **387**.
578 Śvet. 6. 15 c-d [VS. 31. 18] = Śvet. 3. 8 c-d.
579 Śve' 6. 16 *kṣetrajña* see **804**. Śvet. 6. 16 b = 6. 2 b.
580 Śvet. 6. 19 c [Brahma a bridge to immortality] see **98**.
581 Śvet. 6. 21 a [doctrine of *prasāda*] see **354**.
582 Śvet. 6. 22 [restrictions on imparting occult knowledge] see **133**.

Maitri Upanishad[1]

583 Maitri 1. 2 [smokeless fire] see **658**.
584 Maitri 1. 2 [ignorance of Ātman confessed] cf. Chānd. 7. 1. 3.

[1] For an elaborate discussion of parallels between Maitri and MBh. see Hopkins, *Great Epic of India*, pp. 33-46; see also D. pp. 312-313.

585 Maitri 1.2 [question declared difficult; another choice advised] cf. Kaṭha 1.21 b-c.

586 Maitri 1.3 [pessimistic description of the human body] cf. Maitri 3.4; also Manusmṛti 6.76-77 = MBh. 12.329.42-43 (C. 12463-4); Viṣṇusmṛti 96.43-53; Dhammapada 150.

587 Maitri 1.3 [dissatisfaction with aspects of human life] cf. Manusmṛti 6.62; see also Kaṭha 1.26; and cf. in general Viṣṇusmṛti 96.27 ff.; Yājñavalkīya Dharmasūtras 3.63-64.

588 Maitri 2.2 *eṣa samprasādo — etad brahmeti* see **237**.

589 Maitri 2.3-4 [the body like a cart] see **359**.

590 Maitri 2.4 *śuddhaḥ pūtaḥ — sve mahimni tiṣṭhaty* = Maitri 6.28. This passage is referred to in 6.31: *yo 'yaṁ śuddhaḥ pūtaḥ śūnyaḥ śāntādilakṣaṇoktaḥ*. Cf. *sve mahimni [pratiṣṭhitaḥ]* Chānd. 7.24.1; *sve mahimni tiṣṭhamānaṁ* Maitri 6.38.

591 Maitri 2.5 *so 'ṁśo 'yaṁ — prajāpatir* = Maitri 5.2. The group of terms *saṁkalpādhyavasāyābhimāna-* recurs (transposed) in 6.10 and 6.30. On the term *kṣetrajña* see **804**.

592 Maitri 2.6 [Prajāpati alone in the beginning] see **7**.

593 Maitri 2.6 [explanation of *vyāna*] cf. Chānd. 1.3.3.

594 Maitri 2.6 *yo 'yaṁ sthaviṣṭho dhātur annasya* cf. Chānd. 6.5.1.

595 Maitri 2.6 [etymological explanation of *samāna*] cf. Praśna 3.5; 4.4.

596 Maitri 2.6 [universal fire; sound heard on stopping the ears] quoted from Bṛh. 5.9; see esp. **117**.

597 Maitri 2.6 *nihito guhāyām* see **349**.

598 Maitri 2.6 *manomayaḥ — ākāśātmā* = Chānd. 3.14.2. See **656**.

599 Maitri 2.6 *khānimāni bhittvā* cf. Kaṭha 4.1 a.

600 Maitri 2.6 *pañcabhī raśmibhir viṣayān atti* = Maitri 6.31.

601 Maitri 2.6 end [the body as a chariot] see **359**.

602 Maitri 2.6 end [the body like a potter's wheel cf. Maitri 3.3. See also **522**.

603 Maitri 2. 7 *sitāsitaiḥ karmaphalair anabhibhūta iva* see 97.

604 Maitri 2. 7 *prekṣakavad avasthitaḥ svasthaś ca* cf. *prekṣakavad avasthitaḥ susthaḥ* Sāṁkhyakārikā 65.

605 Maitri 3. 1 [pairs of opposites] cf. Maitri 3. 2; 6. 29; BhG. 7. 27-28.

606 Maitri 3. 2 [acts determine one's reincarnate status] see 192.

607 Maitri 3. 2 [water on a lotus-leaf] cf. Chānd. 4. 14. 3; BhG. 5. 10; see also MBh. 3. 213. 20 b (C. 13978 d); 12. 187. 24 d (C. 6922 d); 12. 242. 18 b (C. 8821 b); and Dhammapada 401.

608 Maitri 3. 2 *guṇaughair uhyamānaḥ — khacaraḥ* = Maitri 6. 30.

609 Maitri 3. 2 *nibadhnāty ātmanā "tmānam* cf. *badhnāty ātmānam ātmanā* Sāṁkhyakārikā 63.

610 Maitri 3. 3 *yaḥ kartā so 'yaṁ vai bhūtātmā* etc. cf. Manusmṛti 12. 12.

611 Maitri 3. 3 [analogy of the transformation of iron] cf. Bṛh. 4. 4. 4.

612 Maitri 3. 3 *caturjālaṁ caturdaśavidhaṁ caturaśītidhā pariṇataṁ* see 522.

613 Maitri 3. 3 [wheel driven by the potter] cf. Maitri 2. 6 end.

614 Maitri 3. 4 [pessimistic description of the human body] see 586.

615 Maitri 3. 5 [characteristics of *tamas* and *rajas*] see 810.

616 Maitri 4. 4 end [chariot-rider] see 359.

617 Maitri 4. 5 [Agni, Vāyu, Āditya] see 153.

618 Maitri 4. 6 *brahma khalv idaṁ vāva sarvam* = (var.) Chānd. 3. 14. 1.

619 Maitri 5. 2 *so 'ṁśo 'yaṁ —prajāpatir* = Maitri 2. 5; see esp. 591. The text calls attention to this reiteration: *asya prāg uktā etās tanavaḥ.*

620 Maitri 5. 2 [the Ātman manifold] cf. Chānd. 7. 26. 2; Maitri 6. 26 end.

621 Maitri 6. 1 *atha ya eṣo — puruṣo* = Chānd. 1. 6. 6; see 149.

622 Maitri 6. 3 *dve — rūpe mūrtaṁ cāmūrtaṁ ca* see 32.

623 Maitri 6. 3 *sa tredhā "tmānaṁ vyakuruta* = Bṛh. 1. 2. 3.

624 Maitri 6. 3 *sarvam idam otaṁ protaṁ caiva* see **50.**

625 Maitri 6. 4 *atha khalu — eṣa praṇava* = Chānd. 1. 5. 1.

626 Maitri 6. 4 *praṇavākhyaṁ — vimṛtyuṁ* recurs with the addition of *viśokam* at Maitri 6. 25; 7. 5.

627 Maitri 6. 4 *nihitaṁ guhāyām* see **349.**

628 Maitri 6. 4 [the Lone Fig-tree with root above] see **388.**

629 Maitri 6. 4 [ether, air, fire, water, earth] see **528.**

630 Maitri 6. 4 *tasmād om ity — upāsīta* see **726.**

631 Maitri 6. 4 *etad evākṣaraṁ* [stanza] = (var.) Kaṭha 2. 16.

632 Maitri 6. 5 [the higher and the lower Brahma] quoted from Praśna 5. 2; see **498.**

633 Maitri 6. 6 [Prajāpati produced *bhūr, bhuvaḥ, svar*] see **180.**

634 Maitri 6. 7 [Sāvitrī stanza] see **130.**

635 Maitri 6. 7 [the All-pervader as agent in the bodily functions] cf. Praśna 4. 9.

636 Maitri 6. 7 [duality of knowledge transcended] cf. Bṛh. 2. 4. 14 = 4. 5. 15; also 4. 3. 31.

637 Maitri 6. 8 *eṣa hi khalv ātmeśānaḥ — nārāyaṇo* recurs with the addition of *acyuto* in Maitri 7. 7.

638 Maitri 6. 8 *eṣa vāva jijñāsitavyo 'nveṣṭavyaḥ* ≈ Chānd. 8. 7. 3; cf. Chānd. 7. 23 (etc.); 8. 1. 1.

639 Maitri 6. 8 *viśvarūpaṁ hariṇaṁ* [stanza] = Praśna 1. 8.

640 Maitri 6. 9 *adbhiḥ purastāt* [and infra *upariṣṭāt*] *paridadhati* ≈ Chānd. 5. 2. 2.

641 Maitri 6. 9 ['Hail!' to *prāṇa, apāna*, etc.] cf. Chānd. 5. 19-23.

642 Maitri 6. 10 [the soul called 'the enjoyer'] see **360.**

643 Maitri 6. 10 [fourteenfold course] see **522.**

644 Maitri 6. 10 *saṁkalpādhyavasāyābhimānā* see **591.**

645 Maitri 6. 10 [food and the eater of food] cf. Bṛh. 1. 4. 6.

646 Maitri 6. 11 *na yady aśnāty — draṣṭā bhavati* = (var.) Chānd. 7. 9.

647 Maitri 6. 11 *annād vai — antataḥ* = Tait. 2. 2a-d. See **728**.

648 Maitri 6. 12 *annād bhūtāni — ucyate* = Tait. 2. 2 k-n. See **728**.

649 Maitri 6. 13 with the series *anna, prāṇa, manas, vijñāna, ānanda* cf. the series *annarasamaya* to *ānandamaya* in Tait. 2. 2-5. See also **690**.

650 Maitri 6. 14 end *kālo mūrtir amūrtimān* see **32**.

651 Maitri 6. 15 [two forms of Brahma] see **32**.

652 Maitri 6. 15 [origin, growth, and death of creatures] see **532**.

653 Maitri 6. 15 *kālaḥ pacati bhūtāni* [stanza] = (var.) MBh. 12. 240. 25 (C. 8758). Pāda d = BhG. 15. 1 d. Pāda a recurs at MBh. 11. 2. 24 (C. 69).

654 Maitri 6. 16 *āditya brahmety* = Chānd. 3. 19. 1.

655 Maitri 6. 17 *brahma ha vā idam agra āsīd eko* see **10** and cf. **7**.

656 Maitri 6. 17 (*eṣa*) *ākāśātmā* this epithet is found besides only at Chānd. 3. 14. 2 (quoted Maitri 2. 6) and, in a different application, at Kauṣ. 2. 14 (9). Cf. *ākāśaśarīraṁ brahma* Tait. 1. 6. 2.

657 Maitri 6. 17 [creation and reabsorption of the world] see **532**.

658 Maitri 6. 17 [the Supreme like a smokeless fire] cf. Kaṭha 4. 13 b; MBh. 12. 250. 7 (C. 9044); 12. 306. 20 (C. 11387). The simile occurs in another connection at Maitri 1. 2.

659 Maitri 6. 17 [digestive fire in the stomach] cf. Bṛh. 5. 9 (quoted Maitri 2. 6).

660 Maitri 6. 17 *yaś caiṣo 'gnau — sa eṣa eka* = Maitri 7. 7. Cf. Chānd. 3. 13. 7.

661 Maitri 6. 18-30 [rules for Yoga] see **526**.

662 Maitri 6. 18 *yadā paśyan — vihāya* [stanza, pādas a-c] = (var.) Muṇḍ. 3. 1. 3 a-c; see **449**. On pāda d of this stanza see **464**.

663 Maitri 6. 19 [fourth, or superconscious, state] see **519**.

664 Maitri 6. 19 *tac ca lingaṁ nirāśrayam* [stanza, pāda d] cf. *nirāśrayaṁ lingam* Sāṁkhyakārikā 41.

665 Maitri 6. 20 *tadā "tmanā "tmānaṁ dṛṣṭvā nirātmā bhavati* =○= MBh. 3. 213. 27 c-d (C. 13986 c-d).

666 Maitri 6. 20 *cittasya hi prasādena* [stanza] = (var.) MBh. 3. 213. 24 (C. 13983); 12. 247. 10 (C. 8960); recurs at Maitri 6. 34. (For discussion see Hopkins, *Great Epic of India*, pp. 42-43.)

667 Maitri 6. 21 *ūrdhvagā nāḍī suṣumnākhyā* see **64**.

668 Maitri 6. 21 *prāṇasaṁcāriṇī* see **486**.

669 Maitri 6. 21 *tālvantarvicchinnā* see **266**.

670 Maitri 6. 21 *tayā — ūrdhvam utkramet* see **249**.

671 Maitri 6. 22-23 [the higher and the lower Brahma] see **498**.

672 Maitri 6. 22 [the spider and his thread] see **27**.

673 Maitri 6. 22 [sound heard on stopping the ears] see **117**.

674 Maitri 6. 22 [ether within the heart] see **265**.

675 Maitri 6. 22 [unified condition of honey] see **209**.

676 Maitri 6. 22 *dve brahmaṇī veditavye* [stanza] = MBh. 12. 233. 30 (C. 8540-1); pādas c-d are quoted in Sarvadarśanasaṁgraha p. 147, line 2 (Bibl. Ind., Calcutta, 1858).

677 Maitri 6. 23 *tac chāntam — viṣṇusaṁjñitaṁ* = Maitri 7. 3; the words *acalam — viṣṇusaṁjñitaṁ* recur also in Maitri 6. 38. See also **362**.

678 Maitri 6. 24 [bow and arrow analogy for Yoga] see **430**.

679 Maitri 6. 24 [what is not enveloped in darkness] cf. **156**.

680 Maitri 6. 24 [Brahma shines in sun, moon, etc.] see **387**.

681 Maitri 6. 25 *praṇavākhyaṁ — viśokaṁ* recurs at Maitri 7. 5 and, without the last word, at 6. 4; see also **235**. Cf. Muṇḍ. 3. 2. 9.

682 Maitri 6. 26 *anāmaye 'gnau* see **539**.

683 Maitri 6. 26 *viṣṇoḥ paramaṁ padaṁ* see **362**.

684 Maitri 6. 26 *aparimitadhā cātmānaṁ vibhajya* etc. see **227**.

685 Maitri 6. 26 *vahneś ca yadvat* [stanza] = Maitri 6. 31. On the issuance of sparks from fire as an analogy of creation see **421**.

686 Maitri 6. 27 [warmth of the body as the heat of Brahma] cf. Chānd. 3. 13. 8 and see **117**.

687 Maitri 6. 27 *āviḥ san nabhasi nihitaṁ* cf. Muṇḍ. 2. 2. 1 a; see **535**.

688 Maitri 6. 27, 28 [ether within the heart] see **265**.

689 Maitri 6. 28 [bow and arrow analogy for Yoga] see **430**.

690 Maitri 6. 28 [dispersal of the fourfold sheath of Brahma] ≈ Maitri 6. 38. The adj. *caturjāla* occurs also in 3. 3. On the 'fourfold sheath' see Tait. 2. 1-4 (*annarasamaya, prāṇamaya, manomaya,* and *vijñānamaya ātman*).

691 Maitri 6. 28 *śuddhaḥ pūtaḥ — sve mahimni tiṣṭhati* see **590**.

692 Maitri 6. 28 [looking down on a rolling chariot-wheel] cf. Kauṣ. 1. 4 end.

693 Maitri 6. 28 *ṣaḍbhir māsais* [stanza] ≈ MBh. 14. 19. 66 c-d (C. 598); cf. 12. 241. 32 c-d (C. 8799). With *nityayuktasya dehinaḥ* (pāda b) cf. BhG. 8. 14 d. (For discussion see Hopkins, *Great Epic of India*, pp. 45-46.)

694 Maitri 6. 29 [pairs of opposites] cf. Maitri 3. 1, 2; BhG. 7. 27-2.

695 Maitri 6. 29 [restrictions on imparting occult knowledge] see **133**.

696 Maitri 6. 30 *śucau deśe* see **526**.

697 Maitri 6. 30 [meditation upon the Real, sacrifice to the Real] cf. Maitri 6. 9.

698 Maitri 6. 30 *puruṣo 'dhyavasāyasaṁkalpābhimānaliṅgo* see **591**.

699 Maitri 6. 30 *manasā hy eva paśyati — mana eva* = Bṛh. 1. 5. 3.

700 Maitri 6. 30 *guṇaughair uhyamānaḥ — khacaro* = Maitri 3. 2.

701 Maitri 6. 30 *atra hi sarve kāmāḥ samāhitā* see **234**.

702 Maitri 6. 30 *yadā pañcāvatiṣṭhante* [stanza] see **391**.

703 Maitri 6. 30 [northern course to Brahma] see **127**.
704 Maitri 6. 30 *dīpavad yaḥ sthito hṛdi* see **265**.
705 Maitri 6. 30 *sitāsitāḥ — mṛdulohitāḥ* see **71**.
706 Maitri 6. 30 *ūrdhvam ekaḥ sthitas teṣāṁ* see **64**.
707 Maitri 6. 30 *yo bhittvā sūryamaṇḍalam — parāṁ gatim* see **249**.
708 Maitri 6. 30 *yad asyānyad raśmiśataṁ — prapadyate* see **247**, **250**.
709 Maitri 6. 31 [the soul as agent in the senses] see **333**.
710 Maitri 6. 31 *pañcabhī raśmibhir viṣayān atti* = Maitri 2. 6.
711 Maitri 6. 31 *yo 'yaṁ śuddhaḥ — -lakṣaṇoktaḥ* see **590**.
712 Maitri 6. 31 *vāk śrotraṁ cakṣur manaḥ prāṇa ity eke* cf. Kena 2; see **333**.
713 Maitri 6. 31 *dhṛtiḥ smṛtiḥ prajñānam ity eke* cf. Ait. 5. 2.
714 Maitri 6. 31 *vahneś ca yadvat* [stanza] = Maitri 6. 26. See **421**.
715 Maitri 6. 32 *sarve prāṇāḥ — satyasya satyam iti* = (var.) Bṛh. 2. 1. 20.
716 Maitri 6. 32 [literature-list] see **41**.
717 Maitri 6. 34 [Sāvitrī stanza] see **130**.
718 Maitri 6. 34 *cittam eva hi saṁsāraṁ* [stanza] see **192**. Pādas c-d = (var.) MBh. 14. 51. 27 c-d (C. 1451); see Hopkins, *Great Epic of India*, pp. 42-43.
719 Maitri 6. 34 *cittasya hi prasādena* [stanza] see **666**.
720 Maitri 6. 35 *hiraṇmayena pātreṇa* [stanza] = (var.) Bṛh. 5. 15; Īśā 15.
721 Maitri 6. 35 [Person in the sun] see **149**.
722 Maitri 6. 35 [nectar in the sun] cf. Chānd. 3. 1. 2; Tait. 1. 10.
723 Maitri 6. 35 [simile of the solution of salt] see **210**.
724 Maitri 6. 35 *atra hi sarve kāmāḥ samāhitā ity* see **234**.
725 Maitri 6. 36, stanza [the cosmic egg] see **173**.
726 Maitri 6. 37 *tasmād om ity — tejas* = Maitri 7. 11. *tasmād — upāsīta* recurs also at Maitri 6. 4. Cf. BhG. 17. 24 [see **818**]; also **143**.

727 Maitri 6. 37 *tat tredhā — prāṇe* = Maitri 7. 11.

728 Maitri 6. 37 *agnau prāstā* [stanza] = Manusmṛti 3. 76; = (var.) MBh. 12. 263. 11 (C. 9406-7); ⥲ BhG. 3. 14; cf. Tait. 2. 2 (quoted Maitri 6. 11, 12); Praśna 1. 14.

729 Maitri 6. 38 [cleaving the fourfold sheath of Brahma] see **690**.

730 Maitri 6. 38 *acalam — viṣṇusaṁjñitaṁ* see **677**.

731 Maitri 6. 38 *sve mahimni tiṣṭhamānaṁ* see **590**.

732 Maitri 6. 38 end [person of the size of a thumb] see **541**.

733 Maitri 6. 38 end *atra hi sarve kāmāḥ samāhitā ity* see **234**.

734 Maitri 7. 3 *tac chāntam — viṣṇusaṁjñitaṁ* see **677**.

735 Maitri 7. 5 *praṇavākhyaṁ — viśokam* see **681**.

736 Maitri 7. 7 *ātmā 'ntarhṛdaye 'ṇīyān* see **165**.

737 Maitri 7. 7 *asminn otā imāḥ prajāḥ* see **50**.

738 Maitri 7. 7 *eṣa ātmā — satyakāma* see **235**.

739 Maitri 7. 7 *eṣa parameśvara — setur vidharaṇa* see **98**.

740 Maitri 7. 7 *eṣa hi khalv ātmeśānaḥ — nārāyaṇaḥ* see **637**.

741 Maitri 7. 7 *yaś caiṣo 'gnau — sa eṣa ekaḥ* see **660**.

742 Maitri 7. 9 *dūram ete* [stanza] = (var.) Kaṭha 2. 4.

743 Maitri 7. 9 *vidyāṁ cāvidyāṁ ca* [stanza] = Īśā 11.

744 Maitri 7. 9 *avidyāyām* [stanza] = (var.) Kaṭha 2. 5; Muṇḍ. 1. 2. 8.

745 Maitri 7. 10 [instruction of gods and devils] cf. Chānd. 8. 7-8.

746 Maitri 7. 11 *tat tredhā — prāṇa* = Maitri 6. 37.

747 Maitri 7. 11 [simile of the solution of salt] see **210**.

747a Maitri 7. 11 [the immanent Soul said to be like lightning] see **36**.

748 Maitri 7. 11 *tasmād om ity — tejaḥ* see **726**.

749 Maitri 7. 11, stanza 1 [Indra and Virāj] see **61**.

750 Maitri 7. 11, stanza 2 *samāgamas tayor — suṣau* cf. **265**.

751 Maitri 7. 11, stanza 2 *tallohitasyātra piṇḍa* ⥲ Bṛh. 4. 2. 3.

752 Maitri 7. 11, stanza 3 *hṛdayād āyatā tāvac cakṣuṣy asmin pratiṣṭhitā* see **64**.

753 Maitri 7. 11, stanza 6 *na paśyan — sarvaśaḥ* = (var. Chānd. 7. 26. 2.

754 Maitri 7. 11, stanza 7 [fourth, or superconscious, state] see **519**.

Bhagavad-Gītā [1]

755 BhG. 2. 13 = Viṣṇusmṛti 20. 49.

756 BhG. 2. 17 b *yena sarvam idaṁ tatam* = BhG. 8. 22 d; 18. 46 b; MBh. 12. 240. 20 d (C. 8753 d); cf. BhG. 9. 4; 11. 38.

757 BhG. 2. 19, 20 = (var.) Kaṭha 2. 19, 18. With BhG. 2. 20 d cf. *na vadhenāsya hanyate* Chānd. 8. 1. 5; 8. 10. 2, 4.

758 BhG. 2. 22 ⟜ Viṣṇusmṛti 20. 50.

759 BhG. 2. 23-25, 27, 28 = (var.) Viṣṇusmṛti 20. 51-53 29, 48.

760 BhG. 2. 29 cf. Kaṭha 2. 7.

761 BhG. 2. 46 = (var.) MBh. 5. 46. 26 (C. 1785).

762 BhG. 2. 61 a-b ⟜ BhG. 6. 14 c-d.

763 BhG. 2. 70 = Viṣṇusmṛti 72. 7.

764 BhG. 2. 71 c *nirmamo nirahaṁkāraḥ* = BhG. 12. 13 c; see **803**.

765 BhG. 3. 13 cf. BhG. 4. 31 a and see Manusmṛti 3. 118.

766 BhG. 3. 14 ⟜ Maitri 6. 37, stanza; see **728**.

767 BhG. 3. 23 c-d = BhG. 4. 11 c-d.

768 BhG. 3. 35 a-b = BhG. 18. 47 a-b.

769 BhG. 3. 42 ⟜ Kaṭha 3. 10; see esp. **363**.

770 BhG. 4. 16 d = BhG. 9. 1 d.

771 BhG. 4. 21 c-d *karma kurvan nāpnoti kilbiṣam* = BhG. 18. 47 c-d.

772 BhG. 4. 35 c-d *yena bhūtāny . . . drakṣyasy ātmany* see **402**.

773 BhG. 5. 10 [water on a lotus-leaf] see **607**.

773a BhG. 5. 13 [nine-gated citadel] see **543**.

[1] No note has been taken of the recurrence of a number of pādas of purely formulaic character, and parallels between parts of BhG. are recorded under the first of the passages only.

774 BhG. 5. 18 = (var.) MBh. 12. 240. 19 (C. 8752).

775 BhG. 6. 5 c-d = (var.) MBh. 5. 34. 64 c-d (C. 1158 c-d).

776 BhG. 6. 7 c, d = BhG. 12. 18 c, b.

777 BhG. 6. 10-26 [rules for Yoga] see **526** and note **762.**

778 BhG. 6. 23 a-b = (var.) MBh. 3. 213. 33 c-d (C. 13992 c-d).

779 BhG. 6. 29 ⩦ Īśā 6; see esp. **402.**

780 BhG. 6. 35 cf. Patañjali's Yoga-sūtras 1. 12.

781 BhG. 6. 45 *tato yāti paraṁ gatim* = BhG. 13. 28; 16. 22; cf. 8. 13; 9. 32; Maitri 6. 30 [**707**]; and see **792, 249.**

782 BhG. 7. 4 [earth, water, fire, air, ether] see **528**; cf. also **522.**

783 BhG. 7. 10 d = BhG. 10. 36 b.

784 BhG. 7. 24 *paraṁ bhāvam ajānanto mama* = BhG. 9. 11.

785 BhG. 7. 27-28 [pairs of opposites] cf. Maitri 3. 1, 2; 6. 29.

786 BhG. 8. 5-6 [last thoughts determine state after death] cf. Chānd. 3. 14. 1; Praśna 3. 10. Cf. in general **192, 457.**

787 BhG. 8. 9 d = Śvet. 3. 8 b. The phrase *tamasaḥ parastāt* recurs Muṇḍ. 2. 2. 6; MBh. 5. 44. 29 a (C. 1712 a); cf. *tamasas pāraṁ* Chānd. 7. 26. 2. On *aṇor aṇīyāṁsam* in pāda b see **544.**

788 BhG. 8. 11 ⩦ Kaṭha 2. 15.

789 BhG. 8. 14 d *nityayuktasya yoginaḥ* see **693.**

790 BhG. 8. 17 ⩦ Manusmṛti 1. 73.

791 BhG. 8. 18-19 [creation and reabsorption of beings] see **532.**

792 BhG. 8. 21 b *tam āhuḥ paramām gatim* = Kaṭha 6. 10 d (*tām*); see **391** and cf. **781.**

793 BhG. 8. 21 c-d ⩦ BhG. 15. 6 c-d.

794 BhG. 8. 24-26 [course to the Brahma-world and to the lunar world] see **127, 128.**

795 BhG. 9. 5 b = BhG. 11. 8 d.

796 BhG. 9. 21 [rebirth when merit is exhausted] cf. Muṇḍ. 1. 2. 10 and see **128.**

797 BhG. 9. 32 = (var.) MBh. 14. 19. 61 (C. 593).

798 BhG. 9. 34 ≃ BhG. 18. 65.

799 BhG. 10. 35 b [Gāyatrī meter] cf. Bṛh. 5. 14. 1-7; Chānd. 3. 12.

800 BhG. 11. 18 b = BhG. 11. 38 b.

801 BhG. 11. 25 d = BhG. 11. 45 d.

802 BhG. 11. 34 = Kauṣ. 2. 11 (7).

803 BhG. 12. 13 cf. MBh. 12. 237. 34 (C. 8679-80). BhG. 12. 13 c recurs as 2. 71 c; cf. also 18. 53 [**816**].

804 BhG. 13. 1-2 = (var.) Viṣṇusmṛti 96. 97-98. The term *kṣetrajña* occurs also at Śvet. 6. 16 c; Maitri 2. 5.

805 BhG. 13. 13, 14 a-b = Śvet. 3. 16, 17 a-b. BhG. 13. 13 = MBh. 12. 240. 29 (C. 8762); = (var.) MBh. 12. 302. 17 (C. 11230); 14. 19. 49 (C. 580-1); 14. 40. 4 (C. 1087).

806 BhG. 13. 14-18 = (var.) Viṣṇusmṛti 97. 17-21.

807 BhG. 13. 15 ≃ Īśā 5; cf. Muṇḍ. 2. 1. 2 b.

808 BhG. 13. 19 cf. MBh. 12. 217. 7 c (C. 7848 c).

809 BhG. 13. 30 = MBh. 12. 17. 23 (var. in C. 12. 533); cf. Kaṭha 6. 6.

810 BhG. 14. 5-18 [*sattva*, *rajas*, *tamas*] cf. Maitri 3. 5; see also Manusmṛti 12. 24-40; Yājñavalkīya Dharma-sūtras 3. 137-139; MBh. 12. 194. 29-36 (C. 7094-7102); 12. 219. 25-31 (C. 7955-61).

811 BhG. 14. 18 cf. MBh. 12. 314. 3-4 (C. 11637-8).

812 BhG. 14. 21 [transcending the Guṇas] cf. MBh. 12. 251. 22 (C. 9085) and see Patañjali's Yoga-sūtras 4. 32.

813 BhG. 15. 1-3 [eternal fig-tree with roots above] cf. Kaṭha 6. 1; Maitri 6. 4; see also Śvet. 3. 9 c; 6. 6 a. BhG. 15. 1 d = Maitri 6. 15, stanza, pāda d.

814 BhG. 15. 6, 12 see **387**.

815 BhG. 15. 8 see **320**.

816 BhG. 16. 18 *ahaṁkāraṁ — krodhaṁ* = BhG. 18. 53.

817 BhG. 16. 21 = Viṣṇusmṛti 33. 6.

818 BhG. 17. 24 cf. Āpastambīya Dharma-sūtras 1. 4. 13. 7 and see **143**, **726**.

819 BhG. 18. 67 [restrictions on imparting occult knowledge] see **133**.

SANSKRIT INDEX

References to the principal occurrences of important Sanskrit words, chiefly technical terms, are here given for convenience. For exhaustive citations the reader is referred to G. A. Jacob's *Concordance to the Principal Upanishads and Bhagavad-Gîtâ*, Bombay, 1891.

The sequence of letters is that of the Sanskrit alphabet. Superior numerals refer to the footnotes. A reference is enclosed in parentheses when the word appears on the page in question only in translation, but not in its Sanskrit form. For proper names consult the General Index.

akṣara, imperishable, 118, 182[1], 349[2], 367, 391[1]
akṣiti, indestructibility, 321
atimukti, *atimokṣā*, complete release, 107, 108
advaita, without duality, 138, 392
ananta, infinite, 283
anu-vid, to know well, to foreknow, 299[2]
anṛta, the false, 151, 287
antar-ātman, inner soul, 357, 361, 371, 424
antar-yāmin. inner controller, 114–117, 281[1], 392
apavarga, emancipation, 444
apāna, out-breath, 125, 180, 208, 238, 278, 284, 356, 371, 383, 384, 385, 416
apramatta, undistracted, 360[3], (372)
abhimāna(tva), self-conceit, 415, 418, 440
alakṣaṇa, having no distinctive mark, 392
aliṅga, without any mark, 359
avidyā, ignorance, 37, 346, 368–369, 456
avyakta, unmanifest, 8, 352, 359, 395, 431, 432, 438
asat, non-being, non-existent, 11, 214, 241, 286, 287, 372, 381; unreal, 80, 386, 417
asu, life, 300
asura, devil, 76, 150, 178, 179, 268, 334, 456
ahaṁkāra, egoism, 387, 391[4], 395, 407, 426, 441

ākāśa, ether, space, 256, 257, 273, 283
ācaratha, follow (imperative), 6, 367
ājñāna, perception, 300
ātman, body, embodiment, 73, 76, 86, 200, 278, 279, 284, 285, 286, 355, 359; individual soul, 6, 24, 25, 110, 140, 306, 351, 356, 395, 417, etc.; cosmic soul, *see* 'Ātman' in General Index
ātmanvin, possessing a self, embodied, 74, 75, 94
ātma-śakti, self-power, 394
ātma-saṁstha, present in the self, 396
ānanda-maya, consisting of bliss, 286, 392
āsura, devilish, 269

indrajāla, jugglery, 420
indriya, sense, 351, 359, 370, 384, 389, 394[6]

īs, *īśa*, Lord, 374, 395, 400, 402, 403, 406, 409
īśāna, Lord, 84, 404, 429, 454

uktha, hymn of praise, 92, 154
udāna, up-breath, 125, 208, 239, 384, 416, 430, 446, 453
upaniṣad, mystic doctrine, 100, 127, 131, 146, 178, 207, 282, 289, 293, 339, 397, 406, 445; doctrine, 269, 308, 309; mystic meaning, 18, 34, 95, 190, 276, 445; mystic name, 152

ṛta, world-order, right, 280, 293, 356

enas, sin, 157, 365

karma(n), deeds, action, 54–57, 140, 144, 303, 319, 340, 357, 362, 371, 373, 376, 407, 408, 409, 417, 436, 447; active functions, 90

karmamaya, consisting of works, 310
karmendriya, organ of action, 391[4], 394[3]
kāma, desire, 300
kāraṇa, cause, 394[1], 409
kṛtātman, perfected soul, 273, 375, 376
kevala, absolute, 396
kevalatva, absolute unity, 437
kratu, purpose, 157, 209, 300, 365
kṣatra, power, ruling class, 84[2], 98–99, 154, 351, 381
kṣetra-jña, spirit, 410, 415

kha, space, 370, 389

gandharva, demigod, 74, 111, 113, (138), 199, 359, 413
guru, teacher, 369, 411, 441
guṇa, quality, 9, 394, 403[3], 406, 407, 408, 410, 418, 431, 453

caṇḍāla, outcast, 233, 240
caturtha (= *turīya*), fourth, or superconscious, state, 392[11]
citta, thought, 253-254, 323, 384, 387, 391[4]
cintā, meditation, 421
cetas, thought, 375, 392
caitanya, consciousness, intelligence, 431, 452

jāgarita-sthāna, waking state, 391
jātavedas, all-knowing, 164, 338, 344[3], 354, 379[1], 429[2]
jīva, living individual, 436
jūti, impulse, 300
jñānātman, understanding-self, 352

tat tvam asi, That art thou (32), 246–250
tan-mātra, subtile substance, 418
tapas, austerity, 340, 369, 371, 374, 376, 378, 380, 396, 421
tamas, Dark Quality, 419, 423, 441
tarka, contemplation, 347, 435
turīya (*turya*), fourth, or superconscious, state, 49, 392[11], 393, 436, 458; fourth foot of the Gāyatrī, 155, 156
tejas, brilliance, heat, 74, 386, 387
tya, yon, 97, 121, 287, 306

dama, restraint, 340 (cf. 150)
dīkṣā, initiatory rite, 124, 212, 229, 370
dṛṣṭi, insight, 300
deva, god, 277, 381, 394, 395, 396, 399, 402, 404, 405, 407, 408, 416; power, 381; sense-power, 323, 334, 356, 362, 375, 376, 387, 397
deva-loka, world of the gods, 89, 108, 113, 163
dyaus pitṛ, Heaven-father, 166
dvandva, pair of opposites, 417, 442
dvaita, duality, 101

dharma, law, 84, 91, 103, 456; quality, 355; religiousness, 395[3]
dhātṛ, Creator, (59[1]), 278, 350, 402, 404, 407, 429
dhāraṇā, concentration, 435
dhṛti, steadfastness, 300
dhyāna, meditation, 254, 394, 396, 435

nāka, heaven, 195
nāḍī, channel of the body, 519, 521 (see the references there)
nāma-rūpa, name-and-form, i.e. individuality, 82, 92, 242, 273, 367, 376, 389
nāstikya, atheism, 419
nirguṇa, devoid of qualities, 409
nirvṛtatva, peacefulness, 437
niṣkāmatva, freedom from desire, 442
neti, neti, not thus! not so! 97, 125, 132, 143, 147

pañcāgni-vidyā, five-fire doctrine, 60
parokṣa, cryptic, (132), 298
paly-ayate, he moves around, 6
pāpa, evil, 289, 312
pāpman, sin, 286, 312, 334, 340, 377, 388
putra, son, 90, 315[3]
punarmṛtyu, repeated death, 76, 87, 522
puruṣa, person, 81, 283; cosmic person, *see* 'Person' in General Index
pūrṇa, plenum, 330
prakṛti, Nature, 8, 354[3], 396, 403[3], 404, 418, 430, 431, 442
prajñā, intelligence, 305, 307, 319, 324, 325–326, 350
prajñātman, intelligential self, 318, 321, 322, 328, 334 (cf. 136)
prajñāna, intelligence, 300–301
prajñāna-ghana, cognition-mass, 392

SANSKRIT INDEX

lokya, world-wise, world-procuring, 90[1]

vaṁśa, line of tradition, 7, 105, 148, 167, 174, (207, 274, 366)
vaśa, will, 300
vijñāna, understanding, 95, 254–255, 300, 351, 433
vijñāna-ghana, mass of knowledge, 101
vijñāna-maya, consisting of understanding, 285, 376
vijñānātman, conscious self, 387
vidṛti, sagittal suture, 297, 356[1]
vidyā, knowledge, 421; science, 100, 127, 146, 445
vidhi, law, 371 (cf. 420)
vināśa, destruction, 364
viś, the people, 84, 85, 98[2], 273, 314
viśvambhara, fire-holder (?), 82
viṣaya, object, 444
vedānta, Veda's End, 376, 411
vairāgya, indifference to the world, 412
vaiśvānara, universal, 234, 391
vyāna, diffused breath, 125, 180, 208, 238, 278, 284, 384, 385, 416, 426, 430, 446, 453
vyāhṛti, mystical utterance, 278, 425
vyoman, heaven, 283
vrātya, 382[2]

śakti, power, 402, 409
śarīra, body, 418
śānta, tranquil, 392, 410
śāntatva, tranquillity, 442
śraddhā, faith, 163, 178, 231, 285, 341, 369, 371, (377), 378, 389
śrotriya, versed in the scriptures, 160, 234, (242), 288, 369

saṁsāra, cycle of transmigration, 56, 352, 410, 413, 441, 447
saṁkalpa, conception, 101, 252–253, 264, 300, 321, 339, 407
saṁjñā(na), consciousness, 147, 300
sat, being, (11–12), 241, 265, 287, 372, 381; real, actual, 97, 386, 442
sattva, Pure Quality, 423; pure being, 359, 452
satya, the real, truth, 95, 129, 151, 155, 259, 265, 285, 287, 306, 427, 429
saṁnyāsa-yoga, application of renunciation, 376
saṁnyāsin, ascetic, 432
samādhi, absorption, 435
samāna, equalizing breath, 125, 208, 239, 259, 383, 384, 386, 416, 430, 446, 453
samprasāda, serene, 265, 272, 414
sambhava, origin, 364
sambhūti, becoming, 364
sammoha, stupor, confusion, 323, 441, 451
sarvāpti, all-obtaining, 322–324
sarvāvat, all-containing, 6, (134)
sāṁkhya, discrimination, 410
sādhu, good, 288, 289
sāman, chant, 79, 92, 154, 155, 180–186, 189–199, 201–202, 305, 311, 370, 381, 388
sāmya, identity, 374
sāyujya(tva), complete union, 420, 422, 437
sīman, hair-part, 297, 312[6]
suṣupta, sound asleep, deep sleep, 95, 392
suṣupta-sthāna, deep-sleep state, 392
suṣumnā, name of a channel of the body, 384[5], 437, 519, 521
sthāna, place, state, 98[1]
smṛti, traditional doctrines, 262; memory, 300, (444)
svapna-sthāna, dreaming state, 391
svabhāva, inherent nature, 8, 408
svayam-bhū, the Self-existent, 106, 149, 176, 353, 363
svarāj, autonomous, 64[1], 261
svātantrya, independence, 437
svārājya, self-rule, 64[1], 279; chief sovereignty, (202), 205–206, 334, (450)

haṁsa, name for the individual and the cosmic soul, 44[2], 134, 135, 395, 402, 410, 429, 454
hara, epithet of the soul, 396
hiṅ(-kāra), the sound *hiṅ*, 165, 189, 191–199
hita, channel of the body, 95, 132, 136, 267, 333, 361, 384, (519), 521

GENERAL INDEX

The names and subjects of the Bibliography and the Appendix have not been included here except in a few sporadic instances, and considerations of space have likewise required the omission of proper names of secondary importance.

The numbers refer to pages. Superior numerals refer to the footnotes.

B

GENERAL INDEX

GENERAL INDEX

C

GENERAL INDEX

D

GENERAL INDEX

GENERAL INDEX

P p 2

GENERAL INDEX

GENERAL INDEX

GENERAL INDEX

Y